# Unified Software Engineering with Java™

Georges G. Merx
*San Diego Mesa College*

Ronald J. Norman
*Grossmont College and University of Maryland University College*

PEARSON

Prentice
Hall

Upper Saddle River, NJ 07458

**Library of Congress Cataloging-in-Publication Data**

Merx, Georges G.-
    Unified software engineering with Java / Georges G. Merx, Ronald J. Norman.
        p. cm.
    Includes bibliographical references and index.
    ISBN 0-13-047376-6
    Java (Computer program language) 2. Software engineering. 3. Object-oriented
    Methods (Computer science) I. Norman, Ronald J. II. Title

Vice President and Editorial Director, ECS:
  *Marcia J. Horton*
Executive Editor: *Tracy Dunkelberger*
Associate Editor: *Carole Snyder*
Editorial Assistant: *Christianna Lee*
Executive Managing Editor: *Vince O'Brien*
Managing Editor: *Camille Trentacoste*
Production Editor: *Irwin Zucker*
Director of Creative Services: *Paul Belfanti*
Creative Director: *Juan Lopez*
Art Director and Cover Manager: *Jayne Conte*
Managing Editor, AV Management and Production:
  *Patricia Burns*

Art Editor: *Xiaohong Zhu*
Director, Image Resource Center: *Melinda Reo*
Manager, Rights and Permissions: *Zina Arabia*
Manager, Visual Research: *Beth Brenzel*
Manager, Cover Visual Research and Permissions:
  *Karen Sanatar*
Manufacturing Manager, ESM: *Alexis Heydt-Long*
Manufacturing Buyer: *Lisa McDowell*
Executive Marketing Manager: *Robin O'Brien*
Marketing Assistant: *Mack Patterson*
Cover Image: *Aerial photo of Java islands. Science
Source / Photo Researchers, Inc.*

© 2007 Pearson Education, Inc.
Pearson Prentice Hall
Pearson Education, Inc.
Upper Saddle River, NJ 07458

Pearson Prentice Hall™ is a trademark of Pearson Education, Inc.
All other trademarks or product names are the property of their respective owners.

The author and publisher of this book have used their best efforts in preparing this book. These efforts include the development, research, and testing of the theories and programs to determine their effectiveness. The author and publisher make no warranty of any kind, expressed or implied, with regard to these programs or the documentation contained in this book. The author and publisher shall not be liable in any event for incidental or consequential damages in connection with, or arising out of, the furnishing, performance, or use of these programs.

Printed in the United States of America

10 9 8 7 6 5 4 3 2 1

**ISBN: 0-13-047376-6**

Pearson Education Ltd., *London*
Pearson Education Australia Pty. Ltd., *Sydney*
Pearson Education Singapore, Pte. Ltd.
Pearson Education North Asia Ltd., *Hong Kong*
Pearson Education Canada, Inc., *Toronto*
Pearson Educación de Mexico, S.A. de C.V.
Pearson Education—Japan, *Tokyo*
Pearson Education Malaysia, Pte. Ltd.
Pearson Education, Inc., *Upper Saddle River, New Jersey*

My wife Jin always supports and encourages my projects—even one as major as writing this book—although they take away from our time together. I am deeply grateful for this irrefutable evidence of true love.

I hope that my efforts will serve to provide some inspiration for my daughter London to find her own path to success, wherever that path may lead her.

A good portion of this work was completed at the Fenton Place Starbucks in San Diego. I express my gratitude to the staff there, and to Starbucks as one of the great American companies, for creating an environment where those of us with short attention spans can be productive.

All the people at Prentice Hall—especially our editor, Tracy Dunkelberger, and her indefatiguable assistant, Christianna Lee—with whom I have had the privilege to work are immensely supportive, helpful, and competent: my appreciation is heartfelt. A special note of appreciation to Irwin Zucker, our production editor, for getting us through the production phase of this project with patience and much good will.

Finally, the indefatigable encouragement and contributions of my co-author, Ron, have been indispensable ingredients to making this project workable.

*Georges G. Merx*

There are so many to dedicate this book to that I cannot name them individually. Literally hundreds of software engineers (generic title) and academics/researchers around the globe have contributed to making me the professional I am today through the many publications, conferences, seminars, and workshops that I have either physically or virtually attended or led. Their influence has been profound in my life, and I am deeply grateful for the experiences and interaction with each of these professional women and men.

I also dedicate this book to those who will advance their academic and/or professional knowledge through the use of this book. It is truly a privilege to contribute something back to you, since so many individuals have profoundly influenced me.

Thank you, Georges, for allowing me to take this book journey with you—you are a gifted writer and seasoned professional/academic.

Finally, thank you to my life-partner, wife, and best friend: Caralie.

*Ronald J. Norman*

# Brief Contents

# Contents

# Preface

Creating commercial software requires excellent knowledge and skills in a number of areas, not just programming language syntax and semantics. We have therefore written a book that teaches the fundamentals of Java programming in the context of object-oriented software engineering and a Unified-Process-based software development methodology. Today's programmers need to be software engineers who knw their languages and tools, certainly, but who also understand object-oriented analysis and design, software quality asurance, and software project management. In fact, the best antidote to the *outsourcing* of software development jobs overseas is to elevate the profession above the specialist tasks of code development. Software engineers need to have the skills to deliver quality software on time, on budget, and according to stakeholder requirements. Our book puts the study of Java in this meaningful, valuable context.

## Audience

College students with a previous course in programming or software engineering learning their first or second computer programming language are the primary audience for this textbook. Some previous exposure to principles of information systems and computer science is desirable, but not required. Other likely readers are software development professionals who are looking for a methodical approach to learning object-oriented software development using Java, especially those who only have experience in procedural programming.

## Course Definition

This book is recommended for use in information systems or computer science courses at the college level and targets students pursuing an interest in computer science, information systems, or software engineering. In addition to delivering solid programming language instruction, it lays a broad foundation in object-oriented methodology, based on best practices and proven principles developed by Grady Booch, Jim Rumbaugh, Ivar Jacobson, Peter Coad, Barry Boehm, Kent Beck, and other recognized software engineering thought leaders. Based on a complete, object-oriented life-cycle view of the software design and development process, software engineering as defined and described in this book embraces the use of Java for the development of robust, commercially viable, and eminently usable software solutions.

From initial concept to deployment, all aspects of software engineering project design, development, and management will accompany the students' learning experience. They will understand how rigorous iteration-based requirements management (using stakeholder and use case analysis), conceptual and physical design (using the Unified Modeling Language and Design Patterns), component-based implementation, and well-planned deployment contribute to transitioning software development from an art form to an engineering discipline.

For professors and instructors, this book and accompanying website constitute solid teaching aids, providing not only Java language training, but also work process-based instruction, including a clear and practical introduction to object-oriented design and development. Written with the understanding that the introduction to software engineering and Java can be a daunting experience for many inexperienced readers, this book delivers its instructional content with a strong emphasis on illustrative examples and a firm grounding in real-life applications.

Courses on Java and object-oriented programming are mainstay offerings on many college campuses. This book seeks to support and deepen the interest of students, teachers and administrators in an area of computer science critical to the development of core skills sought after by the high-technology industry. Courses built to leverage the contents of this book will help students advance their understanding of object-oriented software engineering using Java to a level where they can either move on to more advanced course work, or apply their new, practical knowledge in entry-level work positions.

## Another Java Book?

The idea for this book arose originally from my search (Merx) for appropriate textbooks for use in my own Java courses. It appeared that available textbooks either focus on Java syntax and structure at the expense of methodology and process, or emphasize "analysis and design," while lacking the practical context of a modern object-oriented programming language and toolset. Both of us have extensive experience both in academia (SDSU, UCSD, Mesa College, University of Phoenix, National University, Grossmont College, and University of Maryland University College) and in business (Borland, TogetherSoft, NCR, AT&T, QUALCOMM, ICL/Fujitsu, etc.). This background convinces us that as educators we need to do better in training our students for the multi-disciplinary effort required to develop valuable, high-quality software that solves difficult problems in a world-class fashion.

While many excellent text and reference books on Java are available, most are lacking key features deemed essential for practical instruction of effective software engineering using Java. From our perspective, a key area of progress in software development is the recasting of professional programming as a *software engineering discipline*, with its implications of reusability, quality controlled rigor, focus on architecture and process, and project management. Software engineering, as described and standardized in the Carnegie-Mellon University Software Engineering Institute's Capability

Maturity Model, for example, promotes a life-cycle approach to software development projects. The unique features of this book focus on programming language instruction within the framework of a solid, comprehensive, object-oriented methodology, appropriate for implementation in real-world commercial software development projects by inexperienced software engineers.

Both of us have extensive commercial hands-on programming, teaching, and managerial experience in software design and development, architecture, tools, implementation, and project management. Our understanding of industry needs, combined with our teaching experience, have led to this text, which integrates important instructional topics otherwise only available from multiple, unrelated textbooks.

GEORGES G. MERX AND RONALD J. NORMAN

# Introduction to Java in the Context of Software Engineering

## 1.1 Getting Acquainted

Welcome to the study of the Java software programming language! You have elected to invest your learning time wisely: Java is a popular, modern tool used by software engineers around the world to create twenty-first-century computer applications. In this book, we study Java in the context of software engineering principles and best practices in order to ensure that you can apply your newfound knowledge usefully and accurately to the creation of functionality actually needed by your current (or future) clients and customers. Unlike many other textbooks, this book combines software engineering topics with Java language learning throughout; this approach follows the advice of software industry experts who claim that a new generation of software developers needs to have extensive skills in process- as well as technology-oriented disciplines.

## 1.2 What Is Java Programming?

For those of you with no previous programming experience, a definition of software development, or "programming," may be in order. Software programs start their lives as text, written in an English-like language (all major programming language are English-based). This text, saved in a file, is then processed and analyzed ("parsed") by a software program called a "compiler" that converts the English-like commands in the source file into either an intermediary form that an interpreter like the Java Virtual

Machine can interpret, or into machine code, or into machine instructions directly, stored in an executable file (e.g., `.exe` extension on the Microsoft Windows platform) that runs directly on the destination computer. The programming process, therefore, is the creation of statements and commands in a human-comfortable form; because these statements are converted into specific machine-level instructions, they must follow rigorous syntax and structure rules.

---

**Example Java statement:**

```
String response = JOptionPane.showInputDialog
("Enter an integer value");
```

---

While the words in Java source code are based on English meanings, the structure of a statement is not like a typical English sentence. It follows a much more rigorous, scientific organization, which allows the compiler to extract all the significant relationships between the words ("tokens") as it parses the text and translate them into computer-understandable instructions. This is necessary because the compiler can only translate source code devoid of ambiguities.

The Java language is based on C and C++; it is relatively new and therefore incorporates recent advances in computer language design, freeing the developer of management tasks (memory, pointers) that constitute a substantial burden in older languages. Its syntax and structure provide access to advanced computing functions while hiding the complexities of the underlying operating-system programs and hardware components. Java features and functions, implemented in Java classes, are organized into libraries. *Classes* from libraries can be imported into your program, giving you much flexibility in controlling the size and portability of your application.

Next, we introduce the concept of software engineering.

---

**Key Term**

A **class** is an object-oriented concept; it represents the combination of data (characteristics or, more formally, attributes) and functions (behaviors, or, more formally, methods).

---

**Key Term**

**Object-oriented life cycle software engineering methodology** is the process of developing software applications using an engineering approach, combined with the principles of object orientation.

---

### 1.2.1   *What Is Software Engineering?*

Like all engineering disciplines, **software engineering** requires substantial initiation for the novice to become a productive practitioner. Constructing valuable software components that optimize the capabilities of modern information systems involves complex planning, analysis, design, development, and quality-assurance activities.

Over the past fifty years, much progress has been made in advancing the activities of software development from an unstructured, individualized approach to a repeatable, predictable, measurable engineering process. These advances are integrated in today's object-oriented life-cycle software engineering practices.

In order to bridge the gap between the machine code executed by the computer system and the language-based information-processing approach favored by humans, efforts began early in the history of computing to develop software languages that translate English-like commands provided by programmers into machine-code compatible with the computer hardware. Today's object-oriented programming languages are the culmination of these efforts: they provide powerful control over the advanced capabilities of modern distributed computer infrastructures. Java, in particular, developed and released in 1995 by Sun Microsystems Inc.,[1] has been adopted by many software development organizations around the world as the *de facto* standard in object-oriented software development language tools. As an advanced tool, Java has two key benefits:

1. Java provides extensive, powerful, and effective metaphors and models to translate human actions and requirements into code that the computer can process; in particular, the representation of computing functions and data as classes and objects maximizes flexibility and portability.
2. Java supports write-once, run-anywhere technology[2] that integrates today's pervasive distributed, heterogeneous computing environments ("open systems") by allowing compiled Java programs (classes) to run on many platforms without change or even recompilation.

These two benefits alone are often compelling enough to tip the scale of the business-value proposition in favor of using Java for the development of new applications, especially in a distributed, heterogeneous operational environment.

However, just using Java does not solve all the problems in developing high-quality software programs. Following a *proven, effective process* of software development is an essential prerequisite for the successful implementation of *information technology (IT)* solutions using Java. Focusing on software development as a collection of processes and workflows (also called *disciplines*)[3] imparts multiple valuable perspectives on the software development life cycle; this inclusive approach improves the quality of translation of project requirements into efficient and effective IT solutions.

In the early years of software development, programs were simple and provided relatively few functions, constrained by limited hardware and slow networks; therefore, most of the complexity and effort went into actual coding, with not much formal upfront planning or design. In the 1970s and 1980s, large complex software behemoths

---

[1]www.sun.com - www.java.sun.com - Inevitably, much information in this book about Java has its origins directly or indirectly in Sun Microsystems materials; all copyrights and intellectual property rights are rightfully those of their owners.

[2]Trademarks are not identified individually in this book, but all trademarks are rightfully those of their owners.

[3]References to software development process and methodology follow the principles and vocabulary of the **Unified Process,** originally commercialized by the Rational Corporation, now a division of IBM, as the "Rational Unified Process."

were developed for business applications, mostly in COBOL,[4] but they were typically customized creations that remained relatively static, with additional functionality "bolted on" over time, often resulting in hard-to-maintain and sometimes hard-to-use collections of functions. The emergence of ever-more powerful computer hardware and high-speed communications made antiquated software tools a critical liability and led to the development of more advanced software technologies and tools, driven by the principles of *object-orientation,* first introduced as long ago as 1967 in a language called Simula-67 and later promoted in the pioneering, fully object-oriented Smalltalk language developed by Alan Kay at Xerox PARC.[5]

---

**Key Term**

**Information Technology (IT)** represents the hardware, software, and networking technologies and the human services associated with the productive use of computers.

---

Nowadays, with powerful, highly productive tools like Java, the complexity of software application development has shifted to the dynamic process of successfully translating extensive, complex, ever-changing stakeholder requirements into highly productive, flexible, distributed computer-based solutions. Another major trend in computing is the location-transparent integration of physically remote, distributed systems from different vendors. The resulting need for open-systems connectivity and integration often leads to complex, multifaceted software development requirements involving many distinct components.

This book provides a *real-world* introduction to object orientation and software engineering using the Java programming language. You will make your acquaintance with Java through a solid understanding of a success-proven approach to developing software: the software development process described in this book is based on the (Rational) Unified Process, and we call our student-oriented interpretation of this widely accepted methodology the **Extended Unified Process Methodology**.

From an overview perspective (Figure 1.1), the process of software development follows a **life cycle** of activities, from initial project concept to the release of the resulting product and subsequent product support and maintenance. As we look at the details of each stage in the development of a typical software project in the chapters of this book, there are a few underlying principles that guide our study:

1. We interpret all the aspects of a project from an *object-oriented perspective* (requirements, functions, data, users, interrelationships, outcomes).[6]
2. We adopt a *comprehensive view* of our project, focusing on the relationships between components, requirements, and deliverables across all phases.
3. We "divide and conquer" the complexity of the project by organizing functions, activities, resources, and deliverables into components and iterations.

---

[4]COBOL (Common Business Oriented Language), a procedural computer programming language, was developed under the auspices of the U.S. Department of Defense and initially specified in 1960.
[5]**P**alo **A**lto **R**esearch **C**enter.
[6]*Object-orientation* will be explained in detail in upcoming chapters.

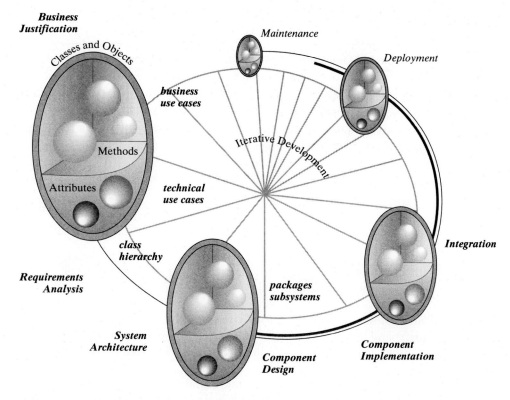

FIGURE 1.1    A High-Level Perspective of the Life Cycle of a Software Development Project

This high-level view of the life cycle of a typical software development project shows the development process as a progression of interrelated activities and deliverables. The class symbol ⬛ used throughout the book indicates that we look at all aspects of this process from an object-oriented viewpoint (seeing the project as a collection of classes and objects with methods and attributes).[7] The process starts with the business justification for the project, followed by the analysis of requirements, which results in the formulation of business and technical use cases. Based on this analysis, a system architecture and class hierarchy can be established as the key components of the design process. Components are then developed, integrated into packages and subsystems, and deployed. In the final stage, field-released software applications enter a maintenance phase where work is limited to minor enhancements and error corrections. Ultimately, the cycle repeats with the next release or the next product. Each major phase is divided into a planned number of manageable *iterations*, which we can think of as subprojects. As we will see in later chapters, this high-level view of our development life cycle will be defined with substantially more detail so that you can apply it in practice.

---

[7]The egg-symbol was chosen to represent the idea that a class should be a reasonably independent, well-integrated, and well-protected unit of functionality. It is inconsistent with UML notation, however, which we will cover in later chapters.

---

### UML DIAGRAM TYPES*

**Behavior Diagrams:** Activity Diagram, State Machine Diagram, Use Case Diagram, and the four interaction diagrams (below).

**Interaction Diagrams:** Communication Diagram, Interaction Overview Diagram, Sequence Diagram, and Timing Diagram

**Structure Diagrams:** Class Diagram, Composite Structure Diagram, Object Diagram, Component Diagram, Deployment Diagram, and Package Diagram

* http://www.agilemodeling.com/essays/umlDiagrams.htm, www.agilemodeling.com, Ambler, Scott, 2003

---

Instead of only learning Java language syntax and structure, you will be guided in this book to apply the unified life-cycle methodology it introduces to the design and development of realistic, high-value software solutions. From your understanding and application of this core methodology, you will be likely, as a professional software engineer, to expand your study of software tools and processes by incorporating variations of the Unified Process, such as Agile Processes and Extreme Programming.

As an object-oriented design modeling approach compatible with the Unified Process methodology, a set of annotated diagram types collectively known as the **Unified Modeling Language (UML)** was developed by *Rational Software Corporation* (which was acquired in 2003 by IBM Corporation)[8] and others and standardized by the *Object Management Group* (OMG).[9] These diagrams collectively describe even the most complex projects before implementation and capture the detailed design of a software solution without having to write code or pseudo-code. We will use these diagrams to illustrate the transformation of business and technical requirements into component designs and, eventually, actual Java code.

## 1.3 Learning Objectives

In this first chapter, as in subsequent chapters, we examine Java software engineering from multiple perspectives. Our understanding of the key stakeholders in a typical development project provides these perspectives as we take on their various viewpoints. One of the key tools in modern software engineering is the **Unified Modeling Language (UML)**, used to visualize the various aspects of a software development project with its components and interfaces. The thirteen UML diagrams (for a more detailed overview,

---

[8]Web site **www.ibm.com/rational/**
[9]Web site **www.omg.org**

please see Chapter 15) illustrate the various elements and relationships associated with a commercial software development project. They fall into three broad categories:

- **Behavior diagrams** illustrate the dynamic interactions between elements over time.
- **Interaction diagrams** are a subset of behavior diagrams that focus specifically on object interactions.
- **Structural diagrams** show the static relationships between design elements.

Multiple examples of various UML diagram types accompany the text to illustrate the different aspects of project control during each phase of a software development project.

### 1.3.1   Learning Layout

This recurring section shows the student-learning objectives for the chapter in a simple diagram (Figure 1.2), using the UML **activity diagram** notation. We will cover UML in more detail, especially in the last chapter. The UML is an industry-standard modeling language that helps visualize software projects and features.

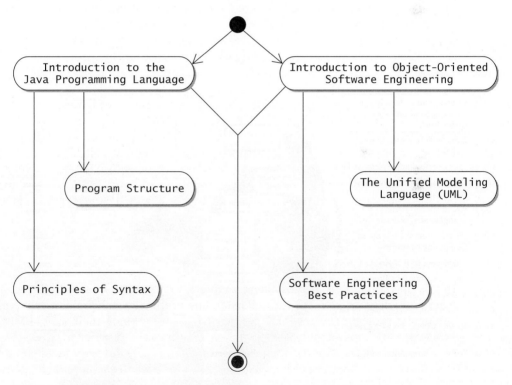

FIGURE 1.2   Chapter 1 Learning Layout (as a UML Activity Diagram)[10]

---

[10]This UML diagram and those in subsequent chapters were created with Visual Paradigm for UML (**www.visual-paradigm.com**).

The recurring theme in this and future chapters is the understanding of Java syntax, structure, and semantics in the context of object-oriented software engineering disciplines. This chapter serves primarily as an introduction to the key topics that the remaining chapters cover.

### 1.3.2  Learning Connections

The Learning Connections diagram (Figure 1.3) shows the content of this chapter from the perspective of the skills and knowledge development recommended for apprentice Java software engineers. The five-spoke software engineering profile is discussed in more detail in Chapter 3. We want you to understand from the beginning that software engineering is an inherently multidisciplinary profession regardless of your chosen development tool (in our case Java). It is not sufficient to be a Java syntax guru. The other areas of development shown here are often equally and sometimes even more important, especially when working on a larger project with a team of professionals belonging to many disciplines.

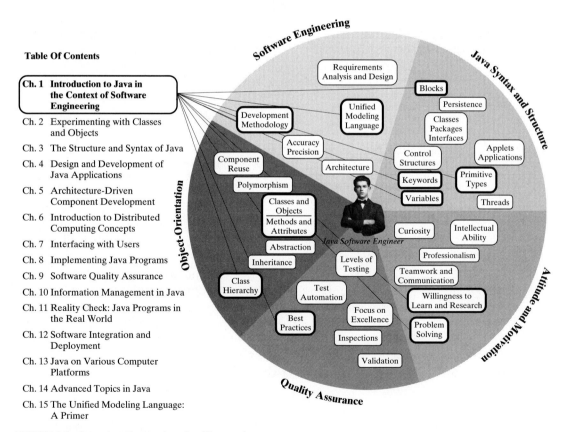

FIGURE 1.3   Learning Connections for Chapter 1

## 1.4 Executive Summary

The essence of software engineering is to develop quality information technology solutions for one or more *stakeholders* (1) *on time,* (2) *within budget,* and (3) according to the stakeholders' *expectations and requirements.*[11] These three core values taken together sufficiently characterize the entire reason for the development of a valuable software project. For too long, programmers have failed in one or more of these areas, often with the result that their customers' urgent, mission-critical expectations are not met, at great cost in money, quality, and professional credibility. The application of engineering principles elevates software development from an erratic "art form" to a repeatable, measurable, and predictable professional endeavor.

---

**Key Term**

**Stakeholders** are all those people (and systems) with a vested interest in the outcome of the project. Their correct and complete identification ensures that all the important sources for project requirements are known.

---

In this chapter, we introduce you to the evolution of the discipline of software engineering, and the practical benefits of applying a predictable, repeatable, quality-driven process to software design and development. We also explain what *object orientation* is and why it has become an important standard in the creation of well-engineered software applications. In Chapter 3, we will take a closer look at the precursor methodologies from which the modern-day Unified Process–based software engineering approach has evolved.

The central benefit of computers over other electro-mechanical systems is that they are *programmable.* The ability to program computers makes them flexible, reusable, and adaptable platforms for a great diversity of information technology solutions. The programming of computers is accomplished with software applications that essentially contain commands that the computer can execute. Software development has evolved over the past fifty years from machine-language control statements to sophisticated English-like, "high-level" programming tools like the Java programming language developed by Sun Microsystems.

At the same time, many software development projects continue to exceed their budgets, are delivered late, and, most painfully, fail to implement the requirements of the customers and users who ordered the system in the first place. In addition, initial releases of new software programs are often unstable, have security loopholes, and may be slow and difficult to use and deploy. The object-oriented software engineering methodology principles guiding this book help you develop productive software engineering skills that implement industry best practices.

---

[11]Implied is that an agreement has been forged between stakeholders and implementers

## 1.5    Learning Modules

The following sections describe the key concepts of this chapter, focused on introducing Java as a premier object-oriented software engineering tool. We use a consistent structure from chapter to chapter, including this segment, to allow you to organize your learning experience in a structured way.

### 1.5.1    Concepts

At this point, we introduce you, the novice Java software engineer, to the fundamental concepts guiding the instruction provided in this book. Obviously, the focus of the book is on teaching you how to competently develop Java software applications. Because software development is often a complex task performed by a team of professionals over an extended period of time, the application of a structured, predictable, repeatable process does much to improve planning and productivity. You will therefore learn to follow a proven object-oriented software engineering approach to software development.

#### Object Orientation Preview

The process of applying software engineering principles to software design and development is called "software development methodology." A methodology signifies the predictable, repeatable, standardized use of work processes, or *disciplines*, which have proven effective and productive. We combine this approach with the principles of **object-orientation,** implemented in a comprehensive fashion in the Java programming language. Object orientation and the methodology disciplines together result in the object-oriented software methodology promoted in this book as the context and foundation of **best practices** in software development.

The main characteristics of Java object-orientation are:

- Component reuse through inheritance, interfaces and polymorphism, following accepted design patterns.[12]
- Controlled access to component attributes and methods through encapsulation.
- Component organization through classes, instantiation of objects, and packages.
- Avoidance of procedural artifacts like pointers and memory management through automatic "garbage collection."
- Transparent multiplatform support through the interpretation of bytecodes by the Java Virtual Machine.

The main technical benefits of object orientation in software design and development are:

- Classes and objects provide a powerful, flexible metaphor for human processes and characteristics.

---

[12]Design patterns will be discussed further in other chapters; the term refers to an approach first promoted by Erich Gamma, Richard Helm, Ralph Johnson, and John Vlissides ("The Gang of Four") in their book *Design Patterns*: *Elements of Reusable Object-Oriented Software* (Addison-Wesley Professional, 1995).

- End-to-end consistency from the initial definition of use cases to the implementation of classes.[13]
- Contextual component abstraction and reuse through *inheritance, polymorphism, and encapsulation* (see Key Terms box).
- Formal detailed design representation using the *Unified Modeling Language* diagrams.
- Elegant high-level support for advanced computing functions, such as multimedia, multithreading, and distributed, heterogeneous, multiplatform applications.

---

**Key Terms**

**Inheritance** is the transfer of attributes, methods, and relationships from parent to child classes/objects.
**Polymorphism** is the ability for methods to take on multiple "roles" under the same name.
**Encapsulation** is the hiding and protection of internal structures from external interface calls.
**The Unified Modeling Language (UML)** is a set of object-oriented modeling diagrams.

---

The integral implementation in Java of these object-orientation features ensures that Java programs, if properly written, fully benefit from the proven strengths of object-orientation. It is impossible, however, to implement coherent, comprehensive object-orientation without a thorough, detailed design based on a comprehensive understanding of project requirements.

### *Process Modeling*

Poorly designed programs are often the result of developers starting the project by "imagining" the features and functions the program should have, instead of studying the underlying work processes. The capturing of real-world work processes is often more difficult than designing features and functions because it involves activities which occur over time, often performed by multiple persons or programs (we will call them "actors" from here on), and not always carried out with the consistency that would make it possible to automate them using information technology.

We therefore use the Unified Modeling Language (UML) diagrams to model the important features of the work processes that we seek to automate using information technology.[14] The UML diagrams are designed and standardized to represent static as well as dynamic behaviors and relationships, at the level of detail and complexity necessary. They are used to model functional and nonfunctional requirements. The diagrams themselves promote "object thinking" and allow for the consistent interpretation of project requirements as object components and relationships.

---

[13]While use cases themselves are not explicitly "object-oriented," their organization and interrelationships to each other lead to a more straightforward conversion of requirements to a viable class hierarchy.
[14]A UML primer is included in Chapter 15 of this book.

### 1.5.2   Unified Process–Based Methodology Overview

We present in this section our interpretation of the standard development process referred to in the software industry as the "Unified Process" in a diagram that takes into account the need for explicit details that most students have for easy understanding and application of a conceptual model.

#### Unified Process

The Unified Process (UP) is a software application development methodology that supports the principles of object-orientation and distributed computing. The methodology includes comprehensive software engineering guidelines for all aspects and stages of program development and integrates into a unifying, life-cycle framework of the process disciplines of software development and its associated participants and deliverables. The original and most recognized implementation of the Unified Process is the Rational Unified Process (RUP) of the Rational Division of IBM Corporation.

Understanding and knowledge of the Unified Process are integral to the skills required of a contemporary software developer because the process governs the best practices in translating project requirements into features and functions that can be developed on time and within the constraints of the project.

#### Extended Unified Process Methodology

The popular UP methodology diagrams and depictions are usually easy to comprehend only when the reader or observer has significant prior experience in software development, perhaps because software engineering methodologies are invariably the empirical generalization of field experience. This practical foundation is certainly desirable but often leads to representations that are difficult to grasp for those with less experience. We believe therefore that software engineering models need to be better tailored to novice students, more explicit and easier to understand and apply, without trivializing the fundamentals.

We embrace the work done by the greats in our domain, including Kent Beck, Martin Fowler, Grady Booch, Ivar Jacobson, and Jim Rumbaugh, Peter Coad and Ed Yourdon, Father and Son Royce, Philippe Kruchten, and James Martin, to name just a few. Our model diagram does not break new ground, but it makes explicit and integrates some of the findings and recommendations of other accepted models and standards. Its main goal is to be clear and inclusive of all the major recommendations we seek to impart to our software engineering students in their quest to develop world-class skills and knowledge in this inherently difficult domain.

Figure 1.4 depicts our **Extended Unified Process Model** diagram, which will hereafter serve as your guide through the major disciplines of a software development project. In its context, you will learn Java structure and syntax.

This methodology comprises nine high-level phases, extended from the core concepts of the Unified Process Model,[15] to provide a complete, explicit, student-friendly depiction of the activities and artifacts associated with the life cycle of a software development project. This model and its associated best practices in software development greatly improve a project's outlook for high-quality and timely construction and

---

[15]Implemented by IBM/Rational as the Rational Unified Process™.

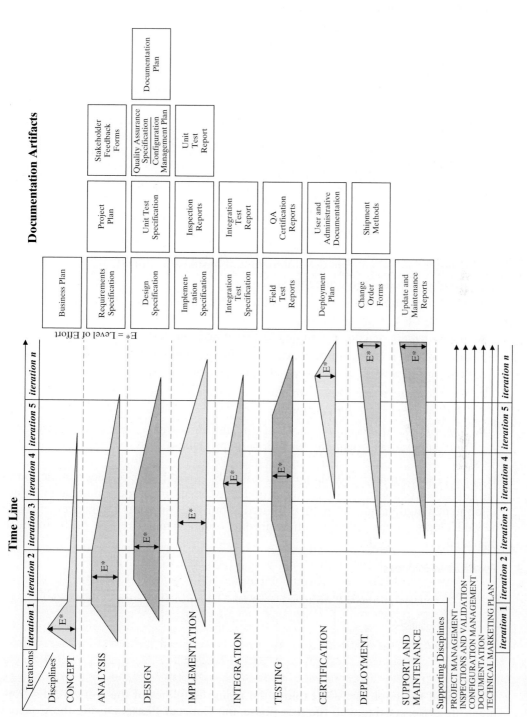

**Documentation Artifacts**

**Time Line**

FIGURE 1.4   Extended Unified Process Model

delivery. Its phases and disciplines lead us through most of this book, one discipline at a time. We examine the process of developing software by mapping our chapters to these major disciplines in the recurring sections called "Position in Process," where we discuss software engineering methodology issues.

At the *macro level*, by necessity, we follow a sequence of phases, but at the *micro level*, we break our development effort into a specific number of iterative subprojects that result in the development of components. This dual view of our project reflects the Unified Process and the reality of short- and long-term planning horizons, which require an overall plan to allocate budgets and project deadlines, and detailed plans for now and the near future to manage specific deliverables while retaining reasonable longer-term flexibility to react to changes in requirements. This duality of planning provides adequate but controlled flexibility in project planning and execution. Figure 1.5 shows an Iteration of the Extended Unified Process.

The disciplines of the **Extended Unified Process Model** will be explained in more detail in the following chapters, but we will provide an overview at this time:

1. *Concept:* initial concept development and business justification.
2. *Analysis:* formal requirements analysis.
3. *Design:* component design, class hierarchy, and creation of a system architecture.
4. *Implementation:* component development and unit test.
5. *Integration:* component integration and integration test.
6. *Testing:* all aspects of testing the developed components.
7. *Certification:* acceptance testing and release certification.
8. *Deployment:* roll-out to customers.
9. *Support and Maintenance:* incident tracking and management; new releases (updates, upgrades)—planning for follow-on product(s).

The last phase, Support and Maintenance, is only entered after project completion in the iterative process. In this phase, the product no longer undergoes significant new development. Ongoing improvement is limited to bug fixes and minor enhancements and new development has shifted to a new product or a new major release of the product, managed as a new cycle.

### 1.5.3 Position in Process

Throughout the book, we will explore the main disciplines of the software development life cycle, starting with the first phase, the **Concept Phase.** During the Concept Phase, the project team concentrates on developing a *Domain Model* and a *Business*

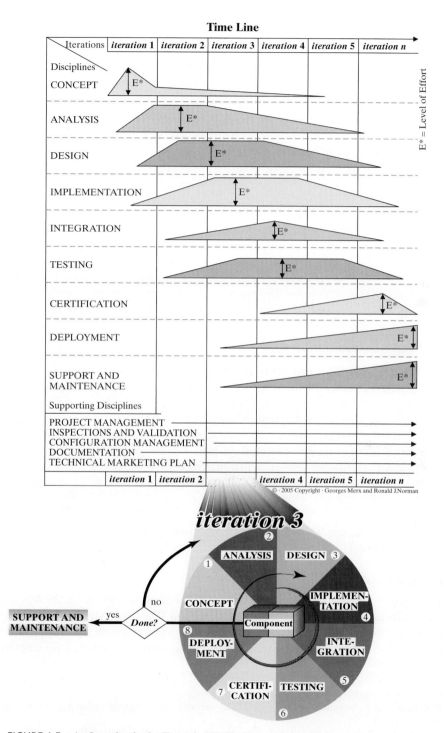

FIGURE 1.5   An Iteration in the Extended Unified Process

*Plan* containing the Business Justification and initial Stakeholder Analysis. During this business analysis phase,[16] we seek to determine the following key information:

- The system vision: a one-or-two sentence high-level strategic description of the project, providing a sense of focus and scope.
- Main business benefits sought (Return on Investment Analysis, Total Cost of Ownership, or similar quantifiable benefit analysis).
- Key stakeholders: all those who are affected by and participate in the project.
- High-level strategic product description.
- Available budget and time frame.
- Organization and management support.
- Marketing plan (target customers, distribution channels, competitive analysis, etc.).
- Risk analysis and management.

---

### PORTFOLIO PROJECT *(see end of chapter)*

We have chosen the following project as the book-spanning portfolio project:

**ModelHomeDesigner™**

The purpose of this project is to help the *HarmonyDesigns®* model home design company efficiently manage its model home design projects. This includes design, material, and vendor selection and management; project planning and deployment; and customer relationship management.

Starting in this chapter and continuing through the rest of the book, we will develop an information technology–based solution for *HarmonyDesigns* to help automate and streamline its work processes and to increase the productivity of its employees, ultimately improving its revenue stream and profitability.

---

The business perspective on the project requirements is best expressed in a **Business Use Case Model**, an organized hierarchy of **Business Use Cases**.

### Business Use Case Model

The Business Use Case Model is a structured representation of the business project and delineates its scope and focus. The Business Use Case Model diagram in UML depicts business actor and the services or functions they request from the business.[17] Each business use case captures an important business process targeted for improvement or automation.

---

[16]"Business" as we use the term encompasses all valuable organizational processes, whether for-profit, non-profit, or public.

[17]Actors are stakeholders who play an active role in the application of the software functionality. Actors do not have to be human; they can also be other systems and components.

**Business Use Cases**

A Business Use Case documents a business process that provides value to project stakeholders; the processes captured are typically those targeted by the project for improvement. These processes are represented as scenarios (primary and secondary) and include functional steps, risk management, interactions with to external resources, and the like.

In use cases, whether business or technical, we describe the key work processes as **scenarios**. We embrace this UML-standard representation as a tool in this book to consistently describe the key workflows associated with each major project requirement and to focus on process rather than function. This is important because the real value in business lies in the work process, not in a particular (software) function or feature.

### 1.5.4   Domain Model

The Domain Model (shown in Figure 1.6) is a high-level, business-centric view of the main conceptual classes that emerge from the Requirements Analysis. Even though use cases are not inherently object-oriented, thinking in terms of conceptual classes early on is helpful in maintaining a streamlined life-cycle view of a software development project, and avoiding an eventual "translation" of concepts from functional to object-oriented.

Figure 1.6 shows how the various early-stage efforts in requirements acquisition and analysis lead to the project Design Model. The Domain Model represents the *decomposition* of the project domain into real-world conceptual classes/objects. The Domain Model is part of the Concept Phase.

### 1.5.5   Scenarios

A **scenario** is a central component of a use case: it provides a systematic description of a workflow. The *story line* of a *theater play* is a good analogy to the software development process, which is why we use terms such as "scenario" and "actor." In this context, we also define the *roles* played by actors participating in the project. The scenarios applicable to the Concept Phase of our model are:

- Developing the system vision from the initial concept.
- Determining key project stakeholders.
- Developing the business case model.
  - Elaborating business use cases.
  - Organizing the business use cases into a hierarchical use case model.
- Summary product or project description.
- Risk analysis.
- Writing the Business Plan.
  - Developing business plan sections, such as a Product Strategy, a Marketing Plan, a Competitive Analysis, a Financial Plan.

---

**Scenario and Other Terms**

Given the abstract nature of software development in general, we use **analogies** and **metaphors** extensively to help practitioners and users more easily understand the capabilities of software and hardware from the vantage point of familiar elements and situations.

---

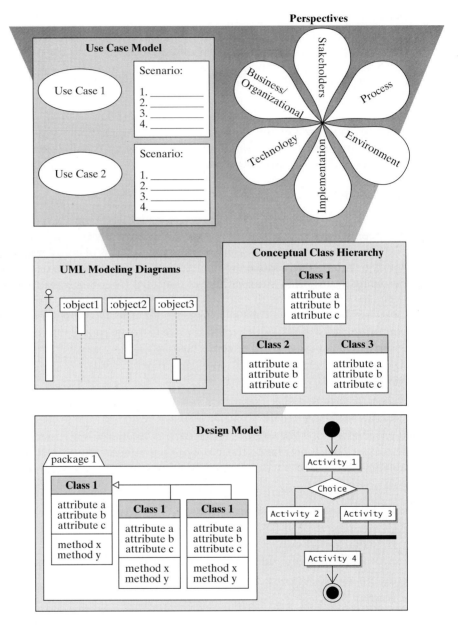

FIGURE 1.6    The Domain Model

Use case scenarios are implemented as *primary* and *secondary scenarios:* the primary scenario (of which there is one per use case) covers the successful progression through the workflow; secondary scenarios deal with alternative paths as well as exceptions, problems, obstacles, and course corrections.

The scenario at this level captures the existing process while highlighting potential problem areas or areas of improvements. It is not intended to capture the proposed solution: this will be done at the design stage.

Next we will examine each one of these plan components in more detail. (An example of each of these elements is provided later in the chapter for **The Voting Program** project.)

### Developing the System Vision

When projects are first conceived, their boundaries are often undefined. The System Vision statement helps focus the reader on the essential project objective and delineates the scope of the project by clearly stating what the project "is about."

### Determining Stakeholders

In order to discover all the requirements (functional and nonfunctional) that define the project, it is essential that all the *stakeholders* influencing the project be known. Stakeholders are those people, individuals and groups, who have a direct or indirect interest in the project, sometimes positive-supportive, sometimes negative-resistant. Stakeholders include the obvious: end-users, system administrators, and managers, but also the less obvious, and often forgotten: developers, employees displaced by the new technology, third-party suppliers, competitors, senior executives, shareholders/investors, customer support specialists, and so on. (Even existing software systems can play the role of stakeholders in the sense that they contribute requirements to the project being defined.)

### Developing the Business Case

The business case justifies investment in the project. If the proposed use of the project is purely internal, this information typically focuses on internal return of investment (ROI); if the product resulting from the project is to be marketed externally, additional market analysis information is needed. In either case, sufficient information for management to make an informed go-ahead decision is needed.

In order to leverage the benefits of our end-to-end development life-cycle process, it is recommended to develop the business case requirements as Business Use Cases and organize them into a hierarchical Business Use Case model, precursors to their technical counterparts, which will be developed in the subsequent stages of the process. The use case format has a number of key benefits:

- Encourages completeness and structure.
- Maps well to subsequent analysis and design activities, including the eventual object-oriented class hierarchy organization central to the project design.
- Is repeatable and reusable.

### Risk Analysis

An important part of the initial decision-making process in a new software development project is the analysis of risk. The purpose of this exercise is not only to identify risks that could impede project progress and success, but also to develop an early plan to address these risks. There are three primary ways of dealing with project risks:

1. *Risk avoidance:* eliminate the risk by not implementing the feature or service that would engender it.
2. *Risk mitigation:* implement an attenuation that will reduce the impact of the risk if it materialized.
3. *Risk replacement:* eliminate the risk by circumventing it with an alternative approach.

For each risk, the project team needs to select a risk-management approach in advance and secure budget and resource commitment for its execution if the risk materializes.

### Writing the Business Plan

In all major phases of the Software Development Methodology, the creation of formal documentation is very important. In this phase, the main tangible outcome, or *artifact,* is the *Business Plan*. This document codifies all the business-related aspects of the project and captures in writing the decisions made in the early phases of the project, as well as their supporting information. It becomes the conceptual foundation for the subsequent work. It also provides a vehicle for organizational and managerial commitment.

The Business Plan itself consists of a number of required sections and more optional information depending on the scope and focus of the project being documented. The required sections are:

1. Project or System Vision
2. Project Description
3. Stakeholder Analysis
4. Customer Profile
5. Market Analysis
6. Risk Analysis
7. Project Description: Business Use Case Model and Business Use Cases
8. Competitive Analysis
9. Distribution: Pricing, Packaging, Promotion, Positioning (Distribution)
10. Financial Plan (Revenue Plan, Budget, Cash Flow Analysis, ROI Analysis)
11. High-Level Project Plan
12. Recommendations

**The Voting Program** example project later in this chapter provides a simple, high-level example of a Business Plan that follows this format. A more detailed discussion of business planning is beyond the scope of this book.

The next section introduces the reader to another key topic and toolset, used to help visualize the main aspects of an object-oriented software engineering project: the Unified Modeling Language.

### 1.5.6   *The Unified Modeling Language*

In order to write high-quality Java programs, the analysis and design process needs to yield an unambiguous, complete design. In the software industry, the Unified Modeling Language (UML)[18] has emerged as the tool of choice for modeling object-oriented software components, packages, and systems. The UML was developed by Rational Software Corporation—now a division of IBM Corporation—and other firms, and has been standardized by the Object Management Group (OMG). In later chapters, we will take a closer look at the various UML diagrams that assist and support us at every stage of the software development process. These diagrams are the precursors to the actual program code, using the Java programming language, tools, and packages. The diagrams represent static and dynamic relationships between project components, actors, and resulting artifacts in sufficient detail that actual code can be derived. This structured visualization approach leads to far more predictable results than relying on unguided "creative" (or haphazard) translation from design to implementation.

## 1.6   The Java Programming Language

Efficient communication between humans and computers is only possible using programmed intermediary translators, given that the two interlocutors speak vastly different "languages." Fundamentally, computers operate based on binary code sequences,[19] whereas humans communicate in a language such as English. Translating from English to zeroes and ones is the job of programming languages like Java.

Because computers need to be explicitly programmed to do anything useful, application software development has been an integral part of the history of computers from its earliest beginnings. Over the years, we have benefited from the development of ever more sophisticated (read *human-friendly*) computer programming tools, culminating in contemporary programming languages like Java.[20] Not only the language syntax, but also its underlying semantic concepts, are more powerful and more accessible than previous software programming languages. This was accomplished by eliminating some esoteric constructs like pointers, replacing the requirement for explicit memory management with automatic "garbage collection," and including the powerful concepts of object orientation as a central theme.

### 1.6.1   *Historical Perspective on Java*

This section takes a brief look at the history of Java, focusing on the important milestones in the development of the language.

James Gosling shown in Figure 1.7 is credited with leading the development of the first version of Java, at the time called "Oak," (after a tree he looked out on from his office window), emerging from the "Green" project at Sun Microsystems Corporation, a study called into existence by the company to examine the next major wave of

---

[18]**http://www.uml.org/**
[19]Zeros and ones.
[20]Developed by Sun Microsystems in Santa Clara, CA.

FIGURE 1.7 James Gosling (© Sun Microsystems)

computing. Java was commercially released in 1995. Details about the early-days evolution of Java can be found in many references on the Web and in other publications.[21]

The more important aspect of Java's history, in the context of this book, is the integration of concepts and technologies developed over the past fifty years, from high-level, structured programming to object orientation, to this still relatively new, state-of-the-art software development language and associated tools and packages. Its extraordinary success almost from the moment of its release is as much the result of the vision of Gosling and his colleagues at Sun as it is the culmination of evolutionary progress in the area of object-oriented software engineering methodology and practice. Java and software engineering methodology are inextricably linked by object-orientation, because the advantages of Java can only be realized effectively through the serious application of object-oriented software engineering principles such as inheritance (e.g., class hierarchy), encapsulation (e.g., public and private modifiers), component reuse (e.g., classes and packages), and polymorphism (e.g., method and type overloading).

---

### SPEAKING OF NEXT LEVEL ...

The OMG has recently released its Model Driven Architecture (MDA) framework specification, which "moves up a level" to concentrate on building models and having code generated from them (see www.omg.org/mda)

The OMG recently merged with the Project Management Institute. This union is likely to lead to other new methodology standards.

---

Java represents a contemporary plateau of programming language development, as proven by the syntactical, structural, and functional similarity of Java with J# and C#, Microsoft's new programming languages for its .NET platform, and even the new version of Microsoft Visual Basic, Visual Basic.NET. *The next generation of general-purpose programming power is yet to be discovered!*

How did all of Java's high-powered usefulness evolve? Its capabilities are not just implemented in its commands; they are intimately connected to the process of software

---

[21]James Gosling's own historical account can be found at http://java.sun.com/people/jag/green/index.html.

engineering and to the representation of workflows and the associated data as classes and objects that follow the principles of component reuse. Because support for object orientation is not optional in Java, as in some other languages, it "forces" the software developer to embrace the prescriptions and advantages of object-oriented software engineering. Over the past decades of software language development, a number of important functions and capabilities have emerged, such as platform independence, extensibility,[22] support for multitasking and distributed computing, especially Web/Internet-based computing, and seamless relational database access. In a more general sense, application components are viewed today ideally as reusable *application services*. Java fully supports this evolution toward advanced, utility-based distributed computing.

### 1.6.2   Java Basics

While the remainder of the book introduces you to the language features of Java in sufficient depth to allow you to regard yourself, by the time you have worked your way through the book and its examples and exercises, as a *Java Software engineering apprentice*, at this point we just want to preview the basic structure and key characteristics of the programming language you are by now hopefully eager to discover.

#### Structure and Basic Syntax Rules

Like all languages, whether for human-to-human or human-machine communication, Java follows a codified, specific syntax and structure: explicit, well-documented rules govern its use. Mastering these rules is not enough to become a proficient Java programmer, but it is an important step in learning how to write useful Java programs. The number and scope of syntax and structure rules are limited, but their combination creates a wide web of flexibility (and, at times, complexity). It is important to understand what syntax is legal and what is not (e.g., results in a compiler error), but it is even more important to clearly understand how to create program logic through the proper sequence and organization of Java statements that reflect project requirements accurately and completely. And finally, the most difficult task is to create programs that not only work as required, but also implement insightful architectural planning, the benefits of object-orientation, appropriate execution and interaction speed, and good user interface design in order to maximize longer-term accessibility, efficiency, reusability, and scalability. In other words, we want to create software in such a way that its components not only meet one-off project requirements, but can also be reused in future similar projects.

But let's start with a simple beginning: *a rudimentary Java program.*

**Step 1: Creating the Program**   Using a text editor or a Java interactive development environment (IDE) like Borland's JBuilder, the open-source Eclipse, or Xinox's JCreator,[23] create a text file named MyFirstProgram with the extension .java.[24]

---

[22]The ability to easily and consistently add new features, supported in Java by the ability to include packages.
[23]It is beyond the scope of this book to provide a tutorial of one or more development tools. It would be difficult to keep this updated, given the frequent new releases provided by tool vendors.
[24]IDEs typically append the .java extension automatically when you save your source file.

Make sure you enter this name exactly, because Java is case-sensitive. Then enter the following text in the editor window:

```java
import javax.swing.JOptionPane;

public class MyFirstProgram {
    public static void main (String args []) {
        JOptionPane.showMessageDialog (null,
        "I am now a Java Software Engineer!",
        "MyFirstProgram", JOptionPane.INFORMATION_MESSAGE);
    }
}
```

**Step 2: Compiling the Program in Order to Create a Runnable Class** Using the Java compiler program javac.exe in the SDK from the DOS command prompt or the compile option in your development tool, create the file MyFirstProgram.class by compiling MyFirstProgram.java. "Compiling" means that the compiler takes your source file and translates the English-like source statements into bytecodes that the Java Virtual Machine program (java.exe on DOS/Windows systems) can interpret into machine codes. The success of this operation depends on error-free source code. When there are syntax errors, no .class file is generated.

**Step 3: Running the Program** Using the java.exe in the SDK (Java SDK or JDK) or the "Run" option in your development tool, execute the bytecode file MyFirstProgram.class:
    For example, at the DOS prompt, type: java MyFirstProgram
    The following dialog window is displayed by the Java Virtual Machine (JVM):

As you can see, writing and compiling simple Java programs require following a specific but simple process. Let's review this procedure:

- Step 1: Create a text file with extension .java that contains the source code.
- Step 2: Compile the source program into a bytecode file with the extension .class that can be executed by the JVM.
- Step 3: Execute the bytecode file using the JVM.

JCreator and other tools are available from a wide range of vendors and with a broad range of capabilities. A screen shot of the JCreator tool is shown in Figure 1.8. The more sophisticated ones, like Borland's Together ControlCenter™ and Together Edition™ for Eclipse, provide UML and Java tool integration and "round-trip" engineering capabilities.

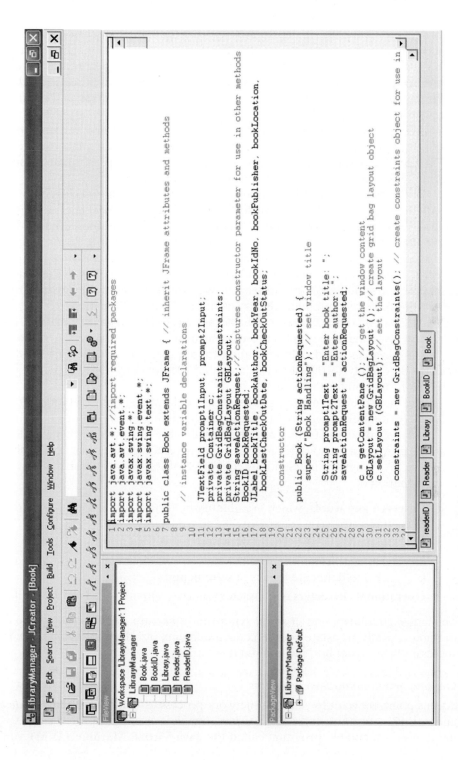

```
1  import java.awt.*; //import required packages
2  import java.awt.event.*;
3  import javax.swing.*;
4  import javax.swing.event.*;
5  import javax.swing.text.*;
6
7  public class Book extends JFrame { // inherit JFrame attributes and methods
8
9      // instance variable declarations
10
11     JTextField prompt1Input, prompt2Input;
12     private Container c;
13     private GridBagConstraints constraints;
14     private GridBagLayout GBLayout;
15     String saveActionRequest;// captures constructor parameter for use in other methods
16     BookID bookRequested;
17     JLabel bookTitle, bookAuthor, bookYear, bookIdNo, bookPublisher, bookLocation,
18             bookLastCheckOutDate, bookCheckOutStatus;
19
20     // constructor
21
22     public Book (String actionRequested) {
23         super ('Book Handling"); // set window title
24
25         String prompt1Text = "Enter book title: ";
26         String prompt2Text = "Enter author: ";
27         saveActionRequest = actionRequested;
28
29         c = getContentPane (); // get the window content
30         GBLayout = new GridBagLayout (); // create grid bag layout object
31         c.setLayout (GBLayout); // set the layout
32
33         constraints = new GridBagConstraints(); // create constraints object for use in
34
```

readerID    Reader    Libary    BookID    Book

FIGURE 1.8    Screen Shot of JCreator by Xinox Software

The problem with simple examples is that they don't show you much about the structure of a Java program. Figure 1.9 therefore illustrates the "generic" structure of a Java source code program. The Name program (class) shown here has no functional statements (yet); it only shows the nesting of variables and statements in methods (procedures), the nesting of methods and instance variables in classes, and the integration of classes in packages.

Figure 1.9 shows an overview of the main structural and syntax elements of a very simple Java program (skeleton) called Voting, leaving out the more complex aspects, which we will cover in later chapters. As you can see, the basic structure is simple and logical. Let's examine this skeleton example in more detail:

The package keyword identifies the package to which this class belongs (if not specified, the classes in the current folder form the default package). In this case, the software application is composed of one or more classes assembled into the package VotingProgram.

The class defined here is the Voting class. Classes are templates for objects. An object of class Voting, called VotingInstance, is declared below in the main method (using the new statement). It is initialized (prepared for use) in the Voting() constructor method, invoked automatically as a result of the object creation.

At least one of the classes in the package has to have a main() method, if the program runs as a stand-alone application (instead of an applet, which runs in a Web browser).

The variables listed right after the class statement are called *instance variables*, because they apply to the object instantiated (derived) from the class. They hold attribute information for the object.

The setValue() method shows an example of a simple method that returns a value anIntNumber of type int (integer) to the calling method (not shown here).

Later chapters will further elaborate on all these functions and capabilities, but this example provides a first overview of the structure of a typical simple Java application.

The Java language is essentially composed of statements consisting of a sequence or combination of:

- **Reserved key words**, which are identifying terms with a special meaning for the Java interpreter.
- **Variable names** created by the programmer to hold information.
- **Structural characters** like semicolons (";") to delineate statements and braces ("{" - "}") to delineate blocks of statements.
- **Operational characters** or character pairs to compare values or to calculate them.

The language follows a strict set of syntax and structure rules that allow the compiler to unequivocally translate source code statements into bytecodes that the JVM can successfully interpret into meaningful functionality.

### Creating and Running Java Programs

At this point, we want to examine the work process associated with Java *code creation* and *execution*, or more correctly, *interpretation*. Java is an interpreted language, meaning that an executable program, called the **Java Virtual Machine (JVM)**, runs *in the*

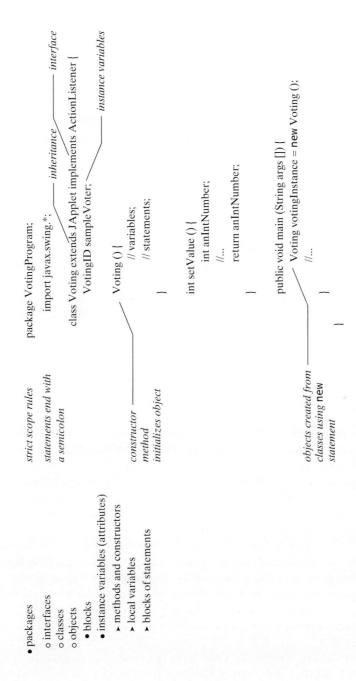

- packages
  - interfaces
  - classes
  - objects
    - blocks
    - instance variables (attributes)
      - methods and constructors
      - local variables
      - blocks of statements

```
package VotingProgram;                                    strict scope rules
import javax.swing.*;              ——— inheritance        statements end with
                                                          a semicolon
class Voting extends JApplet implements ActionListener {  ——— interface
    VotingID sampleVoter;          ——— instance variables

    Voting () {                                           constructor
        // variables;                                     method
        // statements;                                    initializes object
    }

    int setValue () {
        int anIntNumber;
        //...
        return anIntNumber;
    }

    public void main (String args []) {                   objects created from
        Voting votingInstance = new Voting ();            classes using new
        //...                                             statement
    }
}
```

FIGURE 1.9   Java Program Structure

*background* when you execute a Java program and actually interprets (translates) the Java code commands (called **bytecodes**) into computer-readable form.

Figure 1.10 (© Sun Microsystems) shows the components that make up the Java Software Development Kit (SDK or JDK), Standard Edition, Version 1.5 (renamed 5.0).

A number of helper programs are required to develop Java programs. These are available from Sun Microsystems as part of the Java Software Development Kit (SDK). There are multiple kits available, depending on the type of application being developed. Three major categories are: J2SE™ for the development of standard (stand-alone client) applications and applets; J2EE™ for the development of enterprise (server) applications; and J2ME™ for the development of mobile applications. Other special-purpose tools are available for the development of real-time, embedded, JavaCard™ applications.

In addition, most developers use a third-party Integrated Development Environment (IDE), which provides them with a user-friendly environment for code design, development, compilation, testing, debugging, and correction. As we mentioned earlier, Borland's JBuilder, the Eclipse Foundation's Eclipse SDK, and Xinox's JCreator are among the more popular ones.

Figure 1.11 shows the steps that Java source code transverses from its *creation* by a programmer as a text file to its *execution* (well, actually, *interpretation*) on a specific computer system. As we discussed earlier, Java source code (a file with `.java` extension) is compiled into a file of bytecodes (a file with `.class` extension). These bytecodes are interpreted by the Java Virtual Machine (JVM) native to the underlying operating system (there is a JVM available for most important commercial computer systems) and converted to machine-code instructions understandable by the underlying processor.

## 1.7   Relationships

In this recurring section, we help you discover obvious and not-so-obvious relationships between the material covered here and other topics, ideas, systems, technologies, people, and places. As we examine Java software development from the perspective of software engineering, we have established such a relationship between *software application programming* and the discipline of *engineering*. More generically, there is an interdependence in computing between software, hardware, and networking, and between application programs and system software programs.

Other relationships exist between the various disciplines that constitute a successful software project, including *functional* processes (e.g., "writing code") and *nonfunctional* processes (e.g., "managing the project"). There is also a relationship between the end-users and the specialists in an organization who deal with information technology, including administrators and application developers.

These relationships are important because they represent the *processes*, not just the *functions* of a system. It is in the processes that productivity improvements are inherent, where the application of IT can have the most impact. Our challenge as software engineers is to capture and analyze the important work processes and to then develop software that improves these workflows in terms of speed, accuracy, resources needed, quality of output, repeatability, and other benefits.

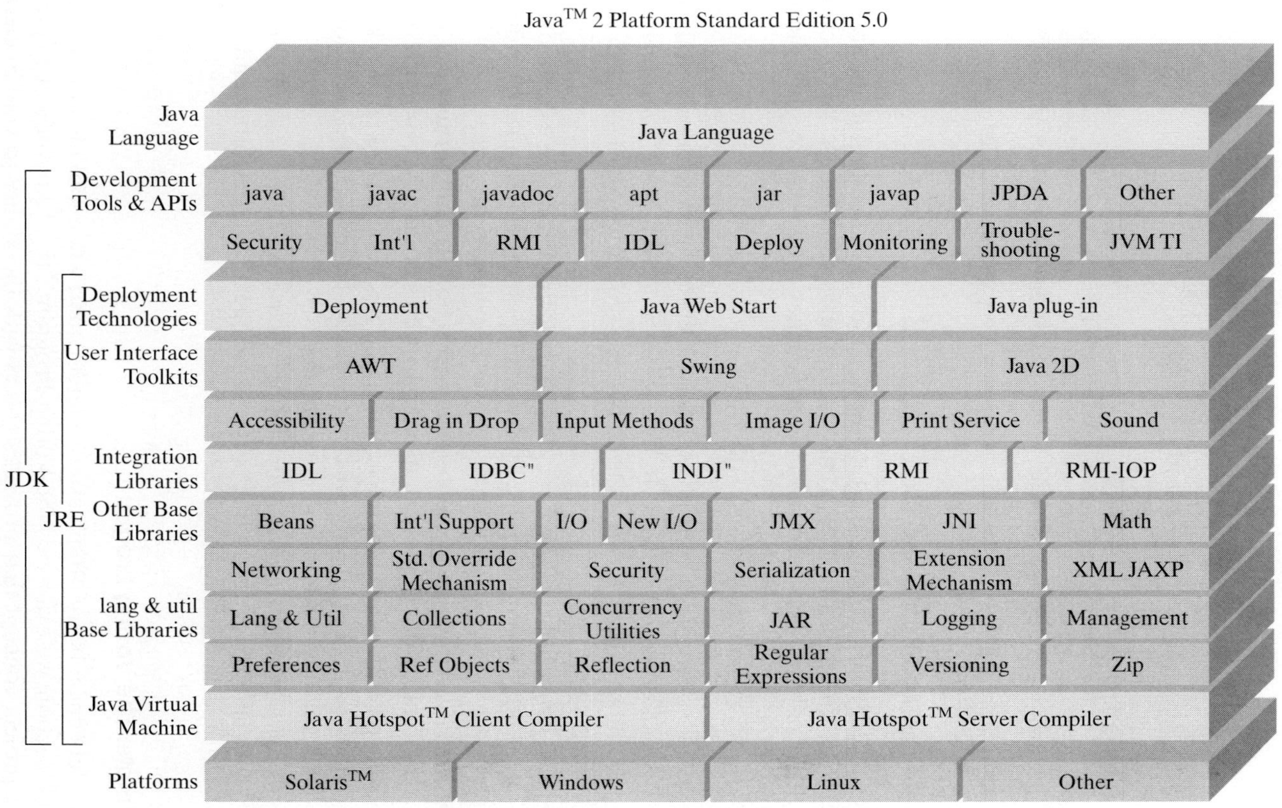

Java™ 2 Platform Standard Edition 5.0

| | | | | | | | |
|---|---|---|---|---|---|---|---|
| **Java Language** | | | | | | | |
| Java Language | | | | | | | |

**Development Tools & APIs**

| java | javac | javadoc | apt | jar | javap | JPDA | Other |
|---|---|---|---|---|---|---|---|
| Security | Int'l | RMI | IDL | Deploy | Monitoring | Trouble-shooting | JVM TI |

**Deployment Technologies**

| Deployment | Java Web Start | Java plug-in |
|---|---|---|

**User Interface Toolkits**

| AWT | Swing | Java 2D |
|---|---|---|
| Accessibility | Drag in Drop | Input Methods | Image I/O | Print Service | Sound |

**Integration Libraries**

| IDL | JDBC" | JNDI" | RMI | RMI-IOP |
|---|---|---|---|---|

**Other Base Libraries**

| Beans | Int'l Support | I/O | New I/O | JMX | JNI | Math |
|---|---|---|---|---|---|---|
| Networking | Std. Override Mechanism | Security | Serialization | Extension Mechanism | XML JAXP |

**lang & util Base Libraries**

| Lang & Util | Collections | Concurrency Utilities | JAR | Logging | Management |
|---|---|---|---|---|---|
| Preferences | Ref Objects | Reflection | Regular Expressions | Versioning | Zip |

**Java Virtual Machine**

| Java Hotspot™ Client Compiler | Java Hotspot™ Server Compiler |
|---|---|

**Platforms**

| Solaris™ | Windows | Linux | Other |
|---|---|---|---|

JDK
JRE

FIGURE 1.10  Sun Microsystems Diagram of the Java SDK[25]

[25]From www.java.sun.com

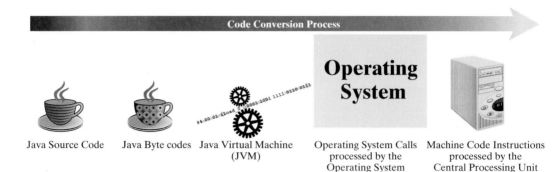

FIGURE 1.11 Transformation of Human-Readable Java Source Code into Machine Code

### 1.7.1 Caveats and Complexities

This subsection describes areas that may require special attention or are especially obtuse or confusing, at least to some readers and practitioners. We also include topics which are potentially controversial or which may require more study outside the scope of this book.

In this chapter, we identify the following areas:

- *Object-oriented life-cycle perspective*—discussed in more detail throughout the book.
- *Translating requirements into scenarios and from there into functions*—arguably the most difficult aspect of software engineering—discussed in more detail in Chapter 3.
- *The nine phases of the Extended Unified Process Model*—these disciplines reappear throughout the book; they warrant your detailed understanding and knowledge as a guide to consistent software development.
- *Effective risk management*—remember that it is important not to just identify risks, but to develop alternative approaches in case they materialize.
- *Project management*—one of the underlying (nonfunctional) workflows that provides control at macro- and micro-levels of project and iterations in terms of time, money, resources, and exceptions.
- *Nonfunctional requirements*—often overlooked, the requirements associated with underlying issues like performance, aesthetics, usability, and availability warrant special attention

## 1.8 Example: The Voting Program

Abstract concepts are often easier to understand when looking at a concrete example. In this section, we examine "the Voting Program," the case study of a (prototype) software project concept that provides voters with the ability to vote in elections using a simple computer-based interface (electronic voting or "e-voting").

What information do we have at this starting point in the project life cycle? Only a very brief description of a future project!

This is often how projects get started. Someone somewhere comes up with an idea—in this case developing software for computer-based voting—and has the power to take it the next level of interest within an organization. The next step is to figure out whether the budding project is worth pursuing. This is usually an informal process involving discussion, persuasion, established relationships, and hope.

Once a preliminary, "back-of-the-napkin," decision is made to investigate the concept further, we embark on the development of the business case and the writing of the Business Plan.[26]

We suggest that the Business Plan contain at least the following sections:

1. Project or System Vision
2. Project Description
3. Stakeholder Analysis
4. Customer Profile
5. Market Analysis
6. Risk Analysis
7. Business Use Case Model and Business Use Cases
8. Competitive Analysis
9. Distribution Plan (Pricing, Packaging, Promotion, Positioning)
10. Financial Plan (Revenue Plan, Budget, Cash Flow Analysis, ROI Analysis)
11. High-Level Project Plan
12. Recommendations

Next, we examine each of these sections from an overview perspective.

### 1.8.1   Project (System) Vision

The very first element of the Business Plan is the Project (or System) Vision. This statement helps define and delineate the scope of the proposed project:

> *The Voting Program allows voters to cast their ballots via computer, using a user-friendly, accessible software program.*

### 1.8.2   Project Description

The project description provides a paragraph of focused statements about the proposed project in terms of its goals and value.

> This program's purpose is to make voting more accessible to the general public, given the rapid proliferation of PCs around the United States. From the comfort of their home, using the familiar Microsoft® Windows™ interface, voters can securely access ballots and vote for their chosen representative or proposition.

---

[26]This also applies, with some modifications, to projects developed for non-profit or public organizations.

### 1.8.3    Stakeholder Analysis

Now that we have a vision and description that will guide our efforts, we need to figure out who the stakeholders for this project are. Stakeholders are all the people directly or indirectly affected by our project and the implementation of our future IT solution.

> A general-purpose voting program has numerous stakeholders, individuals and groups, from voters to politicians to special-interest groups. This analysis may lead us to an early, iterative redefinition of our vision, because we may find that we have to limit the scope of our initial effort to an achievable level. So, instead of listing too many stakeholders and immediately feeling overwhelmed, we redefine our vision as follows:
>
> The initial prototype release of The Voting Program allows the voters of a single district to cast their ballots for one single-candidate election (for example, an election for mayor). (Note that no consideration is given to how to get the voting data off multiple computers for tabulation; the assumption is therefore that for prototype purposes, all the voting will take place on this single computer.)
>
> Now we can envision a reasonably short list of stakeholders:
>
> - Voters in one district (limits the scalability requirements for the program)
> - Election officials
> - Politicians (mayoral candidates)
> - Press
> - Designers and programmers, customer support
> - Funding source (private individual or group, or public agency)
> - Current providers of election materials, equipment, and so on.

### 1.8.4    Customer Profile

Based on this list, our next step is to develop the customer profile.

In our case, where we will develop this product for use by voters, we will assume that our customer is a public agency and that this agency has agreed to fund the project; we will therefore define the profile of the primary users instead:

> Adult eighteen years old or older, registered to vote, with access to a computer with the voting program loaded. The user's skills level will vary from "novice" to "experienced."

### 1.8.5    Market Analysis

Market analysis provides input based on market research about the project's business environment, including issues of positioning (product characterization), promotion (advertising, naming, etc.), pricing, and packaging/placement (distribution channels).

The market research may consist of user surveys, focus groups, online and publication research, competitive analysis studies, and interviews with industry experts and pundits.

Market analysis provides an important source of project requirements as it studies competitors and determines how to create a product that can be sold profitably.

> For the purpose of this example project, we will perform only a limited market analysis by examining some known competing products. In general, we note that this

application can serve a variety of public-service markets, national and international, and that it should be developed to be extensible and support internationalization.

### 1.8.6   Risk Analysis

The risk analysis section covers potential risks and obstacles and documents planned efforts to address these risks, should they arise.

> In developing a system for such potentially widespread use, there are a substantial number of risks. Table 1.1 lists a sampling of them here, limited by the scope of this book example. A real-world project would greatly expand this section.

### 1.8.7   Business Use Case Model and Use Cases

The Business Use Case section consists of business use cases organized into a Business Use Case Model. This formalized approach allows us to follow a coherent, consistent development process from *concept* to *deployment:* the Business Use Cases will translate into technical use cases, which in turn will be the source for classes, interfaces, components, packages, and subsystems. All along this development path, we can go back and validate the component functionality against the business and technical requirements captured in the use cases.

> The Use Case Model for the Voting Program is shown in Figure 1.12. This model and the business use cases are defined in the subsequent sections. They will be expanded into technical use cases in the next chapter.
>
> *The use case model in Figure 1.12 shows the establishment of six business use cases to represent* The Voting Program:
>
> - *Authentication*
> - *Voter Registration*
> - *Ballot Management*
> - *Voting Process*
> - *System Administration*

TABLE 1.1   Risk Management for the Voting Program

| Risk | Risk Management |
| --- | --- |
| Data integrity | Use secure transaction-processing data management to ensure data integrity at all points of the process |
| | Establish safe data-backup procedures (onsite, offsite storage) |
| Functional integrity | Use a mission-critical-validated inspection process |
| | Perform extensive testing at all levels |
| | Roll out in controlled environment with parallel operation for beta testing |
| Budget, resources | Use object-oriented methodology with careful macro/micro-level planning and iterative development |
| User acceptance | Validate ease of use with focus groups |
| Security | Use authentication and transmission security measures (encryption) |

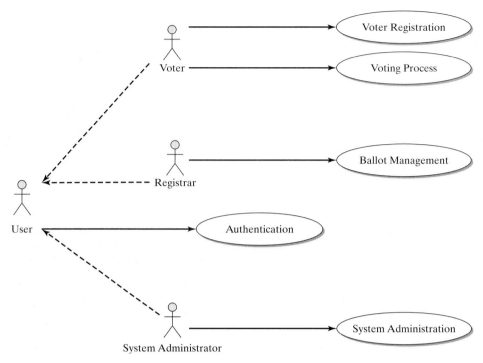

**FIGURE 1.12** Business Use Case Model

### *Business Use Case 1: Voter Authentication*

| | |
|---|---|
| Name: | Voter Authentication |
| Description: | Allowing voters to log in using an identifier and password while ensuring access only by validated voters. Ensuring that voters cannot vote more than once, but that they can change their vote within a certain period of time. |
| Actor(s): | End-user: voter |
| Pre-Conditions: | • The voter must have an identifier and password, possibly provided by mail<br>• The computer must be on, connected to the Internet and a Web browser (program) active |
| Primary Scenario: | 1. Run "The Voting Program"<br>2. At log-on screen or prompt, log-on with id and password<br>3. Validate authentication accepted |
| Secondary Scenarios: | A. Wrong id<br>  - provide message, allow retry (limit retries?)<br>B. Wrong password<br>  - provide message, allow retry (limit retries?)<br>C. Internal, system, or network error<br>  - provide message, exit, notify provider<br>  - reset database to last committed transaction |
| Post-Conditions: | • Arrive on main section screen<br>• Provide way to exit or continue |

## Business Use Case 2: Voter Registration

| | |
|---|---|
| Name: | Voter Registration |
| Description: | Accepting new voters into the system. Updating existing voter information. Deleting voters who pass away or move away. |
| Actor(s): | Registrar—election official |
| Pre-Conditions: | • Administration must be strictly access controlled |
| | • Only operators permitted to manipulate voter database may have access |
| | • This case assumes that an authorized user has been authenticated |
| Primary Scenario: | 1. Select add, change, or delete |
| | 2. Enter information in appropriate fields |
| | 3. Validate, confirm, and save changes |
| Secondary Scenarios: | A. Wrong or incomplete entries<br> - provide message, allow retry (limit retries?) |
| | B. Duplicate record<br> - provide message, force resolution (?) |
| | C. Internal, system, or network error<br> - provide message, exit, notify provider<br> - reset database to last committed transaction |
| Post-Conditions: | • Return to main section screen |
| | • Provide way to exit or continue |

## Business Use Case 3: Ballot Management

| | |
|---|---|
| Name: | Ballot Management |
| Description: | Administrative function to seed the program with the appropriate data for a particular election. This includes the ballot itself and the management of the information associated with ballots and votes collected. Also includes the calculation and display of results. |
| Actor(s): | Registrar—election official |
| Pre-Conditions: | • Administration must be strictly access controlled |
| | • Only operators permitted to create or change a ballot or to collect voting information may have access |
| | • This case assumes that an authorized user has been authenticated |
| Primary Scenario: | 1. Enter Voting Program Administration Functions |
| | 2. a. Create ballot, using input form<br>   b. Modify ballot, using modify form<br>   c. Manage vote tallying and results presentation |
| | 3. Provide option to make changes |
| | 4. Save ballot |
| Secondary Scenarios: | A. Incomplete ballot<br> - save, but mark 'incomplete' – do not allow use |
| | B. Cannot find previously edited ballot<br> - provide message, allow retry |
| | C. Internal, system, or network error<br> - provide message, exit, notify provider<br> - reset database to last committed transaction |
| Post-Conditions: | • Provide way to exit or continue |

### Business Use Case 4: Voting Process

| | |
|---|---|
| Name: | Voting Process |
| Description: | Allowing voters to complete and submit their ballot. |
| Actor(s): | End-user—voter |
| Pre-Conditions: | • The voter must be logged in and authenticated |
| Primary Scenario: | 1. If more than one active ballot, select appropriate ballot |
| | 2. Select candidates/propositions to vote for and select desired button |
| | 3. Complete, submit, provide confirmation, and exit |
| Secondary Scenarios: | A. No ballot<br>  - provide message and exit<br>B. No confirmation or internal, system, or network error<br>  - provide message, exit, notify provider<br>  - reset database to last committed transaction |
| Post-Conditions: | • Return to main menu, allow user to change ballot and resubmit |
| | • Provide way to exit or continue |

### Business Use Case 5: System Administration

| | |
|---|---|
| Name: | System Administration |
| Description: | This use case covers the installation program used to first install and then upgrade the program when new versions are available. Given that the program is Web-based, this only affects the server-based components. |
| Actor(s) | System administrator |
| Pre-Conditions | The installer must have system privileges to install this program. |
| Primary Scenario | 1. Install or upgrade program, using platform-standard installation procedures |
| | 2. Automatic or manual migration of existing data, if needed |
| | 3. Validate security on system to ensure no illegitimate access to any functions |
| Secondary Scenarios | Inability to install, internal, system, or network error |
| | • provide message, exit, notify provider |
| | • reset database, if necessary |
| Post-Conditions | System ready to use, existing data accessible |

## 1.8.8    Competitive Analysis

The competitive analysis section examines existing products, providers, market shares, and other aspects of competition.

*Especially after the Florida debacle in the 2000 presidential election, a number of existing and new companies embarked on the development of computer-based voting programs.*

*Table 1.2 takes a look at some of the competing companies and their products.*[27][28]

---

[27] A genuine competitive analysis would include more extensive information in the areas of pricing, positioning, market share, etc.

[28] From http://www.cs.uiowa.edu/~jones/voting/

TABLE 1.2    Voting Program Competitive Analysis

| Company | Product | Features/Functions (from product Web sites)* | Comparison to the Voting Program |
|---|---|---|---|
| Danaher Controls (Guardian Voting Systems) **http:// www.controls online.com/gvs/vs. html** | **ELECTronic 1242® Voting System** | In setup and ballot preparation, a single Windows 9x/NT database produces all of your election materials, programs machines and prints ballots—eliminating human errors in design, spelling, and typography. | • Appears to be stand-alone system<br>• No Web support |
| | | In the voting process, six redundant memory tables ensure accuracy and security. Each machine continuously monitors its own operation through a self-diagnostic routine performed instantly after each ballot is cast. | |
| | | In tabulating and reporting, vote tallies are completed with the speed and convenience of a PC. Multiple fail-safe audit trails include machine-tables, paper tapes, and final cartridge results. | |
| Diversified Dynamics Inc **http:// www.divdyn.com/** | **System 5 DVRS** | Diversified Dynamics' DVRM is a stand-alone paperless electronic voting machine. It is designed to be completely portable, easy to use, secure, and field-upgradeable. The machines have dual power capability, running on either standard A/C power or D-cell batteries. Weighing only 8 pounds, the DVRM is transportable by just about anybody. It is rugged yet stylishly designed and fits snugly in a handsome briefcase style carrier. | • Appears to be stand-alone system<br>• No Web support |
| | | A single DVRM can store up to 4,000 different ballots with immediate accessibility via a coded smart card. The same ballot can be stored in multiple formats and in various languages and/or visually impaired versions. Ballots from different locations can be stored on a single machine, allowing the vote to be carried to the people—at work, the hospital, nursing home or anywhere where people are immobilized. | |
| | | The DVRM is capable of holding 12,000 individual votes (voted ballots). In cases where more than 12,000 votes are cast on an individual machine, poll workers simply off-load the first 12,000 votes onto a high-capacity smart card and the DVRM is ready to go for another 12,000 votes. This off-loading process takes less than 30 seconds. | |
| Election Systems and Software **www.essvote.com** | **iVotronic** | The proven, patented iVotronic TM Touch Screen voting solution puts leading-edge election technology at the voters' fingertips. Weighing only 9.75 pounds and approximately one foot square in size, the ES&S iVotronic is portable, wireless, and ADA compliant. Its Audio | • Appears to be stand-alone system<br>• No Web support<br>• Seems to focus on impaired voters |

*(Continued)*

TABLE 1.2 (*Continued*)

| Company | Product | Features/Functions (from product Websites)* | Comparison to the Voting Program |
|---|---|---|---|
| | | Ballot feature easily supports voters who are visually impaired, and its portability enables curbside and wheelchair-access voting. | |
| | | Voter intent and ballot correctness are guaranteed prior to ballot casting. Over-votes cannot be accepted by the iVotronic, and the voter is privately alerted to any under-votes during the final ballot-review process. The privacy of all voters—including those visually impaired—is maintained with the iVotronic. Only the voter is informed of the over-vote/under-vote situations, and the involvement of poll officials is not required to replace or correct the ballot. | |
| | | The iVotronic's three independent but redundant memory paths ensure that no votes will ever be lost or altered. Prior to poll opening, one accumulated "zero tape" validates that no votes have been entered into any voter terminal. The precinct level accumulated totals tape provides a double check through verifiable printed documentation of precinct level election results. Also, if an election is ever contested, iVotronic's unique, patented recount system allows replication of the entire election process, including production of all ballot images for re-verification. | |
| | | Each iVotronic unit is, in effect, its own self-contained election system. Thus, any election day malfunction in a single voter terminal has no effect whatsoever on the operation of any other voter terminal in the precinct. | |
| Global Election Systems Inc (Diebold) **www.diebold.com/ solutions/election/ default.htm** | **Diebold Election Systems** | The AccuVote-TS system's integrated components are: The AccuVote-TS Ballot Station: The tabulator is a multifunctional interface that counts and tabulates the ballots at precincts on election day and communicates with the host computer at Election Central for accurate and timely jurisdiction-wide results. | • Appears to be stand-alone system • No Web support |
| | | The Application Software (Global Election Management System or GEMS): GEMS is a powerful multi-user Windows® NT/2000–based software that concurrently and automatically generates: • Appropriate ballot styles for each precinct • Postscript ballot files for postal ballots • Precinct-specific media for tabulation • Vote tally files | |

(*Continued*)

TABLE 1.2   (*Continued*)

| Company | Product | Features/Functions (from product Websites)* | Comparison to the Voting Program |
|---------|---------|----------------------------------------------|----------------------------------|
| | | The Host Computer: The PC-based computer system configured to perform all of the necessary integrated functions of the application software. | |
| Hart InterCivic **www.hartic.com/ solutions/eslate. html** | **eSlate 3000 Judge's Booth Controller™ (JBC 1000)** | The eSlate 3000 has a flexible ballot presentation, durable polycarbonate screen, integrated selector, and is secure and affordable. eSlate's JBC 1000s manage the election process in the precinct. The JBC 1000 issues an access code and manages modem transmission to election central headquarters. The JBC 1000 controls up to twelve eSlate 3000s and enables the election judge to know which booths are in use at any given time. | • Appears to be stand-alone system • No Web support |
| Microvote **www. microvote.com** | **The Infinity Voting Panel MV-464 Voting Machine Internet Ballot Previewing** | Has an Internet-based ballot preview-only system Its other system are stand-alone electronic voting machines | • Appears to be stand-alone system • Web support limited to ballot previewing |
| Safevote **www.safevote.com** | **Delta Delta-Net Remote Voting** | Delta is a software-DRE that can be used as a stand-alone electronic voting machine. Delta includes the Witness-Voting system, which, without paper and paper costs, is able to prove that every vote counts by verifying whether what the voter sees and confirms on the screen is what is actually recorded and counted. However, paper ballot printouts may be added if desired. Delta-Net: networked DREs, for precinct-based Internet or dial-up voting. Remote Voting: Internet and/or dial-up voting systems. | Only vague information available— no comparison possible |
| Sequoia Voting Systems **www. sequoiavote.com** | **AVC Advantage AVC Edge Optech Eagle Optech 400C Integrity TeamWork EDS WinEDS** | AVC Advantage® (direct record electronic full face ballot voting system). AVC Edge® (direct record electronic touch screen voting system). Optech Eagle® (Optical Scan Precinct Count Voting System) Optech 400C® (Optical Scan Central Count Voting System) Integrity (voter registration and election management system). | • Appears to be stand-alone system • No Web support |

(*Continued*)

TABLE 1.2   (*Continued*)

| Company | Product | Features/Functions (from product Websites)* | Comparison to the Voting Program |
|---|---|---|---|
| | | TeamWork (PC based software package capable of reading DataVote® cards, punch cards, and optical scan ballots). | |
| | | SignaScan (signature verification technology). | |
| | | EDS (election database system). | |
| | | WinEDS (Windows election database system). | |
| TrueBallot **www. trueballot.com/ WebVOTE.htm** | **WebVote** | WebVote®, is TrueBallot's vision of how an on-line Voting system should work. An On Line voting system is only as good as the model on which it is based. TrueBallot designed WebVote® based on its knowledge and experience gained in administering ballots for organized labor and associations. The Internet is another election medium. Whether it is the best one depends on the circumstances. TrueBallot's experience in election administration along with its understanding of election media has led to a flexible, secure, and cost-effective approach for the integration of the Internet into the election process. TrueBallot can provide an entirely new way to participate in the voting process that can be used independently or to supplement and enhance a ScanVote® paper ballot or TeleVote® to ensure security, accuracy and efficiency. With a database of eligible voters, TrueBallot can present variable ballots to different segments of the voter base. Each voter sees only those issues (e.g., national, regional or local) on which he or she is entitled to vote. Depending on the needs of the organization, the same issues may appear on each ballot, but do not necessarily have to WebVote® can be used in combination with any or all of TrueBallot's other systems. The TrueBallot database allows for a multilevel security system to make sure that only eligible voters are permitted to vote and vote only once. Tabulation is virtually instantaneous and reporting is unlimitedTrueBallot ensures the accuracy, safety, reliability and confidentiality of organizational voting. TrueBallot offers an integrated approach to voting, by offering a combination of traditional and electronic balloting methods. | • Close competitor |
| VoteHere.net **www.votehere.net** | **VoteHere Gold** | • Secure one-time voter access using VoteHere or custom PIN codes | • Close competitor |

(*Continued*)

TABLE 1.2   (*Continued*)

| Company | Product | Features/Functions (from product Websites)* | Comparison to the Voting Program |
|---------|---------|---------------------------------------------|----------------------------------|
|         |         | • Customized ballot support for graphics, biographies, photographs, Web links and organization logos<br>• Support for write-in candidates<br>• Support for multiple ballot styles<br>• Support for multiple precincts<br>• Support for alternate languages<br>• Real-time monitoring of voter turnout and election statistics<br>• Support for alternate authentication methods<br>• Election audit trail produced at the close of each election<br>• Secure communication over the Internet using SSL | |

*All copyrights are those of their respective owners—the products and companies featured here are shown for example purposes only

### 1.8.9   Distribution Plan

In this section, the Business Plan previews potential product distribution strategies. The four areas typically addressed at this point in the discipline of product marketing are: Pricing, Packaging, Promotion, and Positioning (often referred to as the "Four P's"). *Pricing* addresses product pricing and requires an understanding of the competitive position of the product and the pricing of competing products, as well as the perceived value of the project in development. *Packaging* addresses how the product is presented to customers: examples would be boxed for retail sale, available on the Internet from download sites, and so on. *Promotion* addresses plans for advertising, public relations, marketing alliances, special introductory pricing, and so on. Finally, *Positioning* complements Packaging in terms of the actual presentation of the product, that is, where specifically the product will be offered for sale, and in relation to what products it will be placed. This also includes a decision on distribution channels, such as direct sales via retail or wholesale channels; or indirect sales through third-party vendors, or via alliance agreements (code licensing).

These considerations taken together allow for a thorough analysis of distribution issues and the creation of a viable product distribution plan.

> The Voting Program will be marketed to agencies, public and private, which conduct elections. Software is typically distributed as a **license to use**, not by actually selling the product itself. In this case, election agencies will acquire a general-use license for the product, the size and price of which will depend on the size of the electorate for that agency. Specific pricing will be based on the competitive analysis mentioned earlier. The physical distribution of the product will likely occur on password-protected CD-ROMs with upgrades and updates available over an authentication-protected Web site. Appropriate installation programs for the various supported system platforms and operating systems will be included.

## 1.8.10  Financial Plan

The Financial Plan section in the Business Plan includes the following subsections:

- **Revenue Plan:** two- to five-year revenue plan includes product sales per product line and per market (direct and indirect channels).
- **Budget:** amount of money needed over time to finance operations, technology acquisitions, marketing and sales, etc.
- **Cash Flow Analysis:** amount of funds available in various forms at any point in time.
- **ROI Analysis:** Return-On-Investment Analysis provides a preview of the profitability of investment capital over time and is directly linked to the "Exit-Strategy" pursued by the company.
- The revenue plan is a critical contributor to the decision-making process, because it allows those who provide funding to the development team to ascertain the key aspects of the financial viability of the project and the likely return on their investment.

It is beyond the scope of this example to provide a detailed financial plan at this point. A summary sample plan (start-up operations) is shown in Table 1.3.

TABLE 1.3   Voting Program Financial Analysis

| Revenue Projection | 2005 | 2006 | 2007 | 2008 | Three-Year Totals |
|---|---|---|---|---|---|
| Small licenses (25 seats) | | $ 20,000.00 | $ 40,000.00 | $ 60,000.00 | $ 120,000.00 |
| Large licenses (100 seats) | | $       - | $ 80,000.00 | $ 240,000.00 | $ 320,000.00 |
| *Total license revenue* | | $ 20,000.00 | $ 120,000.00 | $ 300,000.00 | $ 440,000.00 |
| Service revenue | | $   3,000.00 | $ 18,000.00 | $ 45,000.00 | $ 66,000.00 |
| **Total Revenue** | | $ 23,000.00 | $ 138,000.00 | $ 345,000.00 | $ 506,000.00 |
| | | | | | |
| **Expenses** | | | | | |
| Management | $ 15,000.00 | $ 30,000.00 | $ 30,000.00 | $ 45,000.00 | $ 120,000.00 |
| Engineering | $ 30,000.00 | $ 30,000.00 | $ 30,000.00 | | $ 90,000.00 |
| Support | | $ 10,000.00 | $ 10,000.00 | $ 15,000.00 | $ 35,000.00 |
| Sales and marketing | $   5,000.00 | $   7,500.00 | $   7,500.00 | $   7,500.00 | $ 27,500.00 |
| Equipment | $   2,000.00 | $   2,000.00 | $   1,000.00 | $   1,000.00 | $   6,000.00 |
| Facilities | $ 12,000.00 | $ 14,000.00 | $ 16,000.00 | $ 16,000.00 | $ 58,000.00 |
| *Total Expenses* | $ 64,000.00 | $ 93,500.00 | $ 94,500.00 | $ 84,500.00 | $ 336,500.00 |
| | | | | | |
| **Gross Profit** | $ (64,000.00) | $ (70,500.00) | $ 43,500.00 | $ 260,500.00 | $ 169,500.00 |

### 1.8.11  High-Level Project Plan

The macro-level project plan is a first draft, to be populated with greater and more accurate detail later. But it is very important at this early juncture to get an idea of the scope of the project in terms of duration and resources needed, translation into project cost and availability of a finished product. This planning tool will help all parties involved in this project to further develop their contribution and to validate their own predictions and plans.

The sample project plan in Table 1.4 shows how a high-level plan for the Voting Program may look:

Additional charts displaying resources and more detailed milestones would typically be added.

### 1.8.12  Recommendations

This section summarizes the Business Plan from the perspective of a go/no-go decision. Few Business Plans recommend a no-go decision, as we can assume that such a decision would emerge even before the Business Plan was formally pursued. But if the plan was a commissioned effort for another department or an external organization or customer, a negative recommendation is of course possible. Recommendations state clear and unequivocal next steps and provide a confirmation of the size, scope, and key benefits of the project to its stakeholders.

Given the limited scope of this academically motivated example, a credible recommendation for the Voting Program example is hard to formulate. As the competitive analysis in Table 1.2 shows, there are quite a number of well-established competitors, so this product would have to have compelling technical and/or marketing advantages over products already available from alternative suppliers. For the sake of our ongoing study, we do of course at this point recommend the further development of this project, regardless of its competitive challenges.

## 1.9    Harm⊚ny Design Case Study

### 1.9.1    Introduction

This case study has been developed to help the reader see the benefit of methodology-based software engineering from the perspective of a practical project. We will examine the **ModelHomeDesigner** project from its earliest, "back-of-the-napkin" concept to its completion and preparation for field deployment.

TABLE 1.4   High-Level Project Plan

| ID | Task Name | Duration | Start | Finish | Quarter | 3rd Quarter | 4th Quarter | 1st Quarter | 2nd Quarter | 3rd Quarter |
|----|-----------|----------|-------|--------|---------|-------------|-------------|-------------|-------------|-------------|
| | | | | | May Jun | Jul Aug Sep | Oct Nov Dec | Jan Feb Mar | Apr May Jun | Jul Aug Sep |
| 1 | Inception | 15 days | Mon 9/1/03 | Fri 9/19/03 | | | | | | |
| 2 | Analysis | 20 days | Mon 9/22/03 | Fri 10/17/03 | | | | | | |
| 3 | Design | 25 days | Mon 10/20/03 | Fri 11/21/03 | | | | | | |
| 4 | Implementation | 90 days | Mon 11/24/03 | Fri 3/26/04 | | | | | | |
| 5 | Integration | 15 days | Mon 3/29/04 | Fri 4/16/04 | | | | | | |
| 6 | Field Test | 60 days | Mon 4/19/04 | Fri 7/9/04 | | | | | | |
| 7 | Certification | 10 days | Mon 7/12/04 | Fri 7/23/04 | | | | | | |
| 8 | Deployment | 30 days | Mon 7/26/04 | Fri 9/3/04 | | | | | | |
| 9 | Start of Support and Maintenance | 0 days | Fri 9/3/04 | Fri 9/3/04 | | | | | | ◆ 9/3 |

In this chapter, we will examine the **Concept Stage** aspects of this project. The goal is to implement a viable Java solution for **HarmonyDesigns**,[29] an interior design company specializing in model homes, in response to its business and technical requirements, which we will discover and refine over the next several sessions.

### 1.9.2   Initial Concept

The business of model home interior design is project-driven. Model home design companies like HarmonyDesigns specialize in model home design for a number of reasons:

- Unlike residential home interior design clients, model home design clients are professional representatives of construction companies, simplifying and streamlining the process of selection of furniture, fabrics, wall papers, colors, flooring, etc.
- Budgets for model home interior design are substantial, predictable, and pre-approved.
- There is much repeat-business: as builders develop new projects, they tend to use the same model home design companies if they were satisfied with the previous service.

Given that many parameters in this business are semi-static, maximizing profitability in this industry requires the progressive model home interior design company to be efficient. HarmonyDesigns' owner Marianne Solemi ("Marianne") believes that her sixteen-employee operation will benefit greatly from the automation of some of the key work processes in the company, using a custom information technology solution. You and your team have been selected to design, develop, and deploy this software solution.

#### Current Status

Until now, the use of computers at HarmonyDesigns has been limited to simple operational support, such as accounting software to track accounts payable and receivable, spreadsheets to keep track of project status and materials ordered and received, word processing software to generate customer and supplier letters, and e-mail. Internet access is available over a DSL line.

#### Initial Direction

In a first meeting with your team, Marianne describes her business to you:

> "This year, we will design ninety houses for developments in Southern California, Arizona, and Washington (State). Each house has an average budget of $100,000 for materials, labor, and so on. The typical development has three or four model homes. We deal with ten to fifteen different developers/builders.
>
> What I am looking for is a computer program that will streamline the many repetitive tasks we have to run through every time we do a design. Our designers all think they are great artists—and some are. But we can no longer afford to custom-design every aspect of every house. We need to develop efficiencies of "mass production" here.
>
> Our key work processes are the following:
>
> - ***Project analysis:*** What does the client expect, what themes have they selected, what budget do we have?

---

[29]Fictitious name—any similarity with an existing business is purely coincidental.

- **Project design:**  Each piece of furniture, fabric, pillows, flooring, wall covering, etc., has to be selected and designed; detailed specifications and drawings are created.
- **Project execution:**  All the requisite pieces are custom-ordered from a long list of suppliers whom we use regularly, from Tony the Picture Framer to Antiques'R'Us for custom furniture pieces.
- **Project delivery:**  We work with painters, tile and carpet installers, and the builder to prep the model home, and then we truck all these supplies to the job site where our team of installers creates the model home interior design from the plans created in the design phase.
- **Project certification:**  In a final quality-assurance walk-through, the builder accepts our work and certifies its completion.

I believe that a lot of this can be automated, from the third-party ordering process to the repetitive design of pillows used on our furniture pieces. But we need to be careful to preserve our unique image and to have houses appear custom-designed, even if we repeat some items and implementations. Our computers should help us accomplish this. This is your job!"

### 1.9.3   Business Justification

Currently, a typical project generates on average $100,000 in gross revenue for HarmonyDesigns, but this revenue is offset by a long list of costs:

- Labor: direct—designers, project manager, warehouse clerks and truck drivers; indirect—management, office, accounting, contracts.
- Supplies: all furniture and accessory production is outsourced; prices here are often high because of unique custom designs, late orders, and last-minute changes.
- Other overhead: design offices, extensive materials library; presentations to clients (more elaborate because of uniqueness of each design); travel, attendance at trade shows, etc.

In the end, the company's net profit margin is no more than 25–35%. It should approach 50%. Therefore a computerized process management system which allows HarmonyDesigns to do more with less will improve its bottom line: it is looking for at least a 10% gain in profit margin and a 25% gain in revenue without hiring more people, and possibly even reducing its workforce, if possible. For this improvement, it is willing to invest $250,000 for initial software development alone and $15,000/year in maintenance; system and network improvements will be handled separately.

### 1.9.4    Stakeholder Analysis

In order to develop a well-defined set of requirements for this project, we first need to understand who all the key stakeholders are. Stakeholders are all those people who will influence the outcome of our project:

- *Users:* most of HarmonyDesign's employees, from executive management to warehouse clerks, are likely to be users of this system, once installed.
- *System administrator:* HarmonyDesign employs a part-time (50%) system analyst who manages their current network and systems.
- *Software engineers:* all of you, the solution designers and developers.
- *Clients:* the company's clients will be indirectly impacted by this new system, maybe in the use of new forms or online capabilities.
- *Suppliers:* the company's suppliers will also be indirectly impacted by this new system, maybe in the use of new forms or online capabilities.

In the next chapter, we will continue our analysis, but in the meantime, please consider the following assignments for you and your team.

### 1.9.5    Case Assignments

This section provides student opportunities to take ownership of this ongoing case study. Unlike the Voting Program example, which is being developed by the authors, this case study is gradually being turned over to you, our readers, for execution.

**1. Research Interior Design.**   On the Web, find examples (at least three) of interior design companies. Try to find companies that specialize in *model home* interior design. Look for information about their processes (work flows), clients, suppliers, and employees. Alternatively, interview local interior design company staff and management, if you have access to one or more of them.

**2. Start a Business Plan.**   Create a Business Plan document, starting with the following sections for now:

- Project or System Vision
- Project Description
- Stakeholder Analysis
- Customer Profile

Fill in as much information as you can at this time; we will revisit this document frequently as we develop our software solution for HarmonyDesigns.

### 1.10    Resources: Connections • People • Companies

Many companies and individuals are actively involved with object-oriented software engineering using Java. There are thousands of Java programmers worldwide. In this recurring section, we will provide a collection of useful resources and Web links that will give you access to additional information, ideas, cases, and suggestions.[30]

- Xinox® JCreator™
- Borland® JBuilder™
- IBM® Websphere™
- Interior Design Link: Sue Firestone Associates[31]

## 1.11   Summary and Recommendations

In this first chapter, we have not introduced you to as much Java syntax as you may have expected from a Java textbook. But you are now familiar with the basics of software engineering and object-orientation. You are starting to learn the details of the software development life cycle. This contextual knowledge will help you greatly in designing and developing actual software solutions, which your customers (internal or external) will accept and praise. In the more immediate future, it will help you with the next chapters of the book, putting in context the Java skills you will acquire soon enough. We have covered a number of important topics in these first pages:

- Software development methodology and life cycle: the Concept Phase
- Software Engineering Best Practices
- Classes and objects
- The Unified Modeling Language (UML)
- Introduction to Java programs

## 1.12   Review Questions

This section, repeated at the end of every chapter, provides you with a number of questions and assignments that will allow you to check your knowledge.
1. **Life Cycle.** "Invent" your own version of an object-oriented software development life cycle. (This may require some Web research.) List and briefly describe its components.
2. **Object Orientation.** Define object orientation in the context of software engineering and describe five examples of objects that may be implemented in a software program.
3. **Engineering Best Practices.** Select and describe three software engineering best practices. Provide examples of each.
4. **Programming Process.** Explain the process for developing software solutions.
5. **Java Origins.** What languages is Java based on?
6. **Value of Libraries.** What is the value of having Java's features and functions organized into libraries?
7. **Life-Cycle Illustration.** The process of software development follows a life cycle of activities, from initial project concept to the release of the resulting product and subsequent support and maintenance. Draw a picture of this life cycle.

---

[30]Given the volatile nature of business in general and Web links in particular, we cannot warrant that these links and resources will remain accessible over time.
[31]http://sfadesign.com/index.html.

8. **UML Diagrams.** How many diagrams make up the Unified Modeling Language (UML)?
9. **UML Diagram Categories.** Name and describe the three categories of diagrams within the UML
10. **Requirements Analysis (1).** Requirements can be established and tracked within the scope of the project. Where do these requirements come from?
11. **Requirements Analysis (2).** Requirements provide a solid foundation for the follow-on phases of the development process. Discuss how they get started
12. **Requirements Analysis (3).** Describe both functional and nonfunctional requirements.
13. **Software Component Reuse.** List some of the many benefits that arise when software components are reused.
14. **Java Classes.** Define Java classes, objects, attributes, and methods.
15. **Software Quality Assurance.** Describe a key aspect of software quality assurance (SQA) and name one.
16. **Java Object Orientation (1).** What are the main characteristics of Java object-orientation?
17. **Java Object Orientation (2).** What are the main technical benefits of object orientation in software design and development?
18. **The Extended Unified Process Model.** Name and briefly describe the nine disciplines of the Extended Unified Process Model used in this chapter/book.
19. **Business Plan.** Define the Business Plan. What are the required sections of a Business Plan?
20. **Business Use Case Model (1).** Define the concept of a Business Use Case. Define the concept of a Business Use Case Model. Define a use case scenario. Stakeholder analysis: define the concept of a stakeholder.
21. **Domain Model.** Define the concept of a Domain Model.
22. **Vision.** Define the System Vision statement.
23. **Risk Management.** What are the three primary ways of dealing with project risks?

## 1.13    Glossary – Terminology – Concepts

**Best Practices**    A set of work processes designed and validated to represent the best approach to a certain set of activities, problems, or deliverables.

**Closed-Loop Corrective Action (CLCA)**    Figure 1.13 describes the sequence of steps which together constitute a CLCA process:

**Java**    Object-oriented programming language

**Life cycle**    Concept to deployment and support/maintenance process – sequence of phases.

**Object Management Group (OMG)**    Industry standards consortium focused on object-oriented technologies and heterogeneous computing technologies (e.g. CORBA).

**Object-orientation**    A software development technology implemented in a number of programming languages and tools which represents data and functions as combined concepts called "classes" and "objects." Classes are templates for objects that contain attributes (to hold data) and methods (to hold functions). Benefits of object-orientation ("O-O") include component reuse, inheritance, polymorphism, encapsulation, and abstraction, to name just a few.

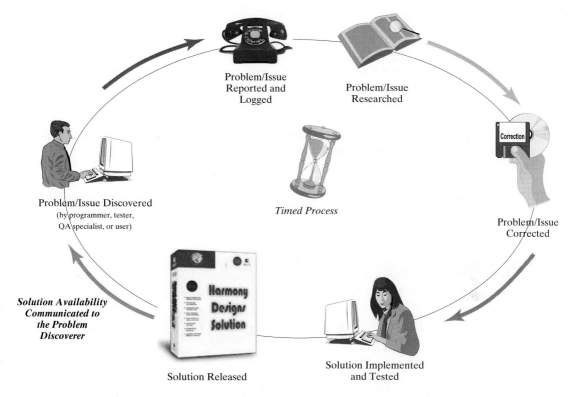

Problem/Issue
Reported and
Logged

Problem/Issue
Researched

Correction

*Timed Process*

Problem/Issue Discovered
(by programmer, tester,
QA specialist, or user)

Problem/Issue
Corrected

*Solution Availability
Communicated to
the Problem
Discoverer*

Harmony
Designs
Solution

Solution Implemented
and Tested

Solution Released

FIGURE 1.13    Closed-Loop Corrective Action Loop

**Software development methodology**    An organized, high-quality, engineering process for developing software in a predictable, repeatable way.

**Software engineering**    Software analysis, design, implementation, and deployment using engineering principles.

**Unified Modeling Language (UML)**    The Unified Modeling Language is a standardized set of modeling diagrams used to represent object-oriented software systems. UML is standardized by the Object Management Group™ (OMG™).

**Use case**    A use case is a structured, comprehensive representation of a requirement. The following categories of information are associated with a use case (reviewed in more detail in a later chapter):

- Use Case Name
- Brief Description
- Actors
- Pre-Conditions
- Primary Scenario (Flow of Events)
- Secondary Scenarios
- Diagrams

- Activity Diagram
- Sequence Diagram
- User Interface Drawing
- Post-Conditions
- Extension Points
- Other Requirements

**Use Case Model**   The UML diagram "Use Case Model" shows an overview of the use cases in a project and their relationships.

## 1.14   Exercises

Instructors are encouraged to construct their own exercises based on the students' level of knowledge and specific interests. The authors recommend a project/case study approach over simple practice exercises. A small number of sample exercises are provided below.

**1. Terminology.**   Research the following terms on the Web and in your book, and define them in writing:
- Unified Modeling Language—UML
- Use case model
- Software engineering—methodologies, tools, providers, standards
- Object orientation
- Software quality assurance
- Java – origins, tools, providers, packages

**2. Stakeholder Analysis.**   Develop a Stakeholder Analysis for the following project: Web-based electronic funds transfer program, to be developed for a nationwide financial institution.

**3. Java Components.**   Describe the relationship between packages, classes, methods, and instance variables.

**4. Authentication.**   For **The Voting Program** example in this chapter, we refer to user authentication. Research this concept and develop one or two ideas about how to implement a secure way for voters to be recognized by the software program.

## 1.15   Setting up a Java Development Environment

A number of well-established Java Interactive Development Environments (IDEs) exist for your use, including JBuilder from Borland, JCreator from Xinox Software, and others. In addition, you can develop Java applications using a simple text editor. After all, Java source files contain nothing but text. We saw the process of Java source code transformation into Java files that can be executed using the Java Virtual Machine (JVM). This **JVM** is a program that runs on a particular operating system and interprets Java bytecodes, themselves therefore platform-independent. The name of the Java program is simply a command-line parameter when executing the JVM program. For example, the following line entered at the DOS command prompt in the Windows operating system, `java MyProgram` will run the `java.exe` program and interpret the `MyProgram.class` bytecode file (see Fig. 1.14).

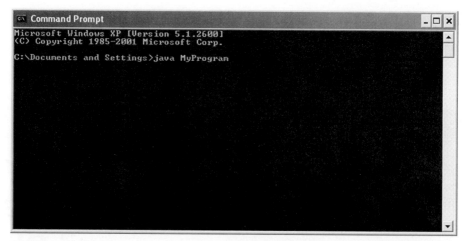

FIGURE 1.14   Running a Java Program "MyProgram" from the DOS Command Prompt

### 1.15.1   *Versions of Java*

The most recent released version of Java is Java 2. The Software Development Kit available at the time of this writing and associated with this release is Java SDK 5.0 (now referred to as JDK 5.0). These release numbers are sometimes confusing for novice programmers. In addition, for Java applets running embedded in Web browsers, we must note that Microsoft® Internet Explorer™ only supports Java 1.1.[32] AOL-TimeWarner® Netscape® Navigator™ Versions 6.1 and up support Java 2.

### 1.15.2   *Class and Classpath Setup*

Installation programs for the Java SDK[33] from Sun Microsystems IDEs normally set the path variable automatically. The Classpath command or command line variable is used to inform the compiler where to find an external package (of classes) that is inserted into a program being compiled into bytecodes (using the import statement). This facility allows for the use of previously developed Java code components (packages and classes) in a new project without having to insert Java source code.

### 1.16   Java Programming Exercises

1. Design and develop a small program which accepts as input the first and last names and social security numbers of voters and displays a list of them on the screen. Use javax.swing.JOptionPane input and output dialogs. Alternatively, use the Scanner class and its character-based input and output methods.

2. Enhance the program you developed for the previous exercise by accepting and displaying voter address information and party affiliation.

---

[32]A plug-in JVM is available from Sun Microsystems to provide Java 2 support in Internet Explorer.

[33]**S**oftware **D**evelopment **K**it, the collection of programs and support files used to create Java-runnable programs.

# Experimenting with Classes and Objects

Classes and objects are central to object-oriented software engineering using Java.

Unlike older programming languages, the object orientation in Java is comprehensive and consistent.[1] In Java, we represent all key components as classes and objects. Objects are created from classes, becoming **members** of classes, or, said differently, classes are **templates** for objects. The concepts of object orientation often take some time to grasp and get used to, especially for novices and for experienced in legacy procedural programming languages like C, Fortran, COBOL, Basic, and the like.

There are two elementary concepts at the core of most computer software programs: **variables** or **data,** and **code** or **functions** (see Fig. 2.1). The former contain specific facts about the topic domain covered by the application; the latter provide computing and other manipulating functions to add value to this data. In fact, most users, especially in business situations,[2] are interested in *data* because they want to extract some useful **information** from this data. This information, in turn, provides new *knowledge*. Knowledge is used to make more accurate and timely **decisions**. Along this data transformation path, **value** is added by the functionality (algorithms) of the software processing the data. It is the role of the software functions to facilitate the transformation of data into better decisions. This progressive transformation is shown in Figure 2.2.

---

[1]Purists will argue that the eight primitive types in Java make its object orientation less than consistent.
[2]Throughout the book "business" includes all profit, non-profit, and public organizations and institutions that use information technology for productive purposes.

```
package myVotingProgram;

import javax.swing.*;

class Voting {
    int voteTally;
    String candidate;
    boolean selected;

    boolean voteSelection () {
        if (selected == true) {
            voteTally++;
            voteSelected = true;
            return voteSelected;
        }
    }
}
```

**Data**

Winston 234 votes
Smith 567 votes
Regis 789 votes
Jarvis 786 votes
Rostov 123 votes
Markus 546 votes
Wilson 669 votes

**Code**

FIGURE 2.1   Data and Code Together Make Up Computer Software Programs

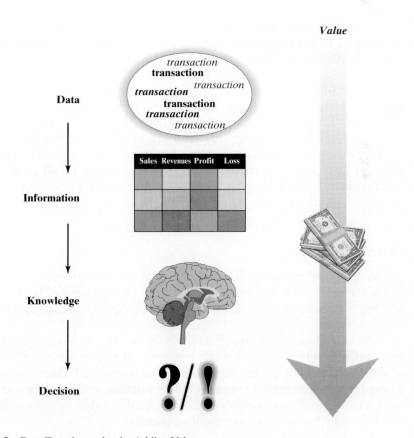

FIGURE 2.2   Data Transformation by Adding Value

Traditionally, data and functions were separated in software applications. Legacy languages have no seamless facility for integrating the two; this is where object orientation contributes its most important benefits. Classes and objects manage to provide an integrated, synergistic representation of data (which can also be thought of as program characteristics) and functions (behaviors) and their interactions. Classes, the templates (on blueprints) for objects, represent data as *attributes* (also called *fields* or properties) and functions as *methods* (also called operations). This chapter will help you understand these *metaphorical* concepts in more detail; it will also describe how classes and object orientation are implemented in Java.

---

**Key Term**

**Metaphors,** in the context of software engineering, are symbolic representations (allegories), using familiar, everyday images and concepts, to illuminate the nature of processes, functions, and contributors in a way that may be easier to understand. We can also think of them as analogies.

---

We will explore ways to leverage this symbolic representation as we develop the architecture and design of typical commercial software solutions. Over the last few years, an object-oriented modeling technique—standardized by the Object Management Group (OMG) as the Unified Modeling Language (UML)—has emerged as a powerful, comprehensive tool for transforming project requirements into detailed designs for software components and systems, using simple, consistent graphical representations. As we began to discuss in the last chapter, the UML definitions and diagrams embrace object-oriented constructs and are explored and applied in this book as a tool for designing high-quality software solutions. We choose to apply this modeling technique because it enjoys high industry acceptance and because it works for all projects, whether small and simple or large and complex. Most valuable software development, in fact, involves complex systems that must be implemented based on extensive planning and design.

## 2.1   Learning Objectives

As you progress in your studies to the level of "junior software engineer," at least within the scope of this book, you need to develop a high level of intimacy with Java. You will begin to build your language skills in this chapter, but always in the context of our object-oriented software engineering methodology.

We use classes and objects as tools for solving "business" problems: more often than not, software applications are developed to improve business processes in terms of their productivity, quality, consistency, cost, and speed. Decision-makers are willing to pay for the often high cost of developing software solutions because they want to realize a substantial gain in productivity and quality, often in support of an improved— and hopefully sustainable—competitive position.

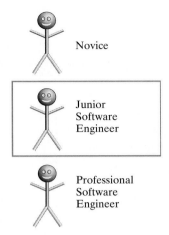

First, we take a look at the benefits of object orientation in software engineering. Software development was predominantly *procedural* until the 1990s, even though the principles of object orientation have been known since the 1960s. While object-oriented systems were attempted in the 1980s—such as Hewlett-Packard NewWave and NCR COOPERATION, both enterprise office automation suites—mainstream support for object orientation only materialized in the nineties. For our profession to make a transition as major as going from procedural to object-oriented software engineering, there must be substantial, sustainable benefits in the new approach.

In this chapter, you will become comfortable with the life-cycle role of classes and objects and the relationship between use cases and classes. You will also encounter a more realistic Java program and are therefore encouraged to start writing small test programs yourself in order to immerse yourself in the Java language until, over time, it becomes a second-nature skill. *Practice makes perfect!*

### 2.1.1  *Learning Layout*

This recurring section shows the learning objectives of the chapter using the notation of the UML Activity Diagram (see Fig. 2.3).

In this chapter, we focus on UML modeling and object orientation, as well as introductory training in Java syntax and structure. Of course, these topics are interrelated; this book is based on an integrated approach to teaching skills in all the five major areas of development appropriate for software engineers:

1. Software Engineering
2. Object Orientation
3. Java Syntax and Structure
4. Software Quality Assurance
5. Attitude and Motivation

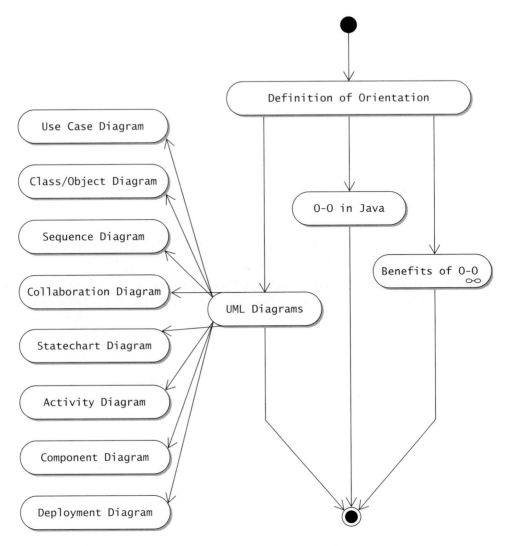

FIGURE 2.3    Chapter 2 Learning Layout (as a UML Activity Diagram)

In combination, skills from these different areas constitute the professional development required for effective execution of software engineering projects. We will discuss these skill-development areas in greater detail in upcoming chapters, under the recurring section "Learning Connections."

### 2.1.2    *Learning Connections*

The Learning Connections diagram in Figure 2.4 shows the content of this chapter in relation to the knowledge and skills development recommended for apprentice Java software engineers.

## Table Of Contents

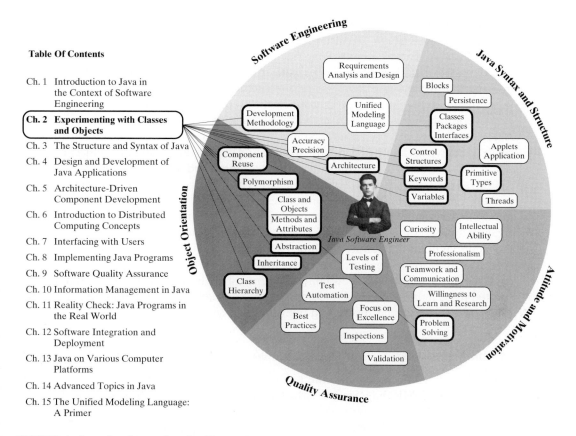

**FIGURE 2.4**   Learning Connections for Chapter 2

## 2.2   Executive Summary

In Java, we identify programs as *classes:* from the start, you learn to think in terms of classes and objects when you develop Java software. In this chapter, we begin to connect the dots: use cases, UML diagrams, objects and classes as concepts, Java objects and classes, attributes, methods. It will all make a lot more sense by the time you reach Chapter 3.

The Unified Modeling Language, or UML from now on, provides us with a comprehensive set of modeling tools to represent all aspects of software methodology, including workflows and processes, functions, and information, or data. We use the diagrams and our own illustrations to ensure that you begin to understand the various aspects of an object-oriented information technology system from a number of key viewpoints. In fact, the **Architectural Perspectives** covered in this chapter will encourage software engineers to look at their problem domain from multiple perspectives, lest they miss key requirements. The **Stakeholder Analysis** introduced in Chapter 1 as part of the Business Plan development process is the first step in ensuring that the various interests of everyone involved with the project are considered. When we identify all the stakeholders in a project, we are more likely not to overlook any requirement areas because we examine requirements with the roles and needs of all the stakeholders in mind.

In our ongoing examination of the Extended Unified Process disciplines, we enter the **Analysis Stage**. We also preview the development of our second key deliverable *artifact*, the **Requirements Specification**, which we will complete in Chapter 3.[3]

Your Java skills will rapidly expand from here onward: in this chapter, you find information about basic Java program structure, syntax, and constructs. Learning a programming language is not that much different from learning any other new language: you familiarize yourself with the meaning of words and phrases (we call them **statements**), and you try to understand how these elements are assembled to make sense and have meaning (we call this **syntax and structure**). In Java, we learn about key words, selection and repetition statements, variables, and algorithms. Our advantage is that Java uses English-based terms, which are chosen to represent their logical function in the program. Also, Java has a limited set of functions, words, and meanings. Keep in mind that a programming language is a helper tool for programmers to more easily interact with the computing machine by translating human-friendly English-like statements into human-unfriendly machine code developed by people who wanted to make software development easier. Therefore, whenever you encounter a difficult concept or construct in Java, keep an open mind and remember that the developer of that feature wanted to be helpful, but had to comply with the exigencies of the underlying capabilities of the computer hardware and operating system.

## 2.3   Learning Modules

The following sections describe the key concepts covered in this chapter, from object orientation, to UML diagrams, to Java language basics. Learning is not based on text alone: it is your responsibility as a prospective Java software engineer to seek knowledge about your new domain from a range of sources, such as other books, magazines, online reports, other Web sites, and subject matter experts.

**Recommendation:** The technical aspects of Java programming involve the learning of new skills best honed through practice and repetition. While most books provide a myriad of specific examples and small exercises, we recommend that you focus your practices on examples and programs that are practical and useful for you in particular. We suggest that you construct your own library of programs (classes), from the very start of your Java software engineering practice. So, for example, if you are involved with accounting work processes, develop accounting-related exercises and components. Similarly, if you are interested or work in medicine, develop components and programs for that field. The same applies to other fields.

### 2.3.1   Concepts

Object orientation, or O-O, is one of the unifying themes of this Java book. (The other is software engineering.) O-O connects the principles of software engineering methodology, from concept to deployment and support, to what makes the Java programming language most valuable in today's software projects, namely, its explicit implementation of reusable, extensible classes and objects. Not only can we implement Java classes and objects in our programs, but we learn here how to evolve these classes and objects from the

---

[3]Recall that the **Business Plan** was the first major artifact produced.

initial requirements provided by the project stakeholders in the form of use cases and their actors and scenarios. We discover how the continuity from the early phases of the process to the implementation of Java code ensures that the code emerges as what project stakeholders expect. We weave the *golden thread* of our object-oriented development methodology through every phase of the software development process, providing a consistent, coherent view of work disciplines, functions, data elements, and computational results, always in support of the business process requirements agreed to by project stakeholders and updated along the way as needed.

### Object Orientation Introduced

We have already mentioned object orientation in Chapter 1. At this point, we want to explore further the conceptual foundation of object orientation in software engineering. Object orientation was first introduced in 1967, in a specialized language: **Simula-67**. Smalltalk followed as the first fully object-oriented language. But all in all, it took another twenty years for O-O to enter the mainstream. Today C++ and Java (and the Microsoft .NET languages) are the dominant object-oriented programming languages. The level of abstraction inherent in O-O requires a great deal of computing resources, which only became available in sufficient abundance in the 1990s.[4] Today, O-O is integral to modern software engineering as a fundamental technological underpinning.

### What Characteristics Make O-O So Compelling?

As software engineers, our challenge is to represent real-world processes and information within the severely confining capabilities of existing ones-and-zeros-based computer systems and networks. Computer technology is very flexible, precisely because it is programmable, but it also has no inherent intelligence or ability to make decisions or to take any human-like actions on its own. All useful, valuable functionality has to be explicitly implemented in software as programming code. This is how software-programming languages evolved in the first place: they provided a symbolic interface between human and computer.

---

## STRUGGLING WITH CONCEPTS

Novice software engineers often struggle with aspects of object orientation, maybe because of its inherent (and highly desirable) conceptual nature. Understanding classes and objects requires adopting a view of the problem domain surrounding the project which incorporates the "translation" of information and data into **attributes**, and of functionality, processes, and workflows into **methods**. Then we have to figure out how to apply the strengths of O-O to the representation of these constructs in computer software code. While this is not an easy intellectual transformation for some to embrace, its ultimate strength and benefit lie in its level of *abstract distance* from the realities of the underlying computer system.

---

[4]In software development, it is usually the case that the more sophisticated the tool and its technology are, the more computing resources they require.

Classes and objects represent the latest great metaphor in software engineering. They are a powerful, humanlike "building block set" for the "real world" and effectively bridge real work processes and contributors and the ones-and-zeros environment of computing. Classes and objects can be programmed to become reusable components, self-contained, efficient building blocks of functionality, which lack nothing, as they combine and integrate both data and functions.

What, then, are classes and objects? Classes are models for objects: they provide templates for objects. Objects, or *instances*, are cookie-cutter copies derived from class templates, but they can also, through *polymorphism*, adjust their behaviors based on their specific use in a particular instance. This flexibility enables objects and classes to represent functionality in a more human-like way than procedural functions ever could; and it is this ability to adjust to their environment and thus become reusable and extensible (through *inheritance*) that makes objects invaluable to modern software engineering. In addition, object orientation allows us to hide complexity and support intricate concepts with simplicity, such as multi-threading, persistence, and multi-platform support and networking.

Before we can successfully program classes and objects in Java, we have to learn how to design them. This is a more difficult task than traditional analysis and design in procedural software development, because the *class hierarchy* becomes the architectural foundation of an O-O-based software solution. Developing a class hierarchy in such a way that it is optimized for simplicity, reuse, extensibility, and performance is a highly conceptual task that involves logical analysis, careful scrutiny, planning, creativity, and, preferably, experience. However, when a good, complete, and detailed *use case model* is in place as a guiding blueprint, a correct, well-balanced, and inclusive class hierarchy is more likely to result from a careful design effort. An overall iterative approach to project development further ensures that continuous improvements are applied to the design throughout the life-cycle phases.

The remainder of this chapter explores these concepts in more detail by examining the components of the **Requirements Specification**, which surround the use case development process. The design process will be covered in later chapters.

The UML diagrams, discussed subsequently in detail, provide an excellent set of tools to support our O-O design activities, starting with the development of a proper **Use Case Model**. The use case model forms the descriptive backbone of the Requirements and Design Specifications. It is necessary, of course, to surround this and other UML diagrams with supportive text that explains how to read, interpret, and apply the diagrams correctly and completely. The entire analysis and design phase of the software development process is an exercise in *communication:* we are engaged in an effort, often complex, of capturing and understanding the requirements of our project stakeholders, interpreting them, and translating them into software components that will not only provide the requisite functionality to support the critical workflows in our client's organization,[5] but to improve these work processes in terms of productivity, quality, and accuracy, taking advantage of the advantages and capabilities of information technology.

After the Business Plan, discussed in the last chapter, the next major document artifact we need to produce is the ***Requirements Specification***. It is the repository of all

---

[5] We will refer to the person, people or organization, which commissions our work as "client" regardless of whether this work is done for an internal or external agency. This will foster your "customer service" mentality.

information about stakeholder and project requirements, developed in a first version in the Analysis Phase of our software development life cycle, but kept up to date throughout the project as new requirements arise or existing ones need adjusting.

### Requirements Specification

While systems analysts have been writing Requirements Specifications for software projects for many years, these documents have often been ad hoc collections of information and flow charts, assembled and organized according to the best judgment of the individual writer. We propose instead to follow a strict outline and consistent format in order to *standardize* this important activity and make it repeatable. Each of the following sections should be included in every Requirements Specification you write.

### Project Description

It is important to provide an accurate, well-crafted project description right up front. This includes a well-chosen name as well as a brief but succinct description of the project's purpose, addressing its main focus and scope.

### System Name

The system name should be considered a "working name," not necessarily a final product marketing name. It should clearly represent the project and its main focus.

---

**Example: The Voting Program**

This name is not particularly unique or attractive, but it clearly states what our sample program is about.

---

### Project Vision and Description

The project vision articulates the strategic orientation of the project. It should be compelling, simple, and focused. The project description does not have to be detailed, but it should give the reader a clear, concise overview over the purpose and value of the project.

---

**Example:**

The Web-based Tempus electronic timecard provides law professionals with a simple, yet complete, project time-tracking solution, with interfaces available to existing accounting packages like Quickbooks™ and Peachtree™.

---

## Risk Management

As we have already discussed for the Business Plan, a Risk Analysis section is required to capture potential problems the project may encounter and offer alternatives for how to deal with them. At this point, as shown in Table 2.1, the Business Plan Risk Management section is migrated to the Requirements Specification and expanded with the analysis and management of additional risks discovered in the Analysis Phase (often of a more technical nature than those first identified in the Business Plan). This also starts to include more project-related and technical risks.

TABLE 2.1    Risk Analysis Revisited

| Risk | Risk Management |
|------|-----------------|
| Data integrity | Use secure transaction-processing data management to ensure data integrity at all points of the process |
| | Establish safe data-backup procedures (onsite, offsite storage) |
| | Use a proven configuration-management system |
| Functional integrity | Use a mission-critical-validated inspection process |
| | Perform extensive testing at all levels |
| | Roll out in controlled environment with parallel operation for beta testing |
| Budget, resources | Use object-oriented methodology with careful macro/micro-level planning and iterative development |
| User acceptance | Validate ease of use with focus groups |
| Security | Use authentication and transmission-security measures (encryption) |
| Platforms supported | Ensure testing on all likely destination platforms (budget impact) |
| Performance | Ensure that the product meets minimum response-time requirements at all times by running stress tests and optimizing code as necessary |

### System-Level Use Case Diagram

For the use case diagram, we adopt the Business Plan Use Case Model and develop from it a more comprehensive technical model with complete requirements-level use cases based on the initial business use cases

The use case (model) diagram shown in Figure 2.5 organizes project use cases into a structured model from which the system architecture and class hierarchy can be derived. Use cases describe each product requirement in detail.[6]

The main constituent elements of a use case model are *actors* and *use cases*. Actors are a subset of the stakeholder group: they are active project participants (or components) that actually perform some function. Use cases describe each requirement workflow from a process perspective and capture the workflows as scenarios. *Primary scenarios* document the normal case of a process; *secondary scenarios* document alternative or abnormal versions of the same process, such as the occurrence of exceptions and their handling.

In the literature and in actual projects, there is a wide range of applications of the *use case concept* in software development. Most practitioners consider use cases primarily as repositories for work process information, tools for the capture and analysis of project requirements; often, technical use cases also describe system features and components, which make them more of a Design Phase tool. We propose to clearly separate requirements use cases and design use cases. We want to capture requirements without hastening the implementation; we want to suspend our commitment to a specific design until we have exhausted our investigation of all the critical project requirements and until we have the proper system architecture in place.

---

[6]This approach is loosely based on the Rational Unified Process™.

**Example:**

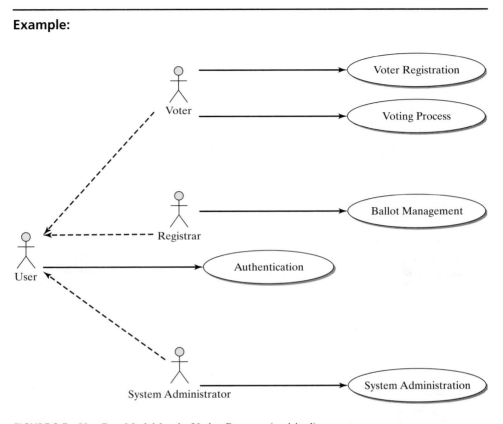

FIGURE 2.5   Use Case Model for the Voting Program (revisited)

### Architecture Diagram

The requirements analysis performed at this stage allows us to establish the project's system architecture. We decide at this point what kind of system we will build, in terms of the major technologies and subsystems. The Architecture Diagram shows the main components of our proposed system and their high-level relationships and interconnections. The architecture also identifies the main underlying systems and technologies.

The example (see Fig. 2.6) shows the simplified client-server architecture for a wireless software solution. We show a variety of architecture diagrams in these pages, because there is no standard for these depictions. Their purpose is to show the solution from a high-level "bird's-eye" perspective to provide a context for the design of subsystems.

### Subsystems Description

As a result of defining a system architecture, it is now possible to describe subsystems, at least in a preliminary, high-level fashion. The detailed design of subsystems will be relegated to the Design Phase of our software development process. A subsystem in Java is typically an agglomeration of one or more packages of classes which contain related functionality, often housed on a particular computer system, while other subsystems may reside on other, network-connected systems. Often subsystems are organized by

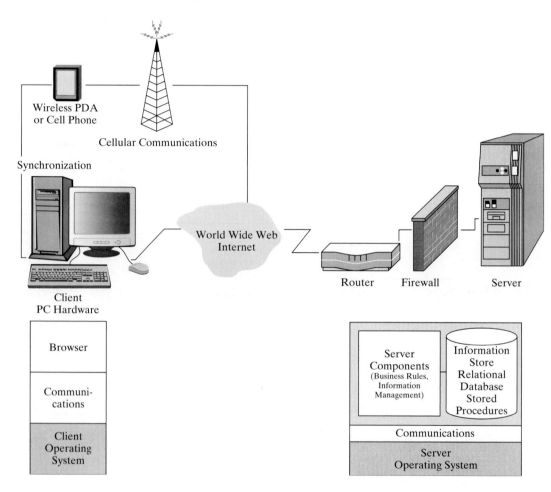

FIGURE 2.6 Sample Client-Server Architecture

function or by where they need to physically reside; in other implementations, the subsystem constituent components are organized by relationship to each other (e.g., based on the system class hierarchy). In a multi-tier architecture, each tier is often implemented as a subsystem. Thus we may have the User Interaction Subsystem; the Business Rule Subsystem; and the Information Management (e.g., database) Subsystem.

### Use Cases

The next major section in the Requirements Specification is the use case description. The following subsection headers represent the headers of this recurring document section: for each use case, each of these subsections needs to be completed.

A use case is foremost a description of a work process. (see Fig. 2.7) It has a well-defined beginning and end, and it contributes tangible value to the overall project.

Before use cases, requirements often ended up expressed as features and functions, blurring the line between analysis and design. Use cases allow us to pay attention to project requirements, and not just from a functional viewpoint, but with a clear focus

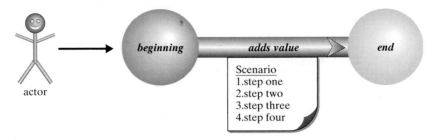

FIGURE 2.7   What Is a Use Case?

on actual workflows. Our goal, after all, is to improve work processes using IT, not just to implement some functions in a program that may or may not have any impact on the quality and speed of the work accomplished. We use the metaphor of *scenarios* to capture work processes as step-by-step descriptions. The more detailed these descriptions, the better foundation they constitute for our subsequent design efforts.

Let us now examine the subsections in the Requirements Specification that document the use case details.

### Use Case Name

Use case names should incorporate the primary action represented by the use case. This action-based labeling makes it easier to capture the core process steps in the primary scenario and accompanying diagrams and descriptions.

---

**Example use case names:**

"User Authentication," "Ballot Creation," "Election Result Determination."

---

### Description

The use case description, like the project description itself, needs to be concise, clear, and provide information about the main intent and scope of this use case. It should clearly outline what process the use case covers.

---

**Example:**

The *User Authentication* use case describes the step-by-step process required to ensure that users logging into the system can be unequivocally validated in terms of their identity and access rights.

---

### Actors

*Actors* are people or software components that play *roles*: they participate in the work process and directly interact with the software being developed.

Human actors represent a subset of *stakeholders*, meaning that every actor is also a stakeholder, by definition; but the reverse does not necessarily hold true. Actors give us a subject for the actions described in the use case scenarios.

### Examples:

"Voter," "Election Official," and "Voter Registration Module" may all be actors in our Voting Program.

### *Pre-Conditions*

Before the scenario in this use case can unfold (see below), certain conditions or circumstances may have to be in place: we call these pre-conditions. Pre-conditions allow us to "set the stage" for the current use case.

### Example:

It is a precondition of this use case that the actor "Voter" is already authenticated at this point.

### *Primary Scenario*

The primary scenario represents the heart of the use case. It provides a step-by-step description of the process being described.[7] If described in sufficient detail, the scenario provides a snapshot of the particular work process represented by this use case. This information proves invaluable when subsequently designing software functionality to support, enhance, or replace the work process. It is the point of origin for all subsequent work and remains a source of validation throughout the project.

### Example:

Electronic Time-Tracking Program: Scenario

1. Employee logs on to the system and is authenticated.
2. Employee enters time spent on various projects today.
3. Employee enters comments about activities, outcomes.
4. System accepts inputs.
5. Employee logs out.
6. System calculates wages for the day, accounting for overtime, differing rates per project.
7. System routes electronic timesheet to supervisor for approval.
8. Supervisor logs in.
9. Supervisor reviews timesheet and approves it.
10. System routes timesheet to payroll department.
11. Supervisor logs out.
12. System tracks employee log-ins and log-outs.

---

[7]We prefer the step-by-step outline-format approach to describing a scenario, even though others may also accept prosaic descriptions or even pseudocode.

### Secondary Scenarios

Secondary scenarios capture all the *alternative workflows* that come into play when the primary scenario cannot be completed for whatever reason. These secondary scenarios often require the lion's share of the documenting effort, given their potential number, scope, and complexity. This is consistent with the phenomenon we will discover in the subsequent coding effort, where most of the work is in handling exceptions, not creating the main (positive) functionality. It is obvious that a detailed, comprehensive description of all the secondary scenarios associated with this use case will later take us a long way toward covering all the potential exceptions our program may encounter and dealing with them effectively.

---

### Example:

Electronic Time Tracking Program: Secondary Scenario 1—Employee Not Authorized for Project:

1. System displays error message and provides options.
   a. Reenter information to correct error.
   b. Request administrator support (online or offline).
2. Exit or continue with permitted functions.

---

### UML Diagrams

UML diagrams were introduced earlier, but we will now examine in detail, those recommended for inclusion in the Requirements Specification. The purpose for these drawings can be traced back to the old saying, "A picture is worth a thousand words!" The combination of UML drawings standardized by the OMG provides a comprehensive consistent way to represent and describe even the most complex information system projects.

### Activity Diagram

Activity Diagrams are the successors of traditional flow charts: they show the activities in a process, including the sequence of events, and the relationships between the activities. The UML notation for activity diagrams includes a number of simple icons that allow for the depiction of process steps. The purpose of an Activity Diagram is to show events in the process being documented by the use case. Remember that the diagram is use-case-specific.[8]

The simple example in Figure 2.8 shows the high-level flow of the Authentication use case in our Voting Program example. Note that Activity Diagrams can be refined over time to contain more and more detail, as needed to make unequivocal design decisions. An iterative improvement approach is recommended, as more information is typically acquired in the course of a project.

---

[8]Students are sometimes tempted to take shortcuts and create one Activity Diagram for the entire project. This is not advisable.

**Example:**

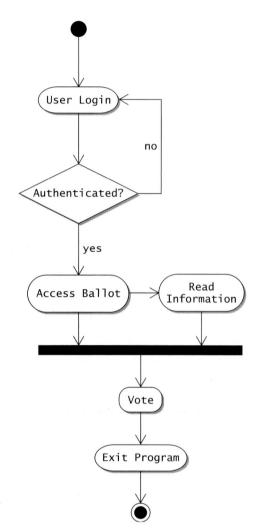

FIGURE 2.8 Sample Activity Diagram (simplified)

### Sequence Diagram

When we want to show events and activities in relationship to time elapsed, we use a Sequence Diagram. This diagram allows us to show the *beginning, end,* and *duration* of the subprocesses in the use case workflow and their temporal relationships to each other.

The example diagram in Figure 2.9 shows a high-level view of the voting subprocess. Again, additional detail is likely to emerge in the course of the project in a real-world scenario.

### User Interface Drawing

While the formal design of the user interface belongs to the subsequent Design Phase in our process, ideas often emerge at this stage in the analysis, about what the user interface

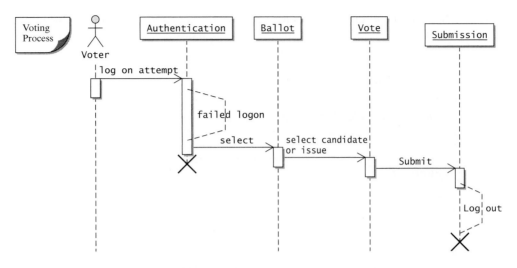

FIGURE 2.9   Sequence Diagram for Voting Program (simplified)

for the proposed IT solution may look like at a high-level. This section provides for the capture of these ideas, without committing the software engineer to a particular implementation. Often, this is simply a hand drawing, or a screen shot of a simulated GUI and is not part of the OMG's UML diagram set.

### Example:

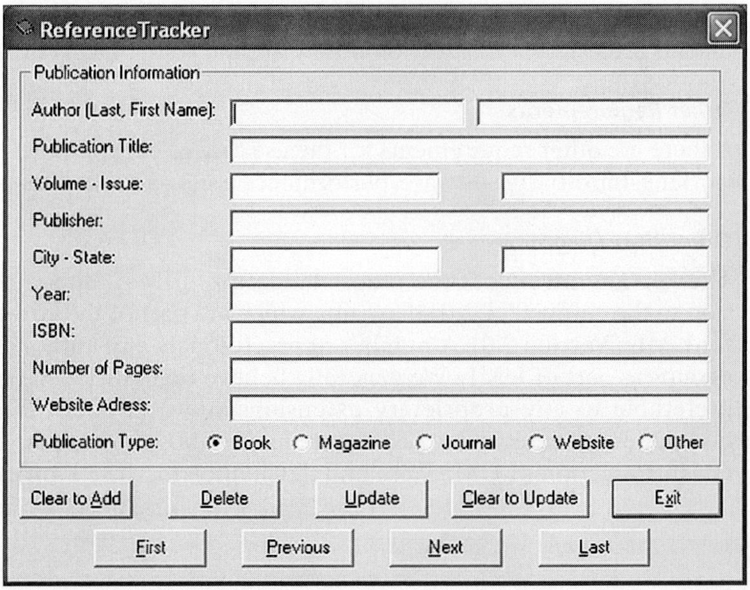

FIGURE 2.10   Sample Screen Layout

The example in Figure 2.10 shows the use of a third-party tool to prototype an application. This GUI sketch is not an adequate final design, but it provides the analyst with an example of what the program functions need to include.

### Post-Conditions

Our scenario may result in certain conditions that need to be addressed after its sequence has concluded. These post-conditions will be addressed in another use case, but they need to be identified here to ensure coverage.

---

### Example:

It is a post-condition of this use case that the voting tally results can be printed on a local or network-connected printer which supports $8.5 \times 11$ inch paper.

---

### Extension Points

Extension points to use cases are possible additional capabilities that are beyond the scope of the current use case but may find future consideration in use case extensions or additional use cases (see Table 2.2).

### Other Use Cases Used

If this use case depends on other use cases, they will be cited in this section. For example, if *Authentication* is a pre-condition, and *Authentication* is a use case, then the *Authentication* use case is listed here.

### Deliverables–Artifacts

Artifacts such as documents, output forms, Web site pages, or other tangible output elements are listed in this section if they are the result of this use case.

### Other Requirements

If there are other requirements for the use case to be workable—hardware, system, networking, third-party software, performance issues, and the like—they are listed here.

### Other UML Diagrams

This section introduces the other standardized UML diagrams. We limit our discussion to the "official" UML diagrams, which are part of the current OMG Specification for UML (Version 2.0). A number of practitioners and authors identify some other diagrams as part of UML. We generally believe that adherence to certified standards is preferable to any proprietary extensions, however meritorious they may be. This book does not seek to be a comprehensive UML tutorial; we only provide a superficial introduction of UML here and in Chapter 15, "The Unified Modeling Language:

TABLE 2.2    Use Case Extension

| Use Case | Extension |
| --- | --- |
| Withdraw money from ATM Machine | Withdraw postal stamps from ATM Machine |

A Primer," to whet your appetite. Please refer to the many excellent books available from other authors for detailed information about UML.

### Class and Object Diagrams

The class diagram and its derivative, the object diagram (which is an instance of the class diagram), are prime *design* artifacts. They are used to establish the class hierarchy. Classes and objects are programming artifacts, meaning that their definition translates directly to code. The example in Figure 2.11 shows a subset of an early design of **The Voting Program** classes. (Note that these diagrams continue evolving in the course of the project.)

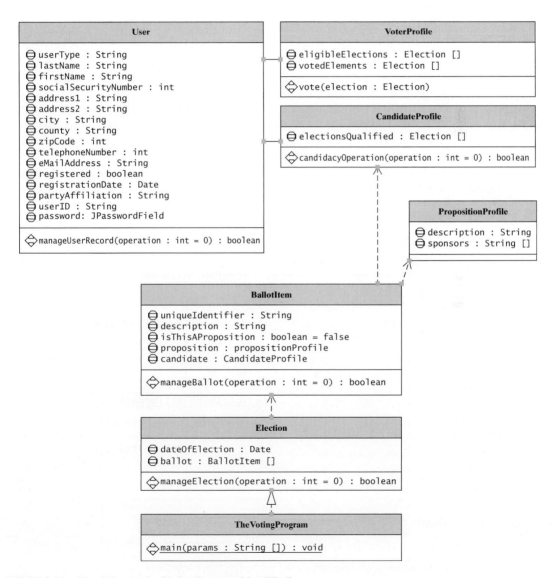

FIGURE 2.11   Class Diagram for Voting Program (simplified)

We can see the obvious advantage of detailed design using graphical representation in these various diagrams. Instead of having to design as we code, as many programmers did in the past with mixed results at best, we focus on figuring out in great detail what our classes (methods and attributes) need to contain, how they are organized and how they interact, and what functionality they implement, all without writing a single line of Java code. The problem with coding too soon, with incomplete designs, is the complexity of the software development process itself; once we start coding, it is increasingly difficult to also design and plan well in concert. The high-level work has to be done beforehand. These diagrams compel us to think through every aspect of our evolving application in detail.

### The Communication Diagram

A Communication Diagram is sometimes substituted for a sequence diagram. It shows the objects contributing to the workflow and their interrelationships and is very useful to show the interaction via message passing between objects. These two UML diagrams are considered isomorphic, which basically means that they are different views of the same information. Automated UML drawing tools can usually convert a sequence diagram into a communication diagram, and vice versa, with the click of a button. Our anecdotal experience has found that about 80% of those who use these diagrams prefer to create and use the sequence diagram rather than the communication diagram, while the other 20% prefer the reverse.

In the simplified communication diagram for the Voting Program shown in Figure 2.12, we see the major objects and associated methods in the process of selecting a ballot and submitting a vote.

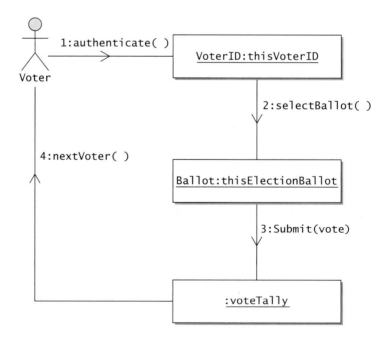

FIGURE 2.12   Communication Diagram for the Voting Program (simplified)

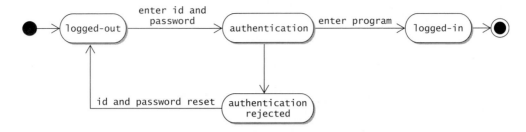

FIGURE 2.13   Statechart for the Voting Program (simplified)

### The Statechart Diagram

A Statechart Diagram is used to show changes of state in a program design. This diagram is usually used to show this state change for one specific object but can be used for multiple objects if desired. A typical example is a turnstile: whenever a person enters a restricted area through a turnstile, the state of the entrant changes from "outside" to "inside."

In business systems, state is often represented as the value of an attribute or a group of attributes at a specific moment in time. For example, a traffic signal object has "color" as one of its attributes. The value of this attribute at any moment in time could be green, yellow, or red. Blinking and broken or burned-out could be represented by another attribute, such as status. State changes are important anchor points in software applications because they represent decision points to execute a set of statements rather than another set of statements, or to begin or stop executing a set of statements repeatedly. A statechart for the Voting Program is shown in Figure 2.13.

### The Deployment Diagram

A Deployment Diagram provides a view of the actual position of program components on different clients, servers, systems, and platforms (see Fig. 2.14).

The various UML diagrams previewed here in a cursory way provide a sufficiently diverse variety of representational capabilities to capture the essential aspects of a software solution, even if it is distributed across multiple systems, uses different tools and interfaces, and provides an extensive set of capabilities.

## 2.3.2   Position in Process

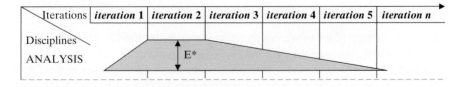

In this chapter, we are moving from the Concept Discipline to the Analysis Discipline in our software development methodology. This is one of the most critical times in the whole process, because it is at this juncture that we collect, document, organize, and analyze the

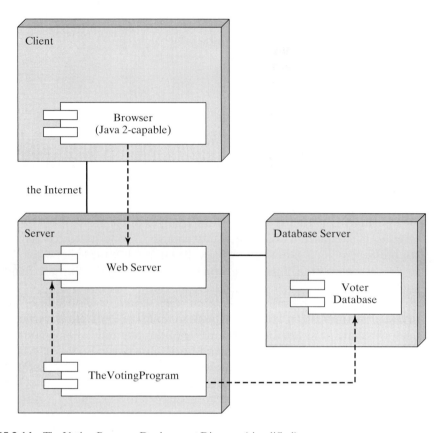

**FIGURE 2.14** The Voting Program Deployment Diagram (simplified)

actual detailed requirements for the software project underway. It is in this phase where we complete the first revision of the Requirements Specification, using the section headers and content recommended earlier in this chapter, including UML activity and sequence diagrams for each use case documented.

In the next sections, we will take a closer look at classes and objects and help you develop a clear understanding of object orientation.

## 2.4 The Purpose of Object Orientation in Software Engineering

The terminology of software engineering is much like the Oracle at Delphi (see Fig. 2.16). In other words, we express the capabilities and features of software systems as metaphors because we have to create a "virtual reality" for users, which typically integrates the display capabilities of the monitor with the input capabilities of keyboard and mouse. Thus when users believe that they are pushing a button on the screen with the mouse pointer and mouse button, the actions displayed on the screen are a mere *simulation* of a button being activated. At a more complex level, virtually all the functionality implemented in a modern graphical software program is a metaphorical simulation of events with which we may be familiar from analogs in the physical world.

---

**METAPHOR: THE ORACLE AT DELPHI**

*Ancient Greek Mythology:* After purifying herself in the water of the Kastalian Fountain, Pythia bent over the Navel of the Earth, ate a laurel leaf and, inhaling the vapors emitted from the chasm, entered a state of ecstasy, uttering incoherent words. The Priest then composed these utterances into verses, while the interpreters attempted to extract some meaning from the prophecy.

---

*Classes* and *objects* are the quintessence of metaphorical representation: while more intangible than traditional procedural program structures, their very abstractness and correlation to the "real world" instills them with great representational power and usefulness. Because they can combine information content and information processing into one conceptual entity, they are self-sufficient functional units that, can operate in ways much more flexible than mere procedural programs.

Classes are *templates:* analogies include architectural blueprints, die cuts, or cookie-cutter stamps. They provide the form or structure for objects but contain no data of their own. Objects (also called instances) are derived from classes in a process called *instantiation*. In this process, characterized by using the Java keyword new, memory is allocated to hold the object, sized and organized based on the structure of the class. Objects are created from classes to hold data about specific instances of the class to which they belong as members.[9]

*Why do we involve ourselves with the complex, esoteric abstraction of classes and objects? Read on.*

## 2.5   Problems with Procedural Programming

We have been building software using *procedural programming* techniques for a long time.[10] Forty-plus years and billions of dollars later, are we now claiming that procedural (structured) programming was all wrong?

In fact, it is actually more accurate to look at object orientation as a powerful evolution of procedural programming.

The software industry has struggled since its inception with problems of quality, cost, and timeliness. The development of software development methodologies, such as W.W. Royce's *Waterfall Method*, attests to the industry's efforts to improve its processes.

Object orientation introduces a new rigor to the process of developing software, legitimizing the precepts of *software engineering*. Java has become a widely adopted object-oriented programming language that explicitly supports the main features of O-O.

---

[9]In procedural programming, the analogy, just for the data aspects of classes and objects, may be how a "type" is related to a "variable of that type."

[10]Procedural programming develops subroutines and functions as procedures. Data is typically stored separately in tables, files or databases. This disconnection easily leads to compatibility and portability problems.

In other words, with object orientation and Java, software development moves from an often unpredictable endeavor based on individual skills to a process that deserves to be characterized as an engineering discipline in terms of adherence to predefined processes and standards, rigor in quality and consistency, ability to repeat and reproduce a particular implementation, and proper documentation and life-cycle manageability.

## 2.6   How O-O Solves Software Development Problems

It is an unfortunate reality that many software developers are notorious for delivering software late, over budget, and containing only a subset of the features expected by the customer, and others never asked for. Object orientation alone only solves some of the long-standing problems in software development. But as part of an overall process, O-O enables major progress. Adhering to an object-oriented life-cycle methodology is the key to improving the reliability of software development. Because our object-oriented software development approach is based on engineering principles, design and development processes become much more predictable, repeatable, and independent of the talents of particular individuals (see Fig. 2.15). The methodology described in this book helps ensure that software development becomes predictable in terms of cost, availability, and feature content reflecting the updated requirements and expectations of the key project stakeholders. Its principles are in concert with the key benefits of the Java programming language. Together, methodology and language provide the committed software engineer with a set of tools that avoid or at least attenuate many of the quality challenges inherent in software development.

FIGURE 2.15   Engineering Precision in Software Development

## 2.7 Understanding Object Orientation

Object orientation can be examined usefully from an architectural perspective. Of course, the notion of "architecture" in software engineering is just another metaphorical concept. We use the analogy of architecture to represent the detailed planning requirements associated with a successful software development project. Just like a blueprint for an office building or a private home, an architectural plan for a software development project provides multiple, coherent perspectives that can be used to completely define the structure of the project (see Figs 2.16 and 2.17).

These images are conceptual analogies that allow us to relate the well-understood process of residential design and construction to the more abstract process of software development. The purpose of this analogy is to help software engineers understand that if they follow a process similar to the one proven to work in building houses, they will gain similar benefits in terms of predictability and repeatability. Just as well-planned buildings are designed to be finished on time and within budget, yet be highly functional and aesthetically pleasing, well-designed software meets all critical customer needs within budget and time constraints.

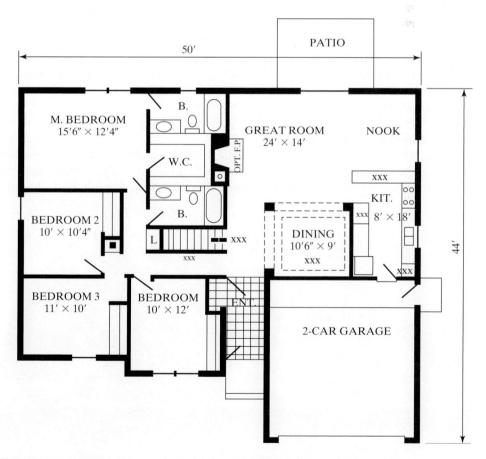

FIGURE 2.16 Sample Architectural Blueprint

FIGURE 2.17 Drawn Perspective of the Architectural Blueprint at Left

In software engineering, *software architecture* realizes the architecture analogy. We identify software architecture as a separate, important step in designing a software solution.

Figure 2.18 shows the different perspectives of an architectural representation of a software development project:

The views in the figure complement our Extended Unified Process Model; they show the various interrelated perspectives that together represent the project at an architectural level. They include the user view, the administrator view, the programmer

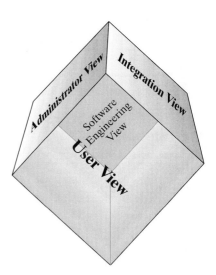

FIGURE 2.18 Architecture Perspectives

view, and the integrator view. Each of these key stakeholders understands the system from a different perspective, and the system has to meet the needs of each viewpoint. The administrator will have a keen interest in the system's installability, for example, while the integrator will want a clear definition of all available interfaces. From these perspectives, software engineers develop the blueprints of their solution, using the requisite UML diagrams and appropriate descriptive paragraphs, even pseudocode.

The combination of use case, component, and deployment diagrams represent the system architecture. From these diagrams, we derive the class hierarchy and all the detailed project designs and implementations. There must be life-cycle consistency between these design diagrams and the Requirements Specification, which represents the stakeholders' requirements.

Object orientation in the life-cycle model translates into implementation specifics in Java-based software applications. The following paragraphs introduce the reader to object orientation in Java and show how software designs based on principles of O-O translate into Java structures and concepts.

## 2.8   Object Orientation in Java

Unlike other programming languages, in particular Visual Basic and C++,[11] object orientation is not "optional" in Java! The very first line in a Java program starts with the O-O keyword "class".[12] Java supports most of the major characteristics of object orientation:

- Abstraction: methods and attributes combined into classes and objects.
- Componentization and component reuse.
- Inheritance (single only):[13] acquiring attributes and methods from a parent class (and its parent, and so on).
- Polymorphism: method and type overloading for flexible reuse of components.
- Strong typing.
- Encapsulation: targeted protection of attributes from external access.

Java provides practical implementations of these features in order to support their benefits in terms of secure, flexible component reuse in the distributed multi-platform computing environment typical of today's IT systems.

### 2.8.1   Java Classes and Objects

As shown in Figure 2.19, the most fundamental characteristic of object orientation is the representation of functionality and data together in *classes,* and in *objects* derived from classes (this derivation is called "instantiation" or "membership"). Program functionality is expressed in *methods*; data is represented by *attributes*. Together, methods and attributes completely define the blueprint for a functional component, a *class.*

---

[11]In C++ and VB, it is possible to write programs without ever using any of the O-O features in the languages.
[12]Keywords are reserved words uniquely identified by the Java compiler to have special meaning.
[13]Interfaces provide an alternative form of "multiple inheritance."

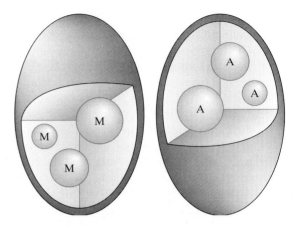

FIGURE 2.19 Attributes and methods together form classes and objects

---

**Example:**

```
/**
 *  which emphasize object interactions.
 *  Structure diagrams  show the static relationships between design elements,
      irrespective of time
 */

public class HelloWorldApp { // class definition
    public static void main(String args[]) {  // method definition
        System.out.println ("Hello World!");
            // Display "Hello World!"
    }
}
```

---

Classes are the templates or blueprints for objects. When there is a need for storing unique data, an object is *instantiated* from a class, so that its methods and attributes can be used to represent specific data and functionality.

This concept is illustrated in Figure 2.20.

As we can see, the object created from the Book class (template) is a specific object (instance) called myBook. In the class, attributes are generic; in the object, they have specific values. Methods remain the same.

Classes are organized into a parent-child structure called a *class hierarchy*. This organization is the basis for the benefits of inheritance, one of the key tenets of object orientation. It is easy to understand how, in a hierarchical structure, *child classes* (also called *subclasses*) inherit methods and attributes from *parent classes* (also called *superclasses*). This makes it possible to create generic functionality only once, for use in multiple places in an application or across multiple applications. The more general methods and attributes simply reside higher in the class hierarchy.

As Figure 2.21 shows, classes have child classes and may be parent classes to other child classes. This organization allows for a well-structured representation of the project architecture as an interrelated system of modular software components. It

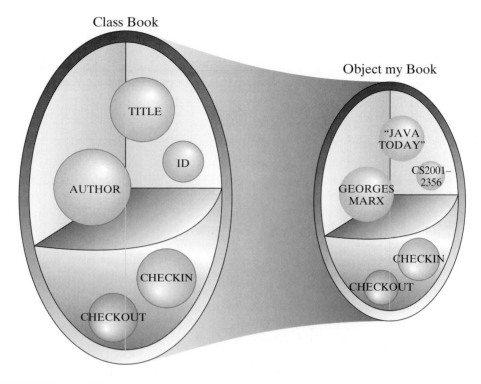

FIGURE 2.20   Simplified Book Class as myBook Object Template

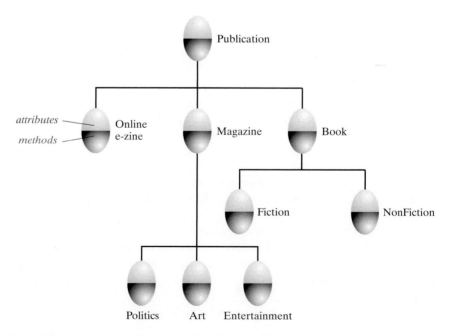

FIGURE 2.21   Representation of a Simplified Class Hierarchy for "Publication"

should become increasingly obvious how the system requirements (from the use cases and use case model of the Requirements Specification) can be converted into classes with methods and attributes in the system class hierarchy, using the various architectural views as guides. This consistency and "translatability" across multiple phases of the development life cycle helps ensure that the development of features is rooted in the system requirements and ultimately satisfies stakeholders' expectations.

## 2.9    Architecture and Class Hierarchy

The different architectural views discussed earlier (see Fig. 2.18) are the scaffold for the conversion of use cases into the class hierarchy. Use cases do not account for detailed technical requirements and software development considerations, so many of the adjustments in creating a class hierarchy from the Use Case Model are related to technical considerations, such as platforms, operating systems, distribution of components, and scalability. While the *User View* is most directly represented by the use cases established during the early phases of the project, the other views will become increasingly important with the progressing implementation of the system. In particular, the **Administrator View** will add requirements for ease of installation and administration. The **Software Engineering View** will influence the distribution and make-up of components. Finally, the **Integration View** will focus architectural and design requirements on interface definitions, and other component-spanning considerations. These views now translate into additional and reorganized classes and subclasses.

One of the main considerations when planning a class hierarchy is to arrange classes for maximum flexibility and reusability. This is important not only in support of actual component reuse, but also to ensure consistency of design and implementation across the entire system. Good reusability fosters a well-balanced design. We will explore this translation of use cases to class hierarchy in more detail in the next chapter, as part of our discussion of Design Phase activities.

## 2.10    Economies of Reuse

There are a number of important considerations associated with the development of reusable software components. They are based on the perspective that building reusable building blocks is preferable to creating one-off software programs. This involves a critical analysis of how each component can be designed and developed for multiple, diverse future uses. This process of abstraction has as a side effect that the resulting software components are more independent, more coherently designed for integration in multiple applications, and more fully functional, especially in the area of error trapping and correction.

Independently functional software components have to work together effectively: the class hierarchy and architectural views are key tools to ensure this cross-component synergy. The definition of *interfaces* has to go hand in hand with the design of the component functionality.[12]

---

[12]"Interfaces" is meant here conceptually, not in terms of the Java-specific implementation of "implements" interfaces.

### 2.10.1   *Quality*

Reusable components tend to get a very good "shakeout" as they are used in multiple applications. The reuse in itself leads to better quality. Also, component developers are aware of the multiple uses of their software and pay increased attention to testing more of the scenarios under which the component may operate. Once a component has been certified, it can be used without retesting its internal workings, as a "black box." This saves on overall testing efforts without compromising quality. (Of course, new integration functionality still has to be validated.)

### 2.10.2   *Consistency*

When a software system is designed as a combination of reusable components, predictable high-quality solutions result from following a consistent pattern in terms of graphical user interface design, naming conventions, interface construction, functional implementation, and logic flow. This is not necessarily true when developing "one-off" programs, in part because these unique efforts often suffer from the "prototyping-turned-product syndrome," in place of a thorough, validated design. Consistency in developing reusable components leads to benefits in usability, installability, maintainability, and scalability.

### 2.10.3   *Implement Once*

The most obvious benefit of reuse is that a given function need only be implemented once and can be reused multiple times. However, in reality, this is usually an iterative process. A component is developed to perform a certain set of functions for a given project. With appropriate foresight and planning, this component is engineered for reuse. More often than not, the additional functionality is added gradually, such as additional overloaded methods,[13] additional interfaces, and so on. Still, as long as the component architecture and its place in the overall system architecture are designed for diverse applications, the principle of "implement once—use many times" is maintained. Because Java is platform-independent, component reuse is easily carried across multiple platforms and operating systems, to run anywhere.

### 2.10.4   *Flexibility*

When designing and developing a component for reuse, it becomes important to think of all the different possible uses of the component even before writing the first line of code. Making components adaptable creates flexibility not only in their various applications, but also in the internal organization of the components in terms of adding functionality later. This added flexibility is a highly desirable side effect of component-based software development, because reworking existing software is a difficult, time- and resource-consuming effort. If the components are engineered for flexible application from the start, their adaptation is faster and easier than with single-purpose software programs.

---

[13]Method overloading refers to the capability of assigning multiple sets of functionality to a function. More on this in a later chapter.

These benefits are maximized if component design and development are executed on the basis of an object-oriented software development methodology like the one advocated in this book, because then the appropriate documentation and supporting information will be readily available whenever additional development work is required.

## 2.11 Use Case Models and Classes

More specifically, how do we convert our Use Case Model into a set of well-organized, related classes?

This conversion is probably one of the most demanding and significant activities in the process of translating stakeholder requirements into information technology–based solutions. It is at this juncture that we take descriptions of requirements and needed functionality and—with an understanding of what computer software can do well—create a blueprint for the implementation we envision. All that we have learned and thought about for a particular project now congeals into a hierarchy of classes. This class hierarchy becomes the scaffold for our IT solution, guided by the system architecture. There is typically not a one-to-one correlation between use cases and classes, because the class hierarchy accounts for all architectural views, as discussed earlier.

In the simple example shown in Figure 2.22, we interpret our Use Case Model with the objective of starting to develop our class hierarchy. This translation process involves the following logical steps:

1. Extract methods and attributes from the use cases.
2. Organize them into logical components (classes).
3. Examine and reorganize classes by extracting *generalizeable* methods and attributes and moving them "up" in the hierarchy.
4. Show relationships between classes (inheritance, interfaces).

This is a simplified preview of an often-complex process, which we will further explore in upcoming chapters.

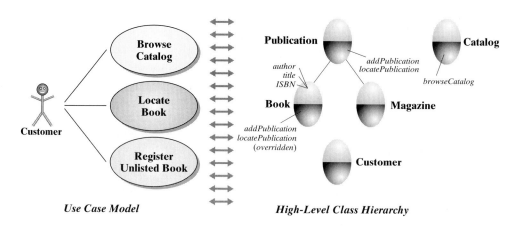

FIGURE 2.22 From Use Case Model to Class Hierarchy (simplified)

## 2.12   "Real-Life" Variations

The development of a class hierarchy is the first major design step in our software development methodology. It is therefore a good idea at this point to ensure that our class hierarchy reflects the project requirements correctly and completely. Our Requirements Specification should be an excellent resource for this validation, but it is also a good idea to include our clients, future users, or any other available project stakeholders in a review of the current state of the project design. While they may not have the technical knowledge to understand software implications of classes and objects, they are the subject matter experts and will have useful intuition about the correct organization of classes.

Also remember that most development projects are impacted by a significant degree of dynamism: an *iterative approach* to software development is an integral component of our methodology because it helps accommodate ongoing refinements and changes. This means that work previously done remains subject to adjustment and improvement as new or changed requirements emerge. It is very important to maintain a lifeline of consistency across all phases of the development project. Especially in the coding phase, developers without a clear plan often go off in one or more directions less and less related to what the project was all about to begin with. It is important to regularly reassess that the project remains on track.

The next step is to understand how conceptual descriptions of classes translate into Java classes.

## 2.13   Translating Generic Class Descriptions into Java Classes

Many Java books introduce classes by having students create a class as a program and then expand it with more functionality. This is a rather "procedural" approach, and we will instead, from the very beginning, look at multiple classes and their interplay. After all, Java is all about component-based, object-oriented programming!

The following example skeleton applies to our earlier Publication example.

**Example:**

```
public abstract class Publication {
    //instance variables – attributes
    private DateFormat: dateAdded, dateRemoved;
    private String: title, author[];
    //methods
    public boolean publicationAdd () {
        // add code to process publication adding
    }

    public boolean publicationRemove () {
        // add code to process publication removing
    }
}

public class Book extends Publication {
```

```
    // instance variables - attributes
    private String: isbnNumber;
    // methods (overridden from Publication
    public boolean publicationAdd () {
        // add code to process publication adding
    }

    public boolean publicationRemove () {
        // add code to process publication removing
    }
}
```

In this example, we create the `Publication` parent class (*abstract*, i.e., no objects will be created from it), and extend it with the `Book` class. The latter class inherits attributes and methods from its parent, but we override the `publicationAdd()` and `publication-Remove()` methods, because we want to handle the book-specific `isbnNumber` attribute in the `Book` version of these methods.

Of course, this early code example is still missing much functional detail, which we will look at in the next chapters, as we develop the requisite Java syntax and structure knowledge.

## 2.14    Unified Modeling Language Perspective

The UML diagrams introduced earlier can be used in certain tools to generate Java code stubs directly. Rational Rose™ from IBM® and Together ControlCenter™ from Borland® Software Corporation are two well-known design products that feature this functionality. These tools also support the reverse process, namely, generating UML diagrams from existing Java code, and thus support *roundtrip engineering*. The latter functionality is useful when acquiring someone else's code and trying to figure out what it does, and how it is organized, in order to bring it into a proper development methodology life cycle.

## 2.15    A Simple Java Program: The Voting Program Prototype

A very basic version of the Voting Program follows. It implements no useful functionality, but shows the basic outline of a simple Java program. (Embedded comments explain functionality.)

```
/**
 * The Voting Program - Basic Version
 *
 * @author Georges Merx, Ph.D.
 * @version 1.00 04/12/07
 */

public class TheVotingProgramBasic { // signature of class
    public static void main(String[] args) {
        // main() method - entry point to program

        String candidate1, candidate2;
```

```
                  // String class variables -> objects
                  int votesCandidate1, votesCandidate2;
                  // primitive type int variables

                  // Display welcome message
                  System.out.println ("Welcome to The Voting Program. " +
                      "Copyright G. Merx.\n");
                  // \n forces newline
                  // Initialize variables with values
                  candidate1 = "Larry Miller";
                  candidate2 = "Lorena Braganza";
                  votesCandidate1 = 2672;
                  votesCandidate2 = 9783;

                  // Display results
                  System.out.print ("The winner of the election is ");
                  // no newline at end of line
                  System.out.println (candidate2 + " with " +
                    votesCandidate2 +" votes!");
                  System.out.println ("\nThank you and good bye!\n");

                  // Exit program
                  System.exit(0);
              }
      }
```

## 2.16    Relationships

In this recurring section, we help readers discover obvious and not so obvious relationships between the material covered here and other topics, ideas, systems, technologies, people, and places.

What we need to keep in mind as we develop software projects are our interpersonal relationships, as much as our understanding of technical issues and connections. Important information about projects is usually found in conversations, informal emails, ongoing discussions and reviews, and generally from sources other than just the formal documents exchanged between stakeholders and implementers. We should regularly review not only our requirements but also our stakeholder analysis, (1) to ensure it is accurate and complete; and (2) to remind ourselves with whom we need to stay in touch.

### 2.16.1    Caveats and Complexities

This subsection in every chapter describes areas that may require special attention or are especially obtuse or confusing, at least for some readers and practitioners. We also include topics which are potentially controversial or which may require more study outside of the scope of this book.

In this chapter, we identify the following areas:

- *Accuracy and completeness of use cases:* superficial use cases are not very useful in developing appropriate designs. In the end, the design requires the specification of attributes and methods; these artifacts are specific and depend on the specificity of the requirement workflows.

- *Documentation:* UML model diagrams are highly useful analysis and design tools, but appropriate notes and information included with each are critical to ensure that the diagrams are interpreted correctly and consistently. As mentioned earlier, these tools are communication devices which must be clear to be useful.

## 2.17 Example: The Voting Program

Let us now pick up our previous example, The Voting Program, introduced in the last chapter. We have progressed to the Analysis Discipline in the development process; the major deliverable of this process step is the Requirements Specification for the Voting Program project. In the next sections, we will take a look at an admittedly skeletal implementation of the Requirements Specification. The Requirements Specification will be based on the conceptual project representation captured in the Project Domain Model, interviews with stakeholders, and other supporting sources of information about functional and nonfunctional requirements.

### 2.17.1 The Domain Model

Figure 2.23 shows the simplified domain model for the Voting Program example.

This domain model diagram shows the main conceptual classes that emerge from the requirements collection and from the conceptualization of the project. This model

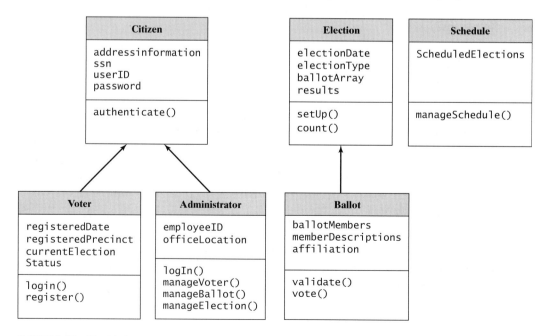

FIGURE 2.23 The Voting Program Domain Model

and the use cases in the Requirements Specification form the foundation for the subsequent design.

### 2.17.2   *Requirements Specification Outline*

As a reminder, the generic outline advocated by the authors for a Requirements Specification follows:

- General Section:
- System Name
- Project Vision and Description
- Stakeholder Analysis
- Risk Management
- System-Level Use Case Diagram
- Architecture Diagram
- Subsystems Description
- For Each Use Case:
- Use Case Name
- Brief Description
- Actors
- Pre-Conditions
- Primary Scenario (Flow of Events)
- Secondary Scenarios
- Diagrams
- Activity Diagram
  - Sequence Diagram
  - User Interface Drawing
- Post-Conditions
- Extension Points
- Other Use Cases Used (including Subordinate Use Cases)
- Deliverables (Artifacts)
- Other Requirements

Following this outline and fleshing out each section with specific information will result in a Requirements Specification with detail complete enough to take the guesswork out of the Design Phase for the Voting Program.

We will expand the Business Use Cases developed in the last chapter and develop an abridged Requirements Specification (shortened to account for the limited space available in these pages):

## *Voting Program Requirements Specification*

| | |
|---|---|
| System Name: | The Voting Program™ |
| Project Vision: | The Voting Program allows voters to securely cast their ballots. |
| Description: | Using a secure computer program (eventually Internet-connected), voters can cast their ballots, following the processes established by the respective registrar of voters. |
| Stakeholder Analysis: | • Voters in one district (initial project)<br>• Election officials<br>• Politicians<br>• Journalists<br>• Software and customer-support engineers<br>• Management, decision-makers<br>• Suppliers of election materials, equipment, etc. |

| Risk Management | Risk | Risk Management Plan |
|---|---|---|
| | Inability to meet election laws | Research requirements carefully |
| | | Focus development on elections approved for this type of product |
| | | Find early-adopter customer to ensure cooperatively that all requirements are met |
| | Security loopholes | Research security technologies and problems and apply from other domains where security is critical (banking, retail) |
| | Lack of acceptance | Do focus group testing, surveys, and investigate other products' success in this market |
| | Limited user access | Work with election officials and communities to ensure computer access for voters at public locations (libraries, schools, etc.) |

System-Level Use
Case Diagram:

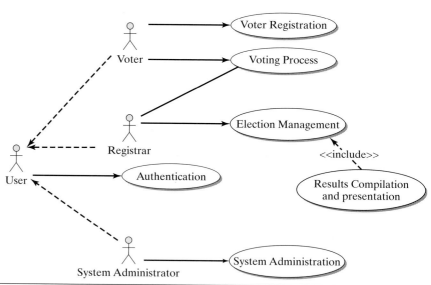

(*Continued*)

Architecture Diagram:

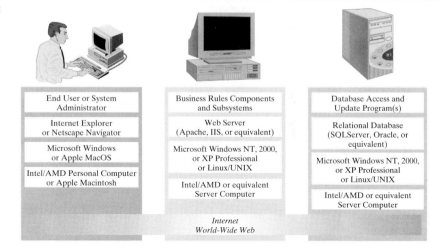

| End User or System Administrator | Business Rules Components and Subsystems | Database Access and Update Program(s) |
|---|---|---|
| Internet Explorer or Netscape Navigator | Web Server (Apache, IIS, or equivalent) | Relational Database (SQLServer, Oracle, or equivalent) |
| Microsoft Windows or Apple MacOS | Microsoft Windows NT, 2000, or XP Professional or Linux/UNIX | Microsoft Windows NT, 2000, or XP Professional or Linux/UNIX |
| Intel/AMD Personal Computer or Apple Macintosh | Intel/AMD or equivalent Server Computer | Intel/AMD or equivalent Server Computer |

*Internet World-Wide Web*

Note: this diagram applies to an eventual Internet-connected implementation, not the prototype implementation covered in this book's example

Subsystems Description:

The complete voting program will consist of three major subsystems:

1. Client subsystem
2. Business Rules subsystem
3. Data Management subsystem

## Use Case 1: Authentication

| | |
|---|---|
| Name: | Voter Authentication |
| Description: | Allowing voters to log in using an identifier and password while ensuring access only by validated voters. Ensuring that voters cannot vote more than once, but can change their vote within a certain time period. |
| Actor(s): | • End user—voter<br>• Election official<br>• System administrator |
| Pre-Conditions: | • The voter must have an identifier and password, possibly provided by mail<br>• The computer must be on |
| Primary Scenario: | 4. Enter URL or pathname of The Voting Program<br>5. At log-on screen or prompt, log-on with id and password<br>6. Validate authentication accepted |
| Secondary Scenarios: | A. Wrong id<br>  - Provide message, allow retry (limit retries?)<br>B. Wrong password<br>  - Provide message, allow retry (limit retries?)<br>C. Internal, system, or network error<br>  - Provide message, exit, notify provider<br>  - Reset database to last committed transaction |

*(Continued)*

Diagrams: Activity Diagram

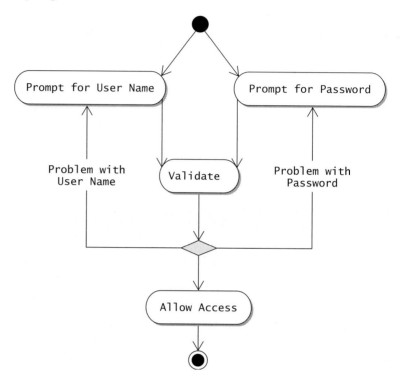

Sequence Diagram

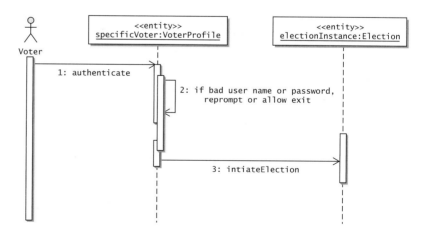

User Interface Drawing

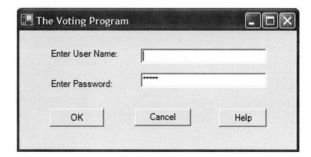

| Post-Conditions: | • Arrive on main section screen<br>• Provide way to exit or continue |
| --- | --- |
| Extension Points: | • Internet-connected Web access<br>• More security—biometrics<br>• Multi-language support<br>• Support for telephone interface |
| Other Use Cases: | • Election Management<br>• Voter Registration<br>• System Administration |
| Other Requirements: | • Access to required platforms (hardware, software, network)<br>• Access to qualified resources<br>• Access to subject matter experts and documentation |

### Use Case 2: Voter Registration

| Name: | Voter Registration |
| --- | --- |
| Description: | This use case covers the addition, deletion, or change of a voter record. |
| Actor(s): | • Registrar—election official |
| Pre-Conditions: | • The registrar must be logged in |
| Primary Scenario: | 1. Select function: add new voter, delete existing voter, modify existing voter record, exit<br>2. Enter relevant information (required and optional), using proper formats<br>   a. Last name, first name, middle name(s)<br>   b. Social security number<br>   c. Address (1, 2, city, county, state, ZIP)<br>   d. Telephone (home, business, cell)<br>   e. Date and location of birth<br>   f. Party affiliation<br>   g. Confirm American citizenship<br>3. Add, delete, change another record or exit |
| Secondary Scenarios: | A. Bad or incomplete input to required fields<br>   - Provide message, allow retry (limit retries?)<br>B. Incorrect input to optional fields<br>   - Provide message, allow retry (limit retries?)<br>C. Internal, system, or network error<br>   - Provide message, exit, notify provider<br>   - Reset database to last committed transaction |

Diagrams:              Activity Diagram

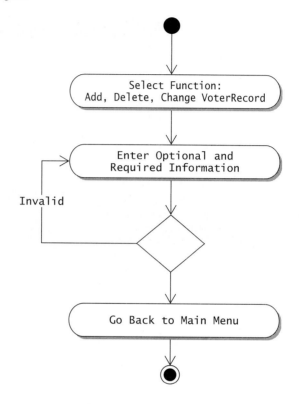

Sequence Diagram

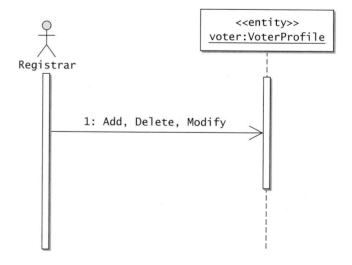

*(Continued)*

User Interface Drawing

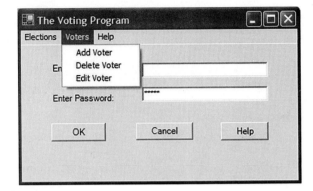

| Post-Conditions: | • Arrive on main section screen<br>• Provide way to exit or continue |
|---|---|
| Extension Points: | • Other voter information—integration with DMV database<br>• Multi-language support |
| Other Use Cases: | • Authentication<br>• Election management<br>• System administration |
| Other Requirements: | • Access to required platforms (hardware, software, network)<br>• Access to qualified resources<br>• Access to subject matter experts and documentation |

## Use Case 3: Voting Process

| Name: | Voting process |
|---|---|
| Description: | Allowing voters to complete and submit their ballot. |
| Actor(s): | End user—voter |
| Pre-Conditions: | • The voter must be logged in and authenticated |
| Primary Scenario: | 4. If more than one active ballot, select appropriate ballot<br>5. Optionally view online information about candidate/proposition<br>6. Select candidates/propositions to vote for and select desired button<br>7. Complete, submit, provide confirmation, and exit |
| Secondary Scenarios: | A. No ballot<br>  - Provide message and exit<br>B. No confirmation or internal, system, or network error<br>  - Provide message, exit, notify provider<br>  - Reset database to last committed transaction |
| Post-Conditions: | • Return to main menu, allow user to change ballot and resubmit<br>• Provide way to exit or continue |

*(Continued)*

Diagrams: Activity Diagram

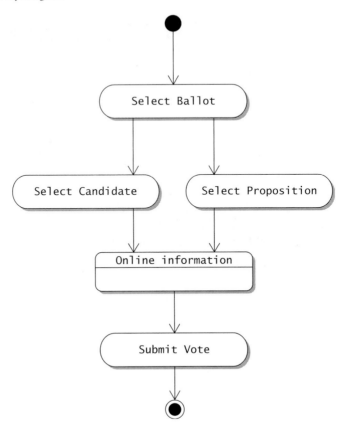

Sequence Diagram

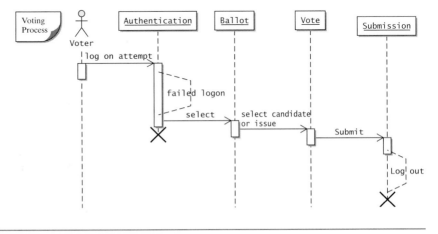

*(Continued)*

User Interface Drawing

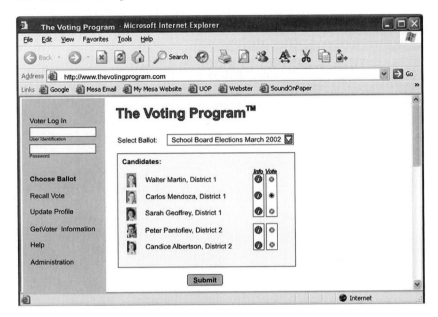

| Post-Conditions: | • Provide way to exit or continue with the next ballot, or option to modify |
|---|---|
| Extension Points: | • Vote change option before a specified deadline (will depend on election laws/regulations) |
| Other Use Cases: | • Authentication, ballot creation |
| Other Requirements: | • Availability of ballot input information (pictures, data, etc.) |
| | • Editor/templates to create ballots |

## Use Case 4: Election Management

| Name: | Election Management |
|---|---|
| Description: | Administrative function to seed the program with the appropriate data for a particular election. This includes the ballot itself and the management of the information associated with ballots and votes collected. |
| Actor(s): | Registrar/election official |
| Pre-Conditions: | • Administration must be strictly access controlled |
| | • Only operators permitted to create or change a ballot or to collect voting information may have access |
| | • This case assumes an authorized user has been authenticated |
| Primary Scenario: | 5. Enter Voting Program administration functions |
| |    A. Create ballot, using input form |
| |    B. Modify ballot, using modify form (variation on input form) |
| | 6. Provide option to make changes |
| | 7. Validate form |
| | 8. Save ballot |

(*Continued*)

| | |
|---|---|
| Secondary Scenarios: | A. Incomplete ballot<br> - Save, but mark "incomplete"—do not allow use/submission<br>B. Cannot find previously edited ballot<br> - Provide message, allow retry<br> - Report problem to administrator<br>C. Internal, system, or network error<br> - Provide message, exit, notify provider<br> - Reset database to last committed transaction |
| Diagrams: | Activity Diagram |

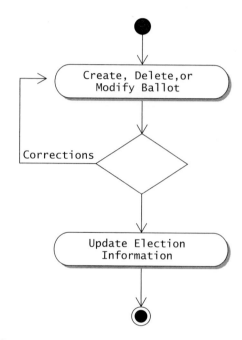

Sequence Diagram

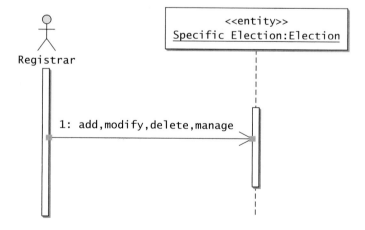

User Interface Drawing

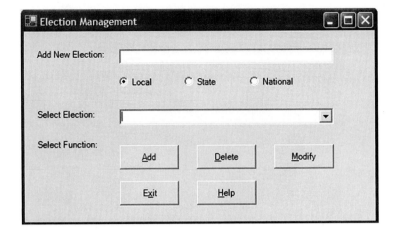

| Post-Conditions: | • Provide way to exit or continue |
| Extension Points: | • Automatic/manual import from other sources<br>• Automatic/manual upload of results to other systems |
| Other Use Cases: | • Authentication—Secure Administration Access |
| Other Requirements: | • Validated system and data security<br>• Ability to effect organized last minute updates<br>• Conservative backup procedures—data loss unacceptable |

## Use Case 5: Results Compilation and Presentation

| Name: | Results Compilation and Presentation |
| Description: | Provides voting results. |
| Actor(s) | Voting official |
| Pre-Conditions | • Administration must be strictly access controlled<br>• Only voting officials permitted to access voting results (future versions may provide access to others)<br>• This case assumes that an authorized user has been authenticated |
| Primary Scenario | 1. Enter Voting Program tallying functions<br>2. Get results info or report<br>3. Provide option to make print or transfer/export |
| Secondary Scenarios | A. Wrong ballot<br>   - Provide message, allow retry (limit retries?)<br>B. No results, wrong results, or internal, system, or network error<br>   - Provide message, exit, notify provider<br>   - Reset database to last committed transaction |
| Post-Conditions | • Return to main menu<br>• Provide way to exit or continue |

*(Continued)*

Diagrams:                    Activity Diagram

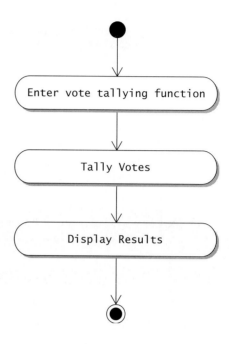

Sequence Diagram

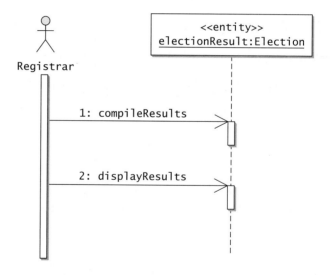

*(Continued)*

User Interface Drawing

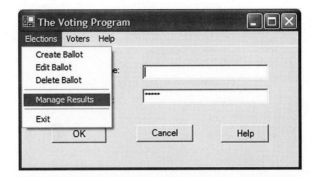

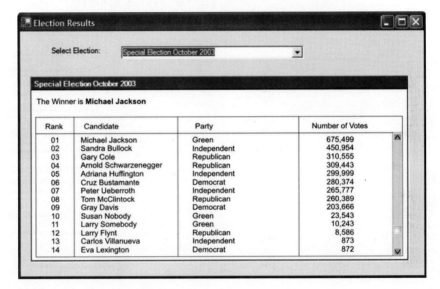

| Post-Conditions: | • Provide way to exit or continue |
| | • Provide way to print results or export to other applications/systems |
| Extension Points: | • Statistical analysis |
| Other Use Cases: | • Authentication |
| Other Requirements: | • Report generator tool or format |

### Use Case 6: System Administration

| Name: | System Administration |
| --- | --- |
| Description: | This use case covers the installation program used to first install and then upgrade the program when new versions are available. Given that the program is Web-based, this only affects the server-based components. |
| Actor(s) | System administrator |
| Pre-Conditions | The installer must have system privileges to install this program. |

*(Continued)*

| | |
|---|---|
| Primary Scenario | 4. Install or upgrade program, using platform-standard installation procedures |
| | 5. Automatic or manual migration of existing data, if needed |
| | 6. Validate security on system to ensure no illegitimate access to any functions |
| Secondary Scenarios | Inability to install, internal, system, or network error |
| | - Provide message, exit, notify provider |
| | - Reset database, if necessary |
| Post-Conditions | System ready to use, existing data accessible |
| Diagrams: | Activity Diagram |

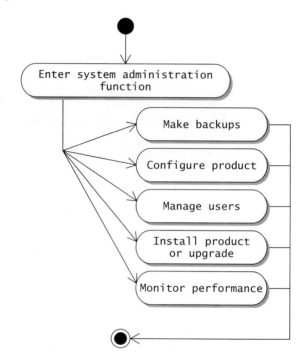

Sequence Diagram

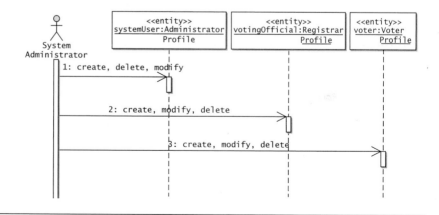

*(Continued)*

User Interface Drawing

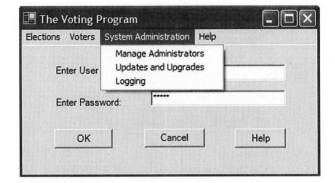

Post-Conditions:     • Provide way to exit or continue, validate and log administration updates

Extension Points:     • Extended logging and monitoring capabilities

                               • Integration with other applications

Other Use Cases:     • Authentication, ballot creation

Other Requirements:     • Installation program

### 2.17.3 *Deliverables*

The additional information deliverables at this time include a High-Level Project/Iteration and Resource Plan, and the revised Business Plan. While detailed project plans will be created for each iteration (subproject), an overall plan is established at this time that covers the scope of the project and the resources and time required to successfully complete it.

### 2.17.4 *Other Requirements*

No other requirements have been identified.

## 2.18 *Harm*  *ny* Design Case Study

We now continue with the Business Case Analysis begun in the last chapter. As you may remember, this case study is your responsibility: we will only provide enough information for you to proceed with your own research to "flesh" out the project. Your assignment in this chapter is to complete the Business Plan for the *ModelHomeDesigner*. Please follow the following outline:[14]

1. Project or System Vision
2. Project Description
3. Stakeholder Analysis
4. Customer Profile
5. Market Analysis
6. Risk Analysis
7. Business Use Case Model and Business Use Cases
8. Competitive Analysis
9. Distribution Plan (Pricing, Packaging, Promotion, Positioning)
10. Financial Plan (Revenue Plan, Budget, Cash Flow Analysis, ROI Analysis)
11. High-Level Project Plan
12. Recommendations

### 2.18.1 Market Analysis

The market analysis will need to look at the overall market for software for interior design, especially the subsegment for model home design. We are interested in market size (total revenue opportunity per year), market window (related to the competitive analysis below), and market growth rate. We are also interested in the process for market penetration and distribution. The analysis needs to focus on the use of IT solutions like **ModelHomeDesigner** and not be overly general. As with everything in business and technology, precision brings value!

### 2.18.2 Risk Management

We begin by establishing a risk-management table for this project (see Table 2.3). Your task is to fill in the rest of the table.

Make sure to include valid risk-management approaches.

TABLE 2.3  Risk Analysis

| Risk | Risk Management |
|------|-----------------|
| • Difficulty creating uniform requirements for diverse target companies … | • … |
| • … | • … |

---

[14]The first four items were completed in the last chapter.

### 2.18.3  Business Use Case Model and Business Use Cases

Based on the example in the previous chapter (The Voting Program), create a set of valid business use cases and organize them in a proper use case model. Possibilities for use cases include:

- Project Description
  - Project Management
- Materials Management
  - Materials Ordering
  - Materials Tracking
- Design Management
- Delivery and Installation Management
- Productivity Analysis

We are positive that you can develop some more use cases and reorganize the ones we have suggested here for optimal integration and flexible reuse.

### 2.18.4  Competitive Analysis

The competitive analysis section of the Business Plan for this project needs to examine other interior design companies, especially those focused on model home interior design. It will be particularly useful to look at the utilization of IT in those companies, and to seek correlations between their use of IT and their productivity. It may also be valuable to look at similar industries that provide a design service like HarmonyDesigns, but in slightly different markets, such as residential interior design companies, advertising companies and their ad campaigns, architectural firms, and other companies with custom projects. Productivity itself is quite straightforward to measure: how many designer and support personnel working hours were required to produce a typical $100,000 project? HarmonyDesigns' own productivity will need to be the obvious yardstick for this comparison.

Establish a list of comparative values, such as:

1. Business profile—type and scope of projects
2. Number of offices, number and job classification of employees
3. Annual revenue, annual profit, revenue and profit per employee, overhead component
4. Use of information technology
5. Strengths and weaknesses

### 2.18.5  Distribution Plan (Pricing, Packaging, Promotion, Positioning)

The distribution of our proposed solution is your concern in this section. Will we have to develop a direct-sales force? Can we distribute through indirect channels (resellers)? Do we deploy via Internet downloads, or do we package the product on CD-ROMs? We also need to consider how we price our product and any services we plan to offer, and need to account for this topic in our competitive analysis. We need to justify our pricing and correlate to our financial plan (see below). Finally, we need to discuss promotion and advertising plans. This may include attendance at trade shows, online or paper ads, and other approaches.

### 2.18.6 Financial Plan (Revenue Plan, Budget, Cash Flow Analysis, ROI Analysis)

While genuine financial planning is beyond the scope of this example, we encourage you to give some thought to the financial side of the project. Even as software engineers, you will be called upon to estimate costs, especially in terms of the time it will take you to complete certain components and features. But other aspects of financial planning are also of interest:

- Revenue planning: When will we receive the first revenue from this project? How much revenue will we receive over time? Per quarter? From where?
- Expense planning (budget): What costs will arise, when, from what?
- How much cash do we need, and exactly when?
- For our investors: What will their Return On Investment (ROI) be? What is our 'exit strategy', meaning when will they get their money back—with gains, of course? What will these gains be?

### 2.18.7 High-Level Project Plan

In order to complete our ambitious project, we need a plan. At this early stage we need to produce a high-level (macro) project plan based on the scope of the project and our understanding of all the key requirements. Available resources and financing provide another key element of information when we develop our project plan, either reducing the amount of functionality possible or lengthening the duration of the overall project. The second project-related planning decision we need to make at this time is to decide on the number of iterations required to complete the project. Each iteration will eventually result in its own (micro) project plan, of course. Our use case model will play a key role in determining our estimate at this point of the number of iterations required to complete this project successfully.

### 2.18.8 Recommendations

Because this is a business plan, one of its key purposes is to convince decision-makers and investors to lend their support to the project. The Recommendations section is therefore the place where we ask for what we want: money, authority, resources, all the people and things we need to produce this project according to requirements, on time, and within budget.

### 2.18.9 Case Assignments

From the outline above, a number of useful student assignments can be derived.

1. Complete the Business Plan.
2. *Marketing Analysis*: Find three more industries with work processes similar enough to warrant a comparison to HarmonyDesigns.

3. *Iteration project plans*: establish micro-level project plans for Iteration 1 (the current one) and 2. Make sure you include the eight phases of the development methodology for each Iteration Plan: *Concept, Analysis, Design, Implementation, Integration, Field Test, Certification, Deployment.* This exercise will be useful not least because it forces you to come up with *tasks* for each of these mini-phases. A good rule of thumb for iterations is that they should cover approximately the work that six people can do in six weeks.

## 2.19   Resources: Connections • People • Companies

Many companies and individuals are actively involved with object-oriented software engineering using Java. There are thousands of Java programmers worldwide. In this recurring section, we will provide you with a collection of useful resources and Web links that will give you access to additional information, ideas, cases, and suggestions.

- Sun® Java™ Tutorial
- IBM Rational® Unified Process
- OMG Unified Modeling Language Standard
- Rational® Rose™
- Borland® Together™

## 2.20   Summary and Recommendations

We have learned much in this chapter about object orientation and about the analysis of software project. It is important to remember that these areas are closely related: in the end, stakeholder requirements captured in text and UML diagrams are sooner or later morphed into features and functions in our software application. We remind you now that the more rigorously you follow the software engineering approach to software development advocated in this book, the better the quality of your resulting software application will be.

## 2.21   Review Questions

This section, repeated at the end of every chapter, provides you with a number of questions and assignments that will allow you to check your knowledge.

1. **Objects and Classes.**  Explain and provide at least five examples of classes and objects and their key components. Choose examples where you can show the relationships between related classes and objects. Provide clear, concise definitions.
2. **Eight UML Diagrams.**  Draw examples of the eight core UML diagrams, all related to a single example: a bank's ATM system.

## 2.22   Glossary – Terminology – Concepts

**Attributes**   Also sometimes called properties; they hold the data components of objects.

**Class hierarchy**  We organize classes as parent and child classes, where child classes inherit attributes and methods from their parents, thus reducing the amount of code in the overall system.

**Classes**  Classes are templates for objects instantiated in Java using the new key word.

**Methods**  Functional components of classes and objects; they contain the executable code of the program.

**Objects**  Instances of classes used to hold specific data in their attributes (instance variables).

**UML Diagrams**  Standardized by the OMG, these diagrams provide representations of all relevant aspects of software engineering projects. There are two types of diagrams. (1) Structural Diagrams: Class/Object Diagram, Component Diagram, and Deployment Diagram; and (2) Behavior Diagrams: Use Case Diagram (used by some methodologies during requirements gathering); Sequence Diagram, Activity Diagram, Communication Diagram, and Statechart Diagram.

## 2.23  Exercises

**1. Terminology.**  Research on the Web and in your book the following terms and define them in writing:

- The 4-Ps in marketing: Pricing, Packaging, Promotion, Positioning.
- System/software architecture.
- Classes and objects, methods and attributes, and their implementation in three programming languages (of your choice).

**2. Creating a Requirements Specification.**  Based on the examples and recommended outlines in this chapter, create a Requirements Specification of the following product:

- Electronic (software-based) time tracking program for law offices Include all recommended sections and diagrams.

**3. Creating UML Models.**  Create the UML models for the above project (Exercise 2) that are *not* part of the Requirements Specification.

# The Structure and Syntax of Java

Like any language, whether for human-to-human or human-to-computer interaction, Java has rules of syntax, structure, and meaning (semantics). In this chapter we begin to explore these rules so that you can become conversant in your new programming language.

When designing and constructing Java code, even software engineering novices need to operate from a clear understanding of Java syntax rules. Vague knowledge is insufficient to conform to the rigors of the language and leads to excessive errors and frustration.

Java is a software development tool composed of many components, some always included, and many optional. From J2SE (Java 2 Standard Edition, for Java client applications and applets), to J2ME (Java 2 Micro Edition, for Java applications on mobile devices), to J2EE (Java 2 Enterprise Edition, for Java applications on enterprise-level systems), Sun Microsystems has developed Java into a vast landscape of packaged classes available from Sun Microsystems and hundreds of third-party vendors.[1] It is therefore almost as important to understand how to find information about components that may be available from an external source, and how to apply these components, as it is critical to

> URLs are provided as references throughout the book. These references may be changed by the site owners over time, leading to inactive links.

---

[1]Sun Microsystems' Java Solutions Marketplace: http://industry.java.sun.com/solutions.

FIGURE 3.1   Kevin Vilay, Java Software Engineer

comprehend the basic Java language syntax rules. Fortunately, these add-on components (packages) normally follow standard formatting and documentation guidelines, making them easily accessible. These add-on packages are available as compiled class structures, so you don't have to become familiar with the internal code; all you have to understand and access are externalized interfaces. There are ample on-line and book resources available that cover all the different capabilities and extensions of Java. It seems most productive to have multiple reference and tutorial resources available, because no single resource cover, every topic equally, an impossible goal that would require thousands of pages per volume.

FIGURE 3.2   Fitting All of Java into One Book
Is Impossible

The following abbreviated list of quality book and online resources will be a good start for your "Java Library."

- Sun Microsystems Java Tutorial
- Core Java Fundamentals and Advanced Features, Seventh Edition (Horstmann and Cornell)
- Java: An Introduction to Problem Solving and Programming, Fourth Edition (Savitch)
- Java: How to Program, Sixth Edition (Deitel and Deitel)
- Java, Java, Java, Third Edition (Morelli and Walde)
- Murach's Beginning Java 2 (Murach)
- The Object of Java (Riley)

Unlike spoken languages, computer programming languages are learned by applying in your code what you read about in books and articles, and in other people's programs. The use of such materials is therefore critical in deepening your knowledge and understanding of Java capabilities and implementations. As in all engineering, most learning is based on the discipline's aggregated experience and knowledge.

## 3.1 Learning Objectives

It is now time to focus our attention on the language features of Java programming. This chapter introduces many of the key concepts in Java syntax, code organization, and logic flow. We will also continue our study of the underlying principles of software engineering methodology, and begin the discussion on the Design Phase and its related deliverables (artifacts), in particular the Design Specification. The design of features is prerequisite to any code development, so before we can usefully apply our emerging Java syntax knowledge, we have to understand how to translate available requirements into properly designed functions and features.

Because this book focuses on the software engineering aspects of Java programming, the coverage detail of language features is neither as comprehensive nor as detailed as other books (e.g., Deitel's Java: How to Program), and it is understood that students will draw from additional resources, especially the vast amount of reference and tutorial information available on the Sun Microsystems Web site (www.java.sun.com) to complement this book's coverage of Java syntax.

### 3.1.1 Learning Layout

This recurring section shows the learning objectives of the chapter in a simple diagram, using the Unified Modeling Language (UML) activity diagram notation (see Fig. 3.3). The diagram shows the student-learning expectations for this chapter. The focus of the chapter is on learning Java syntax and structure, but within the context of *software engineering best practices*. An optional section helps the novice programmer understand basic principles of software development.

### 3.1.2 Learning Connections

The Learning Connections diagram in Figure 3.4 shows the content of this chapter in relation to the knowledge and skills development recommended for apprentice Java software engineers.

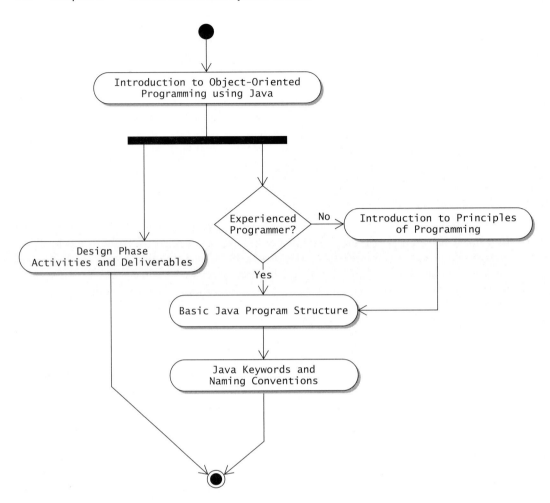

FIGURE 3.3 Chapter 3 Learning Layout (as a UML Activity Diagram)

## 3.2 Executive Summary

Java programs are organized into packages of classes. As you already know, classes are templates for objects. Each package contains one or more classes. If the program is standalone, meaning that it uses the local system's user interface (UI) capabilities (character-based, or graphical windowing system), one class (at least) has to contain the main() method, which tells the Java Virtual Machine (JVM) where the program starts. If the program is an applet, meaning that it is run from a Java Runtime–enabled browser, one class contains the main message-processing methods for the program.

Classes are *templates* for objects; the objects are created as needed within the class code or from other objects/classes (using the keyword new). They become members of the class they instantiate. Objects contain data in the form of attributes defined in the class as instance variables. Classes and, by extension, objects are organized into a hierarchy so that

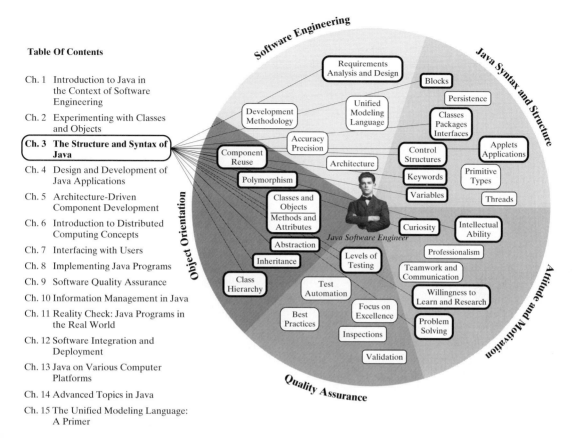

FIGURE 3.4   Learning Connections for Chapter 3

child classes can inherit attributes and methods from parent classes (using the keyword `extends`). In addition, Java provides a facility for defining interfaces, which set up predefined methods coded in our programs (using the keyword `implements`).

This flexible infrastructure, illustrated in Figure 3.5, allows for small, compact programs, which only include the functionality mandated by the program by giving the developer the flexibility to limit the importing of external classes to those needed. At the same time, abstraction, inheritance, polymorphism, and interfaces allow for maximum reuse of existing code, whether from third parties or previously developed for similar purposes by the current development team.

---

## ENUMERATIONS

J2SE 5.0 introduced us to a special class type called **enumerations.** An enumeration is declared using the **enum** keyword and provides a powerful, flexible organization for constant variables and their manipulation.

---

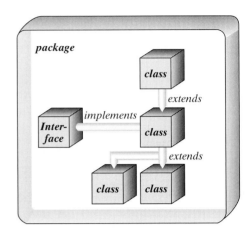

FIGURE 3.5    Concept of Class and Interface Hierarchy

Remember that the purpose of these technologies is to implement stakeholder requirements. It is vital to stay grounded in the software methodology life cycle. In this chapter, we look at the **Design Phase** of the process defined earlier in the book. Arguably the most "creative" aspect of a software development project, the design of the product structure, features, and functions requires a good understanding of how computer technology is applied to solving business problems efficiently and effectively ("process reengineering"). We explore in this chapter proven techniques that ensure that this "translation" from requirements to functional code results in the work process improvements expected by project stakeholders.

## 3.3    Learning a Programming Language

Traditionally, programming languages have been part of the discipline of computer science, itself often viewed as an extension of mathematics. However, learning a software programming language is generally more akin to learning a foreign language than to learning new math skills. From this linguistic perspective, it is easy to understand that *practice, practice, practice* is the straightest path to success. In addition, a foundation in logical thinking and problem-solving is helpful. Math skills are required to implement algorithms and formulas. Most software programs are written to solve more or less complex business or technical problems, using the power of machine computation. The ability, therefore, to logically "translate" business problems into computer functionality is an important and difficult skill for software engineers to develop. (Interestingly, some artists make good software developers; it follows that the ability to think critically and creatively helps in developing high-quality software applications.)

### 3.3.1    For the Novice

If this is the first programming language you learn, take heart: software programming languages are not nearly as complex and extensive as real foreign languages, and their features are repetitive in nature, so that once you learn basic rules and assumptions, understanding additional features is relatively straightforward. That is why we spend so much time building a solid software engineering foundation in the first few chapters of this book: the methodology enables you to populate its rich scaffold with Java features, functions, components, and classes.

Novice programmers often overestimate the "intelligence" of the computer hardware and software at their disposal. Keep in mind that for *everything* you want the computer to do, you have to create program code, or you have to use functionality programmed by someone else and import it into your program!

Most programs are written to manipulate data. As we have discussed previously (see Fig. 3.6), we develop software functions to add substantial value to data by transforming data into information and information into knowledge. Superior knowledge is the key ingredient in better decisions.

Writing programs is an exercise in English, math, and logic, but with very strict additional rules and structure. These strict rules make it possible for the compiler to unequivocally interpret source code statements into bytecodes that translate to specific machine codes. Every source code statement typically contains multiple elements and keywords and incorporates an action to be taken; statements are interpreted first by the compiler (resulting in bytecodes), and ultimately by the JVM as sets of machine instructions. By default, statements are executed (performed) one after another (until some branching instruction is encountered), and the resulting impacts of

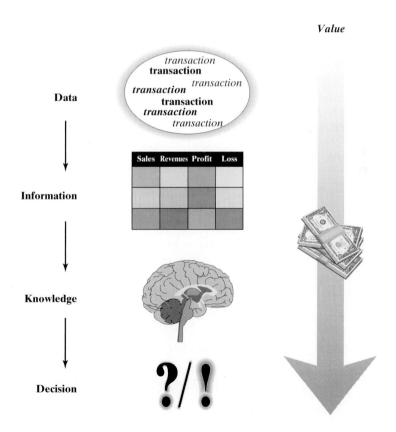

FIGURE 3.6    Software Functions Add Value to Data

each statement on the data manipulated by the program accumulate. This cumulative result is the valuable transformation of data into useful information and therefore hopefully into increased end-user knowledge.

### Out-of-Sequence Statements

While statements are by default executed sequentially, a special set of commands causes the program execution pointer to jump to a specific location in the code and continue executing there or to execute a set of statements repeatedly. To facilitate this type of operation, software source code is organized into blocks, which are not necessarily sequential. Unlike regular English text, Java software code is grouped into blocks of code separated by braces (see Fig. 3.7), and while the statements in these blocks are performed consecutively, the blocks are often not executed in sequence, but are repeated,

```java
1  import java.awt.*; //import required packages
2  import javax.swing.*;
3
4  public class Library extends JFrame { /* extend JFrame class - create
      new window */
5      String name, address, floor, shelf; /* to be used in complete
          program */
6      Container c;
7      JTextArea outputArea;
8
9      public Library() { /* constructor method to initialize program
          block */
10          super ("LibraryManager"); // set window title bar
11
12          String output = "Welcome to the LibraryManager!";
13          c = getContentPane(); /* get the window content and set the
            layout */
14          c setLayout (new FlowLayout());
15          outputArea = new JTextArea (10, 20);
16          c.add (outputArea);
17          outputArea.setText (output): // set the text area's text
18          setSize (300,200); // size the window
19          setVisible (true); // make the window visible
20      }
21
22      public static void main (String [] args) { /* entry point for
          program */
23          Library app = new Library(); /* create a new object of class
              'Library' */
24          app.setDefaultCloseOperation (JFrame.EXIT_ON_CLOSE);
25          // make sure close operation closes window
26      }
27  }
```

FIGURE 3.7 Sample Program to Illustrate a Block of Java Statements

or are selected for execution depending on the result of a conditional test. The Java software engineer must therefore learn not only syntax and statement forms, but also logical flow and the meaning associated with structural elements and block sequencing. This logic flow implements the *semantics*, or useful meaning, of the program.

Traditionally, this information was modeled using flow charts. Today, we use a combination of UML diagrams and descriptions to represent the logic and sequence in software components, as was discussed in the preceding chapters. This represents the Design discipline in our methodology.

---

### TIP FOR NOVICES

*Practice, practice, practice!* Don't start with a "blank sheet," but experiment with existing programs, make sure you understand how they work, and then add functionality a step at a time. Take care to not make small typos or logic mistakes.

---

### Similarities to Foreign Language Learning

While schools teach foreign languages on the basis of grammar and syntax rules, the most effective way to learn a language is through actual practice. Move to Mexico for six months or a year, and your ability to communicate in Spanish will be much greater than if you study Spanish for two semesters in a classroom!

In the same way, novice software engineers who commit themselves from the beginning to write as many Java programs as possible are the ones who succeed most rapidly in mastering this new language. While the analogy between Java and a new foreign language is valid, there are also some differences: in Java and other programming languages, minor mistakes lead to program-stopping compiler or execution errors, whereas a mispronounced Spanish word has few, if any, consequences. In a natural language, even a few words can form an understandable meaning, but in programming, a minimum number of correct statements is required to do anything useful. In general, uncompromising attention to detail is necessary.

### Expectations, Learning Approach

Learning a software programming language is not an easy task, for a number of reasons:

- While Java is English-like, its readability greatly depends on understanding its unique syntax rules, as well as on the programmer's careful use of meaningful variable, method, and class names.
- For the novice, there are many syntax and structure rules to master, and the rigor of a programming language is unfamiliar. The program logic must be accurate and complete.
- Java and similar advanced languages have many different features and capabilities—there is simply *a lot* to learn.
- Software is not forgiving: even seemingly minor errors (like forgetting a semicolon) lead to abnormal program terminations, and, at times, cryptic error messages which are hard to decipher ("debugging" process).

- The novice software engineer has to understand the concepts of translating desired functionality into functioning software code—fundamentally, what lines of code to put where in order to achieve a desired logical-functional result.
- Fully functional programs take many lines of code, leading to a lot of checking and correcting for all the possible error conditions that might occur (hopefully, these have been captured and planned for at design time in the secondary scenarios of the requirements and design use-cases).
- There are multiple interdependencies between components in larger programs. These require extensive testing of interfaces and interactions.

---

### NOVICE TIP

Inexperienced programmers sometimes spend hours trying to fix simple problems associated with careless typing errors.

---

Learning how to develop useful, high-quality software requires commitment, dedication, intelligence, and a significant amount of practice and studying/research time. That is why software engineers typically earn a considerable income, once they have mastered their specialized craft.

But programming languages also have a finite set of features and rules: once you understand them, you can learn them and master them! They follow similar, limited patterns, so your basic understanding of Java syntax and structure will take you a long way toward understanding and quickly grasping the more complex, more advanced capabilities of the language. Your learning will accelerate over time. Also, unlike in foreign language training, you do not need to memorize a large core set of words and sentences for programming languages; it is generally sufficient to know how to find information about these elements in your reference materials.

In addition, the application of a comprehensive, object-oriented software development methodology (as discussed in previous chapters) goes a long way toward helping even inexperienced developers to write code that meets customer requirements and implements stable, resilient functionality.

---

### BACKGROUND

It is important to understand that the program that interprets your Java source statements is just another application, limited in logic and "intelligence" to the rules implemented in its own code. The error messages it generates, for example, are based on its best guess of what you were trying to achieve in your incorrect code ...

### 3.3.2   *For the Experienced Software Engineer*

If you are already a software programmer and you are adding Java to your repertoire, your experience will come in handy—*usually*.

If you are accustomed to procedural programming, you may need to "unlearn" some habits and concepts that do not translate well to object-oriented software engineering. You may also have well-entrenched opinions about object orientation, not always positive ones. But because Java relies on your knowledge and adoption of object orientation, we must encourage you to suspend any negative judgment you may have, and to embrace the benefits of the O-O approach. You can start by "letting go," if necessary, of some of the following "legacy techniques":

- Waterfall method of software design (see Figure 3.8)[2]
- Flow charting as the primary design tool
- "Spaghetti code," often evolved from a prototype-centric programming approach or "heroic programming"
- Separation of functions and data
- Viewing software as a collection of programs or modules and subroutines

The discipline of software development has a long history of good intentions and failed implementations. Many programmers take great pride in their creativity, design talents, and programming prowess. However, these unique, nonstandardized skills and approaches usually do not scale up well to today's larger, more complex projects, and they are difficult to adapt to projects executed by teams of collaborating professionals. Worse yet, these techniques, while possibly resulting in functional programs, often poorly implement the project requirements sought by the primary stakeholders and thus may require extensive reworking.

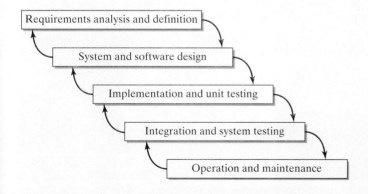

FIGURE 3.8   W.W. Royce's Waterfall Method

---

[2]As Walker Royce points out in *Software Project Management: A Unified Framework* (Addison-Wesley Professional, 1998) the Waterfall Method, developed by his father, W.W. Royce, was visionary for its time and has often been misapplied. We acknowledge its historic contribution to the discipline of software engineering.

Even more important, the concepts of object-orientation in general, and of Java in particular, need to be added effectively to the expert's body of knowledge, given the dominance of these concepts in today's software engineering profession.

Often, the more we know, the more we may resist new knowledge, new approaches to solving old problems. However, approaching object-oriented software engineering with an *open mind* is critical to your success. This is so important a principle that it is embodied in the symbol of the American Institute of Engineers (see Fig. 3.9).

### 3.3.3    Similarities to Other O-O Programming Languages

Java and other modern object-oriented languages share many commonalities, but there are also important differences. The Microsoft languages (C++, C#, Visual Basic) are geared to Microsoft's own .NET Web services strategy, while Sun Microsystems' Java and its supporters promote Java's platform independence and portability to systems from a large number of vendors, from IBM, to Hewlett-Packard, to Apple. C++ is a widely used O-O language that supports advanced features like multiple inheritance, but it suffers from various arcane idiosyncrasies, at least in the opinion of some software engineering experts, mostly because of its compatibility with the original C language. A more comprehensive comparison would also account for proprietary technologies such as Borland's Delphi™ and Compuware's UNIFACE™. However, this brief exploration of other tools is not intended to be complete, just to introduce you to the similarities and differences between Java and other dominant programming tools.

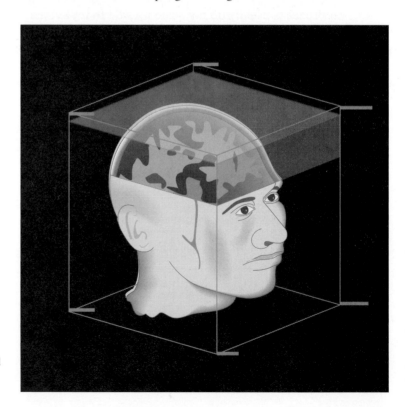

FIGURE 3.9   Open Mind Symbol of the American Institute of Engineers

## C++

C++ may be the most flexible of the dominant contemporary programming languages. Its flexibility has advantages and disadvantages. Unlike Java, C++ allows programmers to write in a wide range of styles, including a C-like procedural programming style.[3] On the other hand, C++ supports all advanced object-oriented features, including multiple inheritance, the latter not available in Java. Also, unlike Java, which is interpreted, C++ is compiled into machine language for the platform on which the program runs, sacrificing portability, but at times yielding much faster execution speeds. C++ is a "lower-level" third-generation language (3GL) in that it requires explicit memory and resource management as well as operating-system-level calls for functions built into Java (e.g., multithreading; support for multimedia, networking). In Java, memory and resource management are handled by the JVM. Syntactically, C++ and Java belong to the same family, sharing a number of similar constructs. Java programmers knowledgeable in C++ may sometimes struggle with the transition from one to the other because of their similarities, expecting one to implement all the other's features.

C++ compilers are available from many sources, including Microsoft, Borland, Watcom, GNU, Intel, and Metrowerks.

### Microsoft® Visual Basic™

Microsoft Visual Basic (VB) programmers will find a lot of O-O similarity between VB and Java. In fact, it often seems as if Sun Microsystems wants to make sure that comparable features are available in Java, and vice versa. Java with a Java Integrated Development Environment (IDE) looks and behaves much like VB, especially when one is developing Microsoft Windows applications.

VB and Java are both high-level, third-generation languages (3GLs) with a full complement of reusable components and support for modern operating system platforms. Java supports many more hardware and operating platforms than VB, however. Java, like VB, manages memory allocation and recovery ("garbage collection") transparently. Both have support for clients and servers, but VB's server support is limited to VBScript, in practice reducing the usefulness of VB to the development of client applications. The most recent version of VB, Visual Basic.NET, has adopted many Java-like features in support of expanded object orientation.

### Microsoft C# and J#

Microsoft has released new object-oriented programming tools as part of its Visual Studio.NET Integrated Development Environment for its .NET platform. These languages follow an architecture similar to Java's, using an intermediary language interpreted during execution, affording improved portability across the various hardware platforms that support Microsoft Windows.NET.

---

[3]"Programming style" is an important concept. It represents an individual's or organization's approach to software development, their internal rules and guidelines, and repeatable ways of implementing software.

---

### ACCORDING TO MICROSOFT

"Microsoft® .NET is the Microsoft XML Web services platform. XML Web services allow applications to communicate and share data over the Internet, regardless of operating system, device, or programming language. The Microsoft .NET platform delivers what developers need to create XML Web services and stitch them together."

---

Microsoft has discontinued all active support of Java. This is not surprising, given its frequently acrimonious competition with Sun Microsystems, which has led to a polarization of the market into the UNIX/LINUX/Java/Sun/IBM/HP camp on one side, and Microsoft on the other. Software engineers now must learn two platforms, languages, and strategies if they want to be able to work on either platform.

## 3.4    Learning Modules

The following sections describe the key concepts of this chapter, focused on further developing your budding knowledge of Java syntax and structure.

### 3.4.1    Concepts

This section introduces the key concepts of Java programming, including variations of program structure, Java keywords and functions, and the overall syntax of Java programs.

#### Building Java Solutions

Programming code is conceptually simple: a program is a collection of structured statements which are processed sequentially, except when the flow of execution is redirected based on a condition or a repetitive clause, or if a call to another function (method) temporarily redirects the course of the program. As always, the devil is in the details.

From the very start, we look at Java programs as well-planned assemblages of classes designed for reuse. Java programs are composed of one or more classes, as we have seen in the simple, earlier examples in this book. These classes represent the use cases described in the (requirements) analysis and design phases of the project and are implemented according to the system architecture established for the product being developed.

The two types of Java programs covered in detail in this book are standalone programs and Java applets, with a focus on applications. The former run on the system using its native user interface (UI).[4] The latter are accessed over the World Wide Web and run as browser clients.

---

[4]User Interface: in this case, the local windowing system, e.g., Microsoft® Windows™, Apple® Mac OS™, or UNIX X-Windows/Motif.

Larger Java programs consist of classes organized into packages for reuse.[5] Classes are used as *templates* for objects, created whenever the storing of object data (instance variables) is required. Using the new keyword, a class creates an object of itself or of another class and thus ensures that memory is allocated and available for data (attributes or instance variables) associated with that object.

### Principles of Java Syntax

As we begin writing more complex Java programs, we need to examine the fundamentals of Java syntax in greater detail. As shown in Figure 3.10, Java statements are composed of words (tokens), just like any other language. These words are keywords, with reserved meanings, or they are words (variables, etc.) created by the programmer to hold specific meaning for the program at hand. Most words either perform a function or they contain information (data). When a word contains data, it is commonly a *variable*; multiple words that together perform specific functions are referred to as *statements*. A variable represents a named storage location allocated in Random Access Memory (RAM) to hold data of a particular type or class.

Java, like all software programming languages, is unforgiving when it comes to syntax errors, so programmers must ensure that they use words and statements with 100% accuracy and consistency, including whether a word is capitalized or not, and including punctuation. This is the case because a software program called a *compiler* analyzes (parses) the Java code you have written, extracts and interprets sequences of tokens ("words") (lexical analysis), and translates them into codes (bytecodes). The JVM then turns the bytecodes into executable (machine language) commands for the computer on which your program executes. There is simply no room for ambiguity!

Let's look at another example to further explore Java structure. As you will see, there are only a few fundamental structural concepts that make up the syntax rules of Java, reducing the level of complexity, as compared to learning a foreign language.

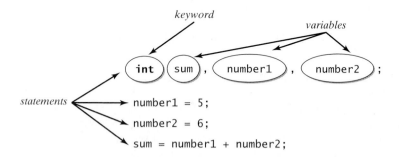

FIGURE 3.10    Java Statements, Keywords, and Variables

---

[5]Creating a package is optional if all the classes developed for the program are accessible in the main class's directory path.

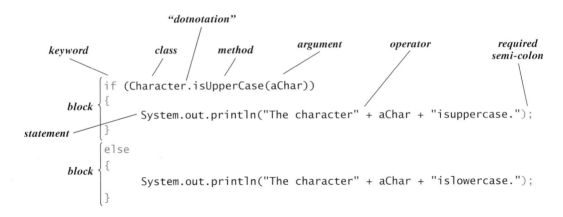

FIGURE 3.11    Java Statement Structure

The structure of a Java statement block generally follows the format shown in Figure 3.11 (of course there are variations). This example shows a conditional statement (expressed as "if ... else" statement blocks), which is used to direct execution of the program through one set of statements or another, depending on a particular condition. The keyword if establishes the test of the condition, and braces are used to enclose the two optional statement blocks, one or the other being executed on the basis of the test result. Conditions are enclosed in parentheses in Java, as are parameters (arguments) passed to methods. (Note that for single statements subordinate to if or else conditions, as shown here, braces are not required.)

As also shown in the figure, the "+" operator is used to string together (concatenate) objects of class String. Whenever the concatenation operator is used with multiple elements of which one is a String member, all other elements in this operation are automatically converted to strings, if possible. (If this automatic conversion is not logically possible, a syntax error ensues.)

In addition to keywords, operators play an important role in a programming language: they allow for calculations (algorithms) as well as comparisons (resulting in true or false conditions). Table 3.1 shows a list of all the operators in Java.

### Java Classes and Objects

Objects are created from classes, taking on their attributes and method definitions in a process called **instantiation**. Objects are representations of items, with their data values expressed as attributes (properties, or instance variables in Java), and their methods (operations) representing their functionality. As noted before, the new keyword is used in Java to instantiate an object from a class. Once an object has been created, its instance values can now take on unique values.

The example in Figure 3.12 illustrates the creation of an object from a class (instantiation). When a new object is created (with the new keyword), its class type is defined to the left of the object variable (in this case myBook), and the constructor for its initialization is invoked with the statement to the right of the equal sign (in this case Book()).

TABLE 3.1   Java Operators.

| Operator | Example | Description |
|---|---|---|
| **Arithmetic Operators** | | |
| + | x + y | Adds the values stored in variables x and y |
| | +x | Promotes x to the next level of primitive type (e.g., from byte to int) |
| ++ | x++ | (Post-)increments x by 1 |
| | ++x | (Pre-)increments x by 1 |
| - | x - y | Subtracts the value stored in y from the value stored in x |
| | -x | Changes the sign on the value stored in x |
| -- | x- | (Post-)decrements x by 1 |
| | --x | (Pre-)decrements x by 1 |
| * | x * y | Multiplies x by y |
| / | x / y | Divides x by y (even if x and y integers, result will be real) |
| % | x % y | Results in the remainder of the division of x by y |
| **Relational Operators** | | |
| == | if (x == y) | Tests equality of x and y (Boolean result of **true** or **false**) |
| != | if (x != y) | Tests inequality of x and y (Boolean result of **true** or **false**) |
| < | if (x < y) | Tests whether x is less than y (Boolean result of **true** or **false**) |
| > | if (x > y) | Tests whether x is greater than y (Boolean result of **true** or **false**) |
| <= | if (x <= y) | Tests whether x is less than or equal to y (Boolean result of **true** or **false**) |
| >= | if (x >= y) | Tests whether x is greater than or equal to y (Boolean result of **true** or **false**) |
| **Conditional Operators** | | |
| & | if (x=0 & y=1) | Tests whether both conditions are true, evaluating both |
| && | if (x=0 && y=1) | Tests whether both conditions are true, evaluating second condition, only if necessary |
| \| | if (x=0 \| y=1) | Tests whether either condition is true, evaluating both |
| \|\| | if (x=0 \|\| y=1) | Tests whether either condition is true, evaluating second condition, only if necessary |
| ! | !x | Returns true if x is false |
| ^ | if (x=0 ^ y=1) | Tests that both conditions are different (tests that one or the other is true, but not both) |
| **Bitwise Operators** | | |
| >> | x >> y | Shifts bits of x right by distance y |
| << | x << y | Shifts bits of x left by distance y |
| >>> | x >>> y | Shifts bits of x right by distance y (unsigned) |

*(Continued)*

TABLE 3.1 *(Continued)*

| Operator | Example | Description |
|---|---|---|
| & | if (x & y) | Bitwise and |
| \| | if (x \| y) | Bitwise or |
| ^ | if (x ^ y) | Bitwise xor |
| ~ | if (x ~ y) | Bitwise complement |

**Assignment Operators**

| | | |
|---|---|---|
| = | x = y | Assigns value of y to x |
| += | x += y | Equivalent to x = x + y |
| -= | x -= y | Equivalent to x = x − y |
| *= | x *= y | Equivalent to x = x*y |
| /= | x /= y | Equivalent to x = x/y |
| %= | x %= y | Equivalent to x = x%y |
| &= | x &= y | Equivalent to x = x&y |
| \|= | x \|= y | Equivalent to x = x\|y |
| ^= | x ^= y | Equivalent to x = x^y |
| <<= | x <<= y | Equivalent to x = x ≪ y |
| >>= | x >>= y | Equivalent to x = x ≫ y |
| >>>= | x >>>= y | Equivalent to x = x ≫ > y |

**Other Operators**

| | | |
|---|---|---|
| . | object.attribute | Refers to a member of a package, class or object |
| ( ) | method (parameter) | List of 0 or more comma-separated parameters on a method call |
| [ ] | array [index] | Create or access an array with 0 or more elements; index is from 0 to n − 1 elements |
| < > | List <Integer> myIntList | Generic class definition |
| ? : | (x == 1) ? y = 0 : y = 1 | If x is 1 y = 0, else y = 1 |
| new | Class object = new Class | Create a new object or array from a class or array specification, respectively |
| instanceof | if (x instanceof Y) | True if x is an instance of Y |
| (cast) | x = (int) y | Converts (casts) y to primitive type int (example); types have to be compatible |

class/type    constructor call*

*) when no constructor is defined,
a default internal constructor is called
when a new object is created

FIGURE 3.12   Constructor Call at Object Creation

The more complex example classes given below show a skeleton of a program used to manage libraries and their inventories.

---

**Example:**

```
public class Book {
    //instance variables
}
class HardcoverBook extends Book {
    // …
}
public class Library {
    // instance variables
    public static void main (String args [])
    {
        Book myBook = new HardcoverBook();
        /* create an object of class Book and initialize it
            using the constructor HardcoverBook */

        // remaining code statements
    }
}
```

These statements play the roles illustrated in Figure 3.13. This example shows how an object can be initialized as HardcoverBook but be a member of the class Book. This construct allows for a form of polymorphism (known as subtype polymorphism), where a method of the same name in a child class will "override" the method in the parent class. We will cover polymorphism in detail in a later chapter.

---

## Methods

Methods are the operational vessels of functionality in Java code. They contain code statements compiled by the Java compiler into bytecodes, which are then interpreted by the JVM on the target system as machine instructions. In a way, they functionally "surround" the attributes and operate on the data they contain. Methods typically extract value from operational data by accepting input, calculating meaningful results, and displaying this information to users, thus helping to create new knowledge.

## Attributes

Attributes (also called fields, properties, or instance variables in Java) hold data values (in objects) or represent the templates for data variables (in classes). When an object is created using the new command, RAM space is set aside for attribute values. While class attributes are generic (Book.bookTitle), object attributes are specific (myBook.bookTitle = "Java Textbook").

```
public class Book {
     //...
}

class HardcoverBook extends Book {
     //...
}

public class Library {

     //...

     public static void main (String args [])
     {
          Book myBook = new HardcoverBook();
          //...
     }
}
```

FIGURE 3.13   Class-Super Class Relationship in Creating New Objects

## Scope

Java is a strongly typed language. This means that all variables are explicitly declared and their types validated. It also means that variable scope is strictly enforced. Simply stated, if a variable is declared in a particular block of code, it is only valid in that block of code.

---

### Example:

```
public class Book {
// ...

     void addBook (String title, String author)
     {
          String bookID;
          // ...
     }
     void removeBook (String title, String author)
     {
          String bookID;
          // ...
     }
}
```

In the preceding example the scope of bookID is limited to the method in which it is declared. The declarations in the two methods of bookID result in two different variables with no relationship between them. A variable declared in one method cannot be used in another. If there is a need to access variables across methods, either an instance variable must be used or a parameter passed.

In the next section, we discuss prototyping, the process of writing a first experimental application to develop a proof of concept for our eventual software solution.

### Prototyping

*Prototyping* means creating a partial application with limited functionality for the sake of experimentation.

At this time, you can begin exercising your Java muscles by learning how to create a simple prototype of a Java application. There are quite a few basic elements to establish before your application will run, especially if it is an application with a graphical user interface. The easiest way to get a program up and running is to start with a working example (selected from those included with this book).[6] Then, when you clearly understand what each statement in the example does, you can begin modifying the code to perform the functions you want, based on your requirements analysis and design. A large part of most modern software applications is the user interface.

### Example Prototype: The Voting Program Basic Plus

The following is the second version of our Voting Program, still a very low-functionality simple prototype to begin exercising some basic Java functionality. This program prompts for inputs using JOptionPane dialog boxes and displays a calculated election result. It does not check for input errors.

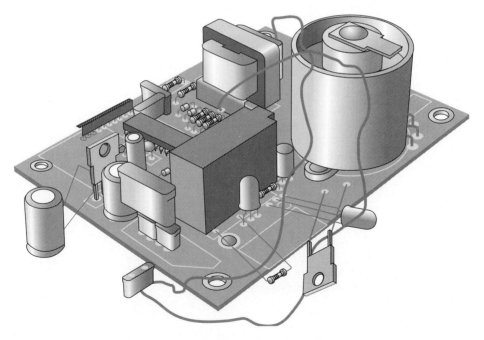

Prototype of some device

---

[6]Available for download on the accompanying Web site.

```java
import javax.swing.JOptionPane;
/**
* The Voting Program - Basic+ Version
* @author Georges Merx, Ph.D.
* @version 1.00 04/12/07
*/

public class TheVotingProgramBasicPlus { // signature of class
    public static void main(String[] args) {
    // main() method - entry point to program
        String candidate1, candidate2;
      // String class variables -> objects
        int votesCandidate1, votesCandidate2;
        // primitive type int variables
        // Display welcome message
        System.out.println(/* Welcome to The Voting Program.
        Copyright G. Merx.\n"*/);
        // \n forces newline

        // Get input from the user
        candidate1 = JOptionPane.showInputDialog
          ("Enter candidate 1 name:");
        votesCandidate1 = Integer.parseInt(JOptionPane.showInputDialog
          ("Number of votes for candidate 1:"));
        // should test for valid int
        candidate2 = JOptionPane.showInputDialog
          ("Enter candidate 2 name:");
        votesCandidate2 = Integer.parseInt(JOptionPane.showInputDialog
          ("Number of votes for candidate 2:"));
        // should test for valid int
        // Display results
        if (votesCandidate1 == votesCandidate2)
          System.out.print("Both candidates," + candidate1 +
             " and " + candidate2 + ", tied with " + votesCandidate1);
        else { // unequal count
          System.out.print("The winner of the election is ");
          // no newline at end of line
          if (votesCandidate1 > votesCandidate2)
            System.out.print (candidate1 + " with " +
              votesCandidate1);
          else // votesCandidate1 < votesCandidate2
            System.out.print (candidate2 + " with " +
              votesCandidate2);
        }

    System.out.println (" votes!");
    System.out.println("\nThank you and good bye!\n");
    // Exit program
    System.exit(0);
    }
}
```

### *Graphical User Interface Components*

As mentioned before, the Java (client) applications covered in this book fall into two major categories:

- Standalone applications
- Applets[7]

It is possible to write character-based Java applications that run in character-mode at the MS-DOS command prompt or on the UNIX console, for example, but most applications today provide a windows-based graphical user interface (GUI).[8]

---

### Example of a character-based application:

```java
import java.util.Scanner; // Java 5.0 Feature
/**
 * Simple Character-Based application
 *
 * @author Georges Merx, PhD
 * @version 1.00 05/02/19
 */
public class SimpleUserInput {
public static void main(String[] args) {
Scanner input = new Scanner (System.in);
    System.out.println
        ("Please enter the voter's first and last names: ");
    String inputLine = input.nextLine();
    System.out.println ("\nYou entered: " + inputLine);
    System.exit(0);
    }
}
```

*Output:*

GUIs contain a number of components, such as text boxes, list boxes, and buttons. Java supports these components through packages that can be imported into your application.

---

[7]In "real-world" applications, Java Server Pages are overtaking applets in popularity.
[8]Microsoft® Windows™, Apple® Mac OS™, UNIX X-Windows, and so on.

*Importing* means making the compiled functions in one or more packaged classes available to your program.[9] Java 2 has an extended set of powerful GUI components collectively known as "Swing."

The structure of most graphical Java programs mirrors the relationship between events that occur when a user interacts with your program and your program's response to these events. We refer to this as event- or message-driven programming.

Most graphical programs fall into this category. A typical event-driven Java program is shown in Figure 3.14. Event-driven programs respond to user input events and other messages. You initialize GUI components at program start-up to declare them as ready for such events. Then, as an action occurs that "belongs" to a particular user interface component, the code in your Java program must be in place to respond to this event by taking an appropriate action (e.g., calculate a result; bring up a new window; terminate the program) The conjoint pair of program elements for event listening and event processing is implemented through the Java interface technology (using the `implements` keyword). An interface implies that the JVM expects methods to be implemented in code that follows the required naming, parameter, and event-handling formats, but customise the event handling to perform the appropriate functions required for your program's functionality.

The simplified example in Figure 3.15 demonstrates how action event handling in a graphical environment involves three areas of coding: implementing the `ActionListener` interface commits us to having a method called `actionPerformed`. Adding the action listener to the component (here a `JButton`) allows us to later know where the action originated, when we process it in the `actionPerformed` method. We typically then want to extract some information from the GUI in response to the action that has occurred (such as retrieving the user input from a `JTextField` text input field).

---

### Graphical Controls

We assume in this text that you will use Swing components to implement your graphical functionality. The obvious reason for using awt components is to support browsers that do not implement Java 2 functionality in their JVM. For learning purposes, it will be helpful to become familiar with the extended capabilities of Swing and all of Java 2, because the previous-release components are a subset of these anyway.

The main Swing components are identified and described in Table 3.2.[10]

These graphical component classes are essential in developing graphical applications with extensive user interaction. Their application is also recommended because they are familiar to most users from their interaction with Microsoft® Windows™ applications and because they simulate many of the information-handling capabilities we have in the real world, such as item and check-off lists, buttons, and labels.

---

[9]Creating a package is optional if all the classes developed for the program are accessible in the main class's directory.

[10]Other Swing components are described on www.java.sun.com.

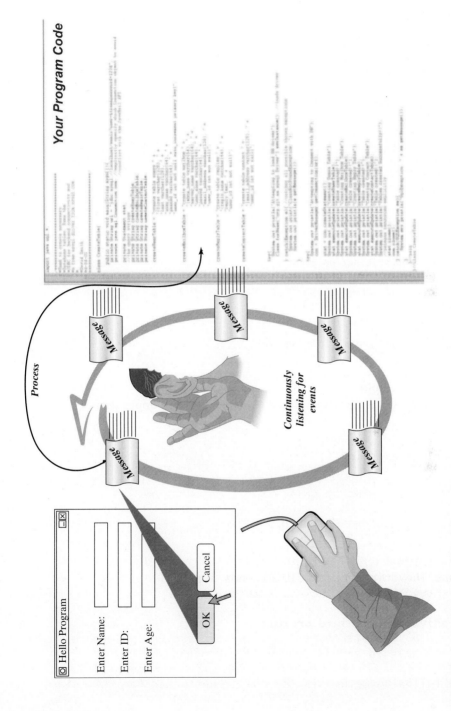

FIGURE 3.14 A Typical Event-Driven Program

```java
import javax.swing.*;

class ATMSimulator extends JApplet implements ActionListener {
    // instance variables
    JTextField accountNbr;

    ATMSimulator () {
        ContentPane currentPane;
        JButton OKButton;

        //...

        currentPane = getContentPane ();
        OKButton = new JButton ("OK");
        currentPane.add (OKButton);
        OKButton.addActionListener (this);

        //...
    }

    public void actionperformed (ActionEvent e) {

        //... handle action event
        validateAccount (accountNbr.getText ());
        //...
    }
}
```

1. *interface defined*
2. *component connected*
3. *action event intercepted*

FIGURE 3.15   Action Event Handling (Code Example)

### Program Example

The following is a highly simplified example of a GUI application.

```java
import java.awt.*;
import java.awt.event.*;
import javax.swing.*;

/**
 * The Voting Program GUI0 - Basic GUI Version
 *
 * @author Georges Merx, Ph.D.
 * @version 1.00 05/02/20
 */

class TheVotingProgramGUI0 extends JFrame {
// extend the JFrame class - inheritance

    private JTextField prompt;
    // object attribute (field) - declare variable here to be
    //     able to access from multiple methods
/**
The following method is the only constructor for this class.
*/
```

Continues on page 138

TABLE 3.2   Swing GUI Components

| Component | Function | Notes | Example |
|---|---|---|---|
| JLabel | Displays a string and/or image for informational purposes | No events generated | Enter library name: |
| JTextField | Provides for a single line of text input | **ActionEvent** generated | |
| JtextArea | Provides for multi-line user or display of text | Place inside **JScrollPane** if expected to exceed size of window | JTextArea Test — this is a text area |
| JList | Displays list of one or more elements; supports single- or multiple-selection | Place inside **JScrollPane** if expected to exceed size of window | JList Test — this is a JList / Item One / Item Two / Item Three |
| JComboBox | Combines functionality of **JList** and **JTextField** | Selection appears in text field; **Item Event** and **ActionEvent** generated | Check Out Book / Check Out Book / Check In Book / Add New Book / Remove Book / Add New Reader / Remove Reader / Update Book Information / Update Reader Information / Help |
| JButton | Rectangular button with text, image, or both | **ActionEvent** generated | Exit |
| JToggleButton | Button that maintains toggle state (pressed, not pressed) | **ActionEvent** generated when clicked; **Item Event** generated when selected/ deselected | Sampling — Hello! / What is your name? Carnlyn Harmon / Male / Married / Continue / Exit |

(*Continued*)

TABLE 3.2 (*Continued*)

| Component | Function | Notes | Example |
|---|---|---|---|
| JRadioButton | Labeled round button; can be selected/deselected– grouped together, selection is made mutually exclusive | **ItemEvent** generated when selected/ deselected |  |
| JCheckBox | Labeled box with check mark when box is selected | **ItemEvent** generated when selected/ deselected | 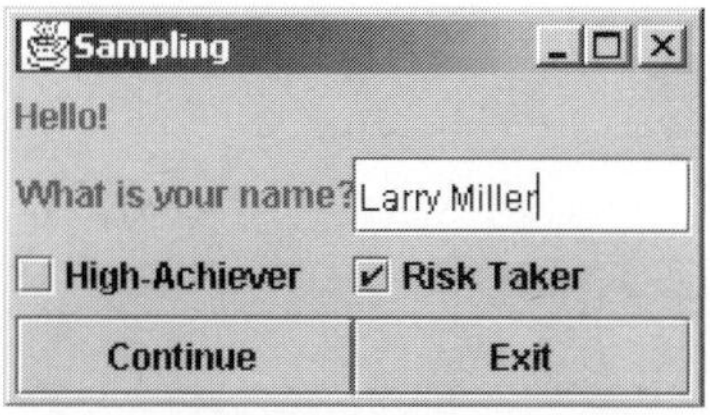 |
| JSlider | Slider bar with labels and major and minor tick marks | **ChangeEvent** generated | 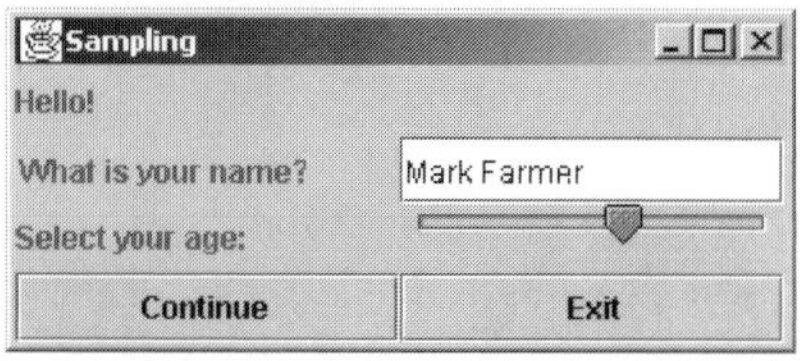 |
| JPassword Field | Same as **JTextField** except that characters entered into input field are immediately replaced by an echo character, usually '*'– used for entering passwords | **ActionEvent** generated | 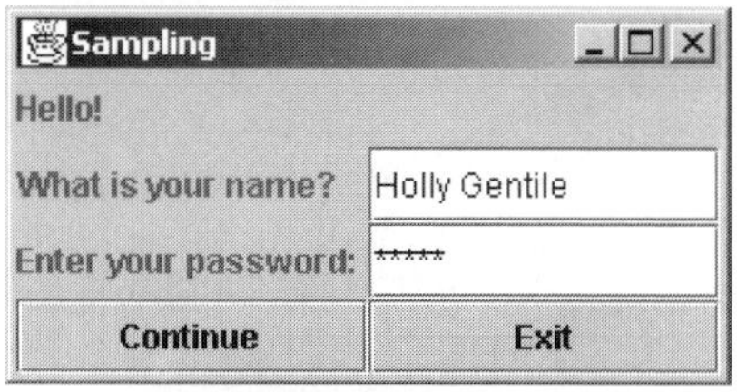 |
| JScrollBar | Horizontal or vertical scrollbar used to select an **int** value between minimum and maximum values | **Adjustment Event** generated | 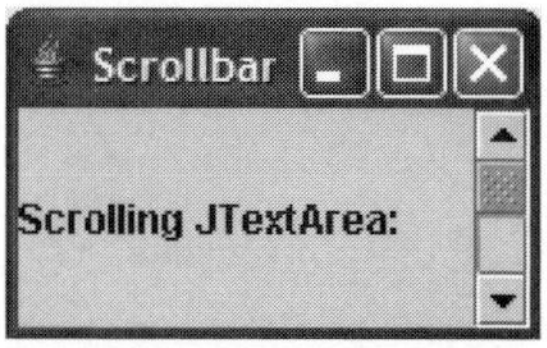 |
| JApplet | Swing container embedded in HTML file for viewing by Web browser | Contains a **JRootPane** | 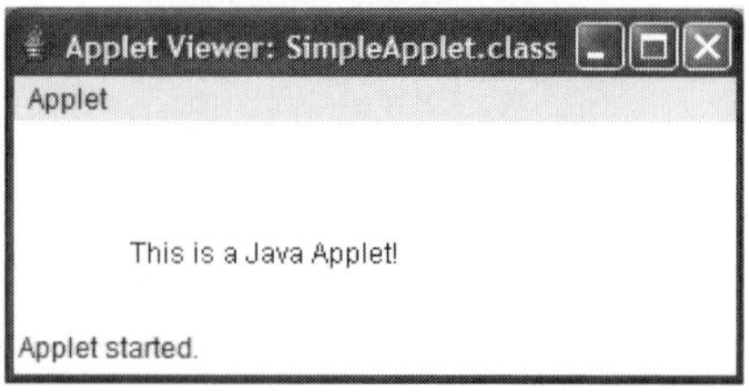 |

(*Continued*)

TABLE 3.2 *(Continued)*

| Component | Function | Notes | Example |
|---|---|---|---|
| JFrame | Top-level window | Contains title, border, and window management buttons; components are added to content pane | |
| JPanel | Simple Swing container | No **JRootPane;** often used for grouping components (*Note: in the example, the red area is a JPanel*) | |
| JTabbedPane | Tabbed Swing container | Each pane is a **JTable** object | |
| JOptionPane | Common pop-up dialog boxes: Input Dialog; Confirm Dialog; Message Dialog; Option Dialog | Can be permanent or temporary | |
| JDialog | Top-level window used to interact with user (usually for confirming an operation) | Components are added to content pane | |
| JFileChooser | Combined directory pane and selection buttons for specifying files to read and write | **ActionEvent** generated | |
| JDesktopPane | Uses **DesktopManager** to control absolute placement of components | No layout manager | |
| JInternal Frame | Contained inside another Java container (often a **JDesktopFrame**) | **InternalFrame Event** generated | |

TABLE 3.2    (*Continued*)

| Component | Function | Notes | Example |
|---|---|---|---|
| JMenuBar | Horizontal menu bar– contains **JMenu** objects | Not required to be at top of container | |
| JMenuItem | Wraps Strings and images used in menu elements | **ActionEvent** generated | |
| JPopupMenu | Menu associated with a GUI component | Usually triggered by a mouse event (right-mouse-button) | |

## Program Example (Continued from page 134)

```
public TheVotingProgramGUIO(String title){ // initializes object
     super (title); // sets window title
     Container c; // variable declaration
     addWindowListener(new WindowAdapter(){
     // handle window being closed by clicking on x box
          public void windowClosing(WindowEvent e)
          dispose();
          System.exit(0); // terminate normally
          }
});

c = getContentPane();

c.setLayout(new GridLayout(3,2));
// set window up as a 3 rows-2 columns grid
c.add(new JLabel("Hello!"));
c.add(new JLabel("")); // skip one cell
c.add(new JLabel("Please enter the voter's name:"));

prompt = new JTextField("... enter name...");
prompt.requestFocus(true);
prompt.selectAll();  // select text for overtyping
c.add(prompt);

JButton continueButton = new JButton("Display");
continueButton.addActionListener(new MyActionListener());
// prepare button for event handling
c.add (continueButton);

JButton exitButton = new JButton("Exit");
exitButton.addActionListener (new MyActionListener());
c.add(exitButton);
```

```
        pack();   // shrink window to miniminum size needed
        setVisible(true);   // make window visible
    }
/**
The following method is the main method and entry point
  for this class.
*/

    public static void main(String args[])   // program entry point
    {
        System.out.println("Starting The Voting Program...");
        // print a message to the console
        TheVotingProgramGUIO mainWindow =
            new TheVotingProgramGUIO("The Voting Program" +
              "Copyright G. Merx");
            // create a new object of class SimpleGreeting
    }

/**
The following inner class and method handle user interaction. This
is not the only approach to event management ...
*/

    class MyActionListener implements ActionListener {

/**
The following method is required by the ActionListener interface and
handles events associated with MyActionListsener objects.
*/

        public void actionPerformed(ActionEvent evt) {
            // determine origin of event -> Display button
            if (evt.getActionCommand().equals("Display")) {
            // validate input - do not accept blank input
                if ((prompt.getText().length() > 0) &&
                  (prompt.getText().compareTo ("... enter name...")
                  != 0)) {
                    // display pop-up message dialog box
                    JOptionPane.showMessageDialog (null,
                        prompt.getText(), "You Entered ...",
                        JOptionPane.INFORMATION_MESSAGE);
                    JButton jb = (JButton)evt.getSource();
                    // get the event's source object
                jb.setEnabled (false); // allow display only once
            }

            else {
                    showMessageDialog (null,
                    "Please enter a name!", "No name provided",
                    JOptionPane.ERROR_MESSAGE);
                    prompt.setText ("...enterName...");
```

```java
                    prompt.requestFocus (true);
                    prompt.selectAll();
            }
        }
        else if (evt.getActionCommand ().equals("Exit")) {
            // Exit button clicked by user
          System.out.println("\nExiting
            TheVotingProgram...\n");
          System.exit(0); // terminate program normally
        }
      }
    }
}
```

*Program output:*

**Start of program**

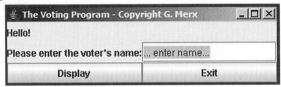

**Entering a name**

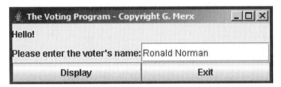

**Pressing "Display"**

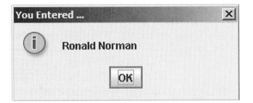

**DOS Console after Program Termination**

### Analysis

This simple program sets up a window (JFrame) and prompts for a voter's name in a JTextField. It has two buttons (JButtons), "Display" and "Exit." The window is created in main() as a JFrame-extended object (since the program class, TheVotingProgramGUIO, is a subclass of JFrame), which invokes the constructor method for the class, TheVoting Program0(). In this method, the window object is set up by populating its window content pane with the above-mentioned swing components.

Since simple graphical application has two program entry points, main() and actionPerformed(). The latter is invoked by the JVM when a user interacts with a swing component with an associated ActionListener object. Class MyActionListener implements the interface's ActionListener to provide the source for these objects that provide the connection between the application's initial state and the user interaction. In this case, when the user clicks the "Display" button, the MyActionListener object's actionPerformed() method handles this event and retrieves the (JTextField) prompt's text content for display using a JOptionPane dialog.

Upcoming chapters show more detailed examples of the use of swing components in implementing graphical user interfaces.

In real-life projects, before you can just "throw GUI components up on the screen," you need to understand how these visual and interactive elements implement the functionality you desire. This is a good time to revisit the use case scenarios in detail and relate functionality expressed as a work process to specific interface components in your program. In this way, we will also start addressing the **Design Phase** activities in our software development process.

### Understanding the Work Process

Efficiently implementing a work process using information technology (IT) is not a simple task. After all, customers do not spend large sums of money on computer equipment and software just to duplicate the manual work processes they have already in place. Instead, they want to *improve* their productivity by leveraging their investment in IT: they want shortener, automated, more efficient, less labor-intensive work processes to result from their implementation of computer solutions. It is the software engineer's primary task to create these productivity improvements through innovative software features. The following principles can be applied in this creative process:

- **Cost reduction** through elimination of human labor for repetitive tasks which can be automated (allowing for the reassignment of workers to higher-value activities).
- **Improvement of accuracy** through computer-aided instead of manual processing.
- **Time reduction** through automation of repetitive processes.
- **New functionality** leveraging computer capabilities: improved analysis and reporting, decision support, knowledge visualization, improved communication.

The design of IT solutions must focus on work process improvements, not just functions and features. Because of the graphical, interactive nature of modern computer environments and the power of software development tools, many junior software engineers develop applications as collections of graphical components and functions, without careful regard for how these windows, buttons, sliders, and lists are going to be used efficiently in everyday business situations. This can be avoided by thoughtfully considering the design so as to connect each program element to specific task requirements.

### Creating Functionality

Competent software engineers always keep in mind that the functionality they create needs to implement the stated and unstated expectations of their project stakeholders. This is only possible if the stakeholders retain an active role in the development process. In real life, requirements change frequently in the course of a project, and the software development organization needs to be responsive to these changes without jeopardizing the overall outcome. As introduced earlier, we use an iterative development approach to retain this flexibility throughout the development life cycle. For each iteration, this process passes through the main phases of the overall development process (defined earlier at the project macro level), emerging into the final phase of Support and Maintenance when the project is complete.

### Validation

From the very start of a new project, software engineers need to pay special attention to *inspection* and *validation*. Feature designs and specific functions need to be evaluated (inspected) by peers and by examining formal and informal documentation (Requirements Specification, Design Specification, system architecture, meeting notes, industry standards, etc.) Ongoing adjustments are made not only at the code level, but also, as needed, to existing documentation, test scripts, and so forth.

Validation also applies to the implementation of program *resilience:* whenever a program obtains data from the outside—whether from user input, sensors, data files, or databases—it needs to ensure that this data is valid for the particular purpose for which it is being acquired. This is a form of error checking, discussed further in the next section.

### Error Checking

The most obvious area of validation is error checking. As we will see in later chapters, Java has a built-in, extensible error-checking mechanism implemented as a hierarchy of error-trapping classes that help software engineers streamline and unify their error handling using object-oriented constructs. What we call "secondary scenarios" in our use cases essentially represents the functional requirements for the various error or exception events that may be encountered in a work process. Unfortunately, many developers treat validation and error checking as an afterthought instead of planning them as part of their functional workflow design. This lack of completeness often leads to unclear, hard-to-understand, brittle code.[11] Adding major unplanned code elements after the fact is often problematic in software development. That is why we spend so much energy on training you in software methodology engineering. In a way, these techniques and their benefits apply nowhere more than in error handling (or the implementation of secondary scenarios, another way of looking at this area of inquiry).

---

[11]The term "brittle" is metaphorical, like so many computer science terms: it refers to software functionality that is not very stable (resilient) under stress conditions and readily terminates abnormally when it should instead recover from minor errors.

*Testing*

A major responsibility of software engineering is testing. We recommend three levels of software testing:

1.  Unit testing, performed by the software engineer who wrote the code.
2.  Integration testing, performed by the software engineering team, or an integration team if available.
3.  Acceptance and *validation* testing, performed by the quality assurance department (which must not be part of the same organization as software engineering in order to preserve impartiality). This often includes *customer acceptance* testing, performed by the recipient organization before final acceptance of the product (may be combined with the previous type).

As it is desirable to perform as many positive and negative tests as necessary to maximize the testing coverage of the application and to stabilize new development quickly, we advocate the use of automated testing tools in order to encourage the frequent execution of regression tests.

It is important to remember that software quality assurance (SQA) is much more than testing, however. SQA is responsible for every quality-related aspect of the software development life cycle. SQA will be discussed in greater detail in a later chapter.

*Systems, Subsystems, Packages, Interfaces, Classes*

Software solutions developed in Java are composed of *classes*, which are related to each other as *parent* and *child* classes (inheritance). However, classes are usually further organized and grouped into *packages*. Package groups form *subsystems*, and we define the complete solution as a *system*. Special class stubs used to define (but not implement) the interactions between classes are called *interfaces* (Figure 3.16).

This organization allows for a flexible, modular use and reuse of components, without overburdening the application with unneeded functionality. Programs only import the classes or packages they require for processing.

## 3.5   The Java Family of Classes and Packages

Java is not a single program, but is organized into an extensive class hierarchy of components comparable to the one we advocate for your own software development.

A list of Java packages and classes can be found on the Sun Microsystems Website at www.java.sun.com.

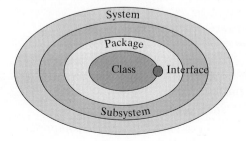

FIGURE 3.16   Classes, Packages, Subsystems, Systems, Interfaces

You can use the functionality available in these classes by including them in your own programs, using the `import` statement. Detailed explanations of each class can be found on Sun's Java Web site. Figure 3.17 shows an overview of the Java 2 Standard Edition Software Development Kit Release 1.5, now called Java 2 JDK Edition 5.0.

In addition, the "Java Family Tree" provides a compelling model of object-oriented design and development: the class hierarchy effectively implements key O-O principles such as encapsulation, inheritance, polymorphism, and component reuse.

## 3.6   Third-Party Components

Thousands of Java programmers around the world are regularly building reusable new, components. Before embarking on the development of new applications, it is wise to research what third-party components may already be available to do the required work, or at least part of it. In the same way, when it is necessary to develop a new component, it is good to ensure that it can be made available for use by others, either internally, for free (ref. "Free Software Foundation"), or for sale, so that the development effort can be leveraged across more than one project. Third-party components are typically packaged as Java Beans™, a format and organization that allows for explicitly defined access to the public attributes and methods of these components without having to understand their internal syntax.

## 3.7   Software Quality Assurance

While the topic of software quality assurance (SQA) will be discussed in detail in a future chapter, we want to introduce you to its main concepts now, because in the development life cycle, it is critical that you make quality assurance part of every aspect of the analysis, design, development, and deployment of software instead of waiting until after most of the development is complete. Many software development organizations mistakenly equate software quality assurance with testing. In reality, testing is only an important part of SQA.

---

### CONCEPT: REAL LIFE

The main purpose of teaching you Java is for you to be able to develop Java programs of value, for yourself or, more likely, for an organization, profit or non-profit. We try in this book to regularly relate your learning to "real-life" experiences and requirements.

---

SQA addresses the following software project deliverables:

- Compliance with project requirements.
- Compliance with software engineering methodology.
- Adherence to internal and external standards.
- Production of all relevant artifacts, such as specifications.
- Inspections, validation, and certification of each deliverable component.

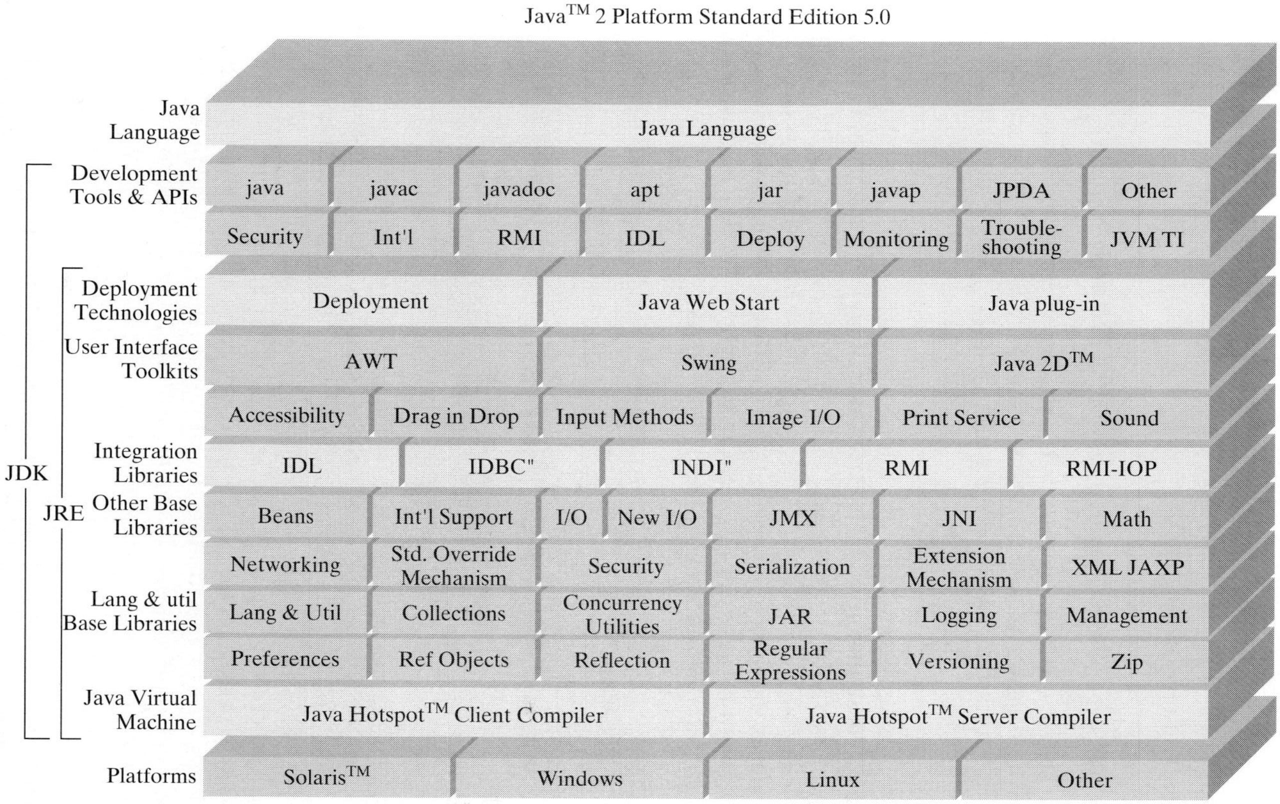

Java™ 2 Platform Standard Edition 5.0

**Java Language**

Java Language

**Development Tools & APIs**

| java | javac | javadoc | apt | jar | javap | JPDA | Other |
|------|-------|---------|-----|-----|-------|------|-------|
| Security | Int'l | RMI | IDL | Deploy | Monitoring | Trouble-shooting | JVM TI |

**Deployment Technologies**

Deployment   Java Web Start   Java plug-in

**User Interface Toolkits**

AWT   Swing   Java 2D™

**Integration Libraries**

| Accessibility | Drag in Drop | Input Methods | Image I/O | Print Service | Sound |
|---------------|--------------|---------------|-----------|---------------|-------|
| IDL | IDBC" | JNDI" | RMI | RMI-IOP | |

**Other Base Libraries**

Beans   Int'l Support   I/O   New I/O   JMX   JNI   Math

**Lang & util Base Libraries**

| Networking | Std. Override Mechanism | Security | Serialization | Extension Mechanism | XML JAXP |
|------------|------------------------|----------|---------------|---------------------|----------|
| Lang & Util | Collections | Concurrency Utilities | JAR | Logging | Management |
| Preferences | Ref Objects | Reflection | Regular Expressions | Versioning | Zip |

**Java Virtual Machine**

Java Hotspot™ Client Compiler   Java Hotspot™ Server Compiler

**Platforms**

Solaris™   Windows   Linux   Other

JDK   JRE

FIGURE 3.17   Java 2 Standard Development Kit (SDK) - © Sun Microsystems Inc.

145

- Adherence to approved project plans (macro and micro)
- Closed-loop corrective action process
- Unit, integration, and acceptance testing and test management
- Acquisition and management of alpha and beta test sites
- Protection of intellectual property
- Configuration management
- Source code management
- Oversight of all issues related to product and process quality

The next step in our learning process is to become acquainted with our first more functional Java program. As with any new language, we have to use some constructs with which you are not yet familiar. We will carry this example forward through the next chapters to ensure that every aspect becomes part of your knowledge base as we examine its various components. We prefer to introduce a "real program" (well, more like a "skeleton real program") instead of only providing short, illustrative code fragments. Over time, this should give you a better idea of how to implement useful functionality and how to use multiple classes and their methods and attributes to maximize the benefits of Java object orientation. Please realize that this program is presented as an example: it lacks the underpinnings of the full software-development life-cycle process. It is not meant to be a complete, practical example of the process, just a vessel for communicating tutorial information about Java syntax and structure.

## 3.8    Position in Process

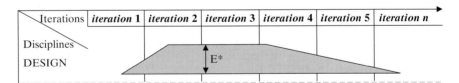

We have progressed through the Analysis Discipline and are entering the **Design Discipline** of our software development process. This phase is characterized by the creation of the **Design Model** and associated design artifacts. We are also engaging in some serious prototyping activities as part of our early iterations, and we will determine the system architecture at this time. The main artifact resulting from this phase is the project's **Design Specification**. We also write the software **Quality Assurance Specification** and **Configuration Management Plan** in this discipline. We will discuss these documents in the next chapter, where we continue the discussion on Design Discipline.

---

**Key Term**

A software **component** is usually a class, collection of classes (package), or a subsystem, which provides a core set of functions. These functions may be end-user functions or supporting (infrastructure) classes.

---

### 3.8.1    *Design Model*

The Design Model captures the main design decisions for our project, using UML diagrams such as the Class Diagram and interaction diagrams such as Activity and Sequence Diagrams. The Design Model results from the inputs of the Domain and Use Case Models. For more information on these analysis and design concepts, read the excellent book by Craig Larman, *Applying UML and Patterns* (Prentice Hall).

### 3.8.2    *Component Design*

In the design phase, we use the information developed earlier as use cases, the use case model, and other detailed descriptions of user requirements to translate these requirements into functional software components, features, and functions.

Of course, this is easier said than done! The design of components is influenced by many considerations, including the other design phase activities described hereafter, such as the definition of a system architecture and of the project's class hierarchy. As we consider the design of components, we keep in mind the various architectural perspectives discussed earlier. We develop functionality not just for end-users, but also for other project stakeholders, such as system administrators. We want to be careful to keep the work process supported by this software implementation at the forefront of our design concepts. Our goal has to be to improve the work process in terms of speed, accuracy, and resources required.

The decisions on what goes into which component depend on our system architecture; our goal is to implement our components for flexible reuse and to organize our components in a well-structured, well-balanced fashion. We want to ensure that it will be easy in the future to add new functionality and additional components. This includes the support of new platforms or other changes in underlying technology. We want to build highly functional software with a long lifespan.

### 3.8.3    *Class Hierarchy*

When developing the design for a software application, the translation of use cases and the use case model into an optimized class hierarchy is a critical step in object-oriented software engineering. When use cases developed in the Analysis Phase map to a well-organized, balanced Use Case Model, the development of a class hierarchy can effectively be based on that model. However, classes do not usually appear "one-for-one" out of use case definitions. Classes often develop out of technical requirements as well as out of stakeholder requirements and scenarios. The development of a comprehensive class hierarchy is the best foundation for well-structured, complete code that satisfies the Requirements Specification closely and accurately.

The **LibraryManager** example discussed in the chapter addendum, and shown in Figure 3.18 provides a good illustration.

The *translation* from use cases to classes is more an *interpretation*: we look at the use cases we have and extract common actors, behaviors, and deliverables (artifacts) from them. We then aggregate these commonalities and interrelationships into our class hierarchy by defining attributes and methods that represent the various actions and artifacts associated with our use case, and by generalizing as many of these methods and attributes as makes sense for our architecture into higher-level parent classes that can

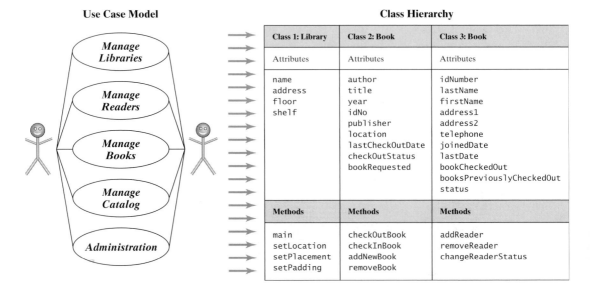

**FIGURE 3.18**   Translation of Use Case Model to Class Hierarchy (LibraryManager Example)

be shared by more specific child classes. This example is too trivial to show much of a hierarchy, but when we expand the list of the publications we track to include magazines, online publications, and CD-ROMs, we can see how an abstract parent class Publication may make a lot of sense, in which we can aggregate all attributes and methods common to all these publication types.[12]

### 3.8.4    System Architecture

Discussed in more detail in a later chapter, the architecture of the system and software solution we are developing provides an essential perspective on the structure, consistency, scalability, and robustness of our program. In the system architecture, we identify the major

---

### "DISCUSSED IN MORE DETAIL LATER"

is a common phrase in these pages. We often introduce topics in advance of their actual detailed description to get you familiar with the scope of Java programming right away. It also helps us use more complex examples without having to bring you "up to speed" on all their technical details. Just accept the overview information presented to you early on, with the expectation to get more details when the time is right.

---

[12]An *abstract* class is one that will never be used to instantiate objects.

components that make up our systems and how they interrelate. In addition, we agree on the underlying systems and networks needed to support our proposed IT solution.

The system architecture addresses the hardware, networking, and software components of the system, that will support our software application. More often than not, modern software solutions consist of multiple subsystems often executing on more than one system. The system architecture design provides a plan for the interrelationship of these components and helps preview how the system will be designed for robustness and scalability and what major technologies it will encompass.

The diagram in Figure 3.19 shows an example of a system architecture description, in this case a three-tier architecture for wireless applications.

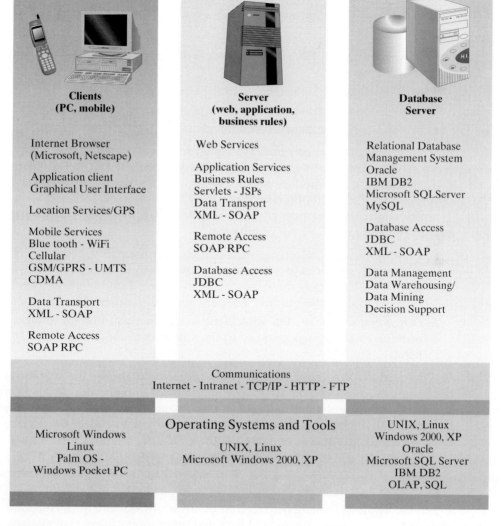

FIGURE 3.19  Example Architecture

One of the client platforms in the architecture may actually be a mobile device. The first tier represents the user interface component(s). Business rules are implemented in the second tier, and data access and management (usually using a relational database) reside on the third tier. It is not necessary for all the tiers to reside on physically different computers, but they are architected so that they can easily span multiple systems across network connections.

Java is particularly adept at supporting multiple platforms and operating systems. One of the reasons for the architectural separation of components is to make it easier to replace one tier without affecting the others. When a new mobile technology emerges, for example, this architecture will enable support for the new device type without extensive reengineering in the other tiers.

### 3.8.5   *Prototyping*

Prototyping can be very useful in the early stages of a project for a range of reasons. It enables you to:

- show your stakeholders your early ideas about solving their business problems in your software.
- develop ideas about the user interface.
- experiment with the structure of your program.
- become familiar with new technology.

However, there are also concerns associated with prototyping. There is a real danger that a good-looking prototype may prematurely become the de facto implementation. Also, prototyping can produce an excessive orientation on graphical user interface-driven functions, instead of retaining a critical focus on work processes.

The way to address these concerns is to develop prototypes under controlled conditions. There are two forms of prototypes:

1. *Proof-of-concept prototype.*  We often create multiple, "throwaway" prototypes to exercise variations of a function or look-and feel (see Fig. 3.20) but with no intention of developing these prototypes into a product. In fact, we may use a prototyping tool for this purpose, not our chosen development environment.
2. *Functional prototype.*  We implement some functions, but not to completion, in order to establish structure and to show how an eventual solution may look and behave.

It is the second form, the functional prototype, that creates the risk mentioned above of unplanned conversion of the prototype into the eventual product. It is important to step back from prototyping and return to the requirements analysis and design activities central to our process. The prototyping experience should be used as simply one more source of information and input in these efforts.

## 3.9     Relationships

In this recurring section, we help readers discover obvious and not so obvious relationships between the material covered here and other topics, ideas, systems, technologies, people, and places.

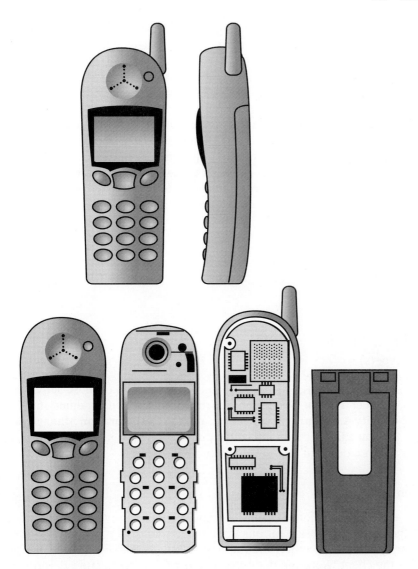

FIGURE 3.20    Example of a Cell Phone Prototype

The practices we promote for software engineering are commonplace in other engineering disciplines. No structural or mechanical engineer would proceed with a project or product without extensive requirements analysis and design, captured in formal written specifications, drawings, and documents. No electrical engineer would build a new integrated circuit without computer-aided design (CAD). Software engineers can learn much from these more mature engineering branches in developing reusable best practices.

The other obvious metaphor in these pages is that of architecture. Just as a good architect plans every intricate detail of a future building in specifications and blueprints, the conscientious software engineer will not leave any aspect of code development to chance or last-minute interpretation of vague requirements or ambiguous design information.

### 3.9.1   Caveats and Complexities

The translation of requirements into design elements is fraught with opportunities for misinterpretation. An assertively iterative approach is required to ensure ongoing stakeholder involvement and validation of requirements.

The use of Swing components in layout managers involves an extensive number of detailed adjustments to line components up as designed. This requires practice and familiarity with how the various layout parameters interact.

## 3.10    Example: The Voting Program

The Design Phase for the Voting Program establishes the following major deliverables:

- Component Design
- Class Hierarchy
- System Architecture
- Prototype(s)

The following sections address these deliverables. As a result of these activities, we will deliver the project **Design Specification** (the primary artifact emerging from this phase), the **Quality Assurance Specification**, and the **Configuration Management Plan**. A **Documentation Plan** should also be produced at this stage. (We will look at these documents in more detail in the next chapter.)

### 3.10.1   Component Design

From the previous work done on business and technical use cases, we can derive the components we need to design for our Voting Program. This is where the use case perspective, the system architecture, and the class hierarchy converge. We will design components for the client, Web, and data server tiers of the architecture described earlier. These components will all be developed in Java, representing one of the key advantages of Java-based software engineering. The following components will need to be designed in detail (note that not all this functionality will be implemented within the limited scope of this book example):

**Program navigation**

- Main form
- Authentication form
- Profile update form
- Ballot form

- Information management form
- *Eventually:* Web interface and server-programs

**Authentication**

- User identification and password acceptance validation
  - Reprompting if necessary
  - Access logging

**Business rules**

- Managing user interface process and interaction
- Error handling and control
- Counting and tabulating votes
  - Importing vote counts from external systems to arrive at totals
  - Providing information summaries and reports
- Database access, update, and validation (secure transaction processing)
- Database secure login and secure table updates
- Database queries and exports
- Database transaction rollback management and logging

### 3.10.2  Class Hierarchy

Figure 3.21 shows the class hierarchy for the Voting Program (simplified version). A more complete version is the subject of an end-of-chapter exercise.

### 3.10.3  System Architecture

The underlying system architecture for the Voting Program consists of subsystems implemented in a three-tier architecture, as shown in Figure 3.22.

### 3.10.4  Prototype

One or more prototypes of the Voting Program can be developed at this time to test the functionality of:

- the user interface components.
- the interaction between the three tiers, including access to the database.
- the interface(s) to external system(s).

These prototypes should be used to show stakeholders the stake of the design, but should be managed carefully to avoid a premature commitment to unproven ideas and concepts.

### 3.10.5  Design Specification, Quality Assurance Specification, and Configuration Management Plan

We will examine these artifacts in the second part of our examination of the Design Phase in the next chapter.

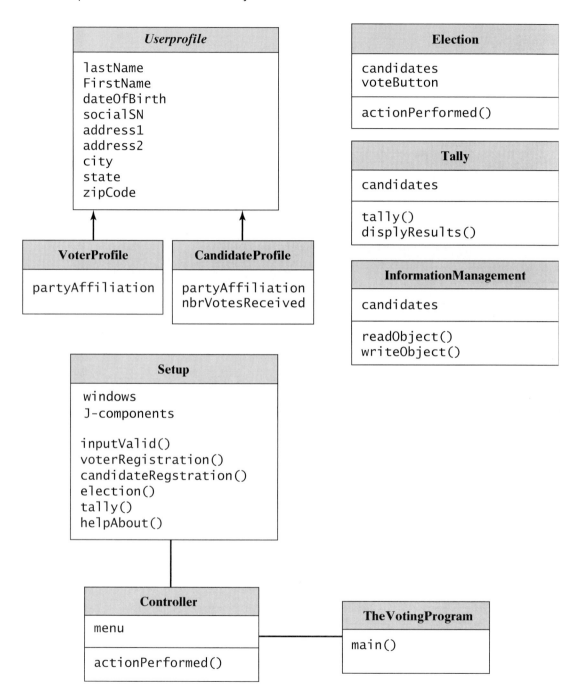

FIGURE 3.21   Voting Program Class Hierarchy (simplified)

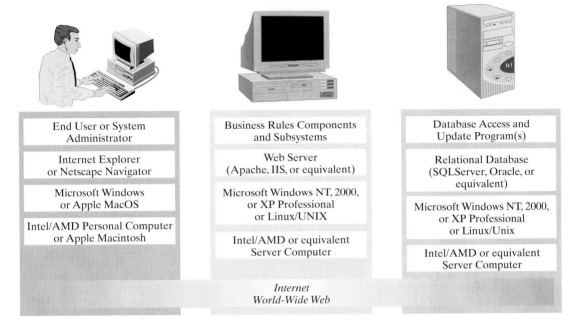

| End User or System Administrator | Business Rules Components and Subsystems | Database Access and Update Program(s) |
|---|---|---|
| Internet Explorer or Netscape Navigator | Web Server (Apache, IIS, or equivalent) | Relational Database (SQLServer, Oracle, or equivalent) |
| Microsoft Windows or Apple MacOS | Microsoft Windows NT, 2000, or XP Professional or Linux/UNIX | Microsoft Windows NT, 2000, or XP Professional or Linux/Unix |
| Intel/AMD Personal Computer or Apple Macintosh | Intel/AMD or equivalent Server Computer | Intel/AMD or equivalent Server Computer |

*Internet*
*World-Wide Web*

FIGURE 3.22   System Architecture for the Voting Program

## 3.11   *Harm ☯ ny* **Design Case Study**

The third phase of our ongoing case study takes us into the Requirements Analysis for our ModelHomeDesigner project. On the basis of the Business Plan completed in the last two chapters, we will embark on a more detailed analysis of the project requirements, including not only business requirements but also technical, environmental, and functional requirements. The following outline, introduced earlier in the book, will guide us in our Requirements Specification development. We will provide some information here to get you started, but it is your job to complete this specification based on your research, ideas, and discoveries.

### General Section

- System Name: ModelHomeDesigner™
- Project Vision:
  - This project streamlines, automates, and improves some of the key work processes in model home interior design projects.
- Project Description:
  - ModelHomeDesigner tracks resources, events, materials, and deliverables throughout the stages of a model home interior design project. It provides up-to-date information to its users about the current state at any time in the course of the project. It also provides workflow-management functions to help streamline sequential activities into repeatable processes.

- Stakeholder Analysis:
    - *Users* (designers, buyers, installer, managers) This category represents the actors or active end-use participants in our projects.
    - *System administrator* The system administrator will be responsible for installation, upgrades, and support and will have requirements of his/her own to support the program without excessive impact.
    - *Software engineers* As the developer of this program, you have requirements of your own as you develop the software; these include technical, environmental, architectural, and functional requirements.
    - *Clients* Clients of our customer, HarmonyDesigns, will be impacted by the use of this software in terms of its impact on their projects.
    - *Suppliers* In a similar way, suppliers of materials and services to HarmonyDesigns will be impacted by the inevitable process changes involved in introducing new systems and technology into existing work processes.
- Risk Management:

| Risk | Attenuation |
| --- | --- |
| • Loss of creativity in automation of repetitive processes | • Process control by design department; beta period of testing and validation with customers |
| • Lack of subject domain knowledge in implementing IT-based processes | • Access to design help from company managers and contributors; research |
| • Budget overruns | • Modular component implementation; iterative design and validation |
| • Quality problems | • Extensive inspection to include client representative(s); stringent QA Best Practices application; careful project planning; methodology-base software engineering process |

- System-Level Use Case Diagram:
    - *Give it your best shot!*
- Architecture Diagram:
    - *Give it your best shot!*
- Subsystems Description:
    - *Given the architectural requirements, the ModelHomeDesigner product is likely to consist of three major logical subsystems:*
        1. Web-based client applet or JSP
        2. Web-Server-based business rule engine
        3. Database-Server-based data access and management subsystem
    - Physically, tiers two and three may reside on the same system, given the relatively small size of the HarmonyDesigns operation.

**For Each Use Case**

- Use Case Name:
  - Enter/Maintain Client Information
- Brief Description:
  - This use case captures the process followed by HarmonyDesigns to capture information about its clients, including all the elements of information it tracks.
- Actors:
  - The main actor in this use case is the CompanyEmployee, a super "class" that includes all company employees. This actor can enter and modify information about clients. (Note that subsets of this use case, e.g., financial information, may have restricted access.)
- Pre-conditions:
  - Authentication. Detailed client information recorded and available for each client.
- Primary Scenario (Flow of Events):
  1. Access Client Information selection (may be a menu option)
  2. Enter personal information
     a. name (last, first, m.i.)
     b. title, role in company
     c. address
     d. phone
     e. e-mail
     f. Web site
     g. Enter company information
     h. past and current projects
     i. appointments
     j. notes
     k. other contacts in organization
- Secondary Scenarios:
  - You do this one.
- Diagrams:
  - Activity Diagram
  - Sequence Diagram
  - User Interface Drawing
- Post-conditions: . . .
- Extension points: . . .
- Other use cases used (including subordinate use cases): . . .
- Deliverables (artifacts): . . .
- Other requirements: . . .
- Next use cases . . .

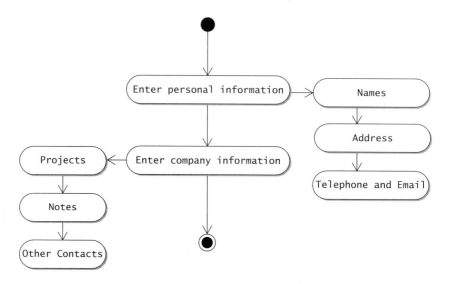

As you continue developing this ModelHomeDesigner program, you will find that the requirements analysis, design, and implementation activities all mesh together and support each other in favor of a superior product. Make sure in the process to keep all these viewpoints and inputs synchronized and actualized, involve subject matter experts on an ongoing basis to the best of your ability, and do your work with a keen focus on high quality.

## 3.12    Resources: Connections • People • Companies

Many companies and individuals are actively involved with object-oriented software engineering using Java. There are thousands of Java programmers worldwide. In this recurring section, we will provide you with a collection of useful resources and Web links that, will give you access to additional information, ideas, cases, and suggestions.[13]

- www.blogger.com - a (partially) free Web site on which you and your team or group can start a discussion group in order to collect and exchange information relevant to your project

## 3.13    Summary and Recommendations

In this chapter, we have jumped into Java programming head-on. You have studied an extensive example, and if you are new to programming, chances are that this example has been a little overwhelming. However, we encourage you to keep studying this and any other examples you find online or in other publications. The more you become familiar with Java code and how it works, the more effective you will be in translating your designs into well-constructed, highly functional code. You will learn the most by doing.

At this point, it is important to realize that not all software engineers follow the same programming style. There are often multiple ways to implement the same

---

[13]Given the volatile nature of business in general and Web links in particular, we cannot warrant that these links and resources will remain accessible over time.

functionality. Hopefully your team, class, or organization follows a common set of style guidelines and internal standards that unify the way your development team implements Java software programs.

On the software engineering side, you have now progressed from the Analysis Phase to the Design Phase, which we will complete in the next chapter with a detailed description of the Design Specification.

## 3.14 Review Questions

1. **Use Cases and Classes.** Describe three examples of use case to class (hierarchy) translation.
2. **Java Structure (1).** In the TheVotingProgramGUI0 example shown earlier, how is the MyActionListener class used?
3. **Java Structure (2).** In the LibraryManager example shown in the chapter addendum, how do the classes interact? Can you suggest structural improvements?
4. **Java Syntax.** Describe all the syntax rules that you can glean from an examination of the **LibraryManager** example.

## 3.15 Glossary – Terminology – Concepts

**Statement**  A "sentence" of Java code, terminated by a semicolon or starting a block of statements, depending on function; typically contains a test, calculation, or variable assignment.

**SQA**  Software Quality Assurance, the discipline of tracking all aspects of quality as an underlying support workflow in the object-oriented software development methodology advocated in this book.

**System Architecture**  The structure of the software system we are developing, including underlying hardware and networking components and any other external components with which our application is connected.

**Variable**  A named memory location for the temporary storing of a value; unless the data is of one of the eight primitive types, the memory has to be set aside by creating an object (new keyword).

## 3.16 Exercises

**1. Terminology.**
- Define and describe an example of a software project's architecture. Draw the components.
- Define and describe the benefits of software quality assurance.
- Compare and contrast a UML class diagram and a Java class format and structure.

**2. Java Packages.**  Research three to five of the packages included with the Java SDK from Sun Microsystems. Describe them in terms of their contents (classes), and highlight some of the key attributes and methods of these classes.

**3. Creating a Class Hierarchy.**  Expand on the class hierarchy shown earlier in the chapter for the Voting Program and develop a more comprehensive display.

## 3.17    Optional Chapter Addendum: LibraryManager, an Application Example

Let us examine **Library Manager,** a simple standalone Java program, composed of three classes. The purpose of this program is to manage books and readers in a public library.[14] (In a real-life implementation, much more functionality, including the use of a relational database for tracking publications, readers, and staff, would be required.)

Classes and, by extension, objects contain all the information required for them to express their roles. This includes data (stored in attributes) as well as functionality or behaviors (implemented as methods). We insist on this point repeatedly, because as a software engineer, you must learn how to leverage the power of objects in your program design.

One of the classes, Library, contains the main entry point to the program. The syntax for this entry point is mandatory, so that the JVM can find it and start interpreting your program:

```
public static void main (String args [])
```

This class creates objects of itself for every instance of a library being managed. The same approach will work for the other classes, with instances (objects) of the book and reader classes created for each book and reader represented.

The program is implemented as a graphical application, using the Java 2 javax.swing package. The swing components extend the standard awt graphics classes; they are enhanced high-level graphics classes that provide application developers with easy access to the native GUI and windowing capabilities available on major platforms such as Microsoft Windows, Apple Mac OS, and UNIX X-Windows/Motif, without having to reimplement the detailed functionality pre-packaged in these sophisticated graphical GUI components.

---

### DEFINITION: ARRAY

An array is a construct available in most programming languages that provides for an indexed list of items of the same type.

---

Note that the String variable args can have any other name, but the rest of the main method signature must follow the format shown.

---

*\*Note: The novice may need to skip this addendum because it previews more advanced features of Java covered in upcoming chapters. This example, like all the examples in this book, is provided for educational purposes; it does not meet the functional robustness or completeness requirements that would apply to a commercial project. It does, however, provide many opportunities for additional assignments in terms of adding functionality or considering improvements.*

[14]In a real-world situation, this program would have to be based on a validated Requirements Specification.

TABLE 3.3   Library Classes (Prototype)

| **Class 1:** Library | **Class 2:** Book | **Class 3:** Reader |
|---|---|---|
| **Attributes** | **Attributes** | **Attributes** |
| Name | author | IdNumber |
| address | Title | lastName |
| floor | year | firstName |
| shelf | idNo | address1 |
| | publisher | address2 |
| | location | telephone |
| | lastCheckOutDate | joinedDate |
| | checkOutStatus | lastDate |
| | bookRequested | booksCheckedOut |
| | | booksPreviouslyCheckedOut |
| | | status |
| **Methods** | **Methods** | **Methods** |
| Main | CheckOutBook | AddReader |
| SetLocation | checkInBook | removeReader |
| SetPlacement | addNewBook | changeReaderStatus |
| SetPadding | removeBook | |

The main classes, **Library**, **Book**, and **Reader** contain attributes (instance variables) to track object characteristics. This approach is especially useful when maintaining lists of items, implemented in Java as arrays of objects).

The following class diagram shows the main *attributes* and *methods* for each class (others may be needed along the way for technical reasons; also, to save space, the Library Manager example only implements a few functions for):

We will now take a closer look at each class, starting with the main class, Library.

## 3.17.1   Program Code

The listing given below shows the code for each class. The program is not fully developed in order to avoid unnecessary complexity at this early stage in your Java learning, and will be expanded in subsequent chapters, but it provides enough functionality to help you understand how to implement basic attributes, classes, and objects. Use this code as a basis for your own experimentation.

### Library Class

The Library class provides the main entry point for the program; it also manages the main navigation through the program (see Fig. 3.23). It can support multiple library locations by creating a new object as needed as a member of itself. The demonstration user interface is kept very simple. More realistic functionality would be added in a commercial version of the program. You are free to experiment with the code yourself, of course, and add features you believe should be available.

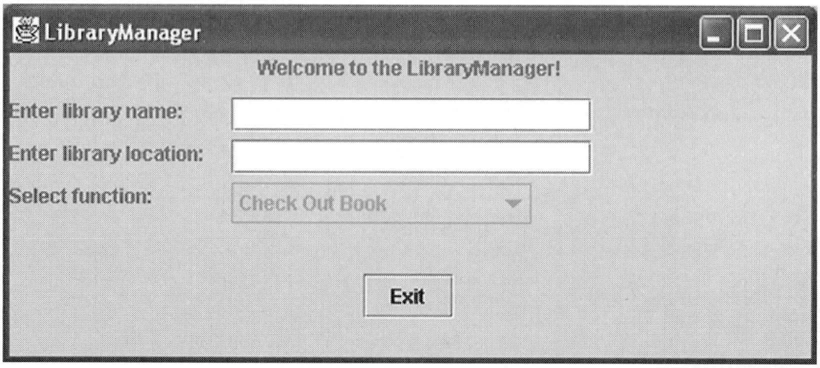

FIGURE 3.23   Library Main Window

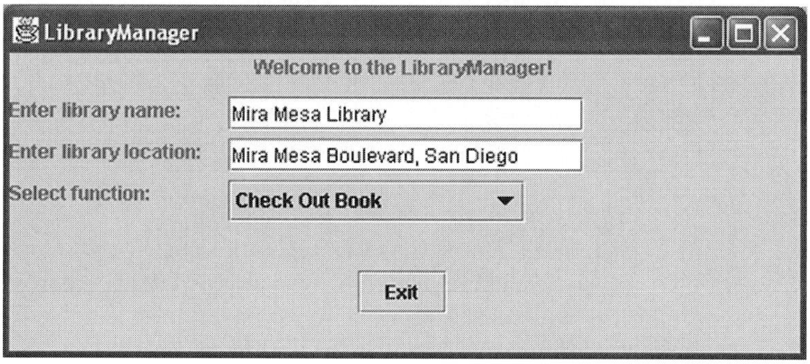

FIGURE 3.24   Library Main Window With Combo Box Enabled

The Library class is a child class (or subclass) of the Java swing class JFrame and prompts the user for the library name and location and the selection of one of a list of functions. The function combo box is only enabled after library and location have been entered (see Fig. 3.24). As both figures show, the requirements assumption here is that the program must support multiple locations.

Next, we provide a copy of the actual Java source code for this class. The comments in grey provide information about particular code components. Remember that this code is incomplete and for illustrative purposes only.

```java
import java.awt.*; //import required external classes
import java.awt.event.*;
import javax.swing.*;
import javax.swing.event.*;
import javax.swing.text.*;
```

```java
public class Library extends JFrame {
    // extend JFrame class - create new window
    private String name, address, floor, shelf; // instance variables
    private JLabel outputField;
    private JTextField prompt1Input, prompt2Input;
    private Container c;
    private GridBagConstraints constraints;
    private GridBagLayout GBLayout;
    private JComboBox combo;
    // defined as instance variable because used in multiple methods
    private JButton exitButton;
    private boolean theOtherIsEmpty = true;
    /* used to ensure that menu selections only available when library
       specified */

    public Library (){ // constructor method to initialize program
        super ("LibraryManager");   // set window title bar
        /* we collect all strings used in the class below for easy
           future modification */
        final String [] sList = {"Check Out Book", "Check In Book",
            "Add New Book", "Remove Book", "Add New Reader",
            "Remove Reader", "Update Book Information",
            "Update Reader Information", "Help"};

        c = getContentPane (); // get the window content
        gblayout = new GridBagLayout ();
        // create grid bag layout object
        c.setLayout (gblayout); // set the layout
        constraints = new GridBagConstraints();

        JLabel outputField = new JLabel (
            "Welcome to the LibraryManager!");
        setLocation (0, 0, 2, 1, "NONE");
        // call method to set constraints
        setPlacement (1.0, 0.0, "NORTH");
        // call method to fine-tune placement
        setPadding (0, 0, 0, 0, 10, 0);
        // call method to fine-tune padding spaces around controls
        gbLayout.setConstraints (outputField, constraints);
        c.add (outputField);

        outputField = new JLabel ("Enter library name: ");
        // let's reuse the outputField variable
        setLocation (0, 1, 1, 1, "NONE");
        // call method to set constraints
        setPlacement (10.0, 0.0, "NORTHWEST");
        // call method to fine-tune placement
        setPadding (0, 0, 0, 0, 5, 0);
        // call method to fine-tune padding spaces around controls
```

```java
gbLayout.setConstraints (outputField, constraints);
c.add (outputField);
prompt1Input = new JTextField (20);
setLocation (1, 1, 1, 1, "NONE");
setPlacement (90.0, 0.0, "NORTHWEST");
gbLayout.setConstraints (prompt1Input, constraints);
c.add (prompt1Input);
TextActionListener textListener = new TextActionListener();
Document document = prompt1Input.getDocument();
document.addDocumentListener (textListener);

outputField = new JLabel ("Enter library location: ");
setLocation (0, 2, 1, 1, "NONE");
setPlacement (10.0, 0.0, "NORTHWEST");
gbLayout.setConstraints (outputField, constraints);
c.add (outputField);
prompt2Input = new JTextField (20);
setLocation (1, 2, 1, 1, "NONE");
setPlacement (90.0, 0.0, "NORTHWEST");
gbLayout.setConstraints (prompt2Input, constraints);
c.add (prompt2Input);
document = prompt2Input.getDocument();
document.addDocumentListener (textListener);

outputField = new JLabel ("Select function: ");
setLocation (0, 3, 1, 1, "NONE");
setPlacement (10.0, 0.0, "NORTHWEST");
gbLayout.setConstraints (outputField, constraints);
c.add (outputField);
combo = new JComboBox ();
combo.setMaximumRowCount (9);
combo.setEnabled (false);

setLocation (1, 3, 1, 1, "NONE");
setPlacement (90.0, 0.0, "NORTHWEST");
gbLayout.setConstraints (combo, constraints);
c.add (combo);
// Populate the combobox list
for (int listCount = 0; listCount < sList.length; listCount++)
    combo.addItem (sList[listCount]);
ComboActionListener comboActionListener =
    new ComboActionListener();
combo.addActionListener (comboActionListener);
exitButton = new JButton ("Exit");
setLocation (0, 4, 2, 1, "NONE");
setPlacement (0.0, 1000.0, "NORTH");
setPadding (0, 0, 25, 0, 0, 0);
gbLayout.setConstraints (exitButton, constraints);
c.add (exitButton);
```

```java
        ButtonActionListener buttonListener =
            new ButtonActionListener();
        exitButton.addActionListener(buttonListener);
        setSize (500,220);  // size the window
        setVisible (true);  // make the window visible
    }
    public static void main (String [] args) {
    // entry point for program
        Library initialLibrary = new Library ();
        /* create a new object of class 'Library' option to instantiate
           other Library objects added in future version */
        initialLibrary.setDefaultCloseOperation
          (JFrame.EXIT_ON_CLOSE);
        // make sure close operation closes window
    }

// The following method sets the location constraints for a control
    public void setLocation (int x, int y, int width, int height,
        String fill) {
        if (fill.equals ("NONE") == true)
            constraints.fill = GridBagConstraints.NONE;
        else if (fill.equals ("VERTICAL") == true)
            constraints.fill = GridBagConstraints.VERTICAL;
        else if (fill.equals ("HORIZONTAL") == true)
            constraints.fill = GridBagConstraints.HORIZONTAL;
        else
            constraints.fill = GridBagConstraints.BOTH;
            constraints.gridx = x;
            constraints.gridy = y;
            constraints.gridwidth = width;
            constraints.gridheight = height;
    }

/* The following method sets the directional placement constraints
   for a control */
    void setPlacement (double x, double y, String anchor) {
        constraints.weightx = x; constraints.weighty = y;
        if (anchor.equals ("NORTH") == true)
            constraints.anchor = GridBagConstraints.NORTH;
        else if (anchor.equals ("NORTHWEST") == true)
            constraints.anchor = GridBagConstraints.NORTHWEST;
        else if (anchor.equals ("NORTHEAST") == true)
            constraints.anchor = GridBagConstraints.NORTHEAST;
        else if (anchor.equals ("SOUTH") == true)
            constraints.anchor = GridBagConstraints.SOUTH;
        else if (anchor.equals ("SOUTHWEST") == true)
            constraints.anchor = GridBagConstraints.SOUTHWEST;
        else if (anchor.equals ("SOUTHEAST") == true)
            constraints.anchor = GridBagConstraints.SOUTHEAST;
        else if (anchor.equals ("CENTER") == true)
```

```java
                constraints.anchor = GridBagConstraints.CENTER;
        }


    // The following method sets the padding space within or around
        control
            void setPadding (int internalPadX, int internalPadY, int insetTop,
                int insetLeft, int insetBottom, int insetRight) {
                constraints.ipadx = internalPadX;  // internal padding
                constraints.ipady = internalPadY;
                constraints.insets.top = insetTop;  // external padding
                constraints.insets.left = insetLeft;
                constraints.insets.bottom = insetBottom;
                constraints.insets.right = insetRight;
            }


            /* The following class captures list selection events and executes
                the command selected by the user for processing */
            final class ComboActionListener implements ActionListener {
                public void actionPerformed (ActionEvent event) {
                        JComboBox cb = (JComboBox)event.getSource();
                        String selection = (String)cb.getSelectedItem();
                        if (selection.equals("Check Out Book"))
                            Book checkOutBook = new Book("Check Out");
                        else if (selection.equals("Check In Book"))
                            Book checkOutBook = new Book("Check In");
                        else if (selection.equals("Add New Book"))
                            Book checkOutBook = new Book("Add New");
                        else if (selection.equals("Remove Book"))
                            Book checkOutBook = new Book("Remove");
                        else if (selection.equals("Add New Reader"))
                            System.out.println (
                            "UNDER CONSTRUCTION - Add New Reader selected!");
                        else if (selection.equals("Remove Reader"))
                            System.out.println (
                            "UNDER CONSTRUCTION - Remove Reader selected!");
                        else if (selection.equals("Update Book Information"))
                            System.out.println (
                            "UNDER CONSTRUCTION - Update Book Info selected!");
                        else if (selection.equals("Update Reader Information"))
                            System.out.println (
                            "UNDER CONSTRUCTION - Update Reader Info selected!");
                        else if (selection.equals("Help"))
                        System.out.println ("UNDER CONSTRUCTION - Help selected!");
                }
            }


            /* The following class waits for the user to click the exit button
                and then exits the program. */
            final class ButtonActionListener implements ActionListener {
                public void actionPerformed (ActionEvent event) {
```

```
                System.exit (0);
        }
}

/* The following class waits for the user to modify one of the two
   text fields in order to determine whether to activate the drop-
   down list of options */
final class TextActionListener implements DocumentListener {
    public voidchangedUpdate(DocumentEvent event) {
            Document document;
            document = event.getDocument();
            if (combo.isEnabled () == true) {
                    if (document.getLength() == 0)
                        combo.setEnabled (false);
            }
            else { // combo greyed
                    if (document.getLength() == 0)
                        theOtherIsEmpty = true; // reset to empty
                    else if (document.getLength() == 1) {
                        if (theOtherIsEmpty == false)
                        combo.setEnabled (true);
                    else
                            theOtherIsEmpty = false;
                    }
            }
    }
    public void insertUpdate(DocumentEvent event) {
            Document document;
            document = event.getDocument();
            if (combo.isEnabled () == true) {
                    if (document.getLength() == 0)
                        combo.setEnabled (false);
            }
            else { // combo greyed
                    if (document.getLength() == 0)
                            theOtherIsEmpty = true;    // reset to empty
                    else if (document.getLength() == 1) {
                    if (theOtherIsEmpty == false)
                                    combo.setEnabled (true);
                            else
                                theOtherIsEmpty = false;
                    }
            }
    }
    public void removeUpdate(DocumentEvent event) {
            Document document;
            document = event.getDocument();

            if (combo.isEnabled () == true){
                        if (document.getLength() == 0)
                            combo.setEnabled (false);
            }
```

```
        else { // combo greyed
                if (document.getLength() == 0)
                    theOtherIsEmpty = true;
            // reset to empty
            else if (document.getLength() == 1) {
                if (theOtherIsEmpty == false)
                    combo.setEnabled (true);
                else
                    theOtherIsEmpty = false;
            }
        }
    }
}
```

Some of the syntax used in this example will be covered in more detail in subsequent chapters. Students should regard these constructs from a preview perspective at this time. We will examine relevant parts of this code in the upcoming "Analysis" Section.

### Book *Class*

The Book class handles adding and removing book records and book check-in and check-out. These functions are implemented as methods in each book object, created from the class template for each unique book. Figure 3.25 shows the prototype user interface for each book-handling procedure. This sample window shows the simplified result of looking up a particular book. At this time, in the prototype stage of our program, this particular example is hard-coded into the statements below. In other words, the look-up function will only work properly for this one book. Real versions will implement a general-purpose look-up capability, of course, based on a database system. But the code shows the way to this future enhancement.

The Java source code for the Book class follows:

```
import java.awt.*; //import required packages
import java.awt.event.*;
import javax.swing.*;
import javax.swing.event.*;
import javax.swing.text.*;
public class Book extends JFrame {
// inherit JFrame attributes and methods
    // instance variable declarations
    JTextField prompt1Input, prompt2Input;
    private Container c;
    private GridBagConstraints constraints;
    private GridBagLayout GBLayout;
    String saveActionRequest;
    // captures constructor parameter for use in other methods
    BookID bookRequested;
    JLabel bookTitle, bookAuthor, bookYear, bookIdNo, bookPublisher,
        bookLocation, bookLastCheckOutDate, bookCheckOutStatus;
```

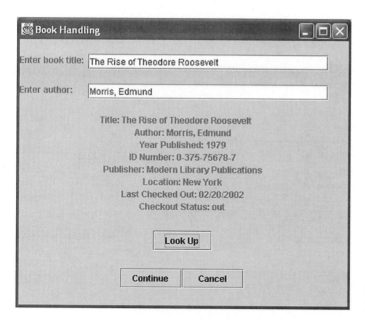

FIGURE 3.25   Book Window, After
Look-Up

```
// constructor
public Book (String actionRequested) {
    super ("Book Handling"); // set window title
    saveActionRequest = actionRequested;
    c = getContentPane (); // get the window content
    gbLayout = new GridBagLayout ();
    // create grid bag layout object
    c.setLayout (GBLayout); // set the layout

    constraints = new GridBagConstraints();
    // create constraints object for use in placing components
    JLabel outputField = new JLabel (Enter book title: ");
    setLocation (0, 1, 1, 1, "NONE");
    // call local method to set constraints
    setPlacement (10.0, 0.0, "NORTHWEST");
    // call local method to fine-tune placement
    setPadding (0, 0, 20, 0, 0, 0);
// call local method to fine-tune padding spaces around controls
    gbLayout.setConstraints (outputField, constraints);
    // set the constraints for this coomponent
    c.add (outputField);
     // add the componet to the content pane
    prompt1Input = new JTextField (30); // accept title
    setLocation (1, 1, 1, 1, "NONE");
    setPlacement (90.0, 0.0, "NORTHWEST");
    gbLayout.setConstraints (prompt1Input, constraints);
```

```
c.add (prompt1Input);
outputField = new JLabel ("Enter author: ");
// accept author - assumption:  enough info to find book
setLocation (0, 2, 1, 1, "NONE");
setPlacement (10.0, 0.0, "NORTHWEST");
gbLayout.setConstraints (outputField, constraints);
c.add (outputField);
setLocation (1, 2, 1, 1, "NONE");
setPlacement (90.0, 0.0, "NORTHWEST");
gbLayout.setConstraints (prompt2Input, constraints);
c.add (prompt2Input);
bookTitle = new JLabel ();
setLocation (0, 3, 2, 1, "NONE");
setPlacement (10.0, 0.0, "NORTH");
setPadding (20, 0, 20, 0, 0, 0);
gbLayout.setConstraints (bookTitle, constraints);
c.add (bookTitle);
// hide these labels until used for lookup
bookAuthor = new JLabel();
setLocation (0, 4, 2, 1, "NONE");
setPlacement (10.0, 0.0, "NORTH");
setPadding (0, 0, 0, 0, 0, 0);
gbLayout.setConstraints (bookAuthor, constraints);
c.add (bookAuthor);
bookAuthor.setVisible (false);
bookYear = new JLabel ();
setLocation (0, 5, 2, 1, "NONE");
setPadding (0, 0, 0, 0, 0, 0);
gbLayout.setConstraints (bookYear, constraints);
c.add (bookYear);
bookYear.setVisible (false);

bookIdNo = new JLabel ();
setLocation (0, 6, 2, 1, "NONE");
setPlacement (10.0, 0.0, "NORTH");
setPadding (0, 0, 0, 0, 0, 0);
gbLayout.setConstraints (bookIdNo, constraints);
c.add (bookIdNo);
bookIdNo.setVisible (false);
bookPublisher = new JLabel ();
setLocation (0, 7, 2, 1, "NONE");
setPlacement (10.0, 0.0, "NORTH");
setPadding (0, 0, 0, 0, 0, 0);
gbLayout.setConstraints (bookPublisher, constraints);
c.add (bookPublisher);
bookPublisher.setVisible (false);

bookLocation = new JLabel ();
setLocation (0, 8, 2, 1, "NONE");
setPlacement (10.0, 0.0, "NORTH");
setPadding (0, 0, 0, 0, 0, 0);
```

```java
gbLayout.setConstraints (bookLocation, constraints);
c.add (bookLocation);
bookLocation.setVisible (false);

bookLastCheckOutDate = new JLabel ();
setLocation (0, 9, 2, 1, "NONE");
setPlacement (10.0, 0.0, "NORTH");
setPadding (0, 0, 0, 0, 0, 0)gb
bLayout.setConstraints (bookLastCheckOutDate,
    constraints);
c.add (bookLastCheckOutDate);
bookLastCheckOutDate.setVisible (false);

bookCheckOutStatus = new JLabel ();
setLocation (0, 10, 2, 1, "NONE");
setPlacement (10.0, 0.0, "NORTH");
setPadding (0, 0, 0, 0, 0, 0);
gbLayout.setConstraints (bookCheckOutStatus, constraints);
c.add (bookCheckOutStatus);
bookCheckOutStatus.setVisible (false);

ButtonActionListener buttonListener =
    new ButtonActionListener();
// create listener object
if (actionRequested.equals ("Add New") != true) {
    JButton lookUpButton = new JButton ("Look Up");
    setLocation (0, 11, 2, 1, "NONE");
    setPlacement (0.0, 0.0, "NORTH");
    setPadding (0, 0, 25, 0, 0, 0);
    c.add (lookUpButton);
    lookUpButton.addActionListener(buttonListener);
}
JPanel twoButtons = new JPanel();
twoButtons.setLayout(new GridLayout(1, 0));

JButton exitButton = new JButton ("Continue");
twoButtons.add (exitButton);
exitButton.addActionListener(buttonListener);
JButton cancelButton = new JButton ("Cancel");
twoButtons.add (cancelButton);
cancelButton.addActionListener(buttonListener);
setLocation (0, 12, 2, 1, "NONE");
setPlacement (0.0, 1000.0, "NORTH");
setPadding (0, 0, 25, 0, 0, 0);
gbLayout.setConstraints (twoButtons, constraints);
c.add (twoButtons);

setDefaultCloseOperation(DISPOSE_ON_CLOSE);
// dispose of window if closed via close box
setSize (460,400);  // size the window
```

```java
        setVisible (true);   // make the window visible
}

/* the following method is called to check out a book -
   it returns false if the book title and author do not match
   an existing book */
boolean checkOutBook (Book book) {
        if (bookRequested.author.equals("Morris, Edmund") ==
          true &
            bookRequested.title.equals(
            "The Rise of Theodore Roosevelt") == true) {
            /* info hard coded for illustration purposes
               future enhancement:  database access */
                bookRequested.year = "1979";
                bookRequested.idNo = "0-375-75678-7";
                bookRequested.publisher = "Modern Library
                Publications";
                bookRequested.location = "New York";
                bookRequested.lastCheckOutDate = "02/20/2002";
                bookRequested.checkOutStatus = "out";
                return true;
}
else return false;
}


/* the following method is called to check in a book -
it returns false if the book title and author do not match an
existing book */
boolean checkInBook (BookID book) {
  if (bookRequested.author.equals("Morris, Edmund") == true &
            bookRequested.title.equals (
                "The Rise of Theodore Roosevelt") == true) {
                bookRequested.year = "1979";
                bookRequested.idNo = "0-375-75678-7";
                bookRequested.publisher =
                "Modern Library Publications";
                bookRequested.location = "New York";
                bookRequested.lastCheckOutDate = "02/20/2010";
                bookRequested.checkOutStatus = "out";
                return true;
        }
        else return false;
}

/* the following method is called to remove a book -
   it returns false if the book can not be added */
boolean addNewBook (BookID book) {
        JOptionPane.showMessageDialog (null, "UNDER CONSTRUCTION",
            "Adding Books Not Yet Implemented",
            JOptionPane.INFORMATION_MESSAGE);
```

```java
            return false;
    }


    /* the following method is called to remove a book -
       it returns false if the book cannot be removed */
    boolean removeBook (BookID book) {
        JOptionPane.showMessageDialog (null, "UNDER CONSTRUCTION",
            "Removing Books Not Yet Implemented",
            JOptionPane.INFORMATION_MESSAGE);
        return false;
    }


    /* The following method sets the component location constraints
       for a control these next three methods together allow complete
       control over the relative placement of a component */
    public void setLocation (int x, int y, int width, int height,
        String fill) {
            if (fill.equals ("NONE") == true)
                constraints.fill = GridBagConstraints.NONE;
            else if (fill.equals ("VERTICAL") == true)
                constraints.fill = GridBagConstraints.VERTICAL;
            else if (fill.equals ("HORIZONTAL") == true)
                constraints.fill = GridBagConstraints.HORIZONTAL;
            else
                constraints.fill = GridBagConstraints.BOTH;
            constraints.gridx = x;
            constraints.gridy = y;
            constraints.gridwidth = width;
            constraints.gridheight = height;
    }


    /* The following method sets the directional placement
       constraints for a control */
    void setPlacement (double x, double y, String anchor) {
            constraints.weightx = x;
            constraints.weighty = y;
            if (anchor.equals ("NORTH") == true)
                constraints.anchor = GridBagConstraints.NORTH;
            else if (anchor.equals ("NORTHWEST") == true)
                constraints.anchor = GridBagConstraints.NORTHWEST;
            else if (anchor.equals ("NORTHEAST") == true)
                constraints.anchor = GridBagConstraints.NORTHEAST;
            else if (anchor.equals ("SOUTH") == true)
                constraints.anchor = GridBagConstraints.SOUTH;
            else if (anchor.equals ("SOUTHWEST") == true)
                constraints.anchor = GridBagConstraints.SOUTHWEST;
            else if (anchor.equals ("SOUTHEAST") == true)
                constraints.anchor = GridBagConstraints.SOUTHEAST;
            else if (anchor.equals ("CENTER") == true)
```

```
                    constraints.anchor = GridBagConstraints.CENTER;
      }


      /* The following method sets the padding space within or around
         control */
      void setPadding (int internalPadX, int internalPadY,
         int insetTop, int insetLeft, int insetBottom, int
           insetRight) {
           constraints.ipadx = internalPadX;   // internal padding
           constraints.ipady = internalPadY;
           constraints.insets.top = insetTop;   // external padding
           constraints.insets.left = insetLeft;
           constraints.insets.bottom = insetBottom;
           constraints.insets.right = insetRight;
      }


      /* The following inner class responds to the user clicking
        one of
         the buttons. */
      final class ButtonActionListener implements ActionListener {
           public void actionPerformed (ActionEvent event) {
                if ((String) event.getActionCommand() == "Cancel"){
                     Book.this.setVisible(false);
                     Book.this.dispose();
                }
                else {
      /* not canceled - process 'Look Up' and 'Continue' buttons
                for each request type */
                     if (saveActionRequest == "Check Out") {
                          bookRequested = new BookID ();
                          bookRequested.title =
                             prompt1Input.getText();
                          bookRequested.author =
                             prompt2Input.getText();

                          if (checkOutBook (bookRequested) == false)
                             JOptionPane.showMessageDialog (null,
                                bookRequested.title + " by " +
                                bookRequested.author,
                          "Book does not exist - cannot be checked out",
                                JOptionPane.ERROR_MESSAGE);


                          else { // book found
                             if ((String) event.getActionCommand()
                                == "Look Up") { // set label
                                bookTitle.setText ("Title: " +
                                   bookRequested.title);
                                bookTitle.setVisible (true);
                                bookAuthor.setText ("Author: " +
```

```
                              bookRequested.author);
                          bookAuthor.setVisible (true);
                          bookYear.setText (
                              "Year Published: " +
                              bookRequested.year);
                          bookYear.setVisible (true);
                          bookIdNo.setText ("ID Number: " +
                              bookRequested.idNo);
                          bookIdNo.setVisible (true);
                          bookPublisher.setText (
                              "Publisher: " +
                              bookRequested.publisher);
                          bookPublisher.setVisible (true);
                          bookLocation.setText ("Location: "
                              + bookRequested.location);
                          bookLocation.setVisible (true);
                          bookLastCheckOutDate.setText
                              ("Last Checked Out: " +
                          bookRequested.lastCheckOutDate);
                          bookLastCheckOutDate.setVisible
                              (true);
                          bookCheckOutStatus.setText
                              ("Checkout Status: " +
                              bookRequested.checkOutStatus);
                          bookCheckOutStatus.setVisible
                              (true);
                  }


                  else JOptionPane.showMessageDialog (null,
                      bookRequested.title +
                      " by " + bookRequested.author,
                      "Book Now Checked Out",
                      JOptionPane.INFORMATION_MESSAGE);
                  }
          /}

          else if (saveActionRequest == "Check In"){
              bookRequested = new BookID ();
              bookRequested.title =
                  prompt1Input.getText();
              bookRequested.author =
                  prompt2Input.getText();

          if (checkOutBook (bookRequested) == false)
                  JOptionPane.showMessageDialog (null,
                      bookRequested.title + " by "
                      bookRequested.author,
              "Book does not exist - cannot be checked in",
                      JOptionPane.ERROR_MESSAGE);
```

```java
        else { // book found
        if ((String) event.getActionCommand() ==
                "Look Up") { // set label
            bookTitle.setText ("Title: " +
                bookRequested.title);
            bookTitle.setVisible (true);
            bookAuthor.setText ("Author: " +
                bookRequested.author);
            bookAuthor.setVisible (true);
            bookYear.setText (
                "Year Published: " +
                bookRequested.year);
            bookYear.setVisible (true);
            bookIdNo.setText ("ID Number: " +
                bookRequested.idNo);
            bookIdNo.setVisible (true);
            bookPublisher.setText
                ("Publisher: "
                + bookRequested.publisher);
            bookPublisher.setVisible (true);
            bookLocation.setText (
                "Location: " +
                bookRequested.location);
            bookLocation.setVisible (true);
            bookLastCheckOutDate.setText
                ("Last Checked Out: " +
                bookRequested.lastCheckOutDate);
            bookLastCheckOutDate.setVisible
                (true);
            bookCheckOutStatus.setText
                ("Checkout Status: " +
                bookRequested.checkOutStatus);
            bookCheckOutStatus.setVisible
                (true);
        }

        else JOptionPane.showMessageDialog (null,
            bookRequested.title + " by " +
            bookRequested.author,
            "Book Now Checked In",
            JOptionPane.INFORMATION_MESSAGE);
        }
    }

    else if (saveActionRequest == "Add New") {
        // will need input fields for all BookID fields
        JOptionPane.showMessageDialog (null,
            "UNDER CONSTRUCTION",
            "Add New Book Requested",
```

```
                                JOptionPane.INFORMATION_MESSAGE);
            }


            else if (saveActionRequest == "Remove") {
                bookRequested = new BookID ();
                bookRequested.title = prompt1Input.getText();
                bookRequested.author = prompt2Input.getText();

                if (checkOutBook (bookRequested) == false)
                    JOptionPane.showMessageDialog (null,
                        bookRequested.title + " by " +
                        bookRequested.author,
                    "Book does not exist - cannot be removed",
                        JOptionPane.ERROR_MESSAGE);

                else { // book found
                    if ((String) event.getActionCommand() ==
                        "Look Up") {
                    // set label
                        bookTitle.setText ("Title: " +
                            bookRequested.title);
                        bookTitle.setVisible (true);
                        bookAuthor.setText ("Author: " +
                            bookRequested.author);
                        bookAuthor.setVisible (true);
                        bookYear.setText ("Year Published: "
                            + bookRequested.year);
                        bookYear.setVisible (true);
                        bookIdNo.setText ("ID Number: " +
                            bookRequested.idNo);
                        bookIdNo.setVisible (true);
                        bookPublisher.setText ("Publisher: "
                            + bookRequested.publisher);
                        bookPublisher.setVisible (true);
                        bookLocation.setText ("Location: " +
                            bookRequested.location);
                        bookLocation.setVisible (true);
                        bookLastCheckOutDate.setText (
                            "Last Checked Out: " +
                            bookRequested.lastCheckOutDate);
                        bookLastCheckOutDate.setVisible
                            (true);
                        bookCheckOutStatus.setText (
                            "Checkout Status: " +
                            bookRequested.checkOutStatus);
                        bookCheckOutStatus.setVisible
                            (true);
                    }
```

```
                                else JOptionPane.showMessageDialog (null,
                                    bookRequested.title + " by " +
                                    bookRequested.author,
                                    "Book Now Removed",
                                    JOptionPane.INFORMATION_MESSAGE);
                        }
                    }

                    if ((String) event.getActionCommand() ==
                            "Continue") {
                        Book.this.setVisible(false);
                        Book.this.dispose();
                    }
                }
            }
        }
    }
```

We see in this code, as in the Library class, that much programming code is dedicated to the GUI components and their organization on the screen. Because of the platform independence of Java, GUI layout programming has to account for the possible multi-platform implementation of the program being developed. This is the reason for the "relative-position" organization of GUI components, instead of more easily placing them into specific x, y-coordinates in the active window. We will cover layout managers in more detail in a later chapter, but we hope that this early exposure to these concepts will encourage you to preview these features as you need to use them, even if they have not been "officially" covered in your current reading. While students often wait to be given the information they may need to complete a particular task, professionals take the initiative to find out what they need to do to succeed.

### Reader *Class*

The Reader class is the template for objects representing the library's customers—the readers. It adds and removes readers and tracks their current status, such as fees-overdue, dormant, paid-up, and so on. At this point, we believe that the Library and Book classes are more than enough for you to digest at this early stage. We will address this Reader class functionality in a later chapter.

```
public class Reader {
    String idNumber, lastName, firstName, address1, address2,
        telephone, joinedDate, lastDate;
    String [] booksCheckedOut, booksPreviouslyCheckedOut;
    int status;

    boolean addReader () {
        return false;
    }
```

```
boolean removeReader () {
      return false;
}


boolean changeReaderStatus () {
      return false;
}


}
```

## 3.17.2  Analysis

By examining this more extensive code example, we find that Java syntax and formatting are English-like and highly structured. Classes are easily created, and the more complex task is to understand the relationship between classes and objects, and between attributes and methods.[15] Another difficulty for the novice is understanding how to use the external Java classes available in the various SDK packages (like awt, swing, etc.).

Much of the code in most applications is devoted to managing the user interface, including the display of windows and prompts, the acceptance and validation of user input, the processing of this input using appropriate calculations or tests for classification, and the display of relevant results. This GUI representation relies on the use of one or more layout manager objects (e.g. GridBagLayout object).

This initial partial implementation only introduces limited graphical user interface manipulations, but can be used as the foundation for developing more extensive functionality. We will revisit this program in later chapters as we add more processing functions, such as arrays of objects, tables, and persistent file and database storage. Let us now look at some of the Java syntax and structure in this code and examine how we can generalize this example.

### Object Creation: Constructors

```
public class Library extends JFrame {
      public Library (){
            super ("LibraryManager");
            // ...
      }
      public static void main (String [] args) {
            Library app = new Library ();
            // ...
      }
}
```

---

[15]You will probably also notice right away how useful the comments are in helping you understand what individual statements do. This should encourage you to comment your own code extensively.

As we see in this code fragment, an object of the class `Library` is created right after the program begins executing in the `main` method. This object is simply called `app`. The software engineer chose this variable name, but could have chosen something more descriptive.

In the class `Library`, the method `Library()` is called a *constructor:* it will execute as part of the initialization of the `app` object; or, in other words, the `Library` constructor sets up the `app` object derived from the `Library` class. This process of object instantiation and initialization using a constructor method is a common and uniquely object-oriented sequence for creating objects from classes.

### Creating and Placing Swing Components

```
c = getContentPane ();
GBLayout = new GridBagLayout ();
c.setLayout (GBLayout);
constraints = new GridBagConstraints();

JLabel outputField = new JLabel ("Welcome to the LibraryManager!");
setLocation (0, 0, 2, 1, "NONE");
setPlacement (1.0, 0.0, "NORTH");
setPadding (0, 0, 0, 0, 10, 0);
GBLayout.setConstraints (outputField, constraints);
c.add (outputField);
```

This code fragment shows the creation of a new `JLabel` called `outputField` and the specification of placement within the framework provided by a Java layout manager, in this case the `GridBagLayout`, which provides for flexible placement in variable-size "cells" subdividing a display panel. When using layout managers, Java code controls the placement of graphical components using relative positions, not absolute coordinates, in order to preserve the platform-independent portability of programs. "Relative" means that components are organized relative to each other and to the display panes in which they are placed.

The code at the beginning of this section shows the sequence of activities required to set up the layout initially and then to place one element, in this case our label `outputField`, in position within the layout associated with the display pane, in this case the interior of the window itself. We have created three helper methods in the class called `setLocation`, `setPlacement`, and `setPadding` to make the setting of the various parameters controlling the exact placement of the component within the `GridBagLayout` grid more transparent and understandable. The first method sets the location of the component, the second fine-tunes the placement within that location, and the third provides internal and external padding control to space components relative to the edge of the pane and to neighboring components.

### Event Handling

```
//...
JTextField prompt1Input = new JTextField(20);
```

```
c.add (prompt1Input);
TextActionListener textListener = new TextActionListener();
Document document = prompt1Input.getDocument();
document.addDocumentListener (textListener);

final class TextActionListener implements DocumentListener {
    public voidchangedUpdate (DocumentEvent event)
    {
        //...
    }
    public voidinsertUpdate (DocumentEvent event) {
        Document document;
        document = event.getDocument();

        if (combo.isEnabled () == true) {
            if (document.getLength() == 0)
                combo.setEnabled (false);
        }
        else { // combo greyed
            if (document.getLength() == 0)
                theOtherIsEmpty = true; // reset to empty
            else if (document.getLength() == 1){
                if (theOtherIsEmpty == false)
                    combo.setEnabled (true);
                else
                    theOtherIsEmpty = false;
            }
        }
    }
    public void removeUpdate (DocumentEvent event) {
        // …
    }
}
```

When we add interactive components, in this case a JTextField called prompt1Input, we need to set up a complementary procedure for handling user interaction with our component. We show in this example one of the three ways of arranging this setup: the creation of a separate internal class to manage the event listener. When we create the component, we add an event listener to it, which creates the connection for the JVM to direct events coming from the component to its associated listener method(s). In our case, we want to capture specific character-level events associated with the input field and therefore use a DocumentListener event listener.

In the event listener class, we intercept event messages meant for our program (coming from our document component) and execute appropriate statements in response to the action our user has initiated by interacting with our component, prompt1Input.

The purpose of our code is as follows: this routine is set up to ungrey (set enabled) another component, a JComboBox named combo (declared as an instance variable in order to be accessible across the entire object), when both input fields contain text (assuming valid input, a "real-life" implementation would first check the input against a stored list of recognized names and locations).

These code fragments are pulled out as examples from the LibraryManager program above.

### Creating New Windows and Closing Them

```java
//...
if (selection.equals("Check Out Book")) {
        Book checkOutBook = new Book("Check Out");
}

public class Book extends JFrame {

        //...

        Book.this.setVisible(false);
        Book.this.dispose();

        //...
```

This code fragment shows how a new instance, in this case a window (JFrame), is created to handle the Book-related inputs and processing, and how it is closed in response to a button event. More details and additional functions for this program will follow in subsequent chapters.

In subsequent chapters, we will explore this example in more detail. We will eventually improve the code to make it more modular and reusable. Meanwhile, we encourage you to study this example in enough detail to gain an understanding of its logic, syntax, and structure.

# Design and Development of Java Applications

This chapter integrates what has been learned up to this point and expands these subjects in order to ground students in the fundamental processes of creating information technology solutions using hardware, software, and networking computer systems and tools. We continue to study our examples and case studies in order to illustrate—from a practical perspective—the components and processes associated with a typical IT-enabled solution. Unlike previous-generation programming languages, Java follows a modular, hierarchical architecture that allows us to integrate components as needed. This flexibility introduces a level of complexity, however, because component integration can occur in many different configurations and combinations. The skills required to build effective, flexible, powerful Java-based software systems extend beyond mere syntax and language structure knowledge. We will begin this chapter with an examination of these multidisciplinary skills.

---

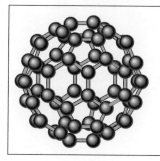

### BUCKYBALLS

These clusters of carbon atoms, nicknamed *buckyballs*, or *fullerenes*, after geodesic dome architect Buckminster Fuller, are among nature's most amazing structures. They represent a form of unique **reuse** of carbon atoms to create a separate unique form, after diamonds and graphite.

We identify five major categories of skills development:

1. Software engineering methodology
2. Java syntax and structure
3. Object orientation
4. Software quality assurance
5. Attitude and motivation ("professionalism")

The image in Figure 4.1 is used in every chapter to show you how the chapter contents and the development of skills in these areas of emphasis correlate.

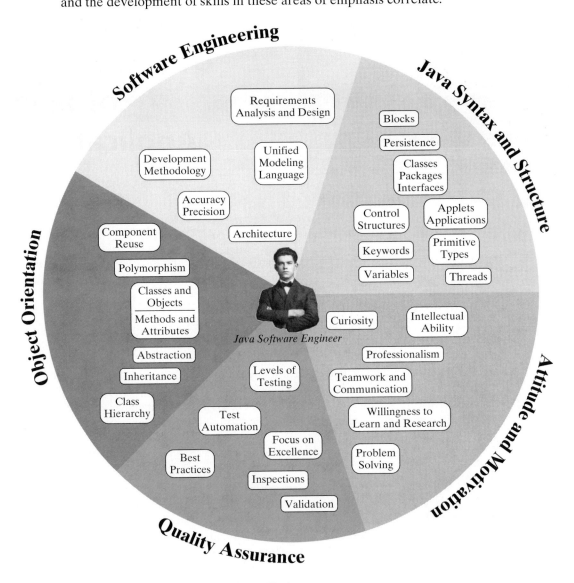

FIGURE 4.1   Becoming a Professional Java Software Engineer

In each of these categories, a combination of talents and skills are required for excellence in the field of software engineering. As you develop these complementary skills, you will gradually become a competent software engineer, capable of carrying a software project through every phase of the development life cycle.

In the remainder of the chapter, we will deepen your knowledge of Java programming in the areas of algorithm and business logic development, and in the use of graphical user interface components from the Swing library.

## 4.1   Learning Objectives

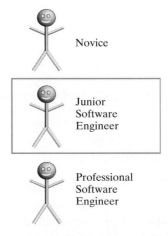

The first three chapters focused on introductory material and start-up language syntax development. In this chapter we establish the discipline of software engineering as a combination of skills development in five related domains (see Fig. 4.2). When software engineers have mastered these five areas, they qualify as professional software engineers. The following sections discuss each of the five areas in more detail.

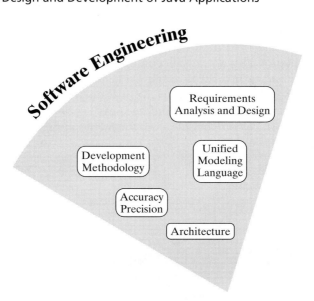

FIGURE 4.2   Key Aspects of Software Engineering

### 4.1.1   *Software Engineering Methodology*

In this first area of the software development skills inventory, we identify the key aspects of software engineering:

- *Development Methodology* Our methodology is an object-oriented, process-driven, end-to-end project life cycle that supports all relevant aspects of software analysis, design, development, and deployment in a comprehensive, internally consistent course of action. In this way, the outcome of a software development project retains a close correlation to the initial analysis and requirements definition and is more likely to meet stakeholder expectations.

- *Documented, Repeatable Processes* Each process and subprocess in this methodology must be duplicatable and follow a documented sequence of proven steps.

- *Use Cases* The collection and organization of stakeholder requirements using the use case format described in an earlier chapter leads to a repeatable process in the all-important requirements-gathering stage of the development methodology.

- *Unified Modeling Language* The use of standard Unified Modeling Language (UML) diagrams in requirements analysis and program design is an integral part of the development methodology advocated in this book.

- *Architecture* Developing object-oriented systems, especially those spanning multiple tiers, requires a thorough analysis and design of the underlying network, system, and software architecture. This architectural perspective involves multiple viewpoints, involving end-users, system administrators, developers, analysts, and other stakeholders.

- *Accuracy, Precision* Like all engineering disciplines, software engineering requires accurate, precise, complete, consistent, and traceable workmanship.

- *Accountability* Software engineers need to take responsibility for the quality, timeliness, cost, and completeness of their work.

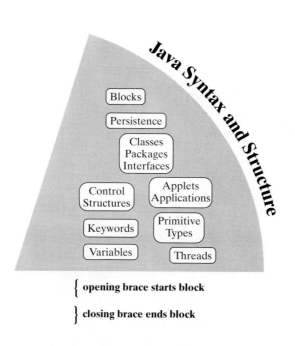

{ **opening brace starts block**

} **closing brace ends block**

FIGURE 4.3   Java Syntax and Structure

### 4.1.2   *Java Syntax and Structure*

Java syntax and structure learning involves a number of categories (see Fig. 4.3), among which we identify:

- *Classes, Packages, and Interfaces* Functionality and data are expressed in object-oriented concepts: classes (program components), objects (instances of classes), and interfaces (providing standard access to repeatable functions).
- *Applets and Applications* The detailed investigation in this book is limited to standalone applications and browser-based applets. However, the book does not ignore the importance of other Java-based formats, such as servlets, Java Server Pages, and (Enterprise) Java Beans.
- *Blocks* Java code is organized into blocks delimited by control statements and braces. Blocks allow the conditional execution of **1** to **n** statements based on a condition being true or false.
- *Control Structures* Control structures provide mechanisms of navigation in Java programs in conjunction with the aforementioned statement blocks. A control structure may involve conditional branching to a particular block of code or repetitive execution of a block of statements as long as a certain condition is true.

- *Keywords* A number of words in Java have special meaning and may not be used as class, attribute or method names:

| | | | | |
|---|---|---|---|---|
| abstract | boolean | break | byte | case |
| cast | catch | char | class | const |
| continue | default | do | double | enum |
| else | extends | final | finally | float |
| for | future | generic | goto | if |
| implements | import | inner | instanceof | int |
| interface | long | native | new | null |
| operator | outer | package | private | protected |
| public | rest | return | short | static |
| super | switch | synchronized | this | throw |
| throws | transient | try | var | void |
| volatile | while | | | |

- *Variables* Sun Microsystems defines a variable is "an item of data named by an identifier." Each variable has a primitive type, such as `int`, or a class type, such as `String`, and a scope. We distinguish class variables, instance variables, and local variables.

- *Primitive Types* Java supports the eight primitive types described in Table 4.1. These primitive types do not have any attributes or methods but represent raw data types, as described in the table.

- *Persistence* Random access memory (RAM) is volatile, meaning that data stored in program variables disappears once the program terminates or the computer is shut off. Since most of the information manipulated by software programs needs to stay around longer than the duration of a single program session, data storage is necessary. Permanent storage of data (in object orientation, this is called "persistence") involves the conversion of data in memory to a format that can be written to a storage medium, such as a floppy or hard disk, or an optical or tape storage device. Once made persistent, data can be retrieved later and reentered into memory when needed, without information loss (see Fig. 4.4).

TABLE 4.1 Primitive Types.

| Keyword | Description |
|---|---|
| byte | Byte-length integer number |
| short | Short integer number |
| int | Integer number |
| long | Long integer number |
| float | Single-precision floating-point real number |
| double | Double-precision floating-point real number |
| char | Single character |
| boolean | Boolean value (true or false) |

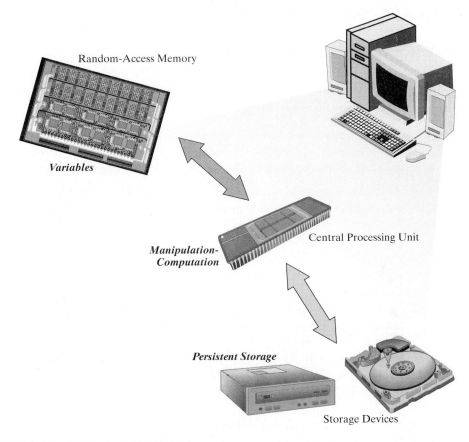

Random-Access Memory

*Variables*

*Manipulation-Computation*

Central Processing Unit

*Persistent Storage*

Storage Devices

FIGURE 4.4   The Notion of Persistence

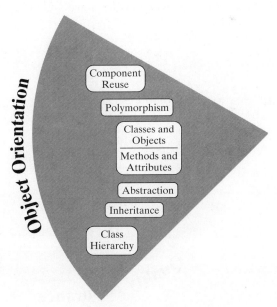

Object Orientation

Component Reuse

Polymorphism

Classes and Objects

Methods and Attributes

Abstraction

Inheritance

Class Hierarchy

FIGURE 4.5   Key Concepts of Object Orientation

### 4.1.3   *Object Orientation*

The next key area of learning for software engineers is a clear and thorough understanding of object orientation (see Fig. 4.5 on page 189). This area can be especially difficult to grasp for novice programmers, as well as for seasoned developers too intimately familiar with procedural programming. The key concepts of object orientation can be understood from two perspectives: conceptual and syntactical. Software engineers need to learn what component reuse means and, more specifically, how it is implemented in Java. As quickly becomes apparent, the main O-O concepts are interrelated and enabled by each other.

- *Abstraction and Component Reuse* Using O-O techniques such as polymorphism, inheritance, and encapsulation to make components reusable in the most flexible way possible.
- *Classes and Objects/Methods and Attributes* Objects are derived (instantiated) from classes (which are like templates), methods hold the functional code, and attributes store object data.
- *Inheritance* Inheritance allows for sub (child) classes to acquire attributes and methods from super (parent) classes. In Java, inheritance is implemented using the `extends` keyword. It transfers methods and attributes from a parent to one or more child classes.
- *Polymorphism* It is a method that can represent more than one set of functions, solely based on the number and/or type of parameters with which it is called. Overloading is one of the ways Java implements polymorphism in support of flexible component reuse.
- *Encapsulation* Protecting attributes and methods from external access using the private and protected keywords provides encapsulation. External access to protected attributes can be provided with syntax- and public `set` and `get` accessor methods.

FIGURE 4.6   Key Aspects of Quality Assurance

- *Class Hierarchy*  Organizing classes into a class hierarchy maximizes the use of inheritance and component reuse: a class hierarchy moves generic, reusable attributes and methods into higher-level super-classes (often abstract classes created solely to be parents to sub/child classes, not to instantiate objects).

### 4.1.4   *Software Quality Assurance*

Often overlooked until (too) late in the development cycle, software quality assurance (SQA) plays a crucial role in delivering quality software on time, within budget, and compliant with stakeholder requirements. We advocate the integration of SQA processes from the very beginning of the project. Quality assurance is not limited to testing: it should be a pervasive mindset and goal in every aspect of project analysis, design, implementation, and delivery. The key aspects are listed in Figure 4.6 on page 190 and explained below:

- *Focus on Excellence*  While hard to quantify, this recommendation refers to an overall attention to detail and a refusal to accept any compromise when it comes to quality in all aspects of product development.
- *SQA Best Practices*  In a subsequent chapter, we provide a detailed review of SQA best practices. The definition of these best practices provides a rigorous set of guidelines for all aspects of software quality assurance.
- *Validation*  Validation and the following item, "Inspections," go hand in hand: the latter is a formal validation process, while the former refers to the ongoing focus on ensuring that all design and code are robust and resilient. This requires ongoing vigilance by all development team members, and an active, respected, empowered role for the quality assurance specialists.
- *Inspections*  Instead of simple design and code reviews, we advocate the process of "inspections." In this approach, the work performed by software engineers at every stage of the development process is scrutinized critically in a peer-review mode, using a formal inspection process where engineers "defend" their work in planned meetings before their work goes on to the next stage. Some commercially available software-development tools provide excellent support in the form of automated audits and metrics, see Borland's Together ControlCenter, for example.
- *Levels of Testing*  New software, even if well designed and developed, typically lacks robustness and resilience. Only extensive, multi-level testing attenuates this risk. Software engineers themselves are the first line of defense with their validated **unit test** process, subject to the above-described inspection process. The next level of testing is **integration testing**, performed by a separate engineering group. The third and final level of testing is the **validation test** performed by the software quality assurance organization, often augmented by a fourth level, the **customer acceptance test**.
- *Test Automation*  An extension of iterative software engineering is incremental development, meaning the frequent stabilization of the current development release to a level of releasability. The frequency of this integration can be as often as daily, but only if unit and integration testing is automated. Many high-quality, very flexible test automation tools are available from reputable vendors, but testability can be designed and built right into the software itself.

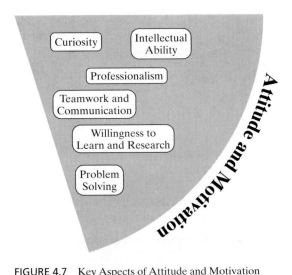

FIGURE 4.7    Key Aspects of Attitude and Motivation

### 4.1.5    *Attitude and Motivation*

Beyond the development of pure skills, the acquisition of the right attitude and motivation for the work of software engineering is a crucial factor in the success of a software engineer's career. Some authors refer to these aspects as *emotional intelligence*. Some key aspects of these "soft skills" are shown in Figure 4.7 and are explained below:

- *Curiosity* An attitude of willingness to explore, progress, and create—character traits indispensable in an engineer of any discipline.
- *Professionalism* This concept encompasses many specific and general attributes, from appearance and presentation to attention to accuracy and detail, reliability, quality, and dependability. Professional software engineers take pride in their work and ensure that what they eventually ship to customers meets their own highest standards.
- *Teamwork and Communication* Most worthwhile projects are larger than one person can manage, resulting in the creation of sizable teams of cooperating professionals. The ability to contribute effectively to a complex team effort is a basic requirement for effective software engineering. This involves collaboration skills, especially effective communication (oral and written).
- *Willingness to Learn and Research* In conjunction with the attitudes and behaviors described above, a basic desire to find out information currently not known is integral to effective software engineering, especially in the early phases of analysis and design. Most software developers lack subject-matter expertise in the industries for which they write software applications, so they need to spend time and energy becoming familiar with the business rules that are unique to the customer's enterprise.
- *Problem-Solving* A "cousin" of curiosity is the desire to solve problems. This proactive exhibition of initiative distinguishes competent software engineers from those who fail to create world-class solutions. Problem-solving takes tenacity, creativity, research, and hard work. Its rewards, however, often exceed the effort required.

---

**LIFELONG LEARNING**

Software engineers, maybe more than any other professional, have to commit to renewing their knowledge on a continuous basis. New hardware, networking, and software technologies emerge so frequently that knowledge is never current for long.

---

- *Intellectual Ability*  Last but not least, but also not the most important, is intelligence—at least an adequate level of intelligence. Software engineering is an intellectually challenging activity, as are most engineering disciplines, requiring cross-disciplinary skills and knowledge and the application of complex, abstract concepts and processes across vast projects often spanning months and sometimes years. However, most of the other attitudes and behaviors listed in this section are more important than pure intelligence. Said another way, a very smart software engineer who lacks the other abilities identified as important in this category will often be less effective and valuable than a software developer with less stellar intelligence, but with well-balanced skills and behaviors across the range of the other required strengths and attitudes.

### 4.1.6   Learning Layout

This recurring section shows the learning objectives of the chapter in a simple diagram using the UML activity diagram notation (see Fig. 4.8). While this diagram is not strictly an interpretation of a use case scenario as it would be in a real application, we hope that it will nevertheless be instructional to the student.

### 4.1.7   Learning Connections

The learning connections diagram in Figure 4.9 shows the content of this chapter in relation to the knowledge and skills development recommended for apprentice Java software engineers.

## 4.2   Executive Summary

It is not enough to learn about Java syntax and structure, or about software engineering, or about object orientation. It is the understanding of the *interrelationships* between these aspects of Java software engineering that provides the most powerful multidimensional foundation for effective software application development. As we have said from the beginning, we are pursuing an end-to-end software development life-cycle methodology, a process, that contains all the elements of software development, from the earliest inception activities to the eventual deployment and support and maintenance phases.

In this chapter, you will learn how to apply your own emerging range of "multi-domain" skills to a conceptual understanding of Java-based software solutions. The skills you will apply include your software engineering analysis and design skills, your understanding of object orientation, and your growing command of Java syntax and

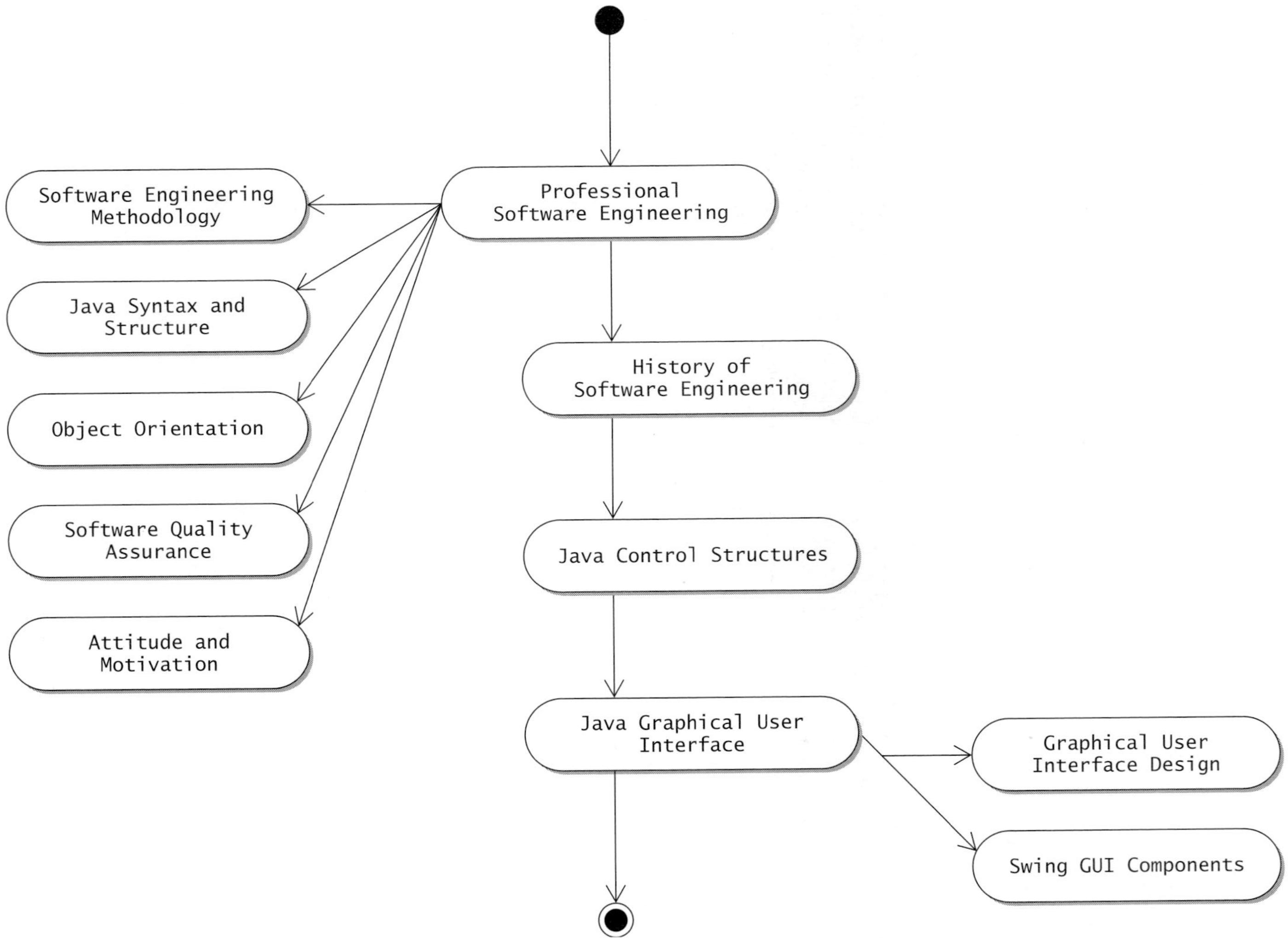

194

FIGURE 4.8   Chapter 4 Learning Layout (as a UML Activity Diagram)

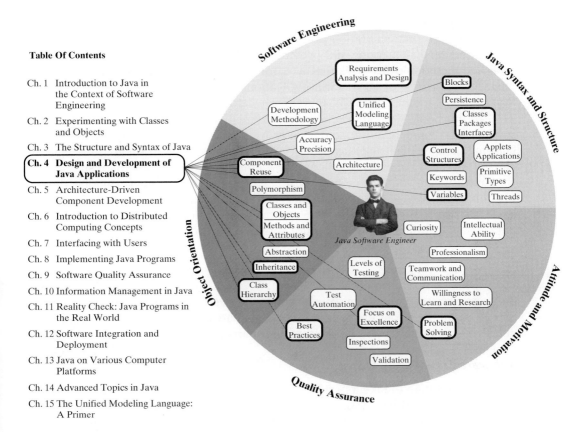

**FIGURE 4.9**   Learning Connections for Chapter 4

navigation structures. You will begin to grasp how to scale your newfound knowledge to the implementation of larger, more complex functionality, but always in the context of validated functional and supporting project requirements.

It is difficult in a textbook to present examples comprehensive enough to give you a feel for the "real world" of Java software engineering. That is why we have had a strong focus from the beginning on examples and case studies that span multiple chapters, like the **LibraryManager** code example introduced earlier. We will pick this example up again in future chapters and examine and develop it further.

Continuing our coverage of the software engineering process, we will complete our examination of the Design Phase. In particular, we are interested in the specifics of prototyping, graphical user interface design, and the detailed translation of requirements into software code design elements and specifications. (**Design Patterns** are a popular technique for reusing proven architecture-based designs and for documenting the process and value of reuse.)[1]

We will begin this chapter with a brief review of the history of software engineering, focusing on developments over the last fifty years that are directly relevant to

[1]See Erich Gamma, Richard Helm, Ralph Johnson, and John Vlissides (The "Gang of Four"), *Design Patterns: Elements of Reusable Object-Oriented Software*, Addison-Wesley, 1994.

present-day processes and tools. Our industry is young enough that most of the gurus in our field are first-generation practitioners. But a new group of second-generation thought leaders is emerging and promoting variations and improvements of well-established methodologies. Walker Royce, for example, who is the director of software engineering process at IBM (formerly Rational Software Corporation), is the son of Waterfall Method pioneer W. W. Royce.[2]

In this book, we take a relatively conservative path, basing our object-oriented software development methodology on proven unified practices and principles and eschewing the latest, untried "fast-track" processes. This is not to say that the emerging class of methods collectively called agile methods is to be summarily dismissed.[3] On the contrary, many of them embody best practices similar to those we endorse throughout this book. Where interesting emerging ideas and methodologies have achieved some real-world traction, we will include them in the discussion and leave their more detailed evaluation and possible future application to you.

## 4.3 Learning Modules

As in every chapter, we present your learning experience as a sequence of *Learning Modules.* Depending on your previous experience and areas of interest, you may find it valuable to seek additional information from third-party resources on the topics covered here.

### 4.3.1 *Software Engineering History*

This is a good time to take a perfunctory look at the history of software methodology. When software and hardware computer systems became sophisticated and powerful enough for software programmers to write more complex applications, the need for a process-driven methodology arose with more and more urgency. Without an organized, repeatable process, the creation of software was excessively dependent on the talents and skills of individual programmers, leading to unpredictability in all aspects of software development. W.W. Royce, Barry Boehm, James Martin, and others developed early techniques, often based on extensive empirical experience with real-life projects, for the organized repeatable execution of complex software-development projects.

Figure 4.10 shows some of the leading theories and methodologies invented over the last five decades, including:

- Waterfall Method (W.W. Royce)
- Spiral Model (Boehm)
- Object-Modeling Technique (Rumbaugh)
- Object-Oriented Software Engineering (Jacobson)
- Object-Oriented Analysis and Design (Booch, Coad and Yourdon)
- Modeling in Color with UML (Coad)

---

[2]W.W. Royce. "Managing the Development of Large Software Systems: Concepts and Techniques." *Proc. IEEE WESTCON*, Los Angeles, 1970.
[3]eXtreme Programming (XP), Feature Driven Development (FDD), Scrum, Crystal, and Dynamic Systems Development Method (DSDM) are all examples of agile methods.

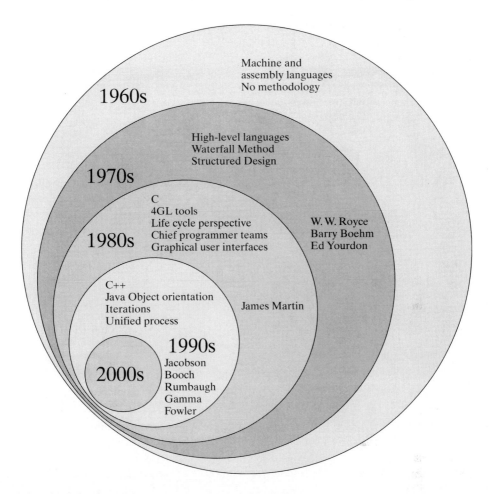

FIGURE 4.10   Software Methodology Genealogy: A Sampling

- Rational Unified Process (IBM)
- Other Unified Process–derived approaches: Design Patterns, Extreme Programming

We will Review all of these in the sections that follow.

### The Waterfall Method

Developed by W.W. Royce in the 1970s, and illustrated in Figure 4.11, the Waterfall Method has stood the test of time. It and its derivatives are still being used throughout the world. Even the most recent innovations in software engineering incorporate the fundamental principles of this methodology, including:

- Step-by-step progression through well-defined project phases
- Validation and verification, with the option for correction
- Requirements-driven analysis and design

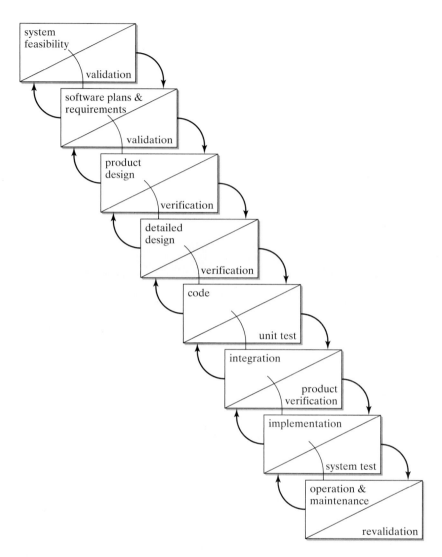

FIGURE 4.11   Waterfall Method

### The Spiral Model

Barry Boehm developed the Spiral Model (see Fig. 4.12) to capture the reality of on-going change throughout the life-cycle of a software-development process and incorporate this variability into the process itself.

### Object-Modeling Technique

As object orientation gained a foothold in the 1980s and 1990s, an urgent need for an object-oriented methodology and modeling capability emerged. This resulted in the development of what would later become the Unified Modeling Language (see Fig. 4.13), pioneered by Jim Rumbaugh, one of the "Three Amigos" (see Fig. 4.14).

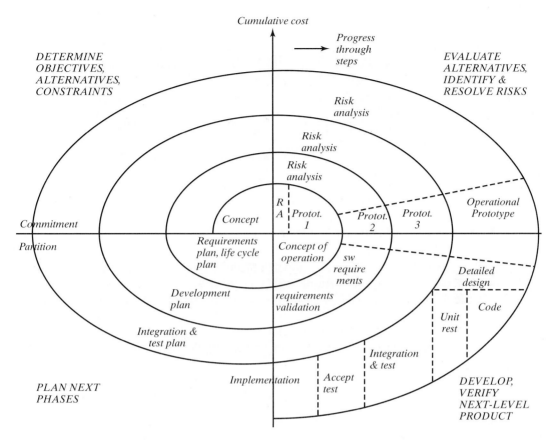

**FIGURE 4.12**   Original Diagram of Spiral Development[4]

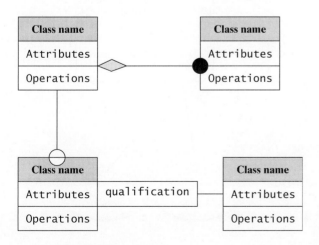

**FIGURE 4.13**   Rumbaugh Object Modeling Technique (OMT)

[4]Barry W. Boehm, "A Spiral Model of Software Development and Enhancement," *IEEE Computer*, May 1988, pp. 61–72.

| James Rumbaugh | Grady Booch | Ivar Jacobson |

**The "Three Amigos"**

**FIGURE 4.14**   The "Three Amigos" Copyright Rational Software Corporation, www.rational.com.


### Object-Oriented Software Engineering

As the dominant thought leader in the domain of object-oriented development methodology, Ivar Jacobson developed object-oriented software engineering, which, combined with Booch's and Rumbaugh's techniques, evolved into what is today probably the dominant approach to modern software development based on software engineering principles.

Object-oriented software engineering (OOSE) includes models for requirements, analysis, design, implementation, and testing (see Fig. 4.15).

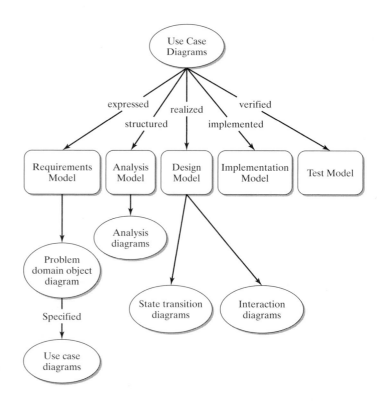

**FIGURE 4.15**   Jacobson Object-Oriented Software Engineering (http://www.smartdraw.com/resources/centers/software/oose.htm).

### *Object-Oriented Analysis and Design*

In addition to the "Three Amigos," Peter Coad and Ed Yourdon are widely recognized as pioneering gurus in the field of object-oriented development methodology and modeling. Figures 4.16, 4.17, and 4.18 show examples of class diagrams by Booch, by Rumbaugh, and by Coad and Yourdon.

Grady Booch's object-oriented design (OOD) is also known as object-oriented analysis and design (OOAD). The Booch model includes six diagrams: class, object, state transition, interaction, module, and process (Figure 4.16).

Jim Rumbaugh's object modeling technique provides support for modeling problem domain objects, along with their attributes, operations, and generalization and aggregation relationships (Figure 4.17).

Coad and Yourdon diagram creation follows five steps (Figure 4.18):

1. Find classes and objects
2. Identify the structures
3. Define subjects
4. Define attributes
5. Define services

### *Modeling in Color with UML*

Taking the modeling paradigm a step further, Peter Coad has been successful with an approach to complex process modeling that uses UML diagrams and a set of colors to add comprehensibility and meaning (see Fig. 4.19).

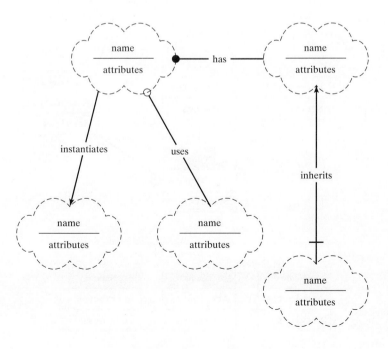

FIGURE 4.16   Booch's Class Diagram

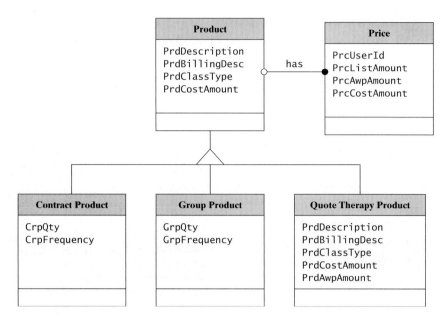

FIGURE 4.17    Rumbaugh's Object Modeler Class Diagram

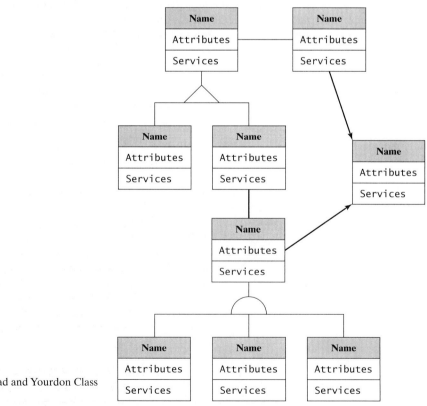

FIGURE 4.18    Coad and Yourdon Class Diagram

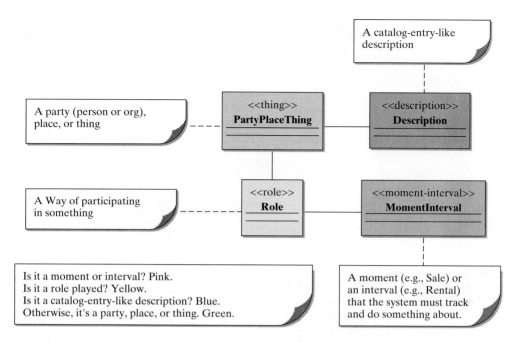

FIGURE 4.19  Modeling with Color. From Coad et al., *Java Modeling in Color with UML*, Prentice Hall, 1999.

### Rational Unified Process

The "Three Amigos" were employed at Rational Software Corporation (now IBM) in senior positions and oversaw the development of the comprehensive set of tools and methodologies available from this company in support of object-oriented software modeling and development. Borland Software Corporation and other companies have developed competing tools and techniques that adhere to the basic tenets of Unified Process–and UML-based software engineering.

The Rational Unified Process depicted in Figure 4.20 has influenced the evolution of object-oriented software engineering for a number of years now. It is a realistic, experience-based depiction of the interplay of processes, time, and emphasis on various activities over time. It clearly shows the nondiscrete ("fuzzy") nature of *real-life* software development and accounts for the need to have a certain controlled degree of adaptability in the process itself. This image usually makes a great deal of sense to experienced software developers, because they recognize their own practice in the humps and bumps of each process. We believe, however, that a more explicit depiction of the process as introduced in an earlier chapter makes more sense for novice practitioners of our complex craft.

### More Recent Developments: Design Patterns and Agile Programming

Kent Beck, one of the founders of the Patterns and Extreme Programming techniques, discovered that the benefits of software component reuse could also be applied to the

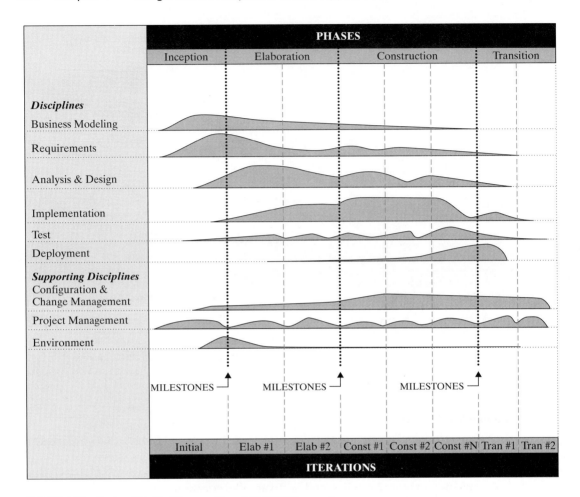

FIGURE 4.20 Rational Unified Process Copyright IBM Corporation.

design stage of the software-development process. Patterns of reusable component designs are originally based on architectural (building) patterns, as described by Christopher Alexander in *The Timeless Way of Building* (1979). Patterns codify existing, tried-and-true knowledge, principles, and approaches to solving particular recurring software engineering problems.

> A **pattern** is a named set of codified principles and idioms that guide software developers in the creation of software solutions. A pattern defines a (recurring) problem and its recommended (generic, reusable) solution.

"A pattern describes a recurring problem in our environment and the core of the solution to that problem in such a way that this generic solution can be used many times without doing it the same way twice."

Christopher Alexander (paraphrased)

**"Listening, Testing, Coding, Designing"** is Extreme Programming as summarized by Kent Beck (http://c2.com/cgi/wiki?ExtremeProgramming). Extreme Programming ("XP") is defined as follows by Ron Jeffries (http://www.xprogramming.com/xpmag/whatisxp.htm): "Extreme Programming is a discipline of software development based on values of simplicity, communication, feedback, and courage. It works by bringing the whole team together in the presence of simple practices, with enough feedback to enable the team to see where they are and to tune the practices to their unique situation." XP comprises the following core practices:

- Whole team
- Planning game, small releases, customer tests
- Simple design, pair programming, test-driven development, design improvement
- Continuous integration, collective code ownership, coding standard
- Metaphor, sustainable pace

The various agile programming techniques popular with experienced programming teams can bring economies in terms of process and documentation, but sometimes at the cost of long-term maintainability and sustainability. Teams change, and all the important information about a project needs to be available in writing, not just in someone's personal "memory bank."

### Synopsis

Thirty years of software-development modeling have resulted in sophisticated, realistic, comprehensive models, perspectives, and representations. From the simplicity of the early efforts (the core values of which survive to this day) to the dramatic dynamic models and techniques collectively known as the Unified Process (UP), object-oriented modeling, representation, and visualization of software engineering projects has become an essential element in improving and stabilizing software-development productivity and accuracy.

### 4.3.2  Process Models

In conjunction with these evolving models and software analysis and design techniques, a number of standard processes have emerged to represent and validate software engineering best practices. A number of these have been codified in accepted industry standards.

We will take a cursory look at some of the major software process models:

- Software Engineering Institute Capability Maturity Model Integration for Systems and Software Engineering (SEI CMMI-SE/SW)
- MIL-STD-498 (Software Development and Documentation for the Department of Defense)

- ISO 9000 (International Organization of Standard Quality Guidelines)
- IEEE Software Engineering Standards
- Model Driven Architecture (MDA) of the Object Management Group (OMG)

### SEI CMMI

The staged version of the software process model developed and promoted by the Software Engineering Institute at Carnegie-Mellon, known as Capability Maturity Model Integration (CMMI), consists of five levels of achievement (see Fig. 4.21).

Alternatively, a continuous-improvement version can be adopted.

Organizations need to meet a comprehensive set of criteria in order to qualify for the upper levels of this hierarchy of certification. Independent inspectors provide certification services. As stated on the CMMI Web site:

> "The purpose of CMM Integration is to provide guidance for improving your organization's processes and your ability to manage the development, acquisition, and maintenance of products or services. CMM Integration places proven approaches into a structure that helps your organization appraise its organizational maturity or process area capability, establish priorities for improvement, and implement these improvements.
>
> CMMI contains and is produced from a framework that provides the ability to generate multiple models and associated training and appraisal materials. These models may reflect content from bodies of knowledge (e.g., systems engineering, software engineering, Integrated Product and Process Development) in combinations most useful to you (e.g., CMMI-SE/SW, CMMI-SE/SW/IPPD).
>
> Your organization can use a CMMI model to help set process improvement objectives and priorities, improve processes, and provide guidance for ensuring stable, capable, and mature processes. A selected CMMI model can serve as a guide for improvement of organizational processes."

### MIL-STD-498

This standard merges DOD-STD-2167A and DOD-STD-7935A to define a set of activities and documentation suitable for the development of weapons systems and automated information systems for the U.S. Department of Defense (DoD). As stated in the MIL-STD-498 standard, "The purpose of this standard is to establish uniform requirements for software development and documentation." This standard is comprehensive

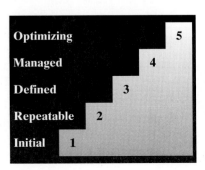

FIGURE 4.21    Five Levels of SW-CMMI (Copyright Carnegie-Mellon)

and strict, because of its application to mission-critical projects that require highly reliable software. Adherence to this standard is required of all organizations developing military software. Both MIL-STD-498 and the CMM support the use of the best practices for software development.

### ISO 9000

The International Organization for Standardization, or ISO, is headquartered in Geneva, Switzerland. ISO-9000, or more precisely, ISO-9001:2000, provides a comprehensive set of standards against which an organization can validate its quality-related processes and procedures. ISO 9000 is concerned with "quality management"—the processes established by an organization to enhance customer satisfaction by meeting customer and applicable regulatory requirements and continually improving the quality of its performance.

The ISO Web site (http://www.iso.ch/iso/en/iso9000-14000/iso9000/selection_use/examplesofiso9000.html) states:

> "ISO 9001:2000 is used if you are seeking to establish a management system that provides confidence in the conformance of your product to established or specified requirements. It is now the only standard in the ISO 9000 family against whose requirements your quality system can be certified by an external agency. The standard recognizes that the word "product" applies to services, processed material, hardware and software intended for, or required by, your customer.
>
> There are five sections in the standard that specify activities that need to be considered when you implement your system. You will describe the activities you use to supply your products and may exclude the parts of the Product Realization section that are not applicable to your operations. The requirements in the other four sections—Quality management system, Management responsibility, Resource management and Measurement, analysis and improvement—apply to all organizations and you will demonstrate how you apply them to your organization in your quality manual or other documentation.
>
> Together, the five sections of ISO 9001:2000 define what you should do consistently to provide product that meets customer and applicable statutory or regulatory requirements. In addition, you will seek to enhance customer satisfaction by improving your quality management system."

### IEEE Software Engineering Standards

The Institute of Electrical and Electronic Engineers (IEEE) has established a Software Engineering Standards Committee (SESC) that provides extensive standards for the practice of software engineering. The manuals for these standards can be ordered directly from the IEEE (http://standards.computer.org/sesc/sesc_geninfo/infondex.htm). The purposes for the standards, as explained by the IEEE, are:

- Codify the norms of professional software engineering practices into standards.
- Promote use of software engineering standards among clients, practitioners, and educators.
- Harmonize national and international software engineering standards development.

### Model Driven Architecture (MDA)

Building upon and leveraging the modeling standards established by the Object Management Group (OMG), the Model Driven Architecture (MDA) provides an open, vendor-neutral approach to the challenge of interoperability of systems and system components (see Fig. 4.22). The applied OMG standards include the Unified Modeling Language (UML), the Meta-Object Facility (MOF), and the Common Warehouse Meta-model (CWM). MDA enables the description of platform-independent applications using the OMG modeling standards. These applications can then be built using any major open or proprietary platform, including CORBA, Java, .NET, XMI/ XML, and Web-based platforms.

According to the OMG Web site on MDA:

"As new platforms and technologies emerge, MDA enables rapid development of new specifications that use them, streamlining the process of integration. In this way, MDA goes beyond middleware to provide a comprehensive, structured solution for application interoperability and portability into the future. Creating Application and Platform Descriptions in UML provides the added advantage of improving application quality and portability, while significantly reducing costs and time-to-market.

The architecture encompasses the full range of pervasive services already specified by OMG, including Directory Services, Event Handling, Persistence, Transactions, and Security. The core logic of many of these services is already available for multiple implementation technologies; for instance, Sun's J2EE platform uses Java interfaces to CORBA's long-established transactions and security services. MDA makes it easier and faster to design similar multiple-platform interfaces to common services. Most importantly, MDA enables the creation of standardized Domain Models for specific vertical industries. These standardized models can be realized

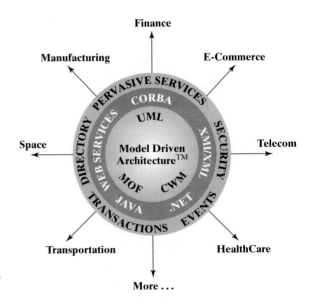

FIGURE 4.22 MDA Enables Interoperability

for multiple platforms now and in the future, easing multiple platform integration issues and protecting IT investments against the uncertainty of changing fashions in platform technology."

These standards are merely introduced here for reference, but we recommend a more detailed study of each one, or at least of a subset likely to apply in your chosen area of current or future practice as a software engineer.

The final major topic in this section will delve more deeply into the key features of object orientation from a structural perspective. We will seek to develop a core set of object-oriented competencies that will make object-orientation "second nature" to you when planning, designing, and implementing a software system.

In our quest to learn Java syntax and structure, we will explore Java Web applets, introduce a few Swing classes, and discover control structures.

### 4.3.3   *"Object Thinking"*

For novices, the concept of objects comes naturally, after some initial puzzling, but for more experienced programmers, it usually takes a modicum of relearning to really embrace object-orientation as a new set of "values" when designing and development software. To promote the adoption of object-orientation principles, we identify a few core value propositions, that will be especially important for those who doubt the value of this approach.

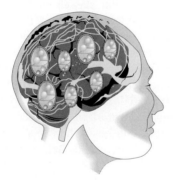

- Think of the information-processing problem at hand in terms of business objects and business workflows.
  - o  Classes and objects are more difficult to develop when they have not been part of the thought process in a project from its inception. If the software engineer views the business case and requirements from the classes-and-objects perspective, the later discovery and definition of classes and objects is derived naturally.
- Perform project analysis from an architecture-centric, object-oriented viewpoint.
  - o  Detailed requirements analysis is object-oriented when it considers stakeholder expectations and requirements from the viewpoint of processes and characteristics. Processes become methods; characteristics become attributes.

- Design features and functions from an architecture-centric, component-based foundation.
  - ○ Architecture is a key component of object-oriented design and construction. Building a proper architectural infrastructure, upon which a well-thought-out class hierarchy design implements subsystems, packages, classes, and objects, leads to a well-balanced, flexible, high-quality O-O implementation.
- Write object-oriented software modules.
  - ○ Code development benefits from all the O-O analysis and design efforts applied in the previous stages only if it also adheres to all the principles of O-O relevant to the project. Using an O-O language like Java to build reusable components is a vitally important aspect of this development process.
- Deploy and maintain components (packages, classes, and objects).
  - ○ Only if the end-to-end O-O software methodology is maintained up-to-date and consistent are the main benefits of this software-development life-cycle approach realized.

### 4.3.4   *Object Orientation*

Once we actively embrace "object thinking," we examine next the central aspects of object orientation in Java software development.

You have already learned that classes and their member objects have *attributes* (properties) and *methods* (behaviors, functions). The class attributes and methods function as templates for the attributes and methods implemented (instantiated) in the objects derived from these classes. This is important because objects can thus contain not only data (stored in attribute variables), but also functions, implemented as methods: they are fully self-contained operational units. This setup allows for a high level of **abstraction** of both function and data, based on the context of their application. The main benefit of abstraction is *generalization:* the less specific and unique a class and its members, the more likely that they can be applied to a larger variety of scenarios and therefore be *reused.* Another O-O characteristic helpful in the flexible application of reusable

---

**OBJECT-ORIENTATION CHARACTERISTICS**

- Classes and objects, attributes and methods
- Abstraction
- Component reuse
- Polymorphism
- Inheritance
- Encapsulation
- Message communication

components is **polymorphism**, which allows the programmer to hide different implementations behind a common interface. When classes and objects are arranged in a logical, meaningful architecture and hierarchy, the benefits of **inheritance**, the passing of shared characteristics to subclasses, comes into play.[5] Another key element in this flexible **reuse** of components is making integration fail-safe and secure: the process of **encapsulation**, which limits access to the inner workings of an object through the use of protective interfaces and simplifies its use for third parties by limiting access to only those attributes and methods needed to apply its functionality in a "black-box" fashion. In the multitasking environment characteristic of all modern graphical user-interface-enabled operating systems, the ability to invoke components not through direct subroutine calls, but by passing messages (**message communication**), is the final key benefit of Java object-orientation.

This brief introduction only covers the very basics of object orientation. Many concepts and principles collectively covered in the Unified Process affect the organization of components in object-oriented systems. Some of these, such as cohesion and coupling, will be discussed in later chapters.

### Java Implementation

Let us now take a closer look at the implementation in Java of these and related object-orientation characteristics. The challenge for the novice or junior Java software engineer is to comprehend how the object-orientation concepts relate to their counterparts in Java and to be able to implement Java programs that implement the best practices of object-oriented software engineering.

### Component Reuse

Java's object orientation is an integral characteristic of the language, promoting component reuse through many different features and functions. However, the most important prerequisites for successful and flexible component reuse are the proper design and architecture of the software system itself. The system has to be planned for component reuse from the beginning, as an interacting, well-ordered collection of building blocks, that can be assembled in different ways for different solutions. In addition, the Java inheritance (`extends`) and interface capabilities (`implements`) provide the foundation for reusable component integration. Java interfaces provide a *de facto* multiple-inheritance capability.

Java provides a special set of facilities called **JavaBeans™** and **Enterprise Java Beans™** (**EJB**) for the specification and "packaging" of reusable components to ensure that they follow a documented standard and that their public attributes and methods can be queried for their access requirements.

### Classes and Objects

The `class` statement in Java is the fundamental structural entity from which we create Java programs and derive objects using the `new` statement. As discussed previously,

---

[5]There is single and multiple inheritance: Java only supports single inheritance, but provides the benefits of multiple inheritance through the use of *interfaces*.

classes are organized into a class hierarchy, with sub (child) classes extended from super (parent) classes, and with abstract and concrete classes.

### Abstraction

The object-oriented best practice of abstraction supports the development of reusable components by pooling behaviors and properties that apply to multiple subclasses into higher-level (more "generic") classes. A carefully designed comprehensive, flexible, and scalable class hierarchy is the fundamental software engineering mechanism driving abstraction (see Fig. 4.23). By generalizing commonly used attributes and methods into superclasses, abstract classes can now be used for a scalable range of additional, similar components.

Abstraction is also supported by polymorphism and encapsulation, by providing flexible, protected reuse capabilities in components.

### Inheritance

The `extends` keyword allows for child classes to inherit attributes and methods from parent classes. A child class can only inherit from one parent class, consistent with the implementation of *single inheritance* in Java. The equivalent of *multiple inheritance* is achieved using Java interface technology (`implements` keyword), with the exception that inherited methods are signatures only—they contain no code.

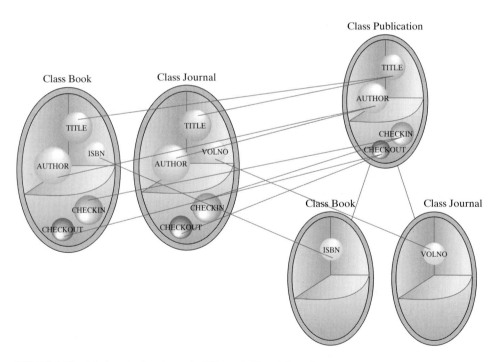

FIGURE 4.23    Abstraction Implemented Through Class Hierarchy

**Examples:**

```
public class Sedan extends Vehicle // inheritance
public class Accounting implements ActionListener // interface
```

### Polymorphism

Method and type overloading provide the implementation for polymorphism in Java. It is possible to create methods with the same name but different signatures (number and/or type of parameters) in the same class or within the class hierarchy. This feature provides polymorphic capabilities by allowing a method to execute different roles depending on how it is invoked. Constructor methods can also be overloaded to provide polymorphic object creation: different constructors are invoked at object creation (new keyword) to initialize different forms of the class instance depending on the parameters passed.

### Encapsulation

The use of `private` and `public` keywords in conjunction with public `set` and `get` methods and the Java scope rules provide the core encapsulation mechanism in Java. Object attributes are declared private so that their access can be controlled through the public `set` and `get` methods, thus *encapsulating* the object in order to protect its data (attributes) from uncontrolled access.

---

### POLYMORPHISM

**a.** The capability of assuming different forms; the capability of widely varying in form

**b.** Existence in many forms; the coexistence, in the same locality, of two or more distinct forms, not connected by intermediate gradations, but produced from common parents.

From www.dictionary.com

---

### CONSTRUCTORS

Constructors are methods that carry the same name as the class to which they belong. A constructor is called when a new object is instantiated from the class. When no constructor has been defined, a hidden constructor is internally generated and invoked.

```
public class BalanceCheck { // encapsulation example
    private double currentBalance;

    public set (String accountNumber, double newBalance) {
        // after validation
        currentBalance = newBalance;
}

    public double get (String accountNumber) {
        // after validation
        return currentBalance;
    }
}
```

***Message-Based Communication***

Events and event handling in Java represent the implementation of message-based communication. Events allow application components to react to requests for action (often initiated by the user by clicking a button) instead of keeping a "stranglehold" on the processor to sequentially run its statements without interruption. In practice, graphical Java applications include GUI object constructor classes to create the user interface and event-response classes to respond to user interactions with the interface. Commercial applications are often composed of cooperating components spread across multiple (sub-)systems (multi-tier architecture). These components collaborate with each other using messages. (Reference: Remote Method Invocation—RMI; Common Object Request Broker Architecture—CORBA.)

In general, when one object requests a service from another object, we say that it *passes a message* to that object, asking it to perform one of its methods.

### 4.3.5    *Java Control Structures*

Essential to the implementation of programming logic is the ability to control the flow of code execution. This is accomplished in a number of different ways:

- Selection: branching to a sequence of code statements based on a specific condition—
  - if/else
  - switch
- Repetition: executing a set of code statements multiple times—
  - for
  - while
  - do/while
- Method call: redirecting the flow of executing to another method
- Event handling: responding—in another method—to an event that has occurred

These features, used alone or in combination, provide complete logical control over the program flow as required by the design of the program functions. The following paragraphs explain each capability in more detail.

### Selection Statements

When deciding to execute a statement (or set of statements) only when a particular condition is true, we use the if statement. This conditional execution of statements mirrors the human decision-making process and allows programs to implement relevant, valuable work flows. For example, the following statement conditionally assigns a letter-grade value to a variable when the numeric grade is at or below a specified level:

```
if (grade <= 60)
    letterGrade = "F";
```

This is the simplest form of the use of if.

We often want to choose between one statement (or set of statements) and another. We use an if/else construct for this purpose:

```
if (grade >= 90)
    letterGrade = "A";
else if (grade >= 80)
    letterGrade = "B";
else if (grade >= 70)
    letterGrade = "C";
else if (grade >= 60)
    letterGrade = "D";
else
    letterGrade = "F";
```

Of course, if we conditionally want to execute multiple statements, all we have to do is enclose them in braces to create a statement block:

```
if (grade >= 90) {
    letterGrade = "A";
    System.out.println ("Good job!");
{
```

When we try to select among multiple sets of one or more statements based on the value of a primitive type variable, we can use the switch statement. For example:

```
class SelectItem {
    public static void main (String args []) {
        String itemSelected = null;
  /* initialized to avoid compile-time error of variable may not
    have been initialized */
            int c = Integer.valueOf (JOptionPane.InputDialog
                ("Enter Number:"));

            switch c {
              case 0:
                  itemSelected = "zero";
                  break;
```

```
              case 1:
                  itemSelected = "one";
                  break;
              case 2:
                  itemSelected = "two";
                  break;
          } //switch
      System.out.println ("Item Selected: " + itemSelected);
      } // end main
} // end class
```

Note that in Java the switch variable has to be of one of the eight primitive types. The break statement ensures that execution continues after the switch statement.

### Repetition Statements

The purpose of repetition structures is to execute one or more statements a number of times, either a specific number of times (for loop) or repeatedly *while* a condition is satisfied or *until* it changes (while and do/while loops).

The following code shows an example of a for loop:

```java
import java.awt.*;
import java.awt.event.*;
import javax.swing.*;
/**
*   Squares application
*
*   @author Georges Merx
*   b@version 1.00 04/06/17
*/

public class SquaresProgram extends JFrame {
    public SquaresProgram() {
        JTextArea localPanel = new JTextArea();
        setTitle("Squares");
        this.addWindowListener (
            new WindowAdapter() {
                public void windowClosing(WindowEvent e) {
                    System.exit(0);
                }
            }
        );

        localPanel.append("Number");
        localPanel.append("\tSquare");
        localPanel.append("\tCube");
```

```
        for (int count = 0; count < 11; count++) {
            localPanel.append("\n" + Integer.toString(count));
            localPanel.append("\t" + Integer.toString((int)
                Math.pow(count,2)));
            localPanel.append ("\t" + Integer.toString((int)
                Math.pow(count,3)));
        }

        this.getContentPane().add(localPanel);
        pack();setVisible(true);
    }

    public static void main(String[] args) {
    // Create application frame
    SquaresProgram frame = new SquaresProgram();
    }
}
```

**Program output:**

This example shows that the for loop provides the way to execute a statement or block of statements a specific number of times, using the syntax given in Figure 4.24.

Java 5.0 introduced an **enhanced for loop**. It is used to iterate through the elements of an array or collection with a counter variable.

**Example:**

```
int votes[] = {211, 334, 667, 887};
int total = 0;

for (int voteNumber:array) {
    total += voteNumber;
    System.out.printf("Current total is %...", total);
}
```

*declare integer variable* counter *and*        *increment variable* counter
*set to 0 at start of loop*                      *by* 1 *after the loop*

```
for (int counter = 0; counter <= 10; counter++) {
    //...
}
```

FIGURE 4.24   for Loop
Syntax

*test* counter *variable; if less than
or equal to ten, continue looping*

Often, we do not know ahead of time how many times to execute a loop. Knowing when a loop is meant to terminate may depend on user input or another external condition that changes within the loop. In this case, we use the `while` loop to execute a set of statements as long as a particular condition is `true`:

```
int counter = 0;

while (++counter <= 10)
    System.out.println(counter + ": Still in the loop ...!)";
```

Note that the `while` loop condition has to be modified in the loop in such a way that the condition eventually becomes `false`, otherwise we are "stuck" in an infinite loop.

If the logic requires that the code in the `while` loop be executed *at least once*, use the `do/while` loop regardless of whether the test is `true` or `false`:

```
int counter = 10;

do
    System.out.println (counter + "in the loop ...!");
while (++counter <= 10); // will run once
```

Two helper statements are available to "break out" of the current loop path or loop (already encountered in the `switch` example above): `break` and `continue.`

`break` is used to break out of a block of statements in a `switch` or repetition sequence. When a label is specified, `break` will exit the labeled block of statements; this functionality is useful with nested loops.

`continue` has functionality similar to `break`, including its optional use of a label, but instead of completely breaking out of a loop, it simply "drops down" to the bottom of the loop, skipping the remainder of statements in that pass through the repetition. Obviously, this functionality only applies to repetition structures, and not to selection blocks (e.g., `switch`).

---

**Example:**

```
//...
int counter = 0;
skipOut: while (counter <= 10) {
    if (counter == 3) continue;
    else if (counter == 5) break skipOut;
    else counter++;
    //...
}
```

Generally, break and continue statements are similar to the GoTo statements in legacy procedural languages: they are disruptive to the natural logic flow and not recommended, except maybe to break out of an error condition (in error logic, break or continue statements are sometimes used to avoid excessive nesting of statements for paths unlikely to ever be taken).

### Example Program

The following updated prototype version of the VotingProgram shows the use of some Java control structures.

```java
/**
 * The Voting Program - Candidates class
 *
 */

class Candidates {
    String firstName, lastName;
    int votesReceived;
}

import javax.swing.JOptionPane;
/**
 * The Voting Program - Control Structures Version
 *
 * @author Georges Merx, Ph.D.
 * @version 1.00 05/12/07
 */

public class TheVotingProgramControlStructures {
// signature of class

    public static void main(String[] args) {
    // main() method - entry point to program
        Candidates candidates[] = null;
        int noCandidates = 0;
        int counter = 0;
        int votes = 0;
        // Display welcome message
        System.out.println(
            "Welcome to The Voting Program. Copyright G. Merx.\n");
        // \n forces newline
        String answer = JOptionPane.showInputDialog
            ("Enter number of candidates (Cancel to exit):");

        if (answer != null) {
            try {
                noCandidates = Integer.parseInt(answer);
            } catch (NumberFormatException e) {
                System.err.println("Invalid number of
                    candidates!");
```

```java
            System.exit (1); // abort program
        }

    if (noCandidates > 0) {
        candidates = new Candidates [noCandidates];
        do {
        // Get input from the user
            answer = JOptionPane.showInputDialog
                ("Enter candidate first name:");

            if (answer == null) {
            // if the CANCEL key has been selected
                System.err.println("Operation canceled (1)!");
                System.exit (0);
            }

            candidates [counter] = new Candidates();
            candidates [counter].firstName = answer;
            candidates [counter].lastName =
            JOptionPane.showInputDialog
                ("Enter candidate last name:");

            if (candidates [counter].lastName == null) {
            // if the CANCEL key has been selected
                System.err.println("Operation canceled (2)!");
                System.exit (0);
            }

            answer = JOptionPane.showInputDialog
                ("Number of votes for " +
                candidates [counter].lastName + ":");

            if (answer == null) {
              // if the CANCEL key has been selected
                System.err.println (
                    "Operation canceled (3)!");
                System.exit (0);
            }

            try {
                votes = Integer.parseInt(answer);
            } catch (NumberFormatException e) {
                System.err.println
                    ("Invalid number of votes!");
                JOptionPane.showMessageDialog (null, "Error",
                    "Please reenter voter information!",
                    JOptionPane.ERROR_MESSAGE);
                counter--; //reenter current candidate
            }
```

```
            candidates [counter].votesReceived = votes;
            counter++;
    } while (counter < noCandidates);

    // Display results
    int winner = 0;
    boolean tie = false;

    for (int count = 0; count < counter; count++) {
        int mostVotes = 0;
        System.out.println (candidates [count].firstName +
            " " + candidates [count].lastName + ": " +
            candidates [count].votesReceived + " votes");
        if (candidates [count].votesReceived > mostVotes)
            winner = count;
        else if (candidates [count].votesReceived ==
            mostVotes)
            tie = true;
    }

    if (tie)
        JOptionPane.showMessageDialog (null,
            There was a tie!", "Results",
            JOptionPane.WARNING_MESSAGE);

    else
        JOptionPane.showMessageDialog (null,
            "The election winner is " +
            candidates [winner].firstName + " " +
            candidates [winner].lastName + " with " +
            candidates [winner].votesReceived + " votes!",
            "Results", JOptionPane.INFORMATION_MESSAGE);
    } // end if for >0 candidates

    System.out.println("\nThank you and good bye!\n");
    // Exit program
    System.exit(0);
    }
}
```

*Analysis*

This simple program uses a **do...while** loop in its **main()** method to prompt for candidate names and number of votes. The **do** loop ensures that the code block governed by the control structure is executed *at least once* (as opposed to a **while** loop). It also uses a **try...catch** block to ensure that the number of votes input is actually an integer, rejecting incorrect input. This process is called *validation*.

This type of exception handling is discussed in more detail in a later chapter. For now, understand that a **try** ... **catch** block suspends the JVM's default error handling and allows the program to deal with specific runtime errors, in this case a potential NumberFormatException.

### *Software Engineering Best Practices*

While many programmers in decades past regarded their profession as a mixture of art and science, we firmly believe that developing software is a serious engineering discipline. We have therefore defined a set of Best Practices that will help standardize your approach to software engineering. Applying software engineering best practices is a proven way to better software development. The concept of Best Practices is useful because it exhorts you to build products that withstand the scrutiny of stringent quality control and competitive comparison. The world of high technology is not constrained by geographic boundaries, but instead is exposed to virtually unlimited global competitive pressure. Only the very best solutions will prevail over time in this international market. By extension, companies that use world-class IT solutions can gain a substantial competitive advantage over their market challengers.

The software engineering Best Practices identified in this book are listed in Figure 4.25. We examine them in greater detail in the next sections and discuss how to apply them to software design and development.

### Life-Cycle Approach to Project Development

Encompassing all other software engineering practices, the Best Practice of life-cycle-driven project development is a key principle of a successful, "end-to-end" product-development process. When the development of software applications is viewed critically from the "bird's-eye" perspective of the overall project, from earliest conception to the maintenance and support process after general release, a coherent, consistent, deliberate approach is much more likely to result.

While a high-level viewpoint is relatively easy to adopt at the beginning of a project, the real challenge is to maintain a healthy distance from the fine details of implementation while writing Java source code. This Best Practice advises us to remain circumspect while passing from phase to phase in the process of developing our software application, always aware of changing requirements, new stakeholders, and other developments that may impact our progress.

### *Understand Problem Domain, Stakeholders, Business Case*

A credible Requirements Specification is the foundation of a successful project. A definition of the problem domain and scope, an examination of the stakeholders (i.e., those groups and individuals directly or indirectly affected by the project), and the business justification for the proposed project are the cornerstones of the development of accurate, complete use cases, which in turn are themselves the essence of the requirements analysis process.

Most of the time, software engineers are not experts in the subject matter for which they are developing a software application. But it is difficult, if not impossible, to

Life Cycle Approach to Project Development

Understand Problem Domain,
Stakeholders, Business Case

Identify and Track Functional and
Non-Functional Project Requirements

Plan and Design for Excellence

Implement and (Re)use Components
(Packages, Classes and Objects)

Deliver and Deploy a Complete
Solution which Meets Functional
and Non-Functional Requirements

Manage Error Corrections and
Change Requests Effectively

Effective Oral and Written Communication

**FIGURE 4.25**   Software Engineering Best Practices

write world-class software without a clear and reasonably deep understanding of the subject area being addressed. Studying and comprehending the key processes and interests of the organization for which you are developing a software application is an important element in systems analysis and design.[6] This may involve observation of work processes, library and Web research, interviews with individual contributors and managers, and documentation and modeling of important facts about the organization and its work practices.

Engineers and programmers generally display little interest in business-related issues and topics, preferring to let the "business people" deal with those subjects. However, business issues (such as budgets, competition, marketing, and profitability) are integral components of development projects and need to be considered with awareness and interest. As seen in Figure 4.26, it is at the *intersection* of business, organizational, and technical issues that the truth about a project lies.

---

[6]We do not perceive these activities as distinct from the tasks associated with software engineering, even though they may in some instances be carried out by specialists different from the core group of programmers. Such an arrangement is not a preferred approach to "holistic" end-to-end software engineering.

### Identify and Track Functional and Non-Functional Project Requirements

Based on the needs expressed by the various project stakeholders and other internal and external information sources, a set of requirements can be established and tracked within the scope of the project. The expression and representation of these requirements follows a predetermined sequence and organization, documented in the Requirements Specification and supported by UML diagrams. The establishment of requirements starts with a careful stakeholder analysis and continues with the development of structured use cases, as will be seen in subsequent chapters. *Functional requirements* represent actual features and functions planned for the application; *non-functional requirements* cover the other supporting aspects of the application, such as performance, scalability, aesthetics, resilience, and supportability (see below). Together all these requirements provide a solid foundation for the follow-on phases of the process, but only if they are well defined in sufficient detail.

### Plan and Design for Excellence

Most software development is done in an economic environment of global competition. Thus the solutions we deliver must pass competitive scrutiny when compared to work done anywhere else in the world. Only a great deal of attention to quality in all aspects of design and implementation can result in world-class, excellent products. We often refer to such products as "best-of-breed" or "best-of-class." Creating excellent products is only possible when every aspect of the product is superior.

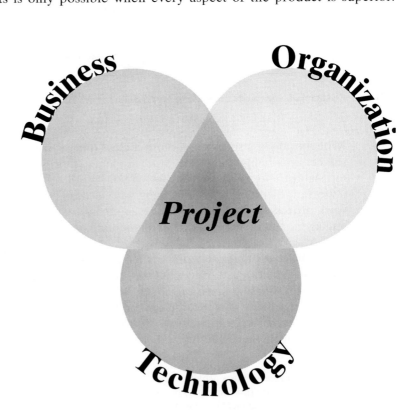

FIGURE 4.26 The Intersection of Business, Organization, and Technology: *The Project*

Weakness in just one area will drag down the perception of high quality for the entire product. An all-encompassing concern for quality is therefore a prerequisite for developing best-of-breed software products. This applies not only to the product's functionality but to its meeting stakeholder requirements accurately, creatively, elegantly, and productively.

## Implement and (Re-)Use Components (Packages, Classes, and Objects)

> **Key Term**
>
> **Scope** delineates the boundaries of the project in terms of a particular version or release level with a defined set of functions and capabilities.

Many benefits arise when software components can be reused. The most obvious advantage—not having to reimplement functionality once developed—is eclipsed by other rewards:

- Consistency from application to application.
- Reusing well-exercised and tested components (i.e., limiting the development of genuinely new code more prone to instability).
- Inherent necessity to properly architect components and coordinate components for maximum flexibility and interoperability.
- Emphasis on constructing solutions from modular, self-contained functional elements.
- Shorter development time and lower cost.

In Java, these capabilities are implemented as classes and objects. Classes are templates for objects, meaning that an object is instantiated (created) from the blueprint represented by the class, containing attributes (instance variables) and methods (code).

The objective of developing reusable components is not limited to classes; the philosophy of reuse should permeate the entire project, from the process of requirements capture and analysis to design[7] and the implementation of classes, packages, subsystems, and systems. The transition from the procedural implementation of a specific solution to the development of reusable components is a difficult one, because it involves a different software engineering philosophy altogether. Software developers are accustomed to finding a singular causal relationship between requirement and feature/function. It is conceptually simpler to solve a given problem with information technology than to create a component that not only solves the problem at hand but can also be used to solve similar problems in the future, in related but different contexts.

---

[7]"Design Patterns" represent an industry-wide trend in design reuse.

For example, in later chapters we will develop a library management program. In this context, it is easy to imagine the development of a "book" class which captures the attributes and processes associated with a book, such as "author," "title," "ISBN-number," "publisher," and so on. But it is slightly more difficult to generalize this class into a general-purpose class, perhaps called "publication," which can be used for all the published materials found in a library. And what about using this same class for other programs, maybe a bookstore? How do we make this component ready and flexible for reuse? This question will be discussed at length in subsequent chapters of this book.

### Deliver and Deploy a Complete Solution That Meets Functional and Non-Functional Requirements

Unfortunately, the word "solution" is overused in marketing collateral materials. In fact, the connotation associated with the term of successfully addressing a customer's problems is very important. The reason for creating a software application is almost always to provide a solution to a challenge and make a task easier, or more consistent, economical, or faster. However, the success of a software development project is dependent on many factors besides software functionality. We therefore differentiate between functional and non-functional requirements.

- Functional requirements address the specification of program capabilities, designed to implement improved work processes using IT. The realization of functional requirements results in program features available to users to perform specific work tasks.

- Non-functional requirements include the environment, platforms, tools, and networking components within which an application is implemented. They include quality-related issues, such as scalability, speed of execution and response time, installability, maintainability, and resilience to failure. These non-functional requirements, in effect, limit or constrain the capabilities of the functional requirements. The analysis and design of a software solution needs to actively account for all requirements, functional and non-functional, and needs to include all aspects of the project, including the packaging, installation, deployment, and maintenance of a software solution.

### Manage Error Corrections and Change Requests Effectively

A key aspect of software quality assurance (SQA) is the process of corrective action. We recommend a *closed-loop corrective action process* in order to ensure that all issues are dealt with completely and effectively. The first step in this process is triage: we need to ensure that we clearly differentiate between errors ("bugs") and requests for enhancements. The point of reference for this decision is the Requirements Specification for the product in question. If a reported malfunction applies to a feature in the Requirements Specification, it is a software error; if the report covers functionality not included in the Requirements Specification, it is a request for an enhancement. We will discuss the process of closed-loop corrective action (CLCA) and other software quality-assurance activities in more detail in a later chapter.

*Effective Oral and Written Communication*

Most useful projects involve a number of contributors working together as a team, sometimes in one location, sometimes in multiple, geographically dispersed locations. In order for people to work well together in a team on a complex technology project, they must be able to communicate effectively face-to-face and over the telephone (orally), and in e-mails, memos, letters, and formal documents and specifications. Unfortunately, many software engineers do not enjoy speaking with others or writing documents and are not very proficient at communication. Lack of communication is often a major problem in failing software development projects. Effective software engineering, therefore, also includes competent oral and written communication, and, by extension, the ability to work effectively in a team.

Next, we will introduce you to the topic of object orientation. Later we will devote more time and study to this key component of Java software engineering, but you will have a chance right now to preview the key aspects of object-oriented software development.

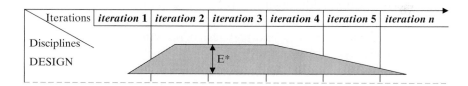

## 4.4 Position in Process

As this point, we are still completing the Design Discipline of our software development process. We have lingered in this phase to ensure that we cover all aspects of proper program architecture and design. The better and more complete the design, the more predictable and easier the code development. In particular, we will take a close look now at the Design Specification (which includes the Software Architecture Document, or SAD), the main artifact resulting from this phase. Associated with the Design Specification is the Unit Test Specification, which documents the test scripts for each of the designed components. Other important documents developed in this phase are the Quality Assurance Plan and the Configuration Management Plan.

### 4.4.1 Design Specification

Our recommended structure for the project Design Specification uses descriptive sections as well as detailed UML diagrams to guide the development of code components and subsystems. The following outline is provided as a guideline for the development of the Design Specification:

- The Design Model: UML-based description of the design classes and their relationships

- The Software Architecture Document (SAD): architectural representation of the software system
- Functional Overview: detailed description of each major component (using UML notation where appropriate)
  - Components, packages, and subsystems
  - Prototype description and evaluation
- Design-Level Use Case Model: update of the use case model described in the Requirements Specification from the design perspective
- Class Hierarchy: overview of all major functional packages and classes with their attributes and methods
  - Patterns: the design patterns used in the design of the individual components and how they are applied
  - UML class and object diagrams: detailed class and object diagrams and descriptions for each package/class/component
- Design-Level Use Cases
  - Scenarios: for each design-level use case, update the scenario descriptions (primary, secondary) to capture all important processing steps
  - UML interaction diagrams (activity, sequence, state): use UML diagrams to support scenario descriptions and clarify attributes, methods, and messages
  - User interface / look-and-feel design: provide detailed pictorial representations of all major screens/forms
- Environment–Non-Functional Requirements
  - Software, hardware, networking required: on the basis of the system architecture, describe all contributing system components required for the application to work properly
  - Other non-functional issues (performance, etc.): how non-functional issues will be addressed in the process and program
- Supporting Disciplines
  - Project plans
    - Macro-level: covers entire project, updates/confirms number of iterations, main milestones, resources, and deadlines
    - Micro-level (per iteration): detailed plan for the current and next iteration
  - Quality Assurance Plan Summary: summarizes all SQA imitative, standards, processes (e.g., inspections, validations, certifications, issues of support)
  - Configuration Management Plan Summary: summarizes all artifact management processes
  - Documentation Plan Summary: summarizes internal and external documentation artifacts (including format, access, scope)

The most important aspect of software design is the translation of requirements to well-structured, well-organized classes, and, ultimately, features and functions. It is especially important that this design process capture the work processes inherent in these functions and find ways to substantially improve their quality and productivity through the application of information technology rather than just replace the current processes with new ones of equal or lesser value. The development of the Design

Specification requires the project team to perform this requirements interpretation in an orderly, iterative manner, creating a product design that is of high quality without requiring extraordinary talent or experience from the team: the process itself helps ensure that all aspects of good design are taken into account.

The UML diagrams introduced in earlier chapters come into full use in the Design Discipline; they play a key role in capturing all the requirements in the context of the proposed computer-based solution.

The process of software design naturally has a strong creative component. However, we advise the novice or junior software engineer to minimize reliance on creativity and to maximize attention to engineering principles, such as adherence to standards and Best Practices, continuous requirements validation involving the key stakeholders, extensive functional validation and testing, peer review (inspections), and complete documentation of all design steps and decisions.

### 4.4.2  Unit Test Specification

The Unit Test Specification documents the unit tests for the components being designed. In their simplest form, unit tests are step-by-step action scripts or scenario descriptions for positive and negative testing of software components and their interfaces. The scripts are developed by the software engineers who "own" the particular components because they know the most about them and thus can develop the most complete, most rigorous tests. The scripts typically document manual testing processes, but may also be the foundation for test automation scripts. The scripts should not only test functionality, but also validate the implementation of requirements documented in the Requirements Specification.

### 4.4.3  Quality Assurance Plan

The quality assurance department or team is responsible for the development of the software quality assurance (SQA) plan. SQA Best Practices are depicted in Figure 4.27. An SQA plan is expected to include the following information:

- SQA guidelines and standards
- SQA organization and roles
  - Empowerment
  - Organizational independence from engineering
- Enforcement Process
  - Participation
  - Inspections
  - Validation and reporting
  - Closed-loop corrective action—incident tracking
- Customer interaction
  - Alpha and beta site testing
  - Deployment control and certification

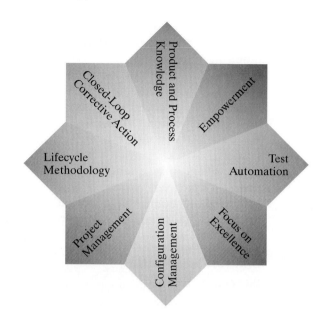

**FIGURE 4.27** Quality Assurance Best Practice.

It is fundamentally the responsibility of SQA to ensure that the solution being developed by engineering considers all the identified stakeholders, meets all their requirements, and follows agreed-upon standards and practices. SQA obviously needs to be organizationally independent from engineering and empowered to "pull the plug" on a deployment or intermediary process when quality requirements are not being met. SQA plays the central role in an organization's ability to produce quality software.

### 4.4.4 Configuration Management Plan

The Configuration Management Plan is the responsibility of the configuration management team, often a group within the quality assurance department. This plan covers the following key topics:

- Source and object code control
- Release and version management
- Intellectual property control
- Environment management, including testing environment and data

### 4.4.5 Documentation Plan

Finally, the Documentation Plan is produced by the technical publication team, a team of technical writers who are responsible for the documentation of the product being developed.[8] This includes hard-copy manuals and electronic documentation, such as

---

[8]The technical publication team is often part of the quality assurance organization.

FIGURE 4.28    Example Tool Tip

on-line help information and tool tip text (see Fig. 4.28). Technical writers should be involved with a new project from early inception: their non-technical, user-oriented viewpoint is invaluable in validating requirements and proposed designs. The documentation plan covers all aspects of external and internal documentation according to the software development model introduced earlier. Technical writers work closely together with software engineering to produce context-specific online help information, tool tips, and other user-oriented help information.

## 4.5    Example: The Voting Program

We will now examine an abbreviated version of the Design Specification for the Voting Program. This specification is based on the software design efforts documented in the preceding chapter. In the interest of space, we will not include SQA and Configuration Management Plans here.

### 4.5.1    Introduction

This Design Specification documents the design of the Voting Program, based on the Requirements Specification outlined in Chapter 2. Given the limited space available in these pages, we will present the specification as an incomplete framework. Figures 4.29 and 4.30 show an overview of the Design Model for the Voting Program project. The Design Model provides a visualization of the use-case realization with interaction and

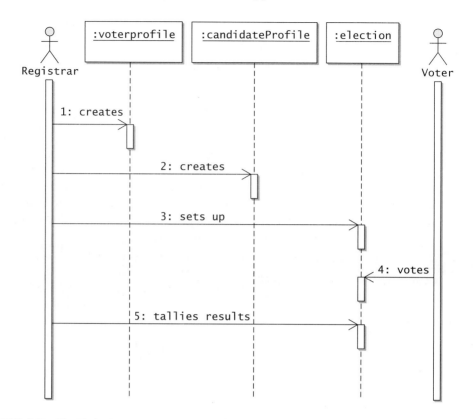

FIGURE 4.29 The Voting Program Design Model (Sequence Diagram)

class diagrams.[9] The interactions between objects and the layout of the class hierarchy are shown as an overview in the Design Model diagrams. Students are encouraged to further develop the UML diagrams presented in these sections. More detailed design diagrams follow.

Figure 4.30 shows the main classes identified for the Voting Program prototype application presented in this book. Of course, the functionality described here is incomplete for a real-life implementation. Note the separation of classes to follow a Model-View-Controller (MVC) design approach:

- **Model:** Election and Tally classes and related
- **View:** Setup class
- **Controller:** The Voting Program and Controller classes

---

[9]See Craig Larman, *Applying UML and Patterns*, Prentice-Hall, 2002.

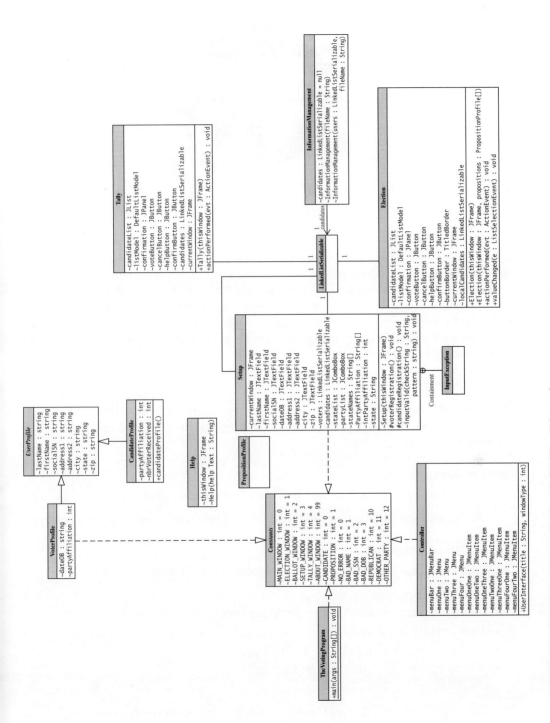

FIGURE 4.30 The Voting Program Design Model (Class Diagram)

233

*Description of Project*

In order to illustrate the principles of software engineering, we are designing the Voting Program as a standalone program, even though a realistic implementation would likely require a distributed architecture, possibly with a Web-based user interface.[10] The program will allow voters to exercise their important civic responsibility using a user-friendly implementation of computer information technology. Election officials have their own access to our program in order to create ballots, legitimatize voters, and receive and tabulate results.

### 4.5.2    Functional Overview

The Voting Program has a number of key functions, divisible into three categories: (1) end user functions; (2) election official functions; (3) program and data administration functions.[11]

*End-User Functions*

The Voting Program's main end-user functions include the following:

- Authentication, registration validation (log-in) [not implemented in the prototype]

*Election Official Functions*

The Voting Program's main election official functions include the following:

- Authentication
- Voter registration initialization (enabling voter authentication)
- Ballot creation and update
- Election information link creation and update
- Voting results tabulation and management

---

[10]The actual implementation of this type of program would likely use Java Server Pages technology.
[11]The scope of the specification given here is the first release of the program. Future features and functions are not considered.

### Administration Functions

The Voting Program's main administrative functions include the following:

- Authentication initialization (enabling election official authentication)
- Data maintenance and back-up
- Program installation, maintenance, and updates

### UML Use Case Diagram

After the iteration(s) of this phase, the development of project use cases should be about 80% complete. Of course, ongoing refinements and adjustments are a natural component of iterative software engineering and will result in specification updates throughout the project life cycle.

We established a number of key UML diagrams as part of our project requirements analysis. It is now time to revisit and revise these diagrams and descriptions to reflect our increased knowledge of the problem domain and to capture the design for the functions and features we are envisaging for our software application. The design is the software engineer's response to the Requirements Specification.

The ongoing UML diagram in Figure 4.31 is a key source for developing the class hierarchy for the Voting Program. It has been updated to reflect corrections, enhancements, and new knowledge acquired since the initial version was developed.

### Other UML Diagrams

As we showed in an earlier chapter, additional UML diagrams, such as component and deployment diagrams, are useful to depict relationships at the system level of components and subsystems, as well as the position of the software system in relationship to the underlying network and hardware platform(s). Figure 4.32 shows a component diagram for the Voting Program.

## 4.5.3   System Architecture

The architecture of the system provides the foundation for the solution being developed. Viewing the system architecture from multiple perspectives is the most useful approach to architectural design. The system architecture can also serve as the basis for an architectural prototype of the planned application.

System architecture should be viewed from a range of perspectives incorporating the viewpoints and interests of the main project stakeholders.

The diagram in Figure 4.33 is a high-level overview of the system architecture. The goal of this graphic is to convey the complete system envisioned for this online voting solution, including its various networking and hardware components (Release 1; the blue-color components are those planned for the *prototype* implementation discussed in this book).

The diagram in Figure 4.33 is limited in terms of comprehensiveness. A more complete diagram (a good class exercise) would incorporate additional details—namely, all the components essential to the successful operation of the future product. These may include:

- Security layer
- Installation and administration components

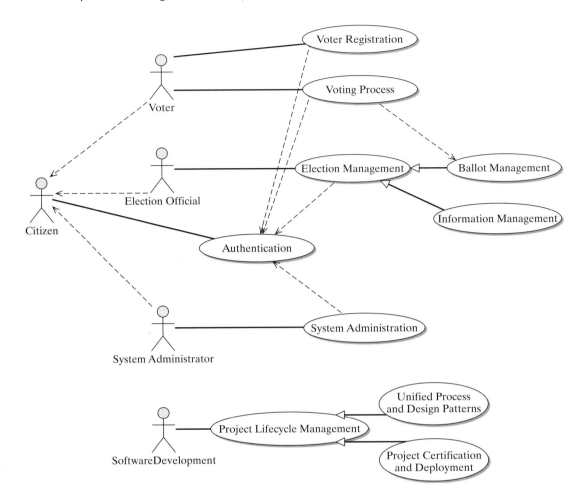

FIGURE 4.31 The Voter Program Use Case Model (updated)

- SQA components for logging and testing
- Specification of third-party components used
- A more explicit specification of inter-component interfaces

### 4.5.4 Class Hierarchy

The class hierarchy of the Voting Program is derived from the domain model, the use case model, and the system architecture.

Please revisit Figure 4.30 for a diagram of the class hierarchy.

#### Fleshing Out the Class Hierarchy

We have previously looked at the mapping of use cases to the system class hierarchy. In our example of the Voting Program, we examine the conceptual classes in the domain

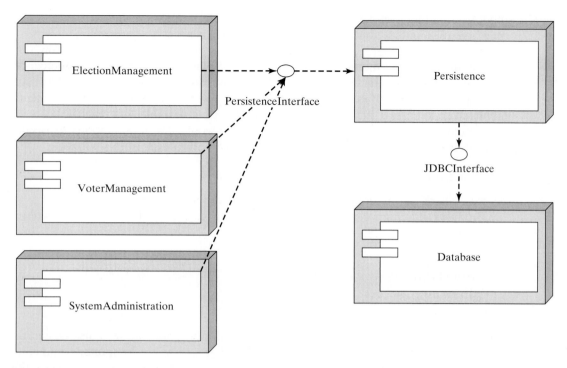

FIGURE 4.32    The Voting Program Component Diagram (simplified)

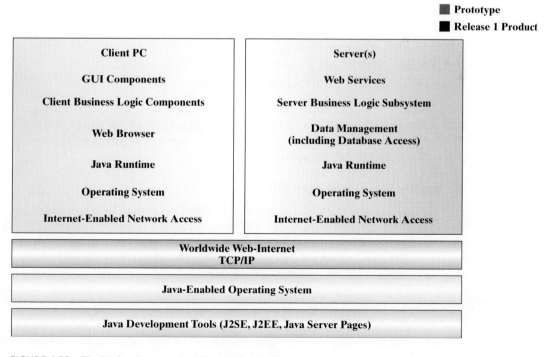

FIGURE 4.33    The Voting Program Architecture (revised)

model and the use cases, from ballot creation to vote submission, and we extract common activities and attributes in order to create our classes. As we develop classes for the program, we recognize, often in an informal incremental or iterative fashion, that certain attributes and methods appear in multiple places. These become prime candidates for inclusion in higher-level super-classes from where they can be shared by multiple subclasses through the process of *inheritance*. We account for the overall project's architecture to ensure that our project remains flexible, scalable, and extensible.

**Note:** In a real-life professional project, we would develop components on the basis of proven Design Patterns, an approach beyond the scope of this book.

### 4.5.5   Component Definition and Design

As we embark on the detailed design of each component of the Voting Program, we use the UML diagrams extensively to cover the specification of design from each important perspective:

- End-users
- Administrators
- Software engineers
- Other stakeholders

A component is a class or a set of classes in a smaller program, but may also be a package, or even a subsystem, in a larger project. The diagrams cover components and component relationships as well as the processing of functions over time (sequence). For each component, we need to develop the following diagrams:[12]

- UML Class and Object Diagrams
- UML Activity Diagram
- UML Sequence or Collaboration Diagram
- UML Statechart Diagram
- User Interface/Look-and-Feel Design Sketch

These diagrams together capture all the important aspects of component design. The last item, User Interface/Look-and-Feel Design Sketch, is not specified in the UML but allows the designer to visually lay out the forms needed to interface the user with the underlying program functionality.

### 4.5.6   Prototype Description and Evaluation

At this point in the Design Phase for the Voting Program, it may be a good idea to develop one or more concept prototypes to begin exploring issues of information capture, processing, and interface usability. *Prototypes* allow us to get users in front of our emerging functionality and to get candid feedback from actual "test voters" in terms of our program's ease of access and use. As software engineers, we are often too close to

---

[12]The explicit presentation of each diagram is beyond the scope of this book, but there are many good publications on the topic of UML diagramming by reputable authors. Visit www.uml.org for more information on the UML Standard.

our product designs to clearly understand how uninitiated users view our functions, and how these functions support or hinder the underlying work process.

When using a prototyping approach at this point, it is important to collect results from prototype testing in an organized, measurable fashion (with the support of the SQA team). Users of your prototype(s) must be carefully observed so that their actions and impressions can be recorded. Any resulting modifications should not only be incorporated in the product design, but also validated against original product requirements.

## 4.5.7   *Environment*

The Voting Program prototype is a standalone Java application, but a releasable version of the program (which we shall call Release 1.00.00) would most likely require a distributed architecture, as shown in Fig. 4.33. The development and deployment of this application require the appropriate infrastructure components for each subsystem (of the complete product). On the client subsystem, this includes a Java-capable browser (assuming that Web-based accessibility is a requirement) and an Internet connection.[13] The business-rule server/Web server needs to support the Java runtime and an Internet connection, but the operating system may be a server version of Windows, UNIX, or Linux.[14] The database server component needs to provide a multi-user relational database and appropriate software (such as JDBC for interfacing the Voting Program with the database).[15]

### Software, Hardware, Networking Required

The prototype's standalone functionality will only require a PC with Java-enabled Microsoft Windows. Alternatively, the program could be implemented as a Java applet and run through a Java-enabled browser. The eventual program follows a distributed architecture with client and server components. These components require Java-enabled operating-system and hardware platforms. Most major non-Microsoft computer vendors offer such systems. Standard Internet networking using the TCP/IP protocol provides the connection between clients and servers. As the content of the information flow is secret, the data will need to be transmitted using a secure technology, such as Secure Socket Layer (SSL).

### Other Non-Functional Requirements

Non-functional requirements (e.g., performance, scalability, adherence to standards, guidelines, etc.) address areas not covered by program functions but instead deal with supporting disciplines. In a realistic implementation of this program, a number of important non-functional requirements should be considered:

- *Performance and scalability:* Can the program support enough concurrent users?
- *Security:* Is the authentication fool-proof? Is the data secured from hackers?

---

[13]Java support is achieved either by using Netscape Navigator 6.1 or above, or by using a Java runtime plug-in, available free of charge from the java.sun.com Web site. (*Note:* In a real-world implementation, we would be likely to use Java Server Pages instead of Java applet technology.)
[14]Other operating systems will work, too, as long as they support Java.
[15]It is beyond the scope of this example to address issues  pertaing to the performance and scalability of this solution.

- Reliability: Is the program error-free to the point where the potential for data corruption is eliminated?

These concerns, which are beyond the scope of the Voting Program prototype covered in this book, are addressed by the implementation of specific technologies and solutions for each point of concern:

- Performance and scalability: Implementation of CORBA- or RMI-supported distributed or distributable components across multiple systems.
- Security: Use of authentication protocols and technology, such as Secure Socket Layer (SSL), and public/private key validation.
- Reliability: enhanced software quality-assurance process, extensive alpha and beta testing, use of transaction-processing methods (atomicity, end-to-end commit, auto-recovery); high-performance, redundant hardware and network systems (RAID disks; redundant backup systems—computers, power).

### 4.5.8    Supporting Disciplines

The supporting workflow disciplines provide various services for the duration of the project. These include:

**Project Management**
As we will discuss in more detail in the next segment, the macro- and micro-level project plans need to be created and kept up to date. The project management workflow provides continuous project control to ensure that the project is delivered on time and on budget.

**Inspections**
At every minor milestone in the project plan, a process of inspection should take place. A peer-level meeting is called and an artifact considered ready by its producer is examined by this peer group for flaws, omissions, and disconnections from the requirements specification. Inspection results are documented and corrections tracked. This process is meant to be a genuine defense by the component's originator, not simply a benign peer review.

**Validation**
Validation is the ongoing process of ensuring that what is being produced meets project requirements. As projects advance, requirements are augmented by technical exigencies that also need to be met.

**Configuration Management**
Discussed in more detail in a later chapter, configuration management ensures that product components are organized and assembled correctly and dependably. In complex systems, dozens or hundreds of components often accumulate to form a solution, which may run on multiple platforms. All the versions and forms of these components (source and object) need to be maintained, catalogued, and assembled as needed. Intellectual property needs to be safeguarded. Test cases and data need to be created, maintained, and refreshed. The Configuration Management Plan (see below) covers all these important activities.

**Documentation**

Documentation includes not only user documentation but also internal documents, such as the various specifications we have been pursuing as part of the software development life-cycle. Documentation also includes the text and format of online help information, even the tool tips associated with each control on the screen.

**Technical Marketing Plan**

While marketing may fall under the dominion of the marketing team, the development of the technical marketing plan is listed here because this plan is an essential component of commercial software development. We advocate the inclusion of marketing talent in the development process because the technical marketing perspective is another source of excellent input into product design. Also, waiting for marketing input until the end of the development cycle makes it impossible to include vital suggestions and recommendations from this important stakeholder source in the initial release of the product.

### Updated Macro-Level Project Plan

While it is beyond the scope of the Voting Program example in this book to provide detailed project plans, it is important to understand that these important planning activities need to take place at this phase in the project. The macro-level project plan maps out the overall project phases and determines the number of iterations needed to complete the project.

An example of a high-level project plan (using Microsoft® Project™) is shown in Figure 4.34.

### Current- and Next-Iteration Micro-Level Project Plan

The micro-level project plans for the current and next iterations cover the detailed tasks, task owners, and timeframes for about six weeks per iteration (rule of thumb).[16] We will not present these detailed plans here, but refer you to appropriate texts or classes on project management to learn how to properly schedule complex projects.

A sample iteration project plan is shown in Figure 4.35. Of course, the plans shown in these pages are mere skeletons of what is required for an actual project. But they may be viewed as starting points for a valuable in-class exercise to develop more detailed project plans.

### Quality Assurance Plan, Configuration Management Plan, Documentation Plan Summaries

The Quality Assurance Plan for the Voting Program covers all aspects of software quality control associated with the project. Quality Assurance Best Practices will be covered in a later chapter. We will not present a complete plan here, for reasons of scope and space, but encourage you to give this important document some thought and

---

[16]The iterative development approach advocated as part of our process stipulates that detailed planning is only possible with a reasonable degree of accuracy for the current and next iteration.

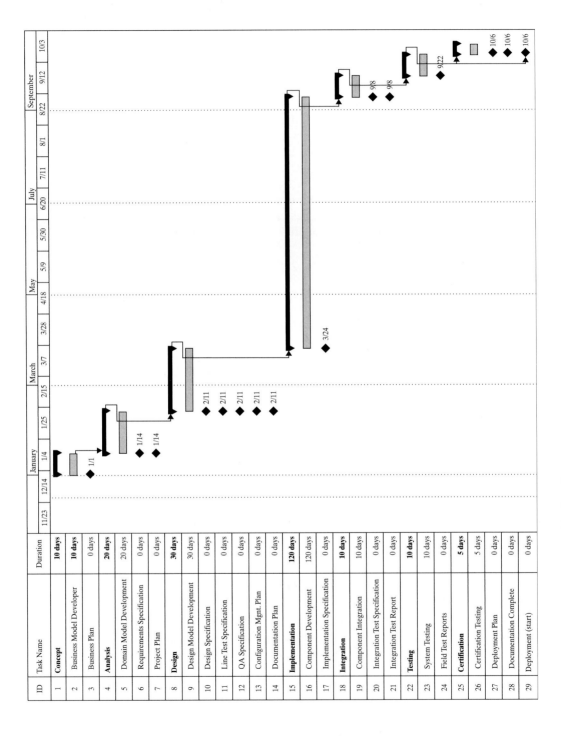

The table portion of the figure reads:

| ID | Task Name | Duration |
|---|---|---|
| 1 | **Concept** | **10 days** |
| 2 | **Business Model Developer** | **10 days** |
| 3 | Business Plan | 0 days |
| 4 | **Analysis** | **20 days** |
| 5 | Domain Model Development | 20 days |
| 6 | Requirements Specification | 0 days |
| 7 | Project Plan | 0 days |
| 8 | **Design** | **30 days** |
| 9 | Design Model Development | 30 days |
| 10 | Design Specification | 0 days |
| 11 | Line Test Specification | 0 days |
| 12 | QA Specification | 0 days |
| 13 | Configuration Mgnt. Plan | 0 days |
| 14 | Documentation Plan | 0 days |
| 15 | **Implementation** | **120 days** |
| 16 | Component Development | 120 days |
| 17 | Implementation Specification | 0 days |
| 18 | **Integration** | **10 days** |
| 19 | Component Integration | 10 days |
| 20 | Integration Test Specification | 0 days |
| 21 | Integration Test Report | 0 days |
| 22 | **Testing** | **10 days** |
| 23 | System Testing | 10 days |
| 24 | Field Test Reports | 0 days |
| 25 | **Certification** | **5 days** |
| 26 | Certification Testing | 5 days |
| 27 | Deployment Plan | 0 days |
| 28 | Documentation Complete | 0 days |
| 29 | Deployment (start) | 0 days |

FIGURE 4.34   Example Macro-Level Project Plan

242

| ID | Task Name | Duration | Start | Finish | Predecessors |
|----|-----------|----------|-------|--------|--------------|
| 1 | **Iteration 4** | **46 days** | **Wed 12/17/03** | **Wed 2/18/04** | |
| 2 | **Concept** | **3 days** | **Wed 12/17/03** | **Fri 12/19/03** | |
| 3 | Revise Business Plan | 3 days | Wed 12/17/03 | Fri 12/19/03 | |
| 4 | **Analysis** | **4 days** | **Mon 12/22/03** | **Thu 12/25/03** | **2** |
| 5 | Update Use Case Management | 3 days | Mon 12/22/03 | Wed 12/24/03 | |
| 6 | Update Specification | 4 days | Mon 12/22/03 | Thu 12/25/03 | |
| 7 | Update Project Plan | 2 days | Mon 12/22/03 | Tue 12/23/03 | |
| 8 | Secure Stakeholder | 3 days | Mon 12/22/03 | Wed 12/24/03 | |
| 9 | **Design** | **4 days** | **Fri 12/26/03** | **Wed 12/31/03** | **4** |
| 10 | Update UML Diagram | 4 days | Fri 12/26/03 | Wed 12/31/03 | |
| 11 | Detailed Design Specification | 3 days | Fri 12/26/03 | Tue 12/30/03 | |
| 12 | **Implementation** | **24 days** | **Thu 1/1/04** | **Tue 2/3/04** | **9** |
| 13 | Component Implementation | 24 days | Thu 1/1/04 | Tue 2/3/04 | |
| 14 | **Integration** | **6 days** | **Wed 2/4/04** | **Wed 2/11/04** | **12** |
| 15 | Component Integration | 6 days | Wed 2/4/04 | Wed 2/11/04 | |
| 16 | Component Testing | 3 days | Wed 2/4/04 | Fri 2/6/04 | |
| 17 | **Testing** | **3 days** | **Thu 2/12/04** | **Mon 2/16/04** | **14** |
| 18 | Validation against Re | 3 days | Thu 2/12/04 | Mon 2/16/04 | |
| 19 | **Certification** | **2 days** | **Tue 2/17/04** | **Wed 2/18/04** | **17** |
| 20 | Component Certification | 2 days | Tue 2/17/04 | Wed 2/18/04 | |
| 21 | **Deployment** | **0 days** | **Wed 2/18/04** | **Wed 2/18/04** | **19** |

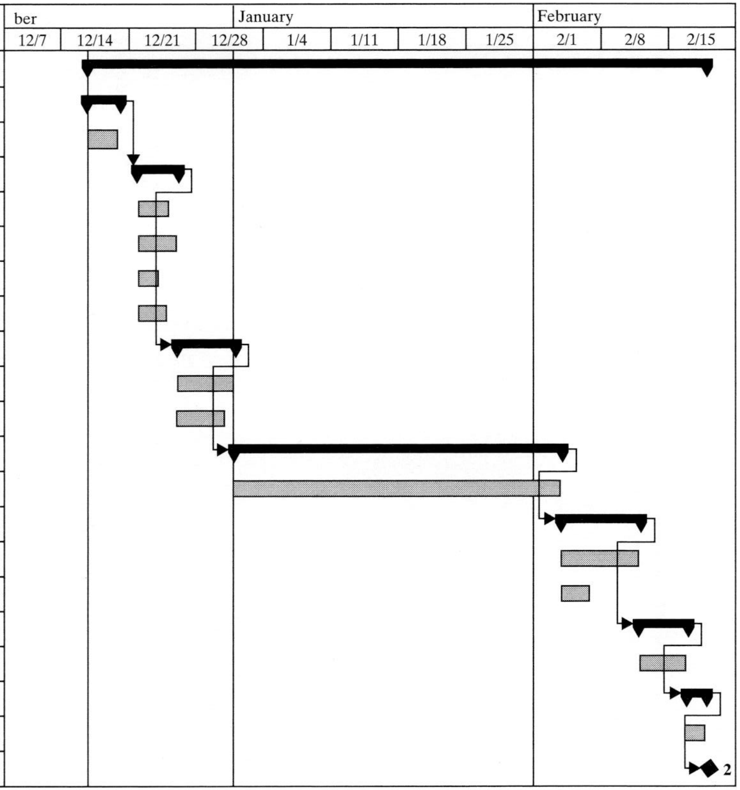

FIGURE 4.35  Example Iteration Project Plan

243

consideration. The Quality Assurance Plan, as outlined below, should include the important issues of testing and incident tracking and resolution.

- Organizational Best Practices
  - Accountability
- Organizational chart
- Approvals
  - Work processes
- Written procedures
- Accepted standards
- Testing process
  - Inspection guidelines
  - Required documents
  - Required reports
- Certification process
  - Validation process
  - Certification accountability

The Configuration Management Plan documents all aspects of intellectual property and component control, in terms of version and release numbers, source and object code control, and management of underlying networks, systems, and platforms. A typical plan of this kind is outlined below.

- Inventory of intellectual property
- Source control procedures
- Build management
- Work process and environment management
  - Check-in/check-out
- Version control
- Authorizations
- Backup and recovery procedures
  - On-site
  - Off-site
- Audit trail

The Documentation Plan addresses all aspects of documentation—internal, external, computer-based, and hard-copy. The following brief outline is a suggestion:

- External
  - Manuals
- End-user
  - Installation and administration
  - Application programming interfaces
  - Online help

- Tutorial
  - ○ Reference
  - ○ Context-specific
- Tool Tips
- Internal
  - ○ Specifications
  - ○ <complete list, based on organizational standards>
- Reports
  - ○ Forms
- Audits

## 4.6   *Harmony* **Design Case Study**

We will now continue with our ModelHomeDesigner case study started earlier in the book. Unlike the Voting Program example, which we are also pursuing across multiple chapters, this case study is yours to complete and fill in. We will continue guiding you in the process, but you are responsible for content and execution.

At this point, we have entered the Design Phase for this project, and we will develop the Design Specification and related specifications, following the outline discussed in this chapter. Obviously, some of the information developed earlier can be transferred to this specification, revised as necessary:

1. *Introduction*  The ModelHomeDesigner™ project is conceived as a tool for model home design companies to help them gain productivity by making work processes traditionally perceived as unique and "artistic" repeatable and predictable, using information technology applications.
   a. Description of Project
      ModelHomeDesigner tracks resources, events, materials, and deliverables throughout the stages of a model home interior design project. It provides up-to-date information to its users about the current state of a workflow at any time in the course of the project. It also provides workflow-management functions to help streamline sequential activities into overt, repeatable processes.

*For you to complete*

2. *Functional Overview*  This section documents the translation from requirements to designs of functions, features, components, and subsystems.
   a. UML Design Model
   b. UML Use Case Diagram (updated to 80% complete)
   c. UML Component Diagrams
   d. UML Package Diagrams
   e. UML Diagrams for Subsystems
   f. UML Deployment Diagram
3. *System Architecture*
4. *Class Hierarchy*
   a. Map of Use Case Model to Class Hierarchy

5. *Component Definition and Design*
   a. For Each Component:
      i. UML Class and Object Diagrams
      ii. UML Activity Diagram
      iii. UML Sequence Diagram
      iv. UML Collaboration Diagram
      v. UML Statechart Diagram
      vi. User Interface / Look-and-Feel Design
6. *Prototype Description and Evaluation (if applicable)*
7. *Environment*
   a. Software, hardware, networking required
   b. Other non-functional requirements[17]
8. *Supporting Workflows*
   a. Updated Macro-Level Project Plan
   b. Current- and Next-Iteration Micro-Level Project Plan[18]
   c. Quality Assurance Plan Summary
   d. Configuration Management Plan Summary
   e. Documentation Plan Summary

## 4.7    Resources: Connections • People • Companies

At this point, we are interested in external information about software design issues. We will find useful information about a number of related fields in the following locations, (all found at http://www.acm.org).

C. Marlin "Lin" Brown, *Human-Computer Interface Design Guidelines*, Norwood, NJ: Ablex Publishing Corp., 1988.

Aaron Marcus, *Graphic Design for Electronic Documents and User Interfaces*, Reading, MA: Addison-Wesley (ACM Press), 1992.

U.S. Department of Defense, *Military Standard: Human Engineering Design Criteria for Military Systems, Equipment and Facilities*, MIL-STD-1472D, Washington, DC: U.S. Government Printing Office; March 14, 1989.

International Standards Organization, *Ergonomic Requirements for Office Work with Visual Displays Units* (ISO 9241).

Hewlett-Packard, IBM, Sunsoft Inc., & USL, *Common Desktop Environment: Functional Specification (Preliminary Draft)*, X/Open Company Ltd., 1993.

Microsoft Corporation, *The GUI Guide: International Terminology for the Windows Interface*, Redmond, WA: Microsoft Press, 1993.

---

[17]Such as performance, scalability, adherence to standards, guidelines, etc.

[18]The iterative development approach advocated as part of our process stipulates that detailed planning is only possible with a reasonable degree of accuracy for the current and next iteration.

Microsoft Corporation, *The Windows Interface: An Application Design Guide*, Redmond, WA: Microsoft Press, 1992.

Open Software Foundation, *OSF/Motif Style Guide*, Englewood Cliffs, NJ: Prentice Hall, 1993.

IBM, *Object-Oriented Interface Design: IBM Common User Access Guidelines*, Carmel, IN: Que, 1992.

## 4.8   Summary and Recommendations

From the software engineering perspective, we have embarked on the crucial process of design modeling, system architecture, class hierarchy, and component design in this chapter. This stage represents the crucial transition from analysis to design, where your role changes from observing and recording to designing and creating. You are making progress in developing your role as a competent, if still inexperienced, software engineer.

As an emerging Java expert, you have learned how to control the flow of your program statements to represent the logic you are seeking to implement from the designs established in the project Design Specification.

## 4.9   Review Questions

1. **Design.** Describe and define software component design. What contributes to a successful design effort? What outcomes do we seek?
2. **Java Structures.** Explain and show examples of selection and repetition structures. Look at the LibraryManager, program introduced in the last chapter for further examples.
3. **Supporting Workflows.** Select and describe two supporting workflows.

## 4.10   Glossary – Terminology – Concepts

**Architecture**   Software architecture and system architecture are related concepts; they provide views of a system from a bird's-eye view that ensures that we consider all the design and development aspects of our system.

**IEEE Software Engineering Standards**   Software engineering standards developed and promoted by the Institute of Electrical and Electronic Engineers.

**ISO 9000 Quality Management Standards**   Software engineering standards developed and promoted by the International Standards Organization, headquartered in Geneva, Switzerland.

**MIL_STD-498**   Software engineering standards developed and promoted by the U.S. government for military software application development.

**SEI CMM/CMMI** Software engineering standards ("Capability Maturity Model") developed and promoted by the Software Engineering Institute at Carnegie-Mellon University.

**Workflow** The sequence of events that together constitute a valuable work process.

## 4.11 Exercises

**1. Structures.** Write a small Java program that uses selection and repetition structures to accept student test scores, but only if they are between 1 and 100. Entering $-1$ should end the program. Use the following Java Swing component and construct:

```
import javax.swing.JOptionPane;

//...
String value = JOptionPane.showInputDialog ("Please enter your
                                             score:");

//...
```

**2. if ... else Statement.** Show the code fragment for the calculation of letter grades ('A' through 'F') from scores between 1 and 100. Use standard grading rules.

**3. Enhanced Voting Program.** Improve the Voting Program example program earlier in the chapter to provide a better user interface (see previous chapter).

**4. Quality Assurance Plan.** Develop and complete a Quality Assurance Plan for the Voting Program.

**5. System Architecture.** Find three examples of system architecture drawings through Web or literature research. Describe each one.

## 4.12 Optional Chapter Addendum: Pattern-Driven Design

This book will not address the topic of Design Patterns in great detail because the available texts on systems analysis and design texts provide ample coverage of the topic. A good example is Craig Larman's *Applying UML and Patterns*, available from Prentice Hall. However, the important design principles captured in popular design patterns deserve cursory coverage at this time, if only to encourage emerging software engineers to expand their knowledge base in this crucial aspect of their future profession.

### 4.12.1 Pattern Principle 1: High Cohesion

**Cohesion** expresses how strongly related the responsibilities of a particular element are to each other. Cohesion represents the degree of focus of a particular design element. Low cohesion is undesirable because it involves the inclusion of unrelated activities and dependencies in a single element. This makes its reuse difficult, its content hard to understand and maintain, and involves a high degree of sensitivity to change.

### 4.12.2  Pattern Principle 2: Low Coupling

**Coupling** is a measure of connectedness to other elements in terms of shared knowledge or mutual reliance. Low coupling reflects low interdependency, a desirable characteristic because change has limited impact and modularity is preserved. Highly coupled design elements are hard to understand in isolation and impact too many other components when they change; this limits component reuse.

### 4.12.3  Most Popular Patterns[106]

The definitions in this section are based on *Design Patterns*, by Erich Gamma, Richard Helm, Ralph Johnson, and John Vlissides, Addison-Wesley, 1995.

#### Creational Patterns

- *Abstract Factory:* Provides an interface for creating families of related or dependent objects without specifying their concrete classes. An abstract factory isolates concrete classes and therefore promotes exchange of components without impacting other parts of an application.
- *Factory Method:* Defines an interface for creating an object, but lets subclasses decide which class to instantiate. The Factory Method pattern applies when a class cannot anticipate the class of objects it must create, or when a class wants its subclasses to specify the objects to create or to localize knowledge about helper subclass delegation.

#### Structural Patterns

- *Adapter:* Converts the interface of a class into another interface that clients expect. Provides a way to connect across incompatible interfaces.
- *Composite:* Composes objects into tree structures to represent "part-whole" hierarchies. This allows for the uniform representation of objects and their aggregations, treating objects and their compositions the same.
- *Decorator:* Dynamically attaches additional responsibilities to an object at runtime by enclosing an object to be extended with another object, a decorator, instead of implementing static inheritance.

#### Behavioral Patterns

- *Observer:* Defines a one-to-many dependency between objects so that state changes are propagated to all dependents. This helps maintain state consistency between cooperating objects. This notification can occur without preceding assumptions.

- *Strategy:* Defines a family of business rules (algorithms), encapsulates them, and makes them interchangeable, providing client-dependent variation. This works well for classes that are related and only differ in their behavior.
- *Template Method:* Defines the skeleton of a business rule (algorithm) in an operation, deferring some steps to subclasses, without changing the algorithm's structure. The Template Method pattern defines operational behavior in terms of abstract operations that operation-specific subclasses override to represent concrete behaviors.

There are many other pattern principles that the interested reader will investigate. Essentially, design patterns capture the proven design principles garnered by our profession over the last decades.

# Architecture-Driven Component Development

In this chapter, you will become more knowledgeable about the close relationship between system requirements, software architecture, component design, and Java software development. You will begin to understand in detail the transitions between the major phases of the development process, and how Java software technology is used to improve productive business processes. This chapter connects the earlier phases of the development process to the actual process of software coding. Illustrations tie requirements analysis and design to Java programming examples and exercises.

We will explore in detail the development of multi-class Java programs and learn about interfaces and packages. Most real-life applications are composed of multiple subsystems, packages, and constituent classes which together provide all the functionality needed in a modern-day graphical, interactive software solution.

## 5.1    Learning Objectives

Through hands-on practice, you are developing your Java programming skills. You are starting to understand how to construct more complex Java statements, how to use existing classes and packages, and how to implement straightforward, powerful programming logic. In this chapter, we will pick up the pace of your Java training without losing sight of the all-important foundation of iterative, architecture-centric, requirements-driven feature design and implementation. While you are becoming proficient in Java

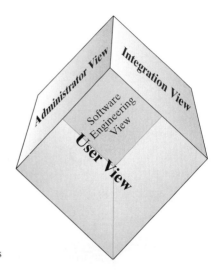

FIGURE 5.1    Software Engineering Architecture Perspectives

programming, in anticipation of more and more implementation work, you are completing your systems analysis and design training, with attention focused on creating a viable class hierarchy and designing and prototyping its constituent components.

The topic of software architecture is inherently advanced because it takes into consideration all the process-related and technical aspects of the particular software development project at hand. As shown in Figure 5.1, the architecture perspective views projects from at least four sides:

- End-user: User View
- Programming: Software Engineering View
- Environment: Administrator View
- Other systems (hardware, software): Integration View

By incorporating these different perspectives, we ensure that the project design accounts for the needs of all the stakeholders.

### 5.1.1    Revisiting System and Software Architecture

Although we have already previewed the topic of system and software architecture, we want to take another look at this important subject here.

The definition of software architecture includes the main subsystems and their interrelationships to one another in the overall system. Larger systems consist of multiple major components, called subsystems, which in turn are composed of subcomponents of their own, such as packages and their constituent classes and interfaces. Software systems are themselves part of an overall integrated system environment composed of hardware, networking, and software components. We use the software engineering subdiscipline of *system architecture* to design and represent the sum total of these interrelated subsystems and components in relationship to each other from multiple relevant perspectives. Stepping back to critically understand the system from this "50,000-foot" viewpoint is an important Best Practice that ensures system integration, scalability, balance, and performance.

An architecture diagram shows the software in the context of the physical and logical environment (hardware—clients and servers in one or more locations; operating systems; network hardware, software, and services). The example in Figure 5.2 shows a client-server system with a PC-based Web browser, a wireless client, and a server with two subsystems, one for business logic, the other for data management. The systems are connected via the Internet; the mobile client uses a high-speed cellular data connection, such as UMTS or CDMA-2000. The benefit of this type of representation is a comprehensive high-level "bird's-eye" view of the entire system.

When software engineers understand the environment in which their application will operate, including hardware, software, and communications subsystems, they can maximize the synergy of their code components with the underlying systems and avoid problems arising from limitations in these infrastructure components.

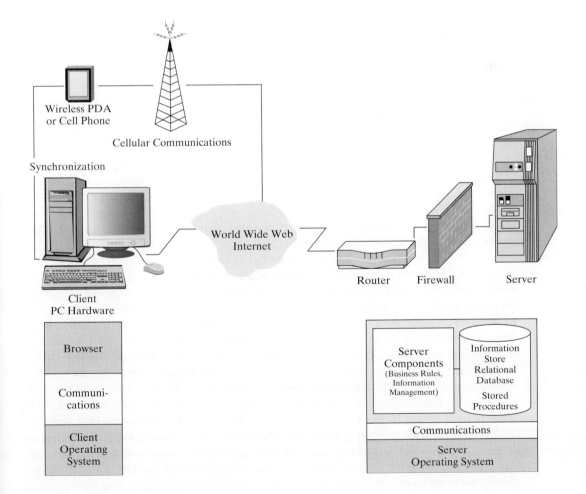

FIGURE 5.2   Example Architecture Diagram

In addition, the application of architectural planning and understanding ensures that major system requirements are not overlooked and that the system is constructed for stability and resilience in a balanced, flexible, and expandable fashion. The benefits of object orientation are directly correlated to the quality of the system architecture: the better the architectural system blueprint is, the more reusable and extensible the system and its components will be. In other words, the architectural view is part of our comprehensive software engineering approach.

### Architectural Perspectives

As mentioned earlier, a well-designed software architecture results from viewing the proposed system from multiple perspectives. These multiple perspectives encourage us to suspend our own biases and assume the perspectives of other key stakeholders. The four viewpoints we will explore further are:

- End-user: User View
- Programming: Software Engineering View
- Environment: Administrator View
- Other systems (hardware, software): Integration View

The *User View* is the one we are most likely to consider by default. This view "looks at" the requirements for the system infrastructure from the user's perspective, including such elements as usability, accessibility, human factors, integration with other applications, and productivity. It drives the attention we give to functional compliance with the Requirements Specification.

The *Software Engineering View* is your perspective and should therefore be easy to adopt. This view drives the technical software engineering requirements for the system architecture. It should include the impact of using certain types of information technology, such as Java. It should also account for functional concerns from an implementation perspective, such as authentication, program navigation, and user access, as well as for non-functional considerations, such as performance, scalability, resilience, and stability.

The *Administrator View* provides a system installation and maintenance viewpoint. This is a vital area often overlooked by system designers because installation and maintenance are activities that do not ramp up until late in the development life-cycle. Programs are typically developed in a specific development environment using a set of software and hardware components connected over a network. Difficulties arise when there are differences between the development environment and the target (customer) environment that were not taken into account as part of the development process. Also, the process of installation itself needs to meet usability requirements, meaning that it should be easy, predictable, repeatable, and error-proof to the greatest extent possible.

Finally, the *Integration View* reminds us to understand our particular solution in the broader context of the IT infrastructure of the target environment. Our software has to interface with existing applications and middleware components. It has to run on various target computer systems, using their resources and connections. Requiring our customers to buy new hardware just to operate our software application is rarely acceptable, so we must be able to integrate our solution into an existing operating environment. In addition, we need to build our software for *interoperability*. This means that we can easily accept data from other applications and in turn can provide our value-added data to other software. (Note that other views can be defined: the important concept here is to adopt multiple perspectives in defining the architecture of a software solution.)

The architectural representation of software systems is particularly important when these systems are large, distributed ("multi-tier") implementations like the one shown in Figure 5.3. The figure depicts a high-level perspective of a multi-tier software infrastructure with multiple clients, application server components, and a database server tier. These layers work collaboratively to provide distributed, reusable computing functions for a range of related business applications. They implement various enterprise-computing Java capabilities (the detailed description of which is beyond the scope of this book), like Enterprise Java Beans™ (EJB™), associated with the J2EE packages available from Sun Microsystems (http://java.sun.com/j2ee/). An application server, JBoss, is an open-source component used to integrate J2EE services.[1] This solution also employs open-systems industry standards like XML and SOAP, described in other texts and references at great lengths.

---

### OPEN SOURCE

Many high-quality software utilities and applications are available through the "open source" movement. Essentially, useful code is contributed for free to a large forum of registered software engineers and then becomes the joint development and maintenance responsibility of the group, resulting in well-tested and–certified code that can be used at no cost by the "community."

---

These architectural perspectives lay the foundation for circumspect, reusable design. When we understand the underlying infrastructure for our project, we can embark with confidence on the design of specific subsystems and components. The challenge here is to develop reusable components, that can be applied again in similar applications.

As explained previously, Design Patterns is the most popular approach to designing reusable components using techniques known to be successful and repeatable.

### 5.1.2  Java Component Interaction and Integration

When we transition from design tasks to software component programming, it is important that we learn to create reusable components, not monolithic, single-use applications. The path to understanding component development is a continuum that reaches back into the analysis and design activities and outcomes discussed in previous chapters, and forward into integration and deployment of finished products (see Fig. 5.4). In addition to careful design and planning, best-of-breed applications require a thorough understanding of the operational domain in which your application will function.[2] A viable, flexible architecture ensures that reusable components "fit together" into a cohesive IT solution.

---

[1]JBoss is a complete J2EE/EJB application server providing enterprise-class security, transaction support, resource management, load balancing, and clustering.

[2]"Best-of-breed" refers to the competitive concept of creating products perceived by a majority of users or customers as significantly superior in key ways to competing products.

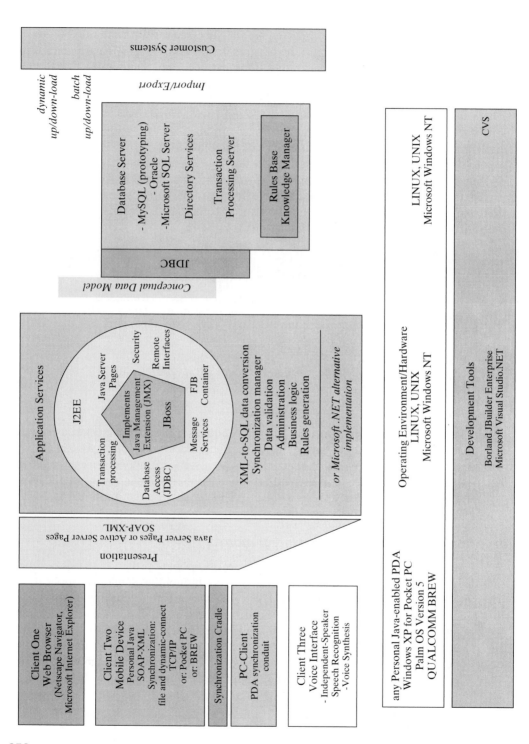

FIGURE 5.3   Another Sample Architecture Diagram

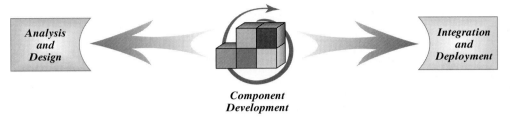

FIGURE 5.4   Iterative Component Development Bridges Analysis and Design and Integration and Deployment

We do not want to be drawn into the technology at the expense of the organizational work processes. The end objective remains to make the core workflows more productive, less expensive, more reliable, and more predictable. The engineering of the software application should be motivated by these goals and not take on a life of its own, as we have witnessed too often in poorly engineered "real-world" applications. Unfortunately, at this stage developers sometimes leave behind—to a lesser or greater degree—the specific, approved project requirements and instead implement what they deem to be useful, desirable features. The resulting product often significantly deviates from what was expected, and these new "features," which were not considered in the project budget, lead to delays and increased risk. They also consume budget funds not allocated in the first place.

Therefore, as we develop Java code modules, we will continue to strive for a close alignment between features and functions, on one hand, and project requirements and design directives, on the other.

The design pattern approach briefly introduced at the end of the previous chapter is a proven methodology for ensuring that system design and implementation Best Practices are employed when translating requirements into application features and functions.

---

## MIDDLEWARE

Programs developed to provide integration and interoperability services not part of the operating system are often referred to as "middleware." This may include networking services, application and Web services, security services, and database services.

---

In real-world, distributed applications, the code elements that together constitute the software solution belong to a range of component categories, and rely on other middleware technologies:

- Client applications
- Applets
- Servlets

- Java Server Pages (JSP)
- Java Server Faces (JSF)
- Java Beans and Enterprise Java Beans (EJB)
- Interfaces
- Packages and subsystems

In this book, we will limit our detailed analysis to Java classes, applications, interfaces, and packages. We will often use existing third-party components in conjunction with our own code. In fact, the Java libraries included by Sun in the Java Software Development Kit (SDK) represent a substantial collection of reusable components at our disposal for integration into our own applications. They also provide a good model for how to optimally organize reusable components. In addition, other commercial and non-profit organizations also make available importable classes and packages that we may choose to license and reuse. We will now take a closer look at how Java components are developed and organized.

### Java Components

In the context of the software engineering and system architecture perspective described so far, you need to understand in detail how components are implemented in Java. One of the key challenges for the novice software developer is to translate work-process steps into Java code structure, and to group and organize Java code into statement blocks, methods, classes, and packages that properly represent the desired functionality. This involves not only a good understanding of the organization's work processes and the functional domain in which our software will operate, but also a level of creative ability to generate functions in software that optimize the workflows in question and can be used efficiently and accurately by the eventual users of our application. The work done in the requirements phase of the project (such as the Domain Model) helps greatly in documenting and formalizing the knowledge necessary to translate the existing workflows into improved, information-technology-supported processes.

In addition to meeting specific project requirements, we seek to develop components that are flexible, reusable, resilient, easy to use, and easy to install and maintain. Altogether, this design and development activity takes substantial knowledge and intellect!

Let us begin with the macro-level perspective of a simple Java software application. In Java, the basic "container" of components is a *package*. Packages are directories and subdirectories containing collections of classes and interfaces. In larger projects, packages are combined to form *subsystems*, which in turn together perform the functions of the total (software) system.

The package is the central container of components, and thus warrants further examination. The generalized diagram in Figure 5.5 shows the relationships between classes in a package: classes are organized hierarchically, connected to each other in a "parent-child" relationship ("`extends`") or as an implemented interface ("`implements`"). This organization enables object orientation benefits, such as inheritance and polymorphism. It also promotes modularization, encapsulation, and component reuse. Packages of classes are optionally included in programs as "pre-packaged" functionality, using an `import` statement at the beginning of a class module.

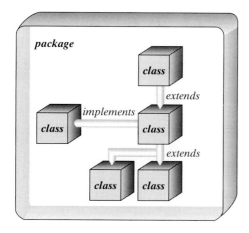

FIGURE 5.5   Class Hierarchy and Interfaces

One of the most challenging design activities is the proper organization of these hierarchies of classes and packages in such a way as to maximize the benefits of this modular approach. Guidelines for the design of a class hierarchy include:

**Decomposition:** Evaluate requirements from a component perspective—the process of extracting essential features and functions from available requirements information. By applying multiple design perspectives or patterns, the detailed description of requirements can be effectively translated into productive, efficient functionality, maximizing the benefit of using information technology top improve important work processes.

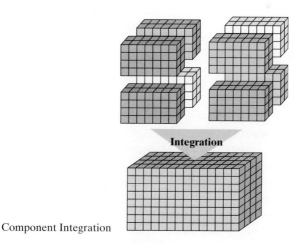

Component Integration

**Component-orientation and reuse:** Develop reusable code modules as self-contained components that can be effectively incorporated in as wide a range of software applications as possible.

**Levels of abstraction:** Avoid repeating the same or similar code functions in multiple parallel places in the hierarchy; extract to a higher level of abstraction functionality used by more than one lower-level class.

**Requirements translation:** Make sure that the design of computer-supported functionality leads to process improvement, not just replacement. Leverage the advantages of computing when implementing the functions on the basis of use case scenarios, and reengineer the process as needed to maximize productivity. Ensure that the class hierarchy resulting from your design efforts complies with the use cases for the project.

**Architecture-centric design:** Develop your components on the basis of a well-defined, "multi-dimensional" architectural blueprint. Ensure that components and their interactions are compliant with the project vision, objectives of component reuse and encapsulation, as well as non-functional requirements, such as performance, scalability, and security.

**Classes, methods, and attributes:** Define classes according to the UML class diagram requirements, specifying return and attribute types completely.

When these Best Practice guidelines are followed, the resulting Java components have a good chance of meeting the requirements of the project in terms of quality, stakeholder expectations, timeliness, and budget.

### 5.1.3    Learning Layout

This recurring section shows the learning objectives of the chapter in a simple diagram using the UML activity diagram notation (see Fig. 5.6).

### 5.1.4    Learning Connections

The Learning Connections diagram in Figure 5.7 shows the content of this chapter in relation to the knowledge and skills development recommended for apprentice Java software engineers. We revisit this dial of learning perspectives in every chapter as a reminder of the multiple facets of professional development required for effective software engineering.

## 5.2    Executive Summary

We have progressed through four chapters and have now arrived at the point where our preparatory efforts allow us to embark with confidence on the final design and initial implementation of the core components of our application. We apply Java syntax and structure to the creation of features and functions that improve the business process or processes for which the application is being developed. Real-world information technology systems tend to involve multiple subsystems, which in turn contain numerous packages composed of even more classes and interfaces. These subsystems may be implemented on multiple clients and servers, connected via local and wide-area networks and the Internet. Given the inherent complexity of these systems, the guidance provided by a thorough, validated system architecture and associated domain and design models provides an indispensable framework for the accurate construction of the interacting components constituting the total system.

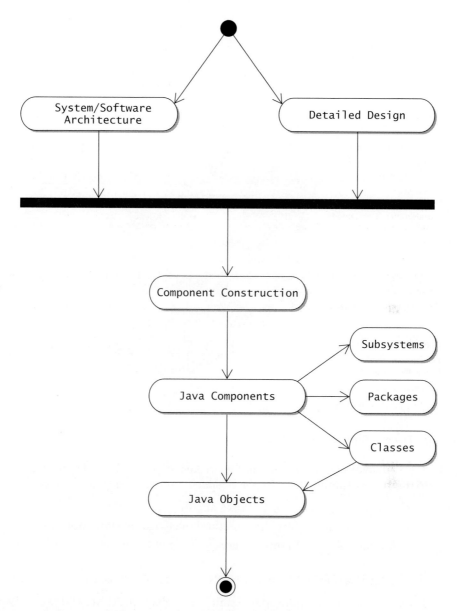

**FIGURE 5.6**   Chapter 5 Learning Layout (as a UML Activity Diagram)

In this chapter, we focus on the construction of components using Java. We base the development of components on the Design Specification, which itself is based on the project's Requirements Specification. As we embark on this code-production work, we need to continuously ensure that we stay "on spec." This means that our specifications must remain "living documents" subject to validated, approved changes as new requirements emerge or existing ones change.

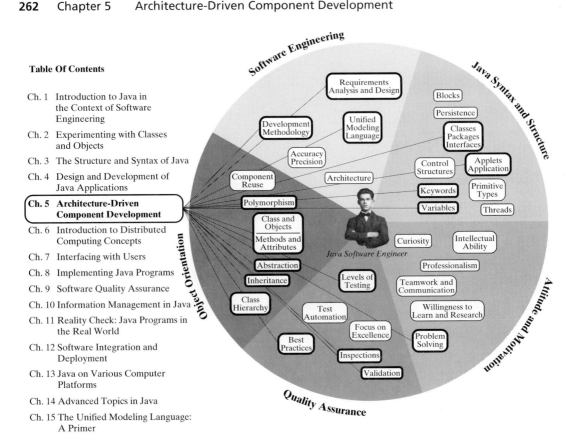

**FIGURE 5.7**   Learning Connections for Chapter 5

An ever deeper understanding of Java capabilities and constructs is fundamental to the successful implementation of specific functionality, including:

- Creating and managing classes and objects
- Methods and constructors, method overloading (polymorphism)
- Extending parent (super) classes into child (sub) classes (inheritance) and using interfaces
- User interface and navigation development and user input validation

These topics will be explored in detail in this chapter. At the end, we will apply our new Java construction knowledge to the example and case study we have been carrying forward from chapter to chapter: the Voting Program and the ModelHomeDesigner.

## 5.3    Learning Modules

As always, your learning experience is laid out as a sequence of *learning modules*. Depending on your previous experience and areas of interest, you may find it valuable to seek additional information from other books, trade magazines, or online resources on one or the other of the topics covered here.

### 5.3.1  *Concepts*

The accurate and complete development of valuable computer software depends on a good plan. In addition to the business- and process-centric project planning efforts associated with a development project, the technical plan, the system blueprint, is developed based on the system architecture (focus on software components). Before any developer starts writing production code, the system architect(s) provide(s) the structural description of the system being developed. The system architecture function monitors adherence to this technical development blueprint; it is a strategic guide to the accurate and efficient implementation of the functions and features derived from the requirements specification.

In addition to good planning, a number of other concepts and practices lead to the development of software that meets high-stakes, critical project requirements. As we write more and more extensive Java code, we will need to follow these software development Best Practices:

**Modularity:** limiting the length and complexity of our components (typically to a singular function or purpose for each); developing components for reuse

**Resilience:** avoiding brittle behaviors by allowing for the graceful handling of exception conditions (fault tolerance)

**Scalability:** ensuring that a larger number of users will not excessively slow down the system; developing modular components that can take advantage of additional hardware and network resources when made available without additional programming being required

**Maintainability:** organizing, documenting, and modularizing code for easy maintenance and enhancement—ensuring extensibility

**Ease of use:** giving attention to user interaction with the system, including installation and administration; consideration for integration, data import/export, migration to new releases, or from other software products to our solution

**Documentation:** implementation notes; keeping documents (e.g., specifications) updated; inline comments to explain coding practices; development of user documentation (electronic and paper); tool tips; online help

**Transparency:** avoiding excessive complexity and obscure coding practices; organizing code for clarity, readability, and maintainability (avoiding "spaghetti code")

**Consistency:** following naming conventions; establishing and maintaining a consistent, repeatable architecture; using standard Java exception handling (see below)

**Verifiability:** designing for testing and validation of functional and non-functional requirements, including validating that features are built according to the Requirements Specification; scalability; ease-of-use; ease-of-maintenance; robustness.

This book seeks to teach you software-development practices valid not only for school tasks and exercises, but scalable to large real-world development projects. Too often, graduating students find that their college education bears little resemblance to the actual practices of the companies they join as entry-level software engineers after completing their degrees. This book attempts to impart actual industry practices rather than limit itself to useful but oversimplified textbook examples (inherently lacking realism). Attention paid to the above recommendations translates directly into improved programming practices and outcomes in the real world.

### 5.3.2    *Architectural Perspectives*

The scenarios we develop as part of the use case description of functional requirements result in step-by-step process descriptions of the organizational workflows that we seek to automate, improve, or reengineer. As each use case represents a major workflow, the organization of the use cases into a model is an important step in the *decomposition* of the system into major design components. However, use cases do not map one-to-one to eventual software components because other requirements, functional and non-functional, influence how we design software components to provide the required functionality efficiently and with flexibility. The next step is to examine the use cases from the perspective of system architecture, taking into account the broader aspects of technology, reuse, scalability, and integration into existing systems (see Fig. 5.8).

With an understanding of this diverse set of influencing requirements, we design components through an *iterative validation process,* where we float an initial concept for review by key stakeholders and improve on that initial decomposition architecture based on feedback and additional discoveries. This process is particularly important in developing object-oriented systems, using tools like Java.

Java applications need to follow an architectural blueprint even more critically than software written in a procedural language because the inherent benefits of object orientation in Java are only realized when components are properly structured, organized, and abstracted. As mentioned earlier, software systems today are typically complex, multi-tier creations with sometimes thousands of classes and components. There is an urgent need for a structured, repeatable approach to component identification and organization. Jia cites *cohesion* and *coupling* as basic criteria for determining the decomposition of a system into appropriate constituent components.[3] We previewed these concepts as design pattern principles in the last chapter.

---

### ELEMENTS OF MODULAR DECOMPOSITION

- High cohesion
- Low coupling
- Abstraction
- Integration

---

"*Cohesion* refers to the functional relatedness of the entities within a module; *coupling* refers to the interdependency among different modules."

(Jia, p. 11)

---

[3]Xiaoping Jia, *Object-Oriented Software Development Using Java*, Addison Wesley Longman, 2000.

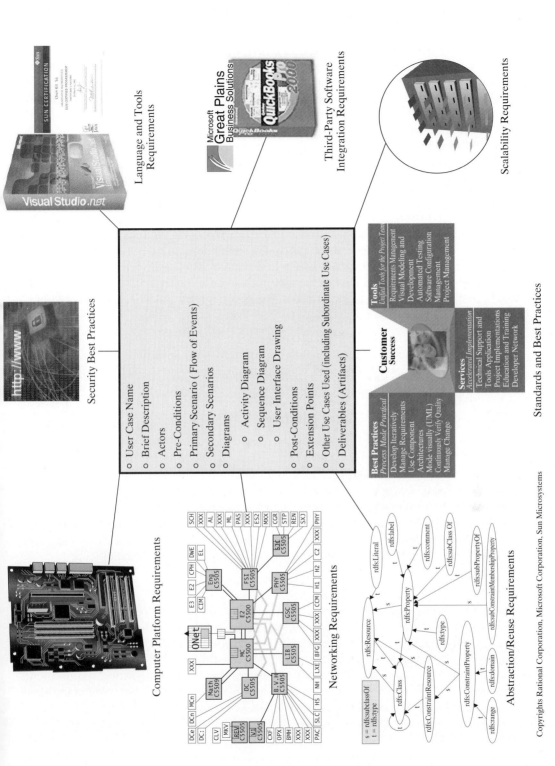

Language and Tools Requirements

Third-Party Software Integration Requirements

Scalability Requirements

Security Best Practices

Computer Platform Requirements

- ○ User Case Name
- ○ Brief Description
- ○ Actors
- ○ Pre-Conditions
- ○ Primary Scenario ( Flow of Events)
- ○ Secondary Scenarios
- ○ Diagrams
  - ○ Activity Diagram
  - ○ Sequence Diagram
  - ○ User Interface Drawing
- ○ Post-Conditions
- ○ Extension Points
- ○ Other Use Cases Used (including Subordinate Use Cases)
- ○ Deliverables (Artifacts)

**Customer Success**

**Best Practices**
*Process Made Practical*
Develop Iteratively
Manage Requirements
Use Component
Architectures
Mode visually (UML)
Continuously Verify Quality
Manage Change

**Tools**
*Unified Tools for the Project Team*
Requirements Management
Visual Modeling and
Development
Automated Testing
Software Configuration
Management
Project Management

**Services**
*Accelerated Implementation*
Technical Support and
Tools Application
Project Implementations
Education and Training
Developer Network

Standards and Best Practices

Networking Requirements

s = rdfs:subclassOf
t = rdfs:type

Abstraction/Reuse Requirements

Copyrights Rational Corporation, Microsoft Corporation, Sun Microsystems

FIGURE 5.8   Requirements Influencing the Decomposition of Use Cases into Software Components

265

In discussing decomposition, we will augment these ideas with the added notions of abstraction and integration. We define *abstraction* as the conceptual distance between hierarchically related entities, and *integration* as the level of uni- and bi-directional functional and data compatibility between entities. These concepts help us design a system architecture that transforms project requirements into components that meet object-orientation standards, in particular component reuse. Note that systems analysis and design practitioners have defined a wide range of design patterns that further codify the decomposition of requirements into high-quality designs. Let us now further examine the basic concepts to which we will limit this text.

### Cohesion

As defined above and in the last chapter, *cohesion* addresses the functional relationship between components. In other words, functional components are more or less cohesive depending on how immediately they belong to the same or related work processes. In programming terms, this may relate to the amount and intensity of interfacing or messaging between components, and to the organization of classes into packages or subsystems.

### Coupling

*Coupling* takes cohesion a level further and describes the interdependencies between components. In an object-oriented class hierarchy, components are ancestors ("parents") of other components or are descendants ("children") of their ancestors. But other relationships exist as well: between packages, between subsystems, between distributed components, between interfaces and classes.

### Abstraction

As we develop a hierarchical structure to promote component reuse, the extraction of elements of *abstraction* is central to the development of components that have broad applicability across a range of software programs. Abstraction entails the discovery of common, reusable elements across a range of specific implementations (or objects) and the amalgamation of these properties (attributes) and behaviors (methods) into super-classes that reflect the model inherent in these multiple, related objects.

### Integration

Software systems rarely operate all by themselves: integration requirements are central to good software design. *Integration* spans a broad range of domains: integration of components (packages, classes, interfaces); integration of subsystems (including those that span platforms/systems); integration into existing systems (hardware, network, software); integration with existing third-party applications. Integration requirements can have a major impact on component design and call for a detailed understanding of connected systems and external components.

### Design Principles

Based on our understanding of cohesion, coupling, abstraction, and integration, we can now derive the following software architecture design principles from these concepts:

---

## CLASS VS. DATA MODEL

In the past, the key representational element in many applications, especially in business software, was the data model, expressed in the database schema and dataflow diagram. This model showed how data migrated through an application and was transformed in the process. The class hierarchy perspective embraces both data and functions and applies the more advanced concepts of object orientation to the representation of the core workflows in a software application.

---

**Intelligent transformation of use cases into software components, organized into efficient, reusable class hierarchies and packages, and subsystems**
This step entails the translation of the relatively "flat" use case view (model) into a flexible, multi-level class hierarchy. The classes are defined in such a way that methods and attributes that apply to multiple components are moved a level up and abstracted into a parent class for use by multiple child classes. Classes are then organized into packages and assembled into subsystems, as dictated by the underlying systems architecture, based on the application of design principles codified in design patterns.

**Attention to the range of functional and non-functional requirements in determining how to extract components and their interrelationships from use cases**
The class hierarchy is the scaffold for the entire software product: its members contain the definitions for both functionality and data types. All relevant use case scenarios are represented in the class hierarchy. In addition, non-functional issues, such as scalability, maintainability, and aesthetics, must also find their places in the class hierarchy.

**Reusability perspective in determining relationships between components "in all directions"**
Components, by definition, are part of a larger system and therefore are connected to other components. This connection can take various forms: local and remote method invocation[4], interfaces, inheritance, or Web services technologies, such as XML/SOAP. As the class hierarchy is formed, the architect must retain a global perspective on the current and future uses of the component being defined, including the flexibility of its position in the class hierarchy structure.

**Attention to workflow and process improvements (as compared to the current system)**
The objective of the software solution is invariably to improve a particular (business) process in one or more ways: making it faster, more reliable, more consistent, less

---

[4]Sometimes referred to as "message passing," a term avoided in this text because it is confusing.

costly, more repeatable, more measurable, requiring less human interaction or skill. The design of the class hierarchy must intelligently implement such improvements if the overall solutions are to be effective in the end. The requirements analysis should list the areas of improvement sought, but additional opportunities for optimization evolve from the creative development of IT-based functions and components.

**Application of flexible technologies for maximum reuse and integration into "surrounding" technologies**

The choice of particular implementation technologies can have a very large impact on the overall flexibility of the components being developed. It is therefore part of the system architecture considerations to select technology components in line with the overall objectives of the projects, its stakeholders, and the target organization. This selection should also account for accepted industry standards, market dominance, total cost of ownership, functional and non-functional requirements adherence, and, if these are third-party components, stability of the supplier and second-source options.

### Modular Programming

The following guidelines support the practical development of reusable components that can be assembled into highly functional, flexible, and productive application systems:

- Careful creation of comprehensive domain and use case models
- Systematic development of a flexible, reusable system architecture
  - Logical and physical organization
- Packages, subsystems
- Creating interfaces and super/subclass relationships which maximize the reuse of components
  - Application of proven design patterns
  - Use of polymorphism and encapsulation
- Method call parameters setup to support flexible component reuse
- Developing a comprehensive, well-designed design model and class hierarchy
  - Abstracting reusable components (attributes and methods)

Modular Programming

⊙ Organizing classes into packages and subsystems
⊙ Support for remote invocation
⊙ Use of available third-party components and technologies that augment system flexibility and extensibility

These guidelines provide a checklist for software engineers and systems architects that allows them to validate the quality of their technical plans. It is at this stage of the project that technical decisions have the most profound and sweeping impact on the subsequent development and deployment phases.

While the software engineering topics covered so far apply to any object-oriented development toolset, the next sections examine the technical specifics of developing **Java components**.

### 5.3.3  *Developing Java Components*

Now that we have some understanding of the conceptual nature of components, we embark on developing additional in-depth knowledge about the practical implementation of Java components. In commercial, distributed Java software applications, a number of Java and Java-related components contribute to the overall solution, but this text only deals in detail with simpler standalone (or client) applications. Other components typically target client-server computing applications and include Java Server Pages for interactions with users in conjunction with a Web server; Java Servlets and (Enterprise) Java Beans; and working in conjunction with an application server, like Sun's iPlanet™ or the open-source JBoss™.

In this chapter, we introduce and examine the following types of Java components:

#### Classes and the Objects Derived from Them

- Sub- and superclasses
- Interfaces
- Enumerations
- Packages

These can be thought of as "code containers" because they hold the Java source code required to implement the desired functionality for an application being developed. In the development process, as discussed in a previous chapter, we write English-like Java source code and store it in files with the .java extension; we then compile this source code into bytecode files with the .class extension (one class per class file). A special type of class file is the enum type, introduced in Java J2SE 5.0. Multiple class files can be organized into packages that in turn together form subsystems. A special type of Java structure is an interface; it will be stored in a normal .java source file and compiled to a .class file.

#### Review: Classes and Objects

As mentioned before, classes are the fundamental components of Java programs. Thus, every Java program is composed of one or more classes. Classes are the templates for objects. As soon as a Java program is required to keep track of specific data, objects

TABLE 5.1  Book Class-Book Object

| Example Class: Book | Instantiated Object: newBookAcquired |
|---|---|
| ```java
public class Book  {
    String title;
    // ...
    public Book()  {
    // ...
    }
    public static void main (String args) {
      // ...
      Book newBookAcquired = new Book();
      //...
    }
    //...
}
``` | ```java
//...
newBookAcquired.title =
"Moby Dick";

//...
``` |

must be created ("instantiated") from the classes to provide unique "containers" for these data elements. Said another way, one or more unique objects can be derived from a class in order to represent a specific *instance* of that class. These objects can be thought of as *members* of that class.

As shown in Table 5.1, the interaction between objects is one of *method invocation* (sometimes referred to as message passing): objects can be thought of as containers that encompass specific property values (fields, attributes) as well as associated functions (methods), the latter being invoked to "self-express" object behaviors. A method call is therefore a form of message, requesting that the object express a certain programmed behavior encoded in the Java statements in the method.

The instantiation of objects in Java can be confusing to novices, because, depending on the circumstances, object creation can take place from within its class code (meaning that a class can instantiate an object of itself) or can be initiated from another class.

One of the difficult challenges inexperienced Java developers encounter is how to organize their design into classes and objects (see Fig. 5.9 and 5.10). The following *decomposition* guidelines will help with this crucial activity:

1. Examine the requirements from the viewpoint of attributes (characteristics) and methods (functionality, behaviors). Logically extract these attributes and methods from the scenario descriptions. Apply "object-thinking" in critically interpreting requirements.

2. Apply proven **design patterns** and/or your own experience to ensure that the principles of object orientation, component independence and reusability (e.g., high cohesion, low coupling, abstraction, encapsulation), and high-performance scalability are upheld.

---

**Key Term**

A *design* pattern is a named set of codified principles and idioms that guide software developers in the creation of software solutions. A pattern defines a (recurring) problem and its recommended (generic reusable) solution.

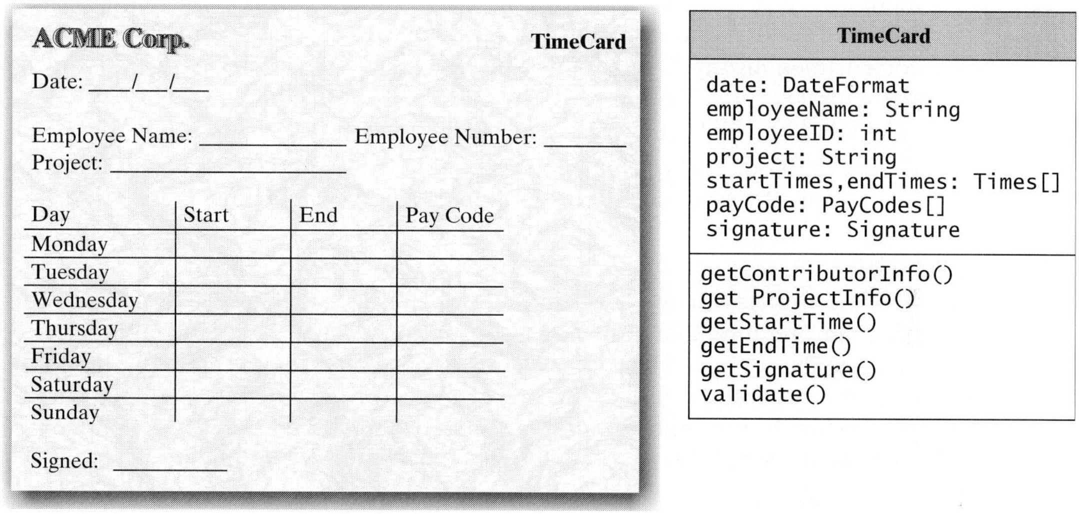

---

**ACME Corp.**                                      **TimeCard**

Date: ____ / ____ / ____

Employee Name: _____  Employee Number: _____
Project: _____

| Day | Start | End | Pay Code |
|-----|-------|-----|----------|
| Monday | | | |
| Tuesday | | | |
| Wednesday | | | |
| Thursday | | | |
| Friday | | | |
| Saturday | | | |
| Sunday | | | |

Signed: _____

| **TimeCard** |
|---|
| date: DateFormat<br>employeeName: String<br>employeeID: int<br>project: String<br>startTimes,endTimes: Times[]<br>payCode: PayCodes[]<br>signature: Signature |
| getContributorInfo()<br>get ProjectInfo()<br>getStartTime()<br>getEndTime()<br>getSignature()<br>validate() |

FIGURE 5.9   Example: The TimeCard Class

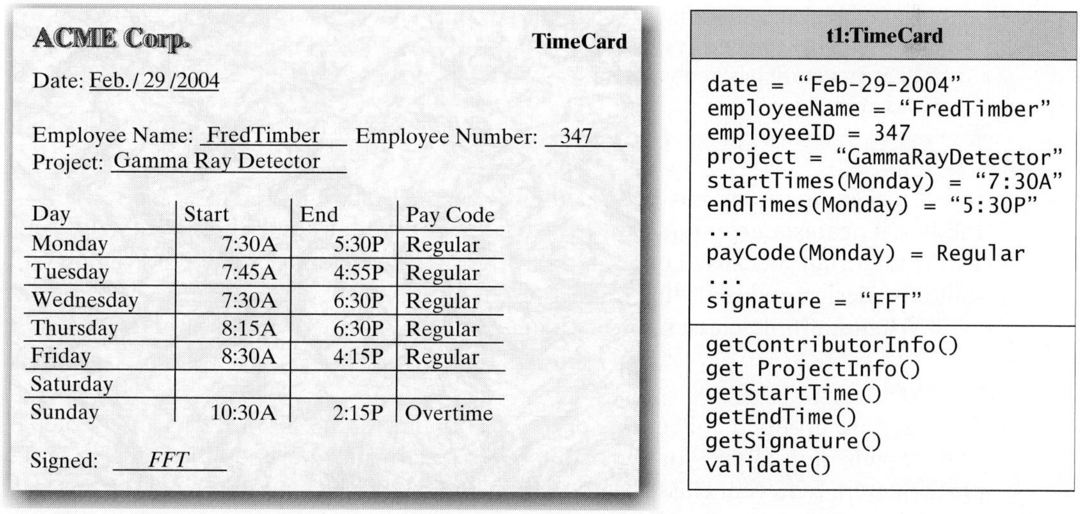

---

**ACME Corp.**                                      **TimeCard**

Date: Feb. / 29 / 2004

Employee Name: FredTimber   Employee Number: 347
Project: Gamma Ray Detector

| Day | Start | End | Pay Code |
|-----|-------|-----|----------|
| Monday | 7:30A | 5:30P | Regular |
| Tuesday | 7:45A | 4:55P | Regular |
| Wednesday | 7:30A | 6:30P | Regular |
| Thursday | 8:15A | 6:30P | Regular |
| Friday | 8:30A | 4:15P | Regular |
| Saturday | | | |
| Sunday | 10:30A | 2:15P | Overtime |

Signed: _____FFT_____

| **t1:TimeCard** |
|---|
| date = "Feb-29-2004"<br>employeeName = "FredTimber"<br>employeeID = 347<br>project = "GammaRayDetector"<br>startTimes(Monday) = "7:30A"<br>endTimes(Monday) = "5:30P"<br>...<br>payCode(Monday) = Regular<br>...<br>signature = "FFT" |
| getContributorInfo()<br>get ProjectInfo()<br>getStartTime()<br>getEndTime()<br>getSignature()<br>validate() |

FIGURE 5.10   A TimeCard Object t1

3. Identify all the attributes and methods relevant for the program's functionality, and then organize them into logical classes (each class should represent one major functional unit). Make sure to name the class in a way that clearly defines its function and purpose (remember: the first letter of the name, by convention, is a capital; concatenate multiple words in an identifier by capitalizing subsequent words, e.g., `myBirthDate`). After a first attempt at class organization, examine the preliminary classes established and look for ways to generalize attributes and methods used in multiple locations into appropriate, flexible parent classes (which will often end up being an abstract class). Optimize class interactions by compartmentalizing functionality and avoiding duplication of code and/or data elements. Use interfaces to provide additional abstraction and flexibility. The development of a high-quality class hierarchy is an iterative process.

4. Define methods and attributes with special attention to maximizing the object orientation of your classes, such as support for abstraction, encapsulation, polymorphism, and inheritance. This naturally leads to well-designed component interaction.

5. Validate the class hierarchy you have established not only against the current program's requirements, but also against other known or possible alternative requirements, perhaps from other clients or customers, or covered by other application project requirements, by comparing the product being developed with the product lines or product families of competitors. Also consider how your components might be reused for future applications in the same domain space.

6. Extensively document design decisions and specifics about the class hierarchy components and their interrelationships.

---

**Key Term**

While not all organizations have a full-time system architect, this role must be staffed in any complex software project. Typically a senior software engineer, the architect establishes the overall architecture based on system requirements and ensures that the evolving solution matches up to it.

---

When a class hierarchy has been defined, it is the system architect's responsibility to validate it against current and future requirements with as much foresight as possible. This is important because later, major changes to the class hierarchy tend to have substantial redesign and rewriting impact on the program code.

When multiple classes form a logical collection, we group them into a package.

### Packages

Packages are grouped collections of classes organized in a hierarchical tree structure. This organization allows for the grouping of one or more classes for reuse as an importable unit. Different classes with the same name can be contained in different packages, because the fully qualified package name is sure to be unique, as long as the Sun Microsystems–recommended conventions are followed. This is sometimes referred to as "name space partitioning," because name collisions are avoided by using the fully qualified name, even in the same class.

The UML representation of a package (in this case for `LibraryManager`) shows it as a container for classes (see Fig. 5.11).

Package organization can be somewhat confusing. In general, the directory structures for source and compiled bytecode files have to match. For programs to use the resulting package, the CLASSPATH has to include its path name.

### Creating Packages

Packages are used to group files into collections of related compiled units. (Files are the compilation units in Java, meaning that each file is compiled separately.)

The convention for naming packages is to use the reverse of the owner's Internet domain as the prefix for the package to ensure its uniqueness. The name should be in all lower-case letters.

### Example:

```
com.sun.java.swing
com.georgesmerx.votingProgram
```

Class membership is file-based, meaning that all the classes in a file belong to the same package, which is optionally declared in the class source file, using the `package` key word.

### Example:

**package** `libraryComponents;`

In the absence of a `package` declaration, the class belongs to an unnamed package encompassing the class files in the local directory path.

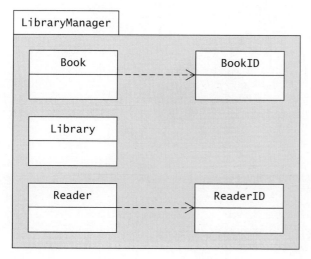

FIGURE 5.11 UML Package Diagram of the LibraryManager Classes

### Using Packages

An unnamed package is used implicitly when the classes in the current directory are involved. In all other classes, packages are included in the current program using the import keyword:

**import** javax.swing.*;
*//import all classes at location javax.swing in the javax package*

The asterisk (*) provides a mechanism for importing all classes at a particular location in the package directory structure. This feature only works on files and will *not* automatically expand subdirectories and import classes in those directories.

In summary, packages provide a mechanism for creating collections of related classes organized into a file hierarchy. This function supports component reuse, a key feature of object orientation. Packages also expand the unique naming options in Java in order to ensure that an organization's class names do not conflict with those of another organization. This is especially important because component reuse is encouraged in Java and therefore has to be flexibly supported.

### Interfaces

Interfaces are a form of inheritance that allows Java programs to implement a limited form of **multiple inheritance**. Interfaces are "stubs" that define the methods for a class and its derived objects, but leave it up to the implementer to populate these definitions with actual code and values. Only constant variables are allowed.[5] Interfaces are

---

**Key Term**

Multiple Inheritance is the creation of a child class from more than one parent class:

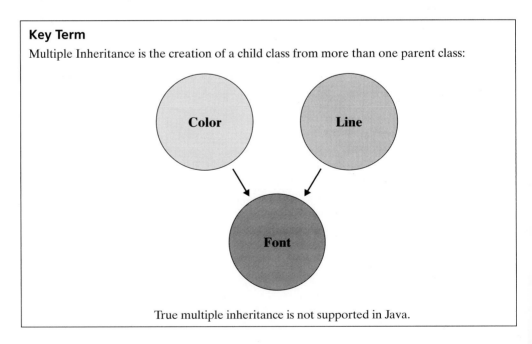

True multiple inheritance is not supported in Java.

---

[5]Enum types are recommended as of J2SE 5.0 to implement constant variable components.

specified on the class signature line using the `implements` keyword; thus, together with the `extends` keyword, a limited, yet powerful, form of multiple inheritance is provided. A particular use of interfaces promotes information hiding (or encapsulation) by providing the mechanism for implementing a level of indirection between related components, making the change or replacement of one component transparent to the other.

The following example shows an interface, `Vehicle`, and a class `Car` that implements the `Vehicle` interface.

```
// Interface code:
interface Vehicle {
    public void trackMiles();
    // method required in class implementing this interface
}
// Class code:

class Car implements Vehicle {
    public void trackMiles(){
    //...
}
```

Interfaces are flexible mechanisms that provide for the clear specification of how classes interact with each other but without imposing a particular internal implementation, thus facilitating polymorphism and encapsulation.

### Enumerations

Enumerations are a special kind of class (key word **enum**) that was added to Java in Release 5.0. In its simplest form, an enumeration declares a set of constants represented by identifiers (enumeration constants). Enumerations can have constructors, fields, and methods like other classes.

---

**Example:**

```
/**
 * The Voting Program - PartyAffiliation enum type
 * Note: this could also be implemented using enum type
 *
 * @author Georges Merx, Ph.D.
 * @version 1.00 04/12/20
 */
public enum PartyAffiliation { // enum type
    NOT_SELECTED("not selected"),
    DEMOCRATIC_PARTY("Democratic Party"),
    REPUBLICAN_PARTY("Republican Party"),
    GREEN_PARTY("Green Party"),
    LIBERTARIAN_PARTY("Libertarian Party"),
    OTHER_PARTY("Other Party");

    private final String partyAffiliation;
    PartyAffiliation (String affiliation) {
```

```
                partyAffiliation = affiliation;
        }
        public String getPartyAffiliation() {
            return partyAffiliation;
        }
    }
```

### 5.3.4  Java Class Interaction

Most software applications are composed of more than one Java class. In fact, a separate Java class is created every time it makes sense to break out a component that can be used again or has a separate function. More important, classes are organized into a class hierarchy in order to maximize componentization and component reuse, thus avoiding code duplication.

The following example shows a very simple example of two classes being used in a program. The first class, Book, defines a simple data-only class; it serves as the type definition of Book objects stored in an array of objects in class Library.

```
public class Book {
        String title;
        String author;
}
public class Library {
public static void main (String args []) {
        Book myBook[]; // declare array of type Book
        myBook = new Book[2];  // create array
        myBook[0] = new Book();  // create an array element
        myBook[0].title = "Moby Dick";
        myBook[0].author = "Herman Melville";
        myBook[1] = new Book(); // create another array element
        myBook[1].title = "Sarah and Jesse";
        myBook[1].author = "Carl Ericson";
        System.out.println (myBook[0].title + " " + myBook[0].author);
        // print string in first array element
        System.out.println (myBook[1].title + " " + myBook[1].author);
        // print string in second array element
        }
}
```

> **Key Term**
>
> An array is a collection of like elements stored under the same name. Individual array elements are addressed using an index.
> For example: MyBook [2] .title = "Einstein";

This program creates a simple two-element **array** of objects of class **Book**. In this fashion, we introduce arrays as tools for storing multiple elements of the same "kind," or "type." Array elements can be of primitive type or class members (objects).

It is important to note that, for an array of objects, the instantiation of the array does not in itself create the array objects to be stored in the array. The objects need to be separately instantiated. Fields and methods in array elements are accessed using dot notation, just as for regular objects.

### More Class Interactions

Classes stored in the same path (package) as the class that contains the `main()` method can access each other's methods and instance variables (attributes) directly, without importing. As discussed earlier, access to classes in other packages requires inclusion in your class through an `import` statement. For example,

```
import javax.swing.*;
```

The separation of an application into classes involves multiple dimensions:

1. *Vertical relationships (inheritance):* parent-child classes (`extends` keyword); interfaces-to-classes (`implements` keyword) (multi-level) ("is-a" relationships)
2. *Horizontal relationships (composition):* helper classes; imported classes ("has-a" relationships) (see Fig. 5.12)
3. *Package grouping:* classes belonging to a particular package, and to a particular directory level in that package
4. *Remote relationships:* Remote Method Invocation (RMI; explained in more detail in a later chapter) and other remote connections (e.g., CORBA, SOAP) between classes in different subsystems

The interaction between classes is governed by these relationships, by the creation of objects from classes (instantiation), and by method invocation—invoking a method in an object instantiated from a class (message passing). As mentioned earlier, interfaces provide a flexible, powerful way to organize the interaction between classes without imposing a specific method implementation, by only defining the interaction protocol itself. In addition, at the point of object instantiation, the form and variety of object constructors provide the requisite flexibility in ensuring polymorphic component reuse across a variety of applications.

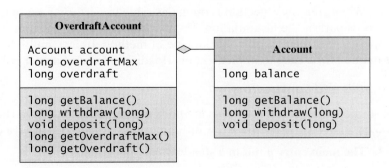

FIGURE 5.12 Example of a Composition

### 5.3.5    Java Objects

At this point, let us take a closer look at the creation of objects from Java classes, and at the role of objects in implementing Java applications according to Object-Orientation Best Practices (see box). The creation of objects is also called *object instantiation,* because we are creating an *instance* of a class, giving life (in the computer's random-access memory) to the realization of the blueprint for attributes and methods provided by the class. An object is created when the new keyword is used to reserve memory for a variable declared to be an object member of the specified class.

---

## OBJECT-ORIENTATION BEST PRACTICES

1. Design the class hierarchy for flexible reuse of components, using proven Design Patterns and applying polymorphism
2. Encapsulate objects to provide stable, secure access (implement information hiding)
3. Implement inheritance to generalize reusable methods and attributes through abstraction

---

**Example:**

```
Book nonFictionBook = new Book (); // create Book object/instance
nonFictionBook.title = "Object-Oriented Software Engineering in 2010";
```

In this example, the object nonFictionBook is created (e.g., memory is allocated) to be of class (type) Book, meaning that it will have the attributes and methods defined in the Book class. The attributes hold data values specific to this instance, such as the title "Object-Oriented Software Engineering in 2010". Note that the names of objects begin, by convention, with small letters. Objects (object variables) can hold specific data (because they have memory allocated, unlike classes). This is fundamentally why we create objects: to store specific data associated with an instance of a class. (Remember that the class is merely a generic blueprint for data objects.)

When creating objects, it is often desirable to perform a set of initialization statements as part of the instantiation. The mechanism of constructors is provided for this purpose. Constructors are a special type of method. In fact, multiple constructors may be defined for a class to implement overloading, a form of object polymorphism.

### 5.3.6    Methods and Constructors

Let us take a look at the various methods we may encounter in a class, and, by extension, in an object. There are a few different types of methods in Java classes/objects:

1. **The main entry point to a standalone application**

   *Example:*
   ```
   public static void main(String args[])
   ```

2. **Regular methods,** with a return value (e.g `int`) or without (`void`). A "regular" method is like a function, but as a component of a class/object; it contains Java statements, which typically manipulate data in variables and interact with other methods. Invoking a method either returns no value (`void`) or a value of a particular type or class.

3. **Overloaded methods.** Overloading is one of the forms of Java polymorphism. Multiple methods of the same name can be defined, distinguished by the number and/or type of the parameters with which the method is invoked. This allows for flexible use of a particular method, or more precisely, a particular version of a method.

4. **Constructor methods.** Constructor methods carry the same name as the class they serve. Their main purpose is to initialize instance variables and other start-up elements, such as GUI components, for that particular class. They are invoked when an object of that class is created. Constructor methods return no values.

5. **Overloaded constructor methods.** A constructor is overloaded when more than one method of the same constructor name is defined, with parameters that differ in type and/or number. The appropriate constructor is invoked at object-creation time based on this parameter signature. This mechanism makes the class flexible because it allows for the creation of objects of the same "type" with different functionality, depending on their utilization.

More on overloading and polymorphism in the next section.

### 5.3.7  Polymorphism: Method Overloading

One of the implementations of polymorphism in Java is method overloading. This technology allows for the definition of multiple methods carrying the same name. This permits multiple implementations of a particular function, providing added flexibility and therefore improved reusability. These methods are distinguished not by their names, but by variations in parameters and/or return value.

---

**Example:**

```
public void setUpBookInfo () {
    // ...
}
public void setUpBookInfo (PubTypes publication; String title) {
    // ...
}
public void setUpBookInfo (String author, title) {
    // ...
}
```

---

Depending on the intended use of the method, one of these three variations is invoked. In the first version, for example, there may be default values for author and title, or this version may prompt for this information, while the other versions take that information from the parameters being passed. (PubTypes is assumed to be a class defined elsewhere.)

A subclass may also replace a method in a superclass, but must implement the same number and type of parameters and return type. We call this "method overriding," as explained next.

### 5.3.8    *Polymorphism: Method Overriding*

A related form of polymorphism is the overriding of methods within the class hierarchy. This type of polymorphism makes inheritance more flexible by providing control over what functionality is inherited and used "as-is," and what functions are customized at the subclass level. A subclass can override a superclass method by implementing it with the same name and parameters; the superclass method remains accessible by using the super keyword to invoke it explicitly. Final methods in superclasses cannot be overridden by subclasses.

---

**Example:**

```
class Election {
    public void determineWinner() {
    //...
    }
}
public class CandidateElection extends Election {
    public void determineWinner() {
    //...
    }
}
public class PropositionElection extends Election {
    public void determineWinner() {
    //...
    }
}
```

---

In this example, determineWinner() is implemented, presumably with some variation for CandidateElection and PropositionElection, respectively, but can be invoked from an Election object where its membership is determined at initialization time. For example,

```
Election currentElection = new CandidateElection();
```

### 5.3.9    *Inheritance: Extending Classes*

Component reuse is exemplified through the object-oriented principle of inheritance. By extending a parent class (superclass) (keyword extends), a child class (subclass) assumes the parent's characteristics and functionality instead of having to recreate them. Combined with abstraction, polymorphism, and encapsulation, this process provides a flexible approach to component reuse under a variety of usage scenarios.

### 5.3.10    *Inheritance: Implementing Interfaces*

A complementary approach to straight inheritance is the implementation of interfaces. An interface is a codeless class that only provides method signatures and constant information. The Java keyword used to apply an interface is implements. When a class implements an interface, it essentially commits "contractually" to include in its code the specific methods(s) defined in the interface. The implementing class fills in the actual code it wants to associate with these declarations.

The ActionPerformed interface, for example, is the method contractually required when a class implements the ActionListener interface. The actual code in the

`ActionPerformed` method, however, is unique to the class using the interface, providing a flexible mechanism for implementing a predefined interface instead of inheriting preexisting code from a parent class.

### 5.3.11  *User Interface: An Introduction*

Most software applications today provide a graphical user interface (GUI). This method of interacting with users is fundamentally different from the original character-based user interface, because instead of explicitly guiding the user through a hierarchical set of menus and submenus mapped to specific functions, the GUI of a typical windowing system like Microsoft® Windows™ is event-driven. This means that the user decides where and how to interact with the system, across multiple applications that may well be running concurrently. (Multitasking is another characteristic of a modern operating system.) *Event-driven* means that programs are now required to be in a waiting state, ready to respond to user interaction. As initially discussed in Chapter 3, we call this waiting state the *event loop*. Fundamentally, this results in having to implement graphical interface components in two places in the code. In one place, they are *created and initialized* (using an `ActionListener`), and in the other, user events associated with the component are processed (by the `actionPerformed` method).

---

### DESIGN PRINCIPLE: SEPARATION OF GUI AND FUNCTIONAL COMPONENTS

It is desirable to separate the user interface from the rest of the application, for the following reasons:

- Option to implement alternative user interface subsystems (e.g., client, Web, mobile)
- Scalability of functional subsystem
- Ability to modify components with minimal impact on other components

---

From a user interface design perspective, the challenge is how to design an interface that provides the flexibility of multiple access points typical of graphical windows applications, but also implements a sequence of functions and actions that represents the workflow being modeled. In addition, a consistent separation between user interface, program control, and functional ("business rules") code should be maintained to preserve flexibility, modifiability, and extensibility. This is referred to as the *Model-View-Controller* architectural design pattern.

All this requires careful planning of the organization of graphical components and their underlying forms or windows. The layout of the windows and GUI components should optimally represent the work process by grouping elements according to their role in the process, by sequencing forms windows to optimize efficiency, ease of access, and ease of use, and by automating whatever functionality can be handled by the computer instead of the human user. Graphical applications must not only be well organized but must also appear to be "smart," alleviating the human user from as many mundane, repetitive chores as possible.

Following the basic rules explained below makes the user interface more accessible and usable.[6]

> The "5- to-7 rule" (from Miller's law, based on research published by Prof. George Miller, a psychologist, in 1956): do not place more than five to seven components in a container, otherwise your form will appear cluttered and difficult to understand. You can use multiple containers on a form (JPanel; JTabbedPane) to accommodate more components. Use default fonts, colors, backgrounds, buttons, sizes, weights, and layouts. Avoid "reinventing the wheel."

> Use default fonts, colors, backgrounds, buttons, sizes, weights, and layouts. Avoid "reinventing the wheel."

> Emulate well-known existing commercial programs in your design. Users will already be familiar with them and will appreciate your application working in a similar way.

> Get extensive feedback from other stakeholders and fine-tune your GUI design in an iterative fashion. This is an engineering task, not a creative process.

> Build the best possible user interface you can—strive for excellence in layout and execution. Pay close attention to detail, including aesthetics.

There are many other valuable user interface design rules that a professional software engineer should learn. The user interface plays a key role in the perceived and actual usefulness of a software solution. From a programming perspective, user interface components must be implemented in a way that flexibly and safely supports the user's interaction with the system rather than impede it. (Ref. GUI consultant Aaron Marcus; Web site http://www.amanda.com.)

### 5.3.12  *User Input and User Input Validation*

Java user interface components are either for display-only purposes (e.g., JLabel) or allow users to interact with the system (e.g., JButton, JList, JTextfield). When a component is interactive, careful input management is required, because human users will not always reliably enter the information expected: they will miss fields, enter strings too long or short, enter numbers where strings were excepted, and vice versa; or they will enter illegal characters. All user input needs to be validated as comprehensively as possible. Some ground rules are:

1. Data integrity is top priority. Ensure that the state of the data is known, and fully recoverable, if at all possible.
2. Whenever possible, use icons, option boxes, or pre-initialized pick lists instead of accepting textual user entry (which is prone to contain input errors).
3. Only provide the user with options that are accessible based on the current workflow context. For example, do not active a "change record" option until an active

---

[6]For more detailed information on the topic of user interface design, please refer to the many excellent books on this subject or peruse Web sites such as Java Look and Design Guidelines (http://java.sun.com/products/jlf/ed1/dg/index.htm).

record is loaded and is allowed to be changed; either exclude a non-active option or gray it out.

4. All entries should be programmatically validated in terms of expected type, length, and, if possible, content. Do not allow your program to accept input which is intrinsically or contextually incorrect.

5. Corrections should be automatic, if contextually possible without ambiguity.

6. As little reentry as possible should be required. The re-prompt should be as localized and quick as possible.

7. If possible, answer hints should be provided.

8. All illegal inputs should be caught and handled as specifically as possible, avoiding generic, catch-all error handling. No user input should ever manage to crash the program.[7]

9. Graphical user interfaces should be flexible to adjust to individual usage situations, foreign language implementations, and other custom adjustments, including support for accessibility options.

As we will see in more detail in the second version of the Voting Program presented in a subsequent chapter, one of the most flexible ways to validate user input is by using the pattern-matching techniques so popular in a number of modern languages and supported in Java.

---

### Example:

```
// ...
inputValid (zip.getText(), "\\d{5}(-?\\d{4})?");
// ...
void inputValid (String checkString, String pattern) throws
  InputException {
      if ((pattern != null) && (!checkString.matches (pattern)))
          throw new InputException();
}
```

---

This code fragment will test an input string for a pattern match and throw an exception if there is no match.

## 5.4    Position in Process

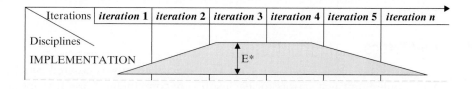

| Iterations | iteration 1 | iteration 2 | iteration 3 | iteration 4 | iteration 5 | iteration n |
|---|---|---|---|---|---|---|
| Disciplines | | | | | | |
| IMPLEMENTATION | | | E* | | | |

---

[7]As a general rule, program crashes or unexpected errors are never acceptable in high-quality software.

At this time, we have transitioned from the Design Discipline to the **Implementation Discipline** in our Unified Process Modified Methodology. In this phase, the focus is on programming, writing actual Java code, and creating the constituent components of the development project in process. Implementation involves production, close attention to ensuring highest quality, extensive testing, and validation against requirements and design imperatives. This is typically the phase with the highest staffing level and the greatest urgency in terms of production of actual functionality according to the requirements and designs established in the previous phases. It is also the time of greatest productivity and therefore of the greatest opportunity for introducing errors and aberrations, so ongoing vigilance is necessary in terms of quality and adherence to requirements and design decisions.

### 5.4.1   Component Implementation

Application components—classes, interfaces, packages, and subsystems—are being coded in this phase, following the detailed design guidelines and patterns documented in the Design Specification. The development team members need to follow a range of professional guidelines, some universally applicable, and some specific to the organization to which they belong:

- Adherence to adopted industry standards (e.g., CMMI, IEEE, ISO 9000)
- Adherence to company-internal standards and styles
- Use of industry Best Practices
- Ongoing stakeholder involvement and validation
- Development for accuracy, resilience, ease of use and installation, maintainability, scalability, and testability
- Team-supported problem-solving, validation, and inspection; management sign-off on all substantial milestones
- Documentation of all design and implementation decisions and corrections (closed-loop corrective action)

#### Documented and Tested Deployment Process and Tools

Disciplined adherence to the highest quality standards is critical in this phase, with a greater number of people typically involved than at any other time, and much production work being accomplished. Regular stringent inspections of components produced by the developers need to be scheduled and managed by the project manager, and resulting improvements have to be documented, implemented and validated. Each component, once developed, needs to undergo detailed unit testing, based on a comprehensive Unit Test Specification.

### 5.4.2   Unit Testing

As part of the Design Phase, a **Unit Test Specification** was created which contains all the detailed unit test scripts for each software component. Careful scripting of detailed instructions for unit testing is one of the factors that differentiates a high-quality software development process from a low-quality process. When unit tests are detailed, comprehensive, and accurate, the validation of product features and functions, and their compliance with requirements, becomes a predictable, measurable, repeatable process. Unit tests typically form the foundation for subsequent testing, since the software engineers who author them, based on their intimate knowledge of the components they are developing, are more familiar with the actual functionality of the components than any other team member is likely to be later on.

In addition, the development of components in this phase and their integration into testable subsystems necessitate a formalized *build management process.* The overall configuration management process is discussed in more detail in a later chapter, but the development build management subprocess is discussed here next.

*Sample Unit Test Specification outline:*

1. Brief system and subsystems description
2. Identification of important interfaces and connections (internal and external)
3. Summary of organizational software quality-assurance Best Practices relevant to unit testing
   a. Risk management
   b. Project management (resources, time, budget)
   c. Error discovery, tracking, reporting: closed-loop corrective action
   d. Expected quality levels—error severity management
4. Unit test descriptions and scripts
   *For each unit test:*
   a. Test title and description
   b. Test prerequisites/preconditions
   c. Set-up needed (e.g., test/data files, database schema/records, test automation tools, reporting tools)
   d. Testing scripts (step-by-test description of unit test)
   e. Expected outcomes (white-box, black-box, recovery)
   f. Areas not covered—dependencies on other components, interfaces
   g. Result documentation
5. Requirements validation and certification

Such a Unit Test Specification ensures that every unit is exposed to substantial engineering scrutiny before it is passed on for integration and further testing.

### 5.4.3   Build Management

In a typical commercial software development organization or company, a good many versions of any software product quickly accumulate. For each version, there are builds for development, and multiple levels of testing, as well as for deployment.

Table 5.3 illustrates the complexity of build management, even for a single product. Most companies concurrently maintain multiple products. If confusion arises about what component belongs to what version, or if it is left to developers to ensure they put the right file in the right location, recurring errors will wreak havoc with

**TABLE 5.3** Sample Table of Builds for an Unspecified Software Product Supported on Multiple Platforms

| Build | Development | Integration | Quality Assurance | Deployment |
|---|---|---|---|---|
| Release 1.01 (Windows) | 1.01.12.36 | 1.01.12 | 1.01.11 | 1.00.24 |
| Release 1.02 (Windows) | 1.02.02.12 | 1.02.02 | 1.02.01 | 1.01.36 |
| Release 1.01 (HP-UX) | 1.01.12.36 | 1.01.12 | 1.01.11 | 1.00.24 |
| Release 1.02 (HP-UX) | 1.02.02.12 | 1.02.02 | 1.02.01 | 1.01.36 |
| Release 1.01 (IBM-AIX) | 1.01.12.36 | 1.01.12 | 1.01.11 | 1.00.24 |
| Release 1.02 (IBM-AIX) | 1.02.02.12 | 1.02.02 | 1.02.01 | 1.01.36 |
| Release 1.01 (Sun Solaris) | 1.01.12.36 | 1.01.12 | 1.01.11 | 1.00.24 |
| Release 1.02 (Sun Solaris) | 1.02.02.12 | 1.02.02 | 1.02.01 | 1.01.36 |
| Release 1.01 (Redhat Linux) | 1.01.12.36 | 1.01.12 | 1.01.11 | 1.00.24 |
| Release 1.02 (Redhat Linux) | 1.02.02.12 | 1.02.02 | 1.02.01 | 1.01.36 |
| R&D Release 2.0 (Windows) | 2.00.00.02 | n.a. | n.a. | n.a. |

product quality and development schedules. Proper build management is therefore an essential Best Practice in software project management. Sophisticated tools exist for this purpose (configuration management tools, discussed in a later chapter). For small organizations, simpler source code management-only tools like CVS (Concurrent Versions System, http://www.cvshome.org/) or Microsoft's SourceSafe™ suffice.

In the past, software-development projects were executed in major consecutive stages (The Waterfall method), resulting in long periods during which the emerging components were non-functional. Today we advocate iterative development where components are put into an internal release cycle on a near-continuous basis, so that functionality can be tested early, and ongoing improvements and integration can take place over time. Many modern software-development organizations have gone to a process of daily builds, where the product is continuously enhanced and stabilized. This is only viable when testing can take place overnight in an automated fashion, making test automation a requirement for unit testing in this kind of progressive development environment. By tightening the build management cycle to as short a period between builds as viable, this approach engenders many benefits:

- Improved product stability and predictability—early discovery of problems
- Inherent support for component modularization and reuse
- Earlier testing—improved use of testing and QA resources
- Exposure of more components earlier to stakeholders for evaluation and validation
- Opportunity for content adjustments based on iterative improvement
- Test automation—efficient, computerized validation; extensive, ongoing regression testing

These implementation process activities together ensure that high-quality code is developed on time, within budget, and according to project (i.e., stakeholder) requirements.

## 5.5    Example: The Voting Program

As we enter the Implementation Phase for the Voting Program, we will develop the components identified in the Design Specification documented in Chapter 4. Given the limited space available in these pages, the program will be presented as a framework, without complete functionality.

You are encouraged to use this example and develop it into a more fully functional program. Some of the functionality incorporated in this program will not be discussed in detail until a later chapter; consider it a "preview."

In order to set up a reasonably useful GUI, the length of the code example exceeds what is typically expected in this type of book. The best way to get the most value from the example is to load it into your IDE and make it work for yourself. In a next step, you can then figure out your own improvements and extensions—the best way to learn how to program!

Note: You may want to "earmark" this chapter for subsequent reference, because the Voting Program as presented here exemplifies most of the major Java syntax and structure elements covered in this book.

The screenshot in Figure 5.13 shows the GUI which presents itself as an electronic form to be completed by the program user. The text input fields contain default

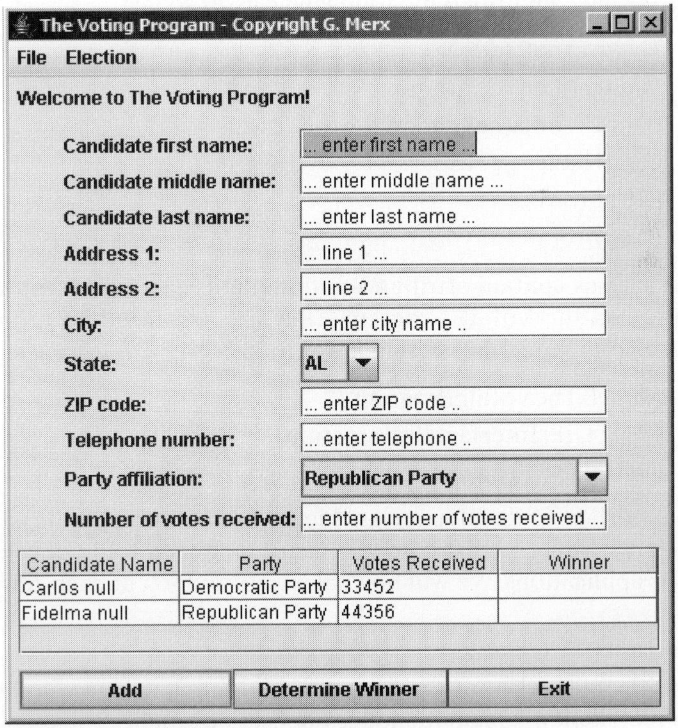

FIGURE 5.13    Screenshot of the VotingProgram Prototype

"prompts," highlighted for automatic overwriting when the user enters actual input. This is not necessarily a standard GUI approach, but it has two benefits:

1. The novice application user receives additional guidance on first-time usage.
2. The program code illustrates the `selectAll()` method.

This "form" is somewhat crowded, in terms of GUI design, but it combines in one window all the main input elements that would go with repetitive data entries for each candidate.

### 5.5.1   Components

This is the time to flesh out the class hierarchy for the Voting Program defined as an initial class diagram in the (incomplete) Design Specification begun in the last chapter, and to more completely define a simple implementation of this program. We look at the program's end-user functions in this chapter, and the administration functions in the next.

Figure 5.14 shows the currently defined classes for our prototype design. This design-level diagram guides the further implementation of class components. Additional updates are likely in the course of actual implementation, as new details are discovered through the iterative process associated with the Extended Unified Process followed in this book.

Note: The code examples shown in these chapters do not implement all the elements of this class diagram. They are merely prototype functions provided to illustrate particular syntax and structure knowledge elements.

We have identified the following classes so far:

- `TheVotingProgram.class`
- `ProgramLogic.class`
- `UserInterfacePresentation.class`
- `Candidates.class`
- `Election.class`
- `PartyAffiliation.class`

These classes contain attributes and methods that represent the functional design of the product the Voting Program. They are organized according to the Model-View-Controller architectural design pattern:

- *Model:* TheVotingProgram
- *View:* UserInterfacePresentation
- *Controller:* ProgramLogic

It is important to develop a class hierarchy that incorporates as much reuse and flexibility as possible, so that components do not need to be developed multiple times for similar applications. We will now take a closer look at each class.

#### Class: TheVotingProgram

This is the main class of the program, containing its entry point (`public void main`). (In a real-life implementation, this application would probably be developed as a Web-based program using Java Server Pages [JSPs], and would not run "standalone" unless targeted for a specialized voting machine.) From here, we set up the main program instance

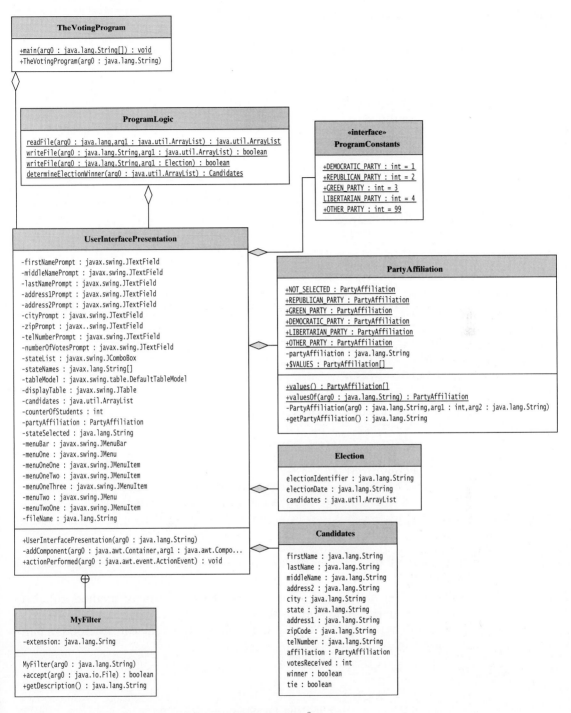

**FIGURE 5.14** Updated Class Diagram for the Voting Program[8]

---

[8]Note that this diagram was generated using Visual-Paradigm from the source code shown on the previous pages. This type of integration of design visualization and code is very helpful in ensuring that the resulting program meets requirements and design guideline.

to run, which in turn instantiates the user interface object from the UserInterface Presentation class.

```java
import java.awt.*;
import java.awt.event.*;
import javax.swing.*;
import java.util.*;

/**
* The Voting Program - Prototype Version
*
* @author Georges Merx, Ph.D.
* @version 1.00 04/12/20
*/

public class TheVotingProgram { // signature of main class
    public TheVotingProgram(String title) { // Object constructor
        UserInterfacePresentation programMainWindow =
        new UserInterfacePresentation (title);
    }

    /** The main() method is the program entry point it is only used
    to invoke the constructor which in turn creates the user
      interface object
    **/

    public static void main(String[] args) {
    // main() method - entry point to program
        // Display welcome message
        System.out.println("Welcome to The Voting Program.
            Copyright G. Merx.");
        TheVotingProgram programInstance = new TheVotingProgram
            ("The Voting Program - Copyright G. Merx");
    }
}
```

- main() method: the main entry point to the program, called by the Java Virtual Machine (JVM).
- TheVotingProgram() constructor method: This constructor method initializes (sets up) the object representing the currently active, just created instance of TheVotingProgram class.[9] We pass the window title to the constructor as a parameter for display.

*Notes:*

- System.out.println() is used to display a welcome message in the console window (on Windows systems, the DOS command).

---

[9]This code fragment, subject to the space constraints in this book, is incomplete and would need to be expanded substantially for a real implementation. You are encouraged to adapt this code and turn it into a more complete, useful application.

- The `main()` method is declared as `void` because it returns no values to the caller (in this case the JVM). It is declared as `static` because it operates at the class level (no time yet to create any objects). It specifies a `String` array as its required argument to accommodate command line parameters, if specified.

### Class: *ProgramLogic*

The ProgramLogic class implements the methods that provide the main program functionality, separate from the user interface. This includes read and write operations to save program execution results to files and a method to determine the election winner. (Subsequent chapters cover file input/output in more detail.)

```java
import java.awt.*;
import java.awt.event.*;
import javax.swing.*;
import java.util.*;
import java.io.*;

/**
The Voting Program - Program Logic class
**
* @author Georges Merx, Ph.D.
* @version 1.00 05/01/01
*/

class ProgramLogic {

/**
The readFile(String fileName, ArrayList<Candidates> candidates)
method reads an object file and returns an ArrayList of candidates
 - probably should be generalized
*/

    static ArrayList<Candidates> readFile (String fileName,
        ArrayList<Candidates> candidates) {
        int count = 0;
        boolean noError = true;
        ObjectInputStream ss = null;

        try {
            ss = new ObjectInputStream (new FileInputStream
              (fileName));
        } catch (IOException e) {
            System.err.println ("I/O Error on opening "+ e.
              toString());
            noError = false;
        }

        if (noError) {
            try {
                candidates = (ArrayList<Candidates>)
                  ss.readObject();
            // cast will cause warning message in compiler --> ignore
```

```
        } catch (EOFException e) {
            noError = false;
            // end of file found
        }

        catch (ClassNotFoundException e) {
            System.out.println ("Class Not Found Error " +
                e.toString());
            noError = false;
        }

        catch (IOException e) {
            System.err.println ("I/O Error on reading " +
                e.toString());
            noError = false;
        }

        catch (ArrayIndexOutOfBoundsException e) {
            System.err.println ("Out of array space");
            noError = false;
        }

        try {
            ss.close();
        } catch (IOException e) {
            System.err.println ("I/O Error on closing " +
                e.toString());
            noError = false;
        }
    }

    if (noError) return candidates;
    else return null;
}
/**
The writeFile(String fileName, ArrayList<Candidates> candidates)
method writes an object file and returns a boolean to indicate
success or failure - probably should be generalized and return
error code
*/

static boolean writeFile(String fileName,
    ArrayList<Candidates> candidates) {
    if (candidates != null) {
        try {
            ObjectOutputStream s = new ObjectOutputStream (new
                FileOutputStream (fileName));
            s.writeObject (candidates);
            s.flush();
```

```java
                s.close();
                return true;
            }catch (IOException e) {
                System.err.println ("I/O Error "+ e.toString());
                return false;
            }
        }

        else {
            System.err.println ("List empty!");
            return false;
        }
    }
```

```
/**
The writeFile(String fileName, Election election) method writes an
object file and returns a boolean to indicate success or
  failure -
probably should be generalized and return an error code
*/
```

```java
static boolean writeFile(String fileName, Election election) {
    if (election != null) {
        try {
            ObjectOutputStream s = new ObjectOutputStream (new
                FileOutputStream (fileName));
            s.writeObject (election);
            s.flush();
            s.close();
            return true;
        }catch (IOException e) {
            System.err.println ("I/O Error "+ e.toString());
            return false;
        }
    }

    else {
        System.err.println ("Election record empty!");
        return false;
    }
}
```

```
/**
The method determineElectionWinner(ArrayList<Candidates>
candidates) is called to find the election winner in the list of
candidates based on most votes received
*/
```

```java
static Candidates determineElectionWinner (ArrayList<Candidates>
    candidates) {
    Candidates winner = null;
```

```
if (!candidates.isEmpty()) {
    for (Iterator<Candidates> count = candidates.
      iterator();
      count.hasNext (); ) {
        Candidates candidate = (Candidates)count.next();
        // object cast to Candidate

        if (winner == null) {
            winner = candidate;
            winner.tie = false;
        }

        else if (candidate.votesReceived ==
            winner.votesReceived)
            winner.tie = true;
        else if (candidate.votesReceived >
            winner.votesReceived) {
            winner = candidate;
            winner.tie = false;
        }
    }
}
return winner;
    }
}
```

- readFile() method: is invoked to read the array list of candidates from a .dat file on disk. We pass in the logical file id (the file is opened in the UserInterface Presentation class) array list of candidates, and the method returns the list filled from the .dat file. The information is stored on disk as objects.
- writeFile() method: is overloaded to write candidate objects and election results, respectively. The method returns a Boolean result to indicate operation success or failure.
- determineElectionWinner() method: compares candidates' votes received to determine an election winner; it returns a winner candidate and indicates whether there was a tie.

*Notes:*

- The file I/O methods write the whole array list as a single object. They could also be implemented to write a Candidates object at a time.
- The determineElectionWinner() method should be upgraded to return a list of tied winners.)

### J2SE 5.0 for Loop

In J2SE 5.0, a new version of the for loop makes traversing a collection easier, as illustrated in the following update of the determineElectionWinner() method.

```java
static Candidates determineElectionWinner (ArrayList<Candidates>
    candidates) {
     Candidates winner = null;

     if (!candidates.isEmpty()) {
         for (Candidates candidate: candidates){ // new for loop
             if (winner == null) {
                 winner = candidate;
                 winner.tie = false;
             }

             else if (candidate.votesReceived == winner.
               votesReceived)
                 winner.tie = true;

             else if (candidate.votesReceived > winner.
               votesReceived) {
                 winner = candidate;
                 winner.tie = false;
             }
         }
     }
     return winner;
}
```

### Class: *UserInterfacePresentation*

The UserInterfacePresentation class provides the view component of the application; it implements the user interface windows and controls. Figure 5.13 shows the main screen displayed by this class.

*Note*: The following code segment is longer than the previous ones, but it contains a lot of similar segments required to set up each of the GUI components seen on the screen when the form is displayed for user input. As you examine the code, keep the image of the GUI in front of you so that you can correlate each line seen on the screen with the code statements that set it up.

```java
import java.awt.*;
import java.awt.event.*;
import javax.swing.*;
import javax.swing.table.*;
import java.util.*;
import java.io.*;

/**
 * The Voting Program - User Interface Presentation class
 *
 * @author Georges Merx, Ph.D.
 * @version 1.00 04/12/20
 */
public class UserInterfacePresentation extends JFrame implements
    ActionListener {
```

```java
// signature of class - ActionListener interface handles GUI events
// Attributes
    private JTextField firstNamePrompt, middleNamePrompt,
        lastNamePrompt, address1Prompt, address2Prompt, cityPrompt,
        zipPrompt, telNumberPrompt, numberOfVotesPrompt;
    private JComboBox stateList;
    private String stateNames [] =
        {"AL","AK","AS","AZ","AR","CA","CO",
        "LA","ME","MH","MD","MA","MI","MN","MS","MO","MT",
         "NE","NV",
        "NH","NJ","NM","NY","NC","ND","MP","OH","OK","OR","PW",
        "PA","PR","RI", "SC","SD","TN","TX","UT","VT","VI","VA",
        "WA","WV","WI","WY" };
    // used for drop-down list of state codes in address block
    private DefaultTableModel tableModel;
    private JTable displayTable; // table used to display candidates
    private ArrayList<Candidates> candidates;
    // an ArrayList is used to accumulate Candidates objects
    private int counterOfStudents = 0;
    private PartyAffiliation partyAffiliation =
        PartyAffiliation.NOT_SELECTED;
    private String stateSelected = null;
    private JMenuBar menuBar;
    private JMenu menuOne;
    private JMenuItem menuOneOne;
    private JMenuItem menuOneTwo;
    private JMenuItem menuOneThree;
    private JMenu menuTwo;
    private JMenuItem menuTwoOne;
    private String fileName;

/** The UserInterfacePresentation(String title) constructor method
    sets up the JFrame object by populating its GUI
*/

public UserInterfacePresentation(String title) {
// Object constructor
    super(title); // sets window title
    addWindowListener(new WindowAdapter() {
    // handle window being closed by clicking on x box
        public void windowClosing(WindowEvent e) {
            dispose();
            System.exit(0); // terminate normally
        }
    });

    Container windowContents; // variable declaration
    windowContents = getContentPane();
    // get a "handle" to the window
    GridBagLayout windowLayout = new GridBagLayout();
    GridBagConstraints windowConstraints =
```

```
      new GridBagConstraints();
// constraint values used with the Gridbag layout manager
windowContents.setLayout(windowLayout);
// set the window up with the Gridbag layout manager
windowConstraints.insets = new Insets(5,5,5,5);
windowConstraints.fill = GridBagConstraints.HORIZONTAL;
      addComponent(windowContents, new JLabel(
      "Welcome to The Voting Program!"), windowLayout,
      windowConstraints, 0,0,1,1);
JPanel personalInfoPanel = new JPanel();
/* panel used to subdivide the GUI into areas with their
   own organization */
GridBagLayout layout = new GridBagLayout();
GridBagConstraints constraints = new GridBagConstraints();
personalInfoPanel.setLayout(layout);
// set the window up with the Gridbag layout manager
constraints.insets = new Insets(3,0,0,3);
int y = 0;
constraints.fill = GridBagConstraints.HORIZONTAL;
addComponent(personalInfoPanel, new JLabel("Candidate first
      name:"), layout, constraints, 0,y,1,1);
firstNamePrompt = new JTextField
      ("... enter first name ...");
firstNamePrompt.selectAll ();  // select text for overtyping
addComponent(personalInfoPanel, firstNamePrompt, layout,
      constraints,  1,y,2,1);  // addComponent helper method
y++; // go down a line
addComponent(personalInfoPanel, new JLabel(
      "Candidate middle name:"), layout, constraints, 0,y,1,1);
middleNamePrompt = new JTextField
      ("... enter middle name ...");
middleNamePrompt.selectAll ();
   // select text for overtyping
addComponent(personalInfoPanel, middleNamePrompt, layout,
      constraints,  1,y,2,1);
y++;
addComponent(personalInfoPanel, new JLabel(
      "Candidate last name:"), layout, constraints, 0,y,1,1);
lastNamePrompt = new JTextField ("... enter last name ...");
lastNamePrompt.selectAll ();  // select text for overtyping
addComponent(personalInfoPanel, lastNamePrompt, layout,
      constraints, 1,y,2,1);
y++;
addComponent(personalInfoPanel, new JLabel("Address 1:"),
      layout, constraints, 0,y,1,1);
address1Prompt = new JTextField ("... line 1 ...");
address1Prompt.selectAll ();  // select text for overtyping
addComponent(personalInfoPanel, address1Prompt, layout,
      constraints, 1,y,2,1);
```

```
        y++;
        addComponent(personalInfoPanel, new JLabel("Address 2:" ),
            layout, constraints, 0,y,1,1);
        address2Prompt = new JTextField ("... line 2 ...");
        address2Prompt.selectAll ();  // select text for overtyping
        addComponent(personalInfoPanel, address2Prompt, layout,
            constraints, 1,y,2,1);
        y++;
        addComponent(personalInfoPanel, new JLabel("City:"), layout,
            constraints, 0,y,1,1);
        cityPrompt = new JTextField ("... enter city name ...");
        cityPrompt.selectAll ();   // select text for overtyping
        addComponent(personalInfoPanel, cityPrompt, layout,
            constraints, 1,y,2,1);
        addComponent(personalInfoPanel, new JLabel("State:"),
          layout,
            constraints, 0,y,1,1);
        stateList = new JComboBox (stateNames);
        stateList.setMaximumRowCount(5);

        stateList.addItemListener (
            new ItemListener () {
                public void itemStateChanged (ItemEvent event) {
                if (event.getStateChange() == ItemEvent.SELECTED)
                    stateSelected = (String)stateList.
                        getSelectedItem();
                }
            });

        addComponent(personalInfoPanel, stateList, layout,
            constraints, 1,y,1,1);
        y++;
        addComponent(personalInfoPanel, new JLabel("ZIP code:"),
            layout, constraints, 0,y,1,1);
        zipPrompt = new JTextField ("... enter ZIP code ...");
        zipPrompt.selectAll ();   // select text for overtyping
        addComponent(personalInfoPanel, zipPrompt, layout,
            constraints, 1,y,2,1);

        y++;
        addComponent(personalInfoPanel, new JLabel(
            "Telephone number:"), layout, constraints, 0,y,1,1);
        telNumberPrompt = new JTextField ("... enter telephone ...");
        telNumberPrompt.selectAll ();
          // select text for overtyping
        addComponent(personalInfoPanel, telNumberPrompt, layout,
            constraints, 1,y,2,1);
        y++;
        addComponent(personalInfoPanel, new JLabel(
            "Party affiliation:"), layout, constraints, 0,y,1,1);
```

```
final JComboBox partyList = new JComboBox();
partyList.setMaximumRowCount(5);
for (PartyAffiliation affiliation:EnumSet.range
    (PartyAffiliation.NOT_SELECTED,
     PartyAffiliation.OTHER_PARTY))
    partyList.addItem (affiliation.getPartyAffiliation());
    // add selections to drop-down box

partyList.addItemListener (
// handle user selection of a particular dropdown list item
    new ItemListener () {
        public void itemStateChanged (ItemEvent event) {
            if (event.getStateChange() ==
                ItemEvent.SELECTED) {
                for (PartyAffiliation
                    affiliation:EnumSet.range
                    (PartyAffiliation.NOT_SELECTED,
                    PartyAffiliation.OTHER_PARTY))
                    if (affiliation.
                        getPartyAffiliation() ==
                        partyList.getSelectedItem())
                        partyAffiliation =
                            affiliation;
        }
    }
});

addComponent (personalInfoPanel, partyList, layout,
    constraints, 1,y,2,1);

y++;
addComponent(personalInfoPanel, new JLabel(
    "Number of votes received:"), layout, constraints,
    0,y,1,1);
numberOfVotesPrompt = new JTextField (
    "... enter number of votes received ...");
numberOfVotesPrompt.selectAll ();
// select text for overtyping
addComponent(personalInfoPanel, numberOfVotesPrompt, layout,
    constraints, 1,y,2,1);
addComponent(windowContents, personalInfoPanel,
  windowLayout,
    windowConstraints, 0,1,1,1);
tableModel = new DefaultTableModel();
// set up the display table
displayTable = new JTable(tableModel);
tableModel.addColumn("Candidate Name");
tableModel.addColumn("Party");
tableModel.addColumn("Votes Received");
tableModel.addColumn("Winner");
```

```java
displayTable.setPreferredScrollableViewportSize
    (new Dimension(0, displayTable.getRowHeight() * 3));
final JScrollPane sp = new JScrollPane (displayTable);
addComponent(windowContents, sp, windowLayout,
    windowConstraints, 0,2,1,1);
JPanel buttonPanel = new JPanel ();
/* create a panel that spans the window and populate it with
   Buttons; this prevents the buttons from aligning with the
   previous controls and instead spaces them out equally */
buttonPanel.setLayout (new GridLayout());
// use the grid layout manager
JButton addButton = new JButton ("Add");
addButton.addActionListener (this);
// prepare button for event handling
buttonPanel.add (addButton);
JButton continueButton = new JButton ("Determine Winner");
continueButton.addActionListener (this);
// prepare button for event handling
buttonPanel.add (continueButton);
JButton exitButton = new JButton ("Exit");
exitButton.addActionListener (this);
buttonPanel.add (exitButton);
windowConstraints.weighty = 1000;
addComponent(windowContents, buttonPanel, windowLayout,
    windowConstraints, 0,3,1,1);
candidates = new ArrayList<Candidates>();
/* create candidates array list to store individual
   Candidates objects */
menuBar = new JMenuBar(); // set up the window menu
menuOne = new JMenu("File");
menuOneOne = new JMenuItem("Open");
menuOneTwo = new JMenuItem("Save");
menuOneThree = new JMenuItem("Exit");
menuTwo = new JMenu("Election");
menuTwoOne = new JMenuItem("Save Election");

// Action listener.for the OPEN selection
menuOneOne.addActionListener(
    new ActionListener() {
        public void actionPerformed(ActionEvent e) {
            JFileChooser chooser = new
              JFileChooser();
            /* use JFileChooser to let the user select a file
                with .DAT extension */
            chooser.addChoosableFileFilter(
                new MyFilter(".DAT"));
            int returnVal = chooser.showDialog
                (UserInterfacePresentation.this,
                "Open File with Candidate Objects");
```

```java
if(returnVal == JFileChooser.
  APPROVE_OPTION) {
  fileName = chooser. getCurrentDirectory()
      + java.io.File.separator +
      chooser.getSelectedFile().getName();
  candidates = ProgramLogic.readFile
      (fileName, candidates);
  if (candidates == null)
      System.err.println
          ("Error loading file!");
  else { // list read
      if (!candidates.isEmpty()) {
          while (tableModel. getRowCount()
              > 0)
              tableModel.removeRow
                  (tableModel.
                  getRowCount()-1);
          for (Iterator<Candidates>
            count =
              candidates.iterator();
              count.hasNext (); ) {
                Candidates
                  localCandidate =
                  (Candidates)count. next();
                // object cast to Candidates
                  tableModel.insertRow(
                  tableModel.getRowCount(),
                      new
                  Object[]{localCandidate.
                      firstName + " " +
                      localCandidate.
                      lastName,
                      localCandidate.
                      affiliation.
                      getPartyAffiliation(),
                      String.valueOf(
                      localCandidate.
                      votesReceived)});
              }
          }

          else System.err.println
          ("Nothing read - nothing to display!");
      }
    }
  }
);
```

```java
// Action listener.for the SAVE selection
menuOneTwo.addActionListener(
    new ActionListener() {
        public void actionPerformed(ActionEvent e) {
            JFileChooser chooser = new JFileChooser();
            chooser.addChoosableFileFilter(new
                MyFilter(".DAT"));
            int returnVal = chooser.showDialog
                (UserInterfacePresentation.this,
                "Save Candidate Objects");
            if(returnVal == JFileChooser.
              APPROVE_OPTION) {
                fileName = chooser.
                  getCurrentDirectory() +
                java.io.File.separator +
                chooser.getSelectedFile().getName();

                if (!fileName.toUpperCase().
                    trim().endsWith(".DAT"))
                        fileName += ".DAT";
                if (ProgramLogic.writeFile(fileName,
                    candidates) == false)
                        System.err.println
                            ("Error saving file!");
            }
        }
    }
);

// Action listener.for the EXIT selection
menuOneThree.addActionListener(
    new ActionListener() {
        public void actionPerformed(ActionEvent e) {
            dispose();
            System.exit(0);
        }
    }
);

// Action listener.for the SAVE ELECTION selection
menuTwoOne.addActionListener(
    new ActionListener() {
        public void actionPerformed(ActionEvent e) {
            Election localElection = new Election();
            localElection.electionIdentifier =
                JOptionPane.showInputDialog
                    ("Name of Election");
            localElection.electionDate =
                JOptionPane.showInputDialog
```

```
                    ("Election Date");
            localElection.candidates = candidates;
            JFileChooser chooser = new JFileChooser();
            chooser.addChoosableFileFilter(new
                MyFilter(".ELE"));
            int returnVal = chooser.showDialog
                (UserInterfacePresentation.this,
                "Save Election Information");
            if (returnVal == JFileChooser.
              APPROVE_OPTION) {
                fileName = chooser.
                  getCurrentDirectory() +
                    java.io.File.separator +
                    chooser.getSelectedFile().
                      getName();
                if (!fileName.toUpperCase().
                  trim().endsWith(".ELE"))
                    fileName += ".ELE";
                if (ProgramLogic.writeFile(fileName,
                  localElection) == false)
                    System.err.println
                        ("Error saving file!");
            }
          }
        }
    );
    menuOne.add (menuOneOne);
    menuOne.add (menuOneTwo);
    menuOne.addSeparator();
    menuOne.add (menuOneThree);
    menuTwo.add (menuTwoOne);
    menuBar.add (menuOne);
    menuBar.add (menuTwo);
    this.setJMenuBar(menuBar);

    pack();    // shrink window to miniminum size needed
    setVisible(true);   // make window visible
  }
```

*(continued below)*

As mentioned earlier, this lengthy code segment sets up the user interface presentation environment when a **UserInterfacePresentation()** object is created. As this class is an extension of **JFrame**, its objects are **JFrame** (i.e. window) objects. Your understanding of the syntax details of this code builds on the previous chapters and your study of Java syntax, structure, and semantics through the available online resources provided extensively by Sun Microsystems (www.java.sun.com), especially the Java tutorial.

- **UserInterfacePresentation()** constructor method: implements the **JFrame**-extended user interface window with all the necessary control, using **JPanels** and the **GridBagLayout** layout manager class. Swing components **JLabels**,

**JTextFields**, a **JComboBox**, a **JTable**, and **JButtons** are used to provide user interaction and information display. A **JMenuBar** is implemented to provide menu actions that are handled in line with dynamically created **ActionListener** objects.

*Notes:*

- While this is the longest method in the program, a lot of its code is repetitive and used to set up individual user interface components
- The window is laid out as a gridbag, as is the panel that holds the candidate's personal-information prompts. The panel that holds the JButtons at the bottom uses a simpler grid layout.
- A **JComboBox** is used to let users select state and party information. It is desirable to use such choice lists rather than text input fields whenever possible to reduce the chance for user input errors.
- The **JTable** used to display candidate information uses a table model to set up the table and specify headers; it resizes the table's viewport to three rows.
- This version of the program does not validate user inputs. In later chapters, we will take a closer look at input validation techniques.

(*to be continued; see end of code segment for further explanations*)

```java
/**
   This method addComponent (Component component, int row,
   int column, int width, int height) simplifies
   populating a GridBagLayout-controlled container.
*/

private void addComponent (Container panel, Component component,
      GridBagLayout layout, GridBagConstraints constraints,
      int column, int row, int width, int height) {
   constraints.gridx = column;
   constraints.gridy = row;
   constraints.gridwidth = width;
   constraints.gridheight = height;
   layout.setConstraints (component, constraints);
   panel.add (component);
}
/**
   This method actionPerformed(ActionEvent guiEvent) handles user
   interaction events
*/

public void actionPerformed (ActionEvent guiEvent) {
   if (guiEvent.getActionCommand ().equals("Add")) {
      // determine origin of event
         Candidates localCandidate = new Candidates();
         localCandidate.firstName = firstNamePrompt.getText();
```

```
localCandidate.middleName = middleNamePrompt.getText();
localCandidate.address1 = address1Prompt.getText();
localCandidate.address2 = address2Prompt.getText();
localCandidate.city = cityPrompt.getText();
localCandidate.zipCode = zipPrompt.getText();
localCandidate.state = stateSelected;
localCandidate.telNumber = telNumberPrompt.getText();
localCandidate.affiliation = partyAffiliation;

try {
    localCandidate.votesReceived = Integer.parseInt
        (numberOfVotesPrompt.getText());
    candidates.add(localCandidate);
    // create Candidates arrayList element object
    tableModel.insertRow(tableModel.getRowCount(),
    new Object[]{localCandidate.firstName + " " +
        localCandidate.lastName,
        localCandidate.affiliation.
        getPartyAffiliation (),
    String.valueOf(localCandidate.votesReceived)});
    // reinitialize input fields
    firstNamePrompt.setText
        ("... enter first name ...");
    middleNamePrompt.setText
        ("... enter middle name ...");
    lastNamePrompt.setText("... enter last name ...");
    address1Prompt.setText("... line 1 ...");
    address2Prompt.setText("... line 2 ...");
    cityPrompt.setText("... enter city name ..");
    stateList.setSelectedIndex (0);
    zipPrompt.setText("... enter ZIP code ..");
    telNumberPrompt.setText("... enter telephone ..");
    numberOfVotesPrompt.setText
        ("... enter number of votes received ...");
    firstNamePrompt.selectAll();
    middleNamePrompt.selectAll();
    lastNamePrompt.selectAll();
    address1Prompt.selectAll();
    address2Prompt.selectAll();
    cityPrompt.selectAll();
    zipPrompt.selectAll();
    telNumberPrompt.selectAll();
    numberOfVotesPrompt.selectAll();
    firstNamePrompt.requestFocus();
} catch (NumberFormatException e) {
    // prompt to reenter
    JOptionPane.showMessageDialog (null,
        "Number of votes must be a whole number!");
    numberOfVotesPrompt.setText
        ("... enter number of votes received ...");
```

```java
                    numberOfVotesPrompt.selectAll();
                    numberOfVotesPrompt.requestFocus();
            }
        }

        else if (guiEvent.getActionCommand().equals
            ("Determine Winner")) {
// determine origin of event
            // Display results
            Candidates winner = ProgramLogic.
              determineElectionWinner
                (candidates);
            if (winner != null) {
                for (int counter = 0; counter <
                    displayTable.getRowCount(); counter++) {
                    if (((String)(tableModel.
                        getValueAt(counter,0))).
                        compareTo (winner.firstName + " "
                            + winner.lastName) == 0){
                        tableModel.setValueAt
                          ("***",counter,3);
                        JOptionPane.showMessageDialog (null,
                            "The winner is " +
                            winner.firstName + " " +
                            winner.lastName + " with " +
                            winner.votesReceived + "!");
                    }
                }
            }
        }

        else if (guiEvent.getActionCommand().equals("Exit")) {
            System.out.println("\nThank you and good bye!\n");
            System.exit(0); // terminate program normally
        }
    }

/** The inner class MyFilter sets up the filter for JFileChooser
 * to limit the display and selection to folders and .DAT files
 **/

class MyFilter extends javax.swing.filechooser.FileFilter {
    private String extension;

    MyFilter (String ext) {
        extension = ext;
    }

    public boolean accept(File file) {
        return (file.isDirectory() ||
```

```
            file.getAbsolutePath().toUpperCase().
                endsWith(extension));
        }

        public String getDescription() {
            return "*" + extension;
        }
    }
}
```

- The class uses `JFileChooser` objects to prompt for file names for reading/writing program data (candidates, election results) (see Figure 5.15).
- `addComponent()` method is a helper function that facilitates the positioning of `swing` controls. It takes as parameters:
  - `Container panel`
  - `Component component`
  - `GridBagLayout layout`
  - `GridBagConstraints constraints`
  - `int column`
  - `int row`
  - `int width`
  - `int height`
- `actionPerformed()` method: as this class `implements` the `ActionListener` interface, it is committed to include this method which deals with events encountered

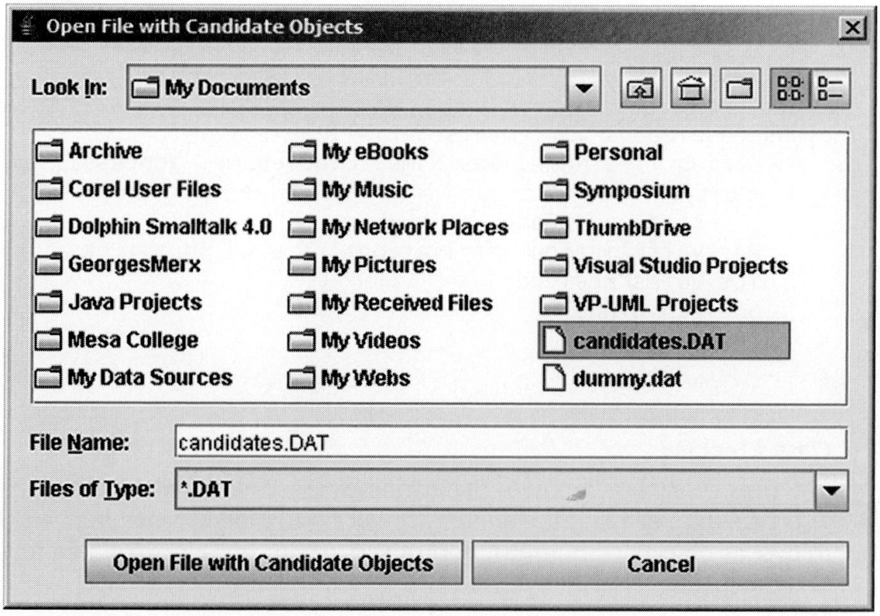

FIGURE 5.15   JFileChooser for Opening Candidates File

by controls that had an **ActionListener** object added to listen for such events; for example,

addButton.addActionListener (**this**);

This method handles user events when they occur, reacting programmatically to the user's interaction with the GUI components. For example, if the user activates the ADD button in the form, this code extracts user-entered text from the text fields and prepares it for persistent storage.

### Class: Candidates

The Candidates class provides the main attributes associated with candidate objects. This class uses the **Serializable** interface because its object members will be written out to disk as objects (serialized). Future versions of this class would add methods for candidate processing. Implementing the **Serializable** interface requires importing **java.io.Serializable**.

---

**Key Concept**

Since objects contain data as well as code references, writing this information to disk involves extracting the data into a format that later allows for the reconstruction of the objects, when read back from disk: this process is called *serialization*.

---

```
import java.io.Serializable;
/**
* The Voting Program - Candidates Class
*
* @author Georges Merx, Ph.D.
* @version 1.00 04/12/13
*/
class Candidates implements Serializable {
    String firstName, lastName, middleName, address1, address2,
      city,
        state, zipCode, telNumber;
    PartyAffiliation affiliation; // uses snum type
    int votesReceived;
    boolean winner;
    boolean tie;
}
```

### Class: Election

The **Election** class provides the attributes associated with election objects. This class also uses the **Serializable** interface because its object members will be written out to disk as objects (serialized). Future versions of this class will add methods for election processing. The **ArrayList** class is provided in **java.util**.

```java
import java.util.*;
import java.io.*;
/**
* The Voting Program - Election Class
*
* @author Georges Merx, Ph.D.
* @version 1.00 05/02/24
*/
class Election implements Serializable {
    String electionIdentifier;
    String electionDate;
    ArrayList<Candidates> candidates;
}
```

### Class: *PartyAffiliation*

This class is an enumeration class (enum type) that demonstrates the use of this J2SE 5.0 functionality. It implements constant values for party affiliation and includes a constructor to set the partyAffiliation attribute (field). It is serializable in that an attribute of this class is included with the Candidates class objects of which are serialized/deserialized in read/write file I/O operations.

```java
import java.io.*;
/**
* The Voting Program - PartyAffiliation enum class
*
* @author Georges Merx, Ph.d.
* @version 1.00 04/12/20
*/
public enum PartyAffiliation implements Serializable {
// enum type must be serializable as it is part of the
  Candidates class
    NOT_SELECTED("not selected"),
    DEMOCRATIC_PARTY("Democratic Party"),
    REPUBLICAN_PARTY("Republican Party"),
    GREEN_PARTY("Green Party"),
    LIBERTARIAN_PARTY("Libertarian Party"),
    OTHER_PARTY("Other Party");

    private final String partyAffiliation;

    PartyAffiliation (String affiliation) {
        partyAffiliation = affiliation;
    }

    public String getPartyAffiliation() {
        return partyAffiliation;
    }
}
```

## 5.6    *Harmny* **Design Case Study**

In our ongoing case study, HarmonyDesigns, you will take your Design Specification from the last chapter and begin program implementation in earnest. You have created detailed UML diagrams representing your classes and the relationships between program components. The implementation of these components is the focus of this phase, during which most of the major code is written. Typically, this is the period of maximum staffing and overall activity; therefore careful control of productivity and quality is essential. The following objectives and guidelines apply to this code production phase:

- Minimize costs by optimizing the use of resources; this is best accomplished through careful macro- and micro-level project management.
- Avoid rework by conducting regular inspections and enforcing individual accountability.
- Achieve good quality rapidly through the efficient development of modular, reusable, testable components, applying good engineering practices in the process.
- Assess releasable product against the project vision and the project requirements specification and its use cases.
- Software Quality Assurance (SQA).

---

**Key Term**

An inspection is a formal review meeting during which the owner of a code component "defends" its implementation to a group of peers who come prepared to challenge any weaknesses in the product.

---

- Apply thorough positive and negative unit and integration testing against defined inspection criteria.
- Introduce test automation, if possible.
- Practice closed-loop corrective action (CLCA).
- Adhere to specific quality standards.
- Identify errors as *critical*, *serious*, **major**, and minor; distinguish between errors and enhancements.
- Implement proper change management, making sure that requests for change are tracked through a proper closed-loop, written or computer-based process.

The last step in the implementation phase is readying the product for delivery. We call this **Initial Operational Capability (IOC)**. In this phase, we ensure that the project has become a complete product ready for shipment and installation, with all the requisite ramifications:

- No critical errors
- All product components available in production form
- All sales and marketing activities in place
- Product supportability ensured
- Quality assurance certification approved

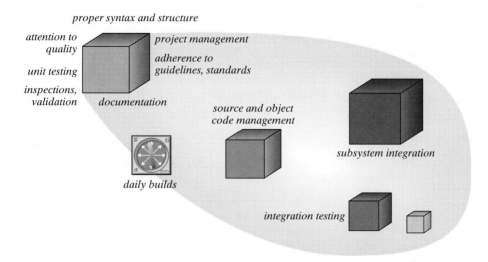

**FIGURE 5.16**   Quality Implementation Process

Figure 5.16 shows the requisite quality-assurance considerations that critically contribute to a product's IOC. As the ModelHomeDesigner software product progresses through the implementation stage of the software development process, detailed attention to quality issues will become the determining factor in ensuring that customer satisfaction and customer expectations converge.

### 5.6.1   Some Notes on the Model Home Interior Design Business

By now you have developed some domain knowledge about the interior design business, and especially the model home industry. Among other things, you have learned the following:[9]

Operation of a model home interior design company involves stringent deadlines and a great plethora of activities and components. Decorating model homes involves off-the-shelf and custom furnishings, from carpeting, tiles, appliances, and large sofas, to the smallest accessory items. All these items need to be thought-out, designed, acquired, inventoried, delivered, installed, and managed. Teams of specialists include designers, shoppers, inventory personnel, project managers, delivery companies, and installers. Many third-party suppliers are involved. All this equipment and activity needs to comply with a pre-established budget, and the difference between the cost of all this work and product and the budget provided by the builder is the company's operating profit.

In many interior design companies, much of this work is managed manually or using relatively simple Excel spreadsheets. It is your responsibility within our defined case study project to harness the power of advanced software capabilities to streamline these core work processes and afford the implementing interior design company a critical competitive advantage through improved productivity, better accuracy, and shorter project cycles.

---

[9]Making the necessary changes in details, the same points apply if you picked an alternative case study based on your personal interests.

## 5.7    Resources: Connections • People • Companies

The implementation of software components benefits from the structure of a formal software development process, but there are instances where agile and rapid application development (RAD) techniques are viable alternatives:[10]

- Conceptual or architectural prototyping—iterative prototyping.
  - Extreme time pressure, small project, experienced team—use of high-level tool such as Visual Basic
  - Well-known problem domain, reimplementation of existing solution
- Proven rapid application development, also known as "Extreme Programming" (www.extremeprogramming.org) approaches, have been documented by Kent Beck, James Kerr, and Richard Hunter.
- Another hot topic in the software development industry is Design Patterns, first described by Erich Gamma, Richard Helm, Ralph Johnson, and John Vlissides (whimsically known as "The Gang of Four"). Design Patterns capture successful Best Practices in designing software components and interactions and make them reusable by codifying them.

## 5.8    Summary and Recommendations

In this chapter, we have explored the process of Java component development. We have approached the topic from an architecture-centric perspective because it is important to view the system being developed as a holistic interplay of components assembled into packages and subsystems interacting through their interfaces. The better thought out the architecture, the more likely genuine component reuse will be successful and valuable across multiple applications.

We have also continued to expand our understanding and knowledge of Java programming concepts in form and structure, delving into The VotingProgram example in earnest. We will further develop this example and our ModelHomeDesigner case study in the next chapters.

## 5.9    Review Questions

1. **Methodology.** How do we achieve component reuse?
2. **Java Structures.** Describe three Swing components.
3. **Layout.** Review the GridBagLayout parameters implemented as three methods in the Voting Manager. Examine how JPanels are used to further control the overall layout in the window.

---

[10]As defined on the whatis.techtarget.com Web site, "RAD (rapid application development) is a concept that products can be developed faster and of higher quality through: Gathering requirements using workshops or focus groups; Prototyping and early, reiterative user testing of designs; The re-use of software components; A rigidly paced schedule that defers design improvements to the next product version; Less formality in reviews and other team communication."

## 5.10 Glossary – Terminology – Concepts

**Agile Programming**  The currently popular term for all forms of rapid application development, using parts of the Unified Process, but seeking accelerations and shortcuts.

**Interface**  A codeless definition of a class, that is available for implementation by other classes.

**Layout Manager**  Java supports application portability across platforms by implementing layout managers. Layout managers impose a structure of relative positions on graphical user interface components.

**RAD**  Rapid Application Development is a technique for shortening a development life-cycle in an especially controlled situation by leaving out certain traditional development steps.

## 5.11 Exercises

**Rapid Application Development.**  Identify and research RAD approaches.

**Implement Field Validation.**  For the voting Program, implement validation for the various user input fields. Examine ways to generalize (e.g., make reusable) field validation for the program.

**Read Election Results.**  For The Voting Program, implement a read function for the saved election results. Add a menu selection and a user interface to display election results saved previously.

# Introduction to Distributed Computing Concepts

As you continue your discovery of additional Java constructs and capabilities, including a preview of the role of Java in distributed computing, our parallel interest in software engineering considerations continues. We will look at the various software development methodologies used in the real world and examine some corporate examples of commercial software development.

While introductory Java textbooks typically focus on Java client application and applet development (using the J2SE platform), we believe that students need to also be exposed from the beginning to the practical applications of Java dominant in the commercial world, and this unavoidably includes distributed computing using more advanced Java concepts and technologies. In fact, industry sources warn that Java applet development—the initial approach to Web-enabling Java applications—has largely been replaced with Java Server Pages technology. On the server side, we see the integration of Java servlets into Web and application services, and the use of XML and SOAP for data packaging and transport. While we will introduce these topics, this book is not intended to give beginning students practical expertise in these advanced, more complex areas. We merely want to present enough information to entice those of you who will continue on this course of study to further investigate interesting and important Java subjects.

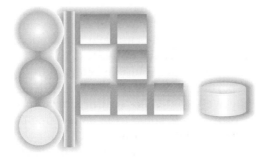

Distributed Computing Symbolized

## 6.1   Learning Objectives

A main goal of this book is to provide software engineering instruction in the context of the real world. But what do we mean by the real world? The skills acquired through this book should translate as directly as possible to projects executed in commercial, governmental, or non-profit software-development organizations. The scope of commercial software projects is typically much larger than what students encounter in the classroom. While fundamentally the same skills and knowledge apply, the substantial difference in scope and depth change the importance of contributing activities, such as project management, configuration management, and software quality assurance. Moreover, they involve a greater degree of complexity that is almost always beyond the scope of a single person's productive ability, thus making teamwork essential. In the classroom, students are accustomed to receiving precise instructions on lab and homework assignments, whereas in the real world, requirements evolve over time and typically start vague and high-level. It is often difficult for computer science graduates to adjust to working as software engineers because their college education prepared them insufficiently for the iterative processes and ambiguities common to real software-development projects. This book proposes to remedy this shortcoming, at least in part.

In practice, real-world projects may involve dozens and hundreds of classes, while your projects in college deal with just a few classes at a time. Keeping track of all these components and understanding their functions and interactions elevate realistic projects to a level of complexity difficult to experience in a classroom setting. Graduating students are therefore often overwhelmed when they enter their initial professional employment and find that commercial software development is much more involved than the simple examples they encountered in their course work.

In this chapter, we overview the Java technologies used to solve problems in these types of projects in larger organizations and see how they are applied from a life-cycle methodology perspective. We will also look at some popular agile software engineering methodologies, such as Extreme Programming (XP), used in experienced organizations to optimize, or substitute for, the resource-intensive Unified Process.

### 6.1.1   Creating Value

The essence of application software programming is to provide a useful service to the project stakeholders, creating value for the organization and individuals who fund the effort. Software engineers focus on substantially improving the productivity of their customers' work processes. Improving productivity and quality often translate directly into financial benefit, but also into improved customer satisfaction, improved product and service quality, and better long-term competitiveness.

Contemporary commercial software solutions often address enterprise-level issues and are not limited to a particular system or location.[1] Given the ubiquity of the Internet and the World Wide Web, companies and organizations have learned that the greatest productivity improvements come from connecting computers for interaction and data integration across physical locations. This allows for the integration of information-processing capabilities between divisions, between suppliers and buyers, between companies and their customers, between companies and their partners, and between financial institutions and brokers, to name but a few possibilities. We commonly refer to this phenomenon as **Distributed Computing**. Distributed business applications often contain three or more tiers:

- **Client components:** Software that interfaces with the user; it may be delivered via a browser from a Web server.
- **Server components:** Software and networking services, such as Web and application services, communications services, database access services, and security services.
- **Database components:** Nominally part of the server tier, this tier houses the relational database typically used in enterprise applications to store information in an organized, centralized, retrievable form.

In the depiction of Distributed Computing shown in Figure 6.1, we see that client services are often delivered on more than one type of device, such as personal computers (desktop and laptop; often now with Web browser programs providing the user interface) and mobile devices, such as data-capable digital cellular telephones and personal digital assistants (PDAs). Server components provide services to clients (as the name implies), meaning that clients share common functionality remotely contained on servers and thus create important synergies among remote users all having simultaneous access to shared functions and data. The database server, a special form of server, hosts a relational database, and its associated tables containing enterprise-available information in an organized, retrievable (table) form. The network connects all these devices, today typically using the TCP/IP protocol and the Internet, over wired and/or wireless connections. While we used to think in terms of local and wide-area connections, the high speeds and low cost of connectivity options available today and the predominance of Internet technology have helped to blur this distinction, making the physical location of a resource almost irrelevant.

The client-server infrastructures discussed here require interoperating software components that present the end-user with a coherent solution optimized to solve the client organization's business problems, typically by improving its workflows. The classes and objects implemented on the various tiers must be able to access each other and to exchange values as needed for the overall solution to appear as one coherent implementation. In fact, since various hardware systems and potentially different operating systems are involved, not all components are always available in one particular technology

---

[1]The term "commercial" is broadly applied and is meant to encompass all projects that provide value to an organization, whether the organization operates for profit or non-profit, or is a government agency.

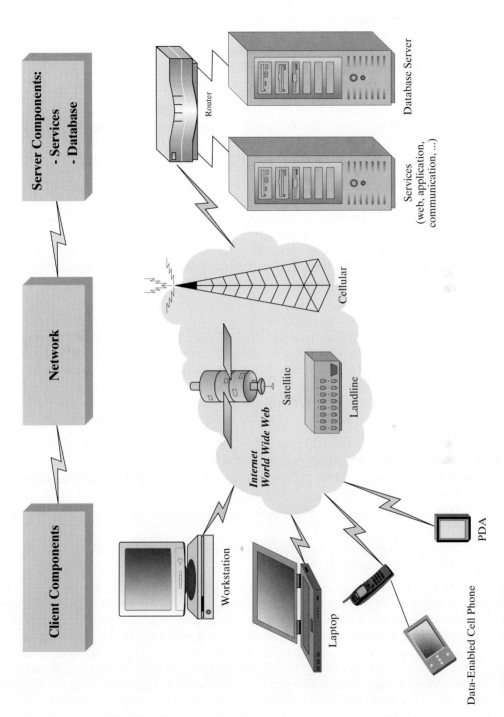

FIGURE 6.1 Example View of a Distributed Computing Solution

317

(e.g., Java), and interoperability between components implemented in different technologies is at times required. Industry-standard representations like XML and SOAP help bridge such interoperability gaps. Java supports most accepted interoperability standards and has numerous ancillary features to support the development of complex, distributed software solutions.

Java technologies in support of these distributed solutions include:

- Remote Method Invocation (RMI) for all-Java applications
- Support for the Object Management Group's Common Object Request Broker Architecture (OMG CORBA) standard
- Java servlets, Java Server Pages (JSP), and Java Server Faces (JSF)

When we implement these often-complex distributed systems (in the interest of brevity, Figure 6.1 shows a substantial simplification of the inherent intricacies of a real-life implementation), the adherence to a proven, well-tested methodology like the Unified Process is the key to success. However, in the twenty-first-century world of fast-paced decisions and short product life-cycles, it is often necessary to pursue a high-efficiency process to accelerate development cycles. The next section examines when it may be acceptable to seek some shortcuts to the formal process advocated in this book.

### 6.1.2   Agile Techniques

The Unified Process–derived methodology advocated in this text is thorough and proven, but it requires a substantial end-to-end commitment of time and resources to develop all the requisite artifacts (e.g., specific components, documents, and validations). There are situations where it may be justifiable to reduce the rigor of the development process in favor of lower cost and/or faster speed. However, such shortcuts always entail certain risks. Let us examine when it may be justifiable to forgo some aspects of the Unified Process:

- When the project is small and well-defined
- When the team working on the project is local, relatively small (ten people or fewer), and quite experienced
- When the technology is well-known, as in a reimplementation or upgrade of an existing product
- When the customers/stakeholders explicitly understand and accept the risks of a streamlined development life-cycle

It must be clear to all concerned that eliminating some of the more formal steps in the process may lead to oversights and suboptimal outcomes. Furthermore, all of the most important aspects of proper software engineering methodology must still be adhered to.

A group of related shortcut methodologies dating back to the early 1990s is collectively known as Rapid Application Development (RAD). These have been surpassed by an emerging set of shortcut methodologies often referred to as **agile methods** in the software engineering literature. Agile methods typically use a focus-group approach, relying on intensive end-user involvement in the project. Prototypes make it possible to visualize the system and to involve users in improvements. Finally, advanced development tools help ensure that proper configuration-management practices are maintained despite the accelerated development timelines inherent in these approaches. More will be said about agile methods later in this chapter.

### 6.1.3   Learning Layout

This recurring section shows the learning objectives of the chapter in a simple diagram, using the Unified Modeling Language (UML) activity diagram notation (see Fig. 6.2). The diagram provides a simple, whimsical view of the learning paths through the chapter.

### 6.1.4   Learning Connections

The Learning Connections diagram in Figure 6.3 shows the content of this chapter in relation to the knowledge and skills development recommended for junior Java software engineers. It is a reminder that software engineering is a multidisciplinary skill set requiring training not only in syntax and structure, but also in other, often "softer," skills critical for successful project completion. As this chapter deals with real-world applications, this perspective is especially relevant.

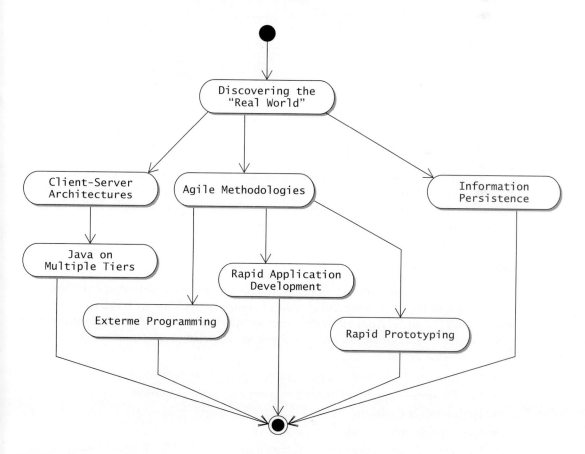

FIGURE 6.2   Chapter 6 Learning Layout (as a UML Activity Diagram)

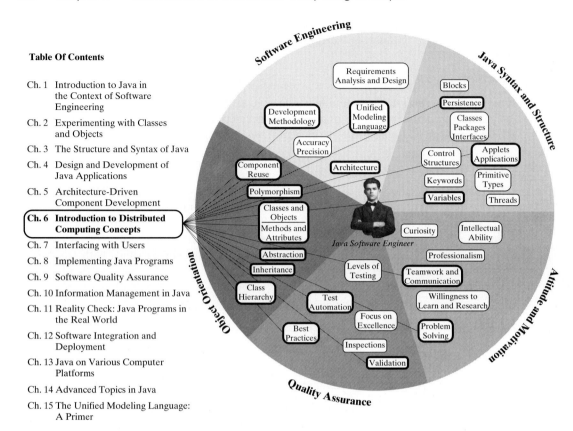

**FIGURE 6.3**    Learning Connections for Chapter 6

Like most of the chapters in this book, Chapter 6 touches on a range of skills in addition to traditional Java syntax skills. We have included this view in every chapter to encourage you to see your profession as an interdisciplinary discipline that benefits greatly from the Best Practices of other domains.

## 6.2    Executive Summary

Software development projects more often than not involve distributed environments, because one of the most powerful aspects of computer technology is the integration of information resources from many different locations and the exchange of information across geographic boundaries. Most of these applications are focused on one or more of the following goals:

- Continuous productivity improvement—process improvement
- Quality improvement, improved support and maintainability
- Better, faster decisions
- Cost or resource savings
- Centralized data management, reduced duplication of data, integration of critical information

- Shorter time to market for products and/or services
- Sustainable competitive advantages

Most of these goals involve the integration of work processes and data from multiple sources in multiple locations. We therefore build distributed applications that bridge these multiple locations and streamline company operations by removing some of the effects of being remote. Today, with the advent of high-speed wireless services, this distributed computing paradigm is being extended to the individual mobile worker, wherever he or she happens to be at a particular moment in time. For many companies, this represents a paradigm shift in terms of work integration and geographic distribution of work.

---

## MOBILE WORKERS

A recent newspaper article cited the example of professionals setting up shop in coffee houses that provide high-speed wireless access (WiFi™) to the Internet, and by extension, networked information resources, such as corporate data and applications, effectively enabling these workers to forgo a fixed office location altogether. At the same time, high-speed cellular data services are becoming commonly available from cellular network providers like Sprint and Verizon.

---

Most introductory Java books and college courses focus on standalone applications and pay lip service to distributed computing through a cursory introduction of Java applets. However, applets are used less and less for commercial projects, and are being replaced by Java Server Pages (JSP) and Java Server Faces (JSF) applications. While this book does not seek to cover distributed Java computing in depth, given the complexity of the subject, we will nevertheless introduce you to the main concepts of Java client and server computing and integrate this important topic with the remainder of the book. Our underlying objective is to introduce you to Java topics from the perspective of real-world software development, so that you can eventually apply your acquired skills and knowledge in the working world or at least know how these technologies are applied.

### What Is The "Real World"?

Many public and private agencies, companies, and individuals develop software. At the most fundamental level, we distinguish between system and application software. *System software* consists of programs written to support an underlying infrastructure, either as part of a particular operating system or in support of peripherals or networking components (e.g., device drivers). While system software ensures that the computer system itself functions properly, *application software* uses system software and the underlying infrastructure to provide valuable, productive "business" functionality to end-users.[2] Many applications are written for business use (profit or non-profit), but there are also innumerable programs for entertainment, personal, and scientific use. In this book, we concentrate on the use of Java for application software,

---

[2]The term "business" is used here in the broadest possible sense.

not system software, which constitutes a special domain, even though system programs are fundamentally similar to application programs. (In fact, Java is typically *not* used for developing system software.)

Real-life application programs, such as those used in commercial enterprises, government agencies, the military, and non-profit organizations, are today often designed for a *multi-tier* infrastructure, where *tier one* represents the clients and *tier two* through *n* the services provided to the clients. One of the strengths of the Java programming language is its support on all the tiers on all the major operating systems that might be installed on the various client and server computers in a distributed computing environment. Three major Java subsystems are available. Together they cover all tiers of a distributed information technology environment:

1. **J2SE**–Java 2 Standard Edition
2. **J2EE**–Java 2 Enterprise Edition
3. **J2ME**–Java 2 Micro Edition

Throughout the book, most of our study focuses on J2SE, but we will examine all three systems in this chapter.

## 6.3   Learning Modules

As in previous chapters, your learning experience is laid out as a sequence of Learning Modules. The context of this chapter is the practical use of Java in commercial applications and the range of software development methodologies applied in larger, distributed development projects.

Figure 6.4 shows client and server software components and technologies for a project that involves a graphical Web-based front-end, various application services, and a back-end database server, all implemented using Java technologies.

### 6.3.1   Concepts

While much progress has been made in developing processes and methods for effective object-oriented software creation, the evolution of these methodologies has so far not resulted in a single, universally accepted approach. While it may be argued that the methodology developed by Jacobson, Booch, Rumbaugh, and others—now generically known as the Unified Process (UP), with its most familiar commercialization, the Rational® Unified Process™—is the dominant commercial methodology, there are a number of popular variations of the process in common use, in particular a collection of recent methods collectively known as agile methods (see www.agilealliance.org) and as rapid application development (RAD). These techniques generally apply certain optimizations to the development life-cycle, taking advantage of special circumstances such as:

- Very experienced staff
- Reduced project scope and resulting small development teams

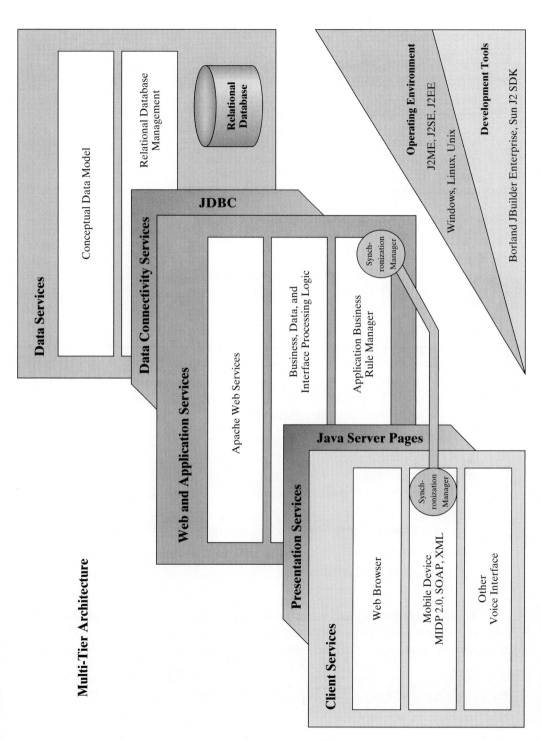

FIGURE 6.4   Example Multi-Tier Software Architecture

- High degree of access and involvement of all project stakeholders
- Well-delineated, reasonably stable problem/requirements domain

Of course, these "optimizations" carry risks:

- Excessive reliance on user-driven design can result in inadequate process improvement because users often have insufficient knowledge of what specific improvements technology can enable
- Prototype-turned-product with inadequate architectural structure
- Quality variations
- Lack of scalability of development process and code
- Lack of proper documentation and traceability

### 6.3.2   *Agile Methods and Rapid Application Development*

While it used to be acceptable to complete major software development projects in eighteen months or more, applying many specialized resources, today's expectations are typically much more stringent. Global competition and an unpredictable economic climate result in much shorter project cycles (often six months) with tight schedules and bare-bones staffing.

---

### DEFINITION

RAD (rapid application development) is the concept that products can be developed faster and of higher quality through:

- Gathering requirements using workshops or focus groups
- Prototyping and early, reiterative user testing of designs
- Reuse of software components
- A rigidly paced schedule that defers design improvements to the next product version
- Less formality in reviews and other team communication

(From whatis.techtarget.com)

---

Under these conditions, software-development organizations look for ways to streamline their software-development life-cycle. Agile methods and RAD are techniques for faster, simpler management of smaller projects with fast-changing requirements. These shortcut methodologies have gained acceptance, especially in the form of Extreme Programming (XP), first promoted by Kent Beck.[3] These techniques are based on some key limiting assumptions, as discussed earlier.

---

[3]Kent Beck, *Extreme Programming Explained: Embrace Change*, Addison-Wesley, 1999.

---

## AGILE METHODS

The *Manifesto for Agile Software Development* states: "We are uncovering better ways of developing software by doing it and helping others do it. Through this work we have come to value:

- **Individuals and interactions** over processes and tools
- **Working software** over comprehensive documentation
- **Customer collaboration** over contract negotiation

---

Some of the more familiar agile methods include eXtreme Programming, Feature Driven Development (FDD), Scrum, Crystal, and Dynamic Systems Development Method (DSDM).

For novice software engineers, however, it is crucial to learn the development methodology without shortcuts, so that eventual later adoption of one of the agile techniques is based on known factors and exemptions.

### 6.3.3 *Distributed Java Applications*

With the Internet as the worldwide backbone for computer communications, most substantive software applications are being developed as distributed applications. This means that users access the application through a client component, implemented either on a local system like a personal computer or through a Web browser interface; this client utilizes application, communications, security, and data services on one or more connected servers. The connection between clients and servers is provided by standard Internet communications using the TCP/IP network protocol, and by standard hardware and operating system components and services.

---

## SOAP

**SOAP (Simple Object Access Protocol):** An XML-based protocol for the message-based exchange of distributed application components and information.

**UDDI (Universal Description, Discovery, and Integration):** A specification composed of SOAP application programming interfaces required to enable a service broker and ultimately simplify inter-enterprise integration.

**WSDL (Web Services Description Language):** An XML vocabulary for describing Web services interfaces, defining the published service operations, and defining the definition, location, and binding details of the service.

(ZDNet: Web Services: Stages of Adoption. SOAP, UDDI, and WSDL Defined. Daniel Sholler. Meta Group. April 9, 2002)

---

### XML

The eXtensible Markup Language (XML) is a standard, simple, self-describing way of encoding both text and data so that content can be processed with relatively little human intervention and exchanged across diverse hardware, operating systems, and applications.

(From the Software AG Web site)

---

On the software side, a number of technologies cooperatively support distributed computing. These include vendor-independent communications protocols like TCP/IP, which work in a standard way across platforms, Web services based on HTML, XML, and SOAP, and remote procedure call mechanisms like Java RMI (Remote Method Invocation) or the cross-platform standard Common Object Request Broker Architecture (CORBA), also supported in Java.

Java was developed from the start to enable distributed computing at a high-level, hiding most of the complexity of the underlying systems and networking components. While distributed Java applications are far from trivial, the benefits of object orientation, such as component reuse, inheritance, and polymorphism, and the platform independence of Java, exert their full power on the development of related components on multiple systems. Figure 6.5 shows the architecture of a distributed Java application. This is a mere example and not the only way to distribute Java application components.

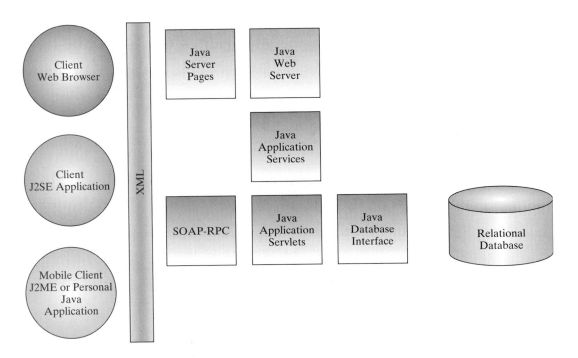

FIGURE 6.5   Generic Distributed Java-Based Architecture

In a distributed environment, Java provides a range of capabilities to make application development easy and components as reusable as possible. The Java system packages J2SE, J2EE (including the Java Server Pages (JSP) technology for Web clients), and J2ME, provide a comprehensive range of development classes for the specific implementation of functions on the various tiers of the distributed environment architecture. In conjunction with modern industry standards like XML (Extensible Markup Language), SOAP (Simple Object Access Protocol), SOAP-RPC, WDSL, and UDDI, distributed Java programs provide flexible, configurable, scalable functionality while generally protecting the application programmer from the system-level complexities of distributed computing. Advanced distributed Java applications can focus on business rules, end-user functionality, and sophisticated information management.

---

### BPEL

**BPEL (Business Process Execution Language)** for Web services is an XML-based language designed to enable task-sharing for a distributed computing or grid computing environment even across multiple organizations, using a combination of Web services. Written by developers from BEA Systems, IBM, and Microsoft, BPEL combines and replaces IBM's WebServices Flow Language (WSFL) and Microsoft's XLANG specification. (BPEL is also sometimes identified as BPELWS or BPEL4WS.)

Using BPEL, a programmer formally describes a business process that will take place across the Web in such a way that any cooperating entity can perform one or more steps in the process the same way. In a supply chain process, for example, a BPEL program might describe a business protocol that formalizes what pieces of information a product order consists of, and what exceptions may have to be handled. The BPEL program would not, however, specify how a given Web service should process a given order internally.

(from www.searchWebServices.com)

---

## 6.3.4   Methodology, Tools, and Distributed Solutions

The Extended Unified Process is illustrated in Figure 6.6. The life-cycle of a distributed software application that touches various parts of the enterprise implementing the solution follows the nine "disciplines" outlined in an earlier chapter (see Fig. 1.5). In the context of multiple subsystems cooperating across multiple computer systems and communications connections, adherence to a formal methodology becomes paramount to a successful implementation, because the required functionality is diverse and complex enough to require careful, detailed planning. In a distributed solution, the quality of the properly validated software architecture plays a key role in ensuring that requirements are translated into a system that meets all stakeholder and technical needs. The software architecture helps determine subsystems and packages, and the related class hierarchies. It also plans for the interaction of these subsystems and components,

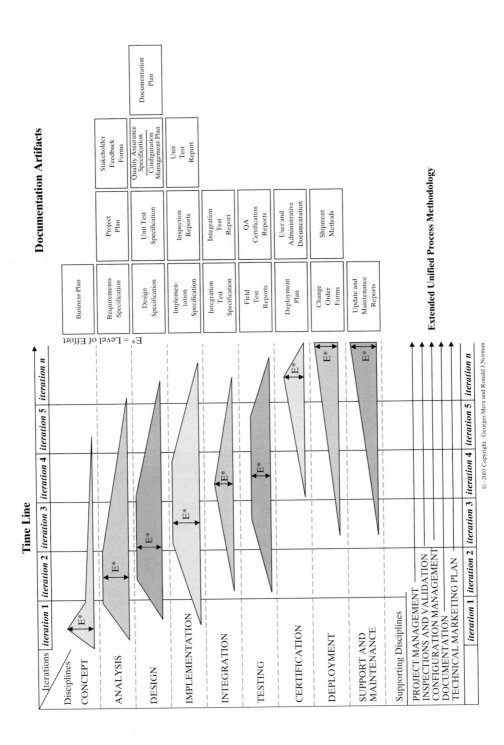

FIGURE 6.6   Extended Unified Process

especially at the interface level (e.g., method arguments and return values). Java-specific technologies can be used with platform-spanning technologies like SOAP and XML to provide data and distributed parameter transportation between subsystems. Underlying the organization of subsystems, components, packages, and classes are the objectives of Best Practices in object-oriented software engineering, especially the focus on robustness, usability, and component reuse. The distribution of reusable classes is often handicapped by slight differences in the capabilities of the individual architecture tiers. For example, J2ME does not support all the same packages and classes as J2SE and J2EE, forcing alternative implementations of similar functionality between Web and mobile clients.

Communication between the tiers and their constituent packages and classes is supported by multiple technologies, depending on the architecture of the solution. These technologies include:

- Java Remote Method Invocation (RMI) (see Figure 6.7)
- Java Database Connectivity (JDBC)
- SOAP and XML
- SOAP-RPC
- CORBA[4]

RMI provides the technology for a Java method to send a message to a remote method, just as if it were available locally. CORBA provides similar capabilities, but across technologies (e.g., between a Java method and a C++ method). SOAP-RPC also provides remote method invocation, but through the intermediary of XML and SOAP, thus also providing tool independence. Since a request for a remote resource is "wrapped" using XML tags, the recipient method does not have to be implemented in the same technology as the requester, as long as it supports the industry-standard XML format. Finally, access to data stored in relational data base tables is facilitated through JDBC, the Java version of general-purpose database access for all major relational database management systems, via the Structured Query Language (SQL).

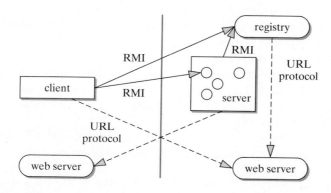

FIGURE 6.7   RMI Example

---

[4]CORBA = Common Object Request Broker Architecture (a standard of the Object Management Group–OMG, www.omg.org).

For user access and interaction, Java now offers two strategies:

- Java Server Pages (JSP)
- Java Server Faces (JSF)

Java Server Pages combined with Java servlets are replacing applets as the preferred interaction mechanism for Web browser clients. JSPs can deliver dynamic HTML page content, providing a powerful mechanism for flexible, extensive user interfacing. Servlets are the server-side classes that interact with and deliver data, communication, and application services required by clients such as JSPs. Servlets are written in Java and executed under a wide range of Web service options, such as iPlanet Enterprise Server, Apache, Microsoft Internet Information Server (IIS), IBM WebSphere, and BEA WebLogic, among others.

Java Server Faces technology includes:

- A set of APIs for representing UI components and managing their state, handling events and input validation, defining page navigation, and supporting internationalization and accessibility
- A JavaServer Pages (JSP) custom tag library for expressing a JavaServer Faces interface within a JSP page

Designed to be flexible, Java Server Faces technology leverages existing, standard graphical user interface and Web-tier concepts without limiting developers to a particular mark-up language, protocol, or client device. The UI component classes included in JSF technology encapsulate the component functionality, not the client-specific presentation, thus enabling JSF UI components to be rendered to various client devices. By combining UI component functionality with custom renderers that define rendering attributes for specific UI components, developers can construct custom tags for particular client devices. As a convenience, Java Server Faces technology provides a custom renderer and a JSP custom tag library for rendering to an HTML client, allowing developers of Java 2 Platform, Enterprise Edition (J2EE) applications to use JavaServer Faces technology in their applications.

Ease of use being the primary goal, the JavaServer Faces architecture clearly defines a separation between application logic and presentation while making it easy to connect the presentation layer to the application code. This design enables individual members of a Web application development team to focus on their respective assignments in the development process, and it also provides a simple programming model to link the pieces together. For example, Web page developers with no programming expertise can use JSF UI component tags to link to application code from within a Web page without writing any scripts.

Developed through the Java Community Process under JSR-127, Java Server Faces technology establishes the standard for building server-side-driven user interfaces. With the contributions of the Community Process expert group, JavaServer Faces APIs are designed to be leveraged by tools that make Web application development even easier.

Several respected tools vendors are contributing members of the JSR-127 expert group and are committed to supporting the JSF technology in their tools, thus promoting the adoption of the JSF technology standard.

### UML Representation

The UML diagrams are powerful, flexible, and scalable enough to represent even complex distributed solutions using these various technologies. The design of these applications depends more than anything on the accurate and detailed translation of detailed requirements (use cases) into class hierarchies for the various packages and subsystems that collaborate to constitute the entire distributed solution.

As we have mentioned, an important goal of this book is to explore Java syntax, structure, and semantics in the context of industry Best Practices in software engineering. A more detailed discussion of advanced distributed software-development technologies is beyond the scope of this book. However, it should be noted that most new commercial software-development projects are implemented in networked, distributed environments (more and more often including wireless clients).

One important aspect of almost any software engineering project is the ability to permanently store data in computer files or databases, a concept called *persistent storage* in object-oriented programming. The next section introduces this important topic, which will be explored in more detail later in the chapter. In this fashion, you can begin incorporating simple file I/O in your programs right away and make the examples more "real-file" useful by saving information to disk.

## 6.3.5 Information Persistence

In the area of Java syntax learning, we are focusing in this chapter on storing information in files for permanent access (writing) and accessing on it from files for use in our programs (reading).

### Writing to Files, and Reading from Files

Making data *persistent* is the object-oriented terminology for writing data to a file or database. A *file* is an organized data structure on a storage device, often a hard disk (HD), which allows for the preservation of information even when a system or device is no longer powered. Files contain data, but also headers with file-management information and some end-of-file indication. File storage, also referred to as secondary storage, contrasts with primary storage in Random Access Memory (RAM), which is volatile, meaning that program data stored in RAM is lost when the program proceeds past the scope of the variables holding the data, when the program terminates, or when power to the computer is cut off. RAM is used only for temporary storage of variables while a program is executing. A more sophisticated form of secondary storage is a database.

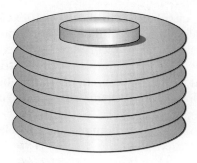

Persistent storage

A *database* is a structured collection of files containing data in tabular form (rows and columns), managed by a set of programs called a database management system. The relational organization of database tables is the dominant form used today.

Java provides a rich environment for file manipulation (we often refer to file operations, file I/O, or file input/output). From, byte-level I/O to reading and writing text files, a number of specific methods are available as part of the `java.io` package to manipulate different kinds of file types. Java files are fundamentally treated as streams of bytes and are preferably attached to buffers for efficient processing. We will introduce persistent storage in this chapter but discuss it in more detail in Chapter 10, "Information Management in Java."

### Overview of Persistence

In order to write to a file or read from a file, a Java program has to establish a logical connection to a physical file (which, we assume for this discussion, resides on a hard disk). We refer to this process as opening the file, even though there is no explicit "open" command in Java.

A file is opened by associating a (logical) file object with the physical file name.

---

### Example:

```
ObjectInputStream ss = new ObjectInputStream (new
FileInputStream(fileName));
```

---

Once the object **ss** is available and initialized ("pointing" to the physical file), it can be used for all subsequent file I/O operations, such as reading or writing and closing the file after all operations are complete.

---

### Example: reading an object from a file:

```
try {
    candidate = (Candidates)ss.readObject();
    } catch (IOException e) {
    // deal with I/O error
}
```

---

Note the mandatory **try...catch** block to check for **IOException** exceptions.

There are various types and levels of file I/O operations, from the lowest level of writing and reading streams of bytes, to record-level I/O, text I/O, and object I/O. Files can be organized randomly (only for primitive type and String fields) or sequentially. In order to write objects out to disk, the class to which they belong must implement the **Serializable** interface. Upon reading them back, the object read must be cast to the proper class type (see the example above).

Database access will be discussed as an overview in a later chapter.

**6.4      Position in Process**

| Iterations | *iteration 1* | *iteration 2* | *iteration 3* | *iteration 4* | *iteration 5* | *iteration n* |
|---|---|---|---|---|---|---|
| Disciplines | | | | | | |
| INTEGRATION | | | | E* | | |

At this point in our software methodology, we have completed the Implementation phase and are entering the **Integration** discipline. The components we implemented in the previous phase now have to "fit together," meaning that they cooperatively provide the functionality set forth in the Design Specification, itself based on the Requirements Specification. The integration of components occurs at multiple levels:

- *Class and object-level integration:* Parameters and return values must match the design expectations.
- *Package-level integration:* Classes are assembled into appropriate, reuse-oriented packages.
- *Subsystem-level integration:* Packages are integrated to provide the functionality of an entire subsystem.
- *System-level integration:* All subsystems together provide the system as specified in the Design Specification.

We will explore these levels of integration in the next few paragraphs. Of course, once integration is progressing, Integration Testing proceeds in parallel.

### 6.4.1    *Class and Object Integration*

The integration of classes and their associated objects is governed by the interaction between their methods and attributes. Methods can receive (primitive) values or objects as parameters and can send back values or objects as return values to the calling (invoking) method.[5] The access limitation of methods and attributes as `private`, `protected`, or `public`, and the equivalent controlled scope of variables provide a way to integrate components without foregoing access control (see Fig. 6.8). The integration of classes needs to follow the application architecture established when the class hierarchy was designed. In conjunction, established design patterns should be applied to optimize how components are integrated, following the previously discussed principles of

- Loose coupling
- Strong cohesion

---

[5]Technically, it would be more accurate to call this the "message sender."

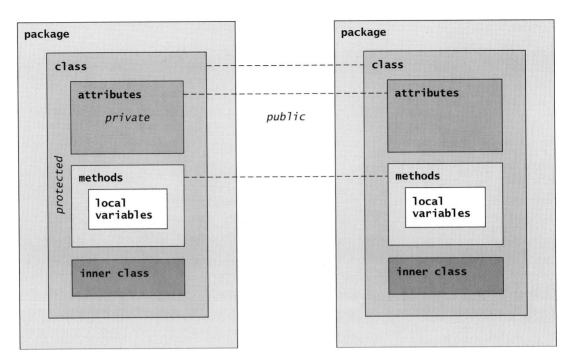

FIGURE 6.8    Illustration of Scope

- Redundancy avoidance
- Abstraction

When components are organized according to these design principles, and assuming excellent technical skills among the team of software engineers, the resulting application follows a predictable, high-quality development path that has proven successful with many commercial software-development projects.

### 6.4.2    Package Integration

Classes are organized into hierarchical file/folder structures and stored in a compressed format (.jar) in packages for ordered integration into programs using the import statement. Please note that the logical class hierarchy and the physical package organization do not have to coincide; that is to say, a class hierarchy can be composed of classes that belong to different packages. Specific classes are referred to with the familiar dot notation when specified for import. An asterisk (*) is used to specify all classes at a given level of the package hierarchy. Note that the asterisk will *not expand packages* at the level where it used, but only reference classes.

Packages make it easy to reuse compiled components in new applications as "black boxes" without having to understand or modify the source code of these components. Through encapsulation, the programmer of a reusable class in a package can limit access to **public** attributes and methods.

**Example:**

```
import javax.swing.JOptionPane;
import java.awt.*;

public class MyGraphicalProgram {
// code
    JOptionPane.showMessageDialog (null, msg, "Information",
        JOptionPane.INFORMATION_MESSAGE);
{
```

### 6.4.3   *Subsystem Integration*

Packages containing class hierarchies are logically/physically integrated into subsystems. Subsystems reside on clients and servers, and together form the complete application system. The client subsystem(s) provide(s) the user access to the system; server subsystems provide the services for the distributed enterprise application environment. Subsystems may be organized by function or location. The integration of subsystems is beyond the scope of this book.

### 6.4.4   *System Integration*

The subsystems integrated together constitute the complete working system, destined to optimally solve the business problems for which the software was conceived in the first place. The integration of the subsystems and the underlying hardware, software, and networking elements, services, and components is determined by the system architecture. Of course, all interactions between subsystems and with external systems "upstream" and "downstream" must be thoroughly tested as part of the formal Integration Test effort.

### 6.4.5   *Integration Testing*

*Integration testing* is an engineering task. The I-Test is the final step completed by the software engineering group or department before turning over the software product to Software Quality Assurance (SQA).[6] Ideally, a separate Integration Test team or group is

---

### ALPHA AND BETA TESTING

*Alpha tests* are conducted with customers who sign up as early adopters of a new software product. The product in alpha stage lacks some capabilities but has others functional enough to undergo field-testing.

*Beta testing* assumes that all functionality is implemented according to spec and that outstanding issues are non-critical.

Some organizations use the term "early access" to refer to either alpha or beta or both types of testing.

---

[6]Organizations may have slightly different activities, phases, and descriptions/names in this phase of the project. The process described here is proven to work in a commercial environment.

responsible for formal integration testing. Functional and non-functional requirements are validated in this phase, and extensive stress and functionality testing is executed.

The beginning of the I-Test is also often the trigger for field **alpha testing** of the emerging software product. Alpha testing puts the emerging products in the hands of early-adopter customers and solicits their feedback on the quality and accuracy of implementation of functional and non-functional requirements. This feedback is then folded in with follow-on development iterations. **Beta testing** follows when all functions have been implemented and prospective users of the product pot it through its paces in at least a simulation of real use (see Chapter 7).

Associated with integration testing, the team develops an **Integration Test Specification**, which documents the specific tests to be executed as part of this important phase in the development process. The test scripts in the I-Test Spec, as this document is often abbreviated, are typically based on tests found in the Unit Test Specification, augmented by tests devised by the I-Test team, perhaps with support from the SQA specialists. While unit tests validate the functionality of individual components, I-tests ensure that these components interoperate properly, and that the software correctly interacts with other, third-party components and products. Evaluating the proper operation of a component is ensured by validating test results against the specification's documented expected results, which in turn are based on the Requirements and Design Specifications.

### Sample Integration Specification Outline

The following outline provides an example skeleton of an Integration Test Specification.

- Introduction and Purpose
- Objectives of the Integration Test Process
- Organization and process description
  - External and Internal Standards
    - Types of tests
    - Error detection, reporting, correction
    - Regression testing
  - Use of testing tools
  - Closed-loop corrective action
- Integration Test Scripts
  - *For each test:*
  - Name and identification of the test
  - Description
  - Resources/set-up required—pre-conditions
  - Step-by-step procedure to exercise program function
  - Expected results
    - Program behavior and displays
    - Error display and recovery
    - Performance and other non-functional requirements
    - Reference to other specifications
  - Any post-conditions
  - Issues not covered by the test

## 6.5   Iterative Improvements

It is important to retain flexibility throughout the project to accommodate changes in requirements or opportunities to apply new technologies. While it is natural that flexibility is reduced as the team advances through the phases, it is often necessary to accommodate changes that have a significant impact on the overall project. As long as all stakeholders are aware of and accept the resulting impacts, this should be a workable situation, rather than a disaster. Martin Fowler has described the process of *refactoring* in terms of an organized approach to implementing changes to a software product.

---

### REFACTORING

This concept has gained popularity in software engineering and represents the organized, iterative reengineering of initial designs and implementations as new information becomes available. Martin Fowler, co-author of the book *Refactoring: Improving the Design of Existing Code* (Addison-Wesley), explains refactoring as follows:

#### WHAT IS REFACTORING?

Refactoring is a disciplined technique for restructuring an existing body of code, altering its internal structure without changing its external behavior. Its heart is a series of small behavior preserving transformations. Each transformation (called a 'refactoring') does little, but a sequence of transformations can produce a significant restructuring. Since each refactoring is small, it's less likely to go wrong. The system is also kept fully working after each small refactoring, reducing the chances that a system can get seriously broken during the restructuring."

---

Next, we examine ongoing improvements to our Voting Program example. In this chapter, we take a look at input validation using *regular expressions*. The latter is a common computer science technique available in many languages, including Java, for describing patterns of allowable inputs and implementing *pattern-matching* code to accept properly formatted input and reject incorrectly entered input.

## 6.6   Example: The Voting Program

In the user input portion of the Voting Program, it is desirable to validate user inputs to the extent possible to ensure that no invalid inputs are allowed. This is important because the data input portion of a program has to ensure that the data collected by the program is "clean," meaning free from invalid entries.

### 6.6.1  The Voting Program—Updated

UserInterfacePresentation Class

The **UserInterfacePresentation** class is updated to include user input valida-tions. The screenshot (see Fig. 6.9) shows the result of running the application with some incorrect inputs. Note the error message that indicates what input fields need correcting.

Updated code for the **UserInterfacePresentation** class follows:

```
import java.awt.*;
import java.awt.event.*;
import javax.swing.*;
import javax.swing.table.*;
import java.util.*;
import java.io.*;

/**
 * The Voting Program - User Interface Presentation class
 *
 * @author Georges Merx, Ph.D.
 * @version 1.00 04/12/20
 */
```

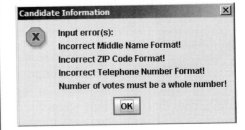

FIGURE 6.9  The Voting Program with Validations

```java
public class UserInterfacePresentation extends JFrame
      implements ActionListener {
// signature of class - ActionListener interface handles GUI events
// Attributes
      private JTextField firstNamePrompt, middleNamePrompt,
          lastNamePrompt, dateOBPrompt, socialSNPrompt,
          address1Prompt, address2Prompt, cityPrompt, zipPrompt,
          telNumberPrompt, numberOfVotesPrompt;
      private JComboBox stateList;
      private String stateNames [] = { "AL","AK","AS","AZ","AR","CA",
          "CO","CT","DE","DC","FM","FL","GA","GU","HI","ID","IL","IN",
          "IA","KS","KY","LA","ME","MH","MD","MA","MI","MN","MS","MO"
          "MT","NE", "NV","NH","NJ","NM","NY","NC","ND","MP","OH","OK",
          "OR","PW","PA","PR","RI","SC","SD","TN","TX","UT","VT","VI",
          "VA","WA","WV","WI","WY" };
      private DefaultTableModel tableModel;
      private JTable displayTable; // table used to display candidates
      private ArrayList<Candidates> candidates;
      // an ArrayList is used to accumulate Candidates objects
      private int counterOfStudents = 0;
      private PartyAffiliation partyAffiliation =
          PartyAffiliation.NOT_SELECTED;
      private String stateSelected = null;
      private JMenuBar menuBar;
      private JMenu menuOne;
      private JMenuItem menuOneOne;
      private JMenuItem menuOneTwo;
      private JMenuItem menuOneThree;
      private JMenu menuTwo;
      private JMenuItem menuTwoOne;
      private String fileName;

  /**
   The UserInterfacePresentation(STring title) constructor method
   sets up the JFrame object by populating its GUI
  */

      public UserInterfacePresentation(String title) {
      // Object constructor
          super(title); // sets window title
          addWindowListener(new WindowAdapter() {
          // handle window being closed by clicking on x box
              public void windowClosing(WindowEvent e) {
                  dispose();
                  System.exit(0); // terminate normally
              }
          });
          // variable declarations
          Container windowContents;
```

```
windowContents = getContentPane();
// get a "handle" to the window
GridBagLayout windowLayout = new GridBagLayout();
GridBagConstraints windowConstraints =
    new GridBagConstraints();
windowContents.setLayout(windowLayout);
// set the window up with the Gridbag layout manager
windowConstraints.insets = new Insets(5,5,5,5);
windowConstraints.fill = GridBagConstraints.HORIZONTAL;
addComponent(windowContents, new JLabel
    ("Welcome to The Voting Program!"), windowLayout,
    windowConstraints, 0,0,1,1);
JPanel personalInfoPanel = new JPanel();
GridBagLayout layout = new GridBagLayout();
GridBagConstraints constraints = new GridBagConstraints();
personalInfoPanel.setLayout(layout);
// set the window up with the Gridbag layout manager
constraints.insets = new Insets(3,0,0,3);
int y = 0;
constraints.fill = GridBagConstraints.HORIZONTAL;
addComponent(personalInfoPanel, new JLabel
    ("Candidate first name:"), layout, constraints,
      0,y,1,1);
firstNamePrompt = new JTextField
    ("... enter first name ...");
firstNamePrompt.selectAll (); // select text for overtyping
addComponent(personalInfoPanel, firstNamePrompt, layout,
    constraints,  1,y,2,1);
y++;
addComponent(personalInfoPanel, new JLabel
    ("Candidate middle name:"), layout, constraints,
    0,y,1,1);
middleNamePrompt = new JTextField
    ("... enter middle name ...");
middleNamePrompt.selectAll ();
  // select text for overtyping
addComponent(personalInfoPanel, middleNamePrompt, layout,
    constraints,  1,y,2,1);
y++;
addComponent(personalInfoPanel, new JLabel
    ("Candidate last name:"), layout, constraints, 0,y,1,1);
lastNamePrompt = new JTextField ("... enter last name ...");
lastNamePrompt.selectAll ();  // select text for overtyping
addComponent(personalInfoPanel, lastNamePrompt, layout,
    constraints, 1,y,2,1);
y++;
addComponent(personalInfoPanel, new JLabel
    ("Candidate date of birth:"), layout, constraints,
    0,y,1,1);
dateOBPrompt = new JTextField ("... enter xx/yy/zzzz ...");
```

```
dateOBPrompt.selectAll (); // select text for overtyping
addComponent(personalInfoPanel, dateOBPrompt, layout,
    constraints, 1,y,2,1);
y++;
addComponent(personalInfoPanel, new JLabel
  ("Candidate SSN:"),
    layout, constraints, 0,y,1,1);
socialSNPrompt = new JTextField ("... enter SSN ...");
socialSNPrompt.selectAll (); // select text for overtyping
addComponent(personalInfoPanel, socialSNPrompt, layout,
    constraints, 1,y,2,1);
y++;
addComponent(personalInfoPanel, new JLabel("Address 1:"),
    layout, constraints, 0,y,1,1);
address1Prompt = new JTextField ("... line 1 ...");
address1Prompt.selectAll (); // select text for overtyping
addComponent(personalInfoPanel, address1Prompt, layout,
    constraints, 1,y,2,1);
y++;
addComponent(personalInfoPanel, new JLabel("Address 2:"),
    layout, constraints, 0,y,1,1);
address2Prompt = new JTextField ("... line 2 ...");
address2Prompt.selectAll (); // select text for overtyping
addComponent(personalInfoPanel, address2Prompt, layout,
    constraints, 1,y,2,1);
y++;
addComponent(personalInfoPanel, new JLabel("City:"),
  layout,
    constraints, 0,y,1,1);
cityPrompt = new JTextField ("... enter city name ...");
cityPrompt.selectAll (); // select text for overtyping
addComponent(personalInfoPanel, cityPrompt, layout,
    constraints,1,y,2,1);
y++;
addComponent(personalInfoPanel, new JLabel("State:"),
  layout,
    constraints, 0,y,1,1);
stateList = new JComboBox (stateNames);
stateList.setMaximumRowCount(5);

stateList.addItemListener (
    new ItemListener () {
        public void itemStateChanged (ItemEvent event){
            if (event.getStateChange() ==
                ItemEvent.SELECTED)
                  stateSelected = (String)stateList.
                    getSelectedItem();
        }
    });
addComponent(personalInfoPanel, stateList, layout,
    constraints, 1,y,1,1);
```

```java
y++;
addComponent(personalInfoPanel, new JLabel("ZIP code:"),
    layout,constraints, 0,y,1,1);
zipPrompt = new JTextField ("... enter ZIP code ...");
zipPrompt.selectAll ();   // select text for overtyping
addComponent(personalInfoPanel, zipPrompt, layout,
    constraints, 1,y,2,1);
y++;
addComponent(personalInfoPanel, new JLabel(
    "Telephone number:"), layout, constraints, 0,y,1,1);
telNumberPrompt = new JTextField(
    "... enter xxx-yyy-zzzz ...");
telNumberPrompt.selectAll ();
  // select text for overtyping
addComponent(personalInfoPanel, telNumberPrompt, layout,
    constraints, 1,y,2,1);
y++;
addComponent(personalInfoPanel, new JLabel
    ("Party affiliation:"), layout, constraints, 0,y,1,1);
final JComboBox partyList = new JComboBox();
partyList.setMaximumRowCount(5);
for (PartyAffiliation affiliation:EnumSet.range
    (PartyAffiliation.NOT_SELECTED,
     PartyAffiliation.OTHER_PARTY))
    partyList.addItem (affiliation.getPartyAffiliation());
    // add selections to drop-down box

partyList.addItemListener (
// handle user selection of a particular
  dropdown list item
    new ItemListener () {
        public void itemStateChanged (ItemEvent event){
            if (event.getStateChange() ==
                ItemEvent.SELECTED) {
                for (PartyAffiliation
                    affiliation:EnumSet.range
                    (PartyAffiliation.NOT_SELECTED,
                        PartyAffiliation.OTHER_PARTY))
                    if (affiliation.
                        getPartyAffiliation() ==
                        partyList.getSelectedItem())
                            partyAffiliation =
                            affiliation;
            }
        }
    });

addComponent (personalInfoPanel, partyList, layout,
    constraints, 1,y,2,1);
y++;
```

```java
addComponent(personalInfoPanel, new JLabel
    ("Number of votes received:"), layout, constraints,
     0,y,1,1);
numberOfVotesPrompt = new JTextField
    ("... enter number of votes received ...");
numberOfVotesPrompt.selectAll();
// select text for overtyping
addComponent(personalInfoPanel, numberOfVotesPrompt, layout,
    constraints, 1,y,2,1);
addComponent(windowContents, personalInfoPanel,
  windowLayout,
    windowConstraints, 0,1,1,1);
tableModel = new DefaultTableModel();
// set up the display table
displayTable = new JTable(tableModel);
tableModel.addColumn("Candidate Name");
tableModel.addColumn("Party");
tableModel.addColumn("Votes Received");
tableModel.addColumn("Winner");
displayTable.setPreferredScrollableViewportSize
    (new Dimension(0, displayTable.getRowHeight() * 3));
final JScrollPane sp = new JScrollPane (displayTable);
addComponent(windowContents, sp, windowLayout,
    windowConstraints, 0,2,1,1);
JPanel buttonPanel = new JPanel ();
/* create a panel that spans the window and populate it with
   Buttons - this prevents the buttons from aligning with the
   previous controls and instead spaces them out equally */
buttonPanel.setLayout (new GridLayout());
// use the grid layout manager
JButton addButton = new JButton ("Add");
addButton.addActionListener (this);
// prepare button for event handling
buttonPanel.add (addButton);
JButton continueButton = new JButton ("Determine Winner");
continueButton.addActionListener (this);
// prepare button for event handling
buttonPanel.add (continueButton);
JButton exitButton = new JButton ("Exit");
exitButton.addActionListener (this);
buttonPanel.add (exitButton);
windowConstraints.weighty = 1000;
addComponent(windowContents, buttonPanel, windowLayout,
    windowConstraints, 0,3,1,1);
candidates = new ArrayList<Candidates>();
// create candidates array list to store individual Candidates
  objects
menuBar = new JMenuBar(); // set up the window menu
menuOne = new JMenu("File");
menuOneOne = new JMenuItem("Open");
```

```java
      menuOneTwo = new JMenuItem("Save");
      menuOneThree = new JMenuItem("Exit");
      menuTwo = new JMenu("Election");
      menuTwoOne = new JMenuItem("Save Election");

      // Action listener.for the OPEN selection
      menuOneOne.addActionListener(
      new ActionListener() {
            public void actionPerformed(ActionEvent e) {
                  JFileChooser chooser = new JFileChooser();
// use JFileChooser to let the user select a file with .DAT
   extension
                  chooser.addChoosableFileFilter(
                        new MyFilter(".DAT"));
                  int returnVal =
                        chooser.showDialog(UserInterfacePresentation.
                              this,
                              "Open File with Candidate Objects");
                  if(returnVal == JFileChooser.APPROVE_OPTION) {
                        fileName = chooser.getCurrentDirectory() +
                              java.io.File.separator +
                              chooser.getSelectedFile().getName();
                        candidates = ProgramLogic.readFile (fileName,
                              candidates);
                        if (candidates == null)
                              System.err.println (
                                    "Error loading file!");
                        else { // list read
                              if (!candidates.isEmpty()) {
                                    while (tableModel.getRowCount
                                        () > 0)
                                          tableModel.removeRow
                                              (tableModel.getRowCount
                                              ()-1);
                                    for (Iterator<Candidates> count =
                                    candidates.iterator();
                                    count.hasNext (); ){
                                          Candidates local
                                              Candidate =
                                              (Candidates)count.next();
                              // object cast to Candidates
                                          tableModel.insertRow
                                              (tableModel.getRow
                                              Count(),
                                              new Object[]{
                                    localCandidate.first Name +
                                              " " +
                                        localCandidate.last Name,
                                              localCandidate.
```

```
                                        affiliation.
                                        getPartyAffiliation
                                          (),
                                        String.valueOf
                                        (localCandidate.
                                        votesReceived)
                                        });
                          }
                    }
                    else System.err.println
                      ("Nothing read - nothing to
                        display!");
                }
            }
        }
});
// Action listener.for the SAVE selection
menuOneTwo.addActionListener(
      new ActionListener() {
          public void actionPerformed(ActionEvent e) {
              JFileChooser chooser = new JFileChooser();
              chooser.addChoosableFileFilter(
                  new MyFilter(".DAT"));
              int returnVal = chooser.showDialog
                 (UserInterfacePresentation.this,
                  "Save Candidate Objects");
              if(returnVal == JFileChooser.APPROVE_OPTION){
                  fileName =
                    chooser.getCurrentDirectory() +
                      java.io.File.separator +
                      chooser.getSelectedFile().
                        getName();

                  if (!fileName.toUpperCase().trim().
                    endsWith(".DAT"))
                      fileName += ".DAT";
                  if (ProgramLogic.writeFile(fileName,
                    candidates) == false)
                      System.err.println (
                          "Error saving file!");
              }
          }
      });
// Action listener.for the EXIT selection
menuOneThree.addActionListener(
      new ActionListener() {
          public void actionPerformed(ActionEvent e) {
              dispose();
              System.exit(0);
          }
      });
```

```java
        // Action listener.for the SAVE ELECTION selection
        menuTwoOne.addActionListener(
            new ActionListener() {
                public void actionPerformed(ActionEvent e) {
                    Election localElection = new Election();
                    localElection.electionIdentifier =
                        JOptionPane.showInputDialog
                            ("Name of Election");
                    localElection.electionDate =
                        JOptionPane.showInputDialog(
                            "Election Date");
                    localElection.candidates = candidates;
                    JFileChooser chooser = new JFileChooser();
                    chooser.addChoosableFileFilter(
                        new MyFilter(".ELE"));
                    int returnVal = chooser.showDialog
                        (UserInterfacePresentation.this,
                        "Save Election Information");
                    if(returnVal == JFileChooser.APPROVE_OPTION){
                        fileName = chooser.
                            getCurrentDirectory() +
                            java.io.File.separator +
                            chooser.getSelectedFile().getName();
                        if (!fileName.toUpperCase().trim().
                            endsWith(".ELE"))
                            fileName += ".ELE";
                        if (ProgramLogic.writeFile(fileName,
                            localElection) == false)
                            System.err.println (
                                "Error saving file!");
                    }
                }
            });

        menuOne.add (menuOneOne);
        menuOne.add (menuOneTwo);
        menuOne.addSeparator();
        menuOne.add (menuOneThree);
        menuTwo.add (menuTwoOne);
        menuBar.add (menuOne);
        menuBar.add (menuTwo);
        this.setJMenuBar(menuBar);

        pack();  // shrink window to miniminum size needed
        setVisible(true);  // make window visible
    }

    /**
     This method addComponent (Component component, int row,
     int column, int width, int height) simplifies
```

```
   populating a GridBagLayout-controlled container.
*/


private void addComponent (Container panel, Component component,
    GridBagLayout layout, GridBagConstraints constraints,
        int column,
    int row, int width, int height) {
     constraints.gridx = column;
     constraints.gridy = row;
     constraints.gridwidth = width;
     constraints.gridheight = height;
     layout.setConstraints (component, constraints);
     panel.add (component);
}

/**
 This method actionPerformed(ActionEvent guiEvent) handles
 user interaction events
*/

public void actionPerformed (ActionEvent guiEvent) {
     if (guiEvent.getActionCommand ().equals("Add")) {
     // determine origin of event
          Candidates localCandidate = new Candidates();
          boolean error = false;
          String errorMessage = "Input error(s): ";

          try {
               inputValid (firstNamePrompt.getText(),
                   "[A-Z][a-zA-Z]*");
          } catch (InputException ie) {
               errorMessage += "\nIncorrect Last Name Format!";
               firstNamePrompt.setText ("--- reenter ---");
               firstNamePrompt.selectAll();
               firstNamePrompt.requestFocus(true);
               error = true;
          }

          try {
               inputValid (middleNamePrompt.getText(),
                   "[A-Z][a-zA-Z]*");
          } catch (InputException ie) {
               errorMessage += "\nIncorrect Middle Name Format!";
               middleNamePrompt.setText ("--- reenter --- ");
               middleNamePrompt.selectAll();
               middleNamePrompt.requestFocus(true);
               error = true;
          }

          try {
               inputValid (lastNamePrompt.getText(),
                   "[A-Z][a-zA-Z]*");
```

```
            } catch (InputException ie) {
                errorMessage += "\nIncorrect Middle Name Format!
                    (Enter complete name.)";
                lastNamePrompt.setText ("--- reenter ---");
                lastNamePrompt.selectAll();
                lastNamePrompt.requestFocus(true);
                error = true;
            }
            try {
                inputValid (socialSNPrompt.getText(),
                    "\\d{3}\\-?\\d{2}\\-?\\d{4}");
                // SSN with or without hyphens
            } catch (InputException ie) {
                errorMessage += "\nIncorrect SSN Format!";
                socialSNPrompt.setText ("--- reenter ---");
                socialSNPrompt.selectAll();
                socialSNPrompt.requestFocus(true);
                error = true;
            }
            try {
                inputValid (dateOBPrompt.getText(),
    "(0[1-9]|1[012])[- /.](0[1-9]|[12][0-9]|3[01])[- /.](19|20)\\d\\d");
            } catch (InputException ie) {
                errorMessage += "\nIncorrect DOB Format!";
                dateOBPrompt.setText ("--- reenter ---");
                dateOBPrompt.selectAll();
                dateOBPrompt.requestFocus(true);
                error = true;
            }

            try {
                inputValid (address1Prompt.getText(), null);
            } catch (InputException ie) {
                errorMessage += "\nAddress1 empty!";
                address1Prompt.setText ("--- reenter ---");
                address1Prompt.selectAll();
                address1Prompt.requestFocus(true);
                error = true;
            }

            // address2 may be empty
            try {
                inputValid (cityPrompt.getText(),
                    "[A-Z][a-zA-Z].*");
                // may be multiple words
            } catch (InputException ie) {
                errorMessage += "\nIncorrect City Name Format!";
                cityPrompt.setText ("--- reenter ---");
                cityPrompt.selectAll();
```

```java
            cityPrompt.requestFocus(true);
            error = true;
    }
    try {
        inputValid (zipPrompt.getText(),
            "\\d{5}(-?\\d{4})?");
    } catch (InputException ie) {
        errorMessage += "\nIncorrect ZIP Code Format!";
        zipPrompt.setText ("--- reenter ---");
        zipPrompt.selectAll();
        zipPrompt.requestFocus(true);
        error = true;
    }

    try {
        inputValid (telNumberPrompt.getText(),
            "(\\d{3}-)?\\d{3}-\\d{4}");
    } catch (InputException ie) {
        errorMessage +=
            "\nIncorrect Telephone Number Format!";
        telNumberPrompt.setText ("--- reenter ---");
        telNumberPrompt.selectAll();
        telNumberPrompt.requestFocus(true);
        error = true;
    }

    try {
        localCandidate.votesReceived = Integer.parseInt
            (numberOfVotesPrompt.getText());
    } catch (NumberFormatException e) {
        // prompt to reenter
        errorMessage +=
            "\nNumber of votes must be a whole number!";
        numberOfVotesPrompt.setText("--- reenter ---");
        numberOfVotesPrompt.selectAll();
        numberOfVotesPrompt.requestFocus(true);
        error = true;
    }

    if (error)
        JOptionPane.showMessageDialog (null, errorMessage,
            "Candidate Information",
            JOptionPane.ERROR_MESSAGE);
    else {
        localCandidate.firstName =
            firstNamePrompt.getText();
        localCandidate.middleName =
            middleNamePrompt.getText();
        localCandidate.lastName =
          lastNamePrompt.getText();
```

```
localCandidate.dateOfBirth =
    dateOBPrompt.getText();
localCandidate.socialSN =
  socialSNPrompt.getText();
localCandidate.address1 =
  address1Prompt.getText();
localCandidate.address2 =
  address2Prompt.getText();
localCandidate.city = cityPrompt.getText();
localCandidate.zipCode = zipPrompt.getText();
localCandidate.state = stateSelected;
localCandidate.telNumber =
    telNumberPrompt.getText();
localCandidate.affiliation = partyAffiliation;

candidates.add(localCandidate);
// create Candidates arrayList element object
tableModel.insertRow(tableModel.getRowCount(),
new Object[]{localCandidate.firstName + " " +
localCandidate.lastName,
localCandidate.affiliation.getPartyAffiliation (),
String.valueOf(localCandidate.votesReceived)});
// reinitialize input fields
firstNamePrompt.setText
    ("... enter first name ...");
middleNamePrompt.setText
    ("... enter middle name ...");
lastNamePrompt.setText("... enter last name ...");
dateOBPrompt.setText("... enter xx/yy/zzzz ...");
socialSNPrompt.setText("... enter SSN ...");
address1Prompt.setText("... line 1 ...");
address2Prompt.setText("... line 2 ...");
cityPrompt.setText("... enter city name ...");
stateList.setSelectedIndex (0);
zipPrompt.setText("... enter ZIP code ...");
telNumberPrompt.setText
    ("...enter xxx-yyy-zzzz ..");
numberOfVotesPrompt.setText
    ("... enter number of votes received ...");
firstNamePrompt.selectAll();
middleNamePrompt.selectAll();
lastNamePrompt.selectAll();
dateOBPrompt.selectAll();
socialSNPrompt.selectAll();
address1Prompt.selectAll();
address2Prompt.selectAll();
cityPrompt.selectAll();
zipPrompt.selectAll();
telNumberPrompt.selectAll();
numberOfVotesPrompt.selectAll();
```

```
                    firstNamePrompt.requestFocus();
                    numberOfVotesPrompt.selectAll();
            }
        }


        else if (guiEvent.getActionCommand().equals
            ("Determine Winner")) {
        // determine origin of event
            // Display results
            Candidates winner =
              ProgramLogic.determineElectionWinner
                (candidates);
            if (winner != null) {
                for (int counter = 0; counter < displayTable.
                    getRowCount(); counter++) {
                    if (((String)(tableModel.getValueAt
                        (counter,0))).
                        compareTo (winner.firstName + " " +
                        winner.lastName) == 0){
                        tableModel.setValueAt("***",counter,3);
                        JOptionPane.showMessageDialog (null,
                            "The winner is " + winner.
                              firstName +
                            " " + winner.lastName + " with " +
                            winner.votesReceived + "!");
                    }
                }
            }
        }


        else if (guiEvent.getActionCommand().equals("Exit")) {
            System.out.println("\nThank you and good bye!\n");
            System.exit(0); // terminate program normally
        }
    }

void inputValid (String checkString, String pattern) throws
    InputException {
    if (checkString.equals("") || checkString.equals
        ("--- reenter ---"))
        throw new InputException();
    else if ((pattern != null) &&
        (!checkString.matches (pattern)))
        throw new InputException();
}

/** The inner class InputException sets up a throwable exception
  for handling input errors
*/
```

```
class InputException extends Exception {
/* declare new Exception class to capture bad user inputs ---
  for demonstration only */
}
/** The inner class MyFilter sets up the filter for JFileChooser
  to limit the display and selection to
  folders and .DAT files
*/

class MyFilter extends javax.swing.filechooser.FileFilter {
      private String extension;

      MyFilter (String ext) {
            extension = ext;
      }

      public boolean accept(File file) {
            return (file.isDirectory() ||
            file.getAbsolutePath().toUpperCase().
                  endsWith(extension));
      }

      public String getDescription() {
            return "*" + extension;
      }
   }
}
```

In this updated version, we have added input validation to ensure that user input follows proper formats. While the checking is limited (more sophisticated pattern matching is possible), it illustrates the basic concepts of input validation. A validation method, `inputValid()`, was created to centralize the pattern-matching process it accepts the `String` object as input to match and the pattern.

## 6.7    *Harm* 🌓 *ny* **Design Case Study**

In the ongoing case study of the *Harm* 🌓 *ny* **Designs** information technology project, we examine the integration issues associated with the implementation of the solution you have been developing over the last few chapters. Most small businesses—and HarmonyDesigns is no exception—already use certain computer products, hardware, software, and networking. HarmonyDesigns has the following existing infrastructure:

- Hardware
  - Seven personal computers, one server, all recent-generation Intel Pentiums
  - 60 GB disk storage on the PCs
  - CD-ROM readers/writers on all PCs
  - 600 GB of RAID storage on the server (server also has a helical-scan tape unit for backup)

- TFT flat-screen monitors (17-inch) for all PC workstations
- Two laser printers
- Three ink-jet printers, including one for large-format printing
- One scanner, three digital cameras
- Software
  - Windows XP operating system on all PCs
  - Windows Server operating system on the server
  - Microsoft Office Professional on all PCs
  - Adobe Photoshop on all PCs
  - Intuit Quickbooks on two PCs
  - Legacy application developed custom by a local vendor to track and manage installation projects
  - All important data files are maintained on the server
- Network
  - Local Area Network set up in the office (100 mbps)
  - Business DSL—all PCs connected to the Internet at broadband speeds

This simple infrastructure is expected to be used with your new application. Your client expects to migrate the server to Linux in order to "open up" the environment. You need to formulate a plan to integrate your components and functions with the client's existing environment; this should include the server migration to Linux. You need to set up an Integration Test to ensure that all components interoperate, and you need to track the results of this testing in an Integration Test Report.

## 6.8 Resources: Connections • People • Companies

The agile programming techniques discussed in this chapter are most extensively associated with Kent Beck. The "Gang of Four" (Gamma, Helm, Johnson, and Vlissides) is credited with the seminal work on the Design Pattern concept, or, more accurately, with its application to software engineering. Martin Fowler is prominently associated with the concept of refactoring.

## 6.9 Summary and Recommendations

While novice programmers need to learn and understand every aspect of a software-development life-cycle methodology like the Extended Unified Process, experienced software engineers often apply optimizations to their projects, generally referred to as agile programming, which allow them to maximize the iterative, hands-on activities of the process and reduce the formality and documentation requirements associated with the full life-cycle approach. Agile programming techniques replace the relative formality of the original Unified Process with extended prototyping and iterative improvements. This approach requires advanced skills as well as active stakeholder involvement, but it keeps the project flexible and adaptable as long as firm project-management discipline is applied throughout.

A number of concepts intrinsic to agile programming are of general benefit to the discipline of software engineering:

- Frequent builds—if possible, daily generation of a running version of the emerging product
- Extensive inspection and testing discipline
- Collaborative design and development; extensive stakeholder involvement
- Iterative improvement (refactoring)
- Careful project management—management of tight deadlines

Variations to the accepted object-oriented software engineering processes emerge regularly. Some are mere blips on the long-term horizon of computer software development; others gradually become mainstays of advanced software design and programming. It is therefore important for engineers in our discipline, as in all engineering branches, to remain informed about new developments and intelligently choose which ones to incorporate into their daily practice.

## 6.10    Review Questions

1. **Unified Process Alternatives.** When may it be justifiable to forgo some aspects of the Unified Process?
2. **Inherent Risks.** What are some of the inherent risks in forgoing some aspects of the Unified Process?
3. **Agile Programming.** Research and describe examples of agile programming techniques.
4. **Design Patterns.** Find an example of a software design pattern and describe how you would apply it to the **Harmony Design** project.
5. **Pattern Matching.** Research the pattern-matching algorithm and the associated grammar; identify the differences (if any) between languages (at least Perl and Java). Show three examples of useful patterns for typical inputs in regular business applications.
6. **Files and Persistence.** Research the New I/O APIs available in the Java Platform since J2SE Release 1.4 (`java.nio` package). Describe their features and compare to the existing file I/O functions. Show a simple example.

## 6.11    Glossary – Terminology – Concepts

**Agile Method**    Unified Process-based techniques that accelerate the traditional development process, in part through intense customer involvement.

**Integration Testing**    Formal testing phase where the interplay of the components constituting the software solution is validated; also tested are the interfaces between the solution and third-party products/components.

**Rapid Application Development**    Shortcut methods for developing software in an iterative fashion.

**Real World**    In contrast to the academic world, refers to profit or non-profit organizations that develop software for monetary and/or organizational value.

## 6.12    Exercises

**1. Agile Methods.**    Research agile methods by reviewing a modern book on the topic (e.g., Beck). Write a two-page summary of the key concepts.

**2. Integration Testing.**    Develop five Integration Test scripts for the Voting Program. Include positive and negative testing.

**3. Integration Testing.**    Develop five Integration Test scripts for the Voting Program. Include positive and negative testing.

**4. Validation.**    Enhance the Voting Program to make the validation more complete and foolproof. Start by identifying all the possible errors and the extent of variations of formats. Then create validation code enhancements to check for all the exceptions you have identified.

C H A P T E R   7

# Interfacing with Users

You have now begun to understand and embrace the project requirements analysis and feature design activities associated with developing high-quality Java software, and have embarked on actual code-development activities. Moving steadily forward, you need to expand your skills in Java and improve your conceptual understanding of this valuable computer language. This chapter explores the development of more sophisticated client programs, with a focus on user access and interface functions, techniques, components, and guidelines. While the functionality of a program—its business rules, algorithms, and information provided—may be the primary determinant of its value, the user's ability to access this functionality efficiently, comfortably, and consistently is a major factor determining how useful and easy to navigate the program will be.

## 7.1    Learning Objectives

Sun Microsystems has invested much effort in the Java programming language, as have other firms in extensions of Java, to enable user interaction with Java applications across the full range of graphical, interactive, and multi-media capabilities available from modern computer operating environments without sacrificing Java's high-level platform and technology independence. This chapter explores the user interface functions in Java, based on the original Abstract Window Toolkit, awt, but implemented most usefully in the Java 2 extensions referred to as javax.swing. Together, these libraries provide (relatively) easy-to-implement, powerful access to a wide range of event-driven user interface components germane to Windows operating environments like Microsoft Windows, UNIX Motif/X-Windows, and Mac O.S.

But before covering the Java user interface components that allow software engineers to implement highly usable graphical applications, we will first discuss the development-methodology considerations for user interface design and development.

### 7.1.1  *User Interface Requirements*

It is tempting for programmers developing graphical applications to first design screens and forms, and then figure out the algorithms associated with the graphical user interface components. However, this is not usually a very productive approach, because the value of the program resides in its functionality, not its interface.

In fact, the Software engineering Best Practice is to design the program user interface *after* the functional components have been determined from a work-process perspective. Productivity improvement does not come from the user interface, it comes from the application of computer technology to work optimization, often by automating repetitive work steps or by improving the quality of a work process by eliminating redundancy and sources of errors.

---

### WORKFLOW

In the 1980s and 1990s, a discipline called **Business Process Reengineering** **(BPR)** emerged. Its goal is to critically examine important workflows in organizations and seek ways to dramatically improve their efficiency. A workflow represents the discrete steps of activity required to accomplish a particular valuable task. Sometimes computer technology can be applied to improve a workflow, usually by automating some of the often-repeated steps or by applying the accuracy and predictability of computation to heretofore imprecise activities.

---

Too many modern graphical applications are poorly designed and developed "from the GUI down," often based on a misunderstood "prototyping" approach. This leads to user interface components (buttons, menus, lists, fields, etc.) populating windows without adequate attention to implementing improved work processes. While this approach may seem to work at first, at least from the programmer's viewpoint, and leads to "pretty forms," it rarely results in an optimal implementation. This is a consequence of the difficulty, if not impossibility, of achieving the primary goal of improving the productivity of the work process being automated from the vantage point of the user interface. When the design of program functions is based on a user interface prototype, the software often ends up with an excessive number and complexity of user interaction screens and artifacts, because the actual workflow was not properly considered. Figure 7.1 illustrates the two approaches to functional design: the undesirable "top-down" approach, and the recommended "bottom-up" approach.

In other words, the designer needs to first translate the requirements from the use case scenarios into software logic that implements optimized business rules and work process functions, and second develop an appropriate user interface to these

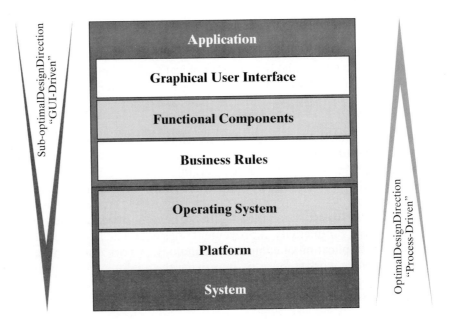

FIGURE 7.1   GUI Design Perspectives

functions. Users need to interface directly and intuitively with the tasks to be completed, instead of having to be excessively aware of the software interface per se. This approach results in a software solution optimized for human use in the context of actual work activities and requirements.

### 7.1.2   *User Interface Design Best Practices*

There are a number of simple rules that software user interface designers should follow in order to ensure that users (end-users and administrators) find interaction with their programs intuitive and familiar:

- Use industry and de facto standards where available. If a program is written for a particular platform, then favor the accepted visualization standards for that platform; otherwise either provide an adaptable graphical user interface (GUI) or use a platform-neutral GUI like Sun's METAL look-and-feel.
- Use familiar, consistently named user interface artifacts; examples: "OK" and "Cancel" buttons with proper shortcuts and organized with correct tab sequences (see Fig. 7.2); consistent menu layouts and menu selections with familiar, consistent shortcuts; tooltips for each artifact; well-organized, naturally sequenced display and interaction components.

FIGURE 7.2   Typical OK-Cancel-Help Button Arrangement

- Activate only logically usable elements—inactivate components that should logically not be accessible, given the sequence of the workflow in process. Inactivation may be implemented as graying out or simply not showing the user an interface component that has no function in the current context.
- Provide context-specific online help for all interactions, components, and functions. Implement function key F1 to access the program Help function and Shift-F1 to change the cursor to a question mark for context-specific help queries.
- Use GUI artifacts conservatively: avoid font changes, colors, icons, and images, unless there is a clear, justifiable purpose for overriding the default look and behaviors. Use the available screen "real estate" sparingly; don't waste space, but organize artifacts logically and consistently according to their work-process function and sequence.
- Avoid cluttering containers; include no more than seven elements in a single container whenever possible ("Miller's law"); use labeled containers (frames) to group related GUI elements.
- Ensure that all GUI components can be localized for other languages and cultures. Account for differences in script direction in certain languages, if necessary.

Adherence to these guidelines helps ensure that the user interface supports the delivery of your program's functions instead of impeding user access.

### 7.1.3  *Java Graphical User Interface Programming*

The architecture of a graphical user interface application is fundamentally different from a character-based application. In the latter, there is a single entry point, the `main()` method, from which all subsequent functionality and interaction flows; in the former, `main()` is the entry point for the initialization phase of the GUI, but `actionPerformed()` (or a similar method) is the entry point to deal with user interactions with GUI components. We refer to this as the event-handling model, because it participates in the Windows metaphor of responding to events (often user interactions) as messages. The connections between these two distinct execution phases are `ActionListener` objects associated with graphical components that expect to be subject to user interaction.

### 7.1.4  *Learning Layout*

This recurring section shows the learning objectives of the chapter in a simple diagram using the Unitied Modeling Language (UML) activity diagram notation. This diagram (see Fig. 7.3) shows the student learning expectations for the chapter. The focus of this chapter is on learning about Java user interface design and development, within the context of software engineering Best Practices.

### 7.1.5  *Learning Connections*

The Learning Connections diagram in Figure 7.4 shows the content of this chapter in relation to the knowledge and skills development recommended for apprentice Java software engineers.

What this view does not capture directly is the need for professionals, and especially software specialists, to keep up with new developments in their field. For example, recent

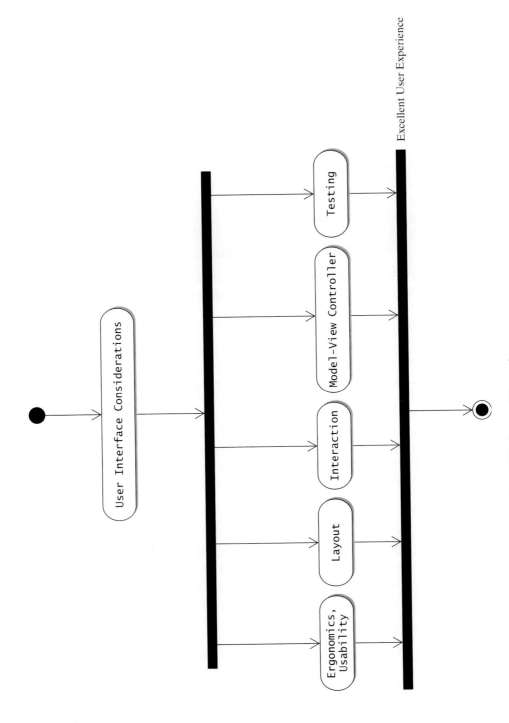

FIGURE 7.3   Chapter 7 Learning Layout (as a UML Activity Diagram)

Table Of Contents

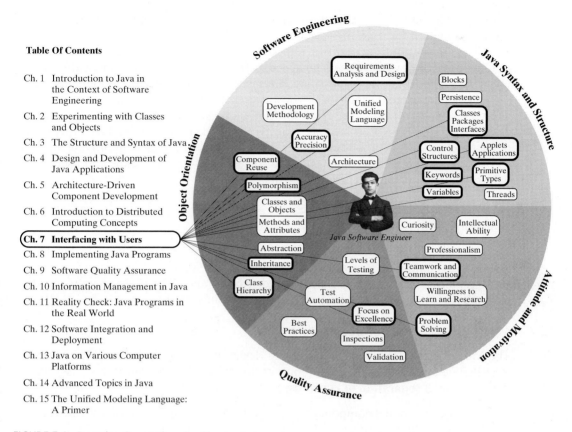

FIGURE 7.4   Learning Connections for Chapter 7

versions of the Java Software Development Kit introduce new file input-output functions (**NIO**) among other enhancements. A new user interface tool called **Java Server Faces** (**JSF**) is available to simplify the development of distributed application clients. By the time you read this book, other new developments are sure to have emerged.

## 7.2    Executive Summary

Java provides a broad range of advanced capabilities to interface human users and their Java software applications. Java 2 augments the graphical user interface features of Java 1.1 (essentially `awt`) with the `swing` library and the lightweight J classes.

   Providing human access to graphical applications involves two key areas of functionality: the initial set-up of the graphical environment, typically using a main or root window containing graphical display and interaction elements, such as panels, buttons, text fields, and list boxes, and the handling of interaction events (which may include the creation of other windows and the subsequent handling of events occurring in them). Technologies are only as good as their application: effective user access to all the application's functions depends fundamentally on effective user interface design. Developing a high-quality user interface is part art, part engineering, and part aesthetics.

A good understanding of cognition, industrial design, and software ergonomics is a useful foundation for user interface design.

The user interface of a software application should provide efficient user access to its functions from a work-process perspective. In other words, the user interface exists to effectively support the work functions. This means that an application should not be designed from the user interface forms "downward," but from the program's key functional requirements "upward" (see Fig. 7.1). The functional code (business rules) should be designed first, and the user interface (forms) should be based on the most efficient use of the functions by the end-user(s) with the goal of accelerating and improving the quality of the work process. An effort should also be made to minimize the end-users' manual work and opportunities for input errors.

## 7.3 Learning Modules

The following sections describe the key concepts of this chapter, focused on developing your understanding of how to "connect" your application and its users. The various Java graphical user interface classes are discussed, and their application to meeting particular user requirements and expectation are illustrated.

### 7.3.1 Model-View Controller Design Pattern

The Model-View Controller architectural design pattern is a well-established design Best Practice governing the distribution of functionality for applications according to the principle of **separation of concerns**:

- *Model:* the model component of the pattern represents the business rules and algorithms, the core functional components
- *View:* the view component provides the user interface and interaction
- *Controller:* the controller component governs the program navigation functions

Separating an application according to these three major components allows for a modular, flexible approach to implementation and enhancement. If a new client interface must be supported (e.g., a mobile telephone client), this can be done with no or only minor impact to the other components. If new functions are added to the model, their support in the other components would follow the established pattern of communications between the components, making the product reasonably extensible and flexible.

### 7.3.2 User Interface Design Principles

Inexperienced programmers often want to design and develop what they think of as "creative" user interfaces, using unique colors, font sizes and weights, and other graphical artifacts to "personalize" the application's graphical user interface, or GUI. Most often, these efforts fail, because the best GUI design almost always involves the conservative use of familiar components and features (see Fig. 7.5). The default colors, fonts, and graphical components and layouts are the best elements to use in most normal situations, not only because users are familiar with them from other applications, but also because the customization of a GUI should occur at the system level, where users can set window look-and-feel schemes based on their personal needs and preferences,

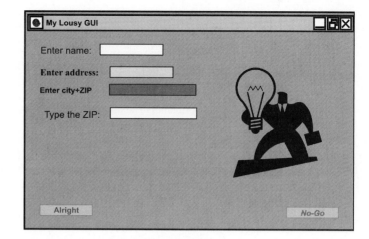

**FIGURE 7.5**   Example of BAD GUI Design

instead of having font sizes and types and colors imposed on them by the software developer. In addition, non-standard fonts and other graphical artifacts may not be available on the destination systems for which the application is targeted.

Table 7.1 provides an overview of other graphical user interface guidelines. This list is non-exhaustive and cursory, because the topic of graphical user interface design is treated in detail in other publications.

**TABLE 7.1**   Basic GUI Design Guidelines

| Stakeholder Requirement | GUI Design | Caveats |
|---|---|---|
| Authentication | • Modal dialog which forces the entry of a valid user id and password before access to program functions (and data) is allowed | • Provide convenient exit for users who cannot remember their user id/ password<br>• Provide easy access to register new users, if appropriate, so that they can continue authentication after registration without delay |
| Entering input data about a particular task | • Process-driven input forms—logical navigation—emphasis on default sequence<br>• 5–7 controls maximum per container<br>• Labeled frames and labeled controls Menu- and control access to key functions<br>• Efficient, smart error handling—error avoidance | • Special attention must be paid to represent the most efficient workflow possible in the user interface artifact and input sequences<br>• Input fields and controls should minimize user error |
| Extracting information from data to obtain new knowledge or make better decisions | • Minimize user intervention required to complete processing—automate process as much as possible, including flexibility todeal with variations | • Avoid over-involving the user in decisions and activities the computer should handle, perhaps after initial defaults are set by an administrator |

*(Continued)*

TABLE 7.1    *(Continued)*

| Stakeholder Requirement | GUI Design | Caveats |
|---|---|---|
| | • Automate the knowledge extraction process as much as possible but give the user easy-to-access opportunities to adjust the process and its associated rules<br>• Include the ability to dynamically reconfigure defaults | • Remember related past operations, allowing your program to be as "smart" as possible—avoid the user having to manually duplicate repetitive processes |
| Obtaining output information in table form | • Display only the information the user needs<br>• Provide flexible variations/reconfiguration of the output and of the columns/rows selected<br>• Allow for flexible report generation, if possible using standard report program as plug-ins (e.g., CrystalReports™ or the like)<br>• Provide export in standard file/data formats for use of information by other programs | • Avoid a "standard" template which leaves it up to the user to extract relevant information |

The topic of user interface design has been intensely discussed ever since graphical user interfaces became available on general-purpose computers. Many excellent books have been written by specialists who have made it their career mission to help software engineers improve the interaction of programs with human users. A few recommended authors and their books are:

M. H. Ashcraft, *Fundamentals of Cognition.* Addison-Wesley, New York, 1998.

R. W. Bailey, *Human Performance Engineering: Designing High Quality Professional User Interfaces for Computer Products, Applications, and Systems,* 3rd ed. Prentice-Hall, Upper Saddle River, NJ, 1996.

P. Bauersfeld, *Software by Design: Creating People Friendly Software.* M&T Books: New York, 1994.

N. S. Borenstein, *Programming as If People Mattered: Friendly Programs, Software Engineering, and Other Noble Delusions.* Princeton University Press, Princeton, NJ, 1991.

S. Fowler, *GUI Design Handbook.* McGraw-Hill, New York, 1998.

S. L. Fowler and V. R. Stanwick, *The GUI Style Guide.* AP Professional, Boston, 1995.

L. Macaulay, *Human-Computer Interaction for Software Designers.* International Thomson Computer Press, London, 1995.

A. Marcus, N. Smilonich, and L. Thompson, *The Cross-GUI Handbook for Multiplatform User Interface Design.* Addison-Wesley, Reading, MA, 1995.

D. Norman, *The Design of Everyday Things.* Doubleday, New York, 1990.

B. Shneiderman, *Designing the User Interface: Strategies for Human-Computer Interaction,* (3rd ed.). Addison-Wesley, Reading, MA, 1998.

C. D. Wickens, S. E. Gordon, and Y. Liu, *An Introduction to Human Factors Engineering*. Addison-Wesley (Longman imprint), New York, 1998.

C. Zetie, *Practical User Interface Design: Making GUIs Work*. McGraw-Hill, London, 1995.

### 7.3.3  *Java User Interface Components*

The vast majority of modern software applications interface with the user via a graphical user interface (GUI). This means that the user's interaction with the software follows an *event-driven model*. In such a model (see Fig. 7.6), an application typically has two main entry points: the start-up entry point (which is the **main()** method in a standalone Java application) and the event-handling entry point (e.g., the **actionPerformed()** method in the **ActionListener** object associated with the control that captured the user interaction being processed). The user interface components are set up when the program first starts running, including appropriate window (e.g., **JFrame**) and GUI (e.g., **JList**, **JButton**) objects. The program then comes to a logical stop, awaiting user interaction with GUI components set up with a "listener" object (data structure) to intercept such inputs. When the interaction occurs, the event-handling object associated with the object receiving the interaction is invoked to react to the user interaction as programmed. The event handler's responsibility is to start the code that executes in response to the user's interaction with the GUI. This is the reason why the **ActionListener** object implements an interface: the application programmer has to provide the logic for handling the action, and only the method signature is needed to provide an entry point for the event-handling program flow.

The following sections discuss in more detail the GUI libraries of classes available to build an easily accessed, interactive user interface in a typical Java application. The most

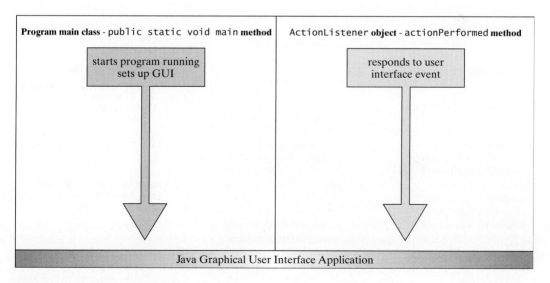

FIGURE 7.6  Java GUI Application Architecture

recent major version of Java extends the initial basic GUI capabilities in the language with a rich set of lightweight, platform-independent components, **javax.swing**, that equip Java with a powerful, easy-to-implement, and very flexible toolset for GUI application development. The benefit of these classes is that all this existing functionality can be imported into new applications, making high-level interfaces available to the programmer. This saves much time and effort making it unnecessary to reimplement these powerful GUI functions.

### awt *Library*

The **awt** library, available in Java 1, contains the core components for creating user interfaces and displaying graphics and images. Some components are for display purposes only, such as labels, and others are interactive. This means that they generate events when activated by the user. **AWTEvent** is the parent class for all possible **awt** events. **awt** also includes the Container class, which provides a receptacle for other **awt** components, including layout managers, which help position components in a graphical environment.

The main **awt** classes categories are listed in Table 7.2. Of necessity, the table only lists some examples of **awt** classes and their associated methods and attributes. The Sun Microsystems Java Tutorial™ covers the functionality of the **awt** library components in detail.

### swing *Library*

In Java 2, Sun Microsystems has added a powerful package of advanced GUI components collectively known as **swing** components. These components (easily identified,

TABLE 7.2   awt Classes

| Component | Purpose | Example |
|---|---|---|
| Layout managers (borders, gridbags, cards, etc.) | Set up the layout of GUI components in relative positions in a window | `Container c;`<br>`c = getContentPane ();`<br>`c.setLayout`<br>` (new GridBagLayout());` |
| Interface components (buttons, textfields, checkboxes, lists, menubars, scrollbars, etc.) | Provide display and interaction graphical 2-D and 3-D metaphorical representations of familiar devices, and lists, buttons, and checkboxes. | `c.add (new JButton ("OK"));`<br><br>`JTextField promptForAnswer =`<br>` new JTextField`<br>` ("-Enter Name-");` |
| Windowing components (windows, frames, dialogs, containers, components, etc.) | Provide graphically enabled containers to host GUI components | `Class MyClass extends JFrame` |
| Graphics components (graphics, canvas, fonts, rectangles, colors, images, cursors, etc.) | Provide GUI components with color, text, and graphics capabilities that allow for a wide range of interactive behaviors and looks | `PromptForAnswer.setFont`<br>` (new Font("Helvetica",`<br>` Font.BOLD, 24));` |
| Output components (printjobs, page attributes, etc.) | Support the creation of output | `PrinterJob printJob =`<br>` PrinterJob.getPrinterJob();` |

because they all start with a "**J**," as in **JRadioButton**, **JLabel**, and **JPanel**) were introduced in Chapter 3 of this book. The majority of these components are "lightweight," meaning that they do not directly interface with underlying operating system calls, and are implemented entirely in Java, making them independent of the underlying operating environment and improving the portability of the resulting application. They extend the core **awt** graphical components. These graphical components provide the typical application with a way to interface with users using the dominant "Windows Look-and-Feel."[1]

In fact, with **swing**, it is possible to change the look-and-feel of an application dynamically. The following short program demonstrates this ability.

```java
/*
 *  @ (#) DynamicLandF.java 1.0 02/12/01
 *
 * Sample application, which shows how to reset the look and
 * feel dynamically.
 */

import java.awt.*;
import java.awt.event.*;
import javax.swing.*;

class DynamicLandF extends JFrame {
    int switchGUI = 0;  // 0 = Metal; 1 = Windows; 2 = UNIX

    public DynamicLandF (String title) { // constructor
        super (title);
        addWindowListener(new WindowAdapter() {
            public void windowClosing(WindowEvent e) {
                System.out.println ("Ending DynamicLandF...");
                dispose();
                System.exit(0);
            }
        });

        Container c = getContentPane ();
        c.setLayout (new FlowLayout());
        c.add (new JLabel ("Enter your name: "));
        JTextField textF = new JTextField (20);
        c.add (textF);
        JButton switchButton = new JButton ("Switch GUI");
        c.add (switchButton);
        switchButton.addActionListener(new ButtonActionListener());

        setSize (400, 100);
        setVisible (true);
    }
```

---

[1]Microsoft Windows, OSF/Motif-X-Windows, Mac O.S., etc.

```java
public static void main(String args[]) {
    System.out.println ("Starting DynamicLandF...");
    DynamicLandF mainFrame = new DynamicLandF
        ("Dynamic Look and Feel Example");
}

final class ButtonActionListener implements ActionListener {
    public void actionPerformed (ActionEvent event) {
    /* change the window layout dynamically, cycling through the
    Java Metal look and feel, the Windows look and feel, and the
    UNIX/Motif look and feel */

        try {
            if (switchGUI == 0) {
                UIManager.setLookAndFeel
            (UIManager.getCrossPlatformLookAndFeelClassName());
                switchGUI++;
            }

            else if (switchGUI == 1) {
                UIManager.setLookAndFeel
            ("com.sun.java.swing.plaf.windows.
              WindowsLookAndFeel");
                switchGUI++;
            }

            else if (switchGUI == 2) {
                UIManager.setLookAndFeel
            ("com.sun.java.swing.plaf.motif. MotifLookAndFeel");
                switchGUI = 0;
            }

            Component c = (Component) event.getSource();
            // get the source of the event
            Component frame = swingUtilities.getRoot();
            // get the parent window
            swingUtilities.updateComponentTreeUI(frame);
            // reset the layout
        } catch (Exception e) {}
    }
}
}
```

The preceding short demonstration program provides a button to switch dynamically between window styles. The screenshots in Figures 7.7, 7.8, and 7.9 show the result of pressing the button marked "Switch GUI." The first window shows the native Java look-and-feel called "Metal." The second window shows the Microsoft Windows look-and-feel,

FIGURE 7.7 Java Native Metal Look-and-Feel

FIGURE 7.8 Microsoft Windows Look-and-Feel

FIGURE 7.9 UNIX/Motif Look-and-Feel

and the third window shows the UNIX/Motif look-and-feel, originally developed by the Open Systems Foundation (OSF), in accordance with IBM System Application Architecture (SAA) standards.

This flexibility further adds to Java's portability of applications across platforms, especially since another method, UIManager.getSystemLookAndFeelClassName(), retrieves the look-and-feel of the current operating platform and thus allows the programmer to let the program dynamically set its look-and-feel according to the platform on which it is currently running. In this way, users interact with the native look-and-feel even though the application did not have to be written specifically for their system environment.

### swing Components

The **swing** components provided by Sun Microsystems deliver a rich collection of metaphors through which users can easily and efficiently interact with and control application functionality. Implementing these components requires only limited knowledge of their inner working because they provide high-level methods and attributes for programmatic control. The **J**-components enable Java software engineers to construct a broad, flexible range of user interface features without dependency on a particular windowing system, such as windows, buttons, drop-down lists, menus, checkboxes, on tables.

Hierarchically, the swing components are children of the swing **JComponent** class and (grand-)children of the Abstract Window Toolkit (AWT) **awt** library. The typical ancestry of a swing component is shown in Figure 7.10.

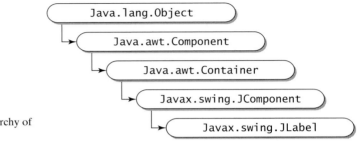

FIGURE 7.10   Class Hierarchy of swing Component JLabel

This class configuration provides a rich inheritance infrastructure that, not only ensures efficient processing of GUI elements, but also provides excellent consistency from component to component. It isolates the application programmer from the complexities of graphics implementation while providing the full range of relevant functionality to develop a rich graphical interaction between the user and the program.

The swing components can be categorized into three groupings:

- Containers, like **JPanel**, **JFrame**
- Display elements, like **JLabel**
- Interactive elements, like **JButtons**, **JTextFields**, and **JTables**

### 7.3.4   Containers

The two main types of containers are top-level container classes like **JFrame**, JDialog, and **JApplet**, and the underlying containment hierarchy, accessible via the container's content pane (see Fig. 7.11), or a container created explicitly by the programmer, such as a **JPanel**. Containers are used to hold other display and interactive components, in logical groupings. Containers are descendants of the **awt Container** class. They provide the graphical background for labels, buttons, text areas, drop-down lists, and the like, thereby allowing users to interact with the program's functions and view its outputs.

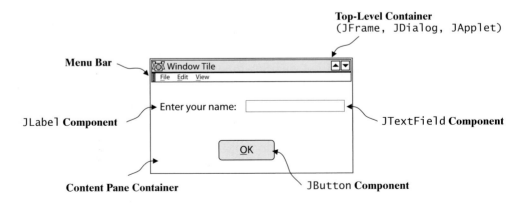

FIGURE 7.11   Container Hierarchy

**JDialog** objects can be modal or modeless dialog boxes. A modal dialog prevents input into any other part of the application; a modeless dialog allows such input while it is up. Dialog boxes are pop-up windows that allow for specific user prompting or input.

With containers, we have the ability to associate layouts, using layout managers. Layouts allow us to control the organization of user interface components; they are described in more detail in the next paragraphs.

### 7.3.5   *Layout Managers*

Because Java supports multiple platforms without requiring the recompilation of source code when an application is moved to a platform different from where it originated, the layout of user interface components has to be more flexible than in a platform-specific development language. Different computer platforms use different coordinate systems or handle windows and fonts in slightly different ways, so Java implements a relative-positioning metaphor in its layout managers that helps to circumvent these differences between platforms. Java layout managers provide for the logical grouping of components, depending on the intended functional layout. The following layout managers are among those available:[2]

- **Flow** layout
- **Border** layout
- **Box** layout
- **Card** layout
- **Grid** layout
- **GridBag** layout

It is also possible to develop custom layout managers or to use absolute positioning if you do not expect any changes related to platform or GUI look-and-feel. This is ***not*** a recommended practice for general-purpose applications. Absolute positioning is set up as follows:

```
Container c = getContentPane();

c.setLayout(null); // -> absolute position
```

Absolute positioning negates the benefits of platform portability in terms of GUI adaptability. We will take a closer look at the standard layout managers next.

#### Flow *Layout*

The default layout manager is the flow layout. The flow layout causes the elements in the container to be aligned left to right, and top to bottom, based on space available. The images in Figure 7.12 show the repositioning of components ("reflowing") when the window is resized.

---

[2]These and others have been implemented by Sun Microsystems; additional layout managers are available from third parties.

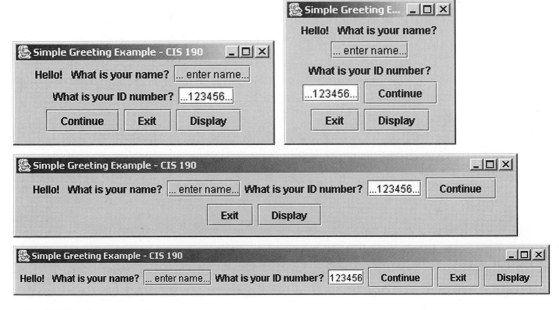

FIGURE 7.12 Flow Layout Example

A flow layout manager is associated with a container as follows:

```
Container c = getContentPane ();

c.setLayout (new FlowLayout());
```

These statements set the layout of a container to **FlowLayout**. Without this statement, all the controls will be superimposed in the center of the panel, resulting in an unacceptable graphical display.

While flow layout works fine for certain basic interfaces, more sophisticated control over GUI component positioning is usually desirable.

### Border *Layout*

The border layout provides a way to orient components in a panel according to geographic directions, *North, South, East,* and *West,* plus *Center.* The following program code excerpt shows an example of Border Layout, illustrated by the screenshot in Figure 7.13.

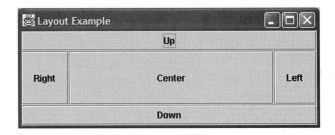

FIGURE 7.13 Border Layout Example

```
// excerpt
c.setLayout (new BorderLayout());
JButton jB1 = new JButton ("Up");
c.add (BorderLayout.NORTH, jB1);
JButton jB2 = new JButton ("Down");
c.add (BorderLayout.SOUTH, jB2);
JButton jB3 = new JButton ("Left");
c.add (BorderLayout.EAST, jB3);
JButton jB4 = new JButton ("Right");
c.add (BorderLayout.WEST, jB4);
JButton jB5 = new JButton ("Center");
c.add (BorderLayout.CENTER, jB5);
setSize(400, 160);
```

This example shows the distribution of buttons according to the directional parameters supported in the **Border** layout manager. This manager is useful for GUIs, which can be organized according to directional indicators.

### Box *Layout*

The **Box** layout manager provides a way to stack user interface components. As with most of the other layout managers described here, modifying methods and properties exist to specify fine-tuning alignment options. The following code snippet provides a simple example of this layout manager, illustrated in Figure 7.14. Component layout details can be further controlled with additional **Box** layout options.

```
// excerpt
Container c = getContentPane ();
c.setLayout (new BoxLayout(c, BoxLayout.Y_AXIS));
JButton jB1 = new JButton ("Button One");
c.add (jB1);
jB1.setAlignmentX(Component.CENTER_ALIGNMENT);
JButton jB2 = new JButton ("Button Two");
c.add (jB2);
jB2.setAlignmentX(Component.CENTER_ALIGNMENT);
```

### Card *Layout*

The **Card** layout manager provides a way to organize GUI panels like a deck of cards through which a user can cycle. The following code fragment and the screenshots in Figure 7.14 illustrate this capability.

FIGURE 7.14   Box Layout Example

FIGURE 7.14   Card Layout Screen Shots - Cycling
Through Card Layers

```
// excerpt
public static void main(String args[]) {
    final LayoutExample mainFrame;
    final CardLayout cLayout;

    System.out.println("Starting LayoutExample...");
    mainFrame = new LayoutExample();
    cLayout = new CardLayout ();
      mainFrame.getContentPane().setLayout
        (cLayout);
    JButton jB1 = new JButton ("Button One");
    mainFrame.getContentPane().add ("First Button", jB1);
    JButton jB2 = new JButton ("Button Two");
    mainFrame.getContentPane().add ("Second Button", jB2);
    ActionListener listener = new ActionListener() {
        public void actionPerformed(ActionEvent e) {
            cLayout.next(mainFrame.getContentPane());
        }
    };

    jB1.addActionListener(listener);
    jB2.addActionListener(listener);
    mainFrame.setSize(140, 80);
    mainFrame.setTitle("Layout Example");
    mainFrame.setVisible(true);
}
```

### Grid *Layout*

The **Grid** layout manager provides a way to organize GUI components in a table format with rows and columns (a "grid"). An example screenshot is shown in Figure 7.15.

### GridBag *Layout*

The **GridBag** layout manager is a more flexible version of the **Grid** layout that provides
flexible row and column sizes and internal and external offsets. The **GridBag** layout allows

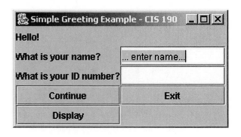

FIGURE 7.15   Grid Layout Example

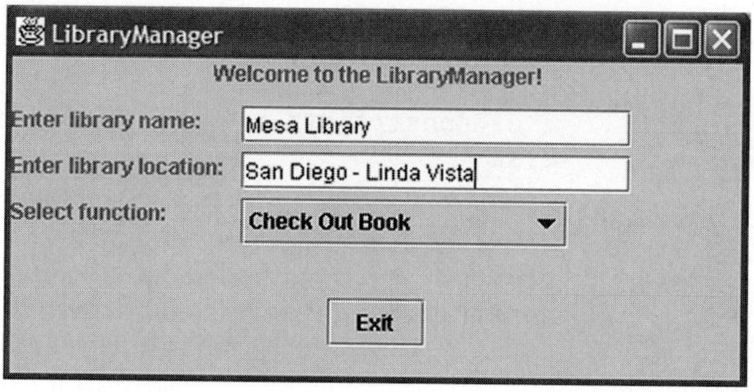

FIGURE 7.16   *GridBag Layout Example*

for the positioning of cell elements in rows and columns of variable heights and widths (see Fig. 7.16). This layout manager provides fourteen separate parameters to adjust the positioning of elements:

- **gridx**—specifies the cell containing the leading edge of the component
- **gridy**—specifies the cell at the top of the component
- **gridwidth**—specifies the number of cells in a row
- **gridheight**—specifies the number of cells in a column
- **weightx**—specifies how to distribute extra horizontal space
- **weighty**—specifies how to distribute extra vertical space
  - **anchor**—determines where to place the component: the absolute values are **CENTER, NORTH, NORTHEAST, EAST, SOUTHEAST, SOUTH, SOUTHWEST, WEST, NORTHWEST**; the relative values are: **PAGE_START, PAGE_END, LINE_START, LINE_END, FIRST_LINE_START, FIRST_LINE_END, LAST_LINE_START, LAST_LINE_END**; the default value is **CENTER**
- **fill**—determines whether to resize the component, and if so, how: **NONE, HORIZONTAL, VERTICAL, BOTH**
- **insets** (**top, left, bottom, right**)—the space a container must leave at each of its edges
- **ipadx**—specifies the internal padding of the component in the horizontal direction
- **ipady**—specifies the internal padding of the component in the vertical direction

The following simple methods, implemented in our Library Manager example, can be used to set the GridBag layout parameters. They are logically separated into three methods because it may be necessary to only set a subset of parameters for a particular look-and-feel and accept the defaults for the remaining parameters.

```
//excerpt
/* The following method sets the location constraints for a control */
public void setLocation (int x, int y, int width, int height,
    String fill) {

    if (fill.equals ("NONE") == true)
        constraints.fill = GridBagConstraints.NONE;
```

```
    else if (fill.equals ("VERTICAL") == true)
        constraints.fill = GridBagConstraints.VERTICAL;
    else if (fill.equals ("HORIZONTAL") == true)
        constraints.fill = GridBagConstraints.HORIZONTAL;
    else
        constraints.fill = GridBagConstraints.BOTH;

    constraints.gridx = x;
    constraints.gridy = y;
    constraints.gridwidth = width;
    constraints.gridheight = height;
}

/* The following method sets the directional placement constraints
   for a control */

void setPlacement (double x, double y, String anchor) {
    constraints.weightx = x;
    constraints.weighty = y;

    if (anchor.equals ("NORTH") == true)
        constraints.anchor = GridBagConstraints.NORTH;
    else if (anchor.equals ("NORTHWEST") == true)
        constraints.anchor = GridBagConstraints.NORTHWEST;
    else if (anchor.equals ("NORTHEAST") == true)
        constraints.anchor = GridBagConstraints.NORTHEAST;
    else if (anchor.equals ("SOUTH") == true)
        constraints.anchor = GridBagConstraints.SOUTH;
    else if (anchor.equals ("SOUTHWEST") == true)
        constraints.anchor = GridBagConstraints.SOUTHWEST;
    else if (anchor.equals ("SOUTHEAST") == true)
        constraints.anchor = GridBagConstraints.SOUTHEAST;
    else if (anchor.equals ("CENTER") == true)
        constraints.anchor = GridBagConstraints.CENTER;
}

/* The following method sets the padding space within or around
control */

void setPadding (int internalPadX, int internalPadY, int insetTop,
    int insetLeft, int insetBottom, int insetRight) {
    constraints.ipadx = internalPadX;   // internal padding
    constraints.ipady = internalPadY;
    constraints.insets.top = insetTop;   // external padding
    constraints.insets.left = insetLeft;
    constraints.insets.bottom = insetBottom;
    constraints.insets.right = insetRight;
}
```

The combination of swing display and interactive elements with layout managers creates broad flexibility in how to interface a Java software program with human users.

### 7.3.6   Display Elements

The JLabel control is a widely used display-only GUI element, often in conjunction with interactive elements. In addition to **JLabel**s, graphical shapes (lines, geometric shapes, and colors), you can use clip art, photo images, and icons to provide graphical information as part of a user interface.

### 7.3.7   Interactive Elements

The main benefit of a graphical user interface is the user's ability to interact with the software in a way similar to the physical world. A GUI is a good simulation of the real, physical world, with its switches, buttons, lists, and forms.

The "**J**" components provided in the swing library are high-level, lightweight components that are easy to implement despite the functional complexity of at least some of them. The basic process is as follows:

1. Create a container, e.g., a **JFrame** object.
2. Create a panel, e.g. a **JPanel** object.
3. Get the content pane object.
4. Create a GUI component, e.g., a **JLabel** object or a **JButton** object.
5. If the component is interactive, associate an action listener with it.
6. Add the component to the content pane.
7. Create the event handler class to handle actions.

Swing provides a range of display and interactive components, including the following (a more detailed list was provided in Chapter 3):

- Labels
  - **JLabel**
- Buttons
  - **JButton**
- Text fields
  - **JTextField**
- Text areas
  - **JTextArea**
- Checkboxes
  - **JCheckBox**
- Radio Buttons
  - **JRadioButton**
- Choice lists
  - **JComboBox**
  - **JList**
  - Multiple-selection lists
- Scroll bars
  - **JScrollPane**
- Other
  - **JPopupMenus**

Most of these components support other useful GUI features, such as tooltip help, a temporary text box that pops up when the user holds the cursor over a component for a few seconds.

### 7.3.8 Event Handling

As previewed in Chapter 3, event handling is an integral part of graphical user interface programming. This section looks at the process of implementing event-handling functionality in more detail. Table 7.3 lists the handlers for the different types of events that may occur.

Event handling requires the implementation of specific code fragments in three different areas of the program:

1. The class that handles events must implement the **ActionListener** interface, or extend a class that does.

```
public class HandleEvents implements ActionListener {
```

2. A statement that adds an action listener object to the interactive graphical component is instantiated from the class that handles the respective action events.

```
myButton.addActionListener (new HandleEvents());
```

3. A method called **actionPerformed()** (as specified in the **ActionListener** interface) responds to events encountered by the registered interactive component.

```
public void actionPerformed (ActionEvent e) {
     // custom code that handles the action ...
}
```

TABLE 7.3   Interactions and Listeners

| Interaction Type | Type of Listener |
|---|---|
| Button click, Return pressed in text field, or menu item selection | ActionListener |
| [X] Main window close button activated | WindowListener |
| Mouse button click while the cursor is over a component | MouseListener |
| Mouse moved over a component | MouseMotionListener |
| Component becomes visible | ComponentListener |
| Component gets keyboard focus | FocusListener |
| A table or list selection changes | ListSelectionListener |

The different event types shown in Table 7.3 are handled by listener objects instantiated from a class that implements that particular action listener interface. There are three different approaches to implementing action listeners:

1. Integrated event handler
2. Inner class
3. Separate class

### Integrated Event Handler

The following example shows the use of an integrated event handler. This means that the same class implements graphical components and their associated event handler(s) and the **actionPerformed()** method.

```
public class SampleInteractiveApplet extends JApplet
    implements ActionListener {
  JButton button;

  public void init() {
       button = new JButton("OK");
       getContentPane().add (button, BorderLayout.CENTER);
       button.addActionListener (this);
  }

  public void actionPerformed (ActionEvent e) {
       //...
  }
}
```

In this example, a button and its event handler are all handled in the same class, **SampleInteractiveApplet**.

### Inner Class

A way to separate out the event handler class without losing the benefit of shared attribute access is to define the event handler calls in an inner class, as the following example illustrates.

```
import java.awt.*;
import java.awt.event.*;
import javax.swing.*;

class SimpleGreeting extends JFrame {
    JTextField prompt;

    public SimpleGreeting(String title) {
        super (title);
        Container c;
        addWindowListener(new WindowAdapter() {
            public void windowClosing(WindowEvent e) {
                dispose();
```

```
                    System.exit(0);
            }
        });

        c = getContentPane();
        c.setLayout(new GridLayout(3,2));
        c.add(new JLabel("Hello!"));
        c.add(new JLabel(""));
        c.add(new JLabel("What is your name?"));

        prompt = new JTextField ("... enter name...");
        prompt.selectAll ();  // select text for overtyping
        c.add(prompt);
        JButton continueButton = new JButton ("Continue");
        continueButton.addActionListener (new MyActionListener());
        c.add (continueButton);
        JButton exitButton = new JButton ("Exit");
        exitButton.addActionListener (new MyActionListener());
        c.add (exitButton);
        pack();  // shrink window to mininimum size needed
        setVisible(true);  // make window visible
    }
    public static void main(String args[]) {
        System.out.println("Starting SimpleGreeting...");
        SimpleGreeting mainWindow = new SimpleGreeting(
            "Simple Greeting Example");
    }
    //inner class handles events
    class MyActionListener implements ActionListener {
        public void actionPerformed(ActionEvent evt) {
            if (evt.getActionCommand ().equals("Continue"))
                JOptionPane.showMessageDialog (null,
                    prompt.getText(), "You entered ...",
                    JOptionPane.INFORMATION_MESSAGE);
            else if (evt.getActionCommand ().equals("Exit"))
                System.exit(0);
        }
    }
}
```

This example provides a nested inner class as the template for event-handling objects. As events manage data associated with a particular instance, an object has to be created for each interactive component.

It is also possible to use an anonymous inner class:

```
public class MyClass extends JApplet {
    //...
    myTextField.addMouseListener(new MouseAdapter() {
        public void mouseClicked(MouseEvent e) {
        // Event handler code
        }
```

```
    });
    //...
    }
}
```

In this example, a temporary anonymous inner class is created "on the fly" in order to supply the template for the event handler object associated with the particular interactive component.

### Separate Class

Finally, it is of course possible to specify the event handler as a separate class, and to provide data access through parameter passing.

```
public class MainProgram {
    //...

    myButton.addActionListener(new EventHandling
        (passingParameter));
        //...
    }
}

class EventHandling implements ActionListener {
    //...
    public EventHandling (String para) {
        //...
    }

    public void actionPerformed (ActionEvent e) {
        // handle event
    }
}
```

There are advantages and disadvantages to each of these approaches. Integrating the event handler class with the class where the interactive component is initialized makes it easier to access shared attributes. The disadvantage is a loss of componentization, as it is desirable to separate user interface components from business logic components, which tend to be associated with event handling.

In the next brief section, we examine the types of applications that a Java software engineer is likely to develop.

### 7.3.9   Types of Applications

While the focus of this book is on standard "business" application development, Java is used for developing a wide range of applications on a variety of computer platforms (even cell phones), including multimedia applications like games and marketing demonstrations, engineering applications, real-time applications, and utility programs. Business applications are the most common category of applications, especially when one considers the amount of investment in software development by private and public

| *Input* | *Process* | *Output* |
|---|---|---|
|  | 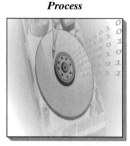 | 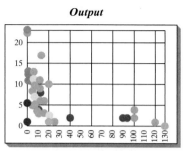 |
| Data entry, data from other application, sensor information | Application of business rules (algorithms, data manipulation, information extraction) | Presentation of results (reports, charts, graphs, database updates, output files) |

FIGURE 7.17 Input → Process → Output Model

institutions and industries. Other applications, such as end-user tools, may have more public visibility (e.g., Microsoft® Office™) than commercial business applications (e.g., Microsoft® Great Plains™), but they involve a much smaller share of the software engineering workforce than business application development, including all the custom application development efforts that companies undertake when they cannot find off-the-shelf solutions for their business problems.

The focus of this book, therefore, is on business application development concepts, albeit most of the learning lessons from this type of application can be directly applied to the other categories cited above. We prefer to anchor student learning in the realm of real applications rather than in program and code examples that have no parallel in the working world.

In a very general sense, most typical applications take the form shown in Figure 7.17. This simple model shows the flow of data and its supreme importance in most applications. We develop software chiefly to manipulate data in order to derive useful information, and ultimately knowledge, from it. This knowledge is most frequently used to make better decisions faster.

## 7.4 Position in Process

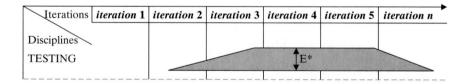

At this point in our software methodology, we have completed the Integration phase of the project life-cycle, which leads us to the **Testing** phase of the process. It is important to understand this as a formal phase of testing at this stage in the development process, not as the first instance of testing overall. Testing activities should permeate the development process from the earliest activities of concept validation to the verification of ongoing maintenance activities after the product is generally released.

In this phase, we begin final product certification. We also expose our emerging product to external users, carefully selected for their willingness and ability to provide ample feedback about what works well and what needs to be improved or corrected. This *field testing* is divided into two phases:

- Alpha testing
- Beta testing

### 7.4.1   Alpha Testing

When significant components of the eventual product are functional enough to constitute a useful, preliminary product set that external users can exercise, we call this an alpha release. Alpha-level products may be missing some promised functions and may not be entirely stable, but they should have sufficient functionality and resilience for external users to use the product for testing purposes, but not in production.

Alpha testing is performed by the external user or by internal testers at an external user's site or on its systems. The tests primarily validate that the functionality implemented meets project requirements, is appropriately functional, and properly improves the target user's process improvement objectives. The outcome of alpha testing is an *alpha field test report.* Alpha testing is managed by the software engineering team under the supervision of the quality-assurance team.

### 7.4.2   Beta Testing

A beta release is a version of the product that has all the required functionality, is stable, and usable, but may be missing some minor production aspects, such as certified scalability, support for extraordinary peripherals, and the like. All the functions should be complete and working at the time of beta release.

Beta testing is performed by the external user under realistic working conditions, sometimes even using the product in live mode, in parallel with existing systems or processes. The outcome of beta testing is a *beta field test report.* Beta testing is managed by the quality-assurance team with support from the engineering team.

### 7.4.3   Early Access Testing

Some organizations refer to alpha testing or beta testing or both as *early access testing.* Early access testing can be with both internal and external customers. Internal customers can be other IT members, field software engineers, field consultants, or even functional area representatives from accounting, marketing, manufacturing, on some other area. External customers generally are individuals and/or organizations that have a special relationship with the organization and have a stakeholder interest in assisting with testing so that the end-product they eventually receive will be more in line with their expectations.

## 7.5   Example

Figure 7.18 shows what areas require post-component testing for an example distributed time-tracking application before it can advance to final certification. This diagrammatic form is a way to show in one picture the various areas of attention required from the test team and can be a helpful visualization tool, especially for more complex, distributed configurations. Of course, in the real world, much more detailed annotation is required. A more complete range of testing strategies is summarized in Table 7.4.

### 7.5.1   *Example Explanation*

The testing required after component certification but before final product release includes a range of quality-assurance-related activities, from Integration Testing (discussed in detail in an earlier chapter), to alpha and beta (customer) testing, to final SQA certification testing. The diagram in Figure 7.18 identifies a variety of areas of testing required to ensure that all components interact with each other and the world

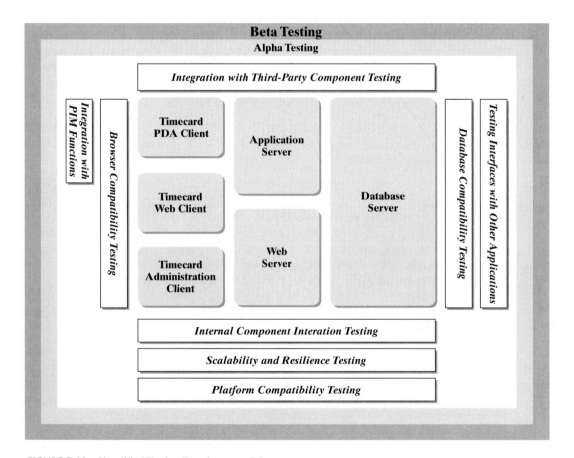

FIGURE 7.18   Simplified Testing Requirements Diagram

TABLE 7.4   Testing Types

| Test | Description |
|---|---|
| *Alpha Testing* | First customer exposure, possibly limited functionality, non-production environment |
| *Beta Testing* | Formal customer testing, parallel production environment, full functionality |
| *Integration with PIM Functions* | If required, integrated data sharing with resident Personal Information Manager (PIM) functions (e.g., calendar, e-mail, PocketWord, PocketExcel™) |
| *Browser Compatibility Testing* | Ensuring that application works in required release level(s) of support browsers; if plug-in(s) required, testing of download process and functionality (attention to release level of plug-in) |
| *Internal Component Integration Testing* | Ensuring that all product component interfaces function as required and designed |
| *Integration with Third-Party Component Testing* | Ensuring that product interfaces with third-party software upstream and downstream as required; include performance and recovery testing; focus on data integrity |
| *Database Compatibility Testing* | Ensuring that product can interface to all supported databases (attention to release levels) |
| *Testing Interfaces with Other Applications* | Ensuring that programmatic interfaces with other applications work as required |
| *Scalability and Resilience Testing* | Ensuring that the number of concurrent users required can be supported without unacceptable degradation of response time |
| *Platform Compatibility Testing* | Ensuring that the product installs and runs as required on all supported platforms, networks, and peripherals; include performance testing |

around them as required. Since few applications operate in standalone mode, the data and program interfaces to other third-party components and products are critical. In addition, testing needs to ensure that the application can be installed and run reliably on all required target platforms.

## 7.6   *Harm●ny* Design Case Study

At this point, the Harmony Designs case study is nearing completion. The solution you have designed and implemented now needs to be tested for "implementability" in a realistic customer environment. If possible, your team should seek an alpha test environment (a real company) where you can test-implement your solution and receive practical feedback from your test partner/customer. You should also examine and certify that your application can interface effectively (at least in terms of data compatibility) with existing products in regular use in interior design firms. An example of such an application may be Intuit®'s Quickbooks™, used by a large number of small businesses worldwide.

## 7.7    Resources

One of the learning challenges in these later phases of the software-development process is the difficulty of simulating the real world: school projects tend to be over-simplifications of the types of projects modern organizations implement. It is therefore most helpful at this stage to seek exposure to real-world programming projects. This can be accomplished through a variety of means:

- Guest speakers
- Company site visits
- Reviews of industry publications such as *InfoWorld*™, *eTimes*™, etc.
- Internships
- Case studies


## 7.8    Summary and Recommendations

In this chapter, we have examined the technologies that Java provides for user interface construction. This is an important area of modern software design and development, because users expect a rich, easy-to-navigate and -use environment where they can efficiently do their work using a graphical environment that effectively simulates real-world interactions and behaviors.

We also explored how graphical user interface interaction is handled as events associated with GUI objects at instantiation time and provided at event time for reactive processing in your application.

On the methodology side, we reviewed the "wrap-up" testing requirements and activities that ensure that our product actually meets practical "productization" requirements. We studied alpha and beta testing and gained an overall understanding of formal testing requirements and test procedures.


## 7.9    Review Questions

1. **Illustrate Event Handling.** Write a brief program that shows how a **JButton** is implemented.

```
import java.awt.*;
import java.awt.event.*;
import javax.swing.*;
/**
 * AButtonTest sample application
```

```
 *
 * @author Georges Merx, Ph. D.
 * @version 1.00 04/10/08Ph. D.
 */

public class AButtonTest extends JFrame implements ActionListener {
    JButton testButton;

    public AButtonTest() { // constructor
        setTitle("Button Test");
        Container c = getContentPane();
        c.setLayout (new FlowLayout());
        testButton = new JButton ("Click Here!");
        testButton.addActionListener (this);
        c.add (testButton);
        pack();
        setVisible(true);
    }

    public static void main(String[] args) {
        // Create application frame
        AButtonTest frame = new AButtonTest();
    }

    public void actionPerformed (ActionEvent e) {
        if  (e.getActionCommand ().equals("Click Here!"))
            testButton.setText ("Exit");
        else if (e.getActionCommand ().equals("Exit"))
            System.exit (0);
    }
}
```

2. **Discuss Areas of Testing.** Using the diagram in Figure 7.18, discuss the various areas of testing recommended for a distributed graphical Java application.

## 7.10   Glossary – Terminology – Concepts

**Alpha and beta testing**   Alpha testing refers to early customer installations in non-production environments to solicit early customer feedback on select functions; beta testing refers to customer installations of the completed but still unreleased product, to perform a final evaluation of the finalized product in a real-world environment before general release certification.

**Layout Manager**   An **awt** Java class type that provides two-dimensional formatting elements to lay out and organize GUI windows (content panes); e.g., **GridBagLayout** class.

## 7.11    Exercises

**1. Layout Manager.**    Compare three layout managers. Create a table and list relevant features. Write a sample program that uses all three.

**2. GUI Guidelines.**    Research the topic of GUI design; provide at least two reputable sources; write a one-page paper.

**3. Event Handling.**    Write a graphical game application that shows a small window with a range of numbers running through it continuously at slow enough speed to be recognizable, a label with a changing target number, and a button that has to be pressed at the right time to "catch", the target number. Display the number "caught," and award points for each hit or near hit.

CHAPTER 8

# Implementing Java Programs

This chapter reviews and integrates the main software-development phases from design to **certification**. The most exciting and creative aspect of software engineering is the successful translation of project requirements into a viable, valuable software application design and product implementation. Now that we have reached the Certification Phase in our step-by-step examination of the software methodology life-cycle, we step back in this chapter to relook at the main phases of the implementation process. Supporting disciplines such as software project management are also discussed. As we approach the release phase of our product, we must redouble our attention to quality: even small errors or oversights lead to the perception of poor quality in software products.

---

**Key Term**

*Certification* is a quality-assurance process that validates that a product meets all productization requirements. Typically, the following areas are reviewed:

- Functionality meets requirements (Requirements and Design Specifications)
- Product has no outstanding major errors
- Product meets quality requirements (functional and non-functional)
- Product is supportable
- All documentation is in place

---

Multiple threads and multimedia are the key technical topics in this chapter in our on-going study of Java syntax, structure, and semantics. These topics are interrelated be-cause multiple concurrent-execution threads support the efficient implementation of multimedia data processing.

## 8.1    Learning Objectives

An all-inclusive, architectural viewpoint that embraces all the phases and activities as-sociated with a project is one of the major anchors of comprehensive quality in soft-ware development. When a project is viewed not as a sequence of distinct phases, but as the tight, validated integration of interrelated activities, the result tends to be of higher quality than in traditional projects and much better matched to the initial and evolving stakeholder requirements. This approach, combined with iterations and a strong commitment to continuous improvement, goes a long way toward making soft-ware-development projects more predictable and avoiding customer dissatisfaction when the final product is delivered.

As shown in Figure 8.1, we recommend that you approach projects from a layered approach (think "onion layers") instead of compartmentalized "vertical" subprojects. Especially when a team of people collaborates on a project, better overall integration is obtained if the work is approached from a layered viewpoint, where all major compo-nents are being worked on together (more or less). While specialization inevitably leads to some compartmentalization, the commitment to bringing components together very regularly leads to earlier stability and better transparency. You can also think of the lay-ers shown as *iterations,* where the first layer may be a prototype, for example.

### 8.1.1    *Learning Layout*

This recurring section shows the learning objectives of the chapter using the UML ac-tivity diagram notation (see Fig. 8.2).

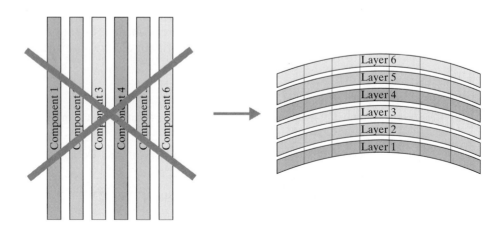

FIGURE 8.1    Perferred Approach to Project Component Development

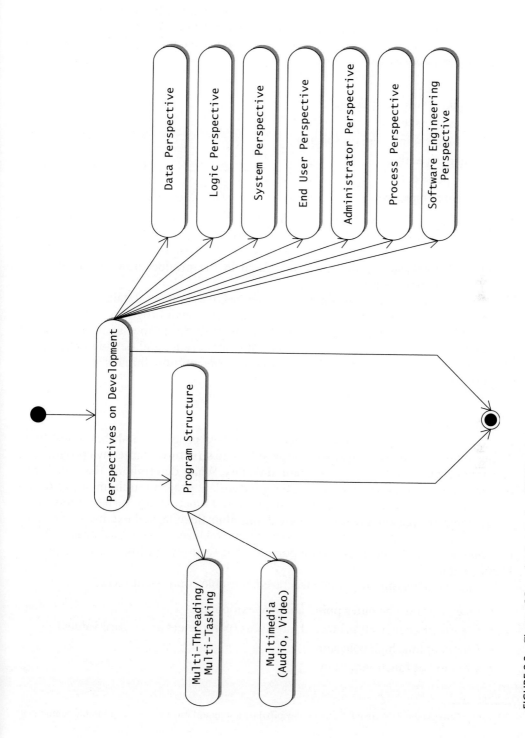

FIGURE 8.2  Chapter 8 Learning Layout (as a UML Activity Diagram)

391

In this chapter, we will revisit the efforts that brought us through implementation and initial field-testing to the point of product certification. We examine how to critically ensure that the product meets its intended functionality requirements from the following perspectives:

- End-user perspective
- Administrator perspective
- Process perspective
- Software engineering perspective
- Data perspective
- Logic perspective
- System perspective

These perspectives are the facets of a multidimensional lens on the project. Taken together they ensure that the project requirements, as captured in the Project Requirements Specification with its detailed use cases, and the design requirements, detailed in the Design Specification, are actually fulfilled in the product now presumably approaching general distribution.

The following sections examine these perspectives in more detail.

On the language side, we will explore how larger Java programs are structured, and what syntax and structure elements contribute to the proper application of the principles of object orientation in ensuring component reuse and flexible extensibility of a program. This includes an overview of how to use multiple threads and also introduces the multimedia capabilities built into Java.

### 8.1.2    *Program Structure*

In the preceding chapters, we examined various Java programs and their constituent classes. At this point, we take a closer look at how to structure a large Java program for maximum reuse, extensibility, and maintainability. When determining the class structure, as we discussed in an earlier chapter, we translate project requirements into a hierarchy of classes which best represent the required functionality such that individual components are reasonably self-contained, reusable, flexible, and extensible. From an object-oriented perspective, we want components (classes, objects, packages, and subsystems) to avoid duplication and be polymorphic, securely encapsulated, and properly documented.[1]

The characteristics of a well-structured, reusable component include:

- One purpose, one entry point, and one exit point
- Clearly defined, well-protected interfaces (parameters and return values)
- Low coupling, high cohesion
- Creation of functional value

---

[1]The Sun Microsystems Java Beans™ technology provides a standard way for creating reusable components.

- Flexibility to use in a variety of scenarios (e.g., polymorphism)
- Simplicity—proper structure and sequencing of class hierarchy and packages (e.g., abstraction)
- Extensibility—flexible ability to create child-class extensions (e.g., inheritance)
- If for external reuse, adherence to Javabean™ packaging and documentation (e.g., Javadoc™) standards

These goals are not always easy to achieve and often evolve over time. This is another important justification for iterative development: in the course of the project, developers realize further opportunities to abstract and generalize components for reuse.

Next, we examine how to take better advantage of the modern computer's processing power by running multiple program tasks concurrently.

### 8.1.3  Multiple Concurrent Tasks

The typical modern computer's central processing unit (CPU) is much faster than the computational needs of most programs. Thus programs often sit idle, waiting for input from a user, sensor, file, or interface. Java provides a standard way to run multiple "threads" (or "tasks") of your program "in parallel" (or virtually in parallel if your computer has only one CPU). This means that your program can accomplish subtasks concurrently rather than sequentially. These concurrent subactivities can be synchronized when there are interdependencies between the threads. The built-in high-level interface support for multitasking makes multithreaded applications much easier to implement in Java than in most other modern languages. These capabilities were further enhanced in Java SDK 5.0. Please refer to java.sun.com for details on the 5.0 enhancements.

The display of multimedia data is a typical application of multithreading. While the data is being continuously loaded in the background (streaming), the application can begin playing the data stream already loaded in the foreground. Background and foreground threads share a buffer that is filled from one side and emptied from the other.

### 8.1.4  Multimedia

The support of multimedia functionality in Java is provided by a collection of classes in different packages, including **awt**, **image**, and **graphics**. The simplest form of multimedia is an animation, or the display in rapid sequence of a related series of frames. More advanced animation is supported by sprites (a subject beyond the scope of this book).

#### Eliminating Flickering

The default repainting behavior is to update graphical components; however, the default updating behavior is to first blank out the respective component with the background color and then to repaint it. This causes flickering in an animation. Animations therefore take control of the repainting of window contents in order to limit repainting to areas that have actually changed. The technique of double-buffering further helps to alleviate this problem.

### Double-Buffering

Double-buffering is accomplished by taking advantage of CPU speed, which is much faster than the storage device that stores the animation frames. Using multi-threading techniques, the next frame is loaded into an off-screen memory buffer so that it is quickly available for display after the current frame.

---

## BUFFERS

**Buffers** are structures allocated in memory to reduce the lag time associated with accessing secondary storage devices. RAM and CPU are orders of magnitude faster than storage devices. Loading large chunks of data into memory at one time, especially if this is done in the background, streamlines the overall program/data interaction.

---

### Video

Sun provides an optional package for media support that includes video. According to Sun Microsystems, "The Java Media Framework API (JMF) enables audio, video and other time-based media to be added to applications and applets built on Java technology.... Heavy weight components are used in JMF as they permit using native rendering methods for higher frame rate video." A future version of Java may well include support for video and other advanced multimedia formats (e.g., speech) in the core JDK.

### Sound

Java provides extensive support for a variety of sound file formats. Additional extensions are available from Sun and third-party software providers for additional formats. The interfaces are high-level and protect the application developer from the complexities of the underlying implementation.

## 8.1.5 Learning Connections

The Learning Connections diagram in Figure 8.3 shows the content of this chapter in relation to the knowledge and skills development recommended for apprentice Java software engineers.

Of course, at this point, the cumulative knowledge from the previous chapters results in almost complete coverage of our learning connections areas. But it is still helpful to view software engineering as a collection of interrelated skills which software engineers must continually develop and expand in order to maintain their competitiveness.

## 8.2 Executive Summary

The implementation, integration, and field test phases of the software-development process are the most labor-intensive stages of a typical software-development project.

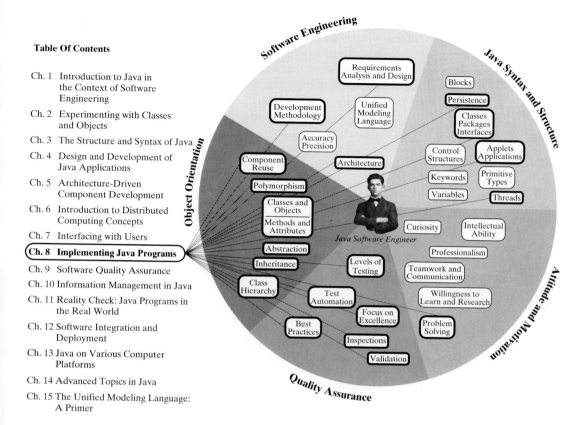

**FIGURE 8.3**  Learning Connections for Chapter 8

Best development practices are critical at this time, because errors and oversights are much more costly during these phases than during Requirements Analysis and Design, when necessary corrections are normally limited to internal documentation. A formal, structured process can now make a major positive difference in productivity, ensuring that rework is minimized and that completed features accurately meet project requirements.

Also, by this time, junior Java software engineers must have cemented and expanded their programming skills to implement the planned features correctly and efficiently. Depending on the planned features, study of extension libraries and experimentation with their contents may be required. Advanced computing capabilities like multithreading may need to be applied to ensure good response time and application scalability. This chapter discusses some of the more advanced features in J2SE, including integrated support for multimedia file formats and multithreaded concurrency.

## 8.3    Learning Modules

The focus of this chapter is on the production aspects of Java code development and completion in preparation for product certification. While many introductory texts do not cover this type of real-world material, the junior software engineer will benefit from at least a cursory understanding of the work processes followed by commercial software-development organizations in generating their products. It is the totality of activities associated with a software-development project of value that results in a high-quality product, but only if every phase and every aspect is pursued from a perspective of excellence.

The synthesis of the requirements analysis, design, and implementation activities is reviewed from the perspective of **Initial Operational Capability** (IOC). IOC is a milestone that encompasses the validation of all the constituent project components as a *product solution* in the context of stakeholder (or market) requirements. This final validation benefits from a multi-perspective approach, just as previous phases have.

Seven perspectives participate in ensuring that a product meets all the requisite functional and support requirements when it is released.

As Figure 8.4 illustrates, these seven perspectives together ensure that the software product being certified meets the requirements of the major categories of stakeholders who play an active role in the implementation, productive application, and maintenance of the product.

### 8.3.1 End-User Perspective

The requirements for end-user functionality typically drive the core features of any given software product. It is important not only to translate these requirements into features and functions, but to consider work-process productivity when designing solutions to requirements. Said in another way, the product features need to improve on existing processes and tools, not just mirror them.

The continued involvement of knowledgeable end-users through the design and development phases ensures that the solutions envisioned by the software engineers actually meet the end-users' goals and needs.

In this validation effort, it is important to critically examine how the product features improve the work-process productivity enough to warrant general implementation. These improvements should be measurable, consistent, and sustainable.

### 8.3.2 Administrator Perspective

End-user requirements are often the most visible input to product design, and they may be the most important in a way, but they should be considered in the context of the other perspectives we have listed. In particular, *software installability* and *maintainability* are key considerations for system and network administration professionals. A software application must be easily installed into the target environment of the client or customer who acquires the program. Software engineers must bear in mind that the environment in which the software was created and tested is often not analogous to the environment where the application will be installed and operated.

This often involves additional programming and documentation, hopefully considered in the design phase as a deliverable. Installation programs and data migration tools are often required to successfully implement a software solution in a customer's particular IT environment.

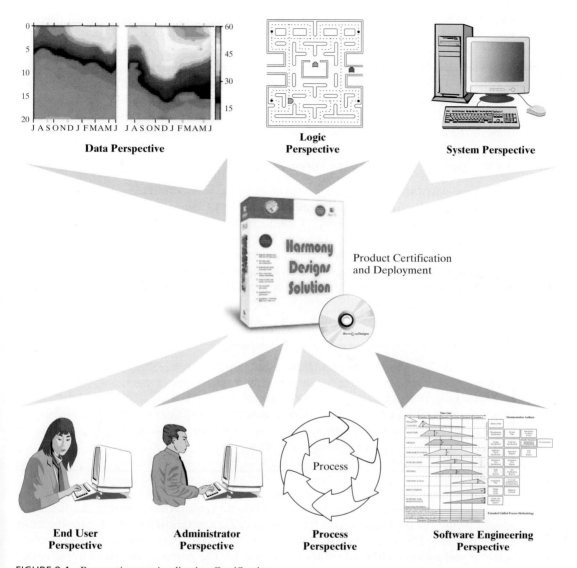

**FIGURE 8.4** Perspectives on Application Certification

### 8.3.3 Process Perspective

In a well-managed project, the requirements are captured from a process perspective; in fact, the main purpose of describing requirements in *scenario* form is to record the underlying work processes. However, it is easy to lose this important viewpoint when designing features and functions. It is, in fact, all too common to disassociate one phase from the next, whether intentionally or accidentally (see Fig. 8.1), and lose the coherence between phases that is so important in ensuring that the eventual product actually implements all the major and minor project requirements.

Translating use case scenarios into appropriate software functions is a special challenge. Using techniques like decomposition and design patterns, this is done most effectively with the extensive involvement of experienced designers as well as project stakeholders. An iterative, "open-mind" approach is crucial in making all the adjustments necessary to implement a superior work process that optimizes the contributions of the computer hardware, networking, and software systems.

### 8.3.4    Software Engineering Perspective

Finally, the software engineering perspective contributes the technical considerations that arise from the strengths and weaknesses of the IT components constituting the solution. It is important to understand the technology at all levels (architectural viewpoint) in order to maximize its benefits and minimize its limitations when designing the functionality that responds to the requirement scenarios. This includes functional requirements, such as specific features, commands, options, and interactive components, but also non-functional (supporting) requirements, such as performance, scalability, security, and usability.

---

### CORRELATION TO REQUIREMENTS

Software engineers have the power to implement features, that were never required in the first place, but which they may find "cool" or necessary. Substantial discipline is warranted to ensure that all features can be traced back to the original or updated Requirements Specification.

---

Software engineers often discover additional requirements during the technical design of the product that result from the specific capabilities of the technologies at their disposal. These additional needs must be folded back into the requirements analysis and validated like any other requirements. The commitment to an iterative development process in the methodology should make this a straightforward process.

### 8.3.5    Data Perspective

Most programming projects involve the transformation of data into useful information, most often in support of making better decisions faster. The application designer therefore should always look at the project requirements and design features from the *data perspective*, and pay special attention to the following considerations:

- Data origin
  - ○ Connection to data source
  - ○ Format compatibility

- Data quality: accuracy, quality, timeliness
  - ○ Need for validation
  - ○ Process for "cleaning"
- Data organization
  - ○ Process for extracting usefulness from the data
- Structure, aggregation, ordering, algorithms
- Data transformation, output and storage of results

These considerations are vital because the quality and accuracy of application data (and associated metadata[2]) essentially determine the usefulness of the program.

### 8.3.6   *Logic Perspective*

Software engineers have to clearly grasp the logic flows associated with the work processes that characterize various project features. This involves understanding the original work process (or lack thereof) and the design of an improved, IT-enabled workflow. Often, complex logic is required to maximize the value extraction from the data available; the complexity comes from the variety of business rules that need to be implemented and the computational intricacy associated with application algorithms.

Implementing proper logic requires skills in logic and knowledge of computer science.

---

### Examples:

- Mathematical notations, formulas, representations, precision, proofs
- Data structures
- Parsing, language processing
- Recursion
- Performance measurement and optimization

---

### 8.3.7   *System Perspective*

Software is never entirely independent of the underlying system environment, including hardware, networking, and other software components (system and application). While Java provides functionality that liberates the typical application from much of the awareness required in the past about underlying system-specific capabilities, issues of precision, optimization, and performance still affect Java applications and require software engineers to understand the limitations of the targeted destination systems.

The astute software engineer has to have sufficient system knowledge and understand the capabilities of the system to use language features efficiently in implementing project requirements.

---

[2]Metadata are data about data (e.g., organizational structure).

These seven viewpoints together ensure that a product is not thrust upon users until all aspects of its functionality have been properly considered. Product functions all too often work well in the lab and then fail in the field. Ensuring that the IOC validation milestone accounts for the requirements of these seven perspectives substantially reduces the likelihood of catastrophic "out-of-the-box" errors.

The discussion in this chapter will now continue to expand your knowledge of Java structure and syntax elements, including the more advanced capabilities, by focusing on support for multiple threads, multimedia, and multilevel exception management.

### 8.3.8   *Multitasking—Multiple Threads*

A **thread** is a part of a program set up to run on its own while the rest of the program does something else. A single program can have lots of threads if that is what is needed to get the job done. Threading is also called *multitasking*. Simply follow the process shown below to create a multithreaded program:

1. Define the class with the interface **Runnable**
   ```
   class MyProgram implements Runnable {
   ```
2. Create a **Thread** object to hold the thread and start it:
   ```
   thread1 = new Thread(this);
   thread1.start();
   ```
3. Create a **run()** method that contains the statements that need to run in their own thread (e.g., redrawing of an animation):
   ```
   public void run() {
   ```
4. Create or override the **stop()** method to terminate the running thread by setting it to null:

   ```
   public void stop() {
        thread1 = null;
   }
   ```

*Notes:*

- Multithreading can also be implemented by extending the **Thread** class.
- J2SE 5.0 implements the Executor framework, an interface that separates thread creation from how each thread is managed.

---

**Example:**

```
class SimpleExecutor implements Executor {
     public void execute(Runnable thread) {
          thread.run();
     }
}
```

The animation program in the next section shows an example of multithreaded execution.

---

### 8.3.9   *Animation Using Multithreading*

Java has built-in and add-on facilities to deal with an extensive variety of multimedia data formats, including still images, audio, animations, and video.

Moving pictures typically fall into two categories:

1. Animation
2. Video

Java provides support for both types of visual multimedia data as well as various sound formats. More advanced video and audio formats, such as AVI and MP3, are supported via the Java Media Framework (JMF).[3]

The following complete Java example simulates a very basic Las Vegas–style slot machine. It demonstrates multithreading using three threads. The output from running the program is shown after the source code, followed by some code explanation.

```java
/**
 * @(#)Slots.java 1.0 02/12/09
 * Author: Georges Merx
 */

import java.awt.*;
import java.awt.event.*;
import javax.swing.*;

class Slots2 extends JFrame {
    MediaTracker tracker;
// use MediaTracker class to manage animation images
    Image anim[] = new Image[5];
    int index;
    Thread animator1, animator2, animator3;
    boolean onOff = false;
    JButton spin;
    ImagePanel slotsPanel1, slotsPanel2, slotsPanel3;

    public Slots2 (String title) {
        addWindowListener(new WindowAdapter() {
            public void windowClosing(WindowEvent e) {
                dispose();
                System.exit(0);
            }
        });

        tracker = new MediaTracker(this);

        for (int i = 0; i < 5; i++) {
            anim[i] = Toolkit.getDefaultToolkit().
                getImage("s-p" + (i+1) + ".gif");
            // load images
```

---

[3]A description of JMF is beyond the scope of this book, but extensive documentation can be found online on the Java Web site provided by Sun Microsystems.

```
                    tracker.addImage(anim[i], 0);
            }

            Container c1 = getContentPane ();
            c1.setLayout (new BorderLayout());
            JPanel slotHolder = new JPanel ();
            slotHolder.setLayout (new GridLayout (1,3));
            slotsPanel1 = new ImagePanel();
            slotHolder.add(slotsPanel1);
            slotsPanel2 = new ImagePanel();
            slotHolder.add(slotsPanel2);
            slotsPanel3 = new ImagePanel();
            slotHolder.add(slotsPanel3);
            c1.add (slotHolder, BorderLayout.CENTER);
            spin = new JButton ("Spin");
            spin.addActionListener (new ButtonListener());
            c1.add (spin, BorderLayout.SOUTH);
            setSize (310,160);
            setTitle("Slots");
            setVisible(true);
    }

    public static void main(String args[]) {
        System.out.println("Starting Slots...");
        Slots2 mainFrame = new Slots2 ("Slots Demo");
    }

    public class ButtonListener implements ActionListener,
      Runnable {
        public void actionPerformed (ActionEvent e) {
            if (onOff == false) {
                onOff = true;
                spin.setText ("Stop");
                animator1 = new Thread(this);
                animator1.start();
                animator2 = new Thread(this);
                animator2.start();
                animator3 = new Thread(this);
                animator3.start();
            }
            else {
                onOff = false;
                spin.setText ("Spin" );
                stop();
            }
        }

        public void stop() {
            animator1 = null;
            animator2 = null;
            animator3 = null;
        }
```

```
        public void run() {
            try {
                tracker.waitForID (0);
            } catch (InterruptedException e) {
                return;
            }

            Thread me = Thread.currentThread();

            while (animator1 == me) {
                try {
                    Thread.sleep (150);
                } catch (InterruptedException e) {
                    break;
                }

                synchronized (this) {
                    index = (int)(4 * Math.random());
                }
                slotsPanel1.repaint();
            }

            while (animator2 == me) {
                try {
                    Thread.sleep (125);
                } catch (InterruptedException e) {
                    break;
                }

                synchronized (this){
                    index = (int)(4 * Math.random());
                }
                slotsPanel2.repaint();
            }

            while (animator3 == me) {
                try {
                    Thread.sleep (175);
                } catch (InterruptedException e) {
                    break;
                }

                synchronized (this) {
                    index = (int)(4 * Math.random());
                }

                slotsPanel3.repaint();
            }
        }
    }
class ImagePanel extends JPanel {
    public void paintComponent(Graphics g) {
        super.paintComponent(g);
```

```
            if ((tracker.statusAll(false)
              & MediaTracker.ERRORED) !=
                0) {
                  g.setColor(Color.red);
                  g.fillRect(0, 0, getSize().width, getSize().
                      height);
                  return;
            }
            if (tracker.statusID(0, false) == MediaTracker.
                COMPLETE) {
                  g.drawImage(anim[index], 10, 10, this);
            }
          }
        }
}
```

The image in Figure 8.5 shows the output from this program. The program consists of one class (**Slots2**), two subclasses (**ImagePanel** and **ButtonListener**) with their own attributes and methods, two methods (**main()**, **Slots2()** constructor), and several attributes (**spin**, **anim**, **index**, **animator1**, **onOff**, etc.). Figure 8.6, created using Borland®'s Together® Edition for Eclipse IDE, shows the UML Class diagram for this program. Several other diagrams in this book also use this IDE.

Figure 8.7 shows a portion of the UML Sequence diagram for the Slots2.main() method. UML sequence diagrams are an excellent way to study the execution behavior of existing class methods or to diagram the proposed execution behavior of new or changes to methods.

The program simulates a basic slot machine loading five versions of a simple star graphic (.GIF extension) and managing them using a **MediaTracker** object:

```
tracker = new MediaTracker(this);
for (int i = 0; i < 5; i++) {
    anim[i] = Toolkit.getDefaultToolkit().getImage("s-p" + (i+1) +
        ".gif"); //load images
    tracker.addImage(anim[i], 0);
}
```

The example uses the **Runnable** interface to allow for three threads of the program's **run()** method to execute quasi-concurrently, one for each slot machine *wheel*:

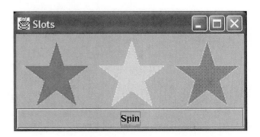

FIGURE 8.5    The Slot Machine Example Program

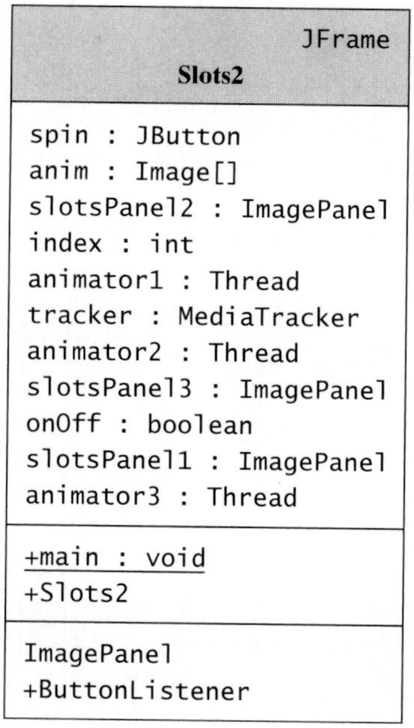

```
                              JFrame
                       Slots2
  ─────────────────────────────────────
  spin : JButton
  anim : Image[]
  slotsPanel2 : ImagePanel
  index : int
  animator1 : Thread
  tracker : MediaTracker
  animator2 : Thread
  slotsPanel3 : ImagePanel
  onOff : boolean
  slotsPanel1 : ImagePanel
  animator3 : Thread
  ─────────────────────────────────────
  +main : void
  +Slots2
  ─────────────────────────────────────
  ImagePanel
  +ButtonListener
```

FIGURE 8.6   UML Class Diagram for the Slot Machine Example Program

```java
public class ButtonListener implements ActionListener, Runnable {
    // The run() method is invoked to run the current thread
    public void run() {
        try {
            tracker.waitForID (0);
        } catch (InterruptedException e) {
            return;
        }
        Thread me = Thread.currentThread();
        // ...
```

The support for animation relies on the use of multiple threads to load images asynchronously (in the background) and uses efficient (double) buffering and painting techniques to minimize flickering and delay in showing smooth motion.

```java
for (int i = 0; i < 5; i++) {
    anim[i] = Toolkit.getDefaultToolkit().getImage("s-p" + (i+1) +
        ".gif"); //load images
    tracker.addImage(anim[i], 0);
}
```

Figure 8.8 shows the activities illustrated in the earlier Java example in terms of their concurrency, using multithreading and buffering. The time-critical activity is the I/O associated with loading images from a storage device. Therefore it is best to have this activity take place in the background, in its own thread, so that drawing images can begin as soon as there are enough images buffered in memory to ensure a smooth sequence.

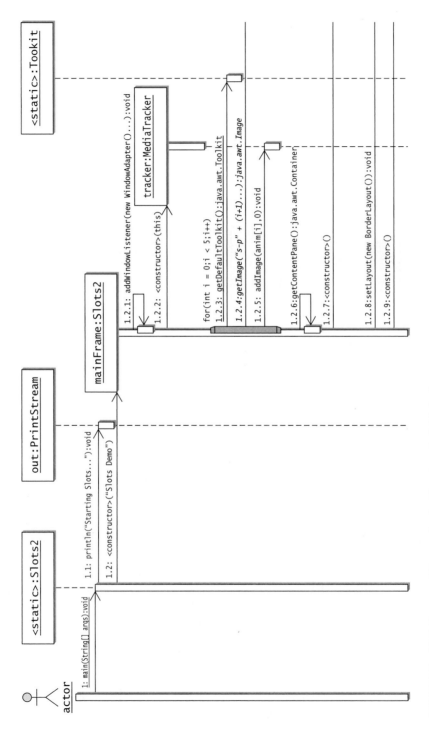

FIGURE 8.7   UML Sequence Diagram for the Slots2.main() Method

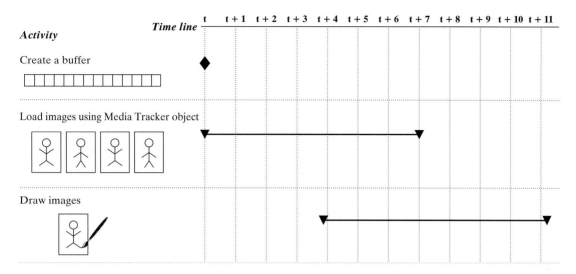

FIGURE 8.8   Overlapping Activities in Animation Handling

Using the **Executor** framework, the same program can be implemented to separate the runnable task (interface **Runnable**) from the task management code. Under J2SE 5.0, this is the preferred approach.

A screenshot of Slots3 is shown in Figure 8.9. The **Slots3** example uses the **Executor** approach:

```
/**
* @(#)Slots.java 1.0 02/12/09
* Author: Georges Merx
*/

import java.awt.*;
import java.awt.event.*;
import javax.swing.*;
import java.util.concurrent.*;
```

FIGURE 8.9   Slots3 Screenshot

```java
class Slots3 extends JFrame {
    private MediaTracker tracker;
    // use MediaTracker class to manage animation images
    private Image anim[] = new Image[5];
    private int index;
    private boolean onOff = false;
    private JButton spin;
    private ImagePanel slotsPanel1, slotsPanel2, slotsPanel3;
    private ExecutorService tExecutor;

    public Slots3 (String title) {
        addWindowListener(new WindowAdapter() {
            public void windowClosing(WindowEvent e) {
                dispose();
                System.exit(0);
            }
        });

        tracker = new MediaTracker(this);

        for (int i = 0; i < 5; i++) {
            anim[i] = Toolkit.getDefaultToolkit().getImage
                ("s-p" + (i+1) + ".gif"); //load images
            tracker.addImage(anim[i], 0);
        }

        Container c1 = getContentPane ();
        c1.setLayout (new BorderLayout());
        JPanel slotHolder = new JPanel ();
        slotHolder.setLayout (new GridLayout (1,3));
        slotsPanel1 = new ImagePanel(tracker, anim[0]);
        slotHolder.add(slotsPanel1);
        slotsPanel2 = new ImagePanel(tracker, anim[1]);
        slotHolder.add(slotsPanel2);
        slotsPanel3 = new ImagePanel(tracker, anim[2]);
        slotHolder.add(slotsPanel3);
        c1.add (slotHolder, BorderLayout.CENTER);
        spin = new JButton ("Spin");
        spin.addActionListener (new ButtonListener());
        c1.add (spin, BorderLayout.SOUTH);
        setSize (310,160);
        setTitle("Slots");
        setVisible(true);
    }

    public static void main(String args[]) {
        System.out.println("Starting Slots...");
        Slots3 mainFrame = new Slots3 ("Slots Demo Using Executor");
    }

    public class ButtonListener implements ActionListener {
    // inner class
```

```java
        public void actionPerformed (ActionEvent e) {
            if (onOff == false) {
                onOff = true;
                spin.setText ("Stop");
                index = (int)(4 * Math.random());
                RunSlots task1 = new RunSlots (150, tracker,
                    anim[index], slotsPanel1);
                index = (int)(4 * Math.random());
                RunSlots task2 = new RunSlots (125, tracker,
                    anim[index], slotsPanel2);
                index = (int)(4 * Math.random());
                RunSlots task3 = new RunSlots (175, tracker,
                    anim[index], slotsPanel3);
                tExecutor = Executors.newFixedThreadPool(3);
                tExecutor.execute (task1);
                tExecutor.execute (task2);
                tExecutor.execute (task3);
            }

            else {
                onOff = false;
                spin.setText ("Spin");
                tExecutor.shutdown();
            }
        }
    }
}
```

---

```java
import java.awt.*;
/**
* @(#)Slots3.java 1.0 05/03/10
* Author: Georges Merx, PhD
*/

class RunSlots implements Runnable {
    private int sleepTime;
    private MediaTracker tracker;
    private ImagePanel slotsPanel;
    private Image image;
    public RunSlots (int sTime, MediaTracker track, Image i,
        ImagePanel s) {
        sleepTime = sTime;
        tracker = track;
        slotsPanel = s;
        image = i;
    }

    public void run() {
        try {
            tracker.waitForID (0);
```

```
        } catch (InterruptedException e) {
            return;
        }

        try {
            Thread.sleep (sleepTime);
        } catch (InterruptedException e) {
            return;
        }

        slotsPanel.repaint(tracker, image);
    }
}
```

```java
import java.awt.*;
import javax.swing.JPanel;
/**
 * The class ImagePanel manages the drawing of the images
 */

class ImagePanel extends JPanel {
    private Image animation;
    private MediaTracker tracker;

    public ImagePanel (MediaTracker track, Image anim) {
        tracker = track;
        animation = anim;
    }

    public void repaint (MediaTracker track, Image anim) {
        tracker = track;
        animation = anim;
        super.repaint();
    }

    public void paintComponent(Graphics g) {
        super.paintComponent(g);

        if ((tracker.statusAll(false) & MediaTracker.ERRORED) != 0) {
            g.setColor(Color.red);
            g.fillRect(0, 0, getSize().width, getSize().height);
            return;
        }

        if (tracker.statusID(0, false) == MediaTracker.COMPLETE) {
            g.drawImage(animation, 10, 10, this);
        }
    }
}
```

You will notice that this approach separates thread creation from thread management, requiring the assignment of arguments to provide access to shared components.

*Notes:*

- The default **repaint()** method is replaced with one that adds these parameters; **super.repaint()** is called to run the repaint functionality.
- The **run()** method performs the thread statements.

## 8.3.10 Handling Sound

What if you could create your own MP3 player in Java?

Well, you can! Java supports a variety of sound formats and provides high-level methods to work with sound files. In the standard J2SE SDK, Java 2 supports the following basic sound-file formats:

- WAVE
- AU
- AIFF
- AIFF-C
- SND

The Java Media Framework supports the MP-3 format, as mentioned earlier.

The support of a Wave (**.wav**) file in a simple Java program is illustrated in the following code example (two classes):

```
/*
* @(#)SounTester.java 1.0 03/05/03
*
* Author:  Georges Merx
*
*/

import java.awt.*;
import java.awt.event.*;
import javax.swing.*;
import java.io.*;
import java.applet.*;

class SoundTester extends JFrame implements ActionListener {
    SoundPlayer sp = null;

    public SoundTester() {
        addWindowListener(new WindowAdapter() {
            public void windowClosing(WindowEvent e) {
                dispose();
                System.exit(0);
            }
        });

        Container c = getContentPane ();
        c.setLayout (new FlowLayout ());
        JButton play = new JButton ("Play" );
```

```
            play.addActionListener (this);
            c.add (play);
            JButton stop = new JButton ("Stop");
            stop.addActionListener (this);
            c.add (stop);
            JButton exit = new JButton ("Exit");
            exit.addActionListener (this);
            c.add (exit);
            pack();
            setVisible (true);
        }
    public static void main(String args[]) {
            System.out.println("Starting SoundTester...");
            SoundTester mainFrame = new SoundTester();
            mainFrame.setTitle("SoundTester");
        }
    public void actionPerformed (ActionEvent e) {
            if (e.getActionCommand().equals("Play")) {
                sp = new SoundPlayer ("EASY RIDER.wav");
            }
            else if (e.getActionCommand().equals("Exit")) {
                System.out.println ("Ending ...");
                System.exit (0);
            }
            else {
                sp.stopIt ();
            }
        }
    }
}
```

This class provides all the basic set-up and control operations. The next class plays and stops the sound file ("clip"). The file **EASY RIDER.wav** provides the sound; substitute your own wave file as needed.

```
import java.awt.*;
import java.awt.event.*;
import javax.swing.*;
import java.io.*;
import java.applet.*;

class SoundPlayer extends JApplet {
    AudioClip clip;

    SoundPlayer (String name) {
            try {
                File file = new File(name);
                clip = Applet.newAudioClip(file.toURL());
                clip.play();
            }
```

```
        catch (IOException e) {
            System.out.println ("IOException reading clip!");
            System.exit (1);
        }
    }

    void stopIt () {
        clip.stop ();
    }
}
```

This brief example plays a specific **.wav** sound file when the PLAY button is activated, stops it when the STOP button is pushed, and ends the program when the EXIT button is selected. Figure 8.10 shows the user interface for the SoundTester program.

Figure 8.11 shows the UML class diagram for the SoundTester program. Being able to visualize the structure and relationships in programs is useful and enlightening, and its value increases as the code becomes more complex. For example, note the relationship line between the **SoundTester** class and the **SoundPlayer** class. You could easily overlook this relationship just scanning the source code, but the UML class diagram makes it obvious. Note too that **SoundTester** extends the Java **swing.JFrame** class and implements the Java **ActionListener** interface, while **SoundPlayer** extends the Java **JApplet** class. Hopefully, you will recall the distinction between **extends** and **implements** from Chapter 3: classes and, by extension, objects, are organized into a hierarchy so that child classes can inherit attributes and methods from parent classes (using the keyword **extends**). In addition, Java provides a facility for defining interfaces that set up predefined method signatures (stubs) coded into our programs (using the keyword **implements**) and we then add the logic (code) necessary for the successful execution of the method in our program.

FIGURE 8.10   The SoundTester Example Program

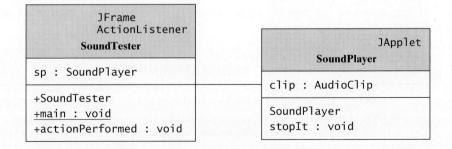

FIGURE 8.11   UML Class Diagram for the Sound Tester Program

Now that you have seen the structure of the **SoundTester** program, let's take a look at the behavior of the **SoundTester.main ()** method via the UML sequence diagram shown in Figure 8.12. Note that as the execution behavior of the **main()** method proceeds, eight objects are involved, as evidenced by the eight vertical dashed lines with rectangles (objects) at their top. Five of the eight objects are created (instantiated) via separate constructor method calls during the execution behavior. Once again, just reading Java source code to follow a method's behavior can be tedious, whereas a sequence diagram can help you to better understand the behavior sequence and can assist with debugging.

### 8.3.11  Handling Exceptions

In most applications, 20% of the code handles the primary scenario where the function works beginning-to-end without error or interruption, while the remaining 80% handles error and exception handling and recovery.

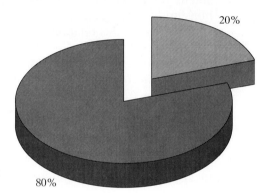

Percentage of code that handles where function works without interruption versus percentage that handles errors and recovery.

20%

80%

Just as obstacles and exceptions are a way of everyday human life—flat tires, traffic delays, car runs out of gas, caught in the rain without an umbrella, and at the beach on a sunny day without a swimsuit—software programs also are subject to the popular "Murphy's law" axiom, and software engineers therefore need to anticipate possible exceptions and address them by incorporating graceful, data-safe recovery mechanisms into their code. For example, when a calculation divides by zero or an array reference is out of bounds, an error occurs. As a programmer, you must anticipate the

---

## PROGRAMMING TIP

It is prudent to test for all possible conditions in selection statements, even those that should never occur. Since it is difficult to imagine every boundary condition, it is good practice to cover all possible values and catch all possible exceptions to increase the program's robustness.

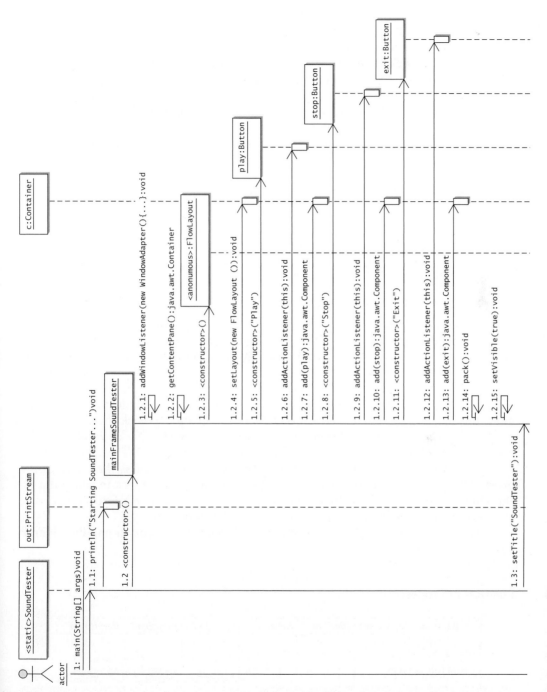

**FIGURE 8.12** UML Sequence Diagram for the SoundTester.main() Method

eventuality of such an error and intercept it so that you can redirect the user to correct any necessary inputs to correct the error. More specifically, instead of allowing your program to terminate abnormally when an error occurs, possibly losing important data in the process as well as upsetting the user, it you must give it the ability to recover from these malfunctions through *exception handlers.*

A Java method *throws an exception* when it encounters an error it does not know how to deal with; if there is an exception handler implemented, it will *catch the exception.* If there is no exception handler for the error in your code, the Java Virtual Machine terminates your program and invokes its default exception handler to display the error in the console window.

```java
public static void main (String args[]) {
    try {
        AllCaps capDemo = new AllCaps (arguments[0]);
    } catch (ArrayOutOfBoundsException e) {
        System.err.println ("No file specified on command line!");
        System.exit(0);
    }
}
```

As illustrated by the preceding example (which sets up the conversion to uppercase of a file specified on the command line), the **try** and **catch** blocks capture specific exceptions (in this case an **ArrayOutOfBoundsException**). One try block can be followed by multiple **catch** blocks, one for each specific exception, so that different errors can be handled uniquely.

The **try** block encloses code that may generate an exception; the **try** block is immediately followed by zero or more **catch** blocks. Each **catch** block specifies the type of exception it can catch and contains an exception handler. An optional **finally** block provides code that always executes, regardless of whether there is an exception (required if there is no **catch** block). The **throws** clause specifies the exceptions a method throws (throw point); once an exception is thrown, the block in which the exception occurred expires (termination model of exception handling). Exception classes can be derived from a common superclass (i.e., polymorphism).

The next chapter covers additional details about the exception-handling hierarchy in Java.

## 8.4    Position in Process

| Iterations | *iteration 1* | *iteration 2* | *iteration 3* | *iteration 4* | *iteration 5* | *iteration n* |
|------------|-----------|-----------|-----------|-----------|-----------|-----------|
| Disciplines | | | | | | |
| CERTIFICATION | | | | | | E* |

At this stage in the life-cycle of our software development methodology, we have reached the **Certification Phase**. At this point, the code should be complete and validated. Early customers have added their feedback, and all errors of any significance have been corrected and released into the most current version. This phase is strictly under the control of quality assurance (QA), which should be set up with enough organizational independence to allow its manager or director to make undisputed go/no-go decisions. A product should not be released for general distribution unless QA certifies that it meets all agreed-upon requirements within agreed-to quality parameters (functional and non-functional). QA issues a **Certification Report** at the end of this phase.

---

### FUNCTIONAL AND NON-FUNCTIONAL REQUIREMENTS

*Functional requirements* cover all the aspects of a program that have to do with functionality, i.e. which perform a work process.

*Non-functional requirements* address supporting issues, such as performance, accessibility, scalability, installability, and maintainability.

---

## 8.5   Example and Explanation

Before certifying a software product, software quality assurance must determine the satisfactory resolution of a broad range of potential shortcomings. Many of these are listed in Table 8.1.

TABLE 8.1   Quality Assurance Issues and Resolutions

| Issue | Resolution |
|---|---|
| Completed testing and test reports:<br>• Component unit testing<br>• Integration testing and test report<br>• Alpha testing and test report<br>• Beta testing and test report<br>• Stress testing and test report<br>• Validation of corrections | Review and validation of all completions and the signed-off availability of all requisite reports |
| Available documentation:<br>• Internal: specifications and reports<br>• External: user documentation, installation documentation, online help | Ensure that all requisite documentation is available, updated to the most current release point, complete, and of high quality; validate that requirements have been met and the design specs followed |
| Deployment readiness:<br>• Product package and distribution<br>• Support<br>• Maintenance<br>• Installation | Verify that product package is complete and adheres to all requirements, standards, and applicable laws; ensure and test the availability of support personnel, processes, and tools (e.g., defect tracking and resolution); ensure process and resources available for ongoing, timely product maintenance; validate that product is installable on target systems (including data-migration support) |
| Issues of intellectual property (IP):<br>• Inventions<br>• Product features<br>• Documentation | Ensure that intellectual property is identified, documented, registered (copyright and/or patents), and securely stored/safeguarded; ensure that appropriate control mechanisms (check-in; check-out) are in place |

## 8.6    *Harm*  *ny* **Design Case Study**

In this chapter, we conclude our case study, *Harm*  *ny* **Designs**. By now you have taken the initiative, over the last few weeks, to construct a realistic project for the model home interior design market. If you have followed through on every assignment and recommendation, you may even have had some "field experience" with your product, even if it is only in prototype form at this time. In "real life," you would now conduct beta testing and initial deployment of your product, having reached initial operational capability (IOC).

## 8.7    Resources

We have many opportunities to learn from other disciplines but rarely take advantage of the wealth of knowledge they have created. When software engineers look beyond the boundaries of their knowledge, they sometimes discover valuable new ideas and approaches. One well-known example of such a cross-disciplinary victory is the adoption of the principles of architectural design into software engineering. Christopher Alexander, a well-known architect, described the concept of "design patterns" in his writings. Software specialists like Kent Beck adapted these perspectives to improve software design processes.

### 8.7.1    *Connections*

Every profession has its own challenges and finds ways over time to meet them. Something that is a minor, secondary challenge in one discipline may be a primary, mission-critical challenge in another. Just think, for example, how much we software engineers can learn in terms of quality Best Practices from examining the procedures in a top-notch emergency room in a major urban university hospital.

### 8.7.2    *People*

- The architect **Christopher Alexander** was born in Vienna, Austria, in 1936. He graduated with degrees in mathematics and architecture from Cambridge University and with a Ph.D. in architecture from Harvard University. Alexander developed an architectural theory in terms of what he called "patterns." This theory suggested a means for creating successful places that blended the application of logic with collective experience.[4] Some of his books:
  - *Notes on the Synthesis of Form*, by Christopher W. Alexander. Harvard University Press, 1970. An early mathematical approach to the logic of good design.
  - *A Pattern Language: Towns, Buildings, Construction*, by Christopher Alexander, Sara Ishikawa, and Murray Silverstein. Oxford University Press, 1977. Beautiful and responsible design and good design thinking at every level of scale.
- **Kent Beck** first discovered patterns as an undergraduate at the University of Oregon. Today, he owns and operates First Class Software, Inc., where he focuses on

---

[4]Muriel Emmanuel, *Contemporary Architects*, New York: St. Martin's Press, 1980, pp. 25–26.

his two greatest interests, patterns and extreme programming. He is the author of more than fifty technical articles and author/co-author of a number of books.

- **Martin Fowler** is the chief scientist for ThoughtWorks, Inc. He is a well-known advocate of using objects in developing business information systems and is particularly known for his work in patterns, the UML, lightweight methodologies, and refactoring. He has written four books: *Analysis Patterns*, *Refactoring*, the award-winning *UML Distilled*, and *Planning Extreme Programming*.

- **Craig Larman** is the author of *Applying UML and Patterns: An Introduction to OOA/D and the Unified Process*, the world's best-selling text on OOA/D and iterative development, translated into many languages, and used in industry and colleges worldwide.

### 8.7.3   Companies

There are many third-party software developers of add-on classes and JavaBeans packages. Depending on your area of interest, you can search for them on the Internet or on the Sun Microsystems Web site. The latter provides a listing of developers and software companies that have registered their product offerings with the site.

## 8.8   Summary and Recommendations

This chapter covered the important topics of multithreaded applications and multimedia support, but these subjects were not discussed at length because an in-depth treatment would go beyond the scope of this book. We also examined seven perspectives on the process of software development (see Table 8.13). The important message here is not a focus on these specific viewpoints, but the need to understand that all complex professional processes benefit from the application of multiple meaningful perspectives to their resolution.

## 8.9   Review Questions

1. **Multithreading.** Describe the two pre-J2SE 5.0 approaches to implementing multithreaded applications.
   Multithreaded applications may be implemented using the `Runnable` interface or by extending the `Thread` class.
2. **Perspectives.** List the seven software engineering perspectives introduced in this chapter and provide an example or description for each one in terms of its relevance in creating quality software.

## 8.10   Glossary – Terminology – Concepts

**Multitasking**   Support for concurrent (multiple-processor) or quasi-concurrent (single-processor) processing of multiple process threads. From an operating system perspective, can also refer to concurrent execution of multiple instances of a program.

**Multimedia formats**   WAVE, AU, AIFF, AIFF-C, SND, MP3, MPEG-2, MPEG-4, WMA

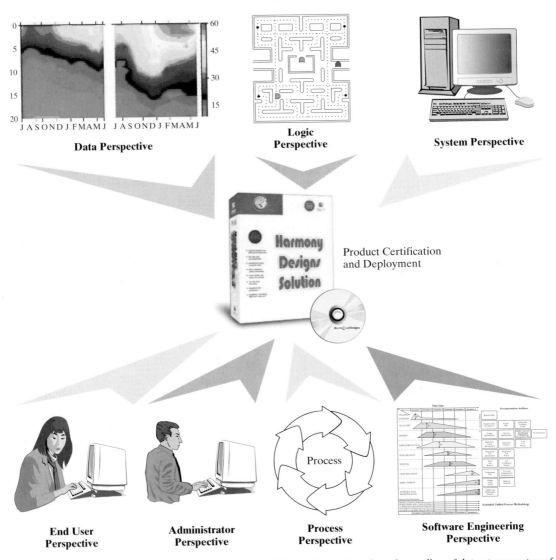

**FIGURE 8.13** Software Development Perspectives on Software Development

**Data:** Focuses on value-added transformation of data to information, and on the safeguarding of data at every step of the processing

**Logic:** Focuses on accurate business-rule and algorithm implementation

**System:** Includes issues of platform, network, portability, installability, and performance

**End-User:** Focuses on usability, accessibility (including disabled-access), and productivity (this can include performance issues, such as response time).

**Administrator:** Focuses on installability, configuration, error handling, error logging, access to support, and turn-around time to obtain corrections.

**Process:** Pays special attention to issues of productivity, workflow, optimization, and accuracy of work results.

**Software Engineering:** accounts for development standards, Best Practices, component reuse, testability, and the like

## 8.11   Exercises

**1. Enhanced Slot Program.**   Add functions to keep track of scores and load alternative images. Add other improvements based on the functioning of commercial slot machines.

**2. Multithreading in J2SE 5.0.**   Compare the pre-J2SE 5.0 approach to multithreading to the post-J2SE 5.0 approach. Use `java.sun.com` as a resource.

**3. Perspectives.**   Reexamine the seven software engineering perspectives introduced in this chapter and provide realistic examples for each in terms of a direct influence on program design for the Voting Program.

**4. Multimedia.**   Research and document recent advances in support for multimedia files in Java programs. Include portable devices and their use of J2ME applications. Also discuss future areas of improvement.

Write a short application using the Java Media Framework (JMF).

# CHAPTER 9

# Software Quality Assurance

Software quality assurance (SQA) is an organization's quality-control discipline implemented organizationally, technically, and procedurally to ensure that all participants assigned to a software engineering project adhere to software quality assurance Best Practices agreed to by project stakeholders. This controlling function is not limited to testing, as it may have been traditionally in many companies and organizations: SQA plays a much broader role in inspection, audit, verification, and validation that spans all phases of the software development life-cycle.

---

### FEELING BUGGED

Software bugs cost the U.S. economy nearly $60 billion a year, with $22 billion of that avoidable if the industry improved testing so that more errors could be detected earlier, says a new study commissioned by the National Institute of Standards and Technology.... The main reason for so many errors is software's increasing complexity, the report said. Whereas software products once consisted of thousands of lines of code, today they are more likely to involve millions of lines.

(From the *Chicago Tribune*, no author) *San Diego Union*, Monday, July 15, 2002

---

Bug . . . ?

In the company, the SQA team and especially its management need to be organizationally independent from the engineering function. Otherwise, conflicts of interest between engineering goals (to get the product finished on time and within budget) and quality assurance (to meet stakeholder requirements, eliminate errors and shortcomings before release, and maximize quality) can easily arise under pressure, with the result that quality is too readily compromised.

Figure 9.1 shows an example organizational chart where the director of QA reports to the vice president of operations. Alternatively, the director may report to the vice president of finance or even to the president directly. This type of organizational structure is recommended because it safeguards QA's independence. (The organizational chart and the role of the lead QA executive are often good indicators of how serious a company is about quality assurance.)

The SQA principles previewed in Chapter 4 are revisited in detail in this chapter and augmented with information about the quality principles established by Dr. W. Edwards Deming.[1] We will also cover Carnegie-Mellon University's Software Engineering Institute's Capability Maturity Model (CMMI),[2] and the IEEE and ISO quality standards and procedures.[3] Direct connections are established to particular design, coding, and testing practices. Quality issues associated with documentation and online help are also covered.

On the software-development side, the issues of robustness, reliability, and testing are examined in detail. Levels and types of testing, testing tools, and test documentation and validation are key topics in software testing.

---

[1]Please visit the W. Edwards Deming Institute at www.deming.org
[2]Please visit the Carnegie-Mellon Software Engineering Institute at www.sei.cmu.edu/cmmi
[3]Please visit the IEEE Software Engineering Standards Zone online at standards.ieee.org/software and the ISO Web site at www.iso.ch/iso/en/iso9000-14000/iso9000/iso9000index.html

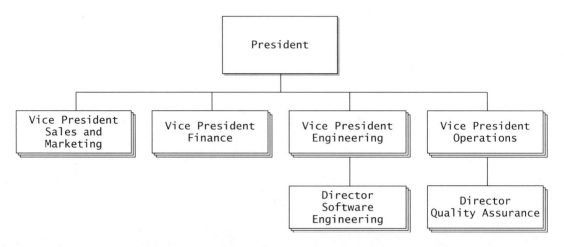

FIGURE 9.1    Proposed SQA Function in a Typical Organization

## 9.1    Learning Objectives

This chapter covers the main quality-related activities associated with software engineering. While software quality assurance (SQA) may once have been viewed as equivalent to software testing, it is recognized today that issues of quality permeate every phase of the software-development life-cycle. SQA responsibilities include:

- *Process control:* Ensuring that all contributors follow agreed-upon software engineering process guidelines established in writing by the company.
- *Adherence to Best Practices and standards:* Establishing and enforcing agreed-upon quality standards, from documentation to testing to certification, following industry Best Practices like CMMI or ISO 9000.
- *Testing:* Appropriate testing according to agreed-upon standards at every phase in the development life-cycle; test automation to ensure regression control.
- *Inspection:* Critical evaluation of completed components; validation against requirements.
- *Closed-loop corrective action:* Exception reporting, tracking, and resolution.
- *Configuration management:* Reliable tracking of all intellectual property (IP), such as all versions of source and object code files, documentation, specifications, test data files, etc.

In addition, we examine in more detail the Best Practices for developing Java software programming logic. In this context, we describe how to develop Java program business logic in relation to the user interface and data management components of a typical application. We also cover issues of software unit testing. Later, in Chapter 12, we will cover integration testing. These areas of learning coincide with the methodology model for this chapter, which covers Product Certification, including Release Management and Quality Measurements.

### 9.1.1  *Learning Layout*

This recurring section shows the learning objectives of the chapter in a simple diagram, using the UML activity diagram notation (see Fig. 9.2).

### 9.1.2  *Learning Connections*

The learning connections diagram in Figure 9.3 shows the content of this chapter in relation to the knowledge and skills development recommended for apprentice Java software engineers.

As we observe in this diagram, the chapter focuses on quality assurance–related issues and learning. However, it should be clear from the start that all aspects of software engineering are directly impacted by issues of quality, and all project participants need to include attention to quality and excellence in their skill development.

## 9.2  Executive Summary

The cost of fixing problems in software projects experiences an exponential increase as the work progresses, peaking when the product is released into production. While this truth is unsurprising, too many software developers nevertheless rush to implementation and release without adequate attention to the fine points of quality. Often they fail to consider aspects of quality which then negatively affect the eventual product user's experience, even though individual features and functions may have been adequately tested.

In this chapter, we also continue the discussion on Java program structure and implementation, including the organization of the various main elements of program logic—user interface, business rules, and information management—but we do so with a special emphasis on the role of software quality assurance.

Many organizations relegate their quality assurance function to a software-testing role, often reserved for the phase after coding is complete, and limited to a validation of previous unit tests performed by engineering. This approach can lead to unpredictable quality and frequent rework. Instead, a consistent focus on quality throughout all phases of the software-development life-cycle is the only way for a high-quality product to emerge at the end.

Figure 9.4 shows all the points of contact between engineering activities and issues of quality. There is an inherent tension between the progress required of an engineering project and the constraints imposed by the quest for perfection. Less-than-perfect software code breaks in operation! Brittle code leads to potentially serious errors and interruptions. For instance, what if this software controls the guidance system of a manned spaceship?[4] The quality assurance function must be empowered to ensure perfection—or near-perfection—with all critical errors eliminated.

Errors or exceptions fall into the following categories:

- *Functional errors:*  A function does not operate as the requirement specifies.
- *Logic errors:*  A function generates an incongruent result, such as incorrect data.

---

[4]A recent far-off-course landing of an "improved" Russian *Soyuz* spaceship was traced to a software problem.

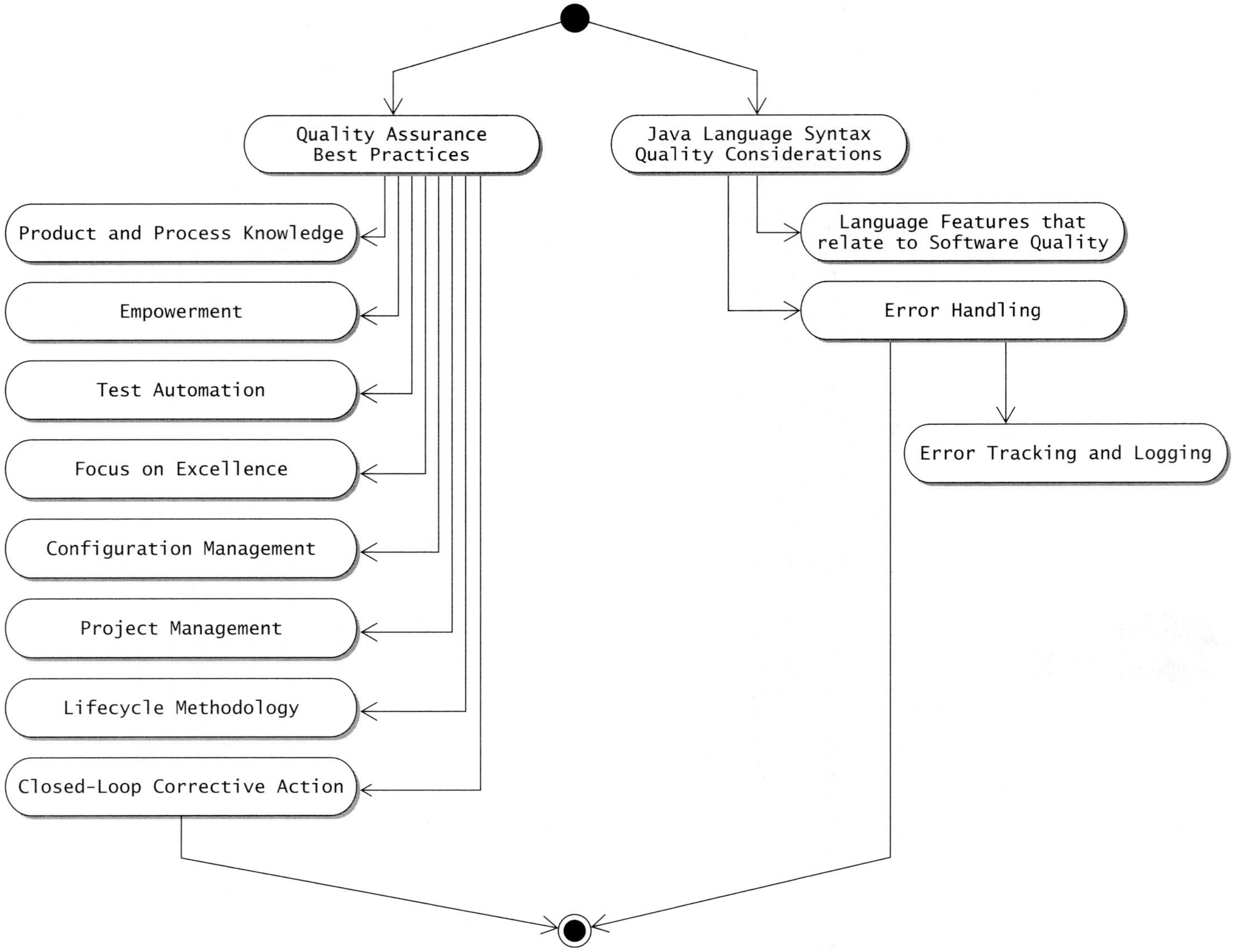

FIGURE 9.2 Chapter 9 Learning Layout (as a UML Activity Diagram)

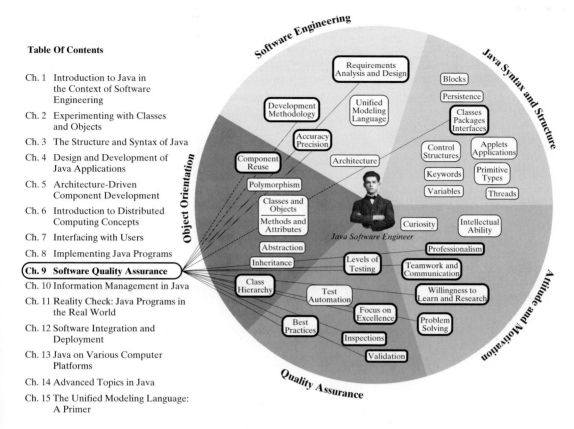

**FIGURE 9.3** Learning Connections for Chapter 9

- *User interface errors:* Access to a function is constrained because of incorrect or inefficient user accessibility.
- *Non-functional problems:* These include excessive lag time, hard to read, poor organization/layout, and the like.

In addition to errors, exceptions, and problems, requirement oversights are often identified along the way: functions that logically should be available are missing or do not work as they should to support the work process optimally. These are tracked as **Requests for Improvement** (RFI).[5]

When developing commercial software applications, competent Java software engineers pursue industry Best Practices that lead to quality software on time, on budget, and compliant with user requirements. The relevant Best Practices are described in

---

[5]Sometimes also called Request for Change (RFC).

| Disciplines | Quality Considerations | |
|---|---|---|
| CONCEPT | *Is high quality achievable economically?* | *Are quality considerations budgeted (organization, tools, time)?* |
| ANALYSIS | *Are all relevant stakeholder requirements captured and documented?* | *Does the requirements analysis follow organizational standards?* |
| DESIGN | *Does the design reflect requirements?* | *Does the design follow software engineering Best Practices?* |
| IMPLEMENTATION | *Is the code stable and robust?* | |
| INTEGRATION | *Are there complete unit tests in place?* | *Is the product tested? (Component, subsystem, system, interfaces)* |
| TESTING | *Is the code inspected and validated?* | *Does the product meet all project requirements?* |
| CERTIFICATION | *Does the product meet all functional and non-functional requirements?* | *Are early users satisfied with the product?* |
| DEPLOYMENT | *Are all known errors corrected?* | |
| SUPPORT AND MAINTENANCE | *Are issues captured, reported, tracked, corrected, tested, and released according to a documented, repeatable process?* | |

FIGURE 9.4 Contact Points for Software Quality Assurance

detail in this chapter. The quality of a software program is determined by a number of qualitative and quantitative factors:

- Complete implementation of requirements
- Improved work process (faster, easier, more reliable)
- Resilience: does not crash, recovers from errors gracefully
- Efficiency: uses system and network resources sparingly, supports as many users as needed (scalability)
- Quality measurements (number of errors per lines of code, severity of errors, etc.)
- Stakeholder satisfaction with the implementation

It is the responsibility of the quality assurance organization to monitor these factors and enforce their implementation, but all project participants must be committed to adhering to standards of excellent quality in their work.

The development of commercial Java applications usually entails the structured design and development of a substantial number of interrelated components, often distributed across multiple logical and/or physical platform "tiers." Here are some basic rules that good design should follow in determining the structure of applications, especially distributed applications:

- Separation of the graphical user interface from the navigation control and business logic
  - ○ Portability of GUI
  - ○ Isolation of navigation and business rules (algorithms) into replaceable components
  - ○ "Model-View-Controller" architecture design pattern
- Portability, extensibility, and scalability of components
  - ○ Developing components for use in diverse implementations and environments without requiring code changes, or at least isolating code changes
  - ○ Structuring the code and its interfaces to make it easy to add more users and functionality

*Design patterns* provide design Best Practices that software engineers should follow in designing and developing code that addresses these and additional design concerns. Many design patterns have been developed since the "Gang of Four" (Vlissides et al.) developed the original set for their seminal book *Design Patterns*. The Abstract Factory pattern, for example, provides a structured, documented approach for governing the creation of similar components based on agreed-upon abstract characteristics.

In our ongoing study of Java software technology, we are focusing in this chapter on what makes code robust, reliable, extensible, and usable. These and other intrinsic qualitative project requirements are determined by design and coding practices that will be illuminated in a later section.

## 9.3   Learning Modules

This section describes the key learning elements in this chapter. Three main topic areas are covered:

- Software quality assurance, including the quality processes inherent in good coding practices
- Java application structure, including the logical distribution of components in distributed solutions
- Java quality coding practices

It is beyond the scope of this book to cover specific Java enterprise capabilities, such as Java Server Pages and Java Servlets, supported in the J2EE product suite. The discussion of distributed computing here will be limited to conceptual considerations. Implementation specifics are covered in other books and in the online tutorials available on the Internet.

### 9.3.1  Software Quality Assurance

We want to introduce the topic of software quality assurance (SQA) in some detail at this point, because SQA must be part of the development life-cycle in every phase and iteration. While it may seem obvious that software is highly quality-dependent, organizations and individual software engineers are sometimes tempted to forgo quality practices, especially under the following circumstances:

- The project is late—pressure is on to finish (maybe a customer has been promised delivery by a certain deadline).
- Quality was not a budget consideration when the project was originally planned.
- Engineering believes that software quality is more the responsibility of the quality assurance department than its own.

Any of these impediments may be fatal to a project; we will therefore explore the role of software quality assurance in software projects from the perspective of a required support discipline.

#### Software Quality Assurance Best Practices

Software quality is determined by a number of soft and hard factors in the software-development organization, ranging from group beliefs, values, priorities, and habits, to budgets, quality measurements, and the use of quality-related tools.[6] Much has been written about SQA over the years, and a number of Best Practices have been identified. Figure 9.5 documents our summary of recommended Best Practices for SQA.

Each of these Best Practices depends on the others to be implemented for maximum effectiveness. A more detailed description of each element follows.

#### Life-Cycle Methodology

The first of our eight SQA Best Practices addresses the development life-cycle itself. High-quality software can consistently emerge only from a high-quality agile ("low-ceremony") or robust ("high-ceremony") development methodology that takes account of every aspect of the software analysis, design, and production process necessary for the project at hand.

---

**Key Term**

*High ceremony* refers to a formal process with extensive documentation and formalized sign-off and tracking procedures. A *low-ceremony* process reduces formality to a minimum and relies on collaboration and iteration to ensure that the resulting product meets requirements.

---

[6]Several of the concepts introduced in the next few pages were originally developed in collaboration between one of the authors (Merx) and Mr. Jesse Martinez for a consulting assignment.

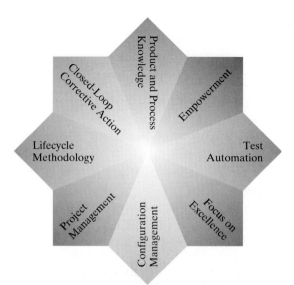

FIGURE 9.5   Software Quality Assurance
Best Practices

Software engineers and methodology specialists have discovered over the years that viewing the process of software development from a "holistic" life-cycle perspective, rather than as a sequence of discrete phases, leads to improved products. In this fashion, all project participants are guided by the driving force of the project requirements, and code writing is governed by a proper design specification resting securely on the foundation of the requirements specification. At the same time, the life-cycle methodology has to provide the development process with the requisite flexibility and agility, which inherently requires ongoing adjustments. The application of iterations to the life-cycle approach enables such adaptability. The inclusion of the principles of object-orientation not only in the coding phases, but also as an underlying approach to analysis, design, and implementation, is a further recommended part of this SQA Best Practice. Effective implementation of object orientation is only possible if its principles are considered in every phase of the project life-cycle.

## SCOPE OF ITERATION

It is a good rule of thumb to set up a project iteration as an effort which a small group can accomplish in four to six weeks.

Another school of thought associated with agile techniques recommends limiting iterations to just two weeks and assembling the project from numerous such mini-project efforts.

The iterative approach introduced in earlier chapters in this book adheres to the principle of an iterative, object-oriented life-cycle methodology.

### Project Management

Structured project management of software-development projects is the second SQA Best Practice. Formal project management has long been part of software engineering projects, but traditional software project management practices have been too detached from the idiosyncrasies of software development and thus not flexible enough to account for the many adjustments typically required in the course of a more complex project. As a Best Practice, we therefore recommend a *two-level* project management approach consistent with the iterative perspective on software engineering methodology. The high-level ("macro-level") project plan covers the main phases and iterations; a low-level ("micro-level"), detailed project plan is developed for each iteration (see Fig. 9.6).

## AGILE PROJECT MANAGEMENT

Some proponents of agile techniques recommend an even more flexible approach that applies bracketing milestones from worst- to best-case to provide management with a range of decision options based on level of risk.

Project management includes the conscientious tracking of tasks, dates, and resources. Corrections are applied as necessary, based on stakeholder approval. Critical path analysis may be performed to ensure efficient use of resources.

### Configuration Management

The organized, efficient tracking of all intellectual property (IP) elements pertaining to a project is covered in the configuration management Best Practice. Software engineering projects often involve thousands of individual files and documents. Configuration management provides the processes for tracking the creation, sorting, storing, updating, and destruction of all these elements of information. It also manages the resources required (hardware, software, networking) for the environment(s) for which the software application is being developed. For example, if an application supports Oracle$^{TM}$ and SQLServer$^{TM}$ relational database management systems, the configuration management process keeps track of all the requisite test database tables required to run the program with one or the other database.

For large projects, specialized configuration management software tools are available from a range of vendors. These tools typically track all required resources in a database and provide access control through an authenticated and logged check-in/check-out mechanism. High-end systems provide distributed project and resource management and sophisticated tracing, audit, and roll-back capabilities.

### Focus on Excellence

Probably the most obvious SQA Best Practice, Focus on Excellence requires that a broad range of specific initiatives and values in an organization be meaningful and consistently produce the desired results. Another view of this category is that of "Focus on

**Project: Online Voting Application**

**Macro-Level Project Plan**

Start: 1/1/2005                                                                 Release: 3/1/2006

| Iteration 1: Business Plan | Iteration 2: Analysis and Design | Iteration 3: Component Implementation | Iteration 4: Initial Deployment | Iteration 4: Commercial Deployment |
|---|---|---|---|---|

**Micro-Level Project Plan**

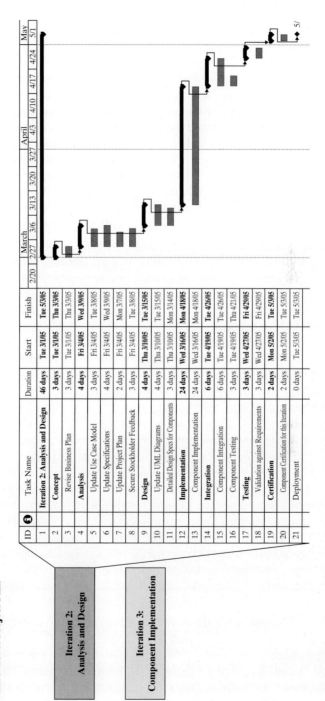

| ID | ⓘ | Task Name | Duration | Start | Finish |
|---|---|---|---|---|---|
| 1 | | **Iteration 2: Analysis and Design** | **46 days** | **Tue 3/1/05** | **Tue 5/3/05** |
| 2 | | **Concept** | **3 days** | **Tue 3/1/05** | **Thu 3/3/05** |
| 3 | | Revise Business Plan | 3 days | Tue 3/1/05 | Thu 3/3/05 |
| 4 | | **Analysis** | **4 days** | **Fri 3/4/05** | **Wed 3/9/05** |
| 5 | | Update Use Case Model | 3 days | Fri 3/4/05 | Tue 3/8/05 |
| 6 | | Update Specifications | 4 days | Fri 3/4/05 | Wed 3/9/05 |
| 7 | | Update Project Plan | 2 days | Fri 3/4/05 | Mon 3/7/05 |
| 8 | | Secure Stockholder Feedback | 3 days | Fri 3/4/05 | Tue 3/8/05 |
| 9 | | **Design** | **4 days** | **Thu 3/10/05** | **Tue 3/15/05** |
| 10 | | Update UML Diagrams | 4 days | Thu 3/10/05 | Tue 3/15/05 |
| 11 | | Detailed Design Specs for Components | 3 days | Thu 3/10/05 | Mon 3/14/05 |
| 12 | | **Implementation** | **24 days** | **Wed 3/16/05** | **Mon 4/18/05** |
| 13 | | Component Implementation | 24 days | Wed 3/16/05 | Mon 4/18/05 |
| 14 | | **Integration** | **6 days** | **Tue 4/19/05** | **Tue 4/26/05** |
| 15 | | Component Integration | 6 days | Tue 4/19/05 | Tue 4/26/05 |
| 16 | | Component Testing | 3 days | Tue 4/19/05 | Thu 4/21/05 |
| 17 | | **Testing** | **3 days** | **Wed 4/27/05** | **Fri 4/29/05** |
| 18 | | Validation against Requirements | 3 days | Wed 4/27/05 | Fri 4/29/05 |
| 19 | | **Certification** | **2 days** | **Mon 5/2/05** | **Tue 5/3/05** |
| 20 | | Component Certification for this Iteration | 2 days | Mon 5/2/05 | Tue 5/3/05 |
| 21 | | Deployment | 0 days | Tue 5/3/05 | Tue 5/3/05 |

FIGURE 9.6   High-Level (Macro)/Low-Level (Micro) Project Planning

433

World-Class" or "Best of Class." Successful attention to excellence requires a focus on issues of quality difficult to achieve for most organizations, whether commercial or nonprofit. Upfront costs for excellence tend to exceed minimums, even though long-term attention to excellence has been proven to achieve higher profits and overall superior business and organizational results. Often, short-term profit motives or schedule delays jeopardize quality—unfortunately, in software engineering, inferior quality leads to dramatically negative results, given the inherent vulnerability of software code. Strict adherence to a high-quality focused development methodology like the one introduced in this text is the best assurance that a focus on excellence is maintained throughout all phases.

Excellence can only be achieved consistently if quality is measured in detail and regularly, and if these measurements form the basis for improvement. Organizationally, all contributors and decision-makers must be committed to continuous quality improvement. Senior management and, by extension, major company stockholders must be prepared to invest in quality-improvement initiatives and must understand and embrace the benefits of prioritizing quality over short-term maximum returns.

### Test Automation

Progressive software-development organizations generally accept the notion that developing software incrementally is more predictable and reliable. Traditionally, applications were developed in large, long-term project cycles following W.W. Royce's Waterfall methodology. This meant that for months no functioning code was available, and that the integration phase brought together disparate components over an extended "shake-out" period. Obviously, this approach led to long periods of instability and many disconnected components needing corrections. Given the state of technology when Royce and his contemporaries initially developed this approach, the Waterfall method was an innovative improvement at the time, but a more flexible approach is warranted today.

---

## UNIT TESTING

Developers are responsible for testing their own software components, including positive and negative testing, usability validation, and proper functioning of programming interfaces (parameters and return values).

The tests developed for these components are documented in a Unit Test Specification consisting chiefly of Unit Test Scripts, step-by-step descriptions of test procedures and expected outcomes.

---

Modern software-development organizations using advanced software engineering tools and processes pursue a "frequent-build" approach where new versions of programs are created often—if possible, daily. Thus a new software product is constructed an "onion layer" at a time, with frequent incremental changes and enhancements. This approach virtually requires test automation, at least with larger projects, because even minimal feature and regression testing against the new build would take too long and tie up human testers too long to execute manually on a sufficiently frequent basis.

Automated software tests involve realistically simulating application interaction in a human-like fashion, as well as programmatically exercising class/object interfaces. Effective test automation must be considered from the beginning as part of the design process, so that all requisite contact points in the code are properly accounted for in the unit and integration test scenarios.

### Empowerment

A chronic problem with software quality assurance in many organizations is the lack of empowerment bestowed upon quality specialists and managers who comprise the SQA organization. If the SQA organization is not able to stop bad code from becoming product, then its efforts are in vain.

While it may seem logical for an organization to trust a group of specialists hired for a particular purpose to do the work in their area of specialization, this is too often not the case for SQA. In organizations that lack quality consciousness, senior managers second-guess SQA reports and override recommendations to delay the release of an untested or defective product. SQA has to be powerful to be effective. That is why we recommended earlier that SQA and engineering should be separated organizationally in order to avoid conflicts of interest. The head of SQA has to be empowered to override decisions made by the head of engineering (even if engineering has a larger staff than SQA). Senior management must be committed to support SQA's quality-driven decisions.

### Product and Process Knowledge

In addition to lack of empowerment, the effectiveness of SQA may be limited by the following two factors:

1. Lack of explicit attention to quality issues in design and development.
2. Lack of product and work-process knowledge on the part of developers and/or SQA specialists.

It is impossible to properly implement effective SQA guidelines and processes without a detailed understanding of the solution domain. This includes the stakeholders' objectives, the purpose of the program, the existing and prospective work processes, the underlying science, math, and technology, and the functional rules ("algorithms") associated with the software application in the context of the underlying work process(es).

### Closed-Loop Corrective Action

As discussed in an earlier chapter, an important aspect of quality management is the tracking of exceptions and errors from discovery to the availability of a working correction in the hands of the problem discoverer. This is called **Closed-Loop Corrective Action (CLCA)** (see Fig. 9.7). Organizations normally institute a call tracking mechanism,[7] which assigns a tracking identifier to a problem report so that its correction, testing, and release can be traced end-to-end. Sophisticated call management systems are available from multiple vendors, either as standalone solutions or in conjunction with configuration management systems. There are some viable open-source products available as well.

---

[7]Common synonyms for "call" include "incident", "bug", "defect", and "case."

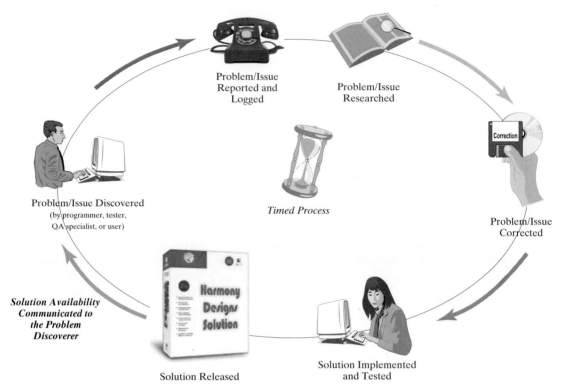

**FIGURE 9.7**    Closed-Loop Corrective Action Process

This approach considers every step of the error-correction process and informs the problem originator of the availability of a solution to the initially reported problem.

### Inspections

Inspections, also referred to as **walk-throughs**, involve a structured process to ensure that a particular component or subsystem meets quality as well as feature/function requirements. An inspection generally follows these steps:

1. The engineer responsible for a component finishes development and unit testing.
2. The engineer calls an inspection and provides appropriate documentation to the inspection participants as far in advance as possible and in accordance with the process being followed. The inspection team should include peers, supervisors, potential customers, quality assurance and technical writing specialists, and anyone else who can make a positive contribution to the inspection process.
3. During the inspection meeting(s), the engineer justifies the validity of the implementation. The team critically inspects every aspect of the deliverable, seeking problems, incorrectly implemented functionality (as compared to the Requirements and Design Specifications), inadequacies, discontinuities, and weaknesses.

**4.** All problems are documented and are then corrected by the engineer, with a follow-up inspection to ensure that all inadequacies have been properly removed, without regressions.

Even if a development team is following less rigorous or less formal software-development processes, such as an agile approach like eXtreme Programming (XP), inspections are still performed, less formally perhaps, by pairs of programmers who work together on code components or on the development of whole-user stories (e.g., requirements).

### Audits

Some organizations incorporate a formalized audit-trail process as a part of their software-development process. Audits tend to occur most often when one organization builds a software product for an entirely different organization. For example, a consulting firm such as Accenture or EDS may have a contract to build a software product for a financial services customer, or a client organization may contract to have a software product built by an overseas provider.

In these cases, the purpose of the audit is to certify that the software product is free of errors and is ready to be placed into production or, in the case of commercial software, made available for purchase. These audits are often performed by an independent third-party organization in order to enhance the integrity of the audit in the eyes of both the supplier and the customer. External audits are also known as independent verification and validation (IV&V), a subject discussed in the next section.

### Verification and Validation

Verification and validation, often referred to as V&V, address two situations: building the correct software product (verification), and building the right software product (validation). Therefore, the major objectives of the software V&V process are to determine whether the software performs its intended functions correctly, ensure that it performs no unintended functions, and provide information about its quality and reliability.[8] V&V is also an aid in ascertaining whether the software requirements are implemented correctly and completely and are traceable back to the requirements. Note, however, that software V&V does not verify the correctness of the requirements, only whether the software functionality can be traced to the requirements.

**Verification** involves the reduction and hopefully elimination of known defects. Verification also tests requirements that are needed for successful deployment and operation of the software product, but are not necessarily functional domain requirements. Performance and throughput, peak-workload processing performance, user interface testing, documentation and procedures testing, and backup and recovery testing are examples of non-functional areas of requirement.

---

[8]*Software Verification and Validation: Its Role in Computer Assurance and Its Relationship with Software Project Management Standards*, NIST Special Publication 500-165, U.S. Department of Commerce/National Institute of Standards and Technology, September 1989.

**Validation** involves the checking of milestones and deliverables against written commitments, typically documented in the project's Requirements Specification. This process also provides for the validation of the work processes associated with the project and its outcomes against agreed-upon standards.

Validation and verification are vital for producing a high-quality software product and mitigating the risk associated with a lesser-quality software product. The more issues and defects that are discovered and rectified before final production and general release, the less costly and frustrating the software product will be for all the stakeholders.

On the technical side, the organization of a program's components has a major impact on its quality characteristics, especially in terms of non-functional (support) requirements such as scalability and maintainability. The next section looks at this topic in more detail.

### 9.3.2 Java Application Structure

The class hierarchy fundamentally determines the structure of Java applications. The most critical design process is, therefore, the translation of the Domain Model (use cases from the Requirements Specification) to the Design Model (especially the class hierarchy), as described in detail in earlier chapters. The determination of what classes to create and how to organize them in relation to each other and to other imported components is determined by a number of factors, including object-oriented design principles. The following practical recommendations should help novice software engineers develop well-structured applications:

- Work within the plan, respect the specifications; if in doubt, get input from stakeholders; use inspection and validation processes
- Use common design patterns that encapsulate object-orientation Best Practices, e.g., Model-View-Controller, Façade, Creator, Pure Fabrication, etc., and implement principles of Low Coupling and high cohesion
- Pursue abstraction and flexible logic; build components to be replaceable
- Use minimal scope for memory components
- Base design decisions on underlying work processes and their optimization
- Account for future changes and scalability
- Standardize input and output interfaces for interoperability
- Document everything; use JavaDoc to create standard-format source documentation; provide online help

Figure 9.8 shows a high-level view of how objects evolve from classes in a multi-tier application.

Abstract classes provide the core methods and attributes for concrete classes; the latter are the templates for objects instantiated using the Java new keyword and initialized by the specific class constructor invoked at object creation. The "connection" between these tiers is via either XML and SOAP or RMI, or CORBA for distributed applications, and via message communication between local objects.

The principles of object orientation remain valid across multi-tier applications, but with some limitations. Networking protocols and databases are not object-oriented, so it is

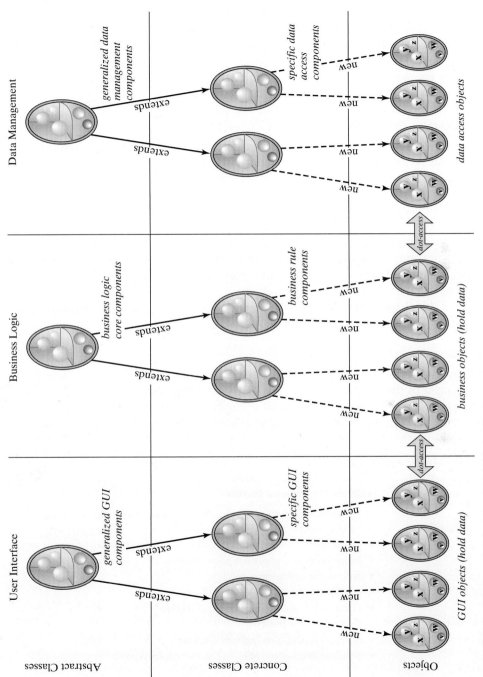

**FIGURE 9.8** Classes and Objects in a Multi-tier Application

necessary to translate between procedural data sequences and objects. Often this is done in well-isolated layers that follow an Adapter pattern.[9]

While the features and functions of the application were captured in the Design Specification, the details of implementation are often determined at this late stage, even though earlier resolution of all architectural issues is highly recommended. Also, the conceptual distribution of components planned in the design stage sometimes has to give way to practical adjustments that account for technology strengths and weaknesses or other factors like costs or reliability.

### Java Quality Coding Processes

From a quality perspective, the distribution of components should naturally support robustness, scalability, testability, maintainability, and consistency. Design-pattern-driven abstraction and polymorphism are key tools in supporting these objectives because they promote modularity and flexibility.

Robustness is achieved by making the Java code resilient and forgiving when external errors occur or users enter wrong information. Extensibility ensures that new features or changes can be easily implemented without having to rewrite (and retest) major portions of existing code. Usability refers to the user's experience in interacting with the software application; both initial/novice use and repetitive/expert use scenarios need to be considered.

Table 9.1 summarizes the coding practices that help ensure optimized software quality.

### Java Error Handling

Many errors can creep into the process of development software applications. Those that are caught by the compiler are the easiest to correct, but logic errors that only appear when the program is running can be difficult to duplicate, diagnose, and correct. Implementing code to deal with potential errors is a key prerequisite for good software engineering.

TABLE 9.1    Development Best Practices

| Quality Attributes | Software Development Practices |
|---|---|
| Usability | • Following established GUI guidelines (using standard GUI components, layouts, fonts, colors, *etc.*)<br>• Designing process functionality before determining the GUI: focus on productivity<br>• Special attention to often repeated interactions—optimization<br>• Alternative access/entry points<br>• Useful, context-specific online help<br>• Localization/internationalization as required |
| Resilience/Robustness | • Extensive error checking<br>• User input validation (pattern matching)<br>• Selection lists instead of input fields wherever possible |

[9]Gamma et al., *Design Patterns*, Addison-Wesley, 1995.

**TABLE 9.1**  (*Continued*)

| Quality Attributes | Software Development Practices |
|---|---|
| | • Careful, comprehensive design and implementation of all alternative scenarios |
| | • Use of standard execption-handling coding techniques, e.g., `Exception` class hierarchy |
| | • Unit testing of all alternative paths through code |
| *Performance* | • Localizing the scope of all data structures |
| | • Use of buffering and multiple threads to minimize I/O delays |
| | • Optimization of code areas that impact performance |
| | • Use of hot-spot compilers for specific destination platforms |
| | • If necessary, implementation of performance-critical components in C++ |
| *Extensibility* | • Use of design patterns to implement separation of concerns (advanced modularity) |
| | • Using abstraction, polymorphism, inheritance, and encapsulation to make components multipurpose and enable the addition of components without impacting parent classes |
| *Maintainability/Supportability* | • Excellent code documentation practices—coding for readability |
| | • Naming conventions—adherence to Sun Microsystems guidelines |
| | • Maintaining an Implementation Specification that documents component interactions, implements UML diagrams, and coding decisions |
| | • Modularization of components—code transparency |
| | • Avoidance of unjustified "clever" or obscure coding practices |
| | • Documentation updating—ensuring that all artifacts are up to date and synchronized |
| *Integration* | • Data import/export support |
| | • Standardized access to public interfaces (encapsulation) |
| | • Support for SOAP and XML to allow for automatic, standard, secure integration with other applications |
| | • Consistency of component interfaces |
| | • Testing of interface functionality and performance |
| *Testability* | • Considering testability as part of feature design/implementation—creating unit tests in conjunction with implementation |
| | • Collaborative SQ effort across project organization |
| | • Ongoing stakeholder involvement—early exposure of project components to eventual users |
| | • Extensive alpha and beta testing |
| | • Creation and support of testing harness to ensure that all interfaces and components are tested in all their permutations |
| | • Documentation and tracking of test results—prioritization of error corrections |
| | • Use of quality metrics |
| *Security* | • Implement proper authentication and encryption for all sensitive components/functions/data |
| | • Ensure that no security leaks are inadvertently implemented in your public interfaces |
| | • Maintain your intellectual property (IP) through proper configuration management practices—copyright your work—safeguard your source code at all times |

Java provides a rich mechanism for handling errors polymorphically and at the various levels of a typical class hierarchy. This streamlines the process of error management without sacrificing granularity and context, a problem endemic to earlier object-oriented software technology.

### Applying the Exception-Handling Class Hierarchy

The exception-handling mechanism in Java provides a class hierarchy of exception classes that allow the software engineer to control the granularity of error management at every calling level in a program and to centralize error management in order to avoid cluttering the code with error-handling code blocks. The **Exception** class has many derived classes, such as **NoSuchFieldException** and **NoSuchMethodException,** and developers can create their own exceptions by extending the parent or any of the defined children exception classes. Components can *throw* excections that are *caught* by the implementing code.

## 9.4     Position in Process

| Iterations | iteration 1 | iteration 2 | iteration 3 | iteration 4 | iteration 5 | iteration n |
|---|---|---|---|---|---|---|
| Disciplines | | | | | | |
| DEPLOYMENT | | | | | | E* |

At this point in the development process, the release management and quality measurement activities begun in the last phase (Integration) are completed and the product is deployed for productive use. The process of **deployment** is critical, because this is the phase where significant customer installations take place and where the product experiences the first extensive exposure to use under operational conditions. Unfortunately, critical errors are often discovered in this phase. They must be corrected very quickly, given that the software is now being used for productive purposes. The organization needs to be set up for customer support in terms of personnel availability and competence and also of support tools.

The maintenance and support work process includes the following activities:

1. Problem acquisition, via telephone, e-mail, or Web site incident report
2. If genuine, problem analysis, categorization, and documentation
3. Assignment for resolution
4. Resolution tracking
5. Inclusion in upcoming release ("point release")
6. Informing incident initiator of solution availability
7. Closing the incident when solution is available

## 9.5     Example

The example in this section examines some of the basic issues of testing and error handling in the Voting Program program.

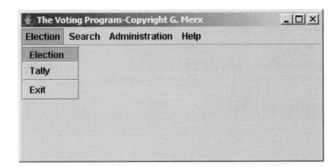

FIGURE 9.9   Election Selection in the Voting Program

```
C:\Program Files\Xinox Software\JCreatorV3\GE2001.exe                _ |□| x |
I/O Error on opening java.io.FileNotFoundException: CANDIDATES.DAT (The system c ▲
annot find the file specified)
java.lang.NullPointerException
        at InformationManagement.<init>(InformationManagement.java:52)
        at Election.<init>(Election.java:49)
        at UserInterface.<init>(UserInterface.java:162)
        at UserInterface$2.actionPerformed(UserInterface.java:82)
        at javax.swing.AbstractButton.fireActionPerformed(AbstractButton.java:17
86)
        at javax.swing.AbstractButton$ForwardActionEvents.actionPerformed(Abstra
ctButton.java:1839)
        at javax.swing.DefaultButtonModel.fireActionPerformed(DefaultButtonModel
.java:420)
        at javax.swing.DefaultButtonModel.setPressed(DefaultButtonModel.java:258
)
        at javax.swing.AbstractButton.doClick(AbstractButton.java:289)
        at javax.swing.plaf.basic.BasicMenuItemUI.doClick(BasicMenuItemUI.java:1
113)
        at javax.swing.plaf.basic.BasicMenuItemUI$MouseInputHandler.mouseRelease
d(BasicMenuItemUI.java:943)
        at java.awt.Component.processMouseEvent(Component.java:5100)
        at java.awt.Component.processEvent(Component.java:4897)
        at java.awt.Container.processEvent(Container.java:1569)
        at java.awt.Component.dispatchEventImpl(Component.java:3615)
        at java.awt.Container.dispatchEventImpl(Container.java:1627)    ▼
```

FIGURE 9.10   Error When Selecting Election

While testing the Voting Program by trying to select the Election option in the menu (see Fig. 9.9), we encounter the error shown in Figure 9.10.

### 9.5.1   Example Explanation

The program abort error in Figure 9.10 is an unacceptable situation in a commercial application where all potential errors should be intercepted by the program code, allowing for recovery or graceful termination. As we examine the error message at the top of those generated by the default exception handler in the Java Virtual Machine, the cause becomes obvious right away: the code attempted to open an internal data file called **CANDIDATES.DAT**, couldn't find it, and had no recovery code in place for that situation.

We then examine the code, tracing program execution from the menu handler in **UserInterface.java** to **Election.java.** By looking more closely at the specific errors we encountered, we find that the interruption actually occurred in the **Information Management.java** class, at (or around) line 52. (This code includes file I/O operations that we will cover in more detail in a subsequent chapter.)

> ## "ERROR ON LINE XXX"
>
> Note that both the compiler and the JVM may not "know" exactly where in your source code and error occurs, because they only recognize the error when he sequence of tokens parsed no longer fits any of their syntax rules. This is often somewhere past the actual point of failure.

In the actual code, we find that we catch an I/O error properly:

```
try {
      ss = new ObjectInputStream (new FileInputStream(fileName));
} catch (IOException e) {
      System.out.println ("I/O Error on opening " + e.toString());
      noError = false;

}
```

When we try to open the file for reading, an error occurs (because the file does not exist), so the file pointer remains null. Our error is that we then try to close this null file:

```
try {
      ss.close();
} catch (IOException e) {
      System.out.println ("I/O Error on closing " + e.toString());
      noError = false;

}
```

This code fails despite the **try ... catch** block, because we only test for an IOException, not a **NullPointerException**.

We then fix the error by moving the close inside the preceding **if (noError)** block. The program now exits in a controlled manner, as shown in Figure 9.11.

While this exit is still far from elegant, it leaves the data in a known state and is programmer-controlled.

This simple example proves demonstrates several points:

- Errors can occur in many different places in your code, especially when you are dealing with external files (persistence).
- The error may be more complex than the initial error message implies.
- Error handling depends on the recognition of specific conditions.
- Extensive careful testing is the only way to ensure product quality.

### 9.5.2 Practical Application

This particular error was found by a student testing the code after not properly following the workflow and ending up with no file of candidates. The programmer should

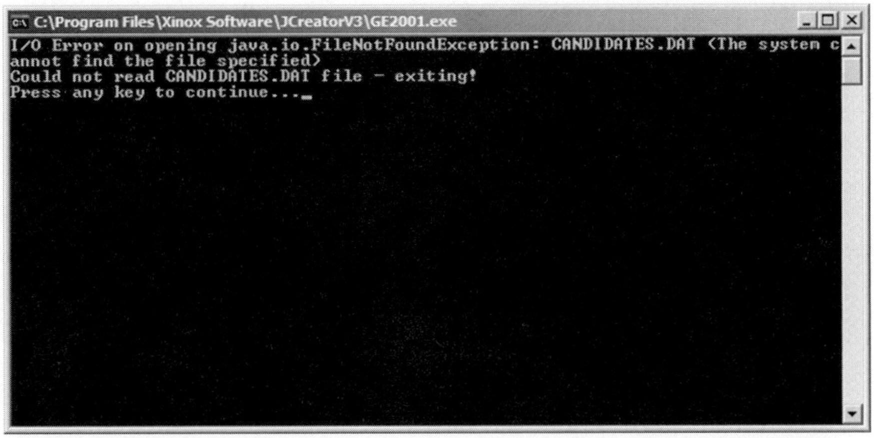

FIGURE 9.11   The Error Corrected

have predicted this scenario and tested for it herself. The process of testing depends on the exhaustive discovery of potential *what..if* error conditions and creating associated test scripts to ensure that these conditions have been handled properly in the code. The review of secondary scenarios on the use cases should help develop all the requisite alternative-execution scenarios to perform exhaustive testing.

## 9.6    Resources

There are many books and numerous organizations that focus on issues of software quality assurance.

### 9.6.1    Connections

One of many examples of an SQ organization is the Southern California Quality Assurance Association (SCQAA). Ref. www.scqaa.org.

Internationally, the International Standards Organization (ISO) maintains the ISO 9000 standard, which covers software quality standards. Ref. www.iso.org.

### 9.6.2    Companies

Many consulting companies specialize in issue of quality assurance. Organizations that have issues with software quality often benefit from bringing in outside consultants to help effect organizational and cultural changes that improve the focus on excellence.

## 9.7    Summary and Recommendations

Issues of software quality were the focus of this chapter. We examined quality assurance Best Practices and discussed the importance of giving constant attention to issues of quality in every phase and discipline of the software-development life-cycle.

## 9.8    Review Questions

**1. SQA Best Practices.** Describe three software quality assurance Best Practices and cite examples of their application (see Table 9.2).

## 9.9    Glossary – Terminology – Concepts

**Best Practice**    Studying the competition and determining what the very best way of doing something is; improving internal processes to meet this new standard; also, applying best-practices industry standards, such as CMMI.

**CMM(I)**    Carnegie-Mellon Maturity Model (interactive); a multilevel software process certification process developed and managed by Carnegie-Mellon's Software Engineering Institute (SEI)

**SQA (Software Quality Assurance)**    The application of quality assurance processes and mechanisms to the development of excellent software products

## 9.10    Exercises

**1. SQA Best Practice.**    Come up with an additional SQ Best Practice, describe it, justify it, and provide an example of its application.

**2. Error Correction.**    Test the Voting Program, find three other errors/shortcomings, and figure out how to correct them.

**3. Quality Software.**    Write a short program that accepts a user name and date of birth and displays that information graphically. Eliminate all possible errors from your code and handle all possible inputs. Document all the errors you find in the course of this exercise and how you handle them.

TABLE 9.2    Software Quality Assurance Best Practices

| SQA Best Practice | Description | Example |
|---|---|---|
| *Empowerment* | Ensuring that the SQA organization and management are independent of the engineering organization and have the power to "stop the presses" when a critical error is discovered | When SQA reports to engineering, the decision-maker has mixed objectives. *Engineering objectives:* deliver product on time, on budget; *QA objectives:* deliver product without errors (even if time and budget limits are exceeded) |
| *Closed-Loop Corrective Action* | Manage error correction from the point of origin all the way back to the point of origin | When customer A discovers a problem in a product module, the maintenance organization needs to correct the problem, test and release it, and make sure to inform A of the availability of a fix for the problem. |
| *Test Automation* | Automate regression testing to shorten the build process, allowing for more frequent, incremental builds | Using test automation tools or building user simulation programs, many functions of the program can be exercised automatically overnight, so that errors can be fixed in the morning and the next build remain on schedule |

# CHAPTER 10

# Information Management in Java

As discussed in previous chapters, most applications are developed to (1) acquire data, (2) process this input by extracting useful information and applying structure and algorithms, and (3) produce value-added information:

$$input \rightarrow process \rightarrow output$$

This information processing cannot be limited to operations in Random Access Memory, because data is not necessarily processed in the same program or timeframe as it is acquired, and the output from an application likewise cannot be allowed to be volatile. Data and results must be permanently storable. In computer systems, we therefore differentiate between *primary* (volatile) storage in RAM, and persistent *secondary* storage on any permanent storage device such as a hard disk. (Please see Figure 10.1 for an example of a JFileChooser object window, used to select a file from a physical file directory location.)

When data is stored on disk, it resides in files. You can think of a file as a named data container on disk. Files are organized according to the information structure they contain, but fundamentally a file is simply a stream of bytes.

This chapter discusses how RAM-based variables (objects) are stored permanently on disk, using the input-output (I/O) process of **serialization**. Object file I/O and other types of file I/O, database access, and access security are discussed for applications and applets. You will learn to consider the dataflow in and out of your application

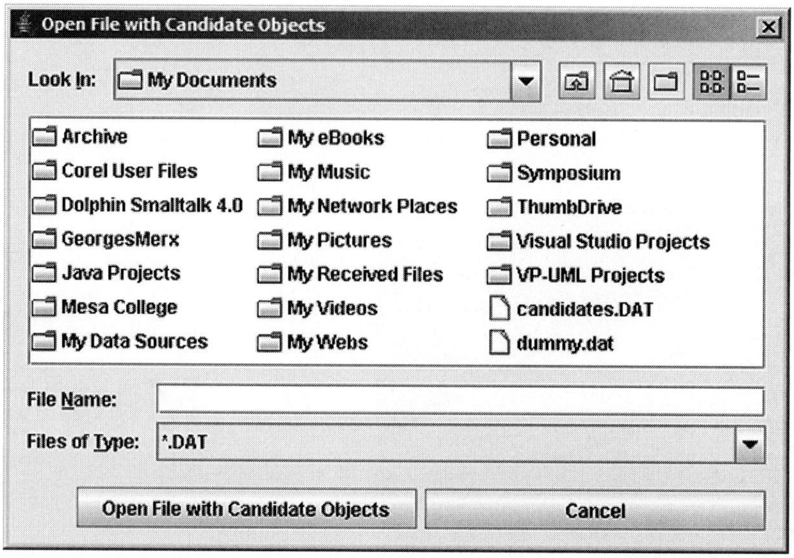

FIGURE 10.1    JFileChooser Screenshot

components (classes). Java interfaces and more advanced object-oriented topics related to data management (packages, serialization) are also included here.

## 10.1    Learning Objectives

Most applications are written to manipulate data input for the purpose of extracting useful information and providing users with knowledge about their operations and processes. Typically, data has to be accumulated over time to provide useful information. This very common functionality requires the permanent storage of data. The volatility of Random Access Memory (RAM) does not lend itself to permanent storage, so other technologies are used to make information permanent, or *persistent,* the term used in object orientation. Converting in-memory objects to storable data elements and back again is the process known as **serialization**: objects are reformatted for storage in files, a process provided by the Java programming language and relatively transparent to the application programmer.

In object-oriented programs, data (attributes) and executable functions (methods) are combined into the structures known as objects. The processes for extracting the data for persistent storage (serialization) and recreating objects with attributes and methods for programmatic access (deserialization) are built into Java using the Serializable interface.

This chapter examines the relationship between Java programs and stored data and the various approaches software engineers can take to provide access to external data sources. In our ongoing review of software engineering methodology, the final phase covers **Support and Maintenance**.

In this phase, the control of the software product often moves to another organization (at least in larger software-development organizations), and the development work is limited to fixing code errors or implementing minor tactical enhancements known as Requests for Change (RFCs), at least in the particular version of the product that enters this phase. For many products, this phase is by far the longest, sometimes up to a decade or more across multiple releases. It also represents the phase of maximum customer exposure, where the business of software development is defined by customer service excellence. Just because a product has reached maturity does not mean that it is invariably stable. Even mature products can be plagued by sporadic critical errors when a user finds a way to exercise code that was not properly quality-assured.

---

**TIP**

The quality of maintenance and support of the current product often determines whether a customer will stay with you as vendor or switch to a different product and supplier when the time comes to upgrade.

---

### 10.1.1  Learning Layout

This recurring section shows the learning objectives of the chapter in a simple diagram, using the United Modeling Language (UML) activity diagram notation (see Fig. 10.2). Of course, the contents of this chapter build on learning achieved in previous chapters. Please remember that while we have used the format of a UML activity diagram, this does not represent the typical software engineering use of this type of visualization.

### 10.1.2  Learning Connections

The learning connections diagram in Figure 10.3 shows the content of this chapter in relation to the knowledge and skills development recommended for apprentice Java software engineers. The categories and labels in the diagram are not immutable; in fact, we encourage you to customize this view for your own goals, activities, and skills. It is simply a way to visualize and be reminded that a great many interrelated skills are needed for successful software engineering.

As this recurring diagram has shown in every chapter, the skills required for any aspect of Java software development are interdisciplinary in nature. Thus focusing on one area at the expense of another will lead to inferior products.

## 10.2  Executive Summary

A process is created when a software application is executed on a computer. This means that the application is loaded into Random Access Memory (RAM) by an operating system routine, and that CPU cycles and memory are allocated for its

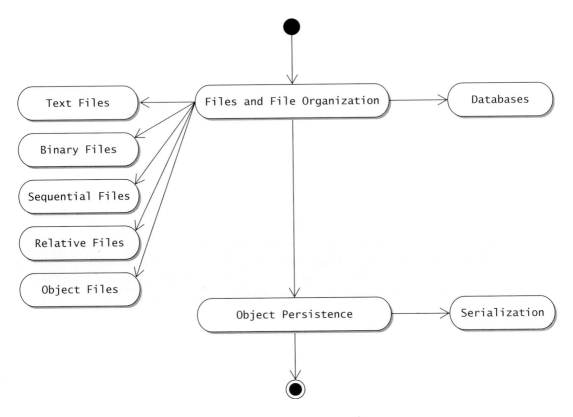

**FIGURE 10.2**    Chapter 10 Learning Layout (as a UML Activity Diagram)

variables.[1] The program is directly "aware" only of CPU and RAM, meaning that all other resources have to logically pass through that CPU/RAM connection. However, these resources are volatile, meaning that they cannot permanently store any information. Practical applications must have access to permanent information (data), of course, so other devices are used to make data permanent (or "persistent"—the term used in object orientation). Information is often stored on hard disks, for example. Other storage devices include:

- CD-ROM/CD-RW disks, DVD-ROM/DVD-RW disks
- Digital tapes
- Solid-state memory devices, such as "thumb-drives" and SD-Cards
- Floppy and ZIP disks
- External hard disks

---

[1]This is a generic description. For a Java class, the process is more complex. It involves the loading of the JVM, which in turn interprets bytecodes. Multiple processes can be involved.

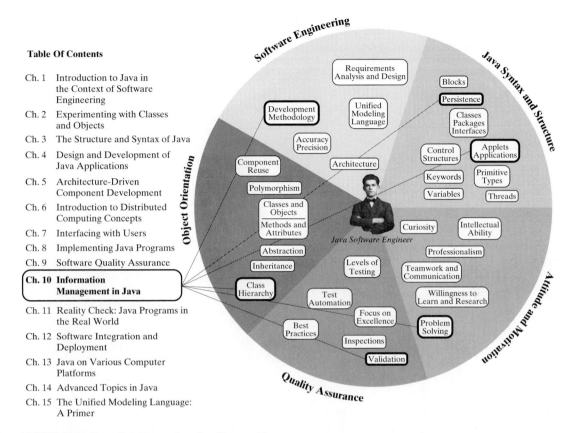

**FIGURE 10.3**   Learning Connections for Chapter 10

These devices are connected to the computer and are managed by operating system utilities that in turn provide interfaces to application programs. Traditionally, programs had to access these low-level operating system interfaces for I/O, but in modern languages like Java, file I/O has been abstracted and implemented at a relatively high level in conceptual classes. This means that as an application programmer you no longer need to know exactly *how* a file is opened or written to: these have become generalized operations.

Java programs (classes) are interpreted by the Java Virtual Machine, an executable on the system, which interfaces with the appropriate operating system programs to provide the Java program with system services as needed, including access to files on storage devices. Technically, Java programs can only interact with the CPU, which in turn accesses data in primary storage (RAM) and secondary storage (file storage devices) on behalf of the program (see Fig. 10.4).

Because data needs to be contained ("packaged") in a way that makes it storable and retrievable, the standard storage mechanism is a *file*. Files provide structure for data on secondary storage devices by preceding them with header fields (metadata)

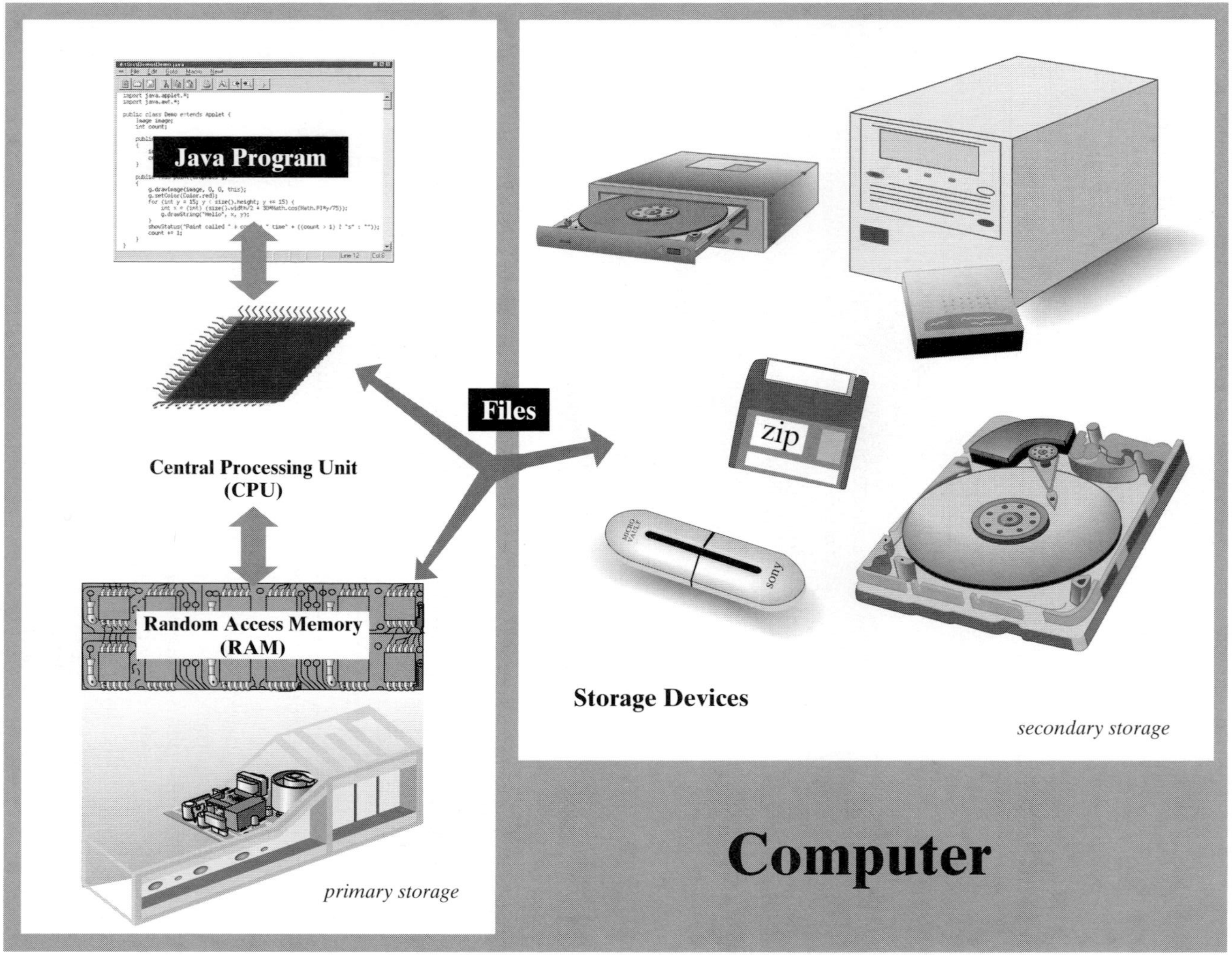

FIGURE 10.4   Java Programs Interact with CPU and RAM (simplification)

that contain information about the contents and length of the file, an end-of-file indicator, and other file-management specifics, including block descriptors for each block of data. This information makes files and the information they contain retrievable. Files can be organized for sequential or random access. At the lowest level, it is necessary to view files simply as a collection of bytes. This is useful when the file operation has nothing to do with the specific contents of the file or when the program subsequently superimposes its own view of the data structure on the stream of bytes read.

Fortunately for Java software engineers, the low-level complexity of physical file input-output (I/O) is managed by the JVM and the operating system of the platform where the program is executed. The programmer can perform these file operations using high-level, English-like statements. Establishing access to a file is described as *opening the file*. By opening a file, a *logical* file identifier is associated with the *physical* file (or path) name, and all subsequent file I/O operations occur when file operation methods interact with the logical file object. Note that there is no open keyword in Java, unlike many other languages. Opening a file in Java results from creating a new (logical) file object from a physical file.

The further challenge is that object-oriented Java programs organize data into objects. Objects also contain methods, but on disk, data and functions are separated, the latter residing in .class files. Data is stored in data files with extensions chosen by the programmer, normally based on the data structure or purpose or the program name. Serialization therefore takes objects of classes that implement the Serializable interface and writes data files with sufficient metadata to reconstruct the object when it is later reloaded (read back) into memory from the file. This chapter discusses the various types and functions of Java file I/O in more detail.

---

**TIP**

In choosing a file extension, try to avoid already-used three-letter sequences, because in Windows, the user can double-click on a data file to launch the associated program, and the operating system determines the program from the extension.

---

The transition of a software product into the **Support and Maintenance** phase is the subject of our final software methodology phase or discipline. In some organizations, this activity is assigned to a team of software engineers specializing in this area, but it is generally advisable to keep the original team involved with support for at least the following two reasons:

1. They know the code well enough to fix urgent problems quickly.
2. They need to understand and learn from the types of problems customers/users encounter in their everyday use of the product.

## 10.3    Learning Modules

The acquisition, manipulation, and delivery of information are central roles for computer systems. Most programs are written to process data into useful information. Data must be storable long-term for this functionality to have meaning as part of normal business and organizational processes. Permanent, or *persistent*, data storage is an integral function of all computer systems, with the possible exception of very small devices that only contain a fixed set of data in read-only memory. In most other computers, persistent data storage is provided by hardware devices, such as hard disks (some as small as a 25-cent coin), digital tape units, and CD-ROM or CD-R/W units, or more recent additions. These include DVD-ROM, DVD-R/W+, and solid-state memory devices, such as USB-connected "thumb-drives," secure digital (SD) storage cards, supporting operating system functions and programs, and application programming interfaces to these operating system input-output functions. In the next section, we will examine in detail how data is acquired, manipulated, and displayed to users.

### 10.3.1    *Information Life-Cycle*

Information usually starts with the acquisition of data. The sources of data are many, among them point-of-sale terminal transactions, forms filled in by operators, scanned images processed by optical character recognition (OCR) programs, sensor data, files or database tables, output files from another software application, and even sound files recorded with a microphone. The program logic takes the data and organizes and manipulates it through a work process that gives the user access to the information and knowledge contained in this data. Access to these results is provided in tables, lists, or graphics on-screen and reports that can be printed. Of course, a significant amount of time may elapse between the various stages, during which data and interim results must be stored in a nonvolatile fashion. Files provide the logical structure for such storage. Files are the way the computer and operating system organize data for storage on secondary storage media and devices for later retrieval and further processing.

Input-Process-Output logic flow

### 10.3.2    *Data and File Structures*

Data follows a hierarchy of organization, from bits and bytes to records and files (see Fig. 10.5). While the contents of Java data files are a stream of bytes, software constructs enable the Java programmer to "superimpose" structure on these byte streams

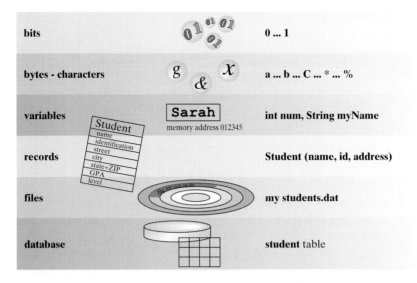

FIGURE 10.5  Data Organization Hierarchy

so that information can maintain structure relevant for program logic (e.g., records). A special type of file is a (relational) database table (actually, the fact that the table is stored as a file is transparent to the application programmer); database access is described later.

Operating systems do not view data from an object-oriented perspective the way Java does. This is what makes necessary the serialization process discussed earlier in order to "convert" from classes and objects to the data structures described above in order to store program data on a secondary storage device. This gives Java programs the ability to sequentially write objects to secondary storage and retrieve them as objects.

In Java programs, data can be stored in any of these formats, or more precisely, can be filtered to any of these levels (all data is stored as bits of zeros and ones, of course).

### Streams, Buffers, and Filters

Files are logical structures with physical manifestations. Magnetic or optical storage devices provide structured mechanisms for permanently recording data, which can later be read back into memory, as needed. Moving files between the relatively fast Random Access Memory (RAM) and the comparatively slow secondary storage devices involves various performance optimization and conversion techniques. Some of these are provided by the hardware (caches), some by the operating system, some by the JVM, and some may be employed by the programmer.

In Java, files are managed for performance reasons as *buffered* streams of data. Streams and their associated buffers and filters are used for different types of input-output (I/O) operations, as described in the sections that follow.

### 10.3.3  16-Bit Character I/O

16-bit Character I/O streams are called character streams and are implemented as *readers* and *writers* (see Fig. 10.6). **8-Bit Byte I/O** streams are called byte streams (see Fig. 10.7).

There are equivalent character and byte streams for each I/O type. The following I/O types are supported:

- Read from, and write to, memory
- Pipe: channeling output from one thread to the input of another thread (in a multithreaded application)
- Reading from, and writing to, a file
- Concatenating multiple input streams into one
- Serializing objects to make them persistent, deserializing them when reading into memory
- Data conversion—read data streams in machine-independent form
- Line-number counting
- Peeking ahead

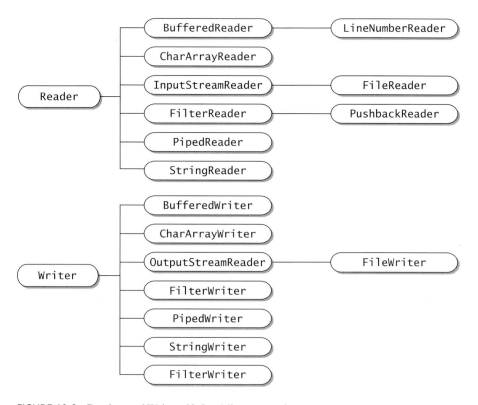

FIGURE 10.6   Readers and Writers (© Sun Microsystems)

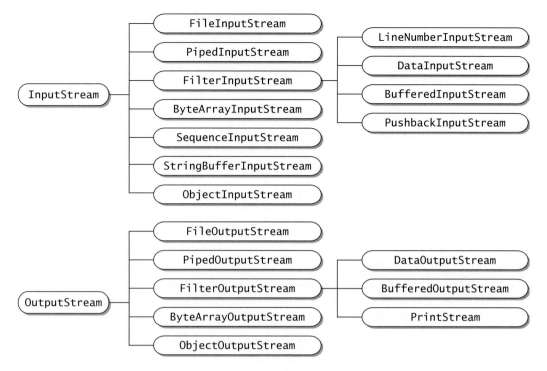

FIGURE 10.7   Input and Output Byte Streams (© Sun Microsystems)

- Buffering I/O to optimize performance
- Filtering to map I/O to specific data structures
- Converting between byte streams and character streams

The following sections describe each stream type and its function. Some of these I/O types are not further covered in this book.

### Type of I/O: File
The streams listed below

- FileReader
- FileWriter
- FileInputStream
- FileOutputStream

are collectively called file streams. They are used to read from, or write to, a file on the file system native to the operating system on which the application is executing.

The FileReader and FileWriter classes are meant for reading and writing streams of characters, respectively. The class hierarchy for FileReader and a sample of the FileReader class are shown in Figure 10.8. The FileWriter class hierarchy and sample are both very similar to these.

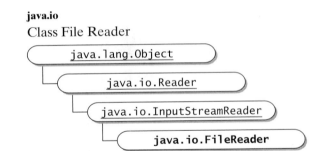

**java.io**
Class File Reader

FIGURE 10.8   Class FileReader Hierarchy
(from Sun Java website)

All of the following examples are based on Java 2 Platform Standard Edition 1.4.2. Minor additions were implemented in J2SE 5.0.

### Example of FileReader:

```
public class FileReader extends InputStreamReader
```

### Sample constructor:

```
public FileReader(String fileName) throws fileNotFoundException
```

### Parameters:

fileName—name of the physical file from which to read

### Throws:

fileNotFoundException—generated if the named file does not exist, is a directory rather than a regular file, or for some other reason cannot be opened for reading

The `FileInputStream` and `FileOutputStream` classes are used to read and write streams of raw bytes such as image data. The class hierarchies for `FileInputStream` and `FileOutputStream` are shown in Figure 10.9.

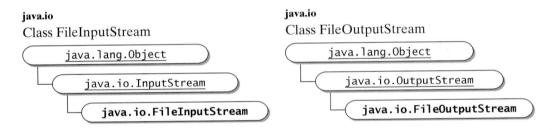

**java.io**
Class FileInputStream

**java.io**
Class FileOutputStream

FIGURE 10.9   Input and Output Streams (from Sun Java Web site)

### Example of FileInputStream:

`public class FileOutputStream extends OutputStream`

### Constructor example:

`public FileOutputStream(String fileName) throws fileNotFoundException`

### Parameters:

`fileName`—the name of the destination file

### Throws:

`fileNotFoundException`—if the file exists but is a directory rather than a regular file, does not exist but cannot be created, or cannot be opened for some reason

---

### *Type of I/O: Memory*

The streams listed below

- `CharArrayReader`
- `CharArrayWriter`
- `ByteArrayInputStream`
- `ByteArrayOutputStream`

are used to read from, and write to, memory. These streams are associated with an array. The `CharArrayReader/Writer` classes read/write a stream of characters to a character array. The `ByteArrayInput/OutputStream` classes perform inputs/outputs to/from a byte array respectively. The read and write methods of each of these streams are used to read from, or write to, the array.

The streams listed below

- `StringReader`
- `StringWriter`
- `StringBufferInputStream`

are used to read from, and write to, string objects. The `StringReader` stream is used to read characters from a String object in memory. The `StringWriter` stream is used to write to a String object. `StringWriter` collects the characters written to it in a `String Buffer`, which can then be converted to a String. The `StringBufferInputStream` is similar to `StringReader`, except that it reads bytes from a `StringBuffer`.

### *Type of I/O: Pipe*

Pipes are synchronized communication channels between threads. They are used to channel the output from one thread into the input of another. The following streams implement the input and output components of a pipe:

- `PipedReader`
- `PipedWriter`

- PipedInputStream
- PipedOutputStream

### Type of I/O: Concatenation

The concatenation stream shown below

- SequenceInputStream is used to concatenate multiple input streams—abstract class InputStream—into one input stream so that the Java program sees the group as one continuous input stream.

### Type of I/O: Object Serialization

The streams listed below

- ObjectInputStream
- ObjectOutputStream

are used for serialization and deserializations ObjectOutputStream is used to convert objects into file-compatible data structures. This process is called serialization for the purpose of making the objects persistent. The opposite function, ObjectInputStream, is used to deserialize objects, meaning to read them back from secondary storage into memory, reconstituting the objects in their previous form.

### Type of I/O: Data Conversion

The streams listed below

- DataInputStream
- DataOutputStream

are used for conversions. These data streams represent Unicode strings and are used to read and write Java primitive data types in a machine-independent format.

### Type of I/O: Counting

The streams listed below

- LineNumberReader
- LineNumberInputStream

are buffered character-input streams that keep track of line numbers while reading.

### Type of I/O: Peeking Ahead

The streams listed below

- PushbackReader
- PushbackInputStream

are input streams with a pushback buffer. When reading data from a stream, it is sometimes useful to peek at the next few bytes or characters in the stream to decide what to do next.

*Type of I/O: Buffering*

The streams listed below

- `BufferedReader`
- `BufferedWriter`
- `BufferedInputStream`
- `BufferedOutputStream`

are used for buffering. It is often efficient to buffer data while reading or writing, thereby reducing the number of accesses required on the original data source. Buffered streams are typically more efficient than similar nonbuffered streams and are often used with other streams.

*Type of I/O: Filtering*

The streams listed below

- `FilterReader`
- `FilterWriter`
- `FilterInputStream`
- `FilterOutputStream`

are abstract classes that define the interface for filter streams that filter data while it is being read or written.

*Type of I/O: Converting Between Bytes and Characters*

The streams listed below

- `InputStreamReader`
- `OutputStreamWriter`

are reader and writer pair that forms the bridge between byte streams and character streams.

An `InputStreamReader` reads bytes from an `InputStream` and converts them to characters, using the default character encoding or a character encoding specified by name.

An `OutputStreamWriter` converts characters to bytes, using the default character encoding or a character encoding specified by name and then writes those bytes to an `OutputStream`.

## 10.3.4 *Persistence and Serialization*

From the perspective of object orientation, the conversion process of taking an in-memory object and storing it on a more permanent storage device is called *persistence*, or *serialization*. The serialized form of an object contains sufficient information to reconstitute the object upon retrieval. The `Serializable` interface[2] must be implemented

---

[2]Or the `Externalizable` interface, which leaves read and write control to the developer through the `readExternal` and `writeExternal` interface methods.

by classes of which the member objects are to be saved in a file. Otherwise, the process is transparent to the programmer and provides the flexible ability to store even complex object types permanently and retrieve them unscathed, provided the class structure is available when the object is read back.

---

| NOTE |
|------|
| XML can be used to store object information long-term, without dependence on specific object formats (ref. XMLEncoder class). |

---

**Example:**

```
import java.io.*; // required for Serializable interface
    public enum PartyAffiliation implements Serializable {
    // enum type must be serializable to be written out to disk
        NOT_SELECTED("not selected"),
        DEMOCRATIC_PARTY("Democratic Party"),
        REPUBLICAN_PARTY("Republican Party"),
        GREEN_PARTY("Green Party"),
        LIBERTARIAN_PARTY("Libertarian Party"),
        OTHER_PARTY("Other Party");
    }
}
```

---

All objects and attributes that are being "persisted" must implement the Serializable interface provided in java.file.io.

The following paragraphs examine two sample file I/O programs. The first reads and writes simple text, the second serializes and deserializes objects.

### 10.3.5 Example File I/O Programs

The file I/O reader and writer StringReader and StringWriter presented earlier in this chapter are often used for simple text file manipulations. The following program implements these two I/O streams.

#### Text I/O

The first class, TextFileFilter, is used to constrain the file type to only display existing files of .txt and .html/.htm types in the file chooser (file open dialog).

```
import java.io.File;

public class TextFileFilter extends javax.swing.filechooser.
  FileFilter {
```

```java
    public boolean accept(File f) {
        if (f.isDirectory())
            return true;
        //get the file extension
        String extension = getExtension(f);
        //check to see if the extension is equal to "html" or "htm"
        if ((extension.equals("txt")) || (extension.equals("html"))
            || (extension.equals("htm")))
            return true;
        return false;
    }

    public String getDescription() {
        return "HTML and Text files";
    }

    private String getExtension(File f) {
        String s = f.getName();
        int i = s.lastIndexOf('.');
        if (i > 0 &&  i < s.length() - 1)
            return s.substring(i+1).toLowerCase();
        return "";
    }
}
```

The second, main class, `FileIO`, allows the user to select input and output files using the standard file dialog of class `JFileChooser`. It then copies the selected file to the new file selected by the user, using a `FileReader` input stream and a `FileWriter` output stream.

```java
import java.awt.event.*;
import javax.swing.*;
import java.io.*;

class FileIO extends JFrame {
    public FileIO() {
        addWindowListener(new WindowAdapter() {
            public void windowClosing(WindowEvent e) {
                dispose();
                System.exit(0);
            }
        });
    }

    public static void main(String[] args) throws IOException {
        JFileChooser chooser = new JFileChooser();
        File inputFile = null;
        File outputFile = null;
```

```
            chooser.setFileFilter(TextFileFilter());

            if (chooser.showOpenDialog(null) ==
                JFileChooser.APPROVE_OPTION) {
                inputFile = chooser.getSelectedFile ();

                if (chooser.showSaveDialog(null) ==
                    JFileChooser.APPROVE_OPTION) {
                    outputFile = chooser.getSelectedFile ();
                    FileReader in = new FileReader(inputFile);
                    FileWriter out = new FileWriter(outputFile);
                    int c;

                    while ((c = in.read()) != -1)
                        out.write(c);
                    in.close();
                    out.close();

                    System.out.println ("File " + inputFile +
                        " copied to File " + outputFile);
                }
            }

            System.exit (0);
        }
}
```

Figure 10.10 shows the UML Class diagram for these two classes.

When this `FileIO` program is launched, the user is prompted to select a file from the File Chooser Dialog box (Open mode) (see Fig. 10.11).

After traversing the folders and selecting your file (`misdir2.txt` in the preceding example), a second File Chooser Dialog box (Save option) appears, asking for the path and name of the file to save (copy) the contents of the file to a user-specified location (see Fig. 10.12).

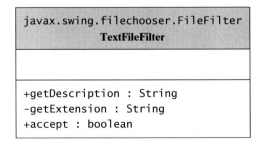
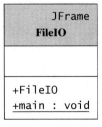

FIGURE 10.10   Class Diagram for File I/O Sample Program

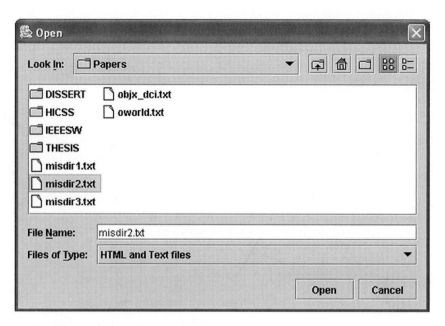

FIGURE 10.11 FileChooser Dialog Box (Open)

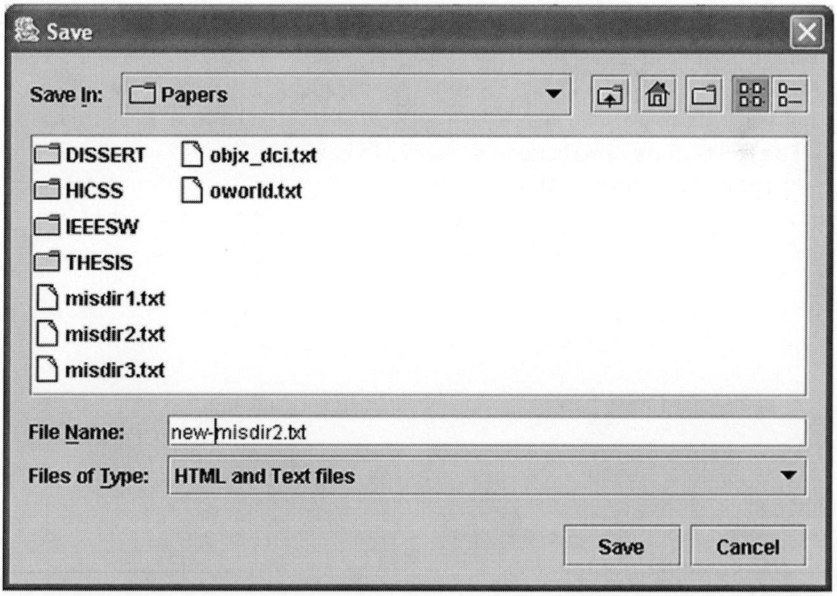

FIGURE 10.12 FileChooser Dialog Box (Save)

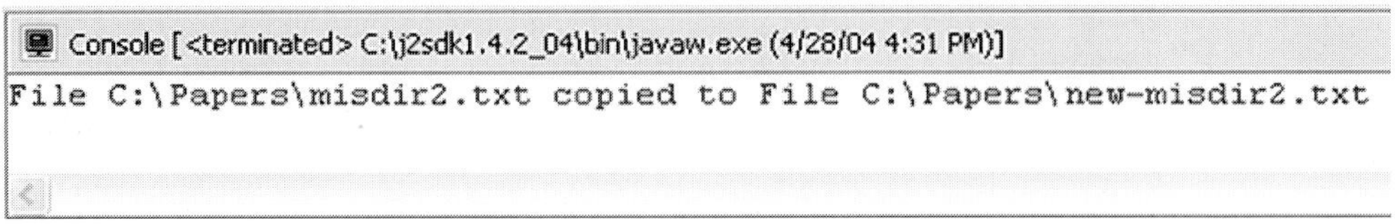

```
File C:\Papers\misdir2.txt copied to File C:\Papers\new-misdir2.txt
```

FIGURE 10.13   Completion Status Message

The user specifies a new filename (e.g., `new-misdir2.txt`) as the destination file into which this program copies the contents of the first file (`misdir2.txt`). When specifying a file name that already exists in this folder, the old contents of the file are deleted and replaced with the contents of the new file, because this simple program does not do any checking to verify that a new, nonexistent file has been specified.

At the completion of the program, a status message is displayed to the command/status (console) window letting the user know that the copy procedure has completed successfully (see Fig. 10.13):

### Object I/O

The following program, `StudentIO`, writes an array of student names and IDs to an object file and optionally reads them back when the program is restarted. This program demonstrates examples of `FileInputStream`, `FileOutputStream`, `ObjectInputStream`, and `ObjectOutputStream` as presented in an earlier section among other features.

```java
import java.io.*;

/** helper class containing Student
  attributes-may also  contain methods */

class Student implements Serializable {
    String name, ID;
}

/**
* @ (#) studentIO.java 1.0 5/12/04
*
* Author:  Georges Merx
* Pu rpose:  CIS 190 Example
*/

import java.awt.*;
import java.awt.event.*;
import javax.swing.*;
import java.io.*;

class StudentIO extends JFrame {  // create a class of type JFrame
    JTextField promptForName, promptForID;
```

```
        JButton continueButton, displayButton;
        static Student studentList [];
// array of Student objects - static because allocated in static main
        String result = ""; // accumulates display string
        static int counterOfStudents = 0;
        // tracks current last element in array
        static int noOfStudents = 0;

        public StudentIO (String title) {
        // constructor method - initializes object
            super (title);  // set window title
            Container c;
            addWindowListener(new WindowAdapter() {
            // handle window being closed by clicking on x box
                public void windowClosing(WindowEvent e) {
                    dispose();
                    System.exit(0); // terminate normally
                }
            });

            c = getContentPane();
            c.setLayout(new GridLayout(5,2));
            // set window up as a simple 5x2 grid
            c.add(new JLabel("Hello!"));
            c.add(new JLabel(""));
            c.add(new JLabel("What is your name?"));
            promptForName = new JTextField ("... enter name...");
            promptForName.selectAll ();  // select text for overtyping
            c.add(promptForName);
            c.add(new JLabel("What is your ID number?"));
            promptForID = new JTextField ();
            c.add(promptForID);

            continueButton = new JButton ("Continue");
            continueButton.addActionListener (new MyActionListener());
            // prepare button for event handling
            c.add (continueButton);
            JButton exitButton = new JButton ("Exit");
            exitButton.addActionListener (new MyActionListener());
            c.add (exitButton);
            displayButton = new JButton ("Display");
            displayButton.addActionListener (new MyActionListener());
            c.add (displayButton);
            pack();  // shrink window to miniminum size needed
            setVisible(true);  // make window visible
        }

        public static void main(String args[]) { // program entry point
            System.out.println("Starting SimpleGreeting...");
            String response = JOptionPane.showInputDialog
```

```java
            ("Enter total number of students you want to enter");
        noOfStudents = Integer.parseInt (response);
        studentList = new Student [noOfStudents];
        // create array of Student objects
        response = JOptionPane.showInputDialog (
            "Show saved records (Y/N)?");
        if (response.equals ("Y") || response.equals ("y")) {
            showRecords ();
            response = "";
        }
        StudentIO mainWindow = new StudentIO
            ("Simple Greeting Example - CIS 190");
        // create new object of class SimpleGreeting
    }


class MyActionListener implements ActionListener {
//inner class to handle button event
    public void actionPerformed(ActionEvent evt) {
        if (evt.getActionCommand ().equals("Continue")) {
        // Continue button pressed
            studentList [counterOfStudents] = new Student ();
            // create Student array element object
            studentList [counterOfStudents].name =
                promptForName.getText();
            studentList [counterOfStudents].ID =
                promptForID.getText();
            counterOfStudents++;
            promptForName.setText ("... enter name...");
            // reinitialize input fields
            promptForName.selectAll ();
            promptForName.requestFocus ();
            promptForID.setText ("");

            if (counterOfStudents >= studentList.length) {
            // do not allow further inputs as array is full
                promptForName.setEnabled (false);
                promptForID.setEnabled (false);
                continueButton.setEnabled (false);
            }
        }

        else if (evt.getActionCommand ().equals("Display")) {
        // Display button pressed
            if (counterOfStudents > 0) {
                try {
                    ObjectOutputStream s = new
                        ObjectOutputStream (new
                        FileOutputStream ("SG.DAT"));
```

```
                        for (int count = 0; count <
                            counterOfStudents; count ++){
                            result = result + studentList
                                [count].name + ": " +
                                studentList [count].ID + "\n";
                            // write array out to disk
                            s.writeObject (studentList
                                [count]);
                        }

                        s.flush ();
                        s.close ();
                    } catch (IOException e) {
                        System.out.println ("I/O Error " +
                            e.toString());
                    }
                    JOptionPane.showMessageDialog (null, result,
                        "Student List", JOptionPane.
                        INFORMATION_MESSAGE);
                    // display pop-up message dialog box
                    displayButton.setEnabled (false);
                    // may press Display button only once
                }

                else
                    JOptionPane.showMessageDialog (null,
                        "No records", "Student List",
                        JOptionPane.ERROR_MESSAGE);
                    // display pop-up message dialog box
            }

            else if (evt.getActionCommand ().equals("Exit"))
            // Exit button pressed
                System.exit(0); // terminate program normally
        }
    }

    static void showRecords () {
        if (noOfStudents > 0) {
            try {
                ObjectInputStream ss = new ObjectInputStream
                    (new FileInputStream ("SG.DAT"));

                for (int count = 0; count < noOfStudents;
                    count++) {
                    studentList [count] = (Student)ss.
                        readObject();
                    System.out.println (studentList [count].
                        name +
                        ": " +
```

```
                                studentList [count].ID);
                }

                ss.close();
        } catch (EOFException eof) { // do nothing…EOF is okay
        } catch (IOException e) {
            System.out.println ("I/O Error "+ e.toString());
        }
          catch (ClassNotFoundException e) {
              System.out.println ("Class Not Found Error " +
                  e.toString());
          }
        }
      }
}
```

Figure 10.14 shows the UML Class diagram for the StudentIO program.

Once launched, this program produces a series of GUI displays. The first prompt (see Fig. 10.15) asks the user how many student names and IDs to enter. The user enters a number greater than zero (e.g., 2) and presses the OK button.[3] Pressing the Cancel button terminates the program.

Another Input Dialog Box is then displayed prompting the user to respond with a yes ("Y" or "y") in order to see the students whose names were entered the last time

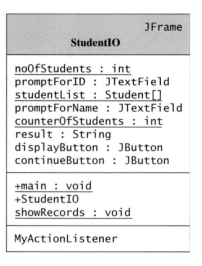

FIGURE 10.14   StudentIO Class Diagram

---

[3]This is, of course, an unattractive design, implemented for simplicity's sake.

FIGURE 10.15   Number of Records Dialog

the program was executed. A user who answers "Y' or "y" and presses OK will see the console display the Input Dialog Box shown in Figure 10.16.

Next, the Simple Greeting Example Input Form appears (see Fig. 10.17). The user enters a student name and student ID in the appropriate text boxes and presses the Continue button. The Continue button cannot be pressed after the user has entered the maximum number of students based on the specification in the previous prompt.

Pressing the Display button results in a list of the student records that have been entered (assuming that there is at least one record) (see Fig. 10.18). It only remains to exit, pressing the Exit button.

The next time the program is run, the user can display in the console window the names and IDs from this execution because the were actually written to the file SG.DAT

FIGURE 10.16   Display of Previous Entries

FIGURE 10.17   Simple Greeting Main Window (Form)

FIGURE 10.18    List of Students

and are read back at that time. (Again, the program will ask for number of students to read, a design that is inflexible and can be improved by using the more advanced techniques applied in the Voting Program, such as `ArrayLists` for flexible growth of the data structure and a `try..catch` mechanism to read objects until the end-of-file is reached.)

### 10.3.6  Database Access

Most modern business applications use relational database technology to store and retrieve data. Commercial relational databases emerged in the early 1970s. Some of the more prominent products on the market today include:

- Oracle (Oracle Corp.)
- DB2 (IBM Corp.)
- Sybase (Sybase Corp.)
- SQL Server (Microsoft Corp.)
- Access (Microsoft Corp.)
- Focus (Information Builders Inc.)
- MySQL (Open Source)

Relational databases conceptually store data in row/column format similar to today's spreadsheet software. Each row is considered a **record** or **tuple** in relational terms, and each column represents a field or attribute.

Since Java is object-oriented and views data as objects belonging to a class, a data structure mismatch exists between these memory-resident data objects and the persistent table records organized into relational data in row/column format. To address this mismatch, a bridging connectivity and translation technology known as **Java Data Base Connectivity (JDBC)**$^{TM}$ interacts with a Microsoft®-originated technology known as **Object Data Base Connectivity (ODBC)**$^{TM}$. There are two techniques available for connecting to a persistent relational data source using JDBC:

1. The **JDBC-ODBC Bridge** (included with the Java SDK) connects to any ODBC-compatible data source.
2. Third-party, vendor-specific bridges are available to connect to specific data sources directly.

When the bridge, most commonly referred to as a **driver**, is loaded, and the data source is available, the Java `getConnection()` method provides the connection using a JDBC URL, name, and password.

An example JDBC URL for Microsoft Access is

$$\texttt{jdbc:odbc:<NAME>}$$

where <NAME> is the name of the data source.

Once connected, Java programs can formulate **Structured Query Language (SQL)** commands, as shown in the following example:

```java
import java.sql.*;   //import JDBC classes

public class DatabaseExample {
    static String[] SQLStatements = {
        "create table JoltData ("+ "cousin varchar (32),"+
        "weekday varchar (3),"+ "cigarettes integer);",
        "insert into JoltData values ('Fidelma', 'Mon', 9);",
        "insert into JoltData values ('Arsène', 'Tue', 0);",
        "insert into JoltData values ('Wilma', 'Wed', 0);",
        "insert into JoltData values ('Norbert', 'Mon', 4);",
        "insert into JoltData values ('Julia', 'Wed', 6);",
        "insert into JoltData values ('London', 'Thu', 2);",
        "insert into JoltData values ('Regina', 'Fri', 1);",
        "insert into JoltData values ('Carl', 'Thu', 0);",
        "insert into JoltData values ('Rhonda', 'Mon', 0);",
        "insert into JoltData values ('Paul', 'Tue', 7);",
        "insert into JoltData values ('Erma', 'Mon', 5);",
    };

    public static void main (String[] args) {
        String URL = "jdbc:odbc:SampleDB";
        // assumes SampleDB available
        String userName = "test";
        String password = "password";

        try {
            Class.forName ("sun.jdbc.odbc.JdbcOdbcDriver");
        } catch (Exception e) {
            System.out.println ("Could not load JDBC/ODBC
                driver!");
            System.exit (1);
        }

        Statement statement = null;
        Connection connection = null;

        try {
            connection = DriverManager.getConnection
                (URL, userName, password);
            // open database connection
            statement = connection.createStatement();
        } catch (Exception e) {
```

```
                    System.out.println("Could not connect to " + URL
                        + "!");
                    System.exit (1);
            }

            try {
                for (int i = 0; i < SQLStatements.length; i++) {
                    statement.execute(SQLStatements [i]);
                    // perform SQL commands
                }

                connection.close();   // close database connection
            } catch (Exception e) {
                System.out.println ("Could not send SQL statement to "+
                    URL + ": " + e.getMessage() + "!");
                System.exit (1);
            }

            System.exit (0);
        }
}
```

This program creates a table using SQL insert statements. The UML class diagram for this DatabaseExample program is shown in Figure 10.19.

In order to run this program, you need to register as an ODBC database the sample database you plan to use. We have a Microsoft Access® database named SampleDB.mdb already created. To register this database as an ODBC database using Windows XP, you must follow these steps:

1. Click on **Start**, and select **Control Panel** followed by **Administrative Tools** and **Data Sources (ODBC)** (see Fig. 10.20).
2. Select the **System DSN** tab followed and press the Add button to bring up the window shown in Figure 10.21.
3. Select the Microsoft Access Driver (*.mdb) and press the **Finish** button. This action displays the next window (see Fig. 10.22).
4. Enter text similar to what is shown above for **Data Source Name** and **Description** and then press the **Select** button to browse to your Microsoft Access SampleDB.mdb file and choose it. After choosing the file, you will see the same window with the actual path and file name for **Database** (see Fig. 10.23).
5. Finally, click the OK button, and the program is ready to use.

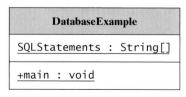

FIGURE 10.19  UML Class Diagram for DatabaseExample

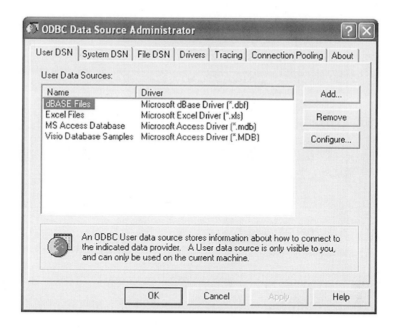

FIGURE 10.20    ODBC Data Source Administrator Dialog (Microsoft Windows™)

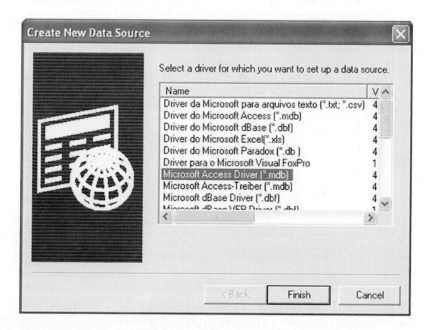

FIGURE 10.21    New Data Source Creation Dialog

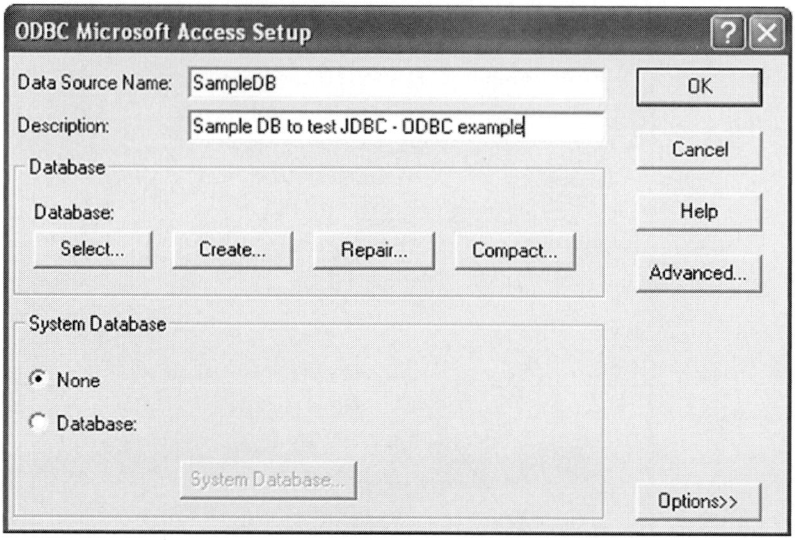

FIGURE 10.22 ODBC Microsoft Access Setup Dialog (1)

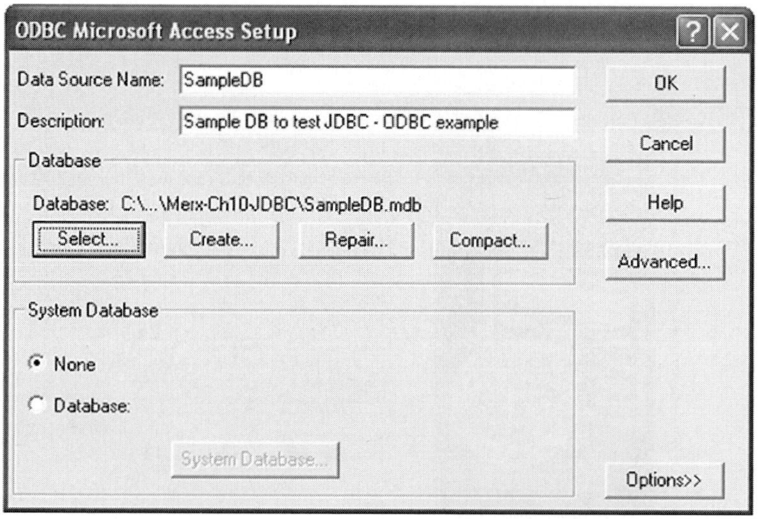

FIGURE 10.23 ODBC Microsoft Access Setup Dialog (2)

After you run the SampleDatabase program successfully, you should be able to view the newly created JoltData table using Microsoft Access™ or Excel™ by entering the database password (which in this example is "password") (Figures 10.24 and 10.25):

FIGURE 10.24   Password Prompt

**JoltData : Table**

| cousin | weekday | cigarettes |
|--------|---------|------------|
| Fidelma | Mon | 9 |
| Arsène | Tue | 0 |
| Wilma | Wed | 0 |
| Norbert | Mon | 4 |
| Julia | Wed | 6 |
| London | Thu | 2 |
| Regina | Fri | 1 |
| Carl | Thu | 0 |
| Rhonda | Mon | 0 |
| Paul | Tue | 7 |
| Erma | Mon | 5 |

FIGURE 10.25   JoltData Table

## 10.4   Position in the Process

| Iterations | iteration 1 | iteration 2 | iteration 3 | iteration 4 | iteration 5 | iteration n |
|------------|-------------|-------------|-------------|-------------|-------------|-------------|
| Disciplines | | | | | | |
| SUPPORT AND MAINTENANCE | | | | | | E* |

We have reached the final phase in the Merx-Norman extended software engineering methodology: the **Support and Maintenance** phase.

This last phase is often the longest-duration period in a project: the years during which a product is supported and in use by customers or internal users. This phase is heavily dependent on the quality of implementation of the previous phases, because in this extended time frame, memories about design decisions fade and original developers are replaced by new ones, considerably increasing the importance of accurate and detailed documentation and records. Now that the product is in productive use, errors discovered "in the field" often take on critical importance because their impact affects organizational capabilities or productivity directly. An efficient and effective *incident-tracking* mechanism is a key work process in support of this phase, so that reported exceptions can be quickly corrected and released as patches or updates. This incident tracking should follow the Closed-Loop Corrective Action (CLCA) process shown in Chapter 1 (see Fig. 10.26).

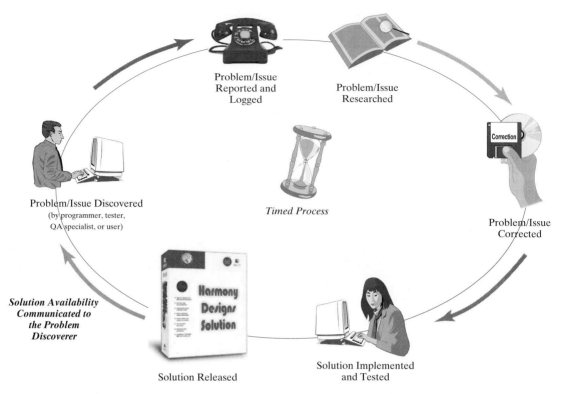

FIGURE 10.26 Review: Closed-Loap Corrective Action process

## 10.5 Example

The following program demonstrates the New I/O (NIO) interfaces and SDK 1.5 support for new language features such as the Scanner class.

```java
import java.util.Scanner;
import java.io.*;
import java.nio.*;
import java.nio.channels.*;
import java.nio.charset.*;

/**
* NIO Sample application
*
* @author Georges Merx, Ph.D.
* @version 1.00 04/10/11
*/

public class NIOSample {
    private static Charset charset = Charset.forName("ISO-8859-15");
    private static CharsetDecoder decoder = charset.newDecoder();
```

```java
public static void main(String[] args) {
    System.out.print ("Please enter a file name and path: ");
    Scanner s= new Scanner(System.in);
    String inputLine = s.next();
    s.close();
    System.out.println ("You entered: " + inputLine);
    File f = new File(inputLine);
    try {
        search(f);
    } catch (IOException x) {
        System.err.println(f + ": " + x);
    }
    System.exit(0);
}

private static void search (File f) throws IOException {
    // Open the file and then get a channel from the stream
    FileInputStream fis = new FileInputStream(f);
    FileChannel fc = fis.getChannel();
    int charCounter = 0;
    // Get the file size and then map it into memory
    int fileSize = (int)fc.size();
    MappedByteBuffer bb = fc.map(FileChannel.MapMode.READ_ONLY,
        0, fileSize);
    // Decode the file into character buffer cb
    CharBuffer cb = decoder.decode(bb);
    // Perform the search
    for (int count = 0; count < cb.limit(); count++)
        if (cb.array()[count] == ';') charCounter++;
            // Close the channel and the stream
            fc.close();

    System.out.println ("We found " + charCounter +
        " semi-colons!");
    }
}
```

### 10.5.1  *Example Explanation*

The simple program shown above is for demonstration puirposes only. It uses J2SE 1.4.2 and 1.5 features such as the Scanner class and the FileChannel NIO technology to search a buffer of characters for a character (in our case, a semicolon) and count instances of this character.

### 10.5.2  *Practical Application*

The NIO interfaces provide a higher-performance file input/output mechanism that is especially relevant to multithreaded applications. The support for C-like character stream interfaces provides more formatted character input/output flexibility. There are many other new features in these recent J2SE update. Visit the Sun Microsystems Java Web site for a comprehensive listing of enhancements.

## 10.6    Resources

Information on file I/O, database access, new I/O interfaces, and related subjects is available from many sources. The major search engines like Google™ continue to be an excellent path to finding online versions of these resources. Major university extension programs (such as University of California Extension, www.extension.ucsd.edu,) offer up-to-date specialized courses in specific areas of Java technology. Such courses are usually taught by practicing professionals and provide a wealth of practical information about the application of these technologies to real-world projects.

### 10.6.1    Connections

Pursuing company internship or part-time job opportunities is the best way for a junior Java software engineer to learn more about the practical use of Java. Alternatively, you can pair up with others at the same level of skill to develop a prototype of a useful, marketable tool or product—either just for the exercise, or even for commercial benefit.

### 10.6.2    Companies

- Sun Microsystems Java Web site—J2SE 1.5 enhancements - `java.sun.com/j2se/1.5.0/docs/relnotes/features.html`

## 10.7    Summary and Recommendations

This chapter covers data persistence, a fundamental requirement for most real-world Java applications. A rich and diverse collection of interfaces and classes exist to help Java programmers interface their software with external (secondary) storage capabilities. Java sees all files as streams of bytes but supports the imposition of further structure, all the way to treating files as text.

We have discussed Support and Maintenance, the last discipline phase in the Extended Unified Process Methodology. Starting in the next chapter, we will examine the supporting disciplines.

## 10.8    Review Questions

1. **Text Files.**  Develop a short program that creates a simple text file and reads it back.
2. **Streams.**  Compare three input/output stream types. Discuss what they are used for and what their limitations are from a design perspective.
3. **NIO Enhancements.**  Study the New I/O interfaces available in Java SDK 1.4 and above. Summarize the new features.

According to Sun Microsystems, the NIO APIs in J2SE 1.4 include the following features:

- Buffers for data of primitive types
- Character-set encoders and decoders
- A pattern-matching facility based on Perl-style regular expressions
- Channels, a new primitive I/O abstraction
- A file interface that supports locks and memory mapping
- A multiplexed, nonblocking I/O facility for writing scalable servers

## 10.9   Glossary – Terminology – Concepts

**I/O**   Input-output; refers to entering data into a program and producing data out of a program. Typical input methods/devices include keyboarding, mouse movements, files, and sensing devices. Typical output devices include printers, displays, and sound speakers.

**NIO**   According to Sun Microsystems, the new I/O (NIO) APIs introduced in J2SE 1.4 provide improved features and performance in buffer management, scalable network and file I/O, character-set support, and regular-expression matching. The NIO APIs supplement the I/O facilities in the `java.io` package.

## 10.10   Exercises

**1. FileIO Program.**   Rewrite the FileIO program introduced earlier to allow for a flexible number of students and not prompt for number of students. Use the Voting Program as an example, if necessary.

**2. Voting Program File I/O.**   Review the Voting Program excerpt below to see how object I/O is implemented. Change the implementation to store an object at a time, instead of a whole `ArrayList` as an object.

```
static boolean writeFile(String fileName, ArrayList<Candidates>
    candidates) {
      if (candidates != null) {
         try {
             ObjectOutputStream s = new ObjectOutputStream (new
                 FileOutputStream (fileName));
             s.writeObject (candidates);
             s.flush();
             s.close();
             return true;
         }catch (IOException e) {
             System.err.println ("I/O Error "+ e.toString());
             return false;
         }
      }
      else {
```

```
            System.err.println ("List empty!");
            return false;
        }
}
```

**3. Voting Program Database Upgrade.**   Replace the file I/O operations in the Voting Program with database storage. A simple example program is shown below (make sure to register the database on your own system):

```java
/** helper class containing Student attributes; can also contain
   methods */

class Student {
    String name, ID;
}

/**
* @ (#) SimpleGreeting5.java 1.0 04/06/16
*
* Author:   Georges Merx
* Purpose:  Database Example
*/

import java.awt.*;
import java.awt.event.*;
import javax.swing.*;
import java.sql.*;

class SimpleGreeting5 extends JFrame {
    // create a class of type JFrame
    JTextField promptForName, promptForID;
    /* object attributes - declare here to be able to access from
       multiple methods */
    JButton continueButton, displayButton;
    // declared here to allow access from multiple methods
    static Student studentList [];
 // array of Student objects - static because allocated in
    static main
    String resultString = ""; // accumulates display string
    static int counterOfStudents = 0;
    // tracks current last element in array
    static int noOfStudents = 0;

    public SimpleGreeting5(String title) {
    // constructor method - initializes object
        super (title);  // set window title
        Container c;
```

```java
addWindowListener(new WindowAdapter() {
// handle window being closed by clicking on x box

    public void windowClosing(WindowEvent e) {
        dispose();
        System.exit(0); // terminate normally
    }
});

c = getContentPane();
c.setLayout(new GridLayout(5,2));
// set window up as a simple 5x2 grid
c.add(new JLabel("Hello!"));
c.add(new JLabel(""));
c.add(new JLabel("What is your name?"));
promptForName = new JTextField ("... enter name...");
promptForName.selectAll ();  // select text for overtyping
c.add(promptForName);
c.add(new JLabel("What is your ID number?"));
promptForID = new JTextField ();
c.add(promptForID);

continueButton = new JButton ("Continue");
continueButton.addActionListener (new MyActionListener());
// prepare button for event handling
c.add (continueButton);
JButton exitButton = new JButton ("Exit");
exitButton.addActionListener (new MyActionListener());
c.add (exitButton);
displayButton = new JButton ("Display");
displayButton.addActionListener (new MyActionListener());
c.add (displayButton);
pack();  // shrink window to miniminum size needed
setVisible(true);  // make window visible
}

public static void main(String args[]) {  // program entry point
    System.out.println("Starting SimpleGreeting...");
    String response = JOptionPane.showInputDialog
        ("Enter total number of students");
    noOfStudents = Integer.parseInt (response);
    studentList = new Student [noOfStudents];
    // create array of Student objects
    SimpleGreeting5 mainWindow = new SimpleGreeting5
        ("Simple Greeting Example - Jsva Book");
    // create new object of class SimpleGreeting
}

class MyActionListener implements ActionListener {
//inner class to handle button event
```

```java
public void actionPerformed(ActionEvent evt) {
    Connection conn = null;
    if (evt.getActionCommand ().equals("Continue")) {
    // Continue button pressed
        studentList [counterOfStudents] = new Student ();
        // create Student array element object
        studentList [counterOfStudents].name =
            promptForName.getText();
        studentList [counterOfStudents].ID =
            promptForID.getText();
        counterOfStudents++;
        promptForName.setText ("... enter name...");
        // reinitialize input fields
        promptForName.selectAll ();
        promptForName.requestFocus ();
        promptForID.setText ("");

        if (counterOfStudents >= studentList.length) {
        // do not allow further inputs as array is full
            promptForName.setEnabled (false);
            promptForID.setEnabled (false);
            continueButton.setEnabled (false);
        }
    }

    else if (evt.getActionCommand ().equals("Display")) {
    // Display button pressed
        if (counterOfStudents > 0) {
            try {
                Class.forName(
                    "sun.jdbc.odbc.JdbcOdbcDriver");
                String url = "jdbc:odbc:Students";
    // now we can get the connection from the DriverManager
                conn = DriverManager.
                    getConnection(url);
            } catch (SQLException e) {
                System.out.println (e.toString());
                System.exit(1);
            } catch (ClassNotFoundException e) {
                System.out.println (e.toString());
                System.exit(1);
            }

            try {
                Statement stat = conn.
                    createStatement();
                stat.executeUpdate
("CREATE TABLE Students (Name CHAR(30), ID CHAR(20))");
```

```
            PreparedStatement pStmt = conn.prepareStatement
                ("INSERT INTO Students VALUES (?,?)");
            pStmt.setString (1,studentList[0].
                name);
            pStmt.setString (2,studentList[0].ID);
            pStmt.executeUpdate();
            ResultSet result = stat.executeQuery
                ("SELECT * FROM Students");
            result.next();
            //moves to the first row of data
            JOptionPane.showMessageDialog (null,
                result.getString("Name"),
                "Student List", JOptionPane.
                INFORMATION_MESSAGE);
            // display pop-up message dialog box
            result.close();
            stat.execute("DROP TABLE Students");
            stat.close();
            conn.close();
        } catch (SQLException e) {
            System.out.println (e.toString());
        } catch (Exception e) {
            System.out.println (e.toString());
        }

    displayButton.setEnabled (false);
    // may press Display button only once
}

else
    JOptionPane.showMessageDialog (null, "No records",
        "Student List", JOptionPane.ERROR_MESSAGE);
    // display pop-up message dialog box
}

else if (evt.getActionCommand ().equals("Exit"))
// Exit button pressed
    System.exit(0); // terminate program normally
}
}
}
```

# Reality Check: Java Programs in the Real World

As a student, you continue to learn more about the features and capabilities of Java as you progress through your course of study. Up to this chapter, we have described software development Best Practices from an educational perspective, including exception handling, component programming, and user interface resiliency, and we have focused mostly on Java applications that run in standalone mode on a local desktop or laptop computer.

In this chapter, descriptive examples from real-world Java programs are used to help you better understand the transition from an educational environment with small, simple examples to the use of Java in actual commercial applications. If you are going to be a programmer in a non-school environment, you should have some notion of what is involved in developing software for use in a real-world organization, whether for-profit or non-profit.

While the real-life application of Java to solving practical business problems typically involves levels of complexity much greater than the classroom can simulate, most of the core knowledge required was covered in earlier chapters and therefore should be familiar territory. Although you may find that the scope of such a program exceeds what you are used to, the basic building blocks are the same or similar. The knowledge provided in this chapter is conceptual rather than covering specific language syntax details, which would in fact exceed the scope of this book. We want you to understand the more realistic distributed applications from a structural perspective without delving into the details of implementation, which must be reserved for a more advanced course on Java enterprise technology.

Most practical software applications today are divided into three architectural tiers with client and server software logically separated. The client tier provides the user interface. The server tier provides services to the client; it is often subdivided into additional service tiers, such as Web server, application server, and the like. The third architectural tier is the database server tier: it provides information management services. The server tiers may be distributed across multiple hardware systems if the software was implemented for full scalability.

A greater diversity of Java classes and packages is required to implement this distributed functionality. Typically you will have to utilize Java 2 Enterprise Edition (J2EE) technology components that support Java servlets, Java Server Pages (JSPs), and Enterprise Java Beans (EJBs). These components add complexity and provide many new capabilities not covered in the text, but in the end, you will simply be using a broader collection of classes that follow now familiar object-oriented behavior patterns.

## 11.1  Learning Objectives

This chapter focuses on topics that will bring you closer to a practical understanding of how Java is used in commercial software engineering. Of course, given that Java is a general-purpose programming language, there are a great many possible applications, from standalone pure Java programs to massively distributed applications using Java with a variety of complementary technologies. These include JSF for graphical user interface (GUI) management, XML and SOAP for data packaging and transport, RMI and CORBA for remote method invocation, and JNI for non-Java component integration.[1] We will not be able to cover the specific coding details of distributed Java solutions here, but we will examine the general characteristics of commercial distributed computing technology choices.

In the area of methodology, this chapter marks our transition from the *action disciplines* to the discussion of *supporting disciplines*, starting with the **Project Management** discipline. The supporting disciplines in the methodology cover all or most of the main phases across the entire project, providing ancillary services that ensure that the overall project stays on track qualitatively and quantitatively. The supporting disciplines are essential to the success of a software-development project.

### 11.1.1  Learning Layout

This recurring section shows the learning objectives of the chapter in a simple diagram, using the Unified Modeling Language (UML) activity diagram notation (see Fig. 11.1). The learning layout for this chapter focuses on real-life software projects. Such projects are typically multi-tier, distributed applications. The first of six supporting disciplines is also covered—the Project Management discipline.

---

[1]You are encouraged to find the appropriate documentation online to make sense of this alphabet soup of abbreviations. A simple search will resolve any confusion you may have.

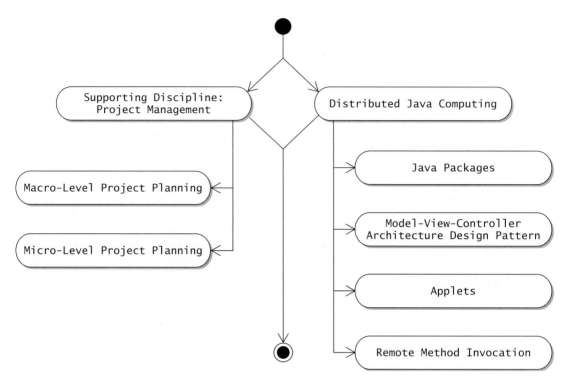

FIGURE 11.1    Chapter 11 Learning Layout (as a UML Activity Diagram)

### 11.1.2  *Learning Connections*

The learning connections diagram (see Fig. 11.2) shows the content of this chapter in relation to the knowledge and skill development recommended for apprentice Java software engineers. This image does not include the advanced skills needed for distributed computing skills development, because we are only introducing these topics in this book, leaving detailed instruction in these technologies for an advanced text.

## 11.2    Executive Summary

The best reason for learning Java is to become competent in creating applications valuable beyond the school environment, whether for commercial or non-profit purposes. While the principles remain the same, the level of complexity and the scope of commercial applications exceed those of the mini-programs written in a classroom setting by orders of magnitude. This chapter will expand your understanding of commercial software application development and broaden your perspective on the scope of activities involved with developing applications that will be used *in production.*

Much productive work is supported by computer systems and software; this is as true for commercial enterprises as for non-profit organizations. Whenever software supports the *creation of value,* its accurate, productive functionality is relevant. It also

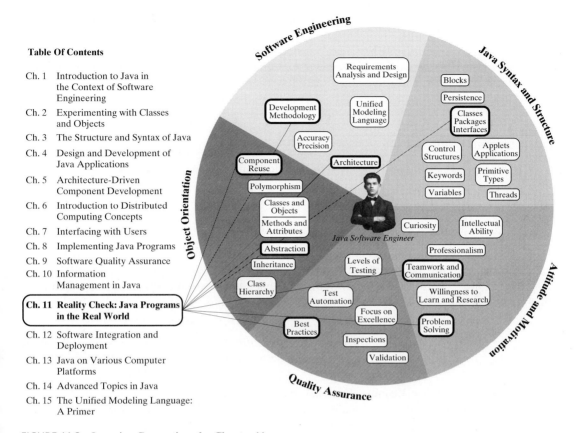

FIGURE 11.2   Learning Connections for Chapter 11

has to work properly in its supported destination environments, which often differ slightly or substantially from installation to installation.

---

**Key Concept:**

Software used in working organizations has to meet all the requirements of the organization, including integration with its work processes and data, acceptance by users, and ongoing support, upgrades, and maintainability. The use *in production* of software is therefore influenced by many factors beyond the pure functionality/feature set.

---

In the twenty-first century, most computer applications are complex, distributed, integrated solutions. Java is a relatively recently developed, well-supported, living programming language that was created, and is regularly enhanced, to efficiently support complex, location-transparent solutions. It includes as standard capabilities many advanced features that in other languages are only available via complicated, direct operating system interface calls. Yet the use of these capabilities is governed by importable classes and therefore does not weigh down individual applications that do not use any specific functionality.

For example, Java has incorporated support for Internet-based distributed application services, advanced platform-independent multimedia capabilities, and relational database access, and it provides seamless integration with optional independent, standardized technologies like CORBA, XML, and SOAP.

## 11.3    Learning Modules

The scope of Java applications can be divided into three major levels:

1. Standalone application
2. Applet
3. Distributed client-server application (thick or thin client)

In addition, there are special-purpose applications and modules, of course, such as mobile clients for Java-enabled cell phones and personal digital assistants (PDAs), or JavaCard™ software for smart cards. For each application level, a number of collaborative technologies come together to help software engineers create a viable, deployable solution. Java technology is subdivided into three major product SDKs:

- *J2SE™ (Java 2 Platform, Standard Edition)* Desktop solutions for standalone applications and browser-based applets
- *J2EE™ (Java 2 Platform, Enterprise Edition)* Enterprise solutions for eCommerce and eBusiness. For example, software developers may create server-side and client-side, large-scale distributed applications, such as a Web shopping cart application for an online retail site
- *J2ME™ (Java 2 Platform, Micro Edition)* Used for resource-constrained consumer solutions for cell phones and other mobile devices (embedded solutions)

### 11.3.1    *Standalone Applications*

The standalone application is the simplest form of Java software. This type of application relies only on the local computer's hardware and operating system resources to provide functionality to its users. No support for networking is required (but it may be desirable, to expand the program's access, functionality, and value). Standalone applications are developed using the J2SE Standard Development Kit, which is the SDK that is the focus of this book.

As shown in Table 11.1, J2SE is composed of a broad collection of packages (documented in more detail on the Sun Website: http://java.sun.com/ j2se/1.5.0/docs/api/overview-summary.html).

These packages and the classes they contain provide a comprehensive range of prefabricated software components that Java software engineers can reuse by incorporating them (**import** statement) in their own applications according to the rules and guidelines described in previous chapters.

Standalone applications, like all others, should adopt a modular structure that enables and promotes component reuse. Fundamentally, the user interface, the business

TABLE 11.1   Java J2SE Standard Development Kit (SDK) Packages (© Sun Microsystems)

| Package | Description |
|---|---|
| **java.applet** | Provides the classes necessary to create an applet and the classes an applet uses to communicate with its applet context. |
| **java.awt** | Contains the classes for creating user interfaces and for painting graphics and images. |
| **java.awt.color** | Provides classes for color spaces. |
| **java.awt.datatransfer** | Provides interfaces and classes for transferring data between and within applications. |
| **java.awt.dnd** | Drag-and-drop is a direct manipulation gesture found in many Graphical User Inerface systems that provides a mechanism to transfer information between two entities logically associated with presentation elements in the GUI. |
| **java.awt.event** | Provides interfaces and classes for dealing with different types of events fired by AWT components. |
| **java.awt.font** | Provides classes and interface relating to fonts. |
| **java.awt.geom** | Provides Java 2D classes for defining and performing operations on objects related to two-dimensional geometry. |
| **java.awt.im** | Provides classes and interfaces for the input method framework. |
| **java.awt.im.spi** | Provides interfaces that enable the development of input methods that can be used with any Java runtime environment. |
| **java.awt.image** | Provides classes for creating and modifying images. |
| **java.awt.image. renderable** | Provides classes and interfaces for producing rendering-independent images. |
| **java.awt.print** | Provides classes and interfaces for a general printing API. |
| **java.beans** | Contains classes related to developing beans—components based on the JavaBeans™ architecture. |
| **java.beans.beancontext** | Provides classes and interfaces relating to bean context. |
| **java.io** | Provides for system input and output through data streams, serialization, and the file system. |
| **java.lang** | Provides classes fundamental to the design of the Java programming language. |
| **java.lang.annotation** | Provides library support for the Java programming language annotation facility. |
| **java.lang.instrument** | Provides services that allow Java programming language agents to instrument programs running on the JVM. |
| **java.lang.management** | Provides the management interface for monitoring and managing the JVM as well as the operating system on which the JVM is running. |
| **java.lang.ref** | Provides reference-object classes that support a limited degree of interaction with the garbage collector. |
| **java.lang.reflect** | Provides classes and interfaces for obtaining reflective information about classes and objects. |
| **java.math** | Provides classes for performing arbitrary-precision integer arithmetic (BigInteger) and arbitrary-precision decimal arithmetic (BigDecimal). |
| **java.net** | Provides the classes for implementing networking applications. |
| **java.nio** | Defines buffers, which are containers for data, and provides an overview of the other NIO packages. |
| **java.nio.channels** | Defines channels, which represent connections to entities capable of performing I/O operations, such as files and sockets; defines selectors for multiplexed, nonblocking I/O operations. |
| **java.nio.channels.spi** | Service-provider classes for the java.nio.channels package. |
| **java.nio.charset** | Defines charsets, decoders, and encoders for translating between bytes and Unicode characters. |

(*Continued*)

TABLE 11.1    (*Continued*)

| Package | Description |
|---|---|
| **java.nio.charset.spi** | Service-provider classes for the java.nio.charset package. |
| **java.rmi** | Provides the RMI package. |
| **java.rmi.activation** | Provides support for RMI Object Activation. |
| **java.rmi.dgc** | Provides classes and interface for RMI distributed garbage-collection (DGC). |
| **java.rmi.registry** | Provides a class and two interfaces for the RMI registry. |
| **java.rmi.server** | Provides classes and interfaces for supporting the server side of RMI. |
| **java.security** | Provides classes and interfaces for the security framework. |
| **java.security.acl** | The classes and interfaces in this package have been superseded by classes in the java.security package. |
| **java.security.cert** | Provides classes and interfaces for parsing and managing certificates, certificate revocation lists (CRLs), and certification paths. |
| **java.security.interfaces** | Provides interfaces for generating RSA (Rivest, Shamir and Adleman AsymmetricCipher algorithm) keys, as defined in the RSA Laboratory Technical Note PKCS#1, and DSA (Digital Signature Algorithm) keys, as defined in NIST's FIPS-186. |
| **java.security.spec** | Provides classes and interfaces for key specifications and algorithm parameter specifications. |
| **java.sql** | Provides the API for accessing and processing data stored in a data source (usually a relational database) using the Java™ programming language. |
| **java.text** | Provides classes and interfaces for handling text, dates, numbers, and messages in a manner independent of natural languages. |
| **java.util** | Contains the collections framework, legacy collection classes, event model, date and time facilities, internationalization, and miscellaneous utility classes (string tokenizer, random-number generator, and bit array). |
| **java.util.concurrent** | Utility classes useful in concurrent programming. |
| **java.util.concurrent. atomic** | A small toolkit of classes that support lock-free thread-safe programming on single variables. |
| **java.util.concurrent. locks** | Interfaces and classes providing a framework for locking and waiting for conditions that is distinct from built-in synchronization and monitors. |
| **java.util.jar** | Provides classes for reading and writing the JAR (Java ARchive) file format, which is based on the standard ZIP file format with an optional manifest file. |
| **java.util.logging** | Provides the classes and interfaces of the Java™ 2 platform's core logging facilities. |
| **java.util.prefs** | This package allows applications to store and retrieve user and system preference and configuration data. |
| **java.util.regex** | Classes for matching character sequences against patterns specified by regular expressions. |
| **java.util.zip** | Provides classes for reading and writing the standard ZIP and GZIP file formats. |
| **javax.accessibility** | Defines a contract between user-interface components and an assistive technology that provides access to them. |
| **javax.crypto** | Provides the classes and interfaces for cryptographic operations. |
| **javax.crypto.interfaces** | Provides interfaces for Diffie-Hellman keys, as defined in RSA Laboratories PKCS #3. |
| **javax.crypto.spec** | Provides classes and interfaces for key specifications and algorithm parameter specifications. |
| **javax.imageio** | The main package of the Java Image I/O API. |

(*Continued*)

TABLE 11.1    (*Continued*)

| Package | Description |
|---|---|
| **javax.imageio.event** | A package of the Java Image I/O API dealing with synchronous notification of events during reading and writing of images. |
| **javax.imageio. metadata** | A package of the Java Image I/O API dealing with reading and writing metadata. |
| **javax.imageio.plugins. bmp** | Package containing public classes used by the built-in BMP plug-in. |
| **javax.imageio.plugins.jpeg** | Classes supporting the built-in JPEG plug-in. |
| **javax.imageio.spi** | A package of the Java Image I/O API containing plug-in interfaces for readers, writers, transcoders, and streams, and a runtime registry. |
| **javax.imageio.stream** | A package of the Java Image I/O API dealing with low-level I/O from files and streams. |
| **javax.management** | Provides the core classes for the Java Management Extensions. |
| **javax.management.loading** | Provides the classes that implement advanced dynamic loading. |
| **javax.management.modelmbean** | Provides the definition of the ModelMBean classes. |
| **javax.management.monitor** | Provides the definition of the monitor classes. |
| **javax.management.openmbean** | Provides open data types and Open MBean descriptor classes. |
| **javax.management.relation** | Provides the definition of the Relation Service. |
| **javax.management.remote** | Interfaces for remote access to JMX MBean servers. |
| **javax.management.remote.rmi** | The RMI connector is a connector for the JMX Remote API that uses RMI to transmit client requests to a remote MBean server. |
| **javax.management.timer** | Provides the definition of the Timer MBean. |
| **javax.naming** | Provides classes and interfaces for accessing naming services. |
| **javax.naming.directory** | Extends the javax.naming package to provide functionality for accessing directory services. |
| **javax.naming.event** | Provides support for event notification when accessing naming and directory services. |
| **javax.naming.ldap** | Provides support for LDAPv3 extended operations and controls. |
| **javax.naming.spi** | Provides the means for dynamically plugging in support for accessing naming and directory services through the javax.naming and related packages. |
| **javax.net** | Provides classes for networking applications. |
| **javax.net.ssl** | Provides classes for the secure socket package. |
| **javax.print** | Provides the principal classes and interfaces for the Java™ Print Service API. |
| **javax.print.attribute** | Provides classes and interfaces that describe the types of Java™ Print Service attributes and how they can be collected into attribute sets. |
| **javax.print.attribute.standard** | Package javax.print.attribute.standard contains classes for specific printing attributes. |
| **javax.print.event** | Package javax.print.event contains event classes and listener interfaces. |
| **javax.rmi** | Contains user APIs for RMI-IIOP. |
| **javax.rmi.CORBA** | Contains portability APIs for RMI-IIOP. |
| **javax.rmi.ssl** | Provides implementations of RMIClientSocketFactory and RMIServerSocketFactory over the Secure Sockets Layer (SSL) or Transport Layer Security (TLS) protocols. |
| **javax.security.auth** | Provides a framework for authentication and authorization. |
| **javax.security.auth.callback** | Provides the classes necessary for services to interact with applications in order to retrieve information (authentication data, including usernames or passwords) or to display information (e.g., error and warning messages). |
| **javax.security.auth.kerberos** | Contains utility classes related to the Kerberos network authentication protocol. |

(*Continued*)

TABLE 11.1    *(Continued)*

| Package | Description |
|---|---|
| **javax.security.auth.login** | Provides a pluggable authentication framework. |
| **javax.security.auth.spi** | Provides the interface for implementing pluggable authentication modules. |
| **javax.security.auth.x500** | Contains the classes that should be used to store X500 Principal and X500 Private Credentials in a *Subject.* |
| **javax.security.cert** | Provides classes for public key certificates. |
| **javax.security.sasl** | Contains class and interfaces for supporting SASL. |
| **javax.sound.midi** | Provides interfaces and classes for I/O, sequencing, and synthesis of MIDI (Musical Instrument Digital Interface) data. |
| **javax.sound.midi.spi** | Supplies interfaces for service providers to implement when offering new MIDI devices, MIDI file readers and writers, or sound bank readers. |
| **javax.sound.sampled** | Provides interfaces and classes for capture, processing, and playback of sampled audio data. |
| **javax.sound.sampled.spi** | Supplies abstract classes for service providers to subclass when offering new audio devices, sound file readers and writers, or audio format converters. |
| **javax.sql** | Provides API for server-side data source access and processing from the Java™ programming language. |
| **javax.sql.rowset** | Standard interfaces and base classes for JDBC RowSet implementations. |
| **javax.sql.rowset.serial** | Provides utility classes to allow serializable mappings between SQL types and data types in the Java programming language. |
| **javax.sql.rowset.spi** | Standard classes and interfaces for use in a third-party vendor's implementation of a synchronization provider. |
| **javax.swing** | Provides a set of "lightweight" (all-Java language) components that, to the maximum degree possible, work the same on all platforms. |
| **javax.swing.border** | Provides classes and interface for drawing specialized borders around a Swing component. |
| **javax.swing.colorchooser** | Contains classes and interfaces used by the JColorChooser component. |
| **javax.swing.event** | Provides for events fired by Swing components. |
| **javax.swing.filechooser** | Contains classes and interfaces used by the JFileChooser component. |
| **javax.swing.plaf** | Provides one interface and many abstract classes that Swing uses to provide its pluggable look-and-feel capabilities. |
| **javax.swing.plaf.basic** | Provides user interface objects built according to the Basic look-and-feel. |
| **javax.swing.plaf.metal** | Provides user interface objects built according to the Java look-and-feel (once codenamed Metal), which is the default look-and-feel. |
| **javax.swing.plaf.multi** | Provides user interface objects that combine two or more look-and-feels. |
| **javax.swing.plaf.synth** | A skinnable look-and-feel in which all painting is delegated. |
| **javax.swing.table** | Provides classes and interfaces for dealing with javax.swing.JTable. |
| **javax.swing.text** | Provides classes and interfaces that deal with editable and noneditable text components. |
| **javax.swing.text.html** | Provides the class HTMLEditorKit and supporting classes for creating HTML text editors. |
| **javax.swing.text.html.parser** | Provides the default HTML parser, along with support classes. |
| **javax.swing.text.rtf** | Provides a class (RTFEditorKit) for creating Rich Text Format text editors. |
| **javax.swing.tree** | Provides classes and interfaces for dealing with javax.swing.JTree. |
| **javax.swing.undo** | Allows developers to provide support for undo/redo in applications such as text editors. |

*(Continued)*

TABLE 11.1   (*Continued*)

| Package | Description |
|---|---|
| **javax.transaction** | Contains three exceptions thrown by the ORB machinery during unmarshaling. |
| **javax.transaction.xa** | Provides the API that defines the contract between the transaction manager and the resource manager, which allows the transaction manager to enlist and delist resource objects (supplied by the resource manager driver) in JTA transactions. |
| **javax.xml** | Defines core XML constants and functionality from the XML specifications. |
| **javax.xml.datatype** | XML/Java Type Mappings. |
| **javax.xml.namespace** | XML Namespace processing. |
| **javax.xml.parsers** | Provides classes allowing the processing of XML documents. |
| **javax.xml.transform** | Defines generic APIs for processing transformation instructions and performing transformations from source to result. |
| **javax.xml.transform.dom** | Implements DOM-specific transformation APIs. |
| **javax.xml.transform.sax** | Implements SAX2-specific transformation APIs. |
| **javax.xml.transform.stream** | Implements stream- and URI- specific transformation APIs. |
| **javax.xml.validation** | Provides API for validation of XML documents. |
| **javax.xml.xpath** | Provides object-model neutral API for evaluation of XPath expressions and access to evaluation environment. |
| **org.ietf.jgss** | Presents a framework that allows application developers to make use of security services like authentication, data integrity, and data confidentiality from a variety of underlying security mechanisms like Kerberos, using a unified API. |
| **org.omg.CORBA** | Provides mapping of OMG CORBA APIs to the Java™ programming language, including the class ORB, which is implemented so that a programmer can use it as a fully functional Object Request Broker (ORB). |
| **org.omg.CORBA_2_3** | Defines additions to existing CORBA interfaces in the J2 SE. These changes occurred in recent revisions to the CORBA API defined by the OMG. The new methods were added to interfaces derived from the corresponding interfaces in the CORBA package. This provides backward compatibility and avoids breaking the JCK tests. |
| **org.omg.CORBA_2_3. portable** | Provides methods for input and output of value types, and contains other updates to the org/omg/CORBA/portable package. |
| **org.omg.CORBA. DynAnyPackage** | Provides the exceptions used with the DynAny interface (InvalidValue, Invalid, InvalidSeq, and TypeMismatch). |
| **org.omg.CORBA. ORBPackage** | Provides the exception InvalidName, which is thrown by the method ORB.resolve_initial_references, and the exception InconsistentTypeCode, which is thrown by the Dynamic Any creation methods in the ORB class. |
| **org.omg.CORBA.portable** | Provides a portability layer, i.e., a set of ORB APIs that makes it possible for code generated by one vendor to run on another vendor's ORB. |
| **org.omg.CORBA. TypeCodePackage** | Provides the user-defined exceptions BadKind and Bounds, which are thrown by methods in in the class TypeCode. |
| **org.omg.CosNaming** | Provides a naming service for Java IDL. |
| **org.omg.CosNaming. NamingContextExtPackage** | Contains the following classes, which are used in org.omg.CosNaming.NamingContextExt: |
| **org.omg.CosNaming. NamingContextPackage** | Contains Exception classes for the org.omg.CosNaming package. |
| **org.omg.Dynamic** | Contains the Dynamic module specified in the OMG Portable Interceptor specification |
| **org.omg.DynamicAny** | Provides classes and interfaces that enable traversal of the data value associated with an any at runtime, and extraction of the primitive constituents of the data value. |

(*Continued*)

TABLE 11.1    (*Continued*)

| Package | Description |
| --- | --- |
| **org.omg.DynamicAny.** **DynAnyFactoryPackage** | Contains classes and exceptions from the DynAnyFactory interface of the DynamicAny module specified in the OMG The Common Object Request Broker: Architecture and Specification |
| **org.omg.DynamicAny.** **DynAnyPackage** | Contains classes and exceptions from the DynAny interface of the DynamicAny module specified in the OMG The Common Object Request Broker: Architecture and Specification |
| **org.omg.IOP** | Contains the IOP module specified in the OMG document The Common Object Request Broker: Architecture and Specification |
| **org.omg.IOP.** **CodecFactoryPackage** | Contains the exceptions specified in the IOP::CodeFactory interface (as part of the Portable Interceptors spec). |
| **org.omg.IOP.CodecPackage** | Generated from the IOP::Codec IDL interface definition. |
| **org.omg.Messaging** | Contains the Messaging module specified in the OMG CORBA Messaging specification |
| **org.omg.PortableInterceptor** | Provides a mechanism to register ORB hooks through which ORB services can intercept the normal flow of execution of the ORB. |
| **org.omg.PortableInterceptor.** **ORBInitInfoPackage** | Contains the exceptions and typedefs from the ORBInitInfo local interface of the PortableInterceptor module specified in the OMG Portable Interceptor specification |
| **org.omg.PortableServer** | Provides classes and interfaces for making the server side of applications portable across multivendor ORBs. |
| **org.omg.PortableServer.** **CurrentPackage** | Provides method implementations with access to the identity of the object on which the method was invoked. |
| **org.omg.PortableServer.** **POAManagerPackage** | Encapsulates the processing state of the POAs it is associated with. |
| **org.omg.PortableServer.** **POAPackage** | Allows programmers to construct object implementations that are portable between different ORB products. |
| **org.omg.PortableServer.** **portable** | Provides classes and interfaces for making the server side of applications portable across multivendor ORBs. |
| **org.omg.PortableServer.** **ServantLocatorPackage** | Provides classes and interfaces for locating the servant. |
| **org.omg.SendingContext** | Provides support for the marshaling of value types. |
| **org.omg.stub.java.rmi** | Contains RMI-IIOP Stubs for Remote types that occur in the java.rmi package. |
| **org.w3c.dom** | Provides the interfaces for the Document Object Model (DOM) that is a component API of the Java API for XML Processing. |
| **org.w3c.dom.bootstrap** | |
| **org.w3c.dom.events** | |
| **org.w3c.dom.ls** | |
| **org.xml.sax** | Provides the core SAX APIs. |
| **org.xml.sax.ext** | Contains interfaces to SAX2 facilities that conformant SAX drivers won't necessarily support. |
| **org.xml.sax.helpers** | Contains "helper" classes, including support for bootstrapping SAX-based applications. |

logic, and the data management functions should be compartmentalized. The Model-View-Controller (MVC) design pattern, augmented with the information management tier (database), supports this modular structure. In addition, appropriate encapsulation should be implemented; for example, **public set()** and **get()** methods should exist for all externally relevant **private** attributes. The class hierarchy should implement a high level of abstraction to ensure flexible reuse of components. Abstraction in this context refers to the generalization of attributes and methods in high-level classes to avoid repetition, and to the use of polymorphism (through method and type overloading) to ensure adaptability. High cohesion and low coupling are the previously discussed, recognized design principles that should govern the use of these object orientation features. Adherence to these Best Practices becomes dramatically more important in the complex, large, multi-tier distributed applications discussed below.

A simple but illustrative example of a standalone application that adheres to the MVC pattern is shown in Figures 11.3 and 11.4. When you launch this application, it

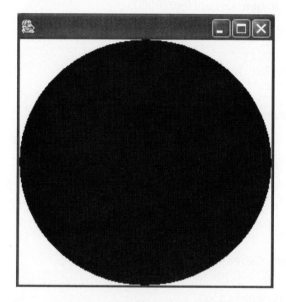

FIGURE 11.3    Window with Black Ball

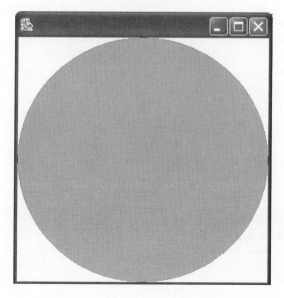

FIGURE 11.4    Window with Red Ball

initially displays a window with a black ball completely filling the window (see Fig. 11.3), and within a few seconds the ball will change color to red (see Fig. 11.4), after which the program ends with the window closing.

### Model Class

```
import java.awt.*;
import java.util.*;

public class Model extends Observable {
    public Color color = new Color(0x010000);
    private int count = 10;

    void doSomething() {
        if (--count <= 0) {
            color = color.brighter();
            count = 10;
            setChanged();
            notifyObservers();
        }
    }
}
```

### View Class

```
import java.awt.*;
import java.util.*;

public class View extends Canvas implements Observer {
    Color color;

    public void paint(Graphics g) {
        if (color == null)
            return;
        g.setColor(color);
        g.fillOval(0, 0, getWidth(), getHeight());
    }

    public void update(Observable observable, Object arg) {
        color = ((Model) observable).color;
        repaint();
    }
}
```

### Controller Class

```
import java.awt.*;

public class Controller extends Frame {
    static Model model = new Model();
    static View view = new View();
```

```java
public static void main(String args[]) {
    Frame f = new Frame();
    f.add(view);
    f.setSize(300, 320);
    f.setVisible(true);

    model.addObserver(view);

    for (int i = 0; i < 200; i++) {
        model.doSomething();
        try {
            Thread.sleep(20);
        } catch (InterruptedException e) {
            // do nothing
        }
    }

    f.dispose();
    }
}
```

The UML class diagram in Figure 11.5 and sequence diagram in Figure 11.6 illustrate the design decisions that led to this implementation.

Note that the Voting Program example introduced in an earlier chapter also subscribes to the basic MVC architectural pattern (see Fig. 11.7).

In this fashion, The Voting Program can implement alternate GUI components, for instance, while only minimally affecting the other tiers.

### 11.3.2  Client-Server Applications

Standalone Java applications like the MVC example in the preceding section interact only with objects within the same application or virtual machine on a single computer.

If several View objects on different computers wanted to interact with single Controller and Model objects running on the same computer or possibly on a computer completely different from the one where the View objects reside, the application would follow the Client-Server model, and Java Remote Method Invocation (RMI) technology would be used. Note that RMI is used when all the components of a distributed application are developed in Java.

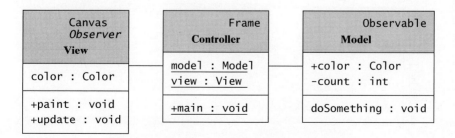

FIGURE 11.5   UML Class Diagram for Model, View, and Controller Classes

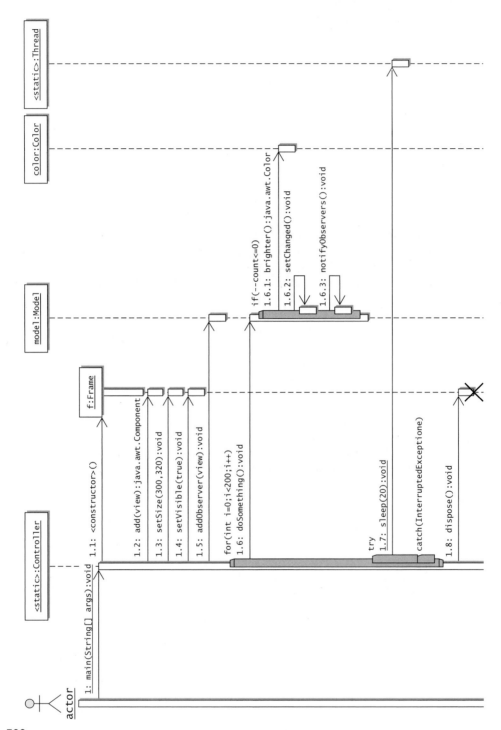

FIGURE 11.6   UML Sequence Diagram—main() Method in the Controller Class

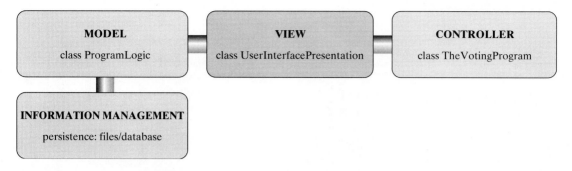

FIGURE 11.7   MVC Classes in the Voting Program

The left side of Figure 11.8 illustrates how multiple View objects become aware of the black circle as they interact with a single Control object. The right side of the figure shows that RMI technology inserts a client stub/proxy for the Control object.

Client-server applications, implementing the distributed computing concept, connect client and server subsystems to provide a distributed, logically connected environment that seems uniform to the end-user (end-users use remote services without awareness of their physical location). In Figure 11.9, based on a real-world example, you see many of the typical components that may contribute to a Java-based distributed application architecture.

The concept of distributed computing emerged many years ago as an approach to moving repetitive aspects of client processing across user workstations (clients) to a single

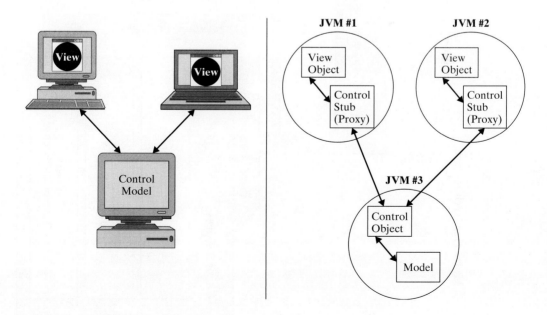

FIGURE 11.8   The Java Remote Method Invocation (RMI) Technology Concept

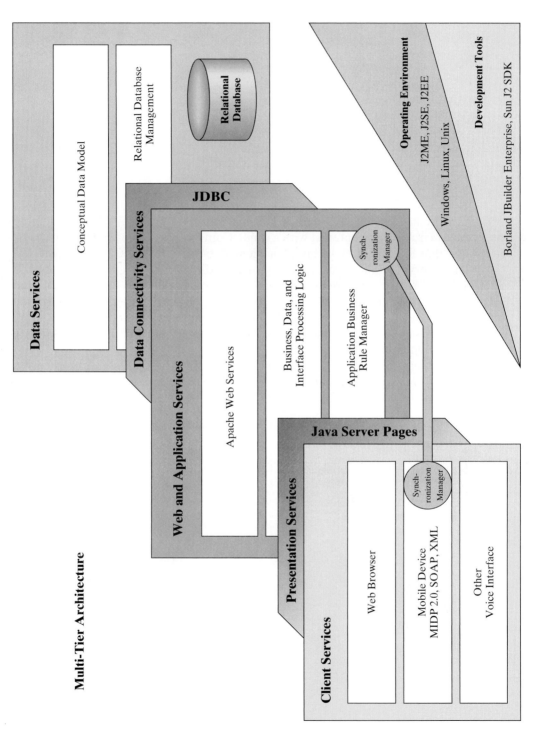

FIGURE 11.9 Example Distributed Computing Environment Architecture

robust computer, referred to as a server, shared by the clients. Early successes with this approach moved file sharing, printer sharing, and then the database used by the program to server computers, turning these functions into services used by clients, originally over proprietary networks, but now typically connected via Internet technology. Eventually, some or all of the common business logic as centralized on a server type referred to as an application server, leaving the user interface (UI) processing and possibly some user input validation on the client. Technologies like JavaServer Pages (JSP) and JavaServer Faces (JSF) even move much of the GUI processing to the server side of distributed computing, allowing for the deployment of *thin clients*, which are essentially Web browser stations.

Today, using Java as the programming language, client-server (distributed) computing is accomplished with J2EE technologies including JSP and servlets. Programmatic access between distributed components uses remote method access via Remote Method Invocation (RMI) and remote database access via Java Database Connectivity (JDBC), among others. CORBA support is available in Java for the integration of heterogeneous, distributed application components. The various forms of communication between clients and servers are discussed in the next section.

### 11.3.3 *Web-Centric Distributed Applications*

Web-centric distributed applications rely on the availability of a client browser on the client computer (e.g., Microsoft Internet Explorer, Netscape Navigator, Apple Safari, Mozilla Firefox). The Java applet was the initial implementation in Java of Web interface technology. Today, more and more applications use JavaServer Pages technology; JavaServer faces are a more recent addition to the server-based GUI delivery services.

A major goal of distributed computing is to accommodate heterogeneous computing environments—both on the client side, such as the many browsers available on client operating systems (e.g., Windows, UNIX, Solaris, Linux, and OS X), and also on the server side—that can also run various operating systems and various Web, database, and application services. This flexibility is important because most customer environments have established IT infrastructures that they are not likely to change just for a new application, however important.

The simplest Web-centric Java application is the **Java applet**. An applet is a program written in Java, stored on a Web server, and delivered via the user computer's Web browser, but otherwise logically very similar to a Java client application run on the client computer. When a user runs a Java technology-enabled browser to view a Web (HTML) page that contains an applet reference, the applet code is transferred to her system and executed by the Java Virtual Machine (JVM) embedded in the browser (assuming appropriate security permissions).

Sample HTML file containing applet reference:

```
<HTML>
<HEAD>
</HEAD>
<BODY BGCOLOR="000000">
<CENTER>
<APPLET
       code  = "TheVotingProgramApplet.class"
       width = "500" height = "300">
```

```
</APPLET>
</CENTER>
</BODY>
</HTML>
```

Applet source code:

```
/**
 * @(#)TheVottingProgramApplet.java
 *
 * @author Georges Merx
 * @version 1.00 o5/03/16
 */

import java.awt.*;
import javax.swing.JApplet;

public class TheVotingProgramApplet extends JApplet {
    public void init() {
    // do nothing
    }

    public void paint(Graphics g) {
        g.drawString(
            "This is the skeleton of a TheVotingProgram applet",
            50, 60 ); // coordinates x=50, y=60
    }
}
```

Of course, as can be seen in the screenshot in Figure 11.10, this overly simple applet example would need to be expanded substantially to provide real usefulness.

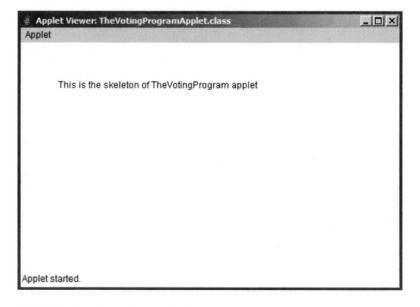

FIGURE 11.10    Voting Program Skeleton

In the area of networking support, the Java 2 Standard Development Kit (J2SE SDK) contains numerous components encapsulating communications facilities at all relevant interaction levels. These include, among others, the Transmission Control Protocol/Internet Protocol (TCP/IP), the File Transfer Protocol (FTP), the Simple Mail Transfer Protocol (SMTP), the Post Office Protocol Version 3 (POP3), and the Network News Transfer Protocol (NNTP). These components provide access to all the necessary communications capabilities, down to the TCP/IP socket level. The implementation details of these communication capabilities are beyond the scope of this book, but ample information about how to program communications-enabled applications is available on the Sun Java Web site and in various advanced Java books.

---

### MIDDLEWARE

When distributed applications use common components for non-business-logic functionality, these functions are often grouped together under the term *middleware*.

---

Modular, distributed computing approaches have emerged over the last few years, grouped around the concept of *services*, such as information management, business logic, naming, security, transaction, event, and message queuing. Server-resident subsystems provide these capabilities to clients, allowing the client subsystems to focus their streamlined functionality on user interaction. This centralization of software services facilitates distributed computing management and control. The technologies participating in Web-centric applications and their development include:

- Web services, e.g., Apache HTTP Server
- Application services, e.g., JBoss, IBM Websphere, BEA Weblogic, Borland Enterprise Server, Microsoft Internet Information Server (IIS), Tomcat
- J2EE (servlets, JavaServer Pages, Enterprise Java Beans, JavaServer Faces)
- XML and SOAP

The screenshot in Figure 11.11 shows the verification page for the **Tomcat** Web server installation. Tomcat is an open-source project of the Apache Jakarta Project. It can be downloaded at http://jakarta.apache.org/tomcat/index.html.

These services provide software engineers with reusable modules that they do not have to implement themselves. Such services, however, require an extensive understanding of the third-party functions and components that contribute to the development of modern distributed applications. Literally thousands of classes are available in the Java distributed computing environment; they provide the necessary range of middleware functions underlying end-user enterprise applications.

Also desirable at this level in most cases are the more advanced software-development tools that provide integrated access to the distributed computing capabilities of J2EE. For example, Sun Microsystems Java Studio Creator provides a drag-and-drop

Apache Tomcat/5.0.25

The **Apache Jakarta Project**
http://jakarta.apache.org/

**If you're seeing this page via a web browser, it means you've setup Tomcat successfully. Congratulations!**

As you may have guessed by now, this is the default Tomcat home page. It can be found on the local filesystem at:

`$CATALINA_HOME/webapps/ROOT/index.jsp`

where "$CATALINA_HOME" is the root of the Tomcat installation directory. If you're seeing this page, and you don't think you should be, then either you're either a user who has arrived at new installation of Tomcat, or you're an administrator who hasn't got his/her setup quite right. Providing the latter is the case, please refer to the Tomcat Documentation for more detailed setup and administration information than is found in the INSTALL file.

**NOTE: For security reasons, using the administration webapp is restricted to users with role "admin". The manager webapp is restricted to users with role "manager".** Users are defined in `$CATALINA_HOME/conf/tomcat-users.xml`.

Included with this release are a host of sample Servlets and JSPs (with associated source code), extensive documentation (including the Servlet 2.4 and JSP 2.0 API JavaDoc), and an introductory guide to developing web applications.

Tomcat mailing lists are available at the Jakarta project web site:

- **tomcat-user@jakarta.apache.org** for general questions related to configuring and using Tomcat
- **tomcat-dev@jakarta.apache.org** for developers working on Tomcat

Thanks for using Tomcat!

Powered by

TOMCAT

**FIGURE 11.11**   Apache Tomcat™ Web Server Installed

environment for creating a robust user interface using JavaServer Faces (see Fig. 11.12). Various other tools from third-party vendors provide similar functionality.

Next, we take a closer look at design patterns. This methodology approach is in common industry use when designing and developing distributed software solutions.

### 11.3.4 Patterns

A **pattern** is a repeatable-solution work sequence to a standard problem. A few simple examples of patterns in everyday life are traffic intersections, cooking recipes, and manufacturing blueprints. In the 1990s, software engineers began to identify and document proven solutions to common software problems. This effort gave rise to the well-documented software-design approach of design patterns. Design patterns can be thought of as codifications of software-design Best Practices. Figure 11.13 shows some line patterns.

Patterns are derived from a specific context and are generalized for application to other, similar scenarios. In fact, a pattern found to be useful in one practical context may well be useful in others. For example, a traffic signal—**green**, **yellow**, and **red**—applies to the control and orderly, safe flow of vehicles and pedestrians on the road. But the same color pattern is more universally applied to mean **proceed—hazard/caution—stop** (respectively).

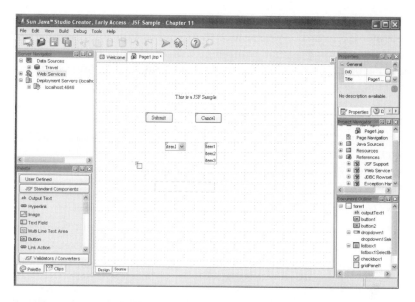

FIGURE 11.12   Sample Screen of Sun Microsystems Java Studio Creator

FIGURE 11.13   Pattern Analogy: Line Patterns

In software engineering, many patterns and pattern classifications have been documented over the years since the Gang of Four first popularized the notion.[2] We are only including a small sampling of these classifications and patterns here, both to endorse their use in software development and to help you become nominally familiar with the pattern concept.

### Separation of Concerns Pattern

The notion of *separation of concerns* is the common thread in all three of the application types described earlier in this chapter—standalone, client-server, and Web-centric. Separation of concerns is a design pattern that partitions the broad types of services that must be provided in almost every type of application. These services deal with:

- *User Interface*—the interaction/dialog with end-users
- *Functional Domain*—the functional area being automated
- *Data Management*—the database or persistent file storage and retrieval
- *System Integration*—the integration points between this application and others, as well as with system software and hardware

Figure 11.14 illustrates the separation of concerns pattern. Note that the User Interface, Data Management, and System Integration components are dependent on the Functional Domain component. This means that primary emphasis is placed on the functional area being automated; the other three services are built subsequently to support the functional domain component or subsystem. The functional domain (functional project requirements) drives the nature and make-up of the other services. Having a stable functional domain architecture is key to the long-term viability of an application, regardless of whether it is a standalone, client-server, or Web-centric application.

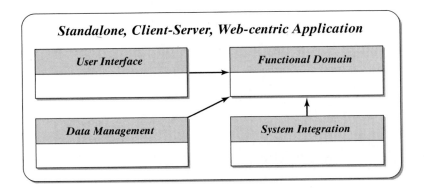

**FIGURE 11.14**    Separation of Concerns Pattern Example[3]

---

[2]See E. Gamma, R. Helm, R. Johnson, and J. Vlissides, *Design Patterns: Elements of Reusable Object-Oriented Software*, Addison-Wesley, 1994.
[3]Adapted from P. Coad, D. North, and M. Mayfield, *Object Models: Strategies, Patterns, and Applications*, © 1995 Object International, Inc., published by Prentice Hall, Upper Saddle River, NJ.

*Scalability* is another reason for following the separation of concerns pattern. Applications sometimes start out as standalone or simple client-server applications and then evolve over time into more complex, multi-tier, Web-services-based solutions. Migration to other application architectures, typically a difficult and expensive task, is easier to accomplish if they are architected and built from the start from the separation of concerns viewpoint.

The Java class hierarchy and packages were engineered from the start to comply with the principle of separation of concerns (as well as numerous other proven design patterns). Recent additions, such as generic classes and methods, add further power and flexibility to the language in support of this design pattern.

### Generic Methods

The most recent release of the Java Software Development Kit, J2SE SDK 5.0, added support for generic methods and classes. Generics further support polymorphism by enabling a generic code component, at runtime, to determine safely the type of a parameter and handle it accordingly.

The following code snippet shows an example change in the Voting Program example that adds *generic* support for saving elections of candidate and ballot measure (proposition) type.

```
/** The saveResults method uses a generic parameter to save any
type of election result */
boolean saveResults (ArrayList <? extends BallotElement> results,
    String extension) {
    JFileChooser chooser = new JFileChooser();
    chooser.addChoosableFileFilter(new MyFilter(extension));
    int returnVal =
      chooser.showDialog(UserInterfacePresentation.this,
        "Save Election Information");

    if(returnVal == JFileChooser.APPROVE_OPTION) {
        fileName = chooser.getCurrentDirectory() +
            java.io.File.separator +
            chooser.getSelectedFile().getName();
        if (!fileName.toUpperCase().trim().
            endsWith(extension)) fileName += extension;
        if (ProgramLogic.writeFile(fileName, results) == false)
            return false;
        else return true;
    }
    else return false;
}
```

*Notes:*

- We have updated the Voting Program to create a simple hierarchy where **BallotElement** is the abstract parent class to **Candidate** and **Proposition**

```java
import java.io.Serializable;

/** The Voting Program - BallotElement Class
 *
 * @author Georges Merx,Ph.D.
 * @version 1.00 04/12/13
 */

abstract class BallotElement implements Serializable {
    int votesReceived;
    boolean winner;
    boolean tie;
}
```

```java
import java.io.Serializable;

/**
 * The Voting Program - Candidate Class
 *
 * @author Georges Merx, Ph.D.
 * @version 1.00 04/12/13
 */

class Candidate extends BallotElement implements Serializable {
    String firstName, middleName, lastName, dateOfBirth,
socialSN,
        address1, address2, city, state, zipCode, telNumber;
    PartyAffiliation affiliation;
}
```

```java
import java.io.Serializable;

/**
 * The Voting Program - Proposition Class
 *
 * @author Georges Merx, Ph.D.
 * @version 1.00 04/12/13
 */

class Proposition extends BallotElement implements Serializable {
    String propositionName, propositionDescription,
propositionAuthor;
}
```

- The first parameter on the **saveResults()** method uses a wildcard to accept any object that is a member of the **BallotElement** class subtree. This enables **saveResults()** to save both candidate- and proposition-type elections.

### Analysis Patterns

Methodology guru Martin Fowler described how analysis patterns reflect conceptual structures of business processes rather than actual software implementations.[4] Analysis patterns are often useful across a many business domains, among them manufacturing, finance, and health care. They can be applied at the start of the **Analysis Discipline** instead of beginning with no concept at all, or they can be compared after the fact to models created through analysis to see how these new models conform or digress from documented model patterns for similar domains.

One of the many conceptual business patterns presented in Fowler's book is the Party pattern, a conceptual illustration of which is shown in Figure 11.15.

A party could be a person or an organization. Each party can have zero or more (**0..***) telephone numbers; a specific telephone number is associated with just one party (either a person or an organization). Likewise, each party can have zero or more (**0..***) addresses; a specific address is associated with just one party (either a person or an organization). Finally, each party can have zero or more (**0..***) e-mail addresses; a specific e-mail address is associated with just one party (either a person or an organization).

You will find many other useful examples of conceptual analysis patterns in Fowler's book as well as in other related books and articles.

### GRASP Patterns

In his book on UML patterns, Craig Larman introduces nine **General Responsibility Assignment Software Patterns (GRASP)**.[5] In Larman's own words:

> "The GRASP patterns are a learning aid to help one understand essential object design, and apply design reasoning in a methodical, rational, explainable way." He further states, that the GRASP patterns "describe fundamental principles of object design and responsibility assignment, expressed as patterns."

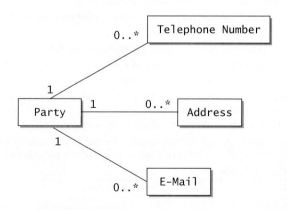

FIGURE 11.15   Party Pattern (Adapted from Fowler)

---

[4]Martin Fowler, *Analysis Patterns: Reusable Object Models*, Addison-Wesley Longman, 1997.
[5]Craig Larman, *Applying UML and Patterns*, 2nd ed., Prentice Hall, 2002.

As Larman explains, objects have responsibilities—obligations or contracts. He suggests that there are two types of responsibilities: *knowing* and *doing*. Peter Coad and one of the authors suggest that are actually three types:[6]

- What an object knows about itself
- What other objects this object know about
- What an object does

Figuring out these responsibilities is a key challenge during analysis, design, and implementation. The GRASP patterns assist with this determination. Table 11.2 lists the nine GRASP patterns and includes a brief description of each. Further details can be found in Larman's book.

### Design Patterns

The seminal book on object-oriented design patterns is *Design Patterns: Elements of Reusable Object-Oriented Software*.[7] Its authors, sometimes referred to as the Gang of Four (GoF), document twenty-three design patterns and classify them as either creational patterns (5), structural patterns (7), or behavioral patterns (11). Table 11.3 presents a few of the patterns described in the book.

Many of the GoF patterns have been implemented in the Java programming language (SDK structure). Various other development tools also support the design-pattern-centric view of the design of software programs. For example, Borland's **Together ControlCenter 6.2**™ allows the user to create these patterns as part

TABLE 11.2    GRASP Patterns (© Copyright Craig Larman)

| Pattern | Description |
| --- | --- |
| *Information Expert* | Assign a responsibility to the information expert—the class that has the information necessary to fulfill the responsibility |
| *Creator* | Who creates? (Note that Factory is a common alternative solution) |
| *Controller* | Who handles a system event? |
| *Low Coupling* | Assign responsibilities so that (unnecessary) coupling remains low |
| *High Cohesion* | Assign responsibilities so that cohesion remains high |
| *Polymorphism* | Who is responsible when behavior varies by type? |
| *Pure Fabrication* | Who is responsible when you are desperate and do not want to violate high cohesion and low coupling? |
| *Indirection* | How to assign responsibilities to avoid direct coupling |
| *Protected Variations* | How to assign responsibilities to objects, subsystems, and systems so that the variations or instability in these elements do not have an undesirable impact on other elements |

---

[6]Peter Coad, and Ed. Yourdon. *Object-Oriented Systems Analysis*, Prentice Hall, 1990; Ronald J. Norman, *Object-Oriented Systems Analysis and Design*, Prentice Hall, 1996.
[7]See above, n.2.

Table 11.3    A Sampling of the GoF Patterns (© Copyright Gamma et al.)

| Pattern | Description |
| --- | --- |
| *Abstract Factory* | Provides an interface for creating families of related or dependent objects without specifying their concrete classes |
| *Singleton* | Ensures that a class only has one instance, and provide a global point of access to it. |
| *Adapter* | Converts the interface of a class into another interface that clients expect. |
| *Façade* | Provides a unified interface to a set of interfaces in a subsystem. Defines a higher-level interface that makes the subsystem easier to use. |
| *Observer* | Defines a one-to-many dependency between objects so that when one object changes state, all its dependents are notified and updated automatically. |

of a project. Figure 11.16 illustrates a generic **Abstract Factory** pattern as a UML class diagram. Each of the classes contains the Java source code to represent the pattern.

Patterns are very useful not only in aiding programmer productivity but also as a guide for reusable analysis and design architecture elements that have been proven helpful in a variety of domains.

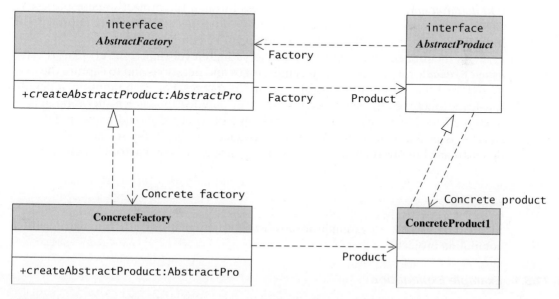

FIGURE 11.16    Abstract Factory Pattern
Borland Together ControlCenter 6.2 Display of an Abstract Factory Pattern

## 11.4 Position in Process

This chapter will cover the first of the supporting disciplines, namely **Project Management**. The supporting disciplines span the entire life-cycle, albeit with varying intensity across the spectrum of iterations. Given that most real-world projects involve complex requirements and extensive design and implementation challenges ("All the easy stuff has already been done!"), the need for smart and flexible project management is critical in completing quality projects on time, on budget, and according to stakeholder requirements.

In projects that span many months, it makes little sense to try to plan all the detail activities for the entire project ahead of time; this archaic approach leads to huge, unmaintainable plans that are out-of-date the moment they are finished. Software development is almost always a dynamic endeavor, with continual requirements updates, new technologies evolving, and the need for change the only constant.

We suggest, therefore, a two-level project-planning approach. We suggest that a macro-level plan should govern the project's major strategic milestones. Planning at this level accounts for the allocated budget and resources. Then, for each iteration of the project, we should have detailed subproject plans that we only finalize *for the current iteration and the next one* as we progress through the project's major phases. We call these micro-level project plans. Our suggested project management approach is illustrated in Figure 11.17 for the Voting Application example.

As mentioned above, in this approach a high-level (macro-level) plan is established to decide on the major project milestones and iterations and to capture the overall scope of the project in terms of time and resources. For each iteration, a detailed low-level (micro-level) plan is established, but only for the current iteration and the next one. This allows for the granular planning of what we should know in detail because it is in the near-future, and it retains adequate flexibility for activities further downstream, but always within the overall constraints of the macro-level plan.

## 11.5 Example

Figure 11.18 shows an example macro-level project plan for a fictitious distributed-computing project.

### 11.5.1 Example Explanation

The plan is shown in Microsoft Project™ as a Gantt chart. In this example plan, iterations are specified with high-level milestones, beginning and end dates, durations, and major resource assignments.

**Project: Online Voting Application**

**Macro-Level Project Plan**

Start: 1/1/2005

Release: 3/1/2006

| Iteration 1:<br>Business Plan | Iteration 2:<br>Analysis and Design | Iteration 3:<br>Component Implementation | Iteration 4:<br>Initial Deployment | Iteration 4:<br>Commercial Deployment |
| --- | --- | --- | --- | --- |

**Micro-Level Project Plan**

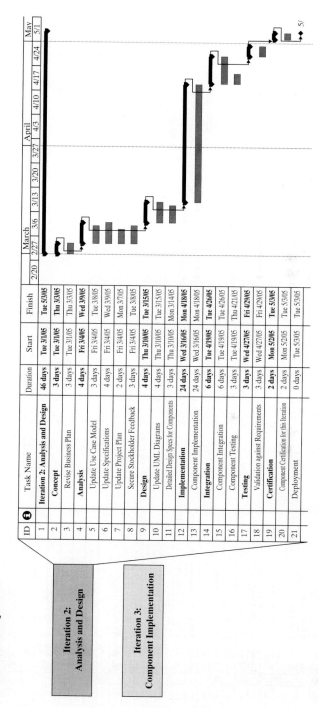

| ID | ⓘ | Task Name | Duration | Start | Finish |
| --- | --- | --- | --- | --- | --- |
| 1 | | **Iteration 2: Analysis and Design** | **46 days** | **Tue 3/1/05** | **Tue 5/3/05** |
| 2 | | **Concept** | **3 days** | **Tue 3/1/05** | **Thu 3/3/05** |
| 3 | | Revise Business Plan | 3 days | Tue 3/1/05 | Thu 3/3/05 |
| 4 | | **Analysis** | **4 days** | **Fri 3/4/05** | **Wed 3/9/05** |
| 5 | | Update Use Case Model | 3 days | Fri 3/4/05 | Tue 3/8/05 |
| 6 | | Update Specifications | 4 days | Fri 3/4/05 | Wed 3/9/05 |
| 7 | | Update Project Plan | 2 days | Fri 3/4/05 | Mon 3/7/05 |
| 8 | | Secure Stockholder Feedback | 3 days | Fri 3/4/05 | Tue 3/8/05 |
| 9 | | **Design** | **4 days** | **Thu 3/10/05** | **Tue 3/15/05** |
| 10 | | Update UML Diagrams | 4 days | Thu 3/10/05 | Tue 3/15/05 |
| 11 | | Detailed Design Specs for Components | 3 days | Thu 3/10/05 | Mon 3/14/05 |
| 12 | | **Implementation** | **24 days** | **Wed 3/16/05** | **Mon 4/18/05** |
| 13 | | Component Implementation | 24 days | Wed 3/16/05 | Mon 4/18/05 |
| 14 | | **Integration** | **6 days** | **Tue 4/19/05** | **Tue 4/26/05** |
| 15 | | Component Integration | 6 days | Tue 4/19/05 | Tue 4/26/05 |
| 16 | | Component Testing | 3 days | Tue 4/19/05 | Thu 4/21/05 |
| 17 | | **Testing** | **3 days** | **Wed 4/27/05** | **Fri 4/29/05** |
| 18 | | Validation against Requirements | 3 days | Wed 4/27/05 | Fri 4/29/05 |
| 19 | | **Certification** | **2 days** | **Mon 5/2/05** | **Tue 5/3/05** |
| 20 | | Component Certification for this Iteration | 2 days | Mon 5/2/05 | Tue 5/3/05 |
| 21 | | Deployment | 0 days | Tue 5/3/05 | Tue 5/3/05 |

Iteration 2:<br>Analysis and Design

Iteration 3:<br>Component Implementation

FIGURE 11.17  Review: Macro/Micro-Level Project Planning

| ID | | Task Name | Duration | Start | Finish | |
|---|---|---|---|---|---|---|
| | | | | | | June / July / August chart |
| | | | | | | 5/30 6/6 6/13 6/20 6/27 7/4 7/11 7/18 7/25 8/1 8/8 8/15 8/22 |
| 1 | | **Iteration 1: Prototype** | **39 days** | **Tue 6/1/04** | **Fri 7/23/04** | Irena[25%],Suzy[25%] |
| 2 | | Add/modify/delete employees, projects, codes | 25 days | Tue 6/1/04 | Mon 7/5/04 | |
| 3 | ▦ | Approvals | 25 days | Wed 6/9/04 | Tue 7/13/04 | Suzy[10%] |
| 4 | | Testing | 8 days | Wed 7/14/04 | Fri 7/23/04 | QA Specialist[25%] |
| 5 | | **Iteration 2: Integrated User Interface (PDA)** | **44 days** | **Tue 6/1/04** | **Fri 7/30/04** | |
| 6 | ▦ | Input validation | 20 days | Mon 6/14/04 | Fri 7/9/04 | Irena[25%] |
| 7 | | SOAP fault management | 20 days | Tue 6/1/04 | Mon 6/28/04 | Suzy[25%] |
| 8 | ▦ | Color coded error handling | 20 days | Mon 6/21/04 | Fri 7/16/04 | Irena[25%] |
| 9 | | Testing | 10 days | Mon 7/19/04 | Fri 7/30/04 | QA Specialist[25%] |
| 10 | | **Iteration 3: Prototype: Business rule manager** | **40 days** | **Tue 6/1/04** | **Mon 7/26/04** | |
| 11 | | Static business rules: validate end-to-end processing | 30 days | Tue 6/1/04 | Mon 7/12/04 | Irena[25%] |
| 12 | | Testing | 10 days | Tue 7/13/04 | Mon 7/26/04 | QA Specialist[25%] |
| 13 | | **Iteration 4: Business rule manager** | **55 days** | **Tue 7/27/04** | **Mon 10/11/04** | |
| 14 | | Dynamic business rules management; interface for creating new business rules | 45 days | Tue 7/27/04 | Mon 9/27/04 | |
| 15 | | Testing | 10 days | Tue 9/28/04 | Mon 10/11/04 | |
| 16 | | **Iteration 5: Administration** | **75 days** | **Mon 7/5/04** | **Fri 10/15/04** | |
| 17 | ▦ | Security | 25 days | Mon 7/5/04 | Fri 8/6/04 | Carl[50%],Irena[25%] |
| 18 | | Testing | 10 days | Mon 8/9/04 | Fri 8/20/04 | Carl[25%],Suzy[25%] |
| 19 | | Audit management | 30 days | Mon 8/23/04 | Fri 10/1/04 | QA Sp... |
| 20 | | Testing | 10 days | Mon 10/4/04 | Fri 10/15/04 | |
| 21 | | **Iteration 6: Customizations** | **60 days** | **Mon 8/2/04** | **Fri 10/22/04** | |
| 22 | ▦ | Per customer | 45 days | Mon 8/2/04 | Fri 10/1/04 | |
| 23 | | Testing | 15 days | Mon 10/4/04 | Fri 10/22/04 | |
| 24 | | **Supporting Disciplines** | **134 days** | **Tue 6/1/04** | **Fri 12/3/04** | |
| 25 | ▦ | Customer Support | 90 days | Mon 8/2/04 | Fri 12/3/04 | Car... |
| 26 | | Configuration and change management | 60 days | Tue 6/1/04 | Mon 8/23/04 | |
| 27 | | Project planning | 120 days | Tue 6/1/04 | Mon 11/15/04 | |
| 28 | | Web site development | 30 days | Tue 6/1/04 | Mon 7/12/04 | Ramon[50%] |
| 29 | | Collateral materials | 30 days | Tue 6/1/04 | Mon 7/12/04 | Ramon[50%] |
| 30 | | Business development | 90 days | Tue 6/1/04 | Mon 10/4/04 | |
| 31 | | General management | 120 days | Tue 6/1/04 | Mon 11/15/04 | |

FIGURE 11.18   Macro-Level Project Plan Summary

### 11.5.2   *Practical Application*

A macro-level project plan needs to be devised for each iteration (see bottom half of Fig. 11.17). When we focus on detailed planning only of the current and the next iteration, we realistically capture short-term deliverables and milestones while maintaining strategic (macro-level) flexibility to deal with the inevitable changes in requirements, priorities, and even technologies. Each iteration should typically be limited to what plus or minus six people can do in plus or minus six weeks.

There are two additional Best Practices that greatly improve the success rate of this type of planning:

- Plan to do the difficult things first, dealing with such matters as new technologies and tools, unknown algorithms, and the resolution of complex dependencies. This allows for early visibility of delays and other difficulties when adjustments are still manageable.

- Allow contributors to provide best-case, typical-case, and worst-case estimates and track milestones accordingly.

### 11.5.3   *Time Boxing*

Another related useful planning approach is "time boxing," where estimates are bracketed into "best-case," "worst-case," and "most-likely," with associated time estimates. The totals for each bracket can be correlated to risk management and can be reevaluated at the end of every iteration cycle.

## 11.6   Resources

The most popular project-planning software product is Microsoft® Project™. The example plan in Figure 11.18 was constructed in MS-Project. However, alternative products are available, such as Primavera., B2B's Time&Money, and many others.

## 11.7   Summary

In this chapter, you learned about client-server strategies using Java, and you were introduced to the concept of design patterns, mentioned earlier but finally covered in introductory detail here.

In our ongoing description of the Extended Unified Process methodology, our attention is now focused on the supporting disciplines. The first one of this group is the Project Management supporting discipline. We covered the concept of macro/micro-level planning, which supports detailed planning, but within a flexible framework.

## 11.8   Review Questions

1. **Distributed Computing.** Research Java Remote Method Invocation and design an example use of the technology. (The ambitious student may attempt an implementation, if infrastructure resources are available.)

2. **Macro-level and Micro-level Project Planning.** Compare macro-level and micro-level project planning. Create a fictitious project or apply your understanding to **the** Voting Program or HarmonyDesigns case study to develop a comprehensive set of plans (macro-level and two micro-level: current and next iteration).

3. **Generics.** Review the various features of generic methods and classes by researching the descriptions on www.java.sun.com.

## 11.9    Glossary – Terminology – Concepts

**Design pattern**    As defined by architect Christopher Alexander:

> *"Each pattern describes a problem which occurs over and over again in our environment and then describes the core of the solution to that problem in such a way that you can use this solution a million times over, without ever doing it the same way twice."*

As defined for software engineering by Erich Gamma, Richard Helm, Ralph Johnson, and John Vlissides ("The Gang of Four"):

> *"A design pattern names, abstracts, and identifies the key aspects of a common design structure that make it useful for creating a reusable object-oriented design."*

**Generics**    Classes and methods that do not resolve the type of a particular parameter or attribute until runtime (introduced as part of the J2SE SDK 5.0).

## 11.10    Exercises

**1. Model-View-Controller Pattern.**    Reorganize the Voting Program code to better reflect the MVC architecture design pattern. As this is a major effort, it is the only programming exercise prescribed in this chapter.

**2. Project Planning.**

   **a.**  Create a macro-level project plan for your **HarmonyDesigns** Case Study project:

   **b.**  Create your choice of two detailed iteration macro-level project plans from that macro-level plan.

**3. Complete the Voting Program.**    Revisit the Voting Program source code discussed in an earlier chapter, make the changes indicated in this chapter, complete the new functionality to create, store, and retrieve election information for both human candidate- and proposition-type elections (ballot measures).

# CHAPTER 12

# Software Integration and Deployment

Continuing the exploration of real-world Java software development practices initiated in the last chapter, this chapter describes how software components are integrated, including testing processes such as inspections and unit, integration, and acceptance testing. These topics are part of the software quality assurance-oriented supporting discipline, **Inspections and Validations.** At this stage in the software-development lifecycle, the quality control activities focus on testing and validation, as the product being developed is almost complete. Before it can be distributed, any and all remaining issues must be identified and corrected.

In our ongoing discovery of additional Java syntax and structure, we examine the more advanced aspects of how data is structured and organized. This topic is not unique to Java, of course. It is a core concern for all programming activities, because most programs are created to manage data and enhance the value of input data through organization and computation. We will therefore examine the support for **abstract data structures** in Java, including some of the new Java SDK 5.0 features.

The chapter concludes with a discussion of project deployment (alpha and beta phases, general release, and transition to the maintenance phase).

The Concept of Integration

## 12.1 Learning Objectives

From the software engineering life-cycle perspective, the validated integration of all the components required to make a software solution operational is the central topic of this chapter. Software-development organizations often have to struggle to ready software applications for general release because of having failed to pay sufficient attention to the productization of the application so that it can run without problems on the target systems the customers have deployed. What works well in the development lab does not necessarily operate error-free on a destination production system!

In addition to the development of viable software features and functions, the validation of integrated operability on all target systems is an important part of a high-quality software-development project. These activities need to be part of the plan and budget from the start; otherwise they cause delays in the critical final phases of the project process. They also need to figure prominently in the system architecture and the overall solution design.

In the area of supporting disciplines (workflows) for the software-development methodology life-cycle, we will take a look at the quality-assurance-related workflows of Inspections and Validation. These critical Software Quality Assurance (SQA) activities span the entire project life-cycle but take on added importance in the phases during which the system components are integrated and prepared for general release.

Java supports eight primitive data types, as described in an earlier chapter.[1] The support for complex data structures in Java centers around classes and objects. Traditional data structures such as lists, stacks, and queues are implemented in Java using specialized classes. In addition, Java programs must interface with relational databases, data files, and network resources, which are not object oriented. The conversion of data from and to objects and the organization and manipulation of structured data elements are discussed in more detail later in this chapter. In addition, we take a closer look at data structure-related enhancements in J2SE Release 5.0.

### 12.1.1   *Learning Layout*

This recurring section shows the learning objectives of the chapter in a simple diagram, using the Unified Modeling Language (UML) activity diagram notation (see Fig. 12.1).

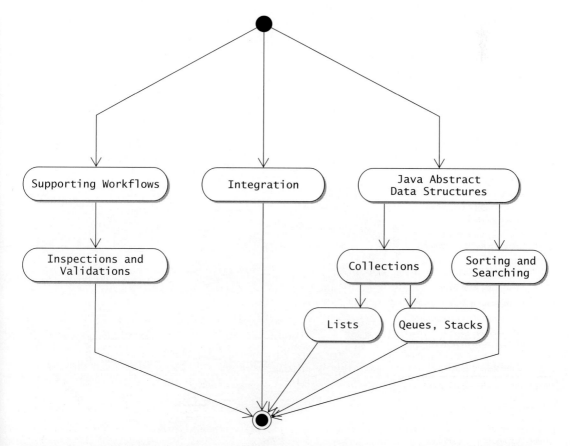

FIGURE 12.1   Chapter 12 Learning Layout (as a UML Activity Diagram)

---

[1]Some pundits cite these types as examples of Java's incomplete object orientation; "pure" object-oriented languages like SmallTalk™ implement all data types as objects.

The learning layout for this chapter continues to focus on real-life software projects. As we saw in the last chapter, these projects are typically multi-tier, distributed applications. In this chapter, we will explore the more advanced data structures that are typically used in commercial applications to deal with the often vast amounts of data processed by an application. The second of the six supporting disciplines is also covered: Inspections and Validations.

### 12.1.2 Learning Connections

The Learning Connections diagram (see Fig. 12.2) shows the content of this chapter in relation to the knowledge and skill development recommended for apprentice Java software engineers. In every chapter, it is intended to remind the reader of the multi-dimensional skills required of software engineers in the twenty-first century and to relate the areas of knowledge addressed in the chapter to these skills.

As holds for most of the chapters, a *cross-disciplinary set of skills* and interests will serve the junior software engineer best. The final phases of the software development process, much like the early ones, involve more system-level considerations than

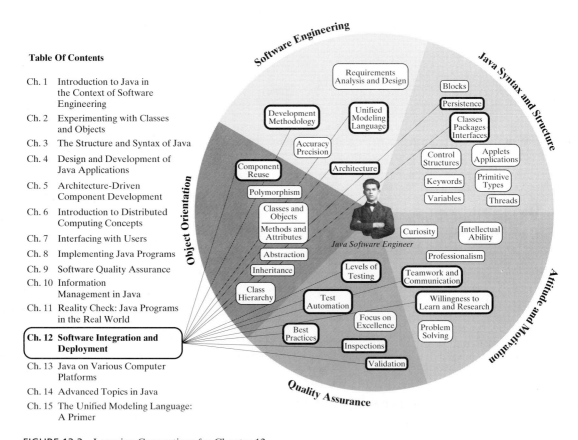

FIGURE 12.2 Learning Connections for Chapter 12

the implementation-focused middle phases. This broader coverage requires that the software engineer understand functional and support requirements and play an active role in the integration and productization of the software solution being developed.

---

### OUTSOURCING/OFFSHORING

Many software developers are concerned about their work being outsourced to a low-cost offshore supplier. It is true that companies have ramped up the movement of skilled ("white-collar") jobs overseas, given the ready availability of large numbers of well-educated professionals in countries like India and China whose labor rates are much lower than U.S. equivalents.

For the ambitious software engineer, no better employment insurance exists than the development of cross-disciplinary skills as described in these "Learning Connections" sections. The combination of these skills and responsibilities cannot realistically be outsourced overseas, because they involve many person-to-person interactions and require a hands-on real-time, detailed understanding of the domain being addressed by the software project.

---

## 12.2   Executive Summary

Among the final steps in a software-development project are the integration of all constituent components and subsystems and the deployment of the complete, integrated system. This chapter provides an overview of all the activities associated with validating a software system for general availability and deployment.

In the area of Java software syntax and structure, you will learn about Java support for abstract data structures. (In the context of object-oriented Java, it might make

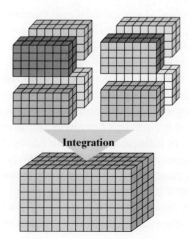

Component Integration

more sense to call them "object structures.") These structures are omnipresent in programming languages, whether procedural or object oriented. In Java, they include members from the primitive types, such as `int`, `double`, and `Boolean`, and complex class types from the Java SDK provided by Sun Microsystems or custom-developed by you or other developers.

The representation of abstract data types in Java involves the use of classes and objects. The structuring of class elements and, by extension, object elements into logical, structural entities allows software engineers to create sophisticated representations of the data intrinsic to their applications. When these representations are organized separately from the specifics of the application, they can be defined as **Abstract Data Types (ADT)**. When creating data structures, the principles of object orientation and design patterns apply: abstraction, component reusability, low coupling, and low cohesion must govern decisions about data structure organization. As discussed in Chapter 10, another key requirement for useful programs is the ability to store data permanently on a secondary storage device. In O-O, we call this capability persistence. Because objects are memory-resident constructs that contain both attributes and methods, they must be converted for persistent storage using a process called serialization.

In this chapter, we provide an overview of the various types of abstract data structures developed by computer scientists and supported in Java to help software engineers organize and manage data elements of primitive and class types.

## 12.3    Learning Modules

This section addresses the major topics in the chapter, one at a time, from a learning perspective. The modules cover the software engineering topics associated with the **Inspection and Validation** support discipline and Java data structures and their implementation.

### 12.3.1    System Integration

One of the important reasons for considering the topic of Java programming from the perspective of software engineering methodology, instead of just syntax and structure, is to account for the thorny issues of component and system integration in producing a deployable software solution. Otherwise, programmers may well develop an interesting collection of software components that fail to result in a well-integrated, deployable solution, and lacks commercial viability.

An integrated solution is made up of validated modules assembled into the desired software solution and tested in the target hardware and software configurations listed as the required environment in the Requirements Specification. While portable technology like Java reduces the number of changes required for deployment on various target systems, many factors influence the functionality and performance of an application in a particular configuration, ranging from memory and storage availability to network connection speed to co-existence with already installed applications (some of which may modify the platform in such a way as to render it incompatible with your application). The generalized perspectives discussed below and shown in Figure 12.3 describe the main contributing views involved with system integration.

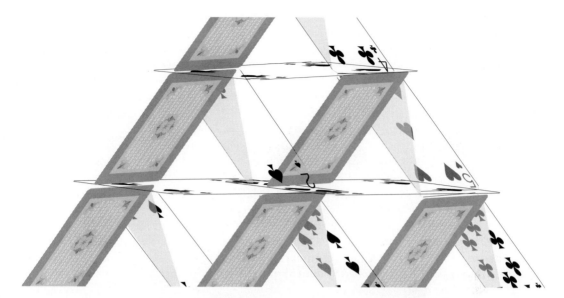

System Integration is Challenging and Volatile.

As can be seen in the figure, many contributing factors impact the quality and readiness of an integrated software system—from the classes created for the program, to the specifications, the underlying infrastructure requirements, such as hardware and networking, software quality assurance (including testing), the project and resource plans, and tools and installation programs and processes. Other contributing factors can be identified for specific projects, such as security considerations, internationalization/localization, and performance. The development organization must account for all these factors and their interactions in ensuring that the complete product solution can be successfully installed and used on customers' systems. Productive, responsive support and maintenance then need to be available to users for the lifetime of the product.

### System Integration Activities

Typically in this phase, extensive integration testing is performed. In smaller development groups, this may be the task of the software engineering team; in larger organizations, a separate integration test team typically owns this responsibility. The testing is performed according to an approved Integration Test Specification and results in an Integration Test Report that must be reviewed and approved by management. In some projects, the final customer may also need to approve these major milestones. The main objectives of these software quality assurance activities are:

- Validate feature content against Requirements and Design Specifications
- Validate interfaces between components
- Validate end-to-end functionality
- Validate program functionality in different configurations

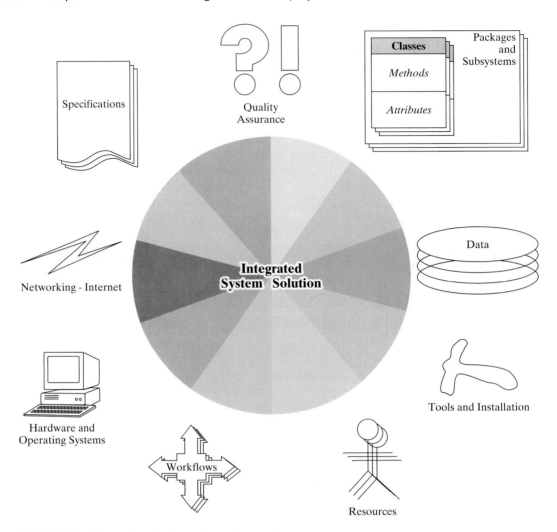

**FIGURE 12.3**   Factors Contributing to System Integration

- Validate usability, accessibility, and resilience
- Ascertain overall quality in terms of error count and error severity: weed out remaining critical issues
- Include regression testing that can be performed every time a new version goes through the integration cycle

Figure 12.4 summarizes the main factors that affect product-release readiness. For every project, other specific factors are likely to be important. Project management planning should include budget and resource allocation for these integration activities as part of the overall project plan.

The integration tests, like all formal tests, must be documented and repeatable; their results are communicated to the engineering team for closed-loop corrective

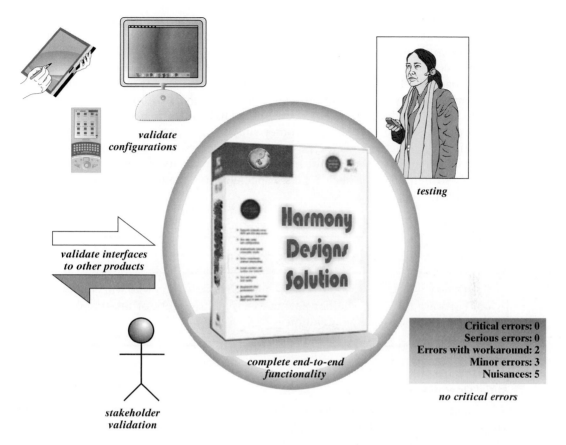

**FIGURE 12.4**   When Is a Product Ready for Release?

action. The Integration Test Specification should contain all the information required to run the entire Integration Test cycle, including test scripts, desired outcomes, environmental variables, test data, and the like. Typically, the Integration Test effort is performed on a build cycle separate from the internal engineering build release. This means that for integration testing, a separate version of the complete product is version-controlled and managed as precursor to the production version. It is at this juncture that engineering and production versions split. (Chapter 6 provides an outline for the Integration Test Specification.)

In addition to testing, a number of other product-release readiness activities take place at this stage, from documentation review to initial customer installations and the processing of feedback from those early field experiences.

### 12.3.2   Solution Deployment

When a solution has been tested and certified for general release, the deployment process tested initially in the beta test phase kicks into full-bore. In this phase, the ability to reliably ship the complete and consistent solution package as required by the targeted customer base becomes a key requirement. In producing products for shipment, no significant regression can be allowed to occur, and release management must be accurate and complete in determining the proper contents of the shipping product package. This is more complicated when the product is available for multiple platforms that may have different requirements, such as different installation routines. In addition, administrative processes need to be in place to support servicing the target customer base, including customer support and product maintenance. Often, it is difficult to anticipate what types of problems users and administrators are going to have with a new software product. It is important for live support personnel to be available to help resolve such issues, especially for products with mission-critical functionality.

---

## CUSTOMERS

In this text, we identify as "customers" all the stakeholders who will end up using our software product, whether paying external customers, or internal organizations that are adopting our solution.

---

### Initial Operational Capability

When a new software product is ready for deployment, a critical stage is reached: **Initial Operational Capability (IOC)**, a major project milestone. This means that the following requirements have been met, at a minimum:

- No outstanding critical errors—operational capability is certified.
- Distribution process and channel(s) are established and ready to go operational.
- Support process and resources are in place.
- Functional requirements have been met and validated.
- Non-functional requirements (scalability, performance, etc.) have been met and validated.
- A viable product maintenance process is in place.

Declaring IOC is the responsibility of the software quality assurance organization and sets in motion subsequent deployment, support, and, if a commercial product, marketing and sales activities.

### Addressing Problems at This Stage

Poorly planned projects all too often encounter serious problems at this stage of the development life-cycle, if not earlier. These are difficult to address because there is so little time left before the general deployment milestone. Many of the procedural suggestions made in previous chapters are geared toward minimizing serious setbacks at this late stage of the game. The types of errors or problems encountered just before product release fall into the following categories:

- *Quality issues:* functional brittleness, scalability issues, performance shortcomings, usability problems
- *Feature issues:* missing features, features that were not required, features operating incorrectly or differently from customer expectations
- *Time problems:* not enough time or resources to perform all the testing and validation required, often leading to problems in the other two categories (typically this problem type originates in inadequate planning and a resulting budget shortfall)

Addressing these issues requires tough decisions, such as reducing the feature set or delaying product availability. If the product was developed in an iterative, modular fashion, with the most important work done earlier, the overall impact of feature reduction is sometimes non-critical. Most important, the errors in process that resulted in these last-minute problems need to be captured and documented so that they can be avoided in the next project.

### 12.3.3 Abstract Data Structures

Most software programs are created to manipulate data and add value to the application's information content. In procedural programming, data and functions are separated; in object-oriented programming, they are integrated in the concept of classes and objects. In either situation, the organization of data into data structures is a key software engineering activity, a prerequisite to extracting process value from data. Unstructured data cannot be processed effectively (imagine a telephone book that is not alphabetized!).

Data structures organized to separate specific content from generic structure are called *abstract*. They provide a template for the concrete implementations of data structures with specific data types and associated operations.

In Java, abstract data structures are implemented using object-oriented concepts. The structures may contain members of class or primitive types. Often, these objects are deconstructed (serialized/deserialized) for persistent storage or transport. The concept of *structure* imposes an organization on the data or objects which allows for powerful data manipulation, typically for one of the following functions:

- Sorting
- Searching
- Storing, retrieving, modifying, and deleting in order within a group
- Extracting mathematical or logical information (relationships)

The computer science constructs typically used to support these types of functions are ordered lists, arrays and vectors, collections, stacks and queues, maps, and hash tables. We will examine the major types of data/object structures in the next paragraphs.

#### Data Structures: A Historical Perspective

Variables of primitive data types such as integers, Booleans, and characters contain no meta-information about the data they hold. Computer scientists have devised ways to store relationships among primitive data types in more complex types, and then to organize variables of the complex types into structures that, in turn, hold even more information about their contents and interrelationships. They behave like connected containers. This is one of the main tenets of *data transformation:* computer programs extract useful information from data by applying structure and algorithms to data elements. In procedural languages, complex data types are typically defined as types or records containing fields. The type becomes the template for variables of that type, a precursor to the object-oriented perspective on data structures.

---

### DEFINITION: METADATA

Metadata is information about data, typically associated with a data container. This may include format, size, name, type, etc.

---

Here is an example format of a structure in generic pseudocode:

```
type Student
      Name: String (36);
      Identifier: String (12);
      Address1:  String (48);
      Address2:  String (48);
      Address3:  String (48);
      Midterm, Final:  Integer;
      GradePointAverage:  Float;
end type
```

This type of organization allows for the definition of variables of this complex type, which can then store the combination of data values in a single named location, using a dereferencing mechanism of some kind to address the individual data values (often the period . character). This creates an efficient method for moving the access to complex data to the logical locations in the program where the value-add processing takes place.

```
Student firstStudent // pseudocode, not Java
firstStudent.Name = "Carlos"
```

While classes and objects readily support this data-centric type of organization through attributes ("Fields" in Sun Microsystems nomenclature), they are actually more flexible if they incorporate the advances of object orientation, specifically the seamless integration of data and functions in the form of objects. But in object orientation, there is still a need to organize data into structures that can be efficiently accessed and processed.

Java incorporates a number of object-organization structures, and others can easily be programmed. The ones most often used are discussed in the next paragraphs.

### Ordered Data Structures

The simplest form of data organization is a *list*. A list may be *unsorted* or *sorted* and typically represents a collection of like items organized in sequence, one following the other. To be useful for data processing, lists are typically organized into sorted sequences so that specific items can be found easily. When a list is sorted, binary searches and other efficient search algorithms can be applied to quickly find a desired item in the list.

In Java, a list can be implemented programmatically in a variety of structures. One of the most common and simplest is the array of variables (if the data is of a primitive type) or objects (for lists of class "types").[2] When the size of a list is static, a simple array will do; when it is meant to be dynamic, an `ArrayList` object used to maintain the list can grow and shrink (semi-) dynamically. Other flexible approaches include the use of vectors and linked lists (discussed later).

In the graphical user interface (GUI) tier of an application, the user view of a list is implemented as a selection or drop-down list (see Fig. 12.5). These display lists are often sorted to make selection easier. They provide parameters to control such features as multiple selection of list items, checkboxes on list items, and even the display of iconic pictures in the list.

It is good design practice to separate the GUI representation of listed items from the internal data structure used to represent and store the associated data/object elements. This approach properly follows the Model-View-Controller architecture pattern.

As noted earlier, arrays are useful for storing a known, fixed number of data elements, but when a need arises for more dynamic storage of sequences of like data, more flexible data structures must be applied. Java supports several dynamic data structures that can grow and shrink while the program runs.

### Collections: Arrays and Vectors, Hash Tables and Maps

The **Collections Framework** available in Java 2 provides a powerful mechanism for managing collections such as arrays, array-lists, and vectors. The Collections Framework

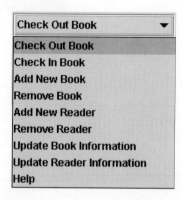

FIGURE 12.5   Example Drop-Down List

---

[2]The term "type" is applied here loosely, it has another meaning in formal Java syntax.

provides an architectural perspective on collection containers and specifies the following key elements:

- *Interfaces:* abstract classes representing collections
- *Implementations:* concrete reusable implementations of the collection interfaces
- *Algorithms:* polymorphic methods used to interact with collection objects and provide administrative functions, such as sorting, searching, adding, and deleting

The Collection interface is the root of the collection hierarchy and is implemented to represent a group of objects. Some Collection subclasses are ordered (e.g., Lists), and others are unordered; some allow duplicate elements, and others do not (e.g., Sets).

Arrays are structures in Java commonly used to represent unordered or ordered lists of like elements (see Fig. 12.6). An array is a structure that holds one or more values of the same type (primitive or class) in one or more dimensions. An array element is one of the values within an array and is accessed by its position (index) within the array. The length of an array is established when the array is created in the program. After that point, the array remains a structure of fixed length. When a memory-based list has to be dynamic in length, an ArrayList object can be used. Both arrays and array-lists are types of collections.

All these data structures belong to the class of structures called *containers.* They typically have one index variable per dimension to keep track of the location of a data element/object in the structure.

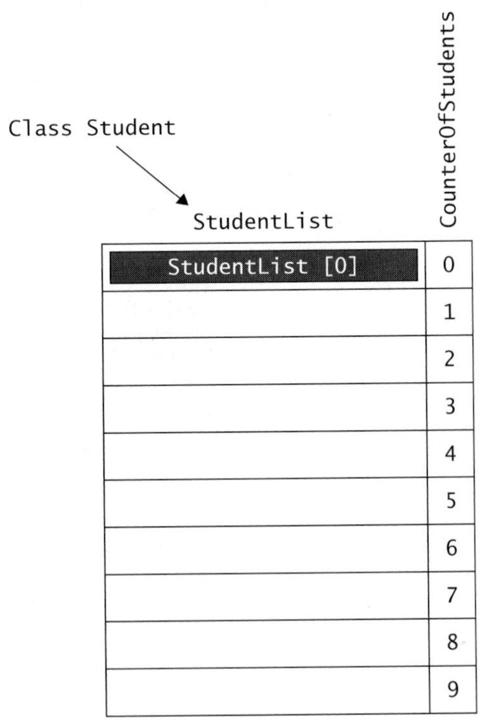

FIGURE 12.6   Illustration of studentList Array Object

Here is an example array of objects:

```
//... program setup assumed
String response = JOptionPane.showInputDialog
    ("Enter total number of students");
Student studentList = new Student [Integer.parseInt (response)];
// create array of class Student
studentList [counterOfStudents] = new Student();
// create Student object and store it as an array element
studentList [counterOfStudents].name = promptForName.getText();
// access object attributes
studentList [counterOfStudents].ID = promptForID.getText();
counterOfStudents++;   // keep track of highest array element
// ... remainder of program
```

Arrays of primitive variables or objects can be single- or multi-dimensional, but their size is fixed at creation. The `ArrayList` class was added to Java to provide more flexible array allocation.

Here is an example `ArrayList` implementation:

```
class Student {
// helper class containing Student attributes
// can also contain methods

String name, ID;
}
```

---

```
/**
 * @ (#) SimpleGreeting6.java 1.0 13/10/02
 *
 * Author:  Georges Merx, Ph.D.
 * Purpose:  ArrayList Example
 */

import java.awt.*;
import java.awt.event.*;
import javax.swing.*;
import java.util.*;

class SimpleGreeting6 extends JFrame implements ActionListener {
// create a class of type JFrame
    JTextField promptForName, promptForID;
    /* object attributes - declare here to be able to access from
       multiple methods */
    JButton continueButton, displayButton;
    // declared here to allow access from multiple methods
    static ArrayList studentList;
    /* array of Student objects - static because allocated in static
       Main */
```

```java
        static int counterOfStudents = 0;
        // tracks current last element in array

    public SimpleGreeting6(String title) {
    // constructor method - initializes object
        Container c;
        setTitle (title);  // set window title
        addWindowListener(new WindowAdapter() {
        // handle window being closed by clicking on x box
            public void windowClosing(WindowEvent e) {
                dispose();
                System.exit(0);  // terminate normally
            }
        });

        c = getContentPane();
        c.setLayout(new GridLayout(5,2));
        // set window up as a simple 5x2 grid
        c.add(new JLabel("Hello!"));
        c.add(new JLabel(""));
        c.add(new JLabel("What is your name?"));
        promptForName = new JTextField ("... enter name ...");
        promptForName.selectAll ();  // select text for overtyping
        c.add(promptForName);
        c.add(new JLabel("What is your ID number?"));
        promptForID = new JTextField ();
        c.add(promptForID);
        continueButton = new JButton ("Save");
        continueButton.addActionListener (this);
        // prepare button for event handling
        c.add (continueButton);
        JButton exitButton = new JButton ("Exit");
        exitButton.addActionListener (this);
        c.add (exitButton);
        displayButton = new JButton ("Display");
        displayButton.addActionListener (this);
        c.add (displayButton);

        pack();  // shrink window to miniminum size needed
        setVisible(true);  // make window visible
    }

    public static void main(String args[]) { // program entry point
        System.out.println("Starting SimpleGreeting...");
        studentList = new ArrayList();
        // create array of Student objects
        SimpleGreeting6 mainWindow = new SimpleGreeting6(
            "Simple Greeting Example");
        // create new object of class SimpleGreeting
    }
```

```java
public void actionPerformed(ActionEvent evt){
    if (evt.getActionCommand ().equals("Save")) {
    // Continue button pressed
        Student localStudent = new Student();
        localStudent.name = promptForName.getText();
        localStudent.ID = promptForID.getText();
        studentList.add(localStudent);
        // create Student arrayList element object
        promptForName.setText ("... enter name ...");
        // reinitialize input fields
        promptForName.selectAll ();
        promptForName.requestFocus ();
        promptForID.setText ("");
    }

    else if (evt.getActionCommand ().equals("Display")) {
    // Display button pressed
        String result = ""; // accumulates display string
            if (!studentList.isEmpty()) {
                for (Iterator count = studentList.iterator();
                    count.hasNext (); ) {
                    Student displayStudent =
                    (Student)count.next();
                    // object cast to Student
                    result = result + displayStudent.name +
                        ": " + displayStudent.ID + "\n";
                }

                JOptionPane.showMessageDialog (null, result,
                    "Student List", JOptionPane.
                    INFORMATION_MESSAGE);
                // display pop-up message dialog box
            }

            else
                JOptionPane.showMessageDialog (null,
                    "No records", "Student List",
                    JOptionPane.ERROR_MESSAGE);
                // display pop-up message dialog box
            }

    else if (evt.getActionCommand ().equals("Exit"))
    // Exit button pressed
        System.exit(0); // terminate program normally
    }
}
```

FIGURE 12.7 Illustration of (Singly) Linked List

This program, a modification of an earlier example, prompts for names and IDs (of students) and stores them in an `ArrayList`-type variable, `studentList`. The `ArrayList` object is a dynamic structure to which you can add elements as needed. (There are some performance implications when you exceed the default size, but the `add()` operation will complete successfully.)

A linked list is a sequence of self-referential class objects. The objects are called nodes and connected by reference links (see Fig. 12.7). Stacks and queues are linked lists with constraints. All support sequences of data where the number of elements is unpredictable in advance of program execution. Class `LinkedList` is provided in `java.util`.

The foundation for the implementation of linked lists in Java is the support for self-referential classes that contain instance variables referring to another object of the same class type ("link" or "node" reference). The `new` keyword is used to dynamically allocate memory as it is needed to add another node. This alleviates the need in Java for the explicit memory allocation characteristic of C and C++.

**Stacks** are ordered lists where new nodes can be added and removed only at the top (LIFO). Class `Stack` is provided in `java.util`. The following simple sample application uses a `Stack` object to add tasks ("push") and remove tasks from the stack in LIFO order ("pop").

```java
import java.awt.*;
import java.awt.event.*;
import javax.swing.*;
import java.util.Stack;

/**
 * Demonstration Application for a Stack Data Structure
 *
 * @ author Georges Merx, Phd
 * @ version 1.00 05/06/05
 */

public class ProjectTracker extends JFrame implements ActionListener {
    JTextField txtTask = new JTextField (20);
    JButton btnAdd = new JButton ("Add");
    JButton btnGet = new JButton ("Get");
    JLabel lblRetrievedTask = new JLabel();
    Stack <String> events = new Stack<String>();

    ProjectTracker(String title) { // constructor
        Container c = new Container();
        setTitle (title);
```

```
            setDefaultCloseOperation(EXIT_ON_CLOSE);
            c = getContentPane();
            c.setLayout (new GridLayout(3,2));
            c.add (new JLabel ("Enter a task:"));
            c.add(txtTask);
            btnAdd.addActionListener(this);
            c.add(btnAdd);
            btnGet.addActionListener(this);
            c.add(btnGet);
            c.add(new JLabel ("Task retrieved:"));
            c.add(lblRetrievedTask);
            pack();
            setLocation (100,100);
            setVisible(true);
      }

      public static void main(String[] args) {
            ProjectTracker frame = new ProjectTracker
                ("Tracking Projects");
      }

      public void actionPerformed (ActionEvent e) {
            if (e.getActionCommand().equals ("Add")){
                  events.push(txtTask.getText());
                  // push element on the stack
                  txtTask.setText("");
            }

            else if (e.getActionCommand().equals("Get")){
                  if (events.empty()) {
                        System.out.println(
                            "Nothing else to pop: exiting!");
                        System.exit(0); // terminate program normally
                  }

                  else {
                        lblRetrievedTask.setText(events.pop());
                        // pop element from stack in LIFO order
                  }
            }
      }
}
```

Running this program produces the output shown in Figure 12.8.

**Queues** are ordered lists where queue nodes are removable (dequeue) only from the top of the list (front/head of the queue) and inserted (enqueue) only at the end/tail (FIFO). Class Queue is provided in java.util.

A **tree** is a non-linear, two-dimensional data structure. The most popular implementation of this structure is the *binary tree*, which contains nodes with two links each. Binary trees are an efficient mechanism for organizing data for fast searches called

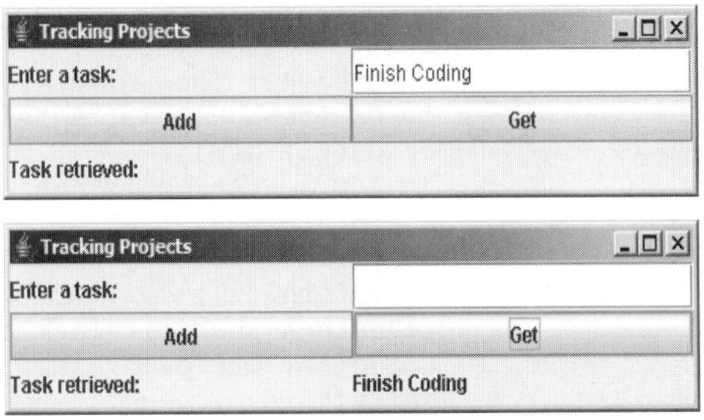

FIGURE 12.8    Using a Stack Object

binary searches. In a binary search tree, all the values in any left subtree are less than the value in that subtree's parent node, and the values in any right subtree are greater than the value in that subtree's parent node.

**Hash tables** and **maps** map keys to values. For example, a map may associate names with colors, describing people's favorite colors. A map is a function from a key set to a value set. A map maintains a one-to-one mapping of a key to an object. This is useful for doing look-ups using a `compareTo()` method, for example.

Any non-null object can be used as a key or as a value in a hash table. A map, on the other hand, cannot contain duplicate keys; each key can map to at most one value. **Hashing** is a technique for quickly finding elements in a data structure. A hash table maintains two arrays, one for keys, one for values. An item is found in a hash table by using a hash function to form the item address (the hash value or code) from the key at the location identified by the function. A **hash function** computes an integer value (hash code) from an object in such a way that different objects are likely to yield different hash codes, converting an input from a large domain into an output having a smaller range (the hash value). The class `Object` defines a `hashCode` method that child classes override: the `String` class, for example, defines an appropriate hash function for `String` objects. The hash code is then used as an array index into a hash table (reduced to a reasonable size). Note that hash collisions need to be dealt with: a collision occurs when two different keys have the same hash value. Duplicate hash codes are handled via link sequences called buckets.

The following code illustrates a very simple implementation of a hash table:

```
import java.awt.*;
import java.awt.event.*;
import javax.swing.*;
import java.util.Hashtable;

/** Demonstration Application for a Hashtable Data Structure
 *
 * @author Georges Merx, PhD
 * @version 1.00 05/06/05
 */
```

```java
public class ProjectTrackerHash extends JFrame implements
    ActionListener {
  JTextField txtTask = new JTextField (20);
  JButton btnAdd = new JButton ("Add");
  JButton btnGet = new JButton ("Get");
  JLabel lblRetrievedTask = new JLabel();
  Hashtable events = new Hashtable();
  int counter = 0;

  ProjectTrackerHash(String title) { // constructor
      Container c = new Container();
      setTitle (title);
      setDefaultCloseOperation(EXIT_ON_CLOSE);
      c = getContentPane();
      c.setLayout (new GridLayout(3,2));
      c.add (new JLabel ("Enter a task:"));
      c.add(txtTask);
      btnAdd.addActionListener(this);
      c.add(btnAdd);
      btnGet.addActionListener(this);
      c.add(btnGet);
      c.add(new JLabel ("Task retrieved:"));
      c.add(lblRetrievedTask);
      pack();
      setLocation (100,100);
      setVisible(true);
  }

  public static void main(String[] args) {
      ProjectTrackerHash frame = new ProjectTrackerHash
          ("Tracking Projects");
  }

  public void actionPerformed (ActionEvent e) {
      if (e.getActionCommand().equals ("Add")){
          events.put("C-" + counter, txtTask.getText());
// put element into the hash table using C-0, C-1, ...counter++;
          txtTask.setText("");
      }

      else if (e.getActionCommand().equals("Get")){
          String localTask = (String)events.get("C-" +
          JOptionPane.showInputDialog("Enter code"));
          /* retrieve element from hashtable using code provided,
          e.g. 0, 1, ... */
          if (localTask != null)
              lblRetrievedTask.setText(localTask);
          else {
```

```
            System.out.println(
                "Nothing to retrieve: exiting!");
            System.exit(0); // terminate program normally
        }
      }
    }
  }
}
```

The hashtable object, events, receives elements paired with an mapping index—in this case "C-0", "C-1", etc.—which allows for the subsequent retrieval of specific elements as needed, using the mapping key.

## 12.4   Position in Process

| Iterations | iteration 1 | iteration 2 | iteration 3 | iteration 4 | iteration 5 | iteration n |
|---|---|---|---|---|---|---|
| Disciplines | | | | | | |
| PROJECT MANAGEMENT | | | | | | |
| **INSPECTIONS AND VALIDATION** | | | | | | |
| CONFIGURATION MANAGEMENT | | | | | | |
| DOCUMENTATION | | | | | | |
| TECHNICAL MARKETING PLAN | | | | | | |

At this stage in our Extended Unified Process life-cycle methodology, we examine the Inspections and Validation support discipline. This supporting workflow provides for software quality assurance and control over every stage of the product life-cycle. The specific approach includes an inspection regime as well as the formal validation of milestones and the management of all deliverables.

The inspection process involves a planned set of activities with the expressed goal of eliminating all critical unknowns from the development of a component or subsystem. Figure 12.9 is a sample project plan for an inspection of a code component.

The plan shows the milestones associated with a formal inspection process initiated by the lead software engineer and supported by a peer-review team. Also included should be key stakeholders, as long as they are technically savvy enough to make a

---

### DOCUMENTATION

Software engineers will at times resist writing documentation; they often prefer the coding work to the writing required for system documentation to be complete and remain up-to-date.

However, documentation is an integral part of engineering best practices in all engineering disciplines; management expectation must include attention to detail in this critical area.

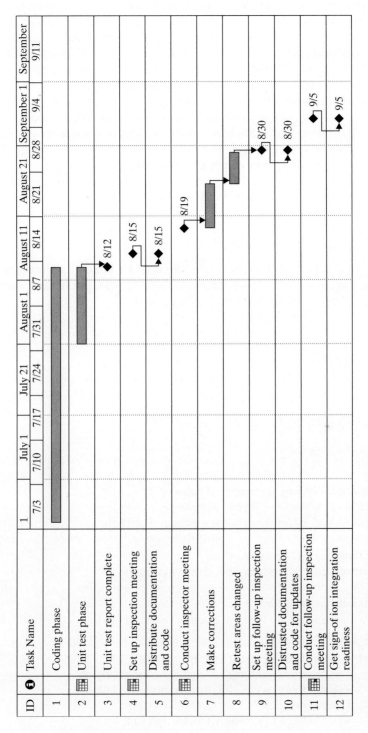

| ID | ❶ | Task Name | 1 7/3 | July 1 7/10 | 7/17 | July 21 7/24 | 7/31 | August 1 8/7 | August 11 8/14 | 8/21 | August 21 8/28 | September 1 9/4 | September 9/11 |
|---|---|---|---|---|---|---|---|---|---|---|---|---|---|
| 1 | | Coding phase | | | | | | | | | | | |
| 2 | ▦ | Unit test phase | | | | | | | | | | | |
| 3 | | Unit test report complete | | | | | | | 8/12 | | | | |
| 4 | ▦ | Set up inspection meeting | | | | | | | 8/15 | | | | |
| 5 | | Distribute documentation and code | | | | | | | 8/15 | | | | |
| 6 | ▦ | Conduct inspector meeting | | | | | | | | 8/19 | | | |
| 7 | | Make corrections | | | | | | | | | | | |
| 8 | | Retest areas changed | | | | | | | | | | | |
| 9 | | Set up follow-up inspection meeting | | | | | | | | | 8/30 | | |
| 10 | | Distrusted documentation and code for updates | | | | | | | | | 8/30 | | |
| 11 | ▦ | Conduct follow-up inspection meeting | | | | | | | | | | 9/5 | |
| 12 | | Get sign-of ion integration readiness | | | | | | | | | | 9/5 | |

FIGURE 12.9   Sample Plan for a Code Inspection Process

positive contribution to the inspection process. The participants in the process of inspection agree to provide critical, constructive feedback about the details of the design and implementation of the component, subsystem, or system being evaluated. An iterative process of improvements results in zero or more follow-up meetings to ensure that all defects are eradicated.

The concept of *validation* permeates all aspects of the software engineering lifecycle. Validation ensures that all work conducted in support of the project is compatible with known requirements and design decisions, and that all documentation is kept up to date. It is not meant to stifle the creative aspects of software development, but it envelops the work with a checks-and-balances system that infuses quality consciousness into all of the software engineer's minor and major decisions.

Validation typically involves peer-reviews of documentation (specifications and reports) and code, including test results.

## 12.5    Data Structure Example Application: Linked List

The code snippet given below illustrates the use of a linked list data structure to track student information in a list that can easily updated, using standard methods associated with the LinkedList class available in java.util.

```java
import java.awt.*;
import java.awt.event.*;
import javax.swing.*;
import java.util.*;

/**
 * @ (#) SimpleGreeting.java   02/09/09
 * @version 6.0
 * @author Georges Merx
 */

class SimpleGreeting extends JFrame {
  // create a class of type JFrame
    JTextField promptForName, promptForID;
    /* object attributes - declare here to be able to access
       from multiple methods */
    JButton continueButton, displayButton;
    // declared here to allow access from multiple methods
    LinkedList studentList;
    String result = ""; // accumulates display string
    int counter = 0;

    public SimpleGreeting(String title) {
     // constructor method - initializes object
        super (title);  // set window title
        Container c;
        studentList = new LinkedList();
```

```
        addWindowListener(new WindowAdapter(){
        // handle window being closed by clicking on x box
              public void windowClosing(WindowEvent e) {
                    dispose();
                    System.exit(0); // terminate normally
              }
        });

        c = getContentPane();
        c.setLayout(new GridLayout(5,2));
        // set window up as a 5x2 grid
        c.add(new JLabel("Hello!"));
        c.add(new JLabel(""));
        c.add(new JLabel("What is your name?"));
        promptForName = new JTextField ("... enter name...");
        promptForName.selectAll ();   // select text for overtyping
        c.add(promptForName);
        c.add(new JLabel("What is your ID number?"));
        promptForID = new JTextField ();
        c.add(promptForID);
        continueButton = new JButton ("Continue");
        continueButton.addActionListener (new MyActionListener());
        // prepare button for event handling
        c.add (continueButton);
        JButton exitButton = new JButton ("Exit");
        exitButton.addActionListener (new MyActionListener());
        c.add (exitButton);
        displayButton = new JButton ("Display");
        displayButton.addActionListener (new MyActionListener());
        c.add (displayButton);
        pack(); // shrink window to miniminum size needed
        setVisible(true); // make window visible
    }

    public static void main(String args[]){ // program entry point
        System.out.println("Starting SimpleGreeting...");
        SimpleGreeting mainWindow = new SimpleGreeting
            ("Simple Greeting Example - CIS 190");
        // create new object of class SimpleGreeting
    }

    class MyActionListener implements ActionListener {
    //inner class to handle button event
        public void actionPerformed(ActionEvent evt) {
              if (evt.getActionCommand ().equals("Continue")) {
              // Continue button pressed
                    Student student = new Student(); student.name =
                        promptForName.getText();
                    student.ID = promptForID.getText();
```

```
            studentList.addLast (student);
            counter++;
            promptForName.setText ("... enter name...");
            // reinitialize input fields
            promptForName.selectAll ();
            promptForName.requestFocus ();
            promptForID.setText ("");
        }

        else if (evt.getActionCommand ().equals("Display")) {
        // Display button pressed
            if (counter > 0) {
                ListIterator iterator = studentList.
                    listIterator();
                while (iterator.hasNext()) {
                    Student student = (Student)iterator.
                        next();
                    result = result + student.name + ": " +
                        student.ID + "\n";
                }

                JOptionPane.showMessageDialog (null, result,
                    "Student List", JOptionPane.
                    INFORMATION_MESSAGE);
                // display pop-up message dialog box
                displayButton.setEnabled (false);
                // may press Display button only once
            }

            else JOptionPane.showMessageDialog
                (null, "No records", "Student List",
                JOptionPane.ERROR_MESSAGE);
            // display pop-up message dialog box
            }

        else if (evt.getActionCommand ().equals("Exit"))
        // Exit button pressed
            System.exit(0); // terminate program normally
        }
    }
}
```

This example implements a linked list to keep track of student records. A new node is added for every new Student object created. A ListIterator object is used to navigate the list and extract the elements for display, using its hasNext() and next() methods.

The list can be visualized as shown in Figure 12.10. Each element in the list has a link to the next element, so it is easy to break a link, insert a new item, and connect it at

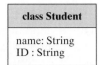

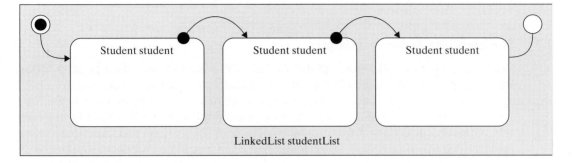

FIGURE 12.10   Linked List Visualization

the desired location into the list. A doubly-linked list is often used to make the insert/delete process even more efficient.

## 12.6   Resources

It is helpful to understand the computer science behind data structures. *Concepts of Programming Languages* by Robert Sebesta (Pearson/Addision-Wesley, 2004) is a helpful text in this area. The implementation of data structures in programming languages follows principles of computer science that span all computer languages; the specific application of these principles in Java provides an interesting illustration of how computer science concepts relate to specific language syntax and structure.

### 12.6.1   Connections

These last chapters in our book often refer to the "real world." It is invaluable for novice software engineers to "get their hands on real code." Internships are the best way to gain this experience, but guest speakers and site visits are also good devices to introduce students to the world of commercial software development.

In the absence of real-world exposure, it helps to develop programs that have *real value*, even if just for class purposes or personal use. When a software program provides features and functions that effectively solve real problems, there is a built-in incentive to properly understand the program's requirements, design its features well, and test it carefully. And if it is really useful, end-users will be available by definition to use the program and provide further feedback.

### 12.6.2   People

Local chapters of professional associations, such as ACM, IEEE, and various special-interest groups (SIGs) are an excellent resource for new software engineers to "rub shoulders" with professionals in their field.

### 12.6.3 *Companies*

Unfortunately, companies rarely post internship opportunities on their human resources Web site pages. It is therefore necessary for interested students to directly call the companies in which they are interested. It is especially helpful to know someone at such a company, hence the suggestion in the preceding paragraph.

## 12.7    Summary and Recommendations

While we have covered almost all the aspects of the Extended Unified Process, focusing on inspection and validation in this chapter, there is always more to learn about Java. In a book like this, we only have room to scratch the surface of Java capabilities. Issues of data structure and organization dominated the Java syntax and structure content of this chapter. These structures may be static or dynamic (in fact, even these terms are insufficiently descriptive, because the nature of a structure's behavior depends on more factors—for example, whether it is allocated from the stack or from the heap).

## 12.8    Review Questions

1. **Linked Lists. Describe the nature of a linked list.** The following picture illustrates the concept of a linked list. A linked list is composed of nodes and fields that point either just to the next node or to the next and previous nodes (doubly-linked list).

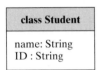

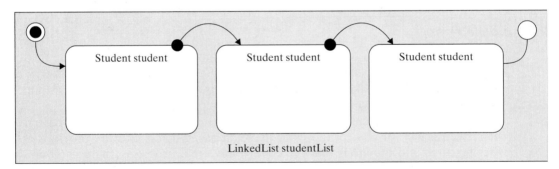

2. **Inspections and Validations. What is the purpose of an inspection and validation regime?** Inspections provide a rigorous, responsible mechanism for peer evaluation and review. The process is focused on finding problems, oversights, and errors, and reliably correcting the errors. The validation aspect verifies that errors are corrected and that all prerequisites and standards established in conjunction with the project are met before product general availability.

3. **Stack, Queues, Trees.** Based on Internet research, describe the similarities and differences between stack, queue, and tree data structures. Be specific about their implementation in Java. Provide an example program for each.

## 12.9 Glossary – Terminology – Concepts

**Dynamic:** Determined at runtime.

**Hash table:** Maps keys to values and tracks elements based on these keys; any non-null object can be used as a key or as a value in a hash table.

**Heap:** A complete tree where every node has a key more extreme (greater or less) than or equal to the key of its parent.

**Stack:** A stack data structure works on the principle of last-in/first-out (LIFO): the last item put on the stack is the first item that can be taken off (analogy: a stack of dishes). The two main stack operations are *push* (an item is put on top of the stack, increasing the stack size by one; as stack size is usually limited, this may provoke a stack overflow if the maximum size is exceeded); and *pop* (the top item is taken from the stack, decreasing the stack size by one); if there was no top item (i.e., the stack was empty), a stack underflow occurs

**Static:** Determined at compile-time.

**Tree:** A non-linear, two-dimensional data structure, the most popular implementation of which is the binary tree that contains nodes with two links each.

## 12.10 Exercises

**1. Arrays and ArrayLists.** Compare and contrast arrays and array lists. Develop two versions of a program to track student results on exams, homework, and attendance to show the use of each. Illustrate the benefits of the array list structure in terms of extensibility.

**2. Linked Lists.** Develop a small program that allows you to track your MP3 music tracks, add new ones, delete old ones, and modify existing ones. Use a linked list.

**3. Binary Tree.** Redevelop the program from the preceding exercise to use a binary tree and implement a fast-search function. (You will need to use Java documentation resources on the Internet, e.g., www.java.sun.com, to complete this exercise.)

**4. Hash Table.** Develop a program that uses a hash table to keep track of employee time cards and records. Include provisions for begin and end time, normal and overtime pay, vacation pay, and project-related information. Implement a search function.

# CHAPTER 13

# Java on Various Computer Platforms

In this chapter, you will learn about the broad support for Java on a range of client and server platforms, including mobile systems. The chapter discusses the differences and similarities between platforms, including customizations introduced by some of the leading vendors, such as IBM, Sun, and HP. We will also take a look at Java development technologies and tools. Networking, Internet, and Web support in Java constitute our key technical topic in this section, and in the area of software methodology, we focus on the Configuration Management support discipline.

## 13.1   Learning Objectives

The ultimate purpose for learning a computer programming language like Java is typically the development of professional software, meaning software that does useful work and that someone is willing to pay for, whether an individual or a commercial, non-profit, or public organization, internal or external.

The computer center of the Extended Studies Department at a major West Coast public university, for example, has a Sun Microsystems mail server running Sun Solaris, an EMC data server running a version of Linux, various Dell servers running Microsoft Windows Server OS, tape backup devices, and over a hundred Microsoft Windows–based client computers, laptops and desktops, as well as a few Apple Macintoshes. Some clients are connected externally, but most are linked to the server computers over a high-speed internal network; they all have controlled access to electronic mail, directory services, and the Internet and World Wide Web. This type of environment is reasonably representative of office environments and organizations anywhere. Other businesses may link manufacturing and other special-purpose equipment and applications into their computer infrastructure. Many companies and organizations also support remote wireless devices, such as personal digital assistants. Outside of the commercial realm, even gaming is now a networked endeavor.

These hardware, networking, and software components form the information technology infrastructure of the customer organizations on which our Java solution has to operate. In this chapter, we examine in more detail the leading platforms that actively support Java solutions, including special enhancements vendors may offer to ensure that Java applications run efficiently and reliably on their systems.

The information technology (IT) environment for any given organization encompasses an often complex, diversified combination of hardware, networking, and software components and tools. The programming language(s) and tools used for the development of applications that support this environment play a central role because they have to not only support the underlying systems but also leverage their capabilities to solve real customer problems. Java has developed a strong following among large and small organizations because it provides a comprehensive range of integrated capabilities, from the portable device technology available on smart cell phones to large, multiprocessor servers running UNIX or Linux, or even Microsoft server technology.

### 13.1.1 Learning Layout

This recurring section shows the learning objectives of the chapter in a simple diagram, using the Unified Modeling Language (UML) activity diagram notation (see Fig. 13.1). As you go back through the chapters, these diagrams provide you with a simple visualization of your learning experience. We have used UML notation in order to impress upon you the usefulness of this type of graphical representation to make complex concepts accessible and capture the essence of design—in this case, the design of your learning.

The learning layout for this chapter focuses on the support for Java on various hardware and operating system platforms, on networked applications developed in Java (e.g., the `java.net` library), and the Configuration Management supporting discipline.

### 13.1.2 Learning Connections

The learning connections diagram in Figure 13.2 shows the content of this chapter in relation to the knowledge and skill development recommended for apprentice Java software engineers. The emergence of new technologies is ongoing, and, as mentioned before, the student is encouraged to seek out as many sources of information as necessary to ensure currency of knowledge.

## 13.2    Executive Summary

Just as the UNIX and Linux computer operating systems have become ubiquitous on numerous (server) hardware system platforms from vendors such as IBM, Sun Microsystems,

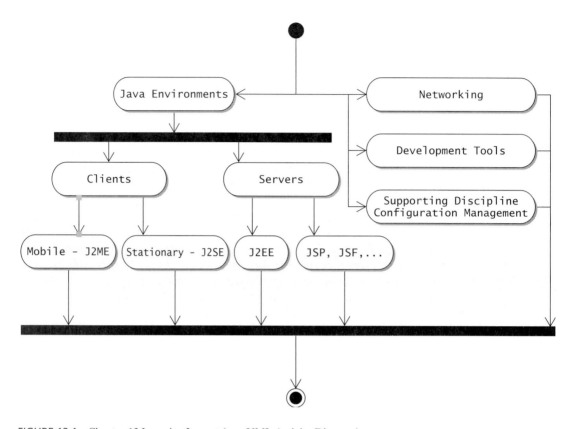

FIGURE 13.1   Chapter 13 Learning Layout (as a UML Activity Diagram)

and Hewlett-Packard, distributed Java applications have proliferated along with these systems. Java is an attractive software-development platform because, in addition to its open-systems centricity, it also supports Microsoft Windows, the dominant client platform. With the decline of new COBOL-based application development, Java continues its rise in the enterprise!

Java offers the right cross between ease-of-use, high productivity, portability, and general-purpose power to develop efficient applications with modern features. As with other cross-platform technologies, system vendors have adapted Java for optimal performance on their systems, typically by providing extended libraries and development tools and ensuring optimal performance for Java applications on their systems. These enhancements optimize the integration of the multiple tier of distributed applications developed for these platforms.

A range of application development environments from various vendors have emerged in support of commercial Java application development (e.g., see Fig. 13.3). The relative platform independence of Java has led to the development of many more third-party tools for the proprietary Microsoft .NET platform than are available for Visual Studio.NET. Some Java development tools provide simple program-editing

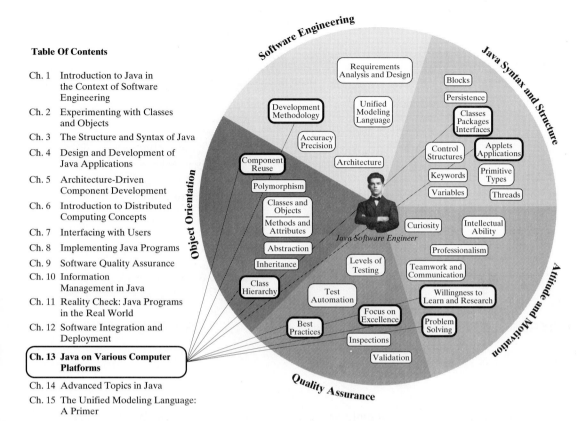

**FIGURE 13.2**   Learning Connections for Chapter 13

functions, while others deliver comprehensive development environments for distributed applications. For professional software development, the selection of the proper tools is a critical first step in establishing a productive development environment. This does include cost as well as functionality: best-of-class tools for distributed Java application development often cost over $2,000 per individual user license!

One of the most popular environments in commercial use, the Borland Development Environment for Java, includes methodology, design, and configuration management functions as well as extensions for various add-ons like Enterprise Java Beans (J2EE).

In a distributed computing environment, Java subsystems communicate with their Java and non-Java counterparts across communication links—typically Internet/TCP-IP-connections, usually using Internet and Web technologies (e.g., HTTP, SOAP). Access to these communication functions is provided through high-level interfaces available in the `java.net` library. The classes in this package encapsulate the complexities of networked interaction so that application programmers do not have to concern themselves with the intricacies of remote communications beyond the requirements of

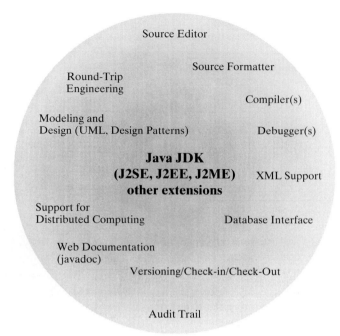

FIGURE 13.3   A Typical Java
Development Environment

their application's functionality and can choose the right level of abstraction, granularity, and control for their particular objectives.

In the area of our object-oriented life-cycle software engineering methodology, we continue our examination of supporting disciplines by learning about **Configuration Management (CM)**, which includes software source code control and product versioning and release management. Projects fail when the **Intellectual Property (IP)** associated with the project—its documentation and code—is not properly organized and managed. CM addresses these issues. In fact, in larger organizations, CM professionals are often responsible for the organizational control and safeguarding of all corporate IP.

## 13.3   Learning Modules

Since 1995, the Java product has rapidly grown into a family of editions and covers a wide range of software engineering requirements, from functions implemented on a small, low-power portable device like a cellular telephone (J2ME), to powerful client applications (J2SE), to server applications developed for the most powerful multiprocessor server systems (J2EE) available for commercial, non-profit, and public use. In this chapter, we take a conceptual tour of some of the successful implementations of Java technologies beyond the core J2SE classes and tools available from Sun Microsystems. (Please note that the information about Java feature availability on the various systems mentioned is as of the time of this writing and will likely have further evolved by the time this text makes it onto bookshelves.)

### 13.3.1 Java HotSpot<sup>TM</sup> Virtual Machines

Rather than the traditional Just-in-Time (JIT) compilation techniques that translate Java application bytecodes into native machine code at runtime, compiling each method the first time it is invoked, the Java HotSpot Virtual Machine interprets and analyzes the program for critical performance "hot spots." A global *native-code optimizer* is then applied to the hot spots, efficiently focusing the Java HotSpot compiler on the performance-critical parts of the program. The monitoring of hot spots is continued as the program runs, optimizing the hot spot performance gains on the fly based on user needs. Figure 13.4 shows the logical position of the Java HotSpot compiler in the J2SE component architecture.

Documentation of Sun's most recent release at the time of this writing that summaraizes the HotSpot features is available at: `http://java.sun.com/products/hotspot/index.html`

The following sections look at the versions of Java available on some of the major client-server platforms from leading vendors.

### 13.3.2 Java on Sun Microsystems Computers

The developer and owner of the Java product suite is Sun Microsystems (see Fig. 13.5). Sun also develops, manufactures, and markets its own computer hardware and software systems (for more information on Sun products and services, please visit www.sun.com). As might be expected, these systems support Java applications and provide the necessary operating system facilities to help optimize the performance of Java solutions on the various Sun computers (see the discussion on HotSpot compilers above).

### 13.3.3 Java on IBM Computers

Implementations of the Java Virtual Machine are available on IBM OS/390 and OS/400 (IBM iSeries), including a number of enhancements to the JVM reference implementation. These included the development of Just-in-Time compilers and various specific mappings of Java features to IBM operating system capabilities in the areas of thread management, memory management, and code execution efficiency.

Developer kits using the IBM WebSphere<sup>TM</sup> Interactive Development Environment are available for AIX, Linux, OS/2, z/OS, and Microsoft Windows. IBM provides its own OSI-certified Java compiler, Jikes<sup>TM</sup>. The IBM Java development tools are very popular in industry and used by substantial numbers of developers who create solutions for IBM platforms.

### 13.3.4 Java on Hewlett-Packard Computers

HP, like IBM, has made a deep commitment to Java technology. HP-UX PA-RISC and HP-UX Itanium® Processor Family systems are supported by the HP-UX Java Software Development Kit, which includes all the standard Java tools and provides HP

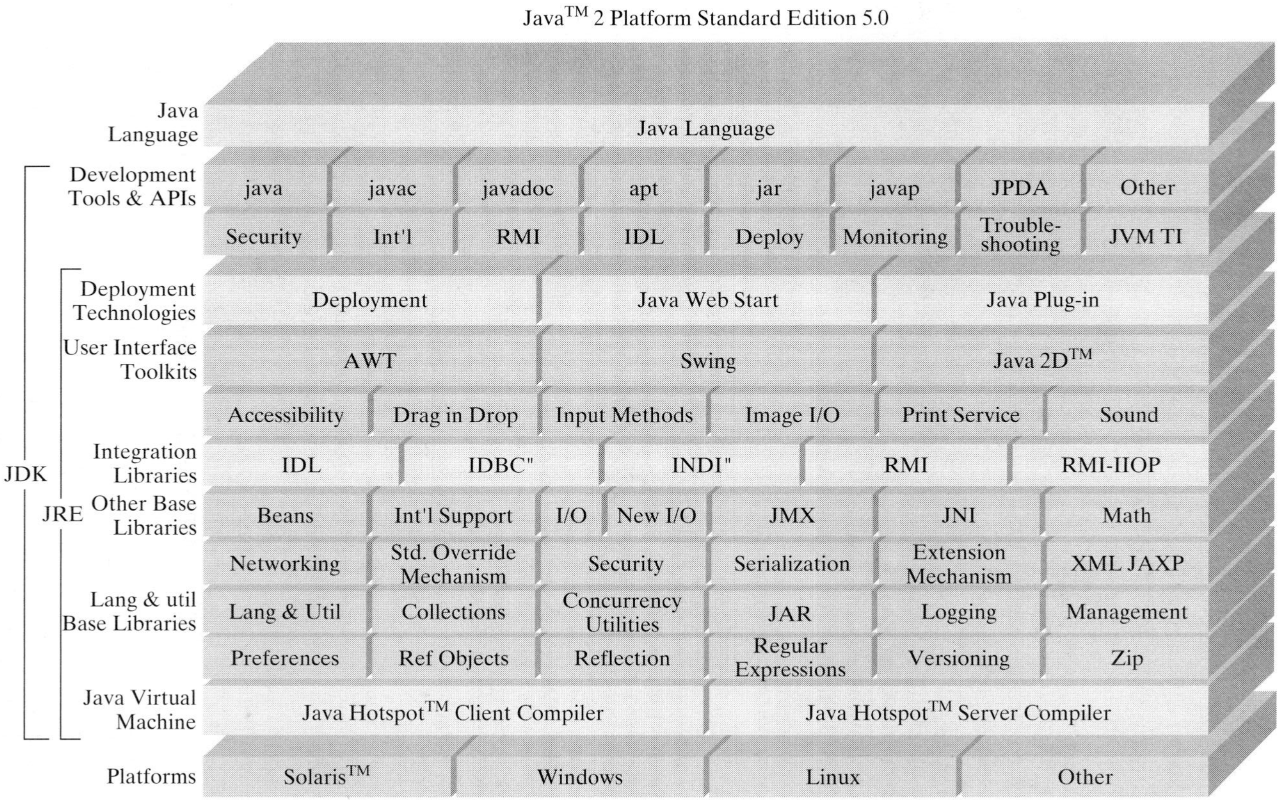

Java™ 2 Platform Standard Edition 5.0

| Java Language | Java Language | | | | | | |
|---|---|---|---|---|---|---|---|
| **Development Tools & APIs** | java | javac | javadoc | apt | jar | javap | JPDA | Other |
| | Security | Int'l | RMI | IDL | Deploy | Monitoring | Trouble-shooting | JVM TI |

| **Deployment Technologies** | Deployment | Java Web Start | Java Plug-in |
|---|---|---|---|

| **User Interface Toolkits** | AWT | Swing | Java 2D™ |
|---|---|---|---|

| **Integration Libraries** | Accessibility | Drag in Drop | Input Methods | Image I/O | Print Service | Sound |
|---|---|---|---|---|---|---|
| | IDL | JDBC" | JNDI" | RMI | RMI-IIOP | |

| **Other Base Libraries** | Beans | Int'l Support | I/O | New I/O | JMX | JNI | Math |
|---|---|---|---|---|---|---|---|
| | Networking | Std. Override Mechanism | Security | Serialization | Extension Mechanism | XML JAXP | |

| **Lang & util Base Libraries** | Lang & Util | Collections | Concurrency Utilities | JAR | Logging | Management |
|---|---|---|---|---|---|---|
| | Preferences | Ref Objects | Reflection | Regular Expressions | Versioning | Zip |

| **Java Virtual Machine** | Java Hotspot™ Client Compiler | Java Hotspot™ Server Compiler |
|---|---|---|

| **Platforms** | Solaris™ | Windows | Linux | Other |
|---|---|---|---|---|

JDK; JRE

FIGURE 13.4  The Java HotSpot Virtual Machine is part of the Foundation for the Java 2 Platform (© Sun Microsystems)

enhancements. The HP-UX HotSpot compiler automatically and efficiently converts bytecode to native machine instructions at runtime.

### 13.3.5  *Java on Other Platforms*

Java is available on a number of additional platforms. A list of platforms and operating supported by Sun Microsystems and/or other vendors is presented in Table 13.1. The information in the table will certainly have changed by the time you read this book, but you can find updated information in the Java section of the Sun Microsystems Web site.

### 13.3.6  *Java on Special Devices*

The Java runtime environment is available on a variety of portable devices, including many cellular telephones, especially those belonging to the so-called third-generation that supports high-speed wireless data transfers. A special version of Java optimized for portable and embedded-systems devices that cannot support a full implementation of J2SE due to power/memory limitations is available under the banner of Java 2 Mobile Edition (J2ME). This version excludes some of the capabilities supported in J2SE but therefore sports a smaller footprint. It also includes awareness of the various types of platforms, because platform transparency is not yet possible at the level of mobile devices, given the great variety of formats and the inherent differences in hardware capabilities.

**TABLE 13.1**   Java SDK Ports (© Sun Microsystems).

| Operating System | CPU | Company/Organization | Ported Technology |
|---|---|---|---|
| AIX | Power4, Intel | IBM | SDK |
| HP-UX | Itanium and PA-RISC | Hewlett-Packard | SDK |
| IRIX | MIPS | Silicon Graphics | SDK, JRE |
| MacOS | PowerPC Gx | Apple | JDK, JRE |
| NetWare chine | various | Novell | Java Virtual Ma- |

| Operating System | CPU | Company/Organization | Ported Technology |
|---|---|---|---|
| NonStop Kernel | MIPS | Hewlett-Packard | SDK |
| OS/2 | Intel | IBM | SDK |
| OS/390, OS/400 | S/390, iSeries (SOI, Power4) | IBM | SDK |
| SCO | Intel | SCO | SDK |
| Tru64 UNIX | Alpha | Compaq Computer Corporation | SDK |
| UnixWare | Intel | SCO | SDK |
| VxWorks chine | Any supported by Wind River Platform | Wind River Systems | Java Virtual Ma- |
| FreeBSD | Intel | The FreeBSD Project | SDK |
| NetBSD | Intel | Quick.com.au | SDK |
| Reliant Unix | MIPS | Siemens Nixdorf Informationssysteme AG | SDK |

This table changes regularly and is likely not current when you read this, but it still provides an idea of the breadth of Java availability on various platforms.

### 13.3.7  Java and Microsoft?

The feud between Sun Microsystems and Microsoft is legendary, so it should be no surprise that their rivalry extends to the domain of Java support. Java applets are supported in Microsoft's dominant browser, Internet Explorer, but, unless you have a special plug-in program from Sun, only at the Java 1.1 level. Sun Microsystems provides free download of all the components necessary to develop and execute Java applications on Microsoft operating system platforms.

Microsoft has developed its own distributed architecture, Windows.NET, which competes head-on with Java enterprise technology. It has also released the programming languages Visual Basic.NET, C#.NET (pronounced "Cee Sharp"), and J#.NET as part of its Visual Studio.NET Microsoft Development Environment (MDE) to compete with the Java programming language and libraries (J2SE, J2E, J2ME). The .NET languages favor a Just-in-Time (JIT) compilation approach to program execution.

The structural, language, and syntax similarities between Java and C# are such that a Java programmer can be become proficient in C# quite quickly. Both languages, of course, belong to the family of C programming languages.

### 13.3.8  Java Development Tools

In addition to the Java SDKs, Sun Microsystems provides a complete collection of Java development tools and libraries known (now) as **Sun Microsystems® Java Studio™**. The Eclipse Foundation (www.eclipse.org), a not-for-profit association, has developed a comprehensive, extensible set of software development tools under the banner of **Eclipse® Interactive Development Environment** (current release: 3.0): the Eclipse Project (Fig. 13.5).

Eclipse is an increasingly popular development tool that can be downloaded free at www.eclipse.org. The Eclipse Development Environment is shown in Figure 13.6.

Commercial software tools companies have issued their own tools for software development, sometimes with special high-performance support for specific platforms. Popular commercial tools include:

- Borland® JBuilder™ and Controlcenter™
- IBM® WebSphere™ Studio™

Many academic labs use JCreator™ from Xinox® Corporation, which is available in multiple versions. We will therefore take a look at this tool:

FIGURE 13.5   Eclipse Logo
(© Eclipse Org.)

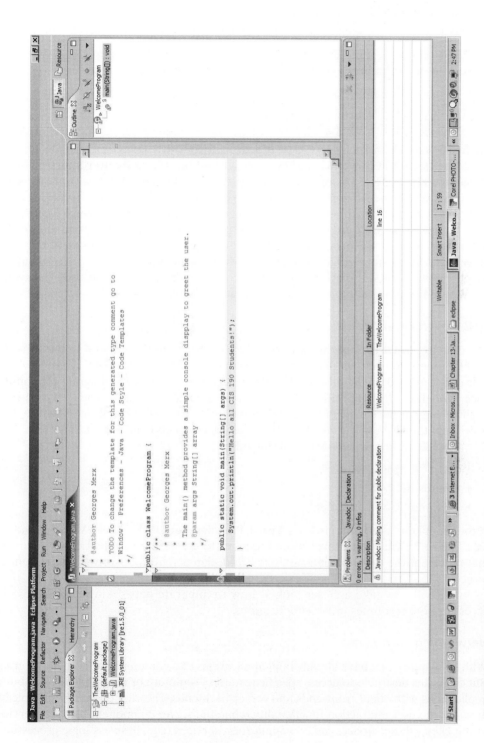

FIGURE 13.6   Eclipse Development Environment

557

- JCreator LE—free community download
- JCreator PRO—commercial version with expanded functionality

In JCreator (as in most Java Interactive Development Environments-IDEs), Java source files are organized into projects that are maintained in workspaces:

- JCreator workspace
  - JCreator project ( → package)
    - Java source file ( → xxx.java)

Figure 13.7 shows the main screen of JCreator PRO with a Java project loaded.

The default access to Java SDK tools is from the character user interface of the respective operating environment, such as the DOS command window (or console) in Microsoft Windows. One of the benefits of a Java IDE is that the relevant SDK tools, such as `java.exe`, `javac.exe`, `appletviewer.exe`, and `javadoc.exe`, are accessible from the graphical user interface, and programs can therefore be compiled and run interactively, without the programmer having to resort to the DOS command line (The preceding statement refers to Microsoft Windows as the development platform but can also be applied to GUI platforms.) Figure 13.8 shows how JCreator is used to execute the Voting Program example used throughout this book.

### 13.3.9 UML Development Tools

The creation of UML tools in support of Java development, is integral to the software development life-cycle, as discussed in previous chapters. Some UML tools only provide support for drawing UML diagrams; others syntax-check the diagram for compliance with the UML specification. The most advanced tools provide "round-trip" engineering support with popular development tools and are able to generate Java code from the UML diagrams, as well as interpret Java code into UML diagrams.

Popular commercial UML tools include:

- IBM® Rational Rose™
- Microsoft® VISIO™
- Borland® ControlCenter™

A tool popular in academic circles is **Visual-Paradigm for UML**™ from Visual-Paradigm (see Fig. 13.9). This tool provides the functions to create the various UML documents that represent the requirements analysis and design activities of software-development projects.

We will now take a closer look at how to integrate networking capabilities and access remote resources in Java applications.

### 13.3.10 Networking with Java

With Java applets, we have already built applications that communicate over the Internet. But often it is desirable to access specific resources remotely, or even to built distributed applications with client front-ends and server back-ends. The client component typically provides the user interaction functionality, while the server component provides services to the client; these services include application services (e.g., business logic processing), communication services (e.g., Web services), and information management services (e.g.,

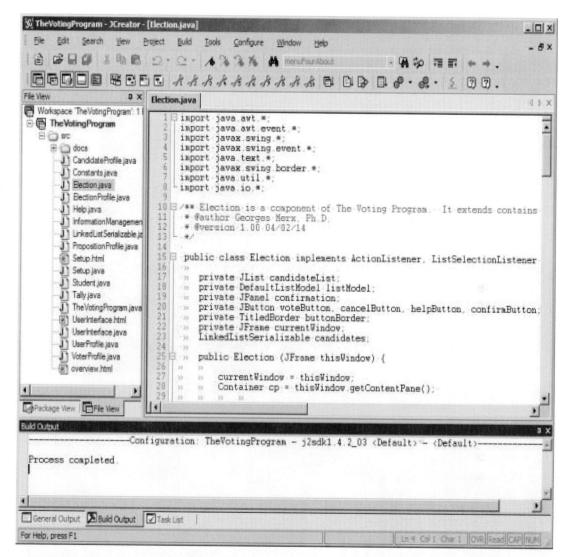

```
import java.awt.*;
import java.awt.event.*;
import javax.swing.*;
import javax.swing.event.*;
import java.text.*;
import javax.swing.border.*;
import java.util.*;
import java.io.*;

/** Election is a component of The Voting Program.  It extends contains
 * @author Georges Merx, Ph.D.
 * @version 1.00 04/02/14
 */

public class Election implements ActionListener, ListSelectionListener
{
    private JList candidateList;
    private DefaultListModel listModel;
    private JPanel confirmation;
    private JButton voteButton, cancelButton, helpButton, confirmButton;
    private TitledBorder buttonBorder;
    private JFrame currentWindow;
    LinkedListSerializable candidates;

    public Election (JFrame thisWindow) {

        currentWindow = thisWindow;
        Container cp = thisWindow.getContentPane();
```

FIGURE 13.7   The Voting Program in JCreator PRO™

database access). Much of the complexity of communicating programmatically across a communications connection is hidden from the Java application developer and, by extension, the application end-user by high-level classes provided in the `java.net` package. More advanced client-server integration is provided by other technologies, not discussed here, that are collectively provided in the framework of J2EE (generally beyond the scope of this book in terms of specific treatment).

With `java.net`, remote files located on a server are accessed from the client just like local files, using Java data streams. The location is specified as a Uniform Resource Locator (URL), and once a connection is established, the file is opened and read from, or written to, using the same type of buffered I/O available with local file streams.

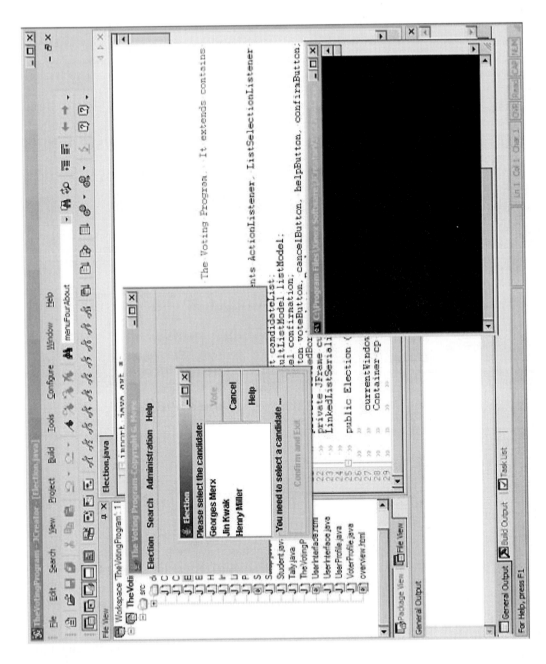

FIGURE 13.8 JCreator Screenshot: Running Program

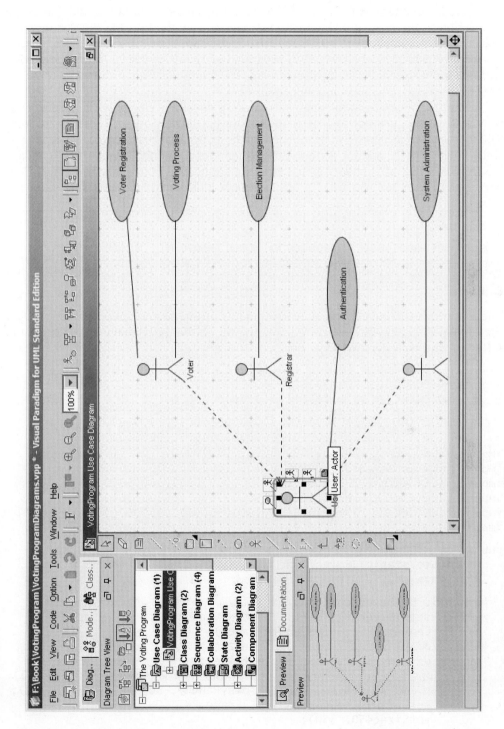

FIGURE 13.9   Screenshot from Visual-Paradigm™

The URLConnection object loads a previously created URL object and makes the connection to the host site. The getInputStream() method of that URLConnection object opens a connection to a URL by creating an InputStreamReader that can read a stream of data from the URL. The program can then associate a BufferedReader with the input stream reader, using standard exception-handling procedures (try ... catch) to handle possible communications or file access errors.

More granular access to communications resources (specific ports, in particular) is provided by Java java.net socket classes, Socket and ServerSocket. These are standard TCP/IP socket connections between clients and hosts, from which a program can read or to which it can write. Socket provides a client-side socket interface similar to a standard UNIX socket. The program uses input/output streams to read from and write to the socket. Server-side sockets listen on a TCP port for a connection and I/O requests from the client.

### Example:

```
Socket connection = new Socket (hostName, portNum);
```

### 13.4    Example

The following example allows a user to input a Uniform Resource Locator to specify a file on a Web server. The program loads the file into a JEditorPane to display the URL content, typically a Web site page.

```
/**
 * java.net Sample application
 * @author Georges Merx, Ph.D.
 * @version 1.00 04/10/16
 */
import java.awt.*;
import java.awt.event.*;
import javax.swing.*;
import javax.swing.event.*;
import java.net.*;
import java.io.*;

public class RemoteAccess extends JFrame {
    private static JEditorPane displayPanel;
    private static String URLName;

    public RemoteAccess(){ // initialize window object
        setTitle("Remote File Access Via URL");
        Container c = getContentPane();
        displayPanel = new JEditorPane();
        displayPanel.setEditable(false);
        displayPanel.addHyperlinkListener(new MyHyperlinkListener());
        c.add(new JScrollPane(displayPanel), BorderLayout.CENTER);
        setDefaultCloseOperation(JFrame.EXIT_ON_CLOSE);
        setSize(450, 350);
        setVisible(true);
    }
```

```
public static void main( String args[] ) {
    URLName = JOptionPane.showInputDialog (null, "URLName",
        "Please enter the URL of a remote file: ",
        JOptionPane.QUESTION_MESSAGE);
    if (URLName == null) System.exit(0);
    RemoteAccess GUIFrame = new RemoteAccess();
    Try {
        displayPanel.setPage(URLName);
    } catch (IOException e) {
        JOptionPane.showMessageDialog(null,
            "Remote File Not Accessible", "Bad URL",
            JOptionPane.ERROR_MESSAGE);
    }
    GUIFrame.setTitle("URL=" + URLName);
}
class MyHyperlinkListener implements HyperlinkListener {
// inner class
    public void hyperlinkUpdate(HyperlinkEvent e) {
        if (e.getEventType() ==
            HyperlinkEvent.EventType.ACTIVATED) {
            //get the data
            try {
                displayPanel.setPage(e.getURL().toString());
                Component c = (Component) e.getSource();
                // get root frame
                Component frame = SwingUtilities.getRoot©;
                JFrame win = (JFrame)frame;
                win.setTitle("URL=" + e.getURL().toString());
            } catch (IOException ioException) {
                JOptionPane.showMessageDialog(null,
                    "Remote File Not Accessible", "Bad URL",
                    JOptionPane.ERROR_MESSAGE);
            } catch (Exception ex) {
                JOptionPane.showMessageDialog(null,
                    "Unspecified Error", ex.toString(),
                    JOptionPane.ERROR_MESSAGE);
            }
        }
    }
}
}
```

### 13.4.1  Example Explanation

This short program sets up a JEditorPane that accepts the contents of a remote file specified as a URL. This remote file would typically be a Web page. It also supports navigation to other URLs by the selection of hyperlinks in the displayed contents by recognizing HyperlinkEvent events. This is a good example of the advanced transparency with which Java supports remote resources: the programmer does not have to implement explicitly any communications support to access a remote resource.

### 13.4.2 *Practical Application*

Support for remote resource access is available at multiple levels, from the "coarse" URL level to the more targeted socket level. This multilevel capability provides for the implementation of many different kinds of remote file access. Java's support for RMI and CORBA support, in turn, provides support for distributed applications with remote method calls. Remote database access is provided via JDBC. The combination of these various remote and distributed computing technologies affords a wide range of high-level flexible capabilities that still do not require the programmer to explicitly program low-level communications code.

This brief look at `java.net` capabilities by no means exhausts the topic, but we hope it will encourage the ambitious Java programming novice to explore distributed computing further and even take a follow-on advanced Java course.

The next section transitions to Supporting Disciplines by discussing source code control.

### 13.4.3 *Source Code Control, a Subset of Configuration Management*

Source code control is a subset of Configuration Management that keeps track of the changes made to programming source files, recording what was changed, when it was changed, and by whom. It provides a version numbering scheme, so that you can tell which version of a file is the most recent. It allows for the controlled, authenticated retrieval of previous versions of files and projects, so that you can roll back to an older version when the new version has become so unstable that a return to the last stable version is warranted. Source control typically provides an "undelete" function, in order to recover the last-saved version. If several people are working on the same file(s), the source code control system ensures coordination across the work group, keeping track of who has worked on what and when.

Examples of popular source control systems are:

- Unix Source Code Control System
  *"The Source Code Control System (SCCS) is an essential tool for any project with multiple source files or which has several people working with multiple source files. It provides a way to keep track of a source file's development and to prevent it from being altered by more than one person at a time."*
- Microsoft Visual Source Safe
- RCS, CVS

### 13.5 Position in Process

| Iterations | iteration 1 | iteration 2 | iteration 3 | iteration 4 | iteration 5 | iteration n |
|---|---|---|---|---|---|---|
| Disciplines | | | | | | |
| PROJECT MANAGEMENT | | | | | | → |
| INSPECTIONS AND VALIDATION | | | | | | → |
| **CONFIGURATION MANAGEMENT** | | | | | | → |
| DOCUMENTATION | | | | | | → |
| TECHNICAL MARKETING PLAN | | | | | | → |

When software projects reach a certain level of complexity, an urgent need arises to manage all the resources and artifacts associated with the project in a very organized fashion. After all, the Intellectual Property contained in the project deliverables is the core value of the project. The process and associated computer software tools used to help manage these resources, deliverables, and artifacts are generically described as Configuration Management. Tools that only help organize and manage source software components are often referred to as Source Code Control tools.

A typical modern Configuration Management tool offers version control for software components, project documents, test data, and other artifacts, software build management, workspace management, and work process customization.

High-end tools scale up from small project teams to large distributed enterprise-level projects. They enable parallel development, even across geographically distributed sites, with secure remote access to projects and components. They integrate software configuration management and unify defect and change tracking. Their workflows are configurable and customizable, so that they can be adapted to existing organizational processes and requirements. All activities managed by the configuration management tool are logged and auditable. Easy-access, secure rollback is supported. User access to the tool should be Web-enabled and graphical. Configuration Management tools should be seamlessly integratable with the leading IDEs and application and Web development tools.

## 13.6    Resources

The newsgroup comp.software.config-mgmt addresses Configuration Management tools issues. Its editor provides a summary of tools on his Web site at www.daveeaton.com/scm.

### 13.6.1  Connections

Searching on "Configuration Management Tools" in one of the popular search engines will return a rich hit list of information on commercial and free solutions available to software-development organizations of all sizes. Beware that many of these sites are product-marketing sites with potentially hyped-up information.

### 13.6.2  Companies

IBM's Rational Division has an enterprise-level Configuration Management solution called **ClearCase**$^{TM}$ that provides a good example of the high-end functionality available to organizations that work with geographically distributed software engineering resources.

## 13.7    Summary and Recommendations

This chapter introduced the support for Java technologies on various computer platforms provided by major computer systems vendors. It also covered development tools, including commercially used Interactive Development Environments (IDEs). Finally, it touched upon the support for remote resource access. In the area of supporting disciplines identified in the Extended Unified Process, we discussed Configuration

Management as a critical process for securing and managing a organization's Intellectual Property, such as its source code and documentation.

## 13.8    Review Questions

1. **Levels of Distributed Access.** Identify and briefly discuss the levels of distributed computing supported in Java.

| Level | Purpose |
|-------|---------|
| *URL* | Access remote files over the Internet |
| *Remote Method Invocation (RMI)* | Access remote Java methods |
| *Common Object Request Broker Architecture (CORBA)* | Access remote non-Java methods |
| *Socket* | Access a specific channel on a remote system |

There are numerous other interfaces and technologies available for protocol-specific remote access.

2. `java.net` Classes. Review the classes and associated methods and attributes of `java.net`; you will find this information on the Sun Java Web site at www.java.sun.com.

3. **Configuration Management.** Review the details of **Rational ClearCase**$^{TM}$ by visiting the www.rational.com Web site. Draw a diagram of the components and their interactions. Use UML notation.

## 13.9    Glossary – Terminology – Concepts

**Configuration Management**    Versioning, access tracking, and intellectual property control of project artifacts

**CORBA**    Common Object Request Broker Architecture, used to access remote non-Java methods

**RMI**    Remote Method Invocation, used to access remote Java methods

## 13.10    Exercises

1. **Configuration Management.**    Research three examples of commercial configuration management (CM) products available on the market, and compare and contrast their features.

2. **Source Code Management.**    Draw a diagram that summarizes the issues of source code management associated with the *Harm* 🌓 *ny* **Designs** case study.

3. **Network Access.**    Write a rudimentary application to simulate a simple Web browser. Make sure to check for possible exceptions.

# CHAPTER 14

# Advanced Topics in Java Software Engineering

This chapter introduces various advanced Java topics, such as mobile computing with Java, programming with XML and SOAP, and developing Web and application services (see Fig. 14.1). In a general sense, advanced topics are beyond the scope of this book, but they are introduced here as concepts for two reasons: (1) in actual real-world industry projects, the more advanced aspects of a language or tool are often the functions in most common use, and (2) in the hope of inspiring you to continue your studies and expand your in-depth knowledge of Java into these domains. Many advanced tutorial and reference Java texts are available to support you in this further study. The good news is that most Java language features are organizationally similar, so as you learn new functions and capabilities, you will begin to recognize the "Java way" of implementing these functions, and your further learning should follow in form and substance the knowledge you have already acquired.

In the area of software engineering, we will discuss **Technical Documentation** and the **Technical Marketing Plan** supporting disciplines. This will conclude the review of the Extended Unified Process that we have followed throughout this book. As you may remember, this methodology is based on the broadly accepted (IBM-Rational) Unified Process; our extensions have been minor clarifications for the benefit of the novice software engineer. We realize that the Unified Process has many critics. It is said to be too documentation-intensive, too burdensome for many real-world applications. While this may be true for projects that are well defined, well scoped, with readily available project stakeholders, and highly skilled, experienced software engineers, we believe that this

FIGURE 14.1    Java Applications on Cell Phones

formal process is a good foundation for the novice software engineer. The decision to streamline software-development processes by applying agile techniques is best made by those with experience who know what formalities they choose to forego.

## 14.1    Learning Objectives

Because the next chapter serves a special purpose, this last regular chapter covers a few final specific topics—like mobile computing with Java, for instance—but it also serves to bring together the topics we have studied throughout the book, especially the pursuit of a well-organized, efficient, and effective object-oriented software engineering process.

By now, you have become a proficient entry-level Java software engineer, and you have developed technical, designer, and organizational skills that together allow you to produce viable, high-quality—albeit simple—client software. Hopefully, this book will be the catalyst for your further learning. Just like learning a new foreign language, the study of a new software-development language requires more than one course and more than one book. Fortunately, a vast array of additional resources is available in book form and online.

### 14.1.1    Learning Layout

This recurring section shows the learning objectives of the chapter in a simple diagram, using the UML activity diagram notation (see Fig. 14.2).

The learning layout for this chapter focuses on advanced Java technologies, especially for mobile applications. The chapter also addresses documentation and the contribution of software engineering to technical marketing.

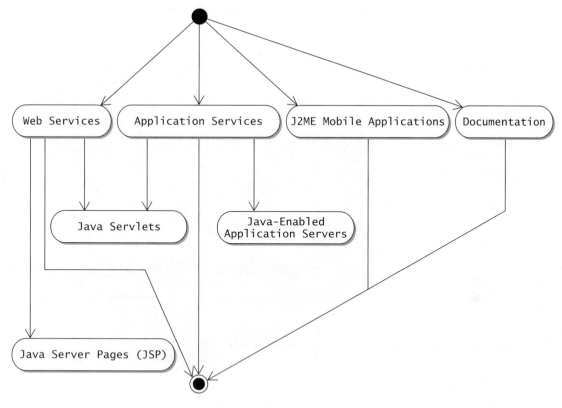

FIGURE 14.2    Chapter 14 Learning Layout (as a UML Activity Diagram)

### 14.1.2  *Learning Connections*

The learning connections diagram shows the content of this chapter in relation to the knowledge and skill development recommended for apprentice Java software engineers. By now, we have covered all the various skills and talents required of a junior software engineer. You are encouraged to take this "skills wheel" and modify it to meet your own values and needs. It is an easy, colorful way to set some specific goals for your further education and development.

## 14.2    Executive Summary

Java has grown in many different directions. In fact, a large component of its attractiveness is its adaptability to different needs, systems, and environments. In this chapter, we explore the use of Java on mobile devices, or, more precisely, the special version of Java, J2ME, custom-tailored to the low-power, low-performance capabilities of small, mobile devices. We will also take an overview look at application and Web services for distributed Java applications. We include the perspective of a service-oriented architecture (SOA). Finally, in concluding our review of the formal object-oriented software-development methodology introduced throughout the book, we look at the

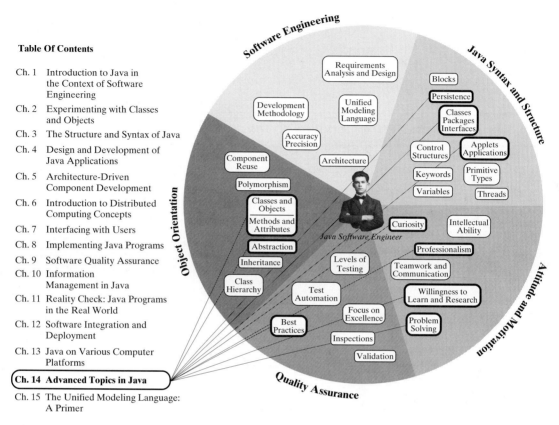

FIGURE 14.3   Learning Connections for Chapter 14

Documentation and Technical Marketing support disciplines. Documentation includes both end-user and administrator documentation, in book form and/or incorporated as online help with the product or online. Technical marketing is included in the software engineering methodology because for all commercial software products there is a direct and strong correlation between their product requirements and functionality and their marketability, competitive position, and characterization for sale. Marketing specialists, like documentation specialists, are excellent sources for requirements that other stakeholders may not have considered.

## 14.3   Learning Modules

In addition to stationary Java client applications developed in the Java 2 Standard Edition SDK, mobile applications and server-based applications (servlets) utilize additional Java classes, packaged as J2ME (Java 2 Micro Edition) and J2EE (Java 2 Enterprise Edition), respectively (see Fig. 14.4). The next sections explore some of these advanced Java features in more detail.

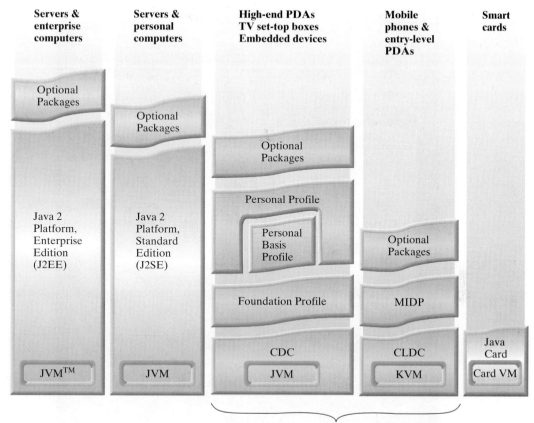

FIGURE 14.4   J2ME, One of the Java 2 SDK Platforms
(© Sun Microsystems)

### 14.3.1  Mobile Applications

Java was actually conceived for low-power, small-footprint services (e.g., set-top control boxes), but subsequently became focused on Web-enabled general purpose computing. Its use in such devices has come into its own with the advent of powerful portable computing devices like personal digital assistants (PDAs) and high-end cell phones.[1] In particular, the recent emergence of powerful cellular telephone platforms has created an ideal environment for mobile Java applications.

The portable version of Java is available from Sun Microsystems as the Java 2 Platform, Micro Edition (J2ME). Because small, portable devices fall into a broad range of power and capability, the J2ME package is subdivided into multiple components, depending on the type of target device platform (see Fig. 14.5). More capable devices are

---

[1]Or at least what used to be "high-end"; these capabilities are now mainstream cell phone features.

FIGURE 14.5   MIDP Test Program for Cell Phones
(© Sun Microsystems)

governed by the Connected Device Configuration (CDC), while lower-end devices run under the Connected Limited Device Configuration (CLDC). Profiles for each configuration further target specific device capabilities, and optional packages are available for specific market/customer/solution requirements.

More recently, application services support (for XML, SOAP, etc.) and relational database access have been added to J2ME.

### 14.3.2   *Web and Application Services*

Web and application services provide functions to software application clients across an Internet connection. They liberate the client side from logic processing, allowing for

FIGURE 14.6 A Service-Oriented Architecture

"thin-client" system architectures. These types of services are today often described within the framework of a service-oriented architecture (SOA; see Fig. 14.6). This is essentially a collection of services that communicate with each other, either by passing data or by coordinating some activity. The origins of SOA go back to Microsoft DCOM and Object Request Brokers (ORBs) based on the OMG's CORBA specification.

In concept, clients request a service over HTTP at a given location on the server (expressed as a Uniform Resource Locator or URL) using the SOAP protocol. The data associated with the interaction across the remote connection is typically packaged in XML. The service receives the request, processes it, and returns a response.

A Web service may provide a price lookup, for example, in which the request asks for the current price of a specified item, and the response returns the price maintained in a shared database. In another example, a mobile user may request an efficient route for the delivery of a particular good or service. The service determines an optimal route based on agreed-upon parameters, such as shortest time or minimal cost.

Web services using XML (Extensible Markup Language), a markup language that makes data portable, allow clients and services to communicate with each other regardless of whether the two sides use the same, or different, computing platforms. This requirement makes the Java platform, with its portable code, an obvious choice for developing XML-based Web services.

In addition to data and code portability, Web-based communication and application services need to be scalable, secure, and efficient. The **Java Platform, Enterprise Edition (J2EE)**, is designed to facilitate the development and deployment of the infrastructure of Web and application services. This infrastructure includes the development of reusable components to meet security, distributed transaction, and connection pool management requirements. A Web service is a server application that provides the methods that clients can call; it is typically implemented in a server-side servlet container based on Web services (e.g., Apache Tomcat) or Enterprise JavaBeans (EJB).

Java Server Pages (JSP) are used for creating dynamic Web content. They typically work with J2EE servlets, and often with Enterprise JavaBeans (EJB) components that are server-based "business logic" components.

The Java platform works with XML seamlessly. The Java APIs for XML and the J2EE platform provide a high-level, flexible technology for the implementation of Web services.

### XML

The Extensible Markup Language, XML, is an industry-standard, system- and platform-independent way of representing data. Like HTML (Hypertext Markup Language), XML encloses data in tags, but XML tags relate to the meaning of the enclosed text, whereas HTML tags only specify how to display the enclosed text. The following XML example shows a price list with the name and price of two laptop computer systems.

```
<priceList>
  <computer>
    <name>JCN Laptop</name>
    <price>1495.00</price>
  </computer>
  <computer>
    <name>Tell Laptop</name>
    <price>1395.00</price>
  </computer>
</priceList>
```

XML tags can be created to describe the content in a particular type of document. XML is a standardized data format that allows platform-independent, structured information interchange between systems and applications. With its platform neutrality and strong industry support, XML is a leading vehicle for linking networked clients with remote enterprise data located on servers in the enterprise and beyond. In Java, these clients may be standard J2SE clients or mobile J2ME clients and devices.

### SOAP

The Simple Object Access Protocol (SOAP) facilitates interoperability among a wide range of programs and platforms by ensuring vendor-independent end-to-end data transport. SOAP combines the proven Web technology of HTTP with the flexibility and extensibility of XML. The HTTP protocol provides the transport for SOAP-based remote procedure calls (RPCs), and XML is its encoding scheme. With a few lines of code and an XML parser, an HTTP server, such as Microsoft Internet Information Server (IIS) or Apache, instantly becomes a SOAP object request broker (ORB). In other words, SOAP codifies the use of XML as an encoding scheme for request and response parameters using HTTP as a transport.

## 14.4    Summary Comments

This book has introduced you to software development using the Java programming language from the perspective of commercial object-oriented software engineering. There are some important reasons why Java has become extremely popular around the world for the development of new software programs:

- Easy-to-learn and -use syntax and structure (no pointers, automatic memory management, support for data persistence, etc.)
- Efficiency and reuse through abstraction and object-orientation, compliance with object-oriented software methodology (e.g., Design Patterns, UML, etc.); support for Design Patterns
- Portability through virtual machine architecture and runtime availability on most platforms (performance optimization using HotSpot technology)
- Distributed computing through support for Internet, Web, application services (RMI, XML, SOAP, CORBA)
- High-level support for advanced computing, such as multithreading and multimedia formats

Java's popularity has pushed its development into many directions, resulting in numerous advanced, sophisticated and complex capabilities and extensions. Java is powerful and general-purpose, with many beneficial features that are most useful if properly channeled. The application of a flexible, scalable development methodology, such as the one advocated in this book, helps ensure from the start that the programs you develop with Java harness its strengths, instead of succumbing to its challenging complexities.

Just learning Java syntax is not enough to become a proficient Java software engineer; especially in a global economy where white-collar outsourcing has become common. Developing competitive software engineering skills includes active participation and leadership in every phase of the software-development life-cycle. As we have seen throughout this book, a comprehensive range of technical engineering, managerial, and communication skills is required to become a professionally competent developer of world-class Java software solutions.

## 14.5   Position in Process

| Iterations | iteration 1 | iteration 2 | iteration 3 | iteration 4 | iteration 5 | iteration n |
|---|---|---|---|---|---|---|
| Disciplines | | | | | | |
| PROJECT MANAGEMENT | | | | | | |
| INSPECTIONS AND VALIDATION | | | | | | |
| CONFIGURATION MANAGEMENT | | | | | | |
| **DOCUMENTATION** | | | | | | |
| TECHNICAL MARKETING PLAN | | | | | | |

The last of the supporting disciplines covered in our Extended Unified Process methodology are the Documentation workflow and the Technical Marketing Plan workflow. The inclusion of the former is reasonably obvious, because documentation is easily understood to be part of the product, but the latter warrants some justification.

Valuable software is often developed for commercial deployment in response to a set of market and/or customer requirements (even if the target customer may not be a commercial organization). If the intention is to market and sell the software product being developed, it is recommended that a Technical Marketing Plan accompany the development of the software product. This ensures that marketability issues flow into the requirements process from the start of the project, and that the characterization of the product and its features for marketing and sales purposes is an integral part of its development. Not only does this create early focus on business-related issues, it also consistently incorporates features that support marketability into the product.

### 14.5.1   Documentation

The Documentation supporting discipline captures all the internal and external documents produced in conjunction with the software-development project, from the earliest concept document to the support and maintenance reports (see Fig. 14.7). Documents associated with a project can be especially difficult to maintain properly because the rigor of source code compilation cannot be applied to documentation. It is up to the individual and the organization to be diligent and accurate in updating and maintaining all the documentation that accompanies a software-development project.

*Disciplines*                    *Documentation Artifacts*

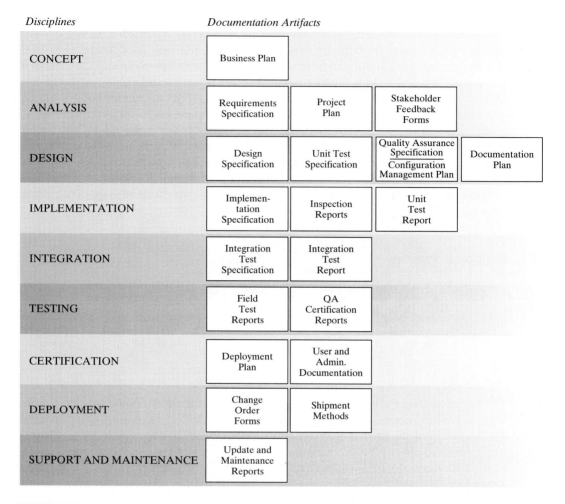

**FIGURE 14.7**  Documents Produced in the Disciplines of the Unified Process Modified Methodology

For example, a change in requirements needs to be reflected in an approved new version of the Requirements Specification, while additional tests need to be added to the appropriate test document(s).

The documents produced by project contributors fall into a number of categories:

- Specifications
- Reports
- Information forms
- User documentation
- Online help and tutorials
- Notes

Each document should follow a format predetermined by internal or external standards or conventions. Version control is just as important for documentation as for source code. In fact, the documents that accompany a software project should be managed by the same Configuration Management (CM) mechanism as the code itself. The quality assurance function in the organization should be in charge of, and empowered to enforce, the production and updating of all documentation resources. As always, these functions are only completed if adequately budgeted and staffed.

As much as possible, standard documentation formats should be followed: use established standards where available, and define company-internal standards as needed. The standards themselves should be subject to updates and improvement.

### *Javadoc Documentation*

The Java SDK includes a documentation-creation utility called **Javadoc**, which is used to produce program documentation in the form of HTML files straight from Java source code files. Javadoc files describe:

- packages
- classes and interfaces
- constructors and methods
- fields/attributes

Generating Javadoc documentation requires special comments in the source code. The Javadoc utility is used to extract these comments and organize them into standard Javadoc-formatted HTML-formatted documentation files.

A **doc** comment has /** at the beginning and */ at the end. Doc comments must be directly above the package, class, or method definition. The first sentence of an introductory Javadoc comment should be a summary statement.

Each doc comment is made up of two parts: a description followed by block tags. Tags begin with the @ sign and are followed by a keyword understood by Javadoc. Tags can be standalone or inline. Some example tags and their uses are shown in Table 14.1.

The `javadoc.exe` utility (on Windows; equivalents available on other platforms) is easily executed from the command prompt:

```
javadoc MyProgram.java or javadoc *.java
```

TABLE 14.1   Selected Javadoc Tags

| Tag | Use |
|---|---|
| @param | method parameter |
| @return | method return value |
| @throws | exception a method may throw |
| @deprecated | compatibility-only feature |
| @see | reference to related documentation |
| @author | class/interface author |
| @version | class/interface version |

This produces a file (or files) `MyProgram.html`.
Execution options:

- `-link` links to another set of Javadoc files, including http://java.sun.com/products/jdk/1.4/docs/api
- `-d` store output in specific directory
- `-classpath` override current **classpath**
- `-sourcepath` override classpath
- `-author`, `-version` include author and version information, otherwise omitted

Creating well-formatted Javadoc documentation is beneficial in many ways:

1. It establishes a culture of documentation in the software engineering organization; after all, source code is only as useful (i.e., maintainable, extensible) as its English-like nature and associated documentation.
2. It creates documentation consistent with a widely accepted format that the reader immediately recognizes and has no problem perusing.
3. It is part of the source code and therefore more readily updates than separate documents.

At the same time, the development organization needs to recognize that Javadoc documentation alone does not sufficiently document the software being developed. This is so because it fails to cover the interrelationships between components and the architectural perspective of the structure of the interconnected subsystems.

## 14.5.2  *Technical Marketing*

A **Technical Marketing Plan** accompanies commercial product development. If your product is destined to be sold, a solid, validated marketing plan is a critical component of the project. The inclusion of the plan's development as a supporting discipline ensures that the specialists involved with this activity are included in the project activities from the beginning. Marketing people bring a useful and different requirements perspective and scrutiny to the development of high-value software: their focus includes the so-called four Ps—packaging, position, price, and promotion. They worry about competitiveness ("sustainable competitive advantages"), feature uniqueness ("unique selling propositions"), presentation, and value. They often present a good sounding board for the engineers, who can get overly enamored with features and functions that may be of little actual value. They also provide a broader perspective than the specific early-customer stakeholders who may have unique wishes not compatible with the market's needs.

There is no industry standard format for this type of plan, but the document should at least include the following information categories:

- Target market, customer profile
- Market segmentation
- Distribution channels (direct, indirect)
- Product description (product and service components)
- Competitive analysis and position (unique advantages)

- Rollout plan, including budget and training required
- The Four Ps:
  - ○ Packaging: online and/or hardcopy sales, name, image
  - ○ Position: characterization of the product against competition
  - ○ Price: pricing of products and services, discounts
  - ○ Promotion: advertising, public relations, third-party alliances

## 14.6   Example

In order to "protect the guilty," we give our start-up example company a fictitious name: LeMans Software Company. LeMans was the brainchild of a brilliant young software developer who had come up with ideas on how to use artificial intelligence in conjunction with then-emerging mobile Java technology to develop a next-generation software product suite. *Sounds good*? Well, it sounded good enough for a group of investors to pledge a multi-million-dollar investment (of course, this was all before the dot-com bust).

Executives were hired, expensive office space acquired, and long sessions held to discuss ideas for the ultimate smart, portable software product. Problem is, no great ideas emerged, no stakeholder analysis was conducted, the market analysis was shallow and unrealistic, and the software engineers were "gung-ho to implement." With money in the bank, the start-up therefore quickly embarked on design meetings, and the engineers impressed everyone with early prototypes. *Prototypes of what*? you may ask. Well, there was a vague agreement to develop some "intelligent messaging software." There was also pressure to show some kind of result—anything—for all the money provided by the impatient investors. The organization therefore rushed through the early stages of the software-development process and focused more and more on feature design and implementation. While marketing planning continued alongside, it was subjugated to the product engineering perspective, and the weak protestations from the marketing manager regarding competitive position, marketability, and value propositions were generally ignored. In the end, LeMans never released a product and went out of business.

### 14.6.1   Example Explanation

While we enjoy reading about the successes of technology companies that started their operations in a brilliant visionary's garage, the failure rate in the software industry is high. This is true for a number of reasons:

1. All the easy projects have been done.
2. The entry barrier is low; anyone can go out and buy a computer and a compiler.
3. Creating truly mission-critical value in software is difficult.
4. Even useful software is often of poor quality.
5. Investors have become much more cautious since the dot-com bust of the 1990s.

LeMans could have been successful if it had planned better and had focused its attention squarely on the needs of its stakeholders. In fact, LeMans was pursuing the development of a horizontal application solution (one that did not address a specific vertical market); this is easier to "think up," and much harder to accomplish, because this space is shared by the largest number of competitors. The moral of this short story is threefold:

1. Pay close attention to all relevant perspectives in a project, including the marketing perspective.
2. Follow a proven methodology in developing a project, and focus on the early phases for as long as it takes to be sure that the subsequent implementation will be right and desirable in every way.
3. Stay flexible and avoid being "pulled" by the implementation effort without being able to make critical adjustments along the way.
4. Do not spend money on surroundings, materials, and people that only marginally add value to the project.

### 14.6.2 *Practical Application*

Whether you are a current or future member of a development organization in a large company or the founder of your own start-up, the same basic principles apply when it comes to developing high-quality software on time, on budget, and according to stakeholder requirements. Successful businesses exist in every domain, but failure is always only a few bad decisions away. A number of simple strategies help avoid failure. These include a humble openness to learning, even outside one's chosen domain; the application of others' experiences and knowledge; a passionate focus on world-class excellence—not just in product development, but in every aspect of the organization and work; a critical, always questioning viewpoint; a detailed understanding of the outside world, including the competition; good listening skills; a culture of always recording and documenting important information; and championing and rewarding others' contributions and accomplishments.

## 14.7   Resources

Visit the web site of IBM Corporation (www.ibm.com) and read the descriptive materials available on the topic of Service-Oriented Architecture (SOA). Also, research SOA on www.infoworld.com, the web site of InfoWorld Online.

### 14.7.1 *Connections*

The major cell phone manufacturers and operators typically provide programs for software developers that include add-on components/classes, support, certification processes, and even product distribution support. Check out the Web sites for Motorola, Nokia, Samsung, Sony-Ericsson, and Nextel.

### 14.7.2 *People*

Alan Kay is one of the inventors of the Smalltalk programming language and one of the originators of object-oriented programming. He conceived of the laptop computer ("Dynabook") and was a key architect of the modern windowing graphical user interface and mouse. His ideas also played a key role in the definition of design patterns and other object-oriented software-development methodology ideas.

## 14.8 Summary

This final regular chapter (before the UML Overview in Chapter 15) provided a high-level overview of popular technologies, from J2ME, to XML, to SOAP. These topics were only briefly introduced, because they exceed the scope of this book. They do, however, provide excellent material for the ambitious Java software engineer's further in-depth study. Many modern distributed applications use Java with XML and SOAP(-RPC). It behooves the clever engineer to know these technologies and how they are implemented in Java.

## 14.9 Review Questions

1. **Origins of XML.** Understand the history of XML in the context of SGML and HTML. Document the evolution.
   Although XML succeeds HTML, its design is based on SGML, which existed before the World Wide Web and HTML. SGML was designed to provide a flexible document markup language: XML supports that principle on the Web through customizable tags.
2. **Distributed Computing with Java.** Describe how the J2SE and J2EE components work together to implement distributed applications. Draw an architectural diagram with labeled components.
3. **Mobile Applications.** Find out more about J2ME support on various cell phone platforms. Compare and contrast J2ME and QUALCOMM BREW.

## 14.10 Glossary – Terminology – Concepts

**SGML**   Standard Generalized Markup Language.
**SOAP**   Simple Object Access Protocol.
**XML**   Extensible Markup Language.

## 14.11 Exercises

**1. Technical Marketing Plan.**   Review the HarmonyDesigns project from the perspective of marketability. Write an abbreviated technical marketing plan for the product. Include a competitive analysis section identify marketing-specific requirements overlooked so far.

**2. XML and SOAP in Java.**   Research how Java supports XML and SOAP. Summarize your findings. For the ambitious: write a prototype application that uses these technologies to track electronic time cards.

**3. Time Tracking.**   Design a simple time-tracking application that would use J2ME and run its client component on a J2ME-enabled cell phone. ***Stretch objective:*** implement a prototype.

# CHAPTER 15

# The Unified Modeling Language: A Primer

Grady Booch, Ivar Jacobson, and Jim Rumbaugh, historically and fondly known in the UML community as the Three Amigos, are often credited with having made the dominant contribution to the Unified Modeling Language. The picture in (Figure 15.1) was taken around 1998, when all three of them were employed by Rational Software Corporation. Rational®, now a division of IBM® Corporation, is a dominant provider of Unified Process and UML technology, tools, and services.

## 15.1    Learning Objectives

In this chapter, readers are introduced to the **Unified Modeling Language**, or UML, the de facto worldwide industry standard for object modeling. As was mentioned in Chapter 1, we use UML as the basis for mapping business requirements to IT solutions.

Because this is only one short chapter on UML, we will limit our discussion to reviewing just the basic elements and aspects of the UML 2.0 specification (books of well over 600 pages have been written on both of these subjects.)

### 15.1.1   Learning Layout

This recurring section shows the learning objectives of the chapter in a simple diagram, using the UML activity diagram notation (see Fig. 15.2).

**FIGURE 15.1**   The Three Amigos

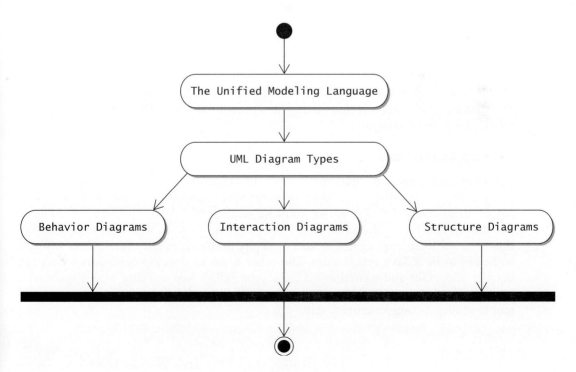

**FIGURE 15.2**   Chapter 15 Learning Layout (as a UML Activity Diagram)

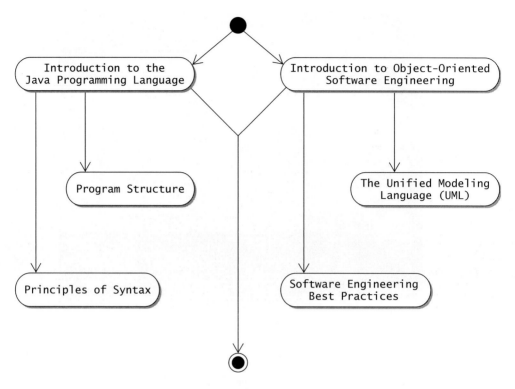

**FIGURE 15.3**    Chapter 1 Learning Layout (as a UML Activity Diagram)

The activity diagram in Figure 15.3 shows the student learning expectations for this chapter. This chapter is intended to be a primer for UML. The specification can be found at http://www.omg.org.[1]

### 15.1.2  Learning Connections

The learning connections diagram (see Fig. 15.4) shows the content of this chapter in relation to the knowledge and skills development recommended for apprentice Java software engineers. The five-spoke software engineering profile is discussed in more detail in Chapter 3. Again, as we stated back in Chapter 1, we want you to understand that Java software engineering is an inherently multidisciplinary profession. It is not sufficient to be a Java syntax guru. The other areas of development shown here are equally important and sometimes critical, especially when working with a team on a larger project. The topic of this chapter, the Unified Modeling Language, is a prime example of such a complementary skill.

---

[1]We do not guarantee exact adherence in this description to the standard, which covers over 600 pages. For details on any particular topic, please refer to the OMG standard documentation.

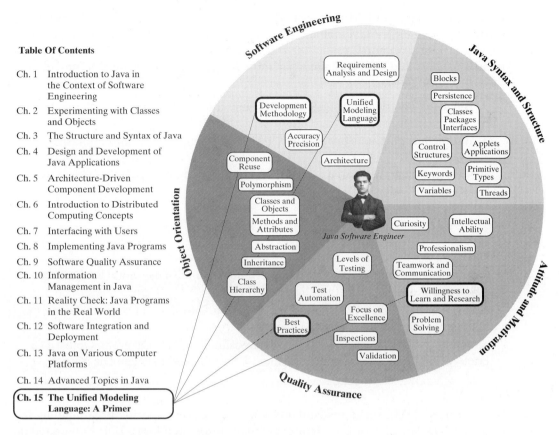

FIGURE 15.4   Learning Connections for Chapter 15

This last installment of the learning connections diagram is a final opportunity
for you to consider your opportunities and responsibilities in developing your software
engineering skills and possibly your career path. Common concerns in our profession
today, such as white-collar outsourcing, are mitigated through broader skills and responsibilities not easily performed remotely. As you find your own path, which hopefully will embrace technical and non-technical, core and supporting skills and
disciplines, you will have the opportunity to maximize your worth to your organization
and for yourself.

## 15.2   Executive Summary

In its current form, the UML defines a **notation** and a **meta-model**. The notation is the
syntax of the modeling language—the graphical icons shown in UML models. The
meta-model is a diagram, usually a class diagram that defines the concept of the language. From the perspective of a member of a software project development team, the

most important part of UML is how to use it to create different diagrams (views) of the software system under development. With that in mind, there are fourteen standard diagrams in UML version 2.0, each of which illustrates the various elements and relationships associated with a commercial software development project.[2] They fall into three broad categories:

- **Behavior diagrams** illustrate the dynamic interactions between elements (over time).
- **Interaction diagrams** are a subset of behavior diagrams that emphasize object interactions.
- **Structure diagrams** show the static relationships between design elements, irrespective of time.

---

### UML DIAGRAM TYPES[2]

*Behavior Diagrams:* Activity Diagram, State Machine Diagram. Use Case Diagram, and the four interaction diagrams (below)

*Interaction Diagrams:* Communication Diagram, Interaction Overview Diagram, Sequence Diagram, and Timing Diagram

*Structure Diagrams:* Class Diagram, Composite Structure Diagram, Object Diagram, Component Diagram, Deployment Diagram, and Package Diagram

---

None of these UML diagrams contains source code for a specific programming language, such as Java, C#, or C++. However, many automated UML IDE (integrated development environment) commercial and research products generate source code directly from some of the UML diagrams. In many of these products, the UML class diagram is simply another view of the source code. This means that if a developer modifies the diagram, the source code changes with it, and if the developer changes the source code using a source code editor, the UML class diagram automatically reflects the coding changes. Basically, model and code are equivalent: this eliminates the historical problem of having models of software become obsolete or stale as project coding proceeds, and no one on the team has the time to go back and update the model.

In this chapter, we briefly introduce the most commonly used UML diagrams and show you samples of them. Remember that each diagram has its purpose, and the diagrams collectively visually communicate all the relevant design information about the software system being built. This chapter is intended to assist those who are new to

---

[2]Go to http://www.omg.org/cgi-bin/apps/doc?ptc/03-08-02.pdf, www.omg.org, Final UML 2.0 Superstructure Specification Document; http://www.agilemodeling.com/essays/umlDiagrams.htm, www.agilemodeling.com; Ambler, Scott. 2003; and http://www.omg.org/gettingstarted/what_is_uml.htm, August 2003. This is a very good overview of UML 2.0 (easy to read), but there are some discrepancies between this document and the 2.0 Specification

UML in applying its basic capabilities. UML is a language with its own syntax. We have used UML diagrams throughout the book to illustrate some of the rigors of the extended unified software development process.

## 15.3   Learning Modules

The following sections describe the key UML concepts, introducing UML as the software industry's accepted approach to the object-oriented modeling of software. Recognizing that the **OMG's UML 2.0 Superstructure Specification** can be overwhelming to the novice practitioner, we provide a cursory summary in this chapter. Martin Fowler suggests that the UML may be used in at least three ways:[3]

> **Sketch mode** is similar to an architectural sketch or drawing that leaves out a significant amount of detail. Software designers use this approach to communicate whatever aspects of a software system they want to emphasize and focus on while ignoring others. UML *selectivity* is the operative word for UML sketching. A white board or flip chart paper and marking pens are often the low-tech UML tools of choice for sketching.
>
> **Blueprint mode** is similar to an office building or home construction blueprint which communicates varying degrees of detail and different views of the structure— top, left, right, inside, electrical, etc.—that correspond to the different UML diagrams. Blueprints have more rigor than sketches because the group creating them is either going to implement the software to match the blueprints (models) or is going to submit the blueprints to another group for implementing the software.
>
> **Programming mode** adds more detail and rigor to the UML diagrams/models, thereby giving the programmer less flexibility in writing the code. In fact, advanced UML-automated tools can auto-generate a significant amount of source code (Java, C#, C++, VB, etc.), allowing the programming team to focus more on business logic for the application and less on "plumbing."

Our approach in this chapter is a combination of sketch mode and blueprint mode. Our rationale should be obvious: we only have a few pages in which to explain UML, so we selectively have chosen the standard diagrams and elements of these diagrams that seem to be used most often in industry practice. We intentionally omit any discussion of the UML Object Constraint Language, Meta-Object Facility (MOF), Action Semantics, Model Driven Architecture (MDA), Executable UML, and similar topics.

Before we begin in earnest, Table 15.1 summarizes an overview of the UML 2.0 diagrams.

The first diagrams we will examine are the UML class and object diagrams—a staple set of diagrams developed in the early days of object-oriented software analysis and design.

---

[3]Martin Fowler, *UML Distilled*, 3rd ed., Addison-Wesley, 2003.

TABLE 15.1    UML 2 Diagram Types[4]

| Diagram Name | Description |
| --- | --- |
| Activity Diagram | Depicts high-level business processes, including data flow, or to model the logic of complex logic within a system. |
| Class Diagram | Shows a collection of static model elements, such as classes and types, their contents, and their relationships. |
| Communication Diagram | Shows instances of classes, their interrelationships, and the message flow between them. Communication diagrams typically focus on the structural organization of objects that send and receive messages. Formerly called a collaboration diagram. |
| Component Diagram | Depicts the components that compose an application, system, or enterprise, including their interrelationships, interactions, and public interfaces. |
| Composite Structure Diagram | Depicts the internal structure of a classifier (such as a class, component, or use case), including the interaction points of the classifier to other parts of the system. |
| Deployment Diagram | Shows the execution architecture of systems, including nodes, hardware or software execution environments, and the middleware connecting them. |
| Interaction Overview Diagram | A variant of an activity diagram that overviews the control flow within a system or business process. Each node/activity within the diagram can represent another interaction diagram. |
| Object Diagram | Depicts objects and their relationships at a point in time, typically a special case of either a class diagram or a communication diagram. |
| Package Diagram | Shows how model elements are organized into packages and the dependencies between packages. |
| Sequence Diagram | Models the sequential logic (in effect, the time ordering) of messages between classifiers. |
| State Machine Diagrams – Behavioral and Protocol | Describes the states an object or interaction may be in, as well as the transitions between states. Formerly referred to as a state diagram, state chart diagram, or state-transition diagram. A behavioral state machine examines the behavior of a class; a protocol state machine illustrates the dependencies among the different interfaces of a class. |
| Timing Diagram | Depicts the change in state or condition of a classifier instance or role over time. Typically used to show the change in state of an object over time in response to external events. |
| Use Case Diagram | Shows use cases, actors, and their interrelationships. |

[4]Adapted from http://www.agilemodeling.com/essays/umlDiagrams.htm, www.agilemodeling.com, Ambler, Scott. 2003.

### 15.3.1  *Class and Object Diagrams*

Class diagrams are at the heart of object-oriented modeling. The OMG's UML 2.0 Specification document defines a class diagram as "a diagram that shows a collection of declarative (static) model elements, such as classes, types, and their contents and relationships."[5] Stated a little differently, class diagrams depict classes with their attributes, operations (methods), associations, and generalizations, among many other detailed notations. Figure 15.5 illustrates some of the more commonly used notations for a sample class diagram.

---

[5]OMG, UML 2.0 Specification dated 03-08-02, p. 6, http://www.omg.org.

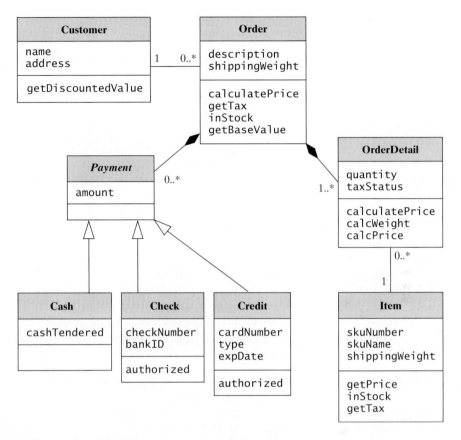

FIGURE 15.5   A Sample Class Diagram in Commonly Used Notation

The chapter uses this **Ordering System** example to illustrate the various diagrams and their notations, starting with Figure 15.5. The explanations progress from the top-left to the bottom-right of this and subsequent diagrams.

Class diagrams help establish the object architecture for the software and serve as a communication vehicle for the domain discussion of requirements with project stakeholders.

In the sample diagram (Figure 15.5), eight classes are shown—**Customer**, **Order**, **Payment**, etc. Class names start with a capital letter and need to be meaningful, indicating their content. Multiple words may be used in class names with no spaces between the words (e.g., "**OrderDetail**.") The use of the underscore character (_) is reserved by convention for constant variables, which are written in all uppercase. The Customer class instantiates customer objects (instances), such as **custIBM**, **custABC**, **custBlockbuster**, **custStarbucks**, and **custTomSmith**, depending on whether customers are companies or individuals or a combination of both. (Note the use of the prefix "**cust**" to avoid writing the first letter of a proprietary name with a small letter, e.g., "**starbucks**.")

The decisions leading to the definition of these classes with the attributes and methods are an important part of understanding the requirements of the domain being developed.

Classes are **concrete** if they can instantiate objects. All of the classes in the diagram except **Payment** are concrete classes. **Payment** is an example of an **abstract** class—a class that cannot instantiate objects. The notation for an abstract class is italics—*Payment*. Abstract classes are used in inheritance hierarchies in which the objects are instantiated from subclasses of the abstract class (keyword **abstract**); in our example, objects can be instantiated for the **Cash**, **Check** and **Credit** child classes of *Payment*.

Class diagram elements are partitioned into three sections—the name of the class, its attributes (fields, instance variables), and its methods (operations, behaviors). Classes often have relationships with other classes, called **associations**. Relationships are shown with lines connecting two classes. Lines may have zero, one, or two arrowheads depicting navigability. No arrowhead means either a two-way connection or undecided/unimportant in this particular diagram. Remember that class diagrams can be drawn in sketch mode to help communicate ideas for the domain, and including notation details may or may not be helpful at that moment.

Associations can have many adornments, the most common one being **multiplicity.** Simply stated, multiplicity expresses how many objects of one class are associated (related) to *one object* of the other class. This is a key concept because association lines are actually relationships between objects instantiated by the classes and not relationships between the classes themselves.

---

**NOTE**

In UML nomenclature, methods are referred to as operations. In order to retain consistency with the Java language and the remainder of this book, we will continue to use the word "method" instead.

---

In our example, a customer object, such as **custTomSmith**, may be associated with none or up to an infinite number of order objects hence the **0..\*** notation next to **Order**. Interpreting the line in the reverse direction, any *one* order object is associated with just one customer, hence the 1 notation next to **Customer**. Thus, when you see associations on a class diagram, interpret them by visualizing objects as illustrated in Figure 15.6.

Inheritance is called **generalization** in UML. Unlike associations, which ultimately relate objects from one class to objects of another class, generalization relationships are between the classes themselves and not the objects instantiated from the classes.

Two types of generalization are possible—**subclass** and **subtype**. Subclass is depicted in Figure 15.5 between the *Payment* superclass and its **Cash**, **Check** and **Credit** subclasses. The subtype is not shown in the figure and is often a relationship between an **interface** (not discussed here) and subtype classes. The subclasses are specializations of the superclass generalization and hence inherit all of the superclass attributes, operations, and associations. In Figure 15.5, the *amount* attribute in **Payment** is automatically inherited by **Cash**, **Check**, and **Credit**, and the *association* between **Payment** and **Order** is also inherited, so that Order objects can be associated with **Cash**, **Check** and **Credit** objects.

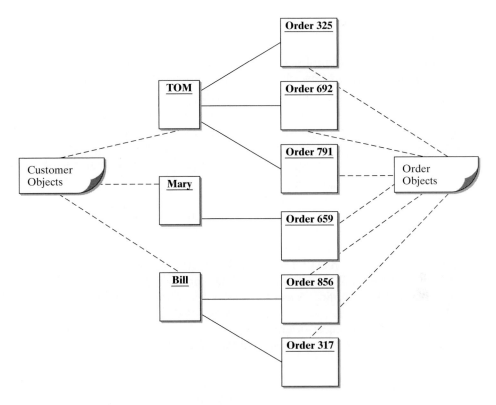

FIGURE 15.6  Sample Object Diagram for Customer and Order Classes

A "stronger" form of association is **composition**—depicted by a black diamond (◆) on one end of the association line. Composition communicates *containment*. Referring to Figure 15.5, what this means is that one **Order** object has a minimum of one (1) and a maximum of infinity (*) **OrderDetail** objects associated with it. The **Order** object lives and dies (is deleted) as a collection of itself and all of its associated **OrderDetail** objects, which is deleted when the Order object is deleted. Within a given domain, this makes logical sense; if an order is deleted, then all of the items on the order (**OrderDetail** objects) should also be deleted. There is a tight coupling between the **Order** object and its **OrderDetail** objects. In fact, a class (actually, object) having a composition relationship with another class (object) may only be related to *one and only one other object*. This is different from the association between **Customer** and **Order** in that if you were to delete a **Customer** object, you would not necessarily delete all of its **Order** objects, and vice versa.

In keeping with the sketch, blueprint, and programming modes commonly used for drawing class diagrams, the amount of detail depicted on the diagram can be varied. For example, you could create a class diagram:

- depicting the classes with just their names.
- depicting the classes with some attributes and/or operations.

- depicting the classes with the above and/or associations, generalizations.
- depicting the classes with navigation and multiplicity and much more.

Figure 15.6 shows a simplified object diagram depicting objects of class **Customer** and class **Order**. It shows how objects are instantiated from these classes; the objects are variables with specific names that hold object-unique data.

### 15.3.2 Use Case Diagram

A use case is the specification of a sequence of actions, including invariants, that a system can perform interacting with actors of the system. A **Use Case diagram** shows the relationship among actors and the subject (system) and the project use cases.[6] The preceding are definitions from the OMG's UML specification document. Others have suggested that use cases are a technique for capturing the functional requirements of the system being built, whereas the use case diagram is an abstract, visual representation of actors and use cases, as shown in Figure 15.7.

   Use cases are mostly textual information describing the functional flow for performing a work flow or action, such as withdrawing money from an ATM machine or purchasing a book online. A use case and its diagram are not object-oriented. This means that any functional requirement can be described via use cases whether it is going to be implemented in a object-oriented language or not. Organizations usually decide on a specific format for the use case textual information, including its name, description,

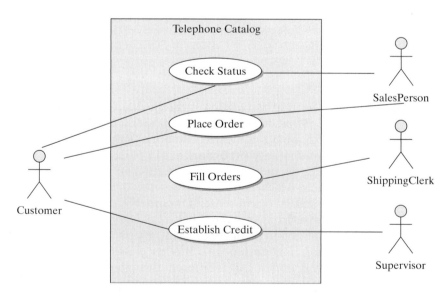

**FIGURE 15.7**   Example Use Case Diagram
(© Object Management Group)

---

[6]OMG, UML 2.0 Specification dated 03-08-02, p. 17, http://www.omg.org.

**TABLE 15.2**   Format for Use Case Textual Information.

| | |
|---|---|
| Name: | Ballot completion and submission |
| Description: | Allowing voters to complete and submit their ballot. |
| Actor(s): | End-user—voter |
| Pre-Conditions: | The voter must be logged in and authenticated. |
| Primary Scenario: | 1. If more than one active ballot, select appropriate ballot |
| | 2. Select candidates/propositions to vote for and select desired button |
| | 3. Complete, submit, provide confirmation, and exit |
| Secondary Scenarios: | A. No ballot |
| | • Provide message and exit |
| | B. No confirmation or internal, system, or network error |
| | • Provide message, exit, notify provider |
| | • Reset database to last committed transaction |
| Post-Conditions: | Return to main menu, allow user to change ballot and resubmit Provide way to exit or continue. |

actor(s), pre-conditions, post-conditions, normal and alternate flows (primary scenario and secondary scenarios), and exceptions (not shown), as illustrated in Table 15.2.

Use cases and use case diagrams have been around for a long time, and their usefulness has been questioned in some organizations, mainly because these organizations have failed to define the structure and granularity of use cases appropriate for their application in the context of the project at hand. For example, one development team member may think that an ATM machine is a use case, whereas another member may think that withdrawing money from an ATM machine is a use case. And the two members do not include the same template of information or sufficient detail in documenting their use case. A further controversy is that creating sufficient use cases is time-consuming and documentation-centric, as opposed to documenting a little in order to produce code sooner. Some authors cite horror stories of projects that wallowed in use case paralysis. We believe that with the proper attention and managerial oversight, the development of use cases serves an effective purpose.

### 15.3.3   Activity Diagram

An activity diagram depicts procedural behavior using a control and data-flow model.[7] Like the use case diagram, activity diagrams are not only for object-oriented development. Their history dates back to the flow charts used in procedural programming design ("Software Development Life Cycle-SDLC"). The principal difference between flow charts and activity diagrams is that the latter can show parallel activities. Activity diagrams are also similar to Petri Nets, another long-standing diagram method for software engineering and other disciplines.

Activity diagrams are highly useful during requirements gathering, organization, and documentation. When there is a need to understand, document, and communicate

---

[7]OMG, UML 2.0 Specification dated 03-08-02, pp. 4–5, http://www.omg.org.

a process in the problem domain, whether we are using use cases, user stories, features, or traditional requirements statements ("The system shall … "), activity diagrams serve a key visualization purpose. For example, if there is uncertainty or lack of understanding about a particular business flow, it is very useful to depict the flow with an activity diagram. (As a simple example, think through the precise details of efficient, safe, multilingual withdrawal of money from an ATM.) In many instances the domain experts may not clearly understand the process flow details, so documenting the workflow is valuable for everyone involved. It can help them "get on the same page" or "level the playing field" of understanding.

Some basic notation for an activity diagram (there is more, of course) is illustrated by the elements in Figures 15.8 and 15.9 below. Figure 15.10 is a sample activity diagram that uses most of these elements.

Activity diagrams can be used effectively to explain a process flow to stakeholders. If you cannot do that, the process described by the activity diagram is probably incorrect in terms of the actual workflow.

As we examine Figure 15.10, we start with the **initial node** (black dot) and then move to the *Receive Order* **activity.** Conditional behavior is delineated by **decisions** and **merges** (both use a diamond as notation). A **decision** (also called a **branch**) has a single incoming flow and several guarded outbound flows. Each outbound flow has a guard—a Boolean condition placed inside square brackets. Each time you reach a decision you can only take one of the outbound flows, so the guards should be mutually exclusive. Using [else] as a guard indicates that the [else] flow should be used if all the other guards on the decision are false.

In Figure 15.10, after an order is received, there is a decision. If you reject the order, you close the order; otherwise, you accept the order and fill it.

A **fork** (black bar/line positioned either vertically or horizontally) has one incoming flow and several outgoing concurrent flows which account for the parallelism within activity diagrams. In Figure 15.10, after an order is filled, two activities are completed—either

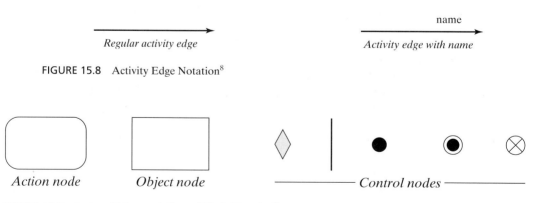

Regular activity edge        Activity edge with name

FIGURE 15.8    Activity Edge Notation[8]

Action node      Object node      ——— Control nodes ———

FIGURE 15.9    Action, Object, and Control Node Notation[9]

---

[8]OMG, UML 2.0 Specification dated 03-08-02, p. 294, http://www.omg.org.
[9]OMG, UML 2.0 Specification dated 03-08-02, p. 303, http://www.omg.org.

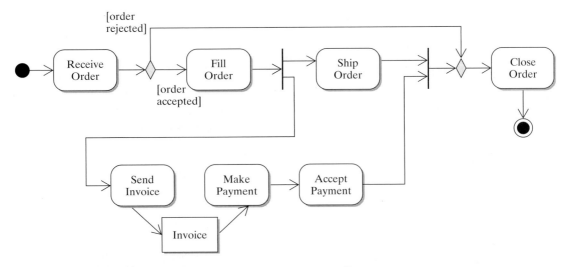

FIGURE 15.10    Sample Order and Payment Process Activity Diagram[10]

in parallel or asynchronously, usually by a different person or group. In our example, someone in the shipping department is responsible for the *Ship Order* activity, and someone in the accounts receivable department is responsible for the *Send Invoice* activity.

The *Close Order* activity is performed either after an order is rejected or after both the *Ship Order* and *Accept Payment* activities have been completed. These two activities come together via a **join** (black bar/line) that has several incoming flows and one outgoing flow. This process is completed as depicted with the **Activity Final node** (bull's-eye notation).

### 15.3.4  *Sequence Diagram*

A sequence diagram depicts an interaction by focusing on the sequence of messages exchanged, along with their corresponding event occurrences on temporal lifelines. Unlike a communication diagram, a sequence diagram includes time sequences but does not include object relationships. A sequence diagram can exist in a generic form (describing all possible scenarios) and in an instance form (describing one actual scenario). Sequence diagrams and communication diagrams express similar information, but show it in different ways.[11]

Sequence diagrams and communication diagrams (discussed in the next section) are grouped together as **interaction diagrams** in UML. Both of these diagrams describe how groups of objects collaborate in some behavior. Each has its purpose and depicts the same information but in a different manner. As stated above, sequence diagrams show ordering or sequencing but do not show object relationships. Communication diagrams do not visually show ordering but do show object relationships.

---

[10]OMG, UML 2.0 Specification dated 03-08-02, p. 303, http://www.omg.org.
[11]OMG, UML 2.0 Specification dated 03-08-02, p. 14, http://www.omg.org.

Although UML 2.0 includes a number of enhancements to the sequence diagram, we only show some basic notations in Figure 15.11. The sample sequence diagram shows the messages used to actually calculate the price of an order—for example, when an online shopper presses a "check out" button after placing items in his shopping cart. The system will do a number of things to prepare the summary for this particular order. Among them might be the operation (method) **calculatePrice**. A message is sent to the order (**aOrder**) to calculate its price (probably the total price for the order). The **aOrder** object delegates the calculation to each of its **aOrderDetail** objects, since each item placed in the shopping cart is represented by one order detail object. The asterisk (**\***) before the **calculatePrice** message being sent to **aOrderDetail** denotes iteration across each order detail object for this order object (**aOrder**).

The calculation of the order price continues with each order detail object sending a **getPrice** message, along with the quantity of the ordered item (e.g., you are purchasing three copies of this textbook from an online book ordering site), to its associated **aItem** object to do the pricing for the given quantity. The **calculatePrice** method in **aOrder** object makes a method call **getDiscountedValue** to **aCustomer** object (e.g., you, as the purchaser of this order) to see if this customer gets a discount, and if so, how much. The discounted value is returned to the calling method in **aOrder**, and the whole process repeats itself for the next **aOrderDetail** object, until there are no more **aOrderDetail** objects for this **aOrder** object.

Sequence diagrams are useful for discovering and understanding the detailed message exchanges between objects for a particular process. In reality, hundreds or thousands of sequence diagrams (or communication diagrams) would be needed to capture all the object interactions in a system. Generally the development team will only create sequence (or communication) diagrams for processes that are so complex or unclear that the diagrams can help clarify design understanding before the coding phase. Another approach to sequence (or communication) diagrams is to create a diagram of the significant method calls, leaving many of the secondary calls off the diagram. This would make it easier to understand the workflow and without getting bogged down in too much detail. The main purpose of these diagrams, after all, is to assist in understanding the needed design elements and communicating within the team.

### 15.3.5 Communication Diagram

A communication diagram focuses on the interaction between lifelines where the architecture of the internal structure and how it corresponds with the message passing are central. The sequencing of messages is documented through a sequence numbering scheme. Sequence diagrams and communication diagrams express similar information but show it in different ways.[12]

Figure 15.12 illustrates the same process as the preceding section's sequence diagram, but the view from the communication diagram perspective is somewhat different. Instead of showing objects with their lifelines and messages being sent in a time-ordered sequence (top to bottom), the communication diagram shows objects in a free-form layout with all of the message calls stacked up between them, showing the direction of the call and a number (e.g., **1.1.1**) indicating the firing order for that message call.

---

[12]OMG, UML 2.0 Specification dated 03-08-02, p. 6, http://www.omg.org.

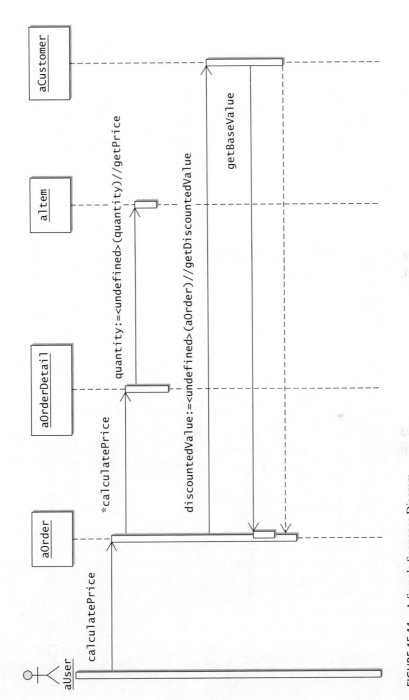

FIGURE 15.11   A Sample Sequence Diagram

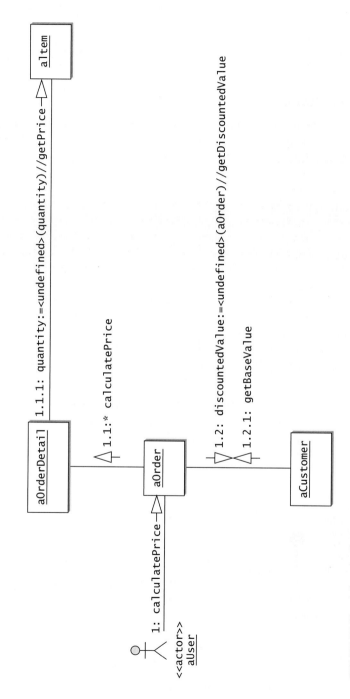

FIGURE 15.12   A Sample Communication Diagram

One of us has presented UML seminars to hundreds of software engineers over the years, and we have found that roughly 80% of them prefer working with sequence diagrams over communication diagrams, with the remaining 20% preferring just the opposite. Most automated UML tools can automatically turn a sequence diagram into a communication diagram, and vice versa, so the team only has to draw one of the two diagrams. This is exactly how Figure 15.12 was created automatically from Figure 15.11.

### 15.3.6  State Machine Diagram

A state machine diagram depicts discrete behavior modeled from a finite state-transition perspective. In particular, it specifies the sequences of states that an object or an interaction goes through during its life in response to events, together with its responses and actions.[13] State machine diagrams were originally developed many years ago, and object-oriented developers adopted them to depict various object behaviors and states. These diagrams quite often represent the various states of a single class (i.e., a behavioral state machine diagram) or the life-cycle of multiple objects (a protocol State Machine diagram). Other names for this diagram are *state chart* and *state transition diagram.*

Although a state machine diagram has a significant amount of notational capability, we will only show a simple example of a behavioral state machine diagram and its notation in this chapter.

Figure 15.13 is a sample of a state machine diagram for a seat on a particular airline flight on a particular day (e.g., from one airport to another airport). According to the figure, the status of the seat objects can either be *Available, Locked, Res[erved],* or *Sold.* The class diagram portion of Figure 15.13 indicates that a particular **FlightLeg** object may have from 20 to 350 **Seat** objects. State machine diagrams use the familiar

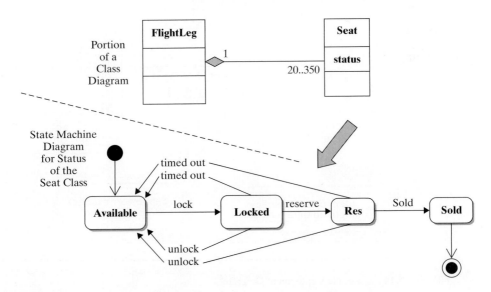

FIGURE 15.13   A Sample State Machine Diagram for an Airline Seat Reservation Process

---

[13]OMG, UML 2.0 Specification dated 03-08-02, p. 15, http://www.omg.org.

**initial node** (black dot) and **final node** (bull's eye). In the diagram, the seat status starts as *Available*. Following the arrow flowing from *Available* to *Locked*, you see that a seat is locked for some reason—a reservation is probably being made, via the Web or a live reservation service representative. Once a transaction is in the *Locked* state, three alternative transitions are possible: follow the outgoing arrows. If a "time-out" occurs, the status reverts to *Available*. If a request to "reserve" occurs, the status state changes to *Res[erved]*. Finally, if an *unlock* event occurs while the status is in the *Locked* state, the status is changed back to *Available*.

Once the status is in the *Res[erved]* state, three different transitions can occur. Two of them are similar to the transitions out of the *Locked* state—time-out and unlock—sending the status state back to *Available,* and the third transition occurs if the seat is actually "sold," in which case the status of the seat becomes *Sold* (or unavailable for purchase).

This sample state machine diagram is quite simple, but it should help you to grasp the value of state machine diagrams for situations when there are dozens or hundreds of states or sophisticated rules for transitioning from one state to another.

### 15.3.7  Deployment Diagram

The final diagram that we discuss in this chapter is the deployment diagram. A deployment diagram depicts the execution architecture of systems. It represents system artifacts as nodes connected through communication paths to create network systems of arbitrary complexity. Nodes are typically defined in a nested manner and represent either hardware devices or software execution environments.[14] Said differently,

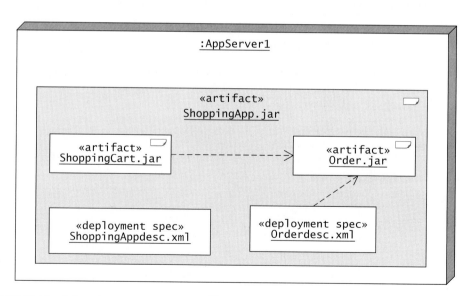

FIGURE 15.14    A Sample Deployment Diagram[15]

---

[14]OMG, UML 2.0 Specification dated 03-08-02, p. 15, http://www.omg.org.
[15]OMG, UML 2.0 Specification dated 03-08-02, Fig. 133, p. 191, http://www.omg.org.

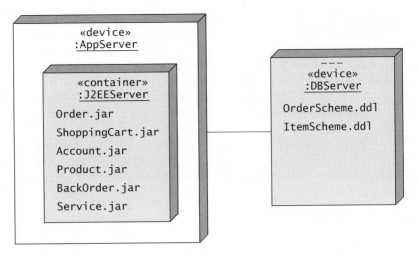

FIGURE 15.15   Sample Deployment Diagram: Device Notation[16]

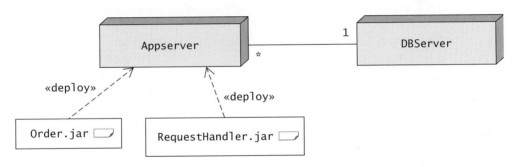

FIGURE 15.16   Sample Deployment Diagram: A Communication Path Between Two Node Types[17]

a deployment diagram shows the physical layout of a system to reveal what pieces of software run on what pieces of hardware.

These diagrams are often quite simple, but they are very useful in depicting complex, distributed environments. Figures 15.14 through 15.17 depict partial deployment diagrams showing various elements that can be documented using the diagram.

## 15.4   Resources: Connections • People • Companies

Many companies and individuals are actively involved with the Unified Modeling Language. The most notable organization is the Object Management Group (OMG), a consortium of companies and individuals working collaboratively to enhance the

[16]OMG, UML 2.0 Specification dated 03-08-02, Fig. 135, p. 192, http://www.omg.org.
[17]OMG, UML 2.0 Specification dated 03-08-02, Fig. 138, p. 196, http://www.omg.org; OMG, UML 2.0 Specification dated 03-08-02, Fig. 139, p. 197, http://www.omg.org.

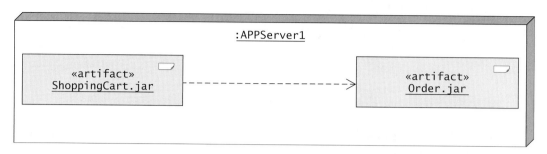

FIGURE 15.17    Sample Deployment Diagram: A Set of Deployed Component Artifacts on a Node

state-of-the-art of object-oriented modeling. The OMG produces the UML specification document. Consequently, various research organizations and commercial enterprises around the world create automated tools that support an approved subset of the UML. (Note that no research or commercial product known to the authors has been 100% compliant with the complete UML specification since the original UML 1.0 spec was published in 1997.) Listed below are some of the commercial and open-source/freeware tools available at the time of this writing:

- Aonix Ameos[TM]
- ArgoUML (open source)
- Borland® Together ControlCenter[TM]
- Compuware® OptimalJ[TM]
- Gentleware® Poseidon[TM]
- JetBrains® IntelliJ IDEA[TM]
- NoMagic® MagicDraw[TM]
- Oracle® JDeveloper[TM]
- IBM® Rational® Rose XDE[TM]
- Telelogic® Tau[TM]
- Visual Paradigm® Visual-Paradigm for UML[TM]
- Omondo® EclipseUML[TM]

## 15.5    Summary and Recommendations

In this chapter, we have presented a limited UML primer as an introduction to UML for those of you who have no previous knowledge of the modeling language. We have made no attempt to be complete, rigorous, or definitive. For that you are referred to the OMG Web site (http://www.omg.org), where you can download the complete UML Superstructure Specification. In addition, many excellent books are available on the subject. Martin Fowler's *UML Distilled*, 3rd edition, is one of the most popular to get you started, but there are dozens of others on the market.

## 15.6   Review Questions

This section, repeated at the end of every chapter, provides a number of questions and assignments that will allow you to check your knowledge.

1. **Class Diagram.** Define a class diagram and discuss its purpose and when it would be appropriate to use one.
2. **Object Diagram.** Define an object diagram and discuss its purpose and when it would be appropriate to use one.
3. **Use Case Diagram.** Define a use case diagram and discuss its purpose and when it would be appropriate to use one.
4. **Activity Diagram.** Define an activity diagram and discuss its purpose and when it would be appropriate to use one.
5. **Sequence Diagram.** Define a sequence diagram and discuss its purpose and when it would be appropriate to use one.
6. **Communication Diagram.** Define a communication diagram and discuss its purpose and when it would be appropriate to use one.
7. **State Diagram.** Define a state diagram and discuss its purpose and when it would be appropriate to use one.
8. **Deployment Diagram.** Define a deployment diagram and discuss its purpose and when it would be appropriate to use one.

## 15.7   Glossary – Terminology – Concepts

Note: Each of the diagram definitions below comes from the OMG's UML 2.0 Specification document.[18]

**Activity diagram**   A diagram that depicts behavior using a control and data-flow model.

**Class diagram**   A diagram that shows a collection of declarative (static) model elements, such as classes, types, and their contents and relationships.

**Communication diagram**   A diagram that focuses on the interaction between lifelines where the architecture of the internal structure and how it corresponds with the message passing is central. The sequencing of messages is given through a sequence numbering scheme. Sequence diagrams and communication diagrams express similar information, but show it in different ways.

**Component diagram**   A diagram that shows the organizations and dependencies among components.

**Deployment diagram**   A diagram that depicts the execution architecture of systems. It represents system artifacts as nodes connected through communication paths to create network systems of arbitrary complexity. Nodes are typically defined in a nested manner, and represent either hardware devices or software execution environments.

---

[18]OMG, UML 2.0 Specification dated 03-08-02, http://www.omg.org.

**Object diagram**   A diagram that encompasses objects and their relationships at a point in time. An object diagram may be considered a special case of a class diagram or a communication diagram.

**Package diagram**   A diagram that depicts how model elements are organized into packages and the dependencies among them, including package imports and package extensions.

**Sequence diagram**   A diagram that depicts an interaction by focusing on the sequence of the messages exchanged, along with their corresponding event occurrences on the lifelines. Unlike a communication diagram, a sequence diagram includes time sequences but does not include object relationships. A sequence diagram can exist in a generic form (describing all possible scenarios) and in an instance form (describing one actual scenario). Sequence diagrams and communication diagrams express similar information, but show it in different ways.

**State Machine diagram**   A diagram that depicts discrete behavior modeled through finite state-transition systems. In particular, it specifies the sequences of states that an object or an interaction goes through during its life in response to events, together with its responses and actions.

**Use Case diagram**   A diagram that shows the relationship among actors and the subject (system), and use cases.

## 15.8    Exercises

**1. Create a Class Diagram.**   Develop a simple class diagram for a video store rental system. Don't get carried away with too many classes—a half-dozen or more should suffice. Be sure to add some of the more important attributes, operations, associations, multiplicities, and generalizations (if any).

**2. Create an Object Diagram.**   Develop a simple object diagram for a couple of the classes from Exercise 1's video store rental system.

**3. Create a Use Case Diagram.**   Develop a simple use case diagram for a video store rental system. Think about the actors and their interactions (use cases), such as checking out a video, checking in a video, etc.

**4. Create an Activity Diagram.**   Develop a simple activity diagram for a *Video Checkout* use case in a video store rental system. Think about all the significant detail activities from the store's perspective that must be performed in order to really check out a video. From your perspective, you walk in, select video, wait in line, pay for the video, and walk out with it. From the store's perspective, additional activity is necessary to properly record information about the check-out activity. Have fun.

**5. Create a Sequence Diagram.**   Create a sequence diagram for one of the use cases for the video store rental system. Be sure to include the message calls and objects involved with providing the information and business logic (methods) necessary to complete the use case.

**6. Create a Communication Diagram.**   Convert the sequence diagram you created in the preceding exercise into a communication diagram.

**7. Create a State Machine Diagram.**   Create a state machine diagram for your potential grade in this course. The possible grade values (status) are A, B, C, D, F, and no grade. If your final whole-number-only score (percent) is $>= 90$, then your grade is A; if between 80 and 89, then B; if between 70 and 79, then C; if between 60 and 69, then D; otherwise if $<= 59$, then F.

**8. Create a Deployment Diagram.**   Create a simple deployment diagram for the video store rental system. Assume that this system will be running on a corporate server hundreds of miles from the store where the actual usage by store employees takes place via Web-based browser capability.

# Index